A critical introduction to twentieth-century American drama

For Herb Blau, whose own book, *Take Up the Bodies*, is one of the finest works of its kind that I know

A critical introduction to twentieth-century American drama

3

Beyond Broadway

C. W. E. BIGSBY

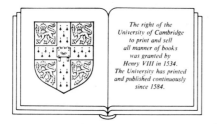

The right of the
University of Cambridge
to print and sell
all manner of books
was granted by
Henry VIII in 1534.
The University has printed
and published continuously
since 1584.

CAMBRIDGE UNIVERSITY PRESS

Cambridge
London   New York   New Rochelle
Melbourne   Sydney

Published by the Press Syndicate of the University of Cambridge
The Pitt Building, Trumpington Street, Cambridge CB2 IRP
32 East 57th Street, New York, NY 10022, USA
10 Stamford Road, Oakleigh, Melbourne 3166, Australia

First published 1985

Printed in Great Britain at the University Press, Cambridge

Library of Congress catalogue card number: 81–18000

British Library Cataloguing in Publication Data
Bigsby, C.W.E.
A critical introduction to twentieth
century American drama.
3: Beyond Broadway
1. American drama – 20th century –
History and criticism
I. Title
812'.52'09   PS351
ISBN 0 521 26256 9 hard covers
ISBN 0 521 27896 1 paperback

CONTENTS

v

Contents

vi

ILLUSTRATIONS

PREFACE

The second volume of this study considered the work of Tennessee Williams, Arthur Miller and Edward Albee. Theirs was a theatre in which the text was central and the writer himself a dominant influence. Though they were fully alive to the capacity for deception contained in the language which they deployed that language was still offered as a primary agent of communication. At the centre of their work was the individual, anxious, suffering, threatened, equivocating, who remained a key to social meaning and cultural achievement. But virtually all of these assumptions were challenged as the American theatre underwent major changes in the 1960s. Institutionally, aesthetically, socially and politically it began to fragment. Theatricality itself became a major concern, the writer was demoted, language distrusted, character disassembled and the relationship between performer and audience redefined. If I begin this book by recapitulating some of the concerns of the immediate post-war world it is so that this subsequent shift of attention and energies can be placed in some kind of context. Often, in what follows, the analysis of texts defers to an account of the activities and philosophies of theatre groups or a description of performances whose texts might seem fragmentary or even inconsequential if submitted to a rigorous critical dissection. But priorities were changing. The theatre, no less than American society itself, was in a state of flux. A new freedom was claimed. Theatre was examined for its interventionist potential. It seemed suddenly, and somewhat surprisingly, a model for social action. In another direction its purely formalist possibilities were explored and this quickly led in the direction of the other arts – dancing, music and painting. What follows, then, is an attempt to chart some of these explorations. Beginning with the major figures who established the post-war reputation of American drama I step off beyond Broadway. I trust that in doing so I can at least suggest something of the variety, originality and energy of this other theatre.

ACKNOWLEDGEMENTS

I would like to thank Jordan Miller for his invaluable help on volumes two and three.

Permission to reproduce the illustrations is gratefully acknowledged: for 1, 2, © Fred W. McDarrah, 1980; for 3, Max Waldman, New York; for 4, 5, 12, 13, 14, 17, 22, Theodore Shank; for 15, Carol Rosegg; for 16, the Dramatic Art Department, University of California, Davis; for 18, 19, 23, the New York Public Library at Lincoln Center; for 20, Gerhard E. Gscheidle; for 21, Jim Crawford.

The appendix is reproduced by kind permission of the Theatre Communications Group, New York.

PART I

Beyond Broadway

INTRODUCTION

On 11 December 1941, at the Music Hall in Kansas City, Alfred Lunt, co-star with Lynn Fontanne in *There Shall Be No Night*, received a phone call from the play's author, Robert Sherwood. He was told that the show was to cease because the plot was now considered contrary to America's war interests. Written in 1939 and receiving its première in 1940, it concerned the plight of a Finnish scientist who had abandoned his pacifism in order to join his country's war against Russia. Now, to Sherwood's evident embarrassment, Russia was fighting against the forces of Nazi Germany; overnight it had become a gallant ally. His phone call was symptomatic. The theatre quickly rallied to the cause. But, if the war inevitably provoked a certain amount of national boosterism, as it also provoked a radical change of direction in the careers of individual writers, evidence of that change, in fact, pre-dated the war. This applied to Sherwood himself. As a pacifist he had still been extolling the virtues of the Sermon on the Mount as late as 1936 in a play called *Idiot's Delight*, although this actually takes place in a Europe menaced by militant fascism, but under the pressure of events that pacifism collapsed and he felt obliged to undertake a radical revision of his position. He did so at first by displacing his concern into the past, in *Abe Lincoln in Illinois* (1938) celebrating the career of a man who had been forced to make a similar decision, and then, in *There Shall Be No Night* with its unfortunate political setting, attempted to confront the issue directly in a contemporary setting.

He was far from alone in this dilemma. Maxwell Anderson had begun to accommodate his own pacifism to the developing situation in Europe by effecting a similar displacement into the past with *Valley Forge* in 1934. Clearly the problem then seemed less acutely threatening. But in 1939 he shifted his ground with *Key Largo* in which he warned of the dangers of a collapse of will in the face of evil, developing his new stance with *Candle in the Wind* (1941) and *The Eve of St Mark* (1942). So, too,

Sidney Kingsley, whose earlier *Dead End* had stressed the betrayal of American values, now chose to celebrate them in *The Patriots* (1943), which, although once again set in the past, proposed the American system as 'the world's best hope'.

Faced with the manifest threat of Nazism the theatre was swiftly enrolled in the battle. In December 1940, Elmer Rice's *Flight to the West* presented a virulent attack on fascism, the actor Paul Henreich, himself a refugee from Hitler's Germany, remarking that, if he could show how 'really rotten' the Nazis were, then he would be doing his 'bit'. It was in that spirit that Lillian Hellman wrote her melodrama of spies and resistance fighters, *Watch on the Rhine*, 1941 (attacked by the Communist Party because its stance was at odds with the Hitler–Stalin pact, and praised as a film in 1942 because by then Hitler had invaded Russia), and Arnaud d'Usseau and James Gow their play *Tomorrow the World* (1943). There were later, to be sure, plays which displayed a rather more tensile realism – such as Arthur Laurents's *Home of the Brave* (1946), John Patrick's *The Hasty Heart* (1945), and William Wister Haines's *Command Decision* (1947) – but for the most part the war generated an idealism which was different in kind from that which had dominated the 1930s but which was no less intense. However, by the same token, it was an idealism which was not likely to survive the events of that war any more than that radical and even sentimental model of human relations which had sustained a number of America's major playwrights through a decade of economic and spiritual collapse. And it did not.

William Saroyan's *My Heart's in the Highlands* (1939), dedicated to the 'pure in heart', the 'poet in the world' who could dominate that world through the sheer force of his spirit, gives way after the war to Tennessee Williams's tortured poets, destroyed by that world. Saroyan's second play, *The Time of Your Life* (1939), which celebrates the 'sorrowful American music' generated by a group of social derelicts transformed into mythic heroes, is succeeded by Eugene O'Neill's *The Iceman Cometh*, whose pessimism led him to postpone its production until after the war. The confident thrust of Clifford Odets's plays, with their conviction that individual action and class solidarity could transform the social system and offer a sense of personal meaning, defers to Arthur Miller's Ibsenesque doubts about idealism, his sense of the fragility of character and the failure of the social impulse. Thornton Wilder's sentimental account of small-town America, his celebration of natural process, is superseded by William Inge's painful realism and by portraits of an urban and suburban America in which national pieties can no longer survive except at the level of parody – as in the work of Edward Albee who saw American idealism only through the prism of historical betrayal.

2

A gulf of experience opened up between the post-war theatre and that of the 1930s and early 1940s, a gulf reflected in the ambiguities which *All My Sons* (1947) identifies in the figure of the idealist whose demands for justice are not untinged with self-interest and cruelty. Because he actually wrote the play in the last months of the war Arthur Miller felt unable then to press the issue any further than simple irony but this figure of the self-interested idealist (derived from Ibsen but with immediate relevance), no less than the near-cliché portrait of a corrupt American businessman, betokened a collapse of confidence which deepened in his work and in that of his contemporaries, the more especially since after the war the major talents who had dominated the scene in the 1920s and 30s quickly faded from the scene. Philip Barry, William Saroyan, Maxwell Anderson, Robert Sherwood, Clifford Odets and even Lillian Hellman were no longer major influences, and though O'Neill's plays continued to dominate individual Broadway seasons for another decade he himself was virtually crippled by illness and died in 1953. For a decade and a half, indeed, serious theatre was represented by the work of only two men, Tennessee Williams and Arthur Miller.

There is a passage in John Updike's novel *Rabbit Redux* (1971) in which the protagonist sits in a Negro bar and listens to the music of a black pianist. As she plays the songs of pre-war America, so he contemplates the collapse of morale and morality of which he is himself an exemplary figure:

> Her hands, all brown bone, hang on the keyboard hushed like gloves on a table; she gazes up through the blue dust to get herself into focus, she lets her hands fall into another tune: 'My Funny Valentine', 'Smoke Gets in Your Eyes', 'I Can't Get Started', starting to hum along with herself now, lyrics born in some distant smoke, decades when Americans moved within the American dream, laughing at it, starving on it, but living it, humming it, the national anthem everywhere. Wise guys and hicks, straw boaters and bib overalls, fast bucks, broken hearts, penthouses in the sky, shacks by the railroad tracks, ups and downs, rich and poor, trolly cars and the latest news by radio. Rabbit had come in on the end of it, as the world shrank like an apple going bad and America was no longer the wisest hick town within a boat ride of Europe and Broadway forgot the tune . . .[1]

It is a passage which, with its sense of loss balanced by nostalgia, its conviction that time and a certain moral failure (easier to detect in its consequences than in its true nature) have destroyed an animating myth no less than a substantial reality, reflects a basic theme of a great deal of post-war American drama. Rabbit Angstrom's shrinking America emerged from the Second World War confident of its own supremacy. But the questioning began early. The explosion of the two atom bombs

3

at Hiroshima and Nagasaki may have been viewed unambiguously at the time but ambiguity began to coalesce early. As Eliott Nugent (co-author with James Thurber of *The Male Animal*) observed: 'The two great flashes over Japan did something to the eyesight and the nerves and spirit of the more civilized, sensitive, thoughtful and humorous people . . . and this change was reflected in literature, drama, music, art and politics.'[2] In 1949, with the detonation of the Russian bomb, America lost its supremacy and its assurance. In Korea it proved less than invincible. It had to come to terms with an unaccustomed sense of insecurity. For the first time in its history its inhabitants had to deal with the fact of total physical vulnerability.

At first the change which Eliott Nugent had identified was oblique and displaced. Apart from a powerful if ironised nostalgia, it seems to have registered as a sense of a disturbance in the social and psychological world, a bafflement over social process – at its most obvious in Miller's *Death of a Salesman* and *The Crucible* or Tennessee Williams's *A Streetcar Named Desire* and *Camino Real*. Something was over. Some view of the world was no longer tenable. Some ultimate security had been destroyed. But there was also an increasing sense of apocalypse in American dramatic writing which was to intensify in the 1960s, 70s and 80s with plays like Edward Albee's *Box*, Tennessee Williams's *The Red Devil Battery Sign*, Sam Shepard's *Icarus's Mother* and Mabou Mines's *Dead End Kids: A History of Nuclear Power*. The very structures of art began to dislocate under the pressure. The sense of consonance implied by the rationality of language, the integrity of character and the coherences of plot began to succumb to what seems at times to be a kind of cultural paranoia. The psychological derangement of characters such as Willy Loman, in *Death of a Salesman* and Blanche Dubois, in *A Streetcar Named Desire*, merely anticipated the more complete collapse of dramatic character to be found in Kenneth Brown's *The Brig* (1963) or, in a different sense, in the work of Robert Wilson or Richard Foreman a decade later.

And during the 1950s the long-deferred question of race forced itself on the political agenda. The image of America was no longer clear. The ideology of self-improvement and material success scarcely seemed adequate as urban decay, crime and racial tension began to impinge more directly. For Arthur Miller, the shift to the right during the 1950s left him culturally stranded, unable to identify an audience which he could address or a model of America which could accommodate both the House Un-American Activities Committee and his own version of American liberalism. For Tennessee Williams, the old South, whose brutal realities he acknowledged but whose myths provided a context for the writer committed to the fragile values of a romantic self, was giving way to a new South whose brutalities and soulless materialism were no longer cloaked by that cavalier myth.

Both Miller's and Williams's early, unpublished plays, written in the 1930s, display an unequivocal morality. They picture the individual fighting back against oppression in concert with others. But their 1940s work tells another story. The confidence has gone and though both implicitly urge the need to reconstitute a morally responsive self they locate that self in a world which no longer allows the individual room in which to define that selfhood, or sustain a sense of identity. Social values seem unrelated to human need. Both are, in effect, pastoralists inhabiting an urban world. Like Miller's ageing cowboy in *The Misfits*, they both feel out of step with their society, living in an age in which money, power and a certain amoral materialism effectively deny the possibility of transcendence. In the 1930s, for all the suffering, there was a commitment to the possibility of social change which could liberate the energies of the individual and preserve a confident selfhood, albeit through submission to the group. In the 1940s and 50s, there is little evidence of this faith in personal or public transformation. In a period of recovery and enormous material advancement, with the Depression and war having given way to rapid expansion and peace (Korea notwithstanding), the values of society were seen as intimately connected with the success of American military might and commercial enterprise rather than inimical to it. As a consequence those values – a fierce individualism, a concern for material advancement and self-improvement – were not so much challenged directly, as they had been by artists a decade earlier, as denounced for their effect on the individual sensibility. This was a psychological theatre in which social issues were reconstituted as private traumas. Indeed the public world was increasingly presented as the source of threat and oppression. In Williams's case, as later in that of Edward Albee, this was perhaps a response to his own publicly menaced sexual identity as well as to his sense of being a poet in an unpoetic culture. In Miller's case it seems to have derived from his early radicalism and subsequently the rise of McCarthyism which made the institutions of his society menacing in a quite literal way.

There is a danger, of course, in too casual an assumption that the theatre simply reflects the state of society. The risk, anyway, is that our model of history will be too simplistic. After all, it is surprising that the 1920s produced *Street Scene* and the early bleak O'Neill plays only if our version of the 1920s is derived from the world which so dazzled Gatsby. For Arthur Miller, it was a decade of unreality, in which paper money was like Fitzgerald's snows of 1929. It was a product of pure imagination.

But for millions it was otherwise. About the next decade there was rather greater agreement. As Miller himself was to suggest, it was one of the few historical realities shared by most Americans, and though it by no means generated a homogeneous drama even the most frivolous Broadway musical invites description in terms of the realities it so studiously sought to evade. The post-war world seems less clear in outline. But in terms of theatre there is one theme that pervades the work of writers as different as Arthur Miller, Tennessee Williams, William Inge, Edward Albee, David Mamet, Neil Simon and many others – loss. For Miller and Williams, I suspect, it is an expression of the failure of that social vision which dominated the world in which they grew up, the notion that reality could be bent to the will of history, that humankind is linked by indissoluble bonds forged out of need and an acknowledged brotherhood. For all of them, however, it was an expression of the collapse of a model of community locatable somewhere in the American past, before the city had destroyed the spirit and the imagination, before the notion of shared values shattered on the hard-edged realities of money and power. Their theme is the need to reconstitute some bond which was presumed, either in the world of myth or reality, to have existed before human relationships came to be perceived in terms of exchange value, before commercial were substituted for human qualities.

The potential for sentimentality is clear – so much so that in many ways it becomes a distinguishing feature of American art, at its most obvious in the movies or television but present in the theatre, too. It is as though the persistence of the family, the reality of community, and the survival of a genuine and undeniable connectiveness between individuals who only think themselves to be alone were all being asserted in the face of overwhelming evidence to the contrary. And the result was a shrill anxiety.

In the 1950s it was not irrational to feel a gulf between the writer and his society. The McCarthy witch-hunts were directed precisely at the old New Dealers, at those of liberal conviction. The writer, the actor, the director were suspect precisely because the theatre had once been so publicly associated with Roosevelt's Works Progress Administration and because for men of no imagination the imagination was perceived as a potent weapon. Publicly oppressed, deeply suspicious of the materialism and the increasing anonymity of society, writers like Miller and Williams tended to dramatise the plight of the individual denied avenues in which to express that individuality. The self was seen as under attack from without and within. Public and private morality were at odds and the conflict between them generated their plays. And these tended to take the form either of existential dramas in which the individual acknowledged responsibilities and claimed rights which defined a problematic but real identity (*The Crucible*), or of romantic gestures by which the individual submitted to the pressure of time or social change, finding a brief epiphany equally in a resistant spirit and in the moment of submission (*Suddenly Last Summer, Sweet Bird of Youth*).

Daniel Bell has argued that the 1950s marked an end of ideology. Those intellectuals who had looked to the Soviet Union in the 1930s and early 1940s no longer had a focus for their convictions. The old utopian dreams had foundered. The new politics had turned out to be merely a version of the old. The apocalypse, which was supposed to have swept away a corruption born of capitalism, had taken a wholly different form. The war had revealed a far more terrifying vision than that offered by a familiar failure of domestic morality. The utopianism of the past had generated only disillusionment and the bland materialism of a post-war economy. In a sense, as Bell has argued, the cultural world was the only one still open to those who felt cut off equally from their own past dreams and the arid conservatism of their immediate political environ-ment. Moral values evacuated from the public world were presumed to have migrated into art or alternatively the arts seemed to constitute the only world sufficiently detached from the social sphere to grant the possibility of perspective. It was, as all too many writers found, only a provisional immunity since an aggressive conservatism quickly set out to disarm political critics who were none the less dangerous for having shifted their base. But, more importantly, it was anyway a deeply insecure refuge for other reasons. The casual moral assurance of the pre-war world could scarcely survive intact in a culture in which the dominant images, for the writer and the sociologist alike, became those of alienation and depersonalisation and in which a profound anxiety, deepening for some into neurosis and psychopathology, seemed the price of continued commitment to values at a tangent to those of the new orthodoxy.

In *The Organization Man* (1956) William Whyte argued that liberal individualism was increasingly deferring to a corporate identity, the individual deriving a sense of personal worth and private meaning only from the institution which granted him a place and a role. David Reisman, in *The Lonely Crowd*, saw a shift from a tradition–oriented model of selfhood, historically located and self-contained, to an 'other directed' model in which identity was a product of peer-group pressure. In *The Hidden Persuaders*, a popularised summary of research on behav-iour patterns, Vance Packard detailed the evidence for the passivity of the consumer public manipulated at a pre-conscious level. And what Packard presented as a vice, B.F. Skinner to some degree presented as a virtue in *Walden Two*, a utopia which struck everyone but Skinner as a chilling view of the loss of personal freedom. Emil Durkheim, writing in

1897, had argued that all people living in a modern political state are simply a 'disorganised dust of individuals'; what differed in the twentieth century was that the very notion of the individual had become problematic.

In the 1940s Erich Fromm had suggested that totalitarian movements appealed to a deep-seated craving to surrender freedom. But by 1955 he was arguing in *The Sane Society* that twentieth-century democracy functions in much the same way. The principal modern experience was thus one of alienation, which he defined as the condition of being estranged from oneself: 'The alienated person is out of touch with himself as he is out of touch with any other person. He, like the others, is experienced as things are experienced; with the senses and with common sense, but at the same time without being related to oneself and to the world outside productively.'[3] That had, to be sure, been a principal theme of O'Neill's *The Hairy Ape*, Elmer Rice's *The Adding Machine* and Chaplin's film, *Modern Times*. It was just that at that time this had seemed little more than an inevitable by-product of capitalism. Now, after the horrors of Auschwitz and Hiroshima, as well as the depersonalising impact of the modern, it seemed more fundamental, so that Arthur Miller and his contemporaries might well have echoed Henry James's appalled remark when confronted with the slaughter of the First World War: 'To have to take it all now for what the treacherous years were all the while making for and *meaning* is too tragic for any words.'[4] Certainly a sense of shock is detectable in his own work. The disturbance is registered in characters who try to trace the origins of their own betrayals, and it is there in a language of resolution and completion so obviously at odds with the fragmenting personal psychologies and social discontinuities of the public world. Indeed, it was to take Miller some twenty years before he could locate those anxieties historically and another fifteen before he could revisit the 1930s of his youth and confront the moment of his own complicity in historic process.

Tennessee Williams was scarcely less apocalyptic. The coercive power of the public world is such that it deforms the self. His characters tread the margin of the social world but when they are pulled into it they are burned out. Their own neurotic energy generates a brief flame but it quickly consumes them just as the only future which he feels able to plot for society is one dominated by the low cunning of a Stanley Kowalski and his far more neanderthal descendants in *The Red Devil Battery Sign*, or ruled over by those literally cancerous representatives of the money powers who provoke the dislocation of public value. His characters are martyrs for a world which has already slipped away unmourned.

The vocabulary of both the absurd and existentialism reached America, but, as ever, very selective items were chosen from the intellectual smorgasbord. The absurd made little obvious headway, except as a European artifact to be admired or rejected as a cultural innovation or, more importantly, as a challenge to acting styles which were largely psychological in theory and naturalistic in practice. Not merely was it at odds with a potent American myth, having to do with purposeful motion and the integrity and centrality of the self, and not only had America not experienced the kind of trauma which Europe had suffered, but a largely Jewish-dominated intellectual world was not about to endorse a view which seemed to annihilate morality just when accusations had to be made.

Existentialism, on the other hand, did strike a spark. It could, without too much difficulty, be accommodated to liberal notions of moral responsibility and in its more acceptable form – the form given to it by Martin Buber in *I and Thou* – be made to endorse that faith in interpersonal relations which was a fundamental theme of American literary and philosophical thought and a useful substitute for that more strictly political solidarity which had been betrayed by Stalin. Thus, in America the loudly announced death of God bred not despair but a kind of desperate humanism. In the words of Yeats's poem:

> Now that my ladder's gone,
> I must lie down where all ladders start,
> In the foul rag-and-bone shop of the heart.[5]

For the former Marxist who had been anxious about an ideology which seemed to require the sacrifice of the concept of self as the price for social advance existentialism seemed to offer a way out. It eliminated determinism and gave meaning to the notion of choice but did so without demanding the dissolution of identity. In America, however, it tended to devolve into a faith in the utility, the power and the reality of personal relationships. Buber's tenets, drained of any theological content, became the substance of a secular faith hawked widely and with varying degrees of conviction by American writers from the Beats to James Baldwin, from Salinger to Carson McCullers. As Fromm put it, 'There is only one passion which satisfies man's need to unite himself with the world, and to acquire at the same time a sense of integrity and individuality, and this is *love. Love is union* with somebody, or something, outside oneself, *under the condition of retaining the separateness and integrity of one's own self.*'[6] This, in effect, becomes an apolitical version of that liberalism which could no longer find adequate political expression. It became Arthur Miller's theme as it did Tennessee Williams's and Edward Albee's. And it became the chief political slogan and theatrical objective of those in the 1960s who mobilised themselves, on the streets and on the stage, against the economic and military machine, who sought to transcend history with a gesture of grace. 'All we need is love' sang the Beatles in a round-the-world television link-up; and the confusion between Eros and Caritas was a feature of a period in which distinction and definition were felt to be egregious.

And the 1950s did offer the 1960s a legacy of sexual transcendence whose theory came from Herbert Marcuse (*Eros and Civilization*, 1955) and Norman O. Brown (*Life Against Death*, 1959), and whose literary model was provided by the Beats. This particular blend of radical politics and sexual exuberance proved a potent one, even if both its ideology and its psychotherapeutic bases were vague in the extreme. But some kind of spiritual sanction seemed available in the form of a domesticated Zen Buddhism whose emphasis on a simple acceptance of the natural world and an acknowledgement of the unity of experience and being was somehow distilled from the essence of a faith from which all religious conviction had been successfully evacuated. Indeed, in the 1960s Zen became little more than the origin of a holistic imagery, or the source of those chance procedures which John Cage employed in the composition of his music, and which creators of 'happenings' chose to use in the creation of their work – that, and a sense of the value of epiphany.

As the 1960s progressed so the refusal of boundaries, the conviction that all peoples meet at the level of the body, became not merely a simple piety but a political assertion. For that conviction tended to be invoked against the divisive authority of national and international policy. Racism and war were to be overcome with a proffered grace to be obtained through abnegation of the rational, which was tainted with scientism and deceit. Truth was presumed to lie beneath the social mask and thus the stripping of social role became a route to authenticity at first symbolised and then achieved by a literal stripping of the individual being.

For Erving Goffman, in *The Presentation of the Self in Everyday Life*, the self was by its very nature performatic. In analysing social process he turned quite naturally to the theatre, as did psychotherapists anxious to trace the path of trauma to its root. And American society was anyway in process of theatricalising itself. The public demonstrations, so much a part of life in the 1960s, were a very self-conscious form of theatre designed for the television screen and offering evidence of authenticity. Presence was all. The insertion of the self into the body politic and the body cultural seemed to offer some kind of guarantee of sincerity. In a public march people mingled with one another; social, economic and racial distinctions dissolved, indeed their dissolution was in part the essence of the occasion. It was only logical, therefore, that the theatre, which suddenly found itself offered as paradigm of social process, psychoanalytic procedure and communitarian ethos, also sought the dissolution of division. For a brief time the theatrical event and the political event genuinely seemed part of a continuum and it was only logical and natural for people to flow freely between them. Thus the Living Theatre spilled onto the streets of New Haven; the Bread and Puppet Theatre took its mute figures to Washington. And they did so in the same spirit in which Norman Mailer went to the Pentagon. To witness, to attend, was to become real. By the same token, theatre, or this particular part of theatre, the one concerned with exploring the nature of performance in a context charged with politics but drained of any precise ideology, became less concerned with re-enacting a pre-existent text than with enactment. And the religious overtones were deliberate if in some fundamental sense fraudulent. In part their claim to significance did not so much lie in the precise configuration of their performance, in the power of their language or gestures, as in the simple fact of their mutual coexistence. To have been there was to have shared a mystery. To have been absent was to have missed the wedding.

For others, though, the emerging issues of race, poverty and the Vietnam war were to be tackled more directly. The theatre became a necessary tool for the reconstruction of identity and the assertion of moral necessities. At first, in the form of a play like Lorraine Hansberry's *A Raisin in the Sun* (1959), this accommodated itself to the orthodoxies of Broadway. This was equally true of James Baldwin's *Blues for Mr Charlie* (1964). But quickly thereafter it sought out its own audience beyond the confines of a theatre which came to be seen as institutional evidence of the very system against which a newly politicised generation was in revolt. Consensus politics had collapsed as had consensus morality and religion. There was no longer a single audience to be addressed, if in truth there ever had been. Now blacks, women, Chicanos, gays, Indians and Chinese addressed themselves, displayed an image of themselves bestriding the stage, the central characters in their own drama rather than marginal figures in some national pageant. And the dramatic form itself began to fragment and re-form. If the question of the real was a social issue it was also a dramatic one. How could language, corrupted by the politicians and the military, redolent with racist and sexist assumptions, be granted any authority? How could character, so easily adjusted to public myths and social stereotypes, be regarded as unproblematic? How could the coherences of plot withstand the deconstructive pressure of experience?

Thus, though the post-war theatre started on a high note, with

O'Neill's flawed masterpieces and the emergence of Arthur Miller and Tennessee Williams, by the end of the 1950s it was apparent that American drama could no longer rest its reputation on the achievement of two writers whose work seemed increasingly to speak to a generation whose perceptions, social priorities and aesthetic criteria were forged in an earlier age; whose conception of theatre, in other words, derived out of Chekhov, Ibsen, and Strindberg rather than Pirandello, Beckett and Artaud, or, perhaps late rather than early Ibsen, early rather than late Strindberg, and the Chekhov of *The Cherry Orchard* rather than the Chekhov of *The Seagull*. By the end of the decade Arthur Miller was four years into what was to become a nine-year silence in so far as the theatre was concerned, and Tennessee Williams had entered an increasingly embarrassing period of decline. Even the posthumous mining of O'Neill's work had finally come to an end. There was, in fact, a real sense of crisis in the American theatre, a crisis which went much deeper than the apparent decline or actual disappearance of its major dramatists. Thus, if it was partly a matter of faltering talent and a growing gulf between the Broadway audience and those who chose to recast their sense of social and spiritual alienation into moral or poetic dramas which seemed to ironise a nostalgia which they otherwise wished to embrace, it was also a question of economics and the destructive hit-or-miss ethos of commercial theatre. In this respect the career of William Inge is perhaps instructive.

Inge was a fragile individual, insecure, prone to rely on alcohol and needing psychiatric help. But a certain amount of his bewilderment derived from his sudden success and the equally sudden failure which followed it. From 1950 to 1957 he had four successful productions on Broadway (*Come Back, Little Sheba*, 1950; *Picnic*, 1953; *Bus Stop*, 1955; *The Dark at the Top of the Stairs*, 1957), but he followed these with a series of commercial and critical disasters. Retreating to the west coast he wrote one successful screenplay (*Splendour in the Grass*) and then again failed to repeat his success. He turned to teaching, writing to fellow playwright William Gibson that, 'I guess it's curtains for me, since my beloved theatre doesn't want me.'[7] In 1973 he committed suicide.

For Gibson, he was in part at least a victim of the Broadway system. Comparing it to the supportive ethos of the pre-war Group Theatre he found it a world without loyalty or enterprise, a world which had abandoned Clifford Odets as readily as it had Inge because, by the commercial standards which it applied, they were no longer felt to be good risks. As Gibson observed, 'Directors are interested in successes . . . Like everybody else in the theatre . . . a director doesn't want to direct a play if he thinks it's going to flop.' It is a 'dollars and cents operation'.[8]

And theatre itself was changing. The economic base seemed to be collapsing. Inge's career folded as Broadway itself approached one of its regular crises. Actor Philip Proctor observed that, 'I went into the theatre because I wanted to do many different parts, attempt different kinds of acting. I wanted to try things beyond my capacity and sometimes shine and sometimes fall on my face . . . And I saw Broadway wasn't built that way any more. It *had* been. Back when it was economically feasible, everybody worked much more, took more risks. But now they couldn't afford it.'[9] Walter Kerr, reviewing for the *Herald Tribune*, dated the decline from 1951 when he joined the paper. For Clive Barnes of *The New York Times*, Broadway, by the 1970s, had become simply 'a commercial shop window' while, for the critic and director Harold Clurman, it was 'the ghetto of the theater' in which there was little room for anything besides comedies, musicals and British imports. It would be wrong to claim that Inge was entirely a victim of the system – in part the wistful sentimentality of his work, the nostalgia for personal and social innocence, no longer seemed credible – but Broadway became increasingly less willing to accommodate anything that did not seem to guarantee a substantial return on investment.

In many ways Inge represented Broadway at its best. It is true that his work is theatrically and socially unadventurous. It is carefully sculpted, moving towards an apparent resolution. Character is ready-formed, close to the stereotype. His work is full of young people on the brink of a maturity which will apparently bring pain and consolation in roughly equal amounts. It is full of appealing drunks, forgiving wives, and men facing middle age and the loss of illusions with such dignity as they can muster. But he was more than this. His power lay in his sensitive evocation of small-town America. In plays like *Come Back, Little Sheba*, *Picnic*, *Bus Stop* and *The Dark at the Top of the Stairs* he examined the petty frustrations and painful determinisms of desperate lives, while for the most part celebrating the simple processes of life much as had Thornton Wilder. His world is not remote from that of Tennessee Williams, in so far as his characters also seem to have been born out of their time, to be terrified of loneliness and of that loss of freedom which stems from the very personal relationships with which they seek to neutralise that loneliness. But where Williams deliberately puts his characters under extreme pressure – breaks them on the rack of time or permits their apocalyptic destruction – Inge holds back. His subject is compromise. Williams has no interest in those who fail to risk everything in their efforts to sustain illusion, to impose the artist's vision on a world resistant to art. Inge has the realist's concern with articulating the plight of those for whom such gestures are impossible or merely ironic. His works offer a series of tableaux. The energy of his plays is generated not so much by the melodramatic gesture (though he is pulled towards melodrama) as by the small change of daily life. His characters have all in some sense or another been betrayed by life. Doc in *Come Back, Little Sheba* and Rubin Flood in *The Dark at the Top of the Stairs* have both been trapped into marriage by an unwanted pregnancy; Dr Lyman in *Bus Stop* is seemingly impelled to molest young girls; Madge in *Picnic* runs off with a young spendthrift, perhaps thereby redeeming herself from a blank existence but perhaps entering into the kind of commitment which entraps so many of Inge's characters. Something of his appeal, indeed, lies precisely in the fact that his plays deal with the familiar processes: young love and disillusionment, the betrayal of youthful aspirations, the imperfections of daily existence, loneliness and the loss of freedom. And if he never presses this to the point of tragedy, then pathos is not without its appeal.

He himself has observed:

> I have never sought to write plays that primarily tell a story; nor have I sought deliberately to create new forms. I have been most concerned with dramatizing something of the dynamism I myself find in human motivations and behavior. I regard a play as a composition rather than a story, as a distillation of life rather than a narration of it. It is only in this way that I feel myself a real contemporary.[10]

What he offers is, in effect, a kind of soft-centred naturalism in which his characters are products of their own inner compulsions and of the small-town environment in which they live. Virtually all of his characters are lower middle class, and feel trapped by their own limited physical and spiritual possibilities. Marriage thus becomes a crucial avenue of escape. But this is liable to resolve itself into a choice between a relationship contracted for pragmatic reasons, and one contracted for love which offers nothing but an endless projection of deprivation.

He adopts no political or social stance. Admittedly, on the whole, Inge's wealthy characters are incorrigibly prejudiced and cruel but his concern is not with the need for reform. He wishes merely to dramatise the ironies of a life which starts with such naive and vigorous hope and seems to end with at best a sad compromise. In *Bus Stop* and *Come Back, Little Sheba* the young couples do opt for love but in both cases the naivety of the partners is such as to threaten a commitment which resolves the action but not the moral dilemma. This is where the interest of Inge lies, for his resolutions are not as secure as they seem and if there is a patent sentimentality in the assumptions which underly his naturalism, no less than in his manipulation of character and plot, there is an irony which undercuts even the assurance of his own logic.

Inge was aware that 'commercial theatre only builds on what has already been created, contributing only theatre back into the theatre. Creative theatre brings something of life itself, which gives the theatre something new to grow on. But when new life comes to us, we don't always recognize it. New life doesn't always survive on Broadway. It's considered risky.'[11] In fact his first Broadway success only survived for six months and that by virtue of the author and actors accepting a salary cut, but his subsequent work in the first half of the 1950s, in which he 'sought breadth instead of depth', was successful and his own description of his objective is perhaps not irrelevant to that success. As he has said, 'Writing for a big audience, I deal with surfaces in my plays, and let whatever depths there are in my material emerge unexpectedly',[12] while even his own descriptions of the characters in *Bus Stop* underline the degree to which those figures can be all too adequately summed up by reference to their plot function: 'The cowboy's eagerness, awkwardness, and naivety in seeking love were interesting only when seen in comparison, in the same setting, with the amorality of Cherie, the depravity of the professor, the casual earthiness of Grace and Carl, the innocence of the schoolgirl Elma, and the defeat of his buddy Virgil.'[13] Inge's plays offer a simple morality. In one sense it is no more than the need to endorse a guileless submission to the processes of life. He dramatises the betrayals, needs and consolations of life in a homely setting rendered disturbing precisely because of its familiarity. But he tends to resist equally the tragic and absurdist interpretation of small-town life, refusing to probe for a more fundamental collapse of meaning and purpose.

Though the persistence of cowboys and harness salesmen perhaps hints at a lost national myth which is never really spelled out, his plays, which are set in the Midwest, are offered less as regional portraits than as universal symbols. His characters, always verging on the stereotype, gain their meaning from the total context of performance. But even thus reassembled theirs is a world deprived of transcendence, with no spiritual dimension, no purpose to serve beyond a sexual impulse which is only momentarily liberating. They have dreams, reach out towards something vaguely perceived, but never realise those dreams or embrace anything but human flesh which turns out to be the springing of a biological trap. His hermetic stage sets (his characters are trapped in their midwestern homes, in backyards which are the reductive residue of frontier, in an isolated bus station) stand as images of the caged world which his characters inhabit. They respond, like Williams's characters, to the call of the wild, the sound of a train whistle. In the case of Hal, in *Picnic*, he even creates a figure who is close kin to Val Xavier in *Orpheus Descending*, or Chance Wayne in *Sweet Bird of Youth*. But there is no other world which he can set out for. He has no resources on which he can draw. He is not destroyed by a vindictive capitalism, though he is pursued by it; he simply has nothing to offer beyond a sexual energy which is apparently redemptive. Since neither he nor the girl he seduces know what to make of what has happened to them their flight is presented as less an escape than another turn of the wheel of fate.

As we see in his other plays, those who keep on the road or seek to opt out of the daily routine are as afflicted with loneliness as anyone else. In *The Dark at the Top of the Stairs* Rubin Flood is a Willy Loman figure, a salesman who, like Willy, buys stockings for his mistress while keeping his wife short of money. But where in Miller's play this betrayal is linked to other more fundamental betrayals, in Inge's it is a function of the loneliness which seems to affect all of his characters, the emptiness against which they battle. As another character in the same play observes, 'I talk all the time just to convince myself that I'm alive. And I stuff myself with victuals just to feel I've got something inside me.'[14] His characters inhabit a world at once familiar and strange. As Rubin says, 'I'm a stranger in the very land I was born in . . . sometimes I wonder if it's not a lot easier to pioneer a country than it is to settle down in it.'[15] This strange land is Inge's subject. For a time it seems to have struck a chord with the American public but, with the exception of his screenplay, *Splendour in the Grass* (1961), he never thereafter recaptured his popular success. The wistful romanticism of his plays – his concern with the minutiae of life, with an unconfident adolescence, a sentimental account of human relationships – seems to have addressed itself to a sense of anxiety in the culture which Miller and Williams similarly acknowledged. The fact that his success did not survive into the 1960s should be seen in the context of their careers, which similarly faltered in a decade when art was more self-consciously experimental, more single-mindedly concerned with social and political issues, more committed to seeing in sexuality a liberating force and in the theatre a model of the perfect society. The 1960s on the whole staged a debate between utopias and dystopias (*America Hurrah!*). It had little room for the ambiguities of small-town America except where, in *Who's Afraid of Virginia Woolf?*, this was presented in apocalyptic terms.

For William Inge, Thornton Wilder, Carson McCullers and Robert Anderson, the small American town offered its own image of alienation, its cultural aridities providing a correlative for a bleak public world, its sentimentalities the only relief from the natural pains of domestic tedium. As writers, they tended to examine the plight of the solitary individual left behind by the tide of American progress to struggle with the intrusive fact of his or her own insignificance, or the distorting

realities of his or her sexual being. It is a theatre which takes as its subject
the baffled, the lonely, the adolescent, the failed. It provides a psychopathology of the American individual but does so, for the most part,
without questioning the nature of that society or the metaphysics of
moral responsibility. With the exception of Wilder's experimentalism, it
is conservative in form and attitude. Life tends to be pictured as the slow
unfolding of a determined pattern. A sentimental consolation is found in
the sheer transmutation of youth into age, the flaring of love, and the
phantoms of nostalgia – the kind of process, in other words, with which
Miller flirts in *Death of a Salesman* but to which be finally refuses to
succumb. It is a theatre, moreover, which could have been written at any
time in the previous thirty years. Yet the affecting images of quiet
desperation found in *Our Town, Come Back, Little Sheba, All Summer
Long*, and *The Member of the Wedding* created a kind of domestic pathos
which proved popular for a while on Broadway and, subsequently, with
provincial audiences. But the peremptory ending of Inge's career was not
unconnected with the increasing economic vulnerability of Broadway.
Delicate studies of human need could no longer command the kind of
audience required to sustain a production over the period needed to
ensure a return on investment while Off-Broadway looked for something rather more aesthetically radical than Inge could offer. His bafflement is clear in his public statements and his letters, and the system cannot
be completely absolved of responsibility for his death.

Of course it was still possible to succeed on Broadway. As the
playwright Robert Anderson once remarked, you may not be able to
make a living on Broadway but you can make a killing. And no one has
proved that more spectacularly than Neil Simon. Simon comes from a
background not dissimilar to that of Arthur Miller. Like him he was born
in New York City, the son of a man in the garment industry. He, too,
graduated from university and began his career writing for the media.
For a number of years he was a comedy writer for CBS and NBC,
writing for Phil Silvers, Tallulah Bankhead and Sid Caesar, among
others. His first Broadway success, *Come Blow Your Horn*, was produced
in February 1961. A master of the one-line gag, his strength lies in
creating familiar situations – a son leaving home (*Come Blow Your Horn*),
a quarrel between husband and wife (*Barefoot in the Park*), a man leaving
his wife (*The Odd Couple*) – which are pressed beyond the point of simple
realism. His drama exists for the moment in which the dull individual,
who can apparently be adequately described by his social and economic
class, is transformed by the writer who himself 'suddenly dashes for
cover behind his protective cloak called skin and peers out unseen . . .
unnoticed, a gleeful, malicious smirk on his face watching, penetrat-

ing . . . probing the movements, manners and absurd gestures of those ridiculous creatures performing their inane daily functions'.[16] It is a moment which could generate an absurdist account but which usually devolves into purest farce. Simon flirts with anarchy; he doesn't finally succumb to it. And the assurance that he won't perhaps accounts for his appeal to Broadway audiences. He offers pathos rather than tragedy, nostalgia rather than guilt. What Miller turns into social drama Simon turns into comedy.

In some moods his characters are terrified of the world which they inhabit but they are, in the end, reconciled with a graceful turn of phrase, a joke, a sentimentality paraded as fundamental truth. His women tend to be mindless blondes, simple *ingénues*, feeble-minded Jewish mothers, but they earn some kind of respect through the writer's sleight of hand and through the sheer pace of the wit. But every now and then a moment of pure pain is enacted, the vacuous life behind the wisecrack momentarily exposed to view and, indeed, taken together, his plays do actually offer an extraordinarily bleak view of American life, a glimpse of a deeply uncommunal people desperately asserting the need for some kind of communality. The system is breaking down; people are breaking down. They are the victims of impulses, neurosis, emotions which they seem incapable of controlling. They inhabit a world which seems to conspire against them, objects asserting some kind of petty will over those who use them. His apartments and his rooms are for the most part cheerless places, scarcely homes for those who find themselves enacting their adulteries, marital conflicts or bachelor existences in them. The urban and suburban world which he dramatises is a place of partial beings, incomplete people, living in a setting to which they feel no connection, but apparently all they need to reconcile themselves to this setting is a gesture of love or companionship, a commitment, often, to the very marriage which he otherwise identifies as the very root of a profound disenchantment — a trap, a snare for the free spirit who nonetheless cannot bear the weight of that freedom. It is a paradox which he does not examine but which in some ways accounts for his fascination as a writer. But the gestures of reconciliation which clearly make him an attractive Broadway writer are never entirely adequate to the alienation which he identifies. Every so often his characters reveal a vulnerability which goes beyond their otherwise patent vacuity. For the most part the product is, to be sure, a kind of ersatz profundity, but from time to time there is a suggestion of something more, and it is this which, for some critics, sustains interest in a man who is otherwise regarded as the master of formula drama. Certainly his plays express precisely that sense of anxiety, guilt and moral ambivalence which writers like Miller and

Williams have equally made the centre of their own work, but he does so in a way and in a context which tends to release the tension which he has created, to deflect into humour and sentimentality what they chose to project to the point of personal and social crisis. The latter, however, the Broadway audience had shown itself increasingly disinclined to accept and hence the Broadway producers increasingly disinclined to stage.

The crisis in the American theatre was, in part at least, a question of economics. In 1929 there were seventy-five Broadway theatres used for legitimate productions; by 1959 the figure was thirty-four. In 1929 there were 233 new productions; in 1959 there were only fifty-six. And costs had increased between six and eight fold. In the 1920s a run of 100 performances (three months) was considered sufficient to recoup investment; by the 1960s it was estimated to require eight months for a play and ten to eleven months of capacity business for a musical. The physical decline of the Broadway area, increasingly given over, in the 1960s and 70s, to blue movie houses, added to the rise in ticket prices, contributed to a sense of crisis. Jack Poggi has pointed out that of the eleven men who started writing plays in the 1920s and whose reputation survives – O'Neill, Barry, Howard, Anderson, Rice, Kelly, Sherwood, Behrman, Green, Kaufman and Connelly (a number of whose stars are, to be honest, somewhat in eclipse) – only O'Neill and Green did not do most of their early work on Broadway. Fewer major figures began their careers on Broadway in the 1930s – Odets, Hellman, Saroyan and Wilder (in the case of Odets, indeed, it was with the Group Theatre, scarcely a typical Broadway company). In the 1940s only Miller and Williams and perhaps William Inge carried the flag.

The American musical might remain a dominant and even innovative form but the non-musical stage seemed to have lost a sense of direction and purpose. And it is worth reminding ourselves that in Europe Beckett and Ionesco had begun writing in the 1940s at about the same time as Miller and Williams were scoring their first successes. If the British rediscovery of naturalism in the mid 1950s was of greater significance in a national rather than an international context, it is still true that for a generation of English writers the theatre was regarded as the centre of cultural life in a way which seemed scarcely credible in the United States. There was little opportunity for the young American writer to emerge. America lacked the German civic theatre tradition. It had no access to federal, state, local or foundation funding on any scale. It had a television service which, after a brief golden age, had mostly ceased to provide the kind of outlet for new writers that the BBC did in Britain, though occasional series like CBS's *East Side/West Side* revealed a potential for serious naturalistic drama which was aborted when the series was discontinued. Arnold Perl's *Who Do You Kill?* (1963), an impressive episode from the series, survives only as a file copy. Unlike many European countries, America had no national theatre, and when one was established at Lincoln Center in 1964, it failed to act as a stimulus for new writing. The universities, many of them better equipped than most commercial theatres in Europe, did nothing to rescue the situation. Renewal, when it came, could scarcely derive from Broadway, with its union problems, high costs, debilitating star system, vulnerability to poor reviews, and deteriorating physical situation.

Touring theatres had long since collapsed. At the turn of the century there had been 327 of them. By 1915 this had shrunk to less than 100 and from 1932 the number never rose above twenty-five. The number of commercial theatres in the country had dropped from 590 in 1927 to barely 200 by the beginning of the 1960s. New regional theatres had been founded but the growth was slow. The first resident professional company (the Barter Theatre in Abingdon, Virginia) was formed in 1932. The second and third (the Alley Theatre, Houston, and the Theatre in the Round at Dallas) did not follow until twenty-five years later. Though to these were added the Arena Stage in Washington (1950), the Actors'. Workshop in San Francisco (1952) and the American Shakespeare Festival in Stratford, Connecticut (1955), by 1959 there were still only eight such theatres.

Nor was the crisis simply a matter of economics and the simple decline of theatre capacity. More crucially it was a matter of attitudes and a basic cultural parochialism.

When Herbert Blau started the San Francisco Actors' Workshop at the beginning of the 1950s the standards were those of Broadway: 'We even used to copy our sets out of old *Theatre Arts* because, give and take a little imaginative revision, that's what designers were taught to do in the schools. We borrowed both plays and performances. There weren't many ideas to pick up, but nobody told us you were supposed to have them.'[17] What began to break this dependent relationship with Broadway in his own case was firstly the emergence of a new European theatre (the Workshop was responsible for the famous production of *Waiting for Godot* presented at San Quentin) and secondly the creative energy not only of Blau and his co-director Jules Irving but also of all those other members of the Workshop who would later contribute to the emergence of a new and varied theatre – R.G. Davis (who founded the San Francisco Mime Troupe within the Workshop), Lee Breuer (of Mabou Mines), Andre Gregory (of Manhattan Project) and Ken Dewey (of Action Events). Blau himself returned from Europe in 1959 determined to create a truly popular theatre in the mode of Jean Vilar's French

20

experiment. This did not mean radical plays but an attempt to adjust the rhythms of theatre to the pulse of history and to reach out beyond the sacred college of the middle class in order to address and move those relegated to the margin of political, economic and cultural life. That European influence proved crucial. Though the theatre of the absurd proved philosophically incompatible it destabilised not merely notions of dramatic coherence but also methods of actor training. And the first appearance in English of Antonin Artaud's *The Theatre and Its Double* in 1958 provided much of the theoretical underpinning for the experiments of the coming decade.

It was also in 1959 and also in San Francisco that Ronnie Davis founded the San Francisco Mime Troupe. He shared Blau's conviction of the need to create a theatre which would reach out to those for whom reprocessed Broadway plays had no relevance. He was also concerned with extending the range of theatrical experiment. In that regard both he and Blau were close kin to Julian Beck and Judith Malina whose own theatrical experiments reached some kind of climax in that same year in New York. The Living Theatre, which like Blau's group had been operating for some time, created, in the form of Jack Gelber's *The Connection*, a play whose social, philosophical and theatrical implications made it seem suddenly central to contemporary experience. This is not to say that it commanded large audiences but that for virtually the first time an original American play, performed off Broadway, had attracted the attention and, in part at least, the respect of drama critics and the interest of theatre practitioners in America and Europe. That latter fact did something to undermine a sense of parochialism on the part of those who had perhaps deferred to foreign models for rather too long, though the impact of Artaud and later Grotowski suggested the degree to which, on the level of theory and actor training, a certain restricting deference remained. But if we add to the success of *The Connection* the emergence, also in 1959 and also off Broadway, of Edward Albee (with *The American Dream* and *The Zoo Story*) and the creation the following year of Cafe La Mama, founded by Ellen Stewart, it is, perhaps, no wonder that suddenly there was a feeling that the American theatre had found itself. The collapse of political consensus at the end of the 1950s had its theatrical correlative. There were now many audiences, some defined racially, some politically, some aesthetically, and Off-Broadway, Off-Off Broadway (which also began to emerge in 1959), and a newly constituted regional theatre were ready to address them. At the beginning of a new decade, with a new young President for whom the arts represented more than an occasional western novel, change seemed in the air. But Off-Broadway did not spring into existence in 1959 fully formed. What it did do was to change its emphasis, to adopt a different series of priorities.

Off-Broadway was born in 1915 with the first production of the Washington Square Players and with the first experiments of the Provincetown Players – the one sturdily professional, the other staunchly amateur. Where they agreed was in their conviction that theatre could aspire to more than technical virtuosity, rhetorical acting and melodramatic displays. Though these were followed by a wide variety of groups, in the 1920s and 30s, they were mostly united in defining themselves in opposition to the theatrical, commercial and, on occasion, political values of Broadway. On the whole such groups performed plays unlikely to receive Broadway production and looked for an audience substantially different from that which patronised the uptown theatre.

In its post-war phase Off-Broadway dates from the production, in 1947, by a group calling themselves New Stages, of *The Lamp at Midnight* by Barrie Stavis. They acquired a cinema in Bleecker Street (Greenwich Village) and, in order to circumvent city building and fire regulations, removed all but 299 seats from the auditorium. As Stuart Little has pointed out, thereafter this became the maximum size of an Off-Broadway audience for purposes of union negotiations. New Stages' policy was to select 'plays by new writers, revivals of classics not frequently seen, first American productions of foreign plays, and new or unproduced plays by established writers'.[18] Though it had only a brief life a number of other groups quickly sprang up, including, in 1948, Interplayers, which launched the careers of Kim Stanley, Michael Gazzo and Anthony Franciosa. Indeed, in 1949, five groups came together and formed the Off-Broadway League of Theatres, partly in order to negotiate an arrangement with Actors' Equity whose members were accepting less than Equity rates in order to work in fringe theatre and who were working with non-union labour. The League, which existed because of 'the obvious inability of the existing commercial theatre to provide a place for serious young theatre people', and which is 'generally recognized as being the precipitating fact for the Off-Broadway theater movement',[19] arrived at a compromise which held until the mid 1960s.

The principal groups, formed within a year or so of one another, were the Living Theatre (1951), the Circle in the Square (1951), the Phoenix Theatre (1953) and the New York Shakespeare Festival (1954), though several others of significance also operated, including the Artists' Theatre which between 1953 and 1956 produced, among other plays, Frank O'Hara's *Try, Try* (1953), John Ashberry's *The Heroes* (1953) and James Merrill's *The Bait* (1953), all verse dramas and hence extremely unlikely to receive Broadway production.

If *The Lamp at Midnight* technically marked the post-war revival of Off-Broadway, it was José Quintero's revival of Tennessee Williams's *Summer and Smoke* at the Circle in the Square which provided its first major success. Originally performed on Broadway during the run of *A Streetcar Named Desire*, it had understandably suffered by comparison. Now, produced in a more intimate setting, its values became apparent. Indeed the intimate nature of these theatres – a consequence of the practical necessities forced on such groups by restricted budgets and the limited availability of suitable premises – became in time the basis of a self-conscious aesthetic practice, as did a production style which of necessity emphasised simplicity. Circle in the Square was born out of the enthusiasm of a group of actors who took over a theatre in Woodstock, New York, in the late 1940s. In 1950, the director, José Quintero, and the group's business manager, Theodore Mann, rented a nightclub in Sheridan Square, Greenwich Village, and transformed the circular dance floor into an arena stage. They lived together, in accommodation above the theatre, and at first solicited donations as other such groups would do in the 1960s and for much the same reason. Their production style and their economic and social organisation were essentially a pragmatic response to their circumstances. But Circle in the Square did mark a significant shift of emphasis and Carlotta O'Neill entrusted her husband's finest work to them.

The Phoenix, by contrast, which declared as its objective the need to 'release actors, directors, playwrights, and designers from the pressures forced on them by the hit-or-flop patterns of Broadway',[20] was hardly the penurious group which we are used to associate with Off-Broadway. Thanks to the efforts of Norris Houghton and Edward Hambleton, assisted by the ubiquitous Roger Stevens, it began with a capital of $125,000 and an 1,100-seat theatre. Nor were its productions particularly adventurous, though it did sustain a commitment to classic theatre. But it was an important alternative centre of creative energy which was not so subject to the peremptory fiat of the businessman and the accountant, though it was scarcely free of such influence.

Joseph Papp, who became an increasingly important figure through the 1960s, 70s and 80s, established a workshop in 1953 in a church basement in order to develop the American actor's technique in playing Shakespeare. It gave its first indoor performance in 1958, following this a year later with its first outdoor production, and, in 1962, moving to a permanent site in Central Park as the New York Shakespeare Festival Theatre. Its announced aim was 'to create a style of acting not too internal, not too bombastic, so that poetic plays could be done on the stage in a highly realistic way, without sacrificing the poetry and the style'.[21] By 1970 Papp had four companies (the Public Theatre being the most important of these) and employed more actors than any other institution in the country. Scarcely modest in his productions or ambitions, he became an increasingly important figure as he set himself to encourage the work of young writers and to develop a theatre which would respond to shifts in social no less than aesthetic concerns.

None of these groups, however, at first set themselves steadfastly to locate new American dramatists, though the Living Theatre, which was of central significance in the 1960s and whose objective was 'to explore untried methods and techniques for the extension of the boundaries of theatrical expression',[22] did produce the work of Paul Goodman, William Carlos Williams and Jackson Maclow, and with the arrival of the new decade Off-Broadway began to shift its emphasis somewhat. The Living Theatre itself launched the careers of Jack Gelber and Kenneth Brown and even the Phoenix produced Arthur Kopit's satiric response to the theatre of the absurd, *Oh Dad Poor Dad Mama's Hung You in the Closet and I'm Feeling So Sad*.

Off-Broadway in the 1950s fulfilled a number of functions. It was a showcase for young actors and actresses (Geraldine Page, George C. Scott, Jason Robards Jr., and Peter Falk). Indeed, to be fair, it has never lost that function, in the 1960s producing Dustin Hoffman, Faye Dunaway, Al Pacino and Stacey Keach, and in the 1970s Judd Hirsch, Meryl Streep, William Hurt and Christopher Reeve. It provided a stage for the revival of American and European classics, and it created an environment in which the commercially unprofitable could survive if not flourish. It was, however, rather less concerned with sponsoring new American writers. It showed little interest in exploring the nature of the theatrical experience and none at all in the possibility of redefining the relationship between the theatre and society. This now began to change. In the 1957–8 season, for the first time, there were more productions Off-Broadway than on and by the 1959–60 season, in which for the first time more than $1 million was invested, there were twice as many productions Off-Broadway as on. In the following year it was three times as many. The sheer volume of productions created a demand for plays by new writers and such writers duly appeared. First, Jack Gelber, Edward Albee and Jack Richardson and then a plethora of others.

In the 1960s, then, the American theatre seemed to stir. It ceased to concern itself quite so much with the dramatisation of the liberal conscience or the plight of the poetic sensibility forced back against the reality of an experience which was hinted at but rarely presented. Suddenly, theatre was forcing a space for itself beyond Broadway. It moved beyond the environs of 42nd Street to the Lower East Side and then to Harlem, to the west coast, to the regions, to the urban centres of

24

the North and the rural areas of the South. As the decade advanced it operated in art galleries, in prisons, on the streets and, in the form of happenings, anywhere. It frequently involved non-professional actors and directors, and writers who were painters, sculptors and dancers. It was partly an aesthetic and partly a social revolt. It was not for the most part a planned revolution. There were occasional commissars energised by a tantalising glimpse of the revolution, just as there were others adding their efforts to those who were fighting to restore America to its principles in the face of racism, exploitation and militarism. But, more than that, the theatre, with its concern with role-playing, its existential thrust, its power to engage the public world, not merely found itself able, literally, to act out the public issues of the day but saw its own procedures being borrowed by psychotherapists, sociologists, teachers and critical theorists. The counter-cultural fascination with communes and a re-newed sense of group identity, in process of being asserted by various sub-groups, found a paradigm in the theatre group. Robert Wilson, a major figure of the 1970s, moved with ease from self-awareness sessions and therapy into theatre and back again.

The arts seemed to interact as seldom before in American life. The energy which invested theatre groups betokened an optimism which was not independent of that which typified the culture. The Kennedy administration, when it was not busy laying down the foundation for future disaster abroad, moved cultural matters closer to the centre of affairs than they had been at any time since the Roosevelt years. And though Johnson's policies placed him increasingly at odds with intellec-tuals no less than with those others who wished to deflect their country from policies which they regarded as immoral and unwise, the Poverty Programme put money into the hands of the community theatre groups as it did into those of assorted crooks and saints. LeRoi Jones's Black Arts Repertory Theatre had been financed through OEO (Office of Eco-nomic Opportunity) money under Kennedy, much to the disgust of Sergeant Shriver, and other groups benefited similarly under Johnson. The urgencies of the political situation – in 1967 and 1968 riots flared across America while in 1968 the Tet Offensive exposed the falsehoods of the American military – provoked a reaction in the theatre as in society at large. The civil rights movement inspired a similar response from Chicanos, Indians, women and gays. And these turned to the theatre as the most public of public arts not subject to the economic exigencies of television and Hollywood. Political activism led on the one hand to the re-emergence of agit-prop as a form – the need for a didactic drama identifying heroes and villains, the raising of political consciousness – and on the other hand to celebratory rituals, the intensified materialism of a booming war economy prompting a renewed interest in the secular ceremonies of theatre.

By 1970, for the first time, both the Pulitzer Prize and the New York Critics' Circle Award had gone to Off-Broadway shows: to Paul Zindell's *The Effect of Gamma Rays on Man-in-the-Moon Marigolds*, and Charles Gordone's *No Place to be Somebody*. This, however, is a useful reminder of the fact that Off-Broadway could successfully accommodate the conventional as well as the innovative. Indeed, not only was Off-Broadway in constant danger of resembling the Broadway which it had set out to reject but it also began to suffer from the same malaise – running into severe financial difficulties. When the Living Theatre, with Marxist leanings and a desire to open itself to something other than the middle-class and student audience, found itself charging $4.75 for a ticket in 1963, it was plainly in trouble – ideological and not simply financial. The very success of Off-Broadway was potentially its undoing, with theatre owners raising their rental and Equity pressing for higher rates. In fact in the 1968–9 season, 92 per cent of investors Off-Broadway lost their money. In his book *New Broadways* Gerald Berkowitz quotes Edward Albee's observation that 'Off-Broadway is a losing proposition. The actors are not in it for the money. The producers are not in it for money. The Off-Broadway theater simply has to be subsidized by the actors, the producers, the playwrights, the directors.'

Thus it was that 1959 also marked the first stirrings of the logical next step from Off-Broadway – Off-Off Broadway. Joe Cino had opened his coffee house just before the turn of the year, in December 1958, while Ellen Stewart's Cafe La Mama (responsible for the emergence of such writers as Paul Foster, Jean-Claude Van Itallie, Lanford Wilson and Sam Shepard) was founded in 1960. Off-Off Broadway consisted of an amazing proliferation of theatre groups who performed in any convenient place and who frequently saw themselves as being in revolt against the aesthetic and political values of the society which they inhabited. They ranged from the Judson Poets' Theatre (which established the careers of Rosalyn Drexler, Maria Irene Fornes and Ronald Tavel), Theatre Genesis and the American Place Theatre, through to the Open Theatre, the Performance Group, the Playwrights' Unit and the Playhouse of the Ridiculous. It was Off-Off Broadway which staged the verse dramas of Robert Lowell, John Ashberry, James Scheville, Kenneth Koch, James Merrill, Frank O'Hara and others, and it was Off-Off Broadway which opened its door to homosexual theatre and to a genuine aesthetic radicalism. Indeed, for Paul Foster, the virtue of Off-Off Broadway was that it 'allows you to set your own pace. It does not have to please the audience – you can test out an idea. It gives you a chance to fail. And if you choose you can be involved with your work – and that of others; twenty-four hours a day.'[23]

The writer no longer necessarily felt compelled to seek the endorsement of Broadway. Lanford Wilson, whose career began Off-Off Broadway with Caffe Cino and Cafe La Mama, moved with ease to the Off-Broadway Circle Repertory Company but, despite his success there, for the most part resisted the blandishments of the Great White Way. His early plays were often sophisticated collages which offered a portrait of rural (*The Rimers of Eldritch*, 1966) and urban (*Balm in Gilead*, 1965) life. But already, there was a lyrical and even a sentimental dimension to his work which made later plays, such as *Lemon Sky* (1970), *The Hot 1 Baltimore* (1973), *Fifth of July* (1978) and *Talley's Folly* (1979) seem securely in a tradition which would include Thornton Wilder and William Inge. Two decades earlier Broadway might have constituted a natural home for such work, and Broadway, in turn, might well have been drawn to his gentle accounts of the outsider, his carefully shaped dramas of human need and resilience. One or two of his plays did eventually appear there, but Off-Broadway seemed to provide a more receptive environment.

And much the same logic applies to Israel Horovitz whose early, somewhat arcane, plays – *The Indian Wants the Bronx* and *It's Called the Sugar Plum* – gave way to rather more accessible work such as *The Alfred Trilogy* (1972–7) and *The Quannapowitt Quartet* (1974–6), which partly celebrated and partly dissected an American rural world. His plays were performed in a wide variety of venues, from the Eugene O'Neill Memorial Centre to the Magic Theatre in San Francisco, the Actors' Studio and the New York Shakespeare Festival. The fact was that the writer now felt free to experiment with styles, to explore ideas and approaches and even to alternate the esoteric and experimental with the consciously popular. Thus Albert Innaurato, who produced what he himself described as the 'frankly crazy' *Wisdom Amok*, was also capable of creating a Broadway success such as *Gemini*, insisting on his right to appeal to radically differing audiences. So, too, with John Guare. Like Lanford Wilson he started his career with Joe Cino (*Something I'll Tell You Tuesday*, 1965, and *The Loveliest Afternoon*, 1966) but he also found a receptive stage with Joe Papp (*Rich and Famous*, 1976; *Landscape of the Body*, 1977; *Marco Polo Sings a Solo*, 1977), with regional theatre (*Bosoms and Neglect* was performed at the Goodman Theatre, Chicago, in 1979) and with Lincoln Center (*In Fireworks Lie Secret Codes*, 1981). Indeed his best-known play – *The House of Blue Leaves* (1970) – though first read at the Eugene O'Neill Playwrights' Conference is familiar Broadway material in its gentle humour and its sentimental assumptions. Certainly his version of *The Two Gentlemen of Verona* proved one of the major successes of 1971 showing that the distinction between Broadway and Off-Broadway was not always a clear one.

Nonetheless, the emergence of this alternative theatre was of critical importance and its rapid expansion a sign of crucial changes in the economics and politics of culture. Between 1960 and 1982 the number of Off and Off-Off Broadway shows increased from nineteen to 132 in an average week, and by 1981 there were eighty-four members of the Off-Off Broadway Alliance and over 200 Off-Off Broadway theatres. By their very nature, however, such groups tend to be transitory. Only eight of the eighty-four had existed prior to 1968, while a third of them were founded during or after 1975. As Joe Papp remarked of Off-Off Broadway, writing in 1981, 'At its best, it is an idea about theatre, a commitment to theatre as an art form and to theatre as a vehicle for responding to that which is contemporary.'[24]

Nor were these developments restricted to New York. The regional theatre which had been sluggishly growing, adding eight new theatres in twenty-five years, now expanded with amazing rapidity. The Guthrie was built in Minneapolis, the Mark Taper Forum in Los Angeles, the Playhouse in Cincinnati, the American Conservatory Theatre in San Francisco, the Mummers in Oklahoma City, the Long Wharf in New Haven, the Hartford Stage Company in Hartford, Connecticut, and so on. And rather than simply restaging Broadway successes they began to create their own work (admittedly itself sometimes indistinguishable from Broadway fare) until in the late 1970s and early 1980s they were providing the year's prize-winning plays. The Mark Taper Forum in Los Angeles was thus the first to stage Michael Christofer's *The Shadow Box* (which won two Tony awards) and Mark Medoff's *Children of a Lesser God*. Indeed, five productions from the 1979–80 season ended up on Broadway. The 1980 Pulitzer Prize winner, Lanford Wilson's *Talley's Folly*, was also a product of regional theatre. There are now an estimated 1,500 professional theatres throughout America and some 200 independent, non-profit, professional companies. By the end of the 1970s the League of Resident Theatres had more than sixty members and, as Gerald Berkowitz has pointed out, the National Endowment for the Arts estimated that there were ten times as many smaller alternative theatres around the country. Between 1962 and 1969 more than 170 theatres and art centres were built.

Now all of this costs money, and another major feature of this period is the emergence, for virtually the first time, of financial subsidy for theatre. Until the 1960s there had been virtually no financial support forthcoming from local, state, or federal government sources; nor had major foundations shown any great interest in this area. President Coolidge had once reportedly asked: Why should we spend money for culture when we can buy all we want from France? And this, or something like it, had been the ruling orthodoxy. Then, beginning in

1959 with the Ford Foundation and thereafter in the late 1960s with the participation of city, state and national cultural agencies, funding became available, sometimes in the most cavalier manner. Ellen Stewart has explained how she landed her first $25,000:

> One day the Ford Foundation called. So this man and his wife came. They asked if I'd like to talk after the performance. I took them to the Fifth Street Deli for hotdogs and sauerkraut. I explained what I was doing. If I had $25,000, I told them, I could put $10,000 down on a building on East 4th Street, fix it up inside for $15,000, and I'd have my own legal premises. I wouldn't always be running. The man nodded and said goodnight. About a week later, I got a call to come to the Ford Foundation. I went up and got an envelope. It had a check for $25,000 in it.

It must have been the sauerkraut. The Ford Foundation, whose first grants to Off-Off Broadway companies were made in 1968, was not always quite so generous, though it had a soft spot for Ellen Stewart. When she was faced with reconstructing the building they once again came to her support: 'The Ford Foundation fixed it up for us. It cost us a few hundred thousand, but they did it.'[25]

In 1959 Ford offered subsidies to the Alley Theatre, to Arena Stage, the San Francisco Actors' Workshop and the Phoenix, rescuing the last from a $350,000 loss in the 1957–8 and 1958–9 season. In 1964–5 the Off-Broadway American Place Theatre received two three-year grants from Ford and Rockefeller totalling $379,000. The finance was essential. In the early 1960s three-quarters of money invested Off-Broadway was lost and in the 1966–7 season only four of fifty-three shows covered their expenses. In 1962 Ford gave over $6 million in grants. In 1966 they were joined by the National Endowment for the Arts. Beginning modestly, its budget had grown by 1982 to $143 million (approximately three-quarters of which went to the arts). And corporations also began supporting selective arts ventures. In 1967 they gave $22 million; by 1981 that figure had risen to $436 million (though much of this went to public television, the opera and other prestige events). In the late 1960s this support extended to the commercial theatre. The Theatre Development Fund, established in 1967, purchased tickets and discounted them to students and others. In 1973 it opened a booth in Times Square where discount tickets could be bought on the day of performance. The fact is that after a long history of neglect money did finally become available, in the 1960s and 70s, to underwrite not merely regional companies but also those groups whose experiments would not otherwise have been able to command box-office support. But money was never the central question. There had always been those who were prepared to make personal sacrifices in order to perform. There were also those who regarded with suspicion financial support offered by representatives of the very forces which they opposed politically and whose lifestyle they chose to oppose with their own style of life and theatre. And that mutual hostility sometimes took concrete form.

In 1963 the Living Theatre had been driven out of the country by the International Revenue Service (and also by their own financial incompetence). Ellen Stewart of La Mama was frequently arrested for the violation of licence laws, Ed Koch, later Mayor of New York, reportedly telling her: 'You will learn to live within the law – or suffer the consequences.'[26] The San Francisco Mime Troupe was harassed by the police while LeRoi Jones's Black Arts Repertory Theatre had its federal grant withdrawn. The theatre, or parts of the theatre, thus found itself in the confrontational position which in a sense it had sought and which was, after all, a logical consequence of its intensifying political commitment.

In 1965 Herbert Blau was invited to New York to rescue an already ailing Lincoln Center. The idea was to apply the new objectives and standards of regional theatre/Off-Broadway (well, Off-San Francisco) to a putative national theatre, as Vilar had taken his ideas to the Palais de Chaillot. The result was a débâcle in which he was attacked by his former colleagues for deserting them and denounced by his new employers for introducing a subversive drama (Büchner's *Danton's Death*). The fact that the move precipitated attacks from former members of Blau's and Irving's group suggests the degree to which a dependent had already changed into an antagonistic relationship in the course of a single decade; the failure of the new venture suggested the extent to which not only the American theatre but American theatre audiences had already begun to fragment.

By no means all attempts to address America's past and present, at this time, were convincing. The ill-named theatre of fact (represented by plays such as *The Trial of the Catonsville Nine*, *Inquest* and *Pueblo*), for example, was neither theatrically nor dramatically compelling. Unlike the novel, which set out to sabotage history by drawing it into the fictive flux, this theatre opted for a more prosaic confrontation with a world which manifested its ethical and structural reality in the form of a simple and unassailable factuality. It also flirted with the assumption that the way to engage the public imagination lay through a denial of that imagination. Television has embraced the same assumption with enthusiasm and the documentary drama is now as close as American television feels it dare come to the dangerous enterprise of releasing the unfettered perceptions of the artist.

Such frontal attacks on the real, such direct attempts to reclaim and reshape the past and hence assert a version of the present, were often touched with naivety. It was not that the theatre of fact was necessarily undramatic; it was that in some disturbing way it felt that the theatre audience, once cast in the role of jury, would fail to examine the writer's own casuistries, that the writer's own manipulations were not themselves fit matters for scrutiny. Fact seemed important because it could most easily be counterposed to the misinformation which had encysted America's blacks in public theories of infantilism and which had clothed the distant conflict in South-east Asia in the language of the very liberalism which it denied. But for the most part these plays tend to offer a simulated dialectic. The debate over the nature of truth is perceived only at a superficial level. Unassailable moral truths are presumed to spring directly from a simple facticity.

Such a presumption was not made by Robert Lowell in his contemplation on history, *The Old Glory*. Neither was it made by Saul Bellow in his liberal parable, *The Last Analysis*, by Kopit in *Indians*, nor by Jules Feiffer in his sardonic images of American reality, *Little Murders* and *The White House Murder Case*. Yet, on occasion, the theatre of fact did have a power which resided as much in the raw material of injustice itself as in the particular shape given to it by the author, as in Martin Duberman's *In White America* or Eric Bentley's *Are You Now or Have You Ever Been?*

Such plays were evidence, however, of a radicalisation of part of the theatre which in time captured much of the avant-garde as the civil rights movement intensified and as Vietnam raised questions of a destructive rationalism, a compromised language, and a false authority implicit in the nature of complex systems. And yet in a sense these had been precisely the kind of issues which had always been implicit in the work of Arthur Miller and which had led Edward Albee to set his tale of moral equivocation and the failure of community in a township with the apocalyptic name of New Carthage. The difference lay in the location of political failure in conflicting dogmas and histories rather than the embattled conscience of the individual; or, alternatively, in an assertion of the pleasure principle over the reality principle, the attempt to counter the collapse of a spiritual and physical sense of community with erotic exuberance and spiritual renewal rather than a restored liberalism.

For those whose purpose was not primarily didactic – for those interested in trying out styles, in bringing together disparate experiences, sometimes in a random and sometimes in a carefully planned manner, but with no social, moral, or even precisely formulated aesthetic purpose – the 'happening' proved a sufficient response to the contemporary fragmenting of experience and the need to test the boundaries of individual arts. Happenings offered an art of surfaces; they were concerned with presentation rather than representation. Drawing on sculpture, music, dance, art, and theatre, the happening was an experiment in an art of the moment which disavowed any metaphoric impulse. Yet, in its unabashed attempts to commandeer the natural world and the familiar environment of parking lots, skyscrapers, and railroad stations, it was not without a sense of self-parody and irony. Its ephemerality and effrontery were part of its purpose. It was a neo-dadaist gesture. Unlike performance theatre, which took itself so seriously at times as to undermine its own premises, the creators of happenings were aware of the humour which could spring from the unlikely disjunctions which they forged. The relevance of happenings to the theatre was, perhaps, tangential but the questions they raised were in many ways precisely those which the Living Theatre, the Open Theatre and the Performance Group addressed in the mid 1960s.

Most of these groups showed a considerable distrust of texts, developing their performances on the basis of improvisation, rehearsal, and a minimum of textual material. Indeed, the whole movement posed a serious problem for the dramatic critic if he was to be anything more than a reporter/reviewer, and criticism did in fact frequently defer to simple description. Nor is it accidental that this theatre should offer such a series of direct challenges to criticism. It is not simply that it became increasingly difficult to isolate a text or that the verbal element became less dominant. The truth is that this theatre was actually an assault on the notion that art is an artifact produced by a unique sensibility and open to interpretation and evaluation in the conventional sense. For both these processes depend upon a rational methodology, and performance drama was in reaction against positivism and rationalism. What it wished to do was reconstitute feeling. For them, as for Hemingway before them, morality was largely a question of feeling good.

And the backwash of 1950s existentialism (now thoroughly processed through the blender of American sentimentality) was still apparent in demands for authenticity which, in terms of the theatre, manifested themselves in a desire to liberate the self or the actor from prescriptive roles. The lies of theatre were to be exposed for what they were so that actor and audience could meet one another in a space purified by this act of self-abnegation to be achieved, paradoxically, through self-assertion. For the Polish director Jerzy Grotowski, whose visits to America in 1967 and thereafter were a major influence on performance theatre groups, there was something of the confessional in such a theatre; for Julian Beck it was the purest form of didacticism, with the priest celebrants of his theatre living and being what they simultaneously advocated and enacted; for Joseph Chaikin, a certain physical strenuousness implied a kind of grace; for Richard Schechner, eclectic to a degree, the theatre space was a kind of crucible in which cultural traditions, myths, public and private ceremonies were rendered down to leave as residue that pure substance of being in which he could not finally believe. Nonetheless, pieties were in the air. The authentic act, the true self, the genuine relationship, the honest gesture, provided an objective – the struggle becoming its own reward. Authority in all its guises was to be distrusted.

Writing in the 1980s, Schechner conceded the dictatorship of the director in the early years, followed by a period in which the actor assumed a central significance. But at the time it was the apparent freedom from dictatorship rather than its protean ability to disguise its essence which seized the imagination. And the distrust of authority extended in particular to the writer. A number of experimental groups actually preferred using texts from the past which were available for transformation, fragmentation and improvisation in the way that contemporary plays, patrolled by their creators, were not. For Schechner, one of the failures of the experimental theatre movement has, however, been its inability to pass on its 'total theatrical text' or to translate its activities into a training programme which would make its activities available for transformation and development. Certainly, a central problem for those wishing to study the American theatre of the 1960s lies in the fact that such texts as were published were allowed to go out of print with the passing of the decade. Its enthusiasms suddenly seemed embarrassing, its urgencies self-deluding. So little residue remained, except at the level of style, that it was apparently more politic and less disturbing to lay the 1960s to rest without benefit of public rites. What followed was more muted, more private, more arcane. The streets were not silent but they gave back fewer echoes. The natural megalomania of theatre practitioners found less support now. The war was over. Love no longer seemed to have the power to dissolve political realities. The problem of race remained. The situation of the Indian and the Chicano was still an affront. The perils of materialism scarcely faded. Unemployment climbed. But the theatre no longer had a taste for the public arena.

By the mid 1970s the new theatre movement had already lost some of its momentum and purpose. The conservatism of post-Vietnam and then post-Watergate America, exacerbated by economic depression, was reflected in the theatre which, having seen itself as something of a resistance movement, had perhaps come to rely rather too much on the implacable fact of American military imperialism and manifest political corruption for its own significance. Radicals in all areas of American life adjusted to the new conservatism, finding God or becoming shirt salesmen or both. Theirs was perhaps an inevitable retreat from the political and aesthetic barricades. The Open Theatre closed, feeling that it had become trapped in its own orthodoxies; the Living Theatre effectively died, or at least fragmented and most recently has been performing the classics in Italy. Jerzy Grotowski seemed to reject theatre in favour of some broader social or spiritual objective. The normal processes of attrition led to the demise of the Manhattan Project, Caffe Cino, Judson Poets' Theatre, Grand Union, the Playhouse of the Ridiculous and many others. The Bread and Puppet Theatre, at the heart of so many political demonstrations in the 1960s, now rarely stirred from its Vermont home. Where in the 1960s and early 1970s Off and Off-Off Broadway avant-garde theatre had seen itself as essentially a public art inviting the full physical participation of the audience, either as a gesture of solidarity with its political objectives or as evidence of a refusal of all restraints (including the special framing of the theatrical event), it now tended to concern itself with the nature of perception and consciousness. It became an expression of intensely private experience, moving from the gnomic tableaux of Robert Wilson and Richard Foreman to the heavily autobiographical pieces of the Wooster Group (the Rhode Island trilogy) and the monologues of Spalding Gray. The audience found itself excluded from the stage onto which it had once been invited and increasingly denied access to meaning.

Indeed Spalding Gray was frank not merely about his privatism but also about the personal utility of his work. 'I am', he admitted in 1979, 'by nature extremely narcissistic and reflective. For as long as I can remember, I have always been self-conscious and aware of my everyday actions . . . I think I began my own work out of a desire to be both active and reflective at the same time before an audience.'[27] Influenced by two decades of avant-garde drama (including the work of the Living Theatre, the Open Theatre, the Performance Group, Robert Wilson and Meredith Monk) he created, in *Sakonnet Point*, a 'series of simple actions . . . that created a series of images like personal, living Rorschachs. These images were not unlike the blank, white wall in Zen meditation, nor were they unlike the mirror reflection of a good therapist. Often, what the audience saw was the reflection of their own minds, their own projections,'[28] And this was ultimately his defence of what was otherwise a 'confessional'. It was, to his mind, equally the aesthetic principle which underlay the work of Robert Wilson and the solo performer Meredith Monk which became 'a kind of therapeutic lesson about how we create our own world through projections'.[29]

But for Richard Schechner this work and that of others implied a regrettable shift not merely from a public to a private art but from a concern with subject to a concern with subjectivity. Thus he insisted that 'Once the war ended and the recession of the mid-seventies hit, artists fell into a formalist deep freeze. Great work was done, but it was cut off: it did not manifest significant content. Instead a certain kind of "high art obscurity" took over.'[30] As the title of his book – *The End of Humanism* – seems to imply he saw this as in some sense a betrayal. And yet in suggesting that form and content are separable he was missing something of the point, as was John Gardner who directed a similar complaint at writers of post-modern fiction in his book *On Moral Fiction*. For though such people were entirely capable of high art obscurity the assumption that the generation of images and the elaboration of new forms takes us outside the moral world is misleading. Indeed, it may well be that in requiring audiences to offer their own completions, in provoking a degree of aesthetic complicity and imaginative collaboration, such theatre practitioners may be reminding them of their capacity to act and to imagine a world beyond the banality of appearance. They may indeed have created a coterie art but that is after all the common fate of the avant-garde. The wonder is that briefly, in the late 1960s and early 1970s, things had seemed otherwise.

If Schechner feared a collapse into privatism, however, he was equally concerned with the fact that an era of experiment might have given way to nothing more than theatrical regression. Thus he suggests that in so far as the theatre had not capitulated to obscurity it had 'slid back to orthodox solutions: the easy solutions of the "Euro-American modern tradition". Frontal staging, passive audiences, sentimental, apolitical texts.'[31] But this is a fear which depends upon its own unstated and unargued premises: that an 'orthodox' solution is necessarily inadequate, unsophisticated and unselfconscious (the theatre of the 1960s, after all, had created its own orthodoxies, rigorously policed by the elaborators of performance theory); that frontal staging is inferior and incapable of subversion (Wilson and Foreman proved otherwise); that an apolitical text is possible and if so inevitably sentimental, and that an audience separated physically from performers is necessarily passive intellectually, imaginatively and emotionally (an assumption specifically attacked by Grotowski). He also assumes that it will be a theatre unmarked by fifteen to twenty years of experiment. The problem, however, is not with the style of production or the nature and degree of moral commitment on the part of writers, directors or theatre groups. It is that the theatre is no longer felt to be at the centre of cultural life as for a time it had seemed to be in a decade in which role was a matter of central concern, the theatrical metaphor was invoked by psycho-historians and sociologists, and political urgencies had transformed America's streets into public stages. The

Vivian Beaumont Theatre at Lincoln Center was closed throughout much of the 1970s and into the 1980s. Inflation began to eat into the value of grants which were anyway being cut back. Foundations began to change their priorities away from the arts and into social programmes. And, for the young, film became a source of greater fascination than the theatre. Why this should be so is more difficult to answer but if the theatre assumed a central role in a decade in which community was a favourite concept, and the nexus between radical politics and radical aesthetics was readily accepted, then perhaps it is only logical that at a time when the dominant concern is with the self, and a new conservative consensus has established itself, the theatre should once more appear marginal and self-regarding.

In the brief lifetime of the Federal Theatre the Negro unit employed 851 people. In October 1936 Sinclair Lewis's *It Can't Happen Here* was staged simultaneously in twenty-one theatres in seventeen states. In New York City alone the play was seen by 300,000 people. Admission rates ranged from 10¢ to $1.10. 65 per cent of audiences attending Federal Theatre productions had never been to the theatre before; 25 per cent of these audiences worked in trades or were office workers. When it was forced to close, its director, Hallie Flanagan, estimated that its audiences in the four years of its existence represented one quarter of the population of the United States.

For all the expansion of regional theatre and the consolidation of Off-Broadway and Off-Off Broadway, forty years later the theatre has in large degree reverted to a minority interest. Its leading writers and directors are for the most part unknown to the public, their experiments seem arcane, their relationship to their culture is problematic. Despite the experimental thrust of the contemporary American novel its major figures still command a large audience: Bellow, Heller, Vonnegut, Mailer. In the 1940s and 50s Miller and Williams could rely on a similar attention. In the 1970s and 80s they had lost those audiences, and few writers had replaced them. After the first few years of his career Albee became a gnomic figure. Robert Wilson, Lee Breuer and Richard Foreman sparked interest in theatre practitioners or followers of the avant-garde. Beyond that they were unknown.

Perhaps a new Federal Theatre could not happen in the 1970s and 80s. However execrable, American television, on the whole, fills the vacuum which the theatre had once briefly occupied (reprocessing history into dramatic packages and consolidating real anxieties into neatly con-structed and reassuring genre shows). That it does so with so little conviction and with such a paucity of imagination, however, is the source of real frustration. Signs of life persist in the theatre. It does now play a significant role in civic life which a decade or so before it did not. There are new and powerful writers such as David Mamet, although another such – Sam Shepard – shows signs of opting for a career as movie actor. It is simply that, in the mid 1980s, it no longer seems quite the vital, energetic and compelling force which it has been at other times in the twentieth century, demanding attention by the brilliance of its authors or the innovative enthusiasm of its practitioners. In January 1983 nearly half of Broadway's theatres were closed while neither Off nor Off-Off Broadway seemed to have much to offer. But then in 1958 few would have given much for the future of theatre beyond Broadway and little for its future on. The following year a detonation of creative talent occurred whose echoes resounded down the following two decades. And the structure of the American theatre is now very different from what it once was. The theatres exist, finance is available, the dominance of Broadway has been eroded. The American theatre is also much more eclectic, much more open to influence from abroad and to interaction with the other arts. Its solemnities have been subverted, its power to reach out to other audiences demonstrated. Undoubtedly much of Off and Off-Off Broadway in the 1960s and early 1970s was overpraised at the time. Its significance was magnified by political turmoil and social change. Its concerns seemed so close to those of many people who felt the need for some public ceremony of solidarity that it perhaps assumed importance beyond its worth. And exclusivist ensembles do encourage cult support. The weakness of Broadway, from which Tennessee Williams (in deep psychological trouble) had all but withdrawn and to which Arthur Miller was an irregular and uncertain contributor, also undoubtedly exaggerated its virtues. Yet at the same time Off and Off-Off Broadway, some regional theatres, and a scatter of small theatre groups across the country did explode established views of the potential and function of the theatre and did provide a stage for those excluded as much from the cultural as from the political and economic system. They explored the limits of language and inspected the assumptions behind their own approach to character and plot. They examined the relationship between the theatrical moment and the historical event. They explored their own space. They posed questions about the self which performs and the self which perceives. They moved theatre closer to the anxieties, the aspirations, the fears, the social and political urgencies of the people they addressed and whom they invited to share their group solidarity.

They made presence not merely the circumstance of drama but also its justification and purpose. More importantly, perhaps, and by degrees, theatre began to examine its own potential for deceit, for manipulation

37

and for coercion, at least at the level of imagination. And this, on the whole, had not typified the American theatre until that time. This was a very considerable achievement in its own right, and despite Richard Schechner's strictures and despite the apparent loss of dramatic and theatrical energy at the present time (a loss equally observable in France, Germany and Italy, for example) the impact of that period remains clear. If we detect a weakness in the theatre of our own day it is anyway perhaps because we are looking for the wrong thing in the wrong place. The contemporary is a country which we all inhabit but there are no reliable maps to this territory. In a sense we are all strangers there and round any corner may lie the object of our journey.

1 Zen, Happenings, Artaud, Grotowski

Off and Off-Off Broadway encompass an enormous range and variety of subjects and approaches. In part this is their justification. In the 1960s and early 1970s some groups sought out audiences on the basis of their racial, sexual or economic composition, while others were motivated by a desire to develop actor training and awareness to a higher pitch or to explore the roots of theatricality. Released from the economic necessities and aesthetic standards of Broadway they were free to explore all aspects of theatre. The erosion of boundaries at every level became a primary objective, including those boundaries which separated the theatre from its allied arts (dance, music, painting and sculpture). Sexuality, whose repressions had been the source of a guilt neatly displaced from the political realm in Arthur Miller's work, was now to be explored as a path to transcendence and analysed for its relationship to social role or archetypal function. And transcendence was on the agenda. The pre-history of the theatrical avant-garde of the 1960s would have to acknowledge the significance of Zen, as it would a fascination with the humanism of Erich Fromm, the psycho-sexual theories of Norman O. Brown and the sexual and political radicalism of Herbert Marcuse. In terms of dramatic theory the chief influences were Antonin Artaud – whose famous cry, 'No More Masterpieces!', was very much in tune with their sense of a caesura in social, political and cultural life – and the Polish director Jerzy Grotowski, whose rigorous attention to actor training shaded over into a concern with a restored unity to being.

The movement away from Broadway was also in part a movement away from formal theatre buildings. Indeed, as the 1960s progressed so this logic was developed further with theatre occurring not merely in churches and coffee shops but also in art galleries and on the streets. It was a shift predicated in part on the desire to take a political message to the people most directly affected, in the environment in which they lived, and in part on a wish to challenge aesthetic presumptions about the special framing of art. Indeed the world of art and that of theatre interacted in ways which seemed for a while to be of equal interest to theatre practitioners and artists.

Perhaps the best place to start an account of the American theatre of the 1960s is, paradoxically, in a small North Carolina university called Black

Mountain College. It may seem an unlikely place to begin precisely because it was not especially known for the quality of its drama. It was, nonetheless, an extraordinary phenomenon, gathering together a group of innovative figures in all areas of the arts who were dedicated to exploring, extending and transcending the boundaries of the given, and it was in part through these people, eclectic, committed to examining the relationship between art and the real, determinedly communitarian and self-consciously experimental, that major influences entered the blood-stream of the American avant-garde. It was the musician John Cage, on the faculty of Black Mountain, who responded to a contemporary interest in Zen Buddhism and applied it to his work. It was at Black Mountain that the first 'happening' was staged and it was through Cage, and his colleague Mary Caroline Richards, that the work of the French theatre theoretician Antonin Artaud was brought to America and thus to the attention of the experimental theatre movement. It was here that the question of artistic performance and its relationship to social perform-ance was debated and in some degree enacted. And it was here that the symbiosis between the arts, which was to be such a feature of the American theatrical scene, was tested.

Originally founded in 1933 as an experimental college, Black Moun-tain was from the start concerned with utopian notions of community, actively discussing whether all members should be required to engage in necessary physical labour. It was appropriate in such a context, therefore, that one of the first members of faculty to be hired was Josef Albers who had worked at the Bauhaus which had equally stressed the interpenetration of art and life. And Albers's philosophy, his conviction that 'Art is concerned with the HOW, not the WHAT; not with literal content, but with the performance of the factual content. The perform-ance – how it is done – that is the content of art',[1] was one enthusiastically embraced by a later generation of Black Mountain faculty and became an essential component of 1960s art.

John Cage did not arrive at Black Mountain until 1948 when he made a brief visit. He had, however, already begun his first experiments with a 'prepared piano' (a piano whose hammers had been modified by the insertion of screws) when he first applied to the college in 1942. And just as it was with Merce Cunningham, the dancer, that he gave his first performance there, so Cunningham also became an essential part of Black Mountain life, his interest in pure movement, his concern with rejecting narrative-based dance as 'melodrama', making clear the degree to which he shared fundamental principles with Cage and again antici-pated many of the ideas of art and performance that are more usually associated with the following decade. Black Mountain was eclectic. The faculty also included at various times Eric Bentley, the theatre director and critic, Paul Goodman, whose plays were performed by the Living Theatre, and Buckminster Fuller, whom Cage claimed as a central influence. It included also Charles Olson, for whom the physical nature of the speech act, the physiological processes of language, became as compelling a concern as the supposed significations of words.

Black Mountain did concern itself directly with drama though this was never a central issue. Thus Wes Hus staged an early performance of *Waiting for Godot*, as well as plays by Zukovsky and Genet. Later, the poet Robert Duncan wrote his *Medea* specifically to incorporate the personalities of the actors as they rehearsed the play over a protracted period, an approach which was to be a favourite tactic of such groups as Richard Schechner's Performance Group, and Julian Beck and Judith Malina's Living Theatre in the late 1960s. It was through Duncan in some degree that a bridge was created between the concerns of the Black Mountain community and those of the San Francisco poets and novelists who were for a while a dominant influence on the 1950s and certainly laid the foundation for many of the assumptions behind 1960s art, music and theatre. As Joel Oppenheimer, the poet, who spent some time at Black Mountain, observed, 'There is a feeling, a texture to . . . the Black Mountain poets that is common . . . distinct as they all are in their own ways . . . They're coming out of the same general attack on language.'[2] That same reaction against language was also apparent in Zen, which fascinated Cage, as it did Kerouac, and which placed a value on physicality which in turn became a central strategy of artists and even political activists in the 1960s. As Alan Watts, principal American interpreter of Zen thought, asserted of the physical universe, 'Words represent it, but if we want to *know* it directly we must do so by immediate sensory contact.'[3]

John Cage derived part of his attitude to art, and more especially to what he called 'this testing of art against life', from attending the lectures of D.T. Suzuki from 1949 to 1951. Through Zen he became interested in experiencing the 'is-ness' of things. Art was to be a celebration of that. Indeed it was to be inherently celebratory. As he remarked in an interview, 'We have spoken of wanting to turn each person into an artist . . . We've spoken of individual anarchy, etc. So, in the case of a performance, we would think of it, wouldn't we, as a celebration of some kind.'[4]

Zen sought to reconcile the individual to experience rather than to stress a gulf between the individual and that experience. In that sense it seemed to address a contemporary sense of alienation. As Alan Watts insisted, 'We need, above all, to disentangle ourselves from habits of speech and thought which set the two apart, making it possible for us to see that *this* – the immediate, everyday, and present experience – is IT, the entire and ultimate point for the existence of a universe.'[5]

Zen's influence in America had been expressed primarily in the work of the Beats, neo-romantics who wandered the country in search of what Jack Kerouac also called 'it' and who burned themselves out on drugs and alcohol, but through those gathered at Black Mountain College it infiltrated the thought of the avant-garde. Among other things there was a revived interest in chance procedures which owed something to the experiments of the dadaists and the surrealists but also something to Zen, for which the order concealed within the contingent was known as *Li*. Hence, the dancer Merce Cunningham created *16 Dances* by chance methods in 1951; John Cage employed chance procedures in his music, composing the score for Cunningham's performance; Jackson Pollock allowed chance to enter the process of creation in painting; Jackson Maclow and others were experimenting with chance procedures in the theatre. Indeed in 1963 La Mont Young and Jackson Maclow edited and published *An Anthology of Chance Operations*.

The desire to open oneself to experience and to appreciate the 'is-ness' of things was of course scarcely a discovery of the 1950s or even necessarily a product of Zen influence. It was securely in the American grain. In 'Self-Reliance' Emerson had insisted that,

> These roses under my window make no reference to former roses or to better ones; they are for what they are; they exist with God today. There is no time for them. There is simply the rose; it is perfect in every moment of its existence. . . . But man postpones or remembers; he does not live in the present, but with reverted eye laments the past, or, heedless of the riches that surround him, stands on tiptoe to foresee the future. He cannot be happy and strong until he too lives with nature in the present, above time.[6]

Watts himself quoted this passage, in his book *In My Own Way*, in the context of an account of his own involvement with Zen. This he saw as meeting some contemporary need for the experiential which was not without its history in American literary and philosophical thought, but which seemed to reach for some external validation.

In terms of film this concern with the 'is-ness' of things was perhaps expressed in Warhol's movie of a man sleeping, while even as late as 1969 Michael Kirby, who replaced Richard Schechner as the editor of *The Drama Review*, could say of his own theatre piece, *Room 706* (the title of a large lecture hall in Saint Francis College, Brooklyn, in which this 'alogical play' was performed) that he was attempting, for one thing, to use acting not for the meaning it could convey, but for its pure experiential qualities – in the same way, so to speak, that paint has been used for *its* qualities of hue, texture, and so forth without the necessity of representing anything. In order to do this I tried to make the basic scene as close to real life as I could. The dialogue was not composed but was 'found' in a situation which appropriated an everyday one. The actors were playing themselves and not characters whose inner natures they would have to imagine or invent.[7]

By this time Zen was perhaps no longer a direct influence but its impact in the 1950s and early 60s had been considerable and had served to shape the cultural environment in which artists, musicians, dancers and theatre practitioners conducted their experiments.

In a popular essay published in 1959, called *Beat Zen, Square Zen and Zen*, Alan Watts accounted for the extraordinary growth of Western interest in Zen in the post-war period by suggesting that it derived from 'the attraction of a non-conceptual, experiential philosophy in the climate of scientific relativism' along with 'the affinities between Zen and such purely Western trends as the philosophy of Wittgenstein, Existentialism, General Semantics, the metalinguistics of B.L. Worf, and certain movements in the philosophy of science and in psychotherapy'.[8] In his view it sprang from a dissatisfaction with the notion of a dichotomy between man and the world. Zen offered the possibility of reintegrating man and nature, of restoring wholeness to a culture in which the spiritual and the material, the conscious and the unconscious, had been cataclysmically split. For Watts, art was an especially apt analogue for the natural world with which it claimed ontological identity:

> Nature is much more playful than purposeful . . . the processes of nature as we see them both in the surrounding world and in the involuntary aspects of our own organisms are much more like art than like business, politics or religion. They are especially like the arts of music and dancing, which unfold themselves without aiming at future destinations . . . The point of music is discovered in every moment of playing and listening to it. It is the same, I feel, with the greater part of our lives.[9]

Zen (which coloured the work of Ginsberg, Snyder and Kerouac) is thus primarily concerned with a world beyond moral and social evaluation. In the words of Hsin-hsin Ming:

> If you want to get the plain truth,
> Be not concerned with right and wrong.
> The conflict between right and wrong
> Is the sickness of the mind.[10]

Peter Brook later responded to *The Connection* precisely because it impelled its audience to confront pure behaviour outside any context of morality. Indeed, he personally looked forward to the creation of a theatre which would be the counterpart of Robbe-Grillet's novels, 'a theatre . . . in which pure *behaviour* can exist in its own right'.[11] But this of course implies the dissolution of a frame between art and experience and Watts found himself at odds with the uses to which the avant-garde chose to put Zen, rejecting those who would argue that they do not want to distinguish between their works and the total universe: 'If this be so they should not frame them in galleries and concert halls. Above all they should not sign them. This is as immoral as selling the moon or signing one's name to a mountain . . . Only destructive little boys and vulgar exhibitionists go around initialling the trees.'[12] To Watts, therefore, John Cage, who composed music according to chance procedures and who drew attention to the music which surrounds us in the environment by amplifying the sound, for example, of a person seated on a chair, and who claimed inspiration in Zen, was creating not art but therapy. He was sensitising his audience to sight and sound but failing precisely to frame his work: 'Cage's work', he insisted, 'would be redeemed if he framed and presented it as a kind of group session in audiotherapy, but as a concert it is simply absurd.'[13] Similarly, he challenged the use to which artists put chance, denying their claim to its origins in Zen. Zen artists did, indeed, employ chance procedures but in a controlled way, and always in relation to a total context. Thus to Watts, 'the formless murmur of night noises in a great city has an enchantment which immediately disappears when formally presented as music in a concert hall. A frame outlines a universe, microcosm, and if the contents of the frame are to rank as art they must have the same quality of relationship to the whole and to each other as events in the great universe, the macrocosm of nature.'[14] This was, however, something of a misjudgement of Cage's work, which was never simply 'sheer caprice', while a decade later Watts himself was happy to be invited onto the stage before the curtain went up on the San Francisco production of *Hair* to lead the cast in mantra chanting.

The impact of Zen was diffuse. In one sense it seems to have fed a latent anti-intellectualism in the American fiction and theatre of the 1950s and 60s, stressing the significance of the irrational and reinstituting a sense of mystery and even mysticism. It seems to have registered as the source of an antidote to alienation, promising the restoration of a harmony between mind and body, the self and a community of selves. Its spiritualism seems to have struck a chord as did its rituals but it was primarily as an image of restored consonance and a celebratory communion with the natural world that it seems to have prompted a response from John Cage as from those in the performance theatre movement of the 1960s. Beyond that, its stress on the need to re-experience the real, to respond to the physical world without an obscuring overlay of 'meaning', was echoed later by theatre practitioners such as Robert Wilson and Richard Foreman as it was more immediately by the creators of 'happenings'.

In 1959 Allan Kaprow coined the word 'happening' to describe a presentation which had its roots in art but which had taken the artist in the direction of theatre. In one sense these were simply extensions of an art-historical development from flat-plane pictures to collages, to environments. The artist shaped the gallery space until it became not merely the location of his art but an essential aspect of it. But when the human form was introduced, either simply as object, whether static or choreographed, or as a more active component, the happening clearly pressed towards theatre, while disavowing any theatrical intent.

The first happening was, in a sense, that staged by John Cage at Black Mountain College in 1952. In this the audience was seated in a hall while activities of various kinds were conducted, either sequentially or simultaneously, in the surrounding space. Cage, in part under the influence of Zen and the *I Ching*, was happy to leave the interactions to chance, co-ordinating the whole event but allowing room for spontaneity. As Martin Duberman (a Black Mountain faculty member who himself later had an impact on the American theatre of the 1960s and 70s) explained:

> Cage invited Olson and Mary Caroline Richards to read their poetry, Rauschenberg to show his paintings and also to play recordings of his choice, David Tudor to perform on the piano any compositions he wanted, and Merce Cunningham to dance. Each person was left free, within his precisely defined time slot, to do whatever he chose to do. Cage's aim, in his own words, was 'purposeless purposefulness': it was purposeful in that we knew what we were going to do, but it was purposeless in that we didn't know what was going to happen in the total.[15]

This is remarkably reminiscent of Dada performances. In one such: 'On the stage of the cabaret tin cans and keys were jangled as music . . . Serner placed a bunch of flowers at the feet of a dressmaker's dummy. Arp's poems were recited by a voice hidden in an enormous hat shaped like a sugar-loaf. Huelsenbeck roared his poems in a mighty crescendo, while Tazara beat time on a large packing case.'[16] And Cage was well aware of the parallel. But where Dada was deliberately deconstructing art, sabotaging coherence, Cage was concerned with the quality of sound and movement, the nature of the interactions and the constructively destabilising intervention of chance.

The man most associated with happenings, however, was Allan Kaprow, an artist who studied with Cage from 1956 to 1958. On 4 October 1959, he created *18 Happenings in 6 Parts*, not the first such event but the one which gave the form its name. It took place in the Reuben Gallery, New York (and New York was to be the principal centre for work of this kind) which, for the occasion, had been divided into three areas by plastic sheeting. The 'audience' were assigned to these rooms with precise instructions as to when to move. The action itself consisted of human figures permitted limited movements while electronic sounds were heard from loudspeakers and slides were projected on a screen. Kaprow has explained that one of the crucial things about this and other happenings was its concern with what he calls the 'suchness' of things, thus echoing the Zen fascination with the 'is-ness' of phenomena. He was concerned, in other words, with presenting action 'with no more meaning than the sheer immediacy of what is going on'.[17]

Happenings were, in the words of Ken Dewey, founder of Action Theatre Inc. (1965) aimed at 'provoking an explosive degree of consciousness'.[18] In that sense they shared something not merely with Zen but with the aesthetics of surrealism (in their concern with an interaction between the arts and the stimulation of the sensibility through a series of juxtapositions), with abstract expressionism (in their concern with pure process), and with the 'new realism' in art (in their concern with forcing an awareness of texture, shape and physical qualities).

Happenings occurred at the intersection point of a number of experiments in different branches of the arts. Most obviously, perhaps, they were a product of painting. Resistance to the flat plane of the painting led to a deliberate desire to violate the frame, as in baroque architecture where the limbs of figures in a conventional relief suddenly threaten to invade the safe space of the observer's own environment. In terms of twentieth-century art this spirit resulted in the collages of the dadaists and surrealists, the environments of Kurt Schwitters (whose collages, begun in 1920, slowly expanded to fill his entire house), and thereafter the 'environmental' art of the 1960s. It generated an art which disturbs both the frame and the field of the picture; an art which displaces, which shapes the space that contains it and which thereby exerts a pressure on the observer.

But, of course, the room which contains this art is also a frame and realisation of this fact led to a desire to violate that determining shape. This resulted, on the one hand, in a conscious attempt to redesign the room, to restructure it with partitions and thereby to deny the geometry of the given, and, on the other, to escape the room entirely – to go out on the street or into the country (as Christo later did when he divided a fair proportion of an entire state with nylon sheeting).

For Kaprow the move from painting to environment was a logical one, for,

> with the breakdown of the classical harmonies following the introduction of 'irrational' or nonharmonic juxtapositions, the Cubists tacitly opened up a path to infinity. Once foreign matter was introduced into the picture in the form of paper, it was only a matter of time before everything else foreign to paint and canvas would be allowed to get into the creative act, including real space. Simplifying the history of the ensuing evolution into a flashback, this is what happened: the pieces of paper curled up off the canvas, were removed from the surface to exist on their own, became more solid as they grew into other materials and, reaching out further into the room, finally filled it entirely. Suddenly, there were jungles, crowded streets, littered alleys, dream spaces of science fiction, rooms of madness, and junk-filled attics of the mind . . .[19]

Space was no longer pictorial but actual and incorporated sound, movement, colour and time.

Kaprow has described the origins of happenings in his own work as deriving from an action collage technique inspired in part by his interest in Jackson Pollock. This began simply as a cluster of variegated materials. To this, however, he added flashing lights and ringing bells in an attempt to stimulate all the senses. These action collages gradually expanded to fill the gallery space until he realised that that space was constricting. Thus he came to feel that it was necessary to break out of the gallery so that the division between his action collages and 'the rest of life' would no longer exist. He even reacted against the sculptor's use of bases and stands which he regarded as 'sculpture's homologue to the frame in painting, serving to separate it more definitely from reality'.[20] His other crucial realisation was that the visitor to the Environment was a part of that Environment and hence could be given work to do other than simply observing. From this came the happening. Both these observations are crucial in terms of the direction which theatre was taking at this time, in particular its concern with the erosion of the barrier between art and reality, the performing space and the performed space (the site chosen for a performance and the space created by the fact of performance).

Clearly when a viewer enters an environment he inevitably theatricalises himself. He becomes a part of the thing which he observes – the more so from the perspective of others so involved. He alters the environment, contributes to the shapes and simultaneously exists as person and object, just as does an actor and just, in a sense, as does the individual in daily life. And that parallel was to be pressed with some force by writers and theatre groups in the 1960s. The whole environment becomes theatricalised through the attention which it now demands. And one consequence of happenings was to stress the theatrical potential of the everyday environment – hardly necessary, perhaps, when the whole of society seemed disposed to enact a series of public performances on the streets of an America all too aware of its political and social dramas.

Claus Oldenburg also chose to emphasise the art-historical dimension of happenings when he observed that, 'The "happening" is one or another method of using *objects in motion*, and this I take to include people, both in themselves and as agents of object motion.'[21] And this was not without its significance for those in the theatre interested in the relationship of audience and performer, for, to Oldenburg, the happening was also a means of incorporating the audience as itself an object, the audience being taken to differ from the players only in so far as 'its possibilities are not explored as far as the players''.[22] There was to be no space between the 'players' and the audience because the objective was to be the painter's desire to find a way of 'unifying a field of divergent phenomena'.[23]

The barrier between art and the real is thus eroded, or rather the dualism which leads to such a distinction is rejected by the deliberate inclusion of everyday objects. The creators of happenings thereby sought to raise this issue by asserting not merely that everything is available for co-option but that in a sense everything is art – art being the moment of realisation. A further eroded barrier, meanwhile, was to be that between high art and popular culture. Not only were the images of popular culture themselves commandeered but they became central mythic reserves of meaning (the circus in particular being invoked by Red Grooms with *The Burning Building* (1959), Robert Whitman with *The American Moon* (1960) and *Water* (1963), and Kaprow with *The Courtyard* (1962)). And happenings shared something else with popular art: they both tended to stress their own inbuilt obsolescence. Happenings were designed, in a sense, to be used up – to render up their sensory charge without asserting pre-emptive rights over the future. In other words, the creators of happenings echoed, on the whole, Artaud's bias against masterpieces. Declaring their independence from the past, they could scarcely claim any rights over the future. Thus, although various happenings were repeated, for the most part they were unique occurrences whose scripts had no real power and were seldom published since to do so would have risked entombment.

Kaprow identified his own rules of thumb with respect to happenings:

(A)   *The line between art and life should be kept as fluid, and perhaps indistinct, as possible.*

(B)   *Therefore, the source of themes, materials, actions, and the relationships between them are to be derived from any place or period except from the arts, their derivatives, and their milieu.*

(C)   *The performance of a Happening should take place over widely spaced, sometimes moving and changing locales.*

(D)   *Time, which closely follows on time considerations, should be variable and discontinuous.*

(E)   *Happenings should be performed once only.*

(F)   *It follows that audiences should be eliminated entirely.*

(G)   *The composition of Happenings proceeds exactly as in Assemblages and Environments, that is, it is evolved as a collage of events in certain spans of time and in certain spaces.*[24]

The fundamental objective, to Kaprow, was 'to release an artist from conventional notions of a detached closed arrangement of time–space. A picture, a piece of music, a poem, a drama, each confined within its respective frame, fixed number of measures, stanzas and stages, however great they may be in their own right, simply will not allow for breaking the barrier between art and life. And this is what the objective is.'[25]

Kaprow's desire to eliminate the audience derived from his desire to exclude 'dead space', a wish to avoid overtones of theatrical performance. He was rightly critical of those happenings which simply manipulated their participants, though it must be confessed that in *A Spring Happening* in 1961 he had those who chose to take part pursued down a corridor by a power lawn mower. But, as he insisted,

> on a human plane, to assemble people unprepared for an event and say that they are participating if apples are thrown at them or they are herded about is to ask very little of the whole notion of participation. Most of the time the response of such an audience is half hearted or even reluctant, and sometimes the reaction is vicious and therefore destructive to the work (though I suspect that in numerous instances of violent reaction to such treatment it was caused by the latent sadism in the action, which they quite rightly resented).[26]

Cage equally attacked Claus Oldenburg for 'the police situation' which he created in *Moviehouse*, in which he had instructed those attending not to sit down, and Kaprow for his manipulation of the audience in *18 Happenings in 6 Parts*. Kaprow was also acutely aware of the capacity for audience response to become formularised and insisted that 'anyone serious about the problem should not tolerate it, any more than the painter should continue the use of dripped paint as a stamp of modernity when it has been adopted by every lampshade and Formica manufacturer in the country'.[27]

Chance became an important element not primarily out of a desire to disconnect moments of experience, though for some creators of happenings this was indeed so, but as a means of destroying customary relationships. Thus Kaprow doubted the possibility of creating an art in which things exist 'for themselves', confessing, however, that the attempt 'is quite respectable', while suspecting, nonetheless, that the real objective, like his own, was involvement in the tangible world. Indeed, in the book which most clearly expressed his convictions about the new art, he insisted on presenting the happening in relation to the wider culture and on acknowledging its intimate relationship with traditional values and ideals:

> Any avant-garde is primarily a philosophical quest and a finding of truths, rather than purely an aesthetic activity; for this latter is possible, if at all, only in a relatively stable age when most human beings can agree upon fundamental notions of the nature of the universe. If it is a truism that ours is a period of extraordinary and rapid change, with its attendant surprises and sufferings, it is no less true that in such a day all serious thought (discursive or otherwise) must try to find in it a pattern of sense . . . I have focussed upon this concept of the real, suggesting a course of action in art that is related to what is likely our experience today, as distinct from what are our habits from the past. I have considered important those aspects of art which have been consciously intended to replace habit with the spirit of exploration and experiment. If some of the past is still meaningful, as it assuredly is, then what is retained in the present work is not archaistic mannerisms, easily recognized and praised for this reason, but those qualities of personal dignity and freedom always championed in the West. In respecting these, the ideas of this book are deeply traditional.[28]

But it was doubtful whether the happening could sustain such a claim for moral significance. It was not that art could not tolerate invasion by the real (in the sense of a heightened sensitivity to sound, colour, movement and so on) but that the theatricalising of the real threatened to turn morality into aesthetics. Thus Jim Dine abandoned happenings precisely because he wished to reintroduce the frame – to re-establish some of the boundaries which the creators of happenings had set themselves so assiduously to destroy: 'I do not feel there was enough of a perspective between art and life in them.'[29] Eventually others began to abandon them precisely because of their non–teleological thrust. Thus Ronald Hunt suggested in 1967: 'None of us feel like doing happenings again. The storming of the Pentagon is much more vital.'[30] In the 1960s, indeed, it was possible to dissolve the barriers between art and reality all too easily simply through the expedient of drugs, so that as Tom Wolfe explained of Ken Kesey and his Merry Pranksters, 'It was more like he had a vision of the forest as a fantastic stage setting . . . in which every day would be a happening, an art form.'[31] And they tried to turn the world on to this truth by serving Kool Aid laced with LSD. But this too had its darker side as, by a terrible assonance, another California-based group a decade and a half later would do the reverse at Jonestown, Guyana, by lacing the Kool Aid with cyanide.

Though the happening flourished for only a relatively brief while and though its status was problematic with regard to theatre, it was clearly part of that process of enquiry, of examining the processes and assumptions of art, which was equally observable in fiction and drama. It raised questions about the nature of the 'frame' which delineated art from the world in which it existed, about the nature of performance and the relationship between performer and audience. It asserted the significance of the real and underlined the generative power of juxtaposition. If it was not theatre, it did at least acknowledge areas which became of increasing concern to theatre practitioners.

Writing in the late 1970s, the artist/performer Carolee Schneeman argued that there was in effect a relationship between what she regarded as the liberation of the imagination through method and those other social, cultural and political liberations which typified the 1960s:

> Happenings made the bridge from painting to multi-media by a unique fusion (and confusion) of script, score, notation, rehearsals, anti-rehearsals, and free spontaneous interactions. For most of us certain formal parameters were to be thrown open, and the risk, unpredictability, and incorporation of random factors presaged burgeoning forms of social protest in our volatile culture.
>
> We were never making 'American Experimental Theatre'. The concerns and impulses that fired painters to subvert *performance* to new ends were different from those of artists brought up with, and perhaps bound to, a reverence for a tradition of theatre. For painters there was no theatre practice to be revised – we were discovering new forms for time and space and 'audience', with no thought that we might ourselves be 'discovered' – at least not by *theatre*. Initially we had no contact with the press, art journals, universities, foundations, theatrical institutions. Our formulations had to do with action painting, movement in found environments, sculpture, waste materials, building from scratch, dreams, and banalities, language used as object, and with confronting taboos inherent in society and its political machinery. All around us were the Viet Nam War Draft Resistance Sit-Ins Be Ins Acid Rock & Roll SDS Weatherpeople The Witches The Diggers . . . assassinations, surveillance of our mail and phones . . . (and the glory mythic light of art-heroism and its reward gathered over certain of our shadowy spaces . . .)[32]

It was an assertion designed to pull happenings closer to the centre of affairs, to situate them on a critical borderline between the public and the private world, to bridge a gap between aesthetic and social revolt which many had eventually come to regard as disabling. And if it is not wholly convincing it is plainly true that form, structure, authority and the presumptive rights of the imagination were of central importance in a decade in which fundamental presumptions were increasingly challenged. If happenings were not themselves the new theatre which many had looked for, they were at least further evidence of that spirit of experimentation which increasingly typified the theatre in the late 1950s and early 1960s.

In 1965 Ken Dewey, himself a creator of happenings, remarked that 'The further out one moves, the simpler becomes one's understanding of what theatre is. I now would accept only that theatre is a situation in which people gather to articulate something of common concern.'[33] Typically vague, this statement was nonetheless in tune with the position of John Cage who regarded all sound as music (and who defined theatre as 'seeing and hearing') and Merce Cunningham who regarded all movement as accommodatable to dance. And, as Richard Kostelanetz has pointed out, the connection between the arts was not simply proposed as theory; in the 1950s and 60s, it was a practical reality. Happenings had merely made this more apparent. Ken Dewey, Michael Kirby and Meredith Monk, all involved in happenings, began in the theatre, while Rauschenberg has designed costumes and sets for the dancer Merce Cunningham as well as being a major painter in his own right. Cunningham himself was once an actor and has conducted Cage's music and directed plays while his fellow dancer Ann Halprin began her career on Broadway.

Indeed the movement in dance largely paralleled that in art. Ann Halprin's first major piece to make a break with her more conventional career as a modern dancer was also a product of that climactic year, 1959 – *Birds of America or Gardens Without Walls*. She has explained that 'The concern in this work was for non-representational aspects of dance, whereby movement, unrestricted by music or interpretative ideas, could develop according to its own inherent principles. The compositional approach allowed for group collaboration and improvisation.'[34] Stillness was an essential ingredient of this dance as silence was of many of John Cage's compositions. The objective likewise was 'the possibility of discovering in chance relationships some new ways of releasing the mind from preconceived ideas and the body from conditioned or habitual responses'.[35] And this itself, as she explained of a subsequent work,

> was a direct attempt to prepare the audience for their own departure from the theatre to the outside – to have opened up their senses and attitudes and

make them able to go outside into the streets with a sharpened awareness of the pure drama all around. Thus, bringing into the theatre itself the everyday real life, merging it with the make-believe or fantasy of theatre, was meant to be a direct invitation to the audience to experience the drama inherent in the 'outside world'.[36]

Ann Halprin was suspicious of uncontrolled improvisation and audience involvement and in that respect she shared something with Robert Rauschenberg who insisted that 'I have never been particularly interested in improvisation because, trusted to improvise, people very rarely move out of their own particular clichés and habits. Or, if they do, they are using their own pre-manufactured disguises of those habits.'[37] It was a perceptive comment and all too applicable to a number of Off-Broadway productions. Nonetheless it is not hard to see the link between her work and that of John Cage or in some degree the creators of happenings. She was above all reacting against meaning and choosing to focus on pure movement, non-mimetic and drained of interpretative weight.

Nor, on one level at least, was it difficult to see a connection between this and the theory of literature then being expounded in France by Alain Robbe-Grillet for whom presence became the central issue and for whom the physical reality of the moment or the object mattered more than any assumed a priori meaning. Robbe-Grillet, of course, was not propounding a sense of mystery or spiritual being. He was in a way proposing the primacy of the 'more immediate world' which would 'take the place of this universe of "meanings"' . . . so that the first impact of objects and gestures should be that of their *presence*, and that this presence should then continue to dominate, taking precedence over any explanatory theory which would attempt to imprison them in some system of reference, whether it be sentimental, sociological, Freudian, metaphysical, or any other.' Apart from anything else this was a rejection of what, in the American context, had constituted the central dramatic tradition while its emphasis on the primacy of existence over signification seemed to chime with Zen's emphasis on the immediate, though Zen, in addition, of course, could offer the consolation of a spiritual dimension all too patently missing from contemporary life.

In 1964 Susan Sontag published an article entitled, 'Against Interpretation', in which she argued that interpretation was 'the revenge of the intellect upon art',[38] a cultural resistance to sensual capacities, to the immediate power of experience. Interpretation, she argued, created a shadow world of meaning which existed to one side of an immediate responsiveness, a world which in asserting its own authenticity implied the inauthenticity of mere experience. She suggested that a great deal of contemporary art derived from a desire to resist interpretation, its concern with abstraction and parody being part of an elaborate strategy to evade emasculation. An art which exists only on the surface is presumably immune to what Robbe-Grillet called cultural 'speleologists', and Robbe-Grillet was the figure who lay behind her remarks. What was needed, she argued, was more attention to form; in place of a hermeneutics, she insisted, we were in need of 'an erotics of art'. In *L'Empire des Signes* (1970) Barthes described various Japanese arts (such as cooking, gardening, gift-wrapping and puppet theatre) and found that they exhibited an 'exemption of the sense', that is a concern for surface over depth, a conviction that the surface is the reality. This was the aesthetic basis of happenings; it also underpinned some of the presumptions of performance theatre. It was equally a concern of Zen.

If John Cage proved a critical figure in the development of the arts in America in the 1950s and 60s through his absorption and recasting of Zen, through his pioneering of happenings and through his concern with probing the relationship between a constructed art and a re-conceived reality, he also played a crucial role by introducing to an English-speaking public what was to prove a major influence on 1960s theatre – Antonin Artaud's *The Theatre and Its Double*. And not the least of the reasons that he personally responded so enthusiastically to Artaud was that writer/director's own fascination with the East.

The path by which Artaud entered American consciousness in the 1950s and 60s is an interesting one. On a visit to Paris, Cage had his attention drawn to the work of Artaud by Pierre Boulez. On his return to America he, in turn, introduced both David Tudor and Mary Caroline Richards at Black Mountain College to Artaud's work and they often read that work together. Mary Caroline Richards then translated *The Theatre and Its Double* into English and it was published by Grove Press, a copy falling into the hands of Julian Beck at the Living Theatre. It had an immediate impact, more especially since many of its ideas seemed to chime so completely with the avant-garde's interest in mysticism, with its suspicion of language, and with its desire to create works in which causality, narrative and character gave way to the power of the image and the liberation of the sensibility.

Artaud, theoretician, actor and director, responded to what he saw as the rupture between 'things and the ideas and signs that are their representation',[39] by desiring to bring art and experience into closer relationship, and this in turn meant circumventing the evasions of a language which was severed from the objects and realities which it purported to describe. His conviction was that 'To break through language in order to touch life is to create or recreate the theatre.'[40] The theatre, indeed, became a primary mechanism in this social and meta-physical recuperation: 'We must believe in a sense of life renewed by the theatre', because 'the theatre takes gestures and pushes them as far as they will go . . . It reforges the chain between what is and what is not, between the virtuality of the possible and what already exists in material-ized nature. It recovers the notion of symbols and archetypes which act like silent blows, rests, leaps of the heart, summons of the lymph, inflammatory images thrust into abruptly wakened heads.'[41] The func-tion of theatre was to 'disturb the senses' repose', free 'the repressed unconscious', and incite 'a virtual revolt' which, however, could only have its full effect 'if it remains virtual'. The value of theatre lies in its power to unmask, its ability to penetrate an experience which lies beyond spoken language. He looked for the substitution of 'a poetry in space' for 'poetry in language'. And this involved music, dance, design, pantomime, mimicry, gesticulation, intonation and lighting. He was determined to move the *mise-en-scène* to the centre of attention. He grants that 'the language of gesture and postures, dance and music, is less capable of analyzing a character, revealing a man's thoughts, or elucidat-ing states of consciousness clearly and precisely than is verbal language', but asks 'whoever said the theatre was created to analyze a character, to resolve the conflicts of love and duty, to wrestle with all the problems of a topical and psychological nature that monopolize our contemporary stage?'[42] Since this was precisely what had concerned the American theatre for half a century it is perhaps not surprising that Artaud was so eagerly received by those in revolt against that theatre. Indeed, his comments on Western theatre in the mid 1930s had a surprising rel-evance to the American theatre of the 1940s and 50s. 'Given the theater as we see it here', he objected, 'one would say there is nothing more to life than knowing whether we can make love skilfully, whether we will go to war or are cowardly enough to make peace, how we cope with our little pangs of conscience, and whether we will become conscious of our "complexes" . . . of if indeed our "complexes" will do us in. Rarely, moreover does the debate rise to a social level, rarely do we question our social or moral system.'[43] For all Miller's ostensible criticism of Ameri-can society this is an accusation which might be levelled at his work, as at that of Tennessee Williams.

Artaud wished not to abandon language but to react against its utilitarian function. He wanted to turn his back on a humanistic, psychological theatre in order 'to recover the religious and mystic'. Nor was he unaware that such an objective was likely to make him an object of some suspicion but insisted that 'If it is enough to pronounce the words *religious* or *mystic* to be taken for a churchwarden or an illiterate priest outside a Buddhist temple, at best good only for turning prayer wheels, this merely signifies and condemns our incapacity to derive the full impact from our words and our profound ignorance of the spirit of synthesis and analogy.'[44]

He reacted against the notion of theatre as a 'performed text'. But at the same time he was not in favour of formalism, a confusion between art and aestheticism. He did not believe that painting should function only as painting, or that dance should 'be merely plastic' because this would 'sever their ties with all the mystic attitudes they acquire in confrontation with the absolute'.[45] The function of theatre was 'to express objectively certain secret truths, to bring into the light of day by means of active gestures certain aspects of truth that have been buried under forms in their encounter with Becoming'.[46] It was 'to create Myths, to express life in its immense, universal aspect, and from that life to extract images in which we find pleasure in discovering ourselves'.[47] He resisted improvisation, because he did not want to leave things at the mercy of the thoughtless imagination of the actor or at the whim of chance, but in a partial contradiction asserted that '*We shall not act a written play, but we shall make attempts at direct staging, around themes, facts, or known works.*'[48]

He claimed that 'to link the theater to the expressive possibilities of forms, to everything in the domain of gestures, noises, colors, movements, etc., is to restore it to its original direction, to reinstate it in its religious and metaphysical aspect, is to reconcile it with the universe'.[49] But at the same time he was not concerned to deny the fact that language, too, held such a potential; merely that this was not how it was used in a Western theatre 'which employs speech not as an active force springing out of the destruction of appearances in order to reach the mind itself, but on the contrary as a completed stage of thought which is lost at the moment of its exteriorization'.[50] To his mind, speech in Western, or what he chose to call Occidental, theatre,

> is used only to express psychological conflicts particular to man and the daily reality of his life. His conflicts are clearly accessible to spoken language, and whether they remain in the psychological sphere or leave it to enter the social sphere, the interest of the drama will still remain a moral one according to the way in which its conflicts attack and disintegrate the characters . . . But these moral conflicts by their very nature have no absolute need of the stage to be resolved. To cause spoken language or expression by words to dominate on the stage the objective expression of gestures and of everything which affects the mind by sensuous and spatial means is to turn one's back on the physical necessities of the stage and to rebel against its possibilities. It must be said the domain of the theater is not

psychological but plastic and physical. And it is not a question of whether the physical language of theater is capable of achieving the same psychological resolutions as the language of words, whether it is able to express feelings and passions as well as words, but whether there are not attitudes in the realm of thought and intelligence that words are incapable of grasping and that gestures and everything partaking of a spatial language attain with more precision than they.[51]

He was in revolt against lucidity, partly because of his conviction that all true feeling is untranslatable and partly because it is a denial of a fundamental truth – the existence and dominating fact of the void. He favoured indirection – the poetic image. As he insisted,

It is not a matter of suppressing speech in the theater but of changing its role, and of reducing its position, of considering it as something else than a means of conducting human characters to their external ends, since the theater is concerned only with the way feelings and passions conflict with one another, and man with man, in life. To change the role of speech in the theater is to make use of it in a concrete and spatial sense, combining it with everything in the theater that is spatial and significant in the concrete domain; – to manipulate it like a solid object.[52]

'Things', he insisted, 'must break apart if they are to start anew and begin afresh . . . Masterpieces of the past are good for the past; they are not good for us.'[53] He opposed psychology because it was rationalist, concerned with reducing the unknown to the known. He opposed a system 'with the spectacle on one side, the public on the other', and looked for a theatre in which an image might 'shake the organism to its foundations and leave an ineffaceable scar'.[54] He also insisted that changes in the public world made it no longer possible to rest with the old idea of theatre: 'there are too many signs that everything that used to sustain our lives no longer does so, that we are all mad, desperate, and sick'.[55] And in this, too, his work struck a chord with those in the American theatre who felt a similar sense of crisis.

They responded, too, to his conviction that the boundary between audience and performer should be destroyed, equally a logical implication of happenings. Thus in *The Theatre and Its Double* he announced,

we abolish the stage and the auditorium and replace them by a single site, without partition or barrier of any kind, which will become the theatre of action. A direct communication will be established between the spectator and the spectacle, between the actor and the spectator, from the fact that the spectator, placed in the middle of the action, is engulfed and physically affected by it.[56]

Artaud, psychologically at odds with the world of the flesh (indeed neurotically disturbed by the natural functions of the body), urged the need to rediscover a sense of the mystical. The crisis of the modern, to his mind, was a crisis of belief and the theatre had a crucial role in restoring this lost capacity. It was to be a ceremony, a world in which the audience was to share. It could short-circuit painful dualisms, as, he believed, did the Balinese dancers he observed at the Colonial Exhibition. The central figure was to become the director. And, since language was to be subordinated to the other aspects of theatre, he thereby became the author or initiator of the play. The theatre was no longer to be structured around the dualisms of actor and audience, stage and auditorium. He proposed the abandonment of existing theatres and the adaptation of informal spaces (realised in America in the form of Off-Off Broadway). If the image of the existing theatre was that of the museum, that of his new theatre was to be the church. And he, too, had turned to the East. His reading included the *Upanishads* and the *Bhagavad-Gita*. In search of theatrical inspiration he travelled to Mexico, as the Beats were to go there in search of mystery, while his revolt against language led him to the creation of his own language – a venture which was ultimately invoked as primary evidence of his insanity (though not of Ted Hughes when he devised a new language for Peter Brook's *Orghast*).

The impact on the American theatre of the 1960s was plain to see. The desire to redefine audience/performer relationships, the revolt against dualism, the suspicion of language, the search for the mystical, the stress on movement and sound released from simple functionalism, the retreat from the psychological, the concern for the spiritual, for a communal experience, all typified, to a greater or lesser degree, the work of the Open Theatre, the Living Theatre, the Performance Group, the San Francisco Mime Troupe, and the Bread and Puppet Theatre as well as a large number of lesser-known groups. It is interesting to contemplate what the nature of American theatre might have been had John Cage not visited Paris and returned with a book first published twenty years before.

It is clear that behind Artaud's desire to breathe life into theatre, to deflect it from what he saw as its stasis, lay a vision of a society similarly transformed and a sensibility reinvigorated by its rediscovery of the spontaneous, the mysterious, the physical reality of existence. His desire to go beyond language, to fill the void with sound and light, to assert an anarchic humour, to stress plenitude, sonority and texture were aspects of a desire to restore man to himself, to close the gaps between conscious and unconscious, form and substance, spirit and body. To Artaud, the playwright's failure stemmed from his desire to present the world as it appeared in its least profound guise, in his acceptance of existence as contained and defined by social and psychological axes. Now the theatre was to be a mechanism of release and primary evidence for the possibility of that release. His own subversive humour was plainly a central strategy at several levels. It was designed to resist criticism and to sustain him in his challenge to orthodoxy, but it was also to be a primary means of short-circuiting conscious and subconscious worlds. So, too, his resort to incantation, to the religious and the mystic; for him, humanism in the theatre was a limiting obsession. For him, space and time were tangible forms and not merely dimensional contexts, simple frames for recreated experience. The key word was to be danger; the primary responsibility to take risks and acknowledge no boundaries. And it was this man who set the tone for the American avant-garde theatre of the 1960s – this man and, in the late 1960s, a Polish theatre director called Jerzy Grotowski, whose theories seemed immediately appealing precisely because they seemed so much a summary of all that the avant-garde had absorbed from Zen, from happenings and from the work of Artaud. The author of an influential book – *Towards a Poor Theatre* – published in 1968, Grotowski appealed in particular to those groups for whom perform-ance was both the method and subject of drama.

As Ludwik Flaszen, theatre critic and one-time literary manager of the Slowacki Theatre in Cracow, remarked when summarising Grotowski's position,

> The performance is not an illusionist copy of reality, its imitation; nor is it a set of conventions, accepted as a kind of deliberate game, playing at a separate theatrical reality. Performance itself is reality; a literal, tangible event. It does not exist outside its own substance. The actor does not play, does not imitate, or pretend. He is himself; he makes a public confession; his inner process is a genuine process, not the work of a deft performer.[57]

Behind this there was a utopian thrust, a yearning for the identity of word and object. The holistic dream dominated. Grotowski looked for a total act from the actor who

> does not tell a story, or create an illusion – he is there in the present . . . If the act is accomplished, the actor, that is to say the human being, transcends the phase of incompleteness, to which we are condemned in everyday life. The division between thought and feeling, body and soul, consciousness and the unconscious, seeing and instinct, sex and brain then disappears; having accomplished this, the actor achieves totality . . . the reaction which he evokes in us contains a peculiar unity of what is individual and what is collective.[58]

Unsurprisingly, this was seized on, when he and his company went to America in 1967 and again in subsequent years, as yet another means of neutralising alienation.

It was in this sense that Grotowski insisted that

> Theatre . . . provides an opportunity for what could be called integration, the discarding of masks, the revealing of the real substance . . . Here we see the theatre's therapeutic function for people in our present-day civilisation . . . We fight them to discover, to experience the truth about ourselves, to tear away the masks behind which we live daily . . . Theatre only has a meaning if it allows us to transcend our stereotyped vision, our conventional feelings and customs, our standards of judgement – not just for the sake of doing so, but so that we may experience the real and . . . discover the real. In this way . . . we are able, without hiding anything, to entrust ourselves to something we cannot name but in which lives *Eros* and *Caritas*.[59]

The problem, of course, is to distinguish between the two and in this the American theatre companies were by no means adept.

What Grotowski was interested in and what those in American performance theatre really seem to have responded to was his desire to aid in the creation of a different sensibility, located in the immediate future but defined in terms which seem reminiscent of romanticism. For Grotowski, a product of a collectivist society, the path to the collectivity lay through the discovery of self; for Richard Schechner and others, products of a society which has enshrined individualism in a myth of *laissez-faire* endeavour, the path to the self lay through the group. It was perhaps no more than a tactical difference but it is worth reminding ourselves that little thought was given to the context from which Grotowski's work emerged, his early production, *Acropolis*, making specific reference to the extermination camps.

In February 1970 Grotowski, of whom Stuart Little in that same month wrote, 'Certainly not since Stanislavsky brought his Moscow Art Theatre to the United States in 1923 has a foreign theatre group had such an impact here',[60] and who had himself just returned from a trip to India, announced that, 'We live in a post-theatre age.'[61] In 1975 his company left the theatre altogether, changing its name to the Institute Laboratory. This ended a period in his work but something had collapsed much earlier in America. A confident if vague radicalism had lost its focus with the ending of America's direct involvement in Vietnam in 1973. The solidarity briefly forged as a political expedient or a psychological and spiritual ideal had fragmented. Economic crisis, political reaction and an altogether insufficiently rigorous aesthetic led to the collapse of morale no less than the loss of audience. Where once the theatre had seemed to express the excitements of a culture in the process of a disturbing re-examination, now it was increasingly relegated to the margin. In a sense, of course, it had always been on that margin, but for a while in the 1960s and early 1970s it could persuade itself otherwise because its concerns seemed to be those of the culture itself. There seemed to be a sympathetic vibration between the age and the stage. For the decade and more that followed it was simply no longer possible to persuade oneself that this was indeed the case.

However, by the same token, for more than a decade the theatre was at the centre of cultural and even political affairs. And the proponents of performance theatre were not the only ones who would have agreed with John Cage's insistence that 'changes in theatre preceded general changes in the lives of people'.[62] As he explained in his book *A Year from Monday*, the important thing was to 'set forth a view of the arts which does not separate them from the rest of life, but rather confuses the difference between Art and Life'. This confusion of realms held throughout the 1960s. For Cage, 'Theatre is obligatory eventually because it resembles life more closely than the other arts do, requiring for its appreciation the use of both eyes and ears, space and time.'[63] And that erosion of the boundary between dramatic and social performance did indeed become a favourite tactic both of the theatre group intent on transforming the nature of political reality and of those whose transformations were more metaphysical than social. They were not, for the most part, intent on leaving an inheritance for future generations which would consist of a series of artifacts, dramas to be re-enacted in other places and at other times. Their art was of the moment. The heritage they hoped to bequeath was a renovated sensibility and hence a renovated world in which the very definition of art would have been changed. Their eclecticism was both method and philosophy. They paraded a vision of an underlying unity to experience and hence responded enthusiastically to those they took to be on the same quest. And because, for a while, the culture seemed responsive to such an objective, theatrical epiphanies seemed to have a potency and a centrality which they could scarcely claim before. Though groups such as the Living Theatre, the Open Theatre and the Performance Group never performed to much more than a coterie audience and though happenings were widely regarded as not much more than a bizarre and marginal activity of an urban avant-garde, those who deployed their energies and creative talents in this direction could feel that theirs was an exemplary art. For all the self-deceit involved, for all the collapse of the social, artistic and metaphysical unity which they sought and for all the naivety of some of their productions, it is by no means clear that they were wrong.

PART II

Performance theatre

INTRODUCTION

In 1949 Paul Goodman, whose plays were later produced by the Living Theatre, observed that, 'the essential present day advance guard is the physical re-establishment of community. This is to solve the crisis of alienation in the simple way: the persons are estranged from themselves, from one another, and from their artist; he takes the initiative precisely by putting his arms around them and drawing them together.'[1] This communitarian impulse strengthened throughout the 1950s and 60s, and to some people the theatre group, sometimes living together as well as performing together, offered a persuasive analogue for this sense of transcendental unity which individuals sought in encounter groups, communes and images of a simplified physical environment. Thus, following the prescripts of Artaud, Julian Beck, one of the co-directors of the Living Theatre, came to reject that kind of theatre in which individuals are required to sit isolated from one another in the dark and live by proxy, surrendering their freedom and their imagination to those on the stage who alone can move and act. This, he suggested, was to be reduced to less than life, to reject the potential for physical contact and spiritual unity which the theatre could and should offer. Over the process of a decade he came to feel that even the avant-garde theatre had become detached from people; that in posing questions of a social or psycho-logical kind, or even in its modernist concern with its own status as fiction, it had ceased to exercise a function which should properly be seen as part celebration, part therapy, part ecstasy and part almost a religious sense of mystery at the heart of the self and of the universe. By the early 1960s he had begun to try to create a theatre in which, as he said, the public could examine its own physical self, examine its being, its own physical being, its own 'holy' body, individually and collectively.

The Living Theatre was founded in 1951 and dedicated itself to the production of experimental works by writers like Gertrude Stein, Kenneth Rexroth, Paul Goodman, Jarry and Picasso. In this respect it was dedicated to the literary avant-garde. But even at this time it was open to influences of a broader kind. In 1952 John Cage wrote a programme note for one of the group's performances which in some ways predicted the direction of some of their later work and of performance theatre itself, as he also anticipated the rationale behind happenings. His piece read:

> instantaneous   and unpredictable
>
> nothing is accomplished by writing a piece of music
>
> nothing is accomplished by hearing a piece of music
>
> nothing is accomplished by playing a piece of music

our ears are in excellent condition[2]

It was some time before Beck pursued the logic behind this, a logic which called for an artless art, for the dissolving of the barrier between art and life, for the abandonment of direction and of metaphoric intent. Indeed his work has never been modelled on Cage's more severe strictures in the way that, say, Rauschenberg's single colour washes are, or Warhol's films. Nonetheless, by the end of the 1950s he was producing plays which simulated improvisation and which were sometimes scripted according to chance procedures and hence mimicked what he saw as the process of life itself – plays like Pirandello's *Tonight We Improvise*, William Carlos Williams's *Many Loves*, Jack Gelber's *The Connection* and Jackson MacLow's *The Marrying Maiden*. But Beck rapidly became discontented with this work precisely because the improvisations were simulated and not real, because the plays were re-enactments and not enactments. For this reason the 1964 production of Kenneth Brown's *The Brig* became crucially important, for this, within given constraints, did allow for genuine improvisation; it also concerned itself with sound rather than language, proving possibly the most complete embodiment of Artaud's theories. *The Brig* followed his prescription in that it created stunning images and effects which assaulted the senses of the audience. The words were virtually impossible to distinguish, characters scarcely existed; there was no attempt at psychological depth, no obvious link between linear time and logical process. It was a crucial production but if it identified a sense of community this was only a community of suffering. Its image of dehumanisation, of the victory of the machine, was an absurdist symbol. The improvisation of the actors, though real enough, was invisible to the audience and hence the freedom which the actors discovered was suffocated by the severe constrictions of the text. In his subsequent work Beck has chosen to foreground technique in the belief that this is content

– the freedom of the actor offering a paradigm of freedom itself, the freedom no longer to act but to be. As Beck has said, 'It would never again be possible for us not to improvise!'[3] He came to see fiction as a parenthesis in the history of art and asserted that from then on the members of his group 'were no longer playing characters, but our-selves'.[4] The writer now largely disappears and the play's dialogue is created through improvisation and through examining the internal dynamic of the group.

What followed were the Living Theatre's most important works, *Mysteries* (1964), *Frankenstein* (1965) and *Paradise Now* (1968), and during these years Beck concerned himself with creating a theatre which would itself become a model for his anarchist/pacifist/communitarian principles and which would hence destroy what he saw as the dictatorship of the director, the writer, and even the autonomous dramatic work as it would seek to subvert the dominating and destructive power of society. And this was to be done in a quest for spiritual unity of the kind he had found extolled by Goodman, Cage and Ginsberg while employing theatre as a means to therapeutic revelation which would bypass the intellectual defences of a puritan society. Scatological language, nudity and at times drugs were to be used not to shock society but as a sign that they refused any of the petty constraints which limited self-perception. Indeed performance theatre chose to de-emphasise language, partly because of its emphasis on rationalism and partly because, as Pinter, Handke and Albee, among others, have indicated, it is a means for structuring and hence controlling experience. To change consciousness therefore is to change language. For, as Beck remarks, 'Breakdown of language equals breakdown of values, of modes of insight, of the sick rationale. Break-down of language means invention of fresh forms of communication.'[5] These groups thus tended to emphasise movement and the body. Some of them showed an interest in proxemics and the techniques of non-verbal communication and, because they were interested in seeing the self in terms of relationships with other selves, in transactional analysis and gestalt psychology. Members of Ann Halprin's San Francisco Dance Theatre and Richard Schechner's Performance Group actually under-went therapy.

The resistance to language manifested by groups from the Living Theatre, the Performance Group and the Open Theatre in the 1960s, to Mabou Mines, and Robert Wilson's theatre in the 1970s had, I suspect, a number of causes, not all of them conscious. Besides the impact of Artaud, linguistics was showing an increasing concern with non-verbal communication. The problematics of language were very much on the intellectual agenda. In sociology, language was regarded in simple, even simplistic terms, both as an agent of a manipulative capitalism and a means of post facto rationalisation. Books like Nancy Mitford's *The American Way of Death* exposed the American love of euphemism while the bland animadversions of the military in the Korean war and later in the Vietnam war, and the newspeak of the House Un-American Activities Committee (whose very title was delightfully paradoxical) scarcely encouraged faith in the identity of language and meaning. Besides, for a country deeply stained by versions of Freud, distrust of language was perhaps engrained. O'Neill had made it the whole basis for his play *Strange Interlude* in the late 1920s.

And the American theatre has been deeply marked by Freud not least in its concern with the price to be paid for the supremacy of the reality over the pleasure principle. The battle between the two was staged in its purest form by O'Neill in *The Great God Brown* but it became the essential theme of both Tennessee Williams and Arthur Miller. For all Williams's responsiveness to the sensual being not only does he show that libidinal self being subordinated to the rational demands of a positivist society but he acknowledges the legitimacy of the demands which society makes. This was the essence of the tragic spirit which he, no less than O'Neill and Miller, aspired to. And since to Freud art itself was a result of sublimation it was perhaps inevitable that art, and specifically the theatre, would turn to a contemplation of its own procedures.

For both John Proctor in *The Crucible* and Willy Loman in *Death of a Salesman* it is a failure to control the sexual impulse which is a primary source of guilt. It is seen as a betrayal. It is such also in *After the Fall* and *A View from the Bridge*. Indeed, Miller's plays operate on the model of psychoanalysis – that is, they work from the assumption that self-consciousness has a vital curative function and the plays tend to consist of a slow examination of the past, a revelatory probing of suppressed experience in an attempt to understand its meaning. Indeed, *After the Fall* seems to consist of a literal psychoanalytic session, though, predictably perhaps, this is blurred so that it could be a religious confession or even a story told to a friend. The objective is freedom. The past has to be faced in order to be transcended; the repressions have to be acknowledged in order to destroy a sense of alienation. Thus his characters are left, for the most part, committing themselves to a new life having liberated themselves from their neurosis, having abandoned all concealments. It is in this sense, however, that he is in a way a profoundly conservative writer. Despite gestures against modernity or a conformist society he is fundamentally concerned with reconciliation – with returning his characters to a world untransformed, unregenerate, its momentum scarcely stilled by the passage of a troubled conscience which is revealed as little more than a self at war with itself. Their neuroses are the product of a failed repression – a simple denial of experience, rather than its transmutation or transcendence.

But if Miller's theatre was Apollonian the new theatre was to be Dionysian. If Miller's was Platonic, if it was intellectual, suspicious, thematically and theatrically, of the body (nearly always sexuality is linked with betrayal), then the new theatre was to be concerned not with the shadow but the substance, the physical being rather than the anguished world of thought and emotion.

Indeed Norman O. Brown offered a neo-Freudian reading of theatre itself, in *Love's Body* (1968):

> The exhibitionism of the phallic personality . . . is fraudulent; an imposture, or imposition on the public theater. The actor needs the audience to reassure him he is not castrated . . . To force the audience to give this reassurance is to castrate, have coitus with the audience: the phallic personality needs a receptive audience or womb. Separately, both actor and audience are incomplete, castrated; but together they make up a whole: the desire and pursuit of the whole in the form of the combined object, the parents in coitus.[6]

What Brown offered as image, performance groups were prone to offer as reality but the pursuit of holistic models of experience was one of the more persistent phantoms of the 1960s. The object was to deny boundaries, destinations, and thereby to deny the reality principle.

Where O'Neill, Miller, Williams and Albee had been concerned with the steadily shrinking physical, moral and psychic space of contemporary life, this was a theatre which sought to create space or to recognise its persistence. As John Cage remarked, 'WHERE THERE DOESN'T SEEM TO BE ANY SPACE, KNOW WE NO LONGER KNOW WHAT SPACE IS. HAVE FAITH SPACE IS THERE, GIVING ONE THE CHANCE TO RENOVATE HIS WAY OF RECOGNIZING IT, NO MATTER THE MEANS, PSYCHIC, SOMATIC, OR MEANS INVOLVING EXTENSIONS OF EITHER.'[7] What was called for, in other words, was a redefinition of space and an increased sensitivity to the physical qualities of the real, though this did not, for the most part, apply to language which increasingly tended to be distrusted or at least subordinated to the supposed authenticity of experience.

To the solemn moralising of the American dramatic tradition, then, performance theatre counterposes a vital, energetic, non-teleological world, a Dionysian celebration of the liberated body and soul. The threats of modern existence are not to be neutralised through desperate illusion, as they were for O'Neill's or Miller's or Williams's characters. Performance art is not a tragic art. For Arthur Miller the paramount need had been to embrace the past, to acknowledge guilt and responsibility, and to commit oneself to an endlessly repeated and perhaps doomed engagement with a fallible human nature. For Tennessee Williams the answer frequently lies in solitary flight or a sexuality which is his imperfect objectification of compassion. For O'Neill it is a tolerant understanding of the need for self-deception and the necessity of grace. But performance theatre rejects this puritan vision of life. It is concerned with celebration.

Where Freud was convinced that civilisation was founded on a necessary suppression of the instincts, with a naturally consequent sense of guilt, this theatre sought to liberate the instincts, to destroy repression and revert to that stage of erotic and sensual spontaneity which is a characteristic of childhood in the individual, and primitive and largely pre-literate physicality in the race. Performance theatre was in effect neo-Freudian. Its adherents were not concerned with delineating the moral burdens implied by necessary sublimations but with liberating the individual and art from social and mimetic constraints. For them the theatre was no longer to be a part of that system which placed the mind over the body, the reality principle over the pleasure principle. It was to be a revolutionary force returning man to a prelapsarian state of grace. It was not to be a reflection of life; it was to be life itself. This was saying no more than Cage had said when he remarked that 'Theatre takes place all the time wherever one is and art simply facilitates persuading one this is the case.'[8] Thus his interest in hearing music in the day-to-day sounds of the environment, in destroying the distinction between art and life, between the performer and the audience, between the mind and the body became the basis of performance theory and it should be no surprise to discover Julian Beck saying in his book on theatre, 'Everything ought to be theatre',[9] or Peter Brook, in his 1968 book, *The Empty Space*, 'theatre and life are one'.[10]

For performance theatre, despite its reliance on mythical structures, action is always contained in the present. It is a theatre of manifestation, of enactment rather than re-enactment. The only past is a mythical one, an archetypal one. The present is not explained by the past. This is the method of the realistic, liberal, theatre. The novel, of course, had inevitably dragged the reader back into the past by virtue of the tense which even now, and even in self-consciously fictive literature, threatens to establish an inevitable sense of causality and rational structuring of events and character. The theatre has always had the special advantage of speaking in the present tense, dramatising the past through the *mise-en-scène* or through the pressure of action and expressed memory. In performance theatre that present is more fully utilised, even celebrated. The physical contact between audience and performer which was a feature of the Living Theatre's *Paradise Now*, the Open Theatre's *Viet Rock* and the Performance Group's *Dionysus in 69*, was an enactment of this connectiveness, a refusal of the moral restraint and the rational concealment which Beck sees as the membrane dividing not only one individual from another but each individual from his or her authentic self.

In the words of Norman O. Brown in *Life Against Death* (1959), 'The life instinct, or sexual instinct, demands activity of a kind that, in contrast to our current mode of activity, can be called play. The life instinct demands a union with others and with the world around us based not on anxiety and aggression but on narcissism and erotic exuberance.'[11] Brown called for a 'Dionysian body mysticism'[12] as Marcuse had urged what he called 'polymorphous sexuality . . . the opportunity to activate repressed or arrested organic biological needs: to make the human body an instrument of pleasure rather than labour'.[13] And it is no accident that Dionysus, bi-sexual, uniting east and west, linking the races, connecting terror and release, standing for the supreme importance of the erotic and the necessity for breaking boundaries, should, historically, be the god of the theatre – a theatre which in Greece began with improvisation, obscene language and celebratory revels.

If this version of theatre, indeed this vision of human activity, should seem regressive, as many of the movements of the 1960s seemed to be (from the establishment of rural communes to a renewed interest in astrology and demonology), this was freely acknowledged not only by Beck but by writers like Brown and Marcuse. In his 1966 preface to *Eros and Civilization*, which had initially appeared a decade earlier, Marcuse even argued that the Vietnam war was a symbol of the body's fight back against the machine – the political and corporate machine. Indeed, in asking the question, 'Does guerilla warfare define the revolution of our time?', he was in fact implying, as he said, that 'historical backwardness may again become the historical chance of turning the wheel of progress in another direction'.[14] But despite his political sympathies this was offered as an image, a metaphor. He explained, 'The spread of guerilla warfare at the height of the technological century is a symbolic event: the energy of the human body rebels against intolerable repression.'[15] So, he suggests, 'as cognition gives way to recognition, the forbidden images and impulses of childhood begin to tell the truth that reason denies. Regression assumes a progressive function.'[16] Performance theatre, in its emphasis on the body, on the feelings, was also, in a Freudian sense, reverting to an earlier stage of development, to the spontaneous, physical and erotic style of the self before it is conditioned by social institutions and of man before he subordinates those instincts to the constraints of rationality. It looked for and affected to find authenticity in feelings liberated from the constraining power of rationality, language and moral structure. And in that, of course, it was by no means the first.

Wagner had called for what he called the 'emotionalising of the intellect'. He had said that 'an action which is to justify itself before and through the feeling, busies itself with no *moral*; its whole moral consists precisely in its justification by the instinctive human feeling . . . from relations such as can spring only from a human society intrinsically at one with itself . . . a society belonging to itself alone, and not to any past'.[17] But here is the root of a very European worry I have about such presumptions, for the belief that the feelings are in some way authentic and necessarily moral and that the mind is deceptive and inauthentic seems to me not merely facile but dangerous (and I am not unaware that something akin to this assumption was held by the dadaists except that their scepticism extended even to the emotions). Totalitarianism is as likely to spring from the feelings as from the mind and the dark romanticism of some aspects of the Third Reich should remind us of this. After all some of the most impressive and monumental examples of total theatre seen in the last half century were staged at Nuremberg and Julian Beck has never succeeded in blurring the line between performer and audience so thoroughly as did Goebbels who provided precisely that sense of secular ritual and ceremony which Beck had struggled to attain. There are some people involved in performance theatre who are aware of this danger and perhaps it is not so surprising that one of them should be a Pole, Jerzy Grotowski. Beck himself has recognised the problem from time to time but has defended what he himself has called 'fascist' methods as in some way necessary in order to coerce people in the direction of truth. I do not want to overplay this point but it seems a necessary one to make because of the curiously anti-modernist conviction which animates this theatre, and which implies that beneath the carapace of positivist existence is a warm, communal spirit which can be released under the pressure of a Dionysian rite. Schechner could see the casuistry of such an assumption, Beck could not. It is perhaps no wonder that though drawn to politics in the general sense of urging life as opposed to death, and echoing the old surrealist cry to open the jails and release those trapped in the constraints of bourgeois society, performance art proved hopelessly ineffectual when confronted in 1968 with the not insubstantial realities of the bourgeois power structure and a radicalised youth which found its pacifist convictions incapable of deflecting the path of the social system. That is perhaps debatable. Possibly the Living Theatre and others did play their part in changing consciousness and hence provoking the politicisation which left them so completely stranded, but my point is rather different. It is that this new theatre was in the end curiously dated. It was also a theatre which one could argue was signally unqualified to tackle the issue of Vietnam since unlike the absurdist and liberal writers of the 1950s and 60s it had responded to the problems raised by the Second World War by ignoring them or simply writing them off as a by-product of a corrupt rationalism. If men had listened to their hearts, it was suggested, then Auschwitz and My Lai wouldn't have happened. It is a presumption which is chilling in its simplicity. But Beck's vision of an ideal community has always been tinged with naivety. Take his own description: 'What we're looking for is a system in which people take care of themselves without abstract forms to control them – small communities in which we can get to communicate with each other and tell each other what our needs are. Obviously with the help of cybernetic automation to process these needs, and then to produce what's necessary – food, clothing, heat – and to distribute them free.'[18]

There is moreover another interesting confusion in Beck's work which derives from his presumption that once one has stripped off the actor one is left with a definable self. As Julian Beck says of *Mysteries*, it 'taught us the pleasure of just being ourselves . . . the courage not to be cast in a role'.[19] Ann Halprin similarly talks about an 'authentic' self.[20] Yet as one of the actors in Schechner's *Dionysus in 69* discovered when she tried to step out of character in the play, refusing to collaborate in a stage murder, 'I found that I could not shed the actor, no matter how you try to escape the bounds of the theatrical you find yourself inside one or another succession of symbolic acts.'[21] Similarly, when Beck says that he is after a simple presentation of 'things as they are', he assumes an empirically defined reality which is perhaps no longer persuasive. He presumes the existence of a hard impenetrable self on the one hand and a cluster of artificial roles on the other, the existence of fiction on the one hand and truth on the other – the one a product of the mind, the other of the sensibility. It scarcely needs sociologists, transactional psychologists or even metaphysicians to suggest that this is something of an over-simplification. Certainly for writers like Pynchon, Coover or Kosinski this is not a formulation which makes any sense. The Living Theatre prefers a simpler version of metaphysics; its references to truth, reality, identity and authenticity make it look especially vulnerable and its attack on cerebral theatre seem like a kind of special pleading.

Its Eden (specifically denoted in the play *Paradise Now*) is not unlike those other Edens being identified by Norman O. Brown, Marcuse, R. D. Laing, Charles Reich or Alvin Toffler but it lacks the rigour of some at least of these visions. Marcuse, for example, had warned that 'in a world of alienation, the liberation of Eros would necessarily operate as a destructive, fatal force . . . relaxed sexual morality within the firmly entrenched system of monopolistic controls itself serves the system'.[22] This of course is a Marxist assumption while those in performance theatre worked from the other end but the totalitarian nature of their methodology (they on occasion physically assaulted their audience and frequently failed to respond to interventions from the audience which they considered hostile and inauthentic) undermined their own efforts. Meanwhile their own didacticism undercut their professed desire to liberate the imagination. The dictatorship of the writer/director/actor was broken only to be replaced by the dictatorship of the group. Shocked by the viciousness of a social world which was, sure enough, revealing a fairly unsophisticated ripple of muscle at the time, they tended to huddle together in cosy groups where their shared language and unsullied love for man and a co-operative economy could create a microcosm of the new new world, a new world which apparently differed from the old new world by virtue of having understood the danger implicit in liberal individualism and a naive presumption that God was located anywhere except in the human heart. The potential for self-deceit in such cabals, however, was clear enough, and when other models of society intruded, as in 1968 at Berkeley they did, the shock could be traumatic.

There were clear limits to the freedom which their style seemed to advocate. The caress, in the Performance Group's production of *Dionysus in 69*, an action in which the actors physically caressed members of the public, was abandoned when one of the actresses, who had encountered a particularly enthusiastic member of the public all too willing to accept the dissolving of barriers between audience and performers, quite properly objected that, 'I didn't join the group to fuck some old man.'[23] Nor were these groups without a disturbing contempt for the audiences with whom they were supposedly establishing a human connection. Schechner remarked that 'the caress depended on an innocence which a long-run play cannot have. And a willingness to participate within the terms of the production that audiences do not have.'[24] There is in fact a disturbing and destructive smugness in Schechner's admission of the play's ultimate failure to communicate its vision. He says:

> When Dionysus throws his buttons down to the spectators, many scramble for them as if a button were a gold coin, so strong is the habit and hold of acquisitiveness. I sit smug and detached and watch a double scene of genuine horror and poignancy. Here, Dionysus turned tyrant and fascist. There, spectators jostling each other for a cheap (but free) souvenir. Their behaviour means they have not understood the play. Instead, they

participate in it with the same unthinking power with which they validate their congressmen, bosses, priests, and presidents. The people deceive and betray themselves even as they listen to a warning against deception and betrayal.[25]

This truculence was perhaps one reason for the decline of these theatres; the unfocussed work an explanation for the return of the writer who made his reappearance in the Performance Group at the end of the 1960s. Performance drama is very much a phenomenon of the 1960s and early 1970s, with its concern with the free expression of the senses, its communitarian impulse, its search for personal transcendence, its optimistic and even naively sentimental presumption about the essential goodness and even holiness of human nature. And in its naivety, like other groups in the 1960s equally dedicated to the propagation of personal freedom and self-perception, it developed at times a dangerously programmatic and exclusivist version of freedom. Its methods became in some ways as coercive as those they sought to displace. It was not inappropriate, therefore, that by the late 1970s the movement should have effectively run its course. The suspicion of theatre which had created the pressure which led to their own experiments eventually expanded to include those experiments. Chaikin moved on because he recognised a new orthodoxy which he had himself created. Grotowski announced that theatre was dead or alternatively was everywhere so that the necessity for a special framing of experience was perhaps thereby obviated. Broadway of course took whatever it considered usable in Off-Off Broadway, especially the nudity, the scatological language and the naive vitality. But since it did so without understanding the impulse behind elements which were rooted in a broader philosophy it did little more than consumerise those elements – proof, if such were needed, that Off-Off Broadway experimentation was not a question of testing new forms but seeking a redefinition of the purpose and possibilities of theatre. That process of redefinition brought an energy to the American theatre it had formerly lacked. Seeking no validation beyond the immediate authenticity of the moment, the magic of the performance, it remains in some final sense immune to critical attack. Its naiveties were its strengths as well as its weaknesses. And for a decade performance theatre commanded a respect and interest on an international scale which had not always typified the American theatre while its major groups merit a more detailed attention. The crucial event was perhaps the Living Theatre's production of Jack Gelber's *The Connection* – not merely because this signalled a renewed interest in the work of young American dramatists but because it raised fundamental questions about the nature of theatre, the role of the actor and the substance of reality.

2 The Living Theatre

The Connection was perceived by critics as hyper-realism, a kind of dramatic *trompe l'œil* in which the *frisson* of the occasion derived from the reality value of what was observed. The power was presumed to lie in a violation of theatrical convention as apparently real drug addicts enacted their own compulsions, and even if this proved a factitious performance the achievement of the play was located in its powerful simulation of reality. What was mostly denied was a symbolic dimension since it was presumed that that very realism precluded the symbolic as it destroyed the transcendent. And yet, as Meyerhold had observed, 'The object does not exclude the symbol; on the contrary, as reality becomes more profound, it transcends its own reality. In other words, reality, in becoming supra-natural, is transformed into a symbol.'[1] However, Gelber's grotesques, whose lives are radically simplified by their supposed dependencies, were offered less as a renovated realism, less as a study of the collapse of character into caricature and the social into the pathological, than as potent images. Again, as Meyerhold had insisted in his acting classes, 'The grotesque helps the actor to portray the real as symbolic and to replace the caricature with exaggerated parody.'[2]

The response to the play was the more surprising given Gelber's careful framing of events. He underlines the fictionality of the work as carefully as Robert Coover was to do in his short stories. The play is itself introduced by Jim Dunn, supposedly the co-producer, who, immediately after insisting on its literal authenticity, identifying the actors as real addicts and introducing Jaybird as the supposed author whose personal research is the guarantee of the play's authenticity, announces that, 'This word musician here has invented me for the sole purpose of explaining that I and this entire evening on stage are merely a fiction.' The play, he insists, 'has no basis in naturalism'.[3] And though the subsequent action is an attempt to destabilise this view, the apparent filming of events by two cameramen creates a multi-layered effect which moves performance itself to the very centre of the piece.

The Connection is ostensibly concerned with a group of drug addicts brought together to perform an improvised play. They await the arrival of their connection – Cowboy – who will supply them with drugs. A Salvation Army sister, of doubtful status, arrives with Cowboy, who has used her as cover for his activities. When the connection duly arrives they inject themselves with heroin, one of them coming dangerously close to taking an overdose. The play is apparently filmed by two men who are themselves drawn into the action and who offer an authentication of the action – 'That's the way it really is.'[4] – which becomes progressively more ironic.

The promise of improvisation is realised only in the music, of which there is approximately thirty minutes in each of the two acts. Indeed, part of the irony of the play derives from the fact of a factitious freedom, a liberty claimed but not realised. It was not an irony which Julian Beck perceived, though it seems clear enough in a play which offers itself as a patent image of social and metaphysical absurdity. As Kenneth Tynan observed, its theme was reminiscent of *Waiting for Godot*, and certainly its central situation of a group of people waiting for the arrival of someone who will satisfy their need for relief from the pain of their situation is familiar enough. The drug, like Camus's sense of the absurdity of routine existence or the familiar god of Beckett, has the quality of satisfying a need which it has itself created.

The connection is not only the man who will bring them drugs, it is also the drug which will connect the fragmenting parts of their experience, and, beyond that, the desire to locate a principle of order, to discover a sense of purpose. As one of the addicts remarks, 'If you don't find it there you look some place else. And you're running, man. Running. It doesn't matter how or why it started.' And lest the general applicability should be lost, he concludes, 'I used to think that the people who walk the streets, the people who work every day, the people who worry so much about the next dollar, the next new coat, the chlorophyll addicts, the aspirin addicts, the vitamin addicts, those people are hooked worse than me.'[5] But this is not offered simply as a comment on America. The play is plainly not only the social drama which Jim announces it to be and which a number of critics were happy to regard it as being. It is, as Solly, the most philosophical of the addicts, observes, about the absurd gulf between desire and fulfilment, the persistent faith in a principle of order with the power to redeem a sense of incoherence. It is about the belief that meaning is external and in definitional relationship to the self. As Solly observes of his fellow addict, 'like the rest of us you are hungry for a little hope. So you wait and worry. A fix of hope. A fix to forget. A fix to remember, to be sad, to be happy, to be, to be. So we wait for the trustworthy Cowboy to gallop in upon a white horse.'[6]

The plot of their lives is that they have no plot. This is precisely the paradox as well as the dramatic strategy of the play, as it had been of *Waiting for Godot*. Hence the irony which lies in the intervention of the supposed author who interrupts to complain that the 'actors' have failed in their responsibility to establish their individual characters and the nature and progression of the plot (this is, of course, precisely the objection raised by critics of Beckett's work on its first appearance). Besides serving to draw attention to the performed quality of conventional life this highlights the paradox involved in creating a carefully constructed and ordered work in order to insist on the absence of such qualities in experience. The suggestion that the play is improvised is a means of both sidestepping the issue and providing a paradigm of a possible response. For Beck, indeed, the suggestion that the play was improvised was a deception, a retreat from authenticity which increasingly bothered him.

The static nature of the play and of the characters is less realistic detail than metaphysical observation. Except in the musical passages they do little but wait. They are supposedly part of 'something infinitely larger', the play which they are to enact, and, beyond that, the underlying meaning of the play, grasped fully only by the author who is abandoned half-way through the first act. The image is an obvious one. They have been abandoned by the man who is, in effect, their creator. And lest the point should not be clear there follows a discussion of the drug syndicate during which the photographers argue, in mock theological fashion, that the existence of the organisation implies the existence of a 'big connection'. 'If you have an organization, somebody must be in charge.'[7] To which Solly replies, 'it is a mystery where Cowboy goes. Anyone coming to Leach feels that he is the central actor in his own drama. An artificial and melodramatic organization. But that is the set up . . . The man is you. You are the man. You are your own connection. It starts and stops here.'[8]

It is a world without transcendence, an absurd world on the social no less than the metaphysical level. 'We are waiting', observes Solly. 'We have waited before. The connection is coming. He is always coming. But so is education, for example. The man who will whisper the truth in your ear. Or the one who will shout it among the people.' It is, he acknowledges, a 'pretty miserable microcosm', chosen by the author, he presumes, 'because of its self-annihilating aspects'.[9] As he confesses, 'There is something perverse in me looking for meaning all the time.'[10] This is reflected in the supposed author's desperate interventions as he tries to impose shape on the play, to introduce a chorus, to precipitate an appropriate ending. And this is Gelber's central metaphor. The writer, after all, creates characters and thereby endorses the assumption of character as a constant; he imposes structure, implies a level of concealed meaning, sculpts experience into form. But if he is a kind of god he is also an apt image of that individual who works on the same assumptions, who encounters dissonance and struggles to hear harmony, who sees disorder and whose brain insists on imposing form. The absurd is born out of these contradictions as, in Freudian terms, it exists in the tension between the instinct for life and that for death. As Solly observes, 'When I talk I'm a pessimist. Yet, I want to live.'[11] The subject of the play is absurdity; the fact of the play its denial. Jaybird, the supposed author, comments that 'one thing I've learned about the theatre. I believe it all fits together . . . We wouldn't be on stage if it didn't fit',[12] a desperate conviction but nonetheless an essential paradox of absurd art. It is a paradox, moreover, which Gelber seeks to resolve by foregrounding it, by insisting on the contingency of art, but also by suggesting a limited transcendence in the fact of Solly's realisation that 'It doesn't have to fit.'[13] Beyond that lies only the fragile consolation of shared experience.

The music, which plays such a significant part in the play, is itself a powerful image of the way in which spontaneous individual freedoms can be merged into a form which is generated rather than imposed. When a silent character, Harry McNulty, interrupts the action to play a Charlie Parker record, it inspires the musician addicts to play, a process which Gelber, in a stage direction, calls 'cementing their feelings'.[14] And that is precisely its function. As the black writer Ralph Ellison remarked of jazz,

> The deliberate balance struck between strong individual personality and the group . . . was a marvel of social organization. I had learned too that the end of all this discipline and technical mastery was the desire to express an affirmative way of life through its musical tradition and that this tradition insisted that each artist achieve his creativity within its frame . . . and when they expressed their attitude toward the world it was with a fluid style that reduced the chaos of living to form.[15]

Though Gelber is more tentative in his affirmation, it clearly does exist within the harmonies of the music and in the fact of abandonment which, if acknowledged as the source of an absurd irony, is also presented as the basis for an existential responsibility. The absolute becomes the self and that in turn becomes the basis for a new possibility. As Sartre had remarked,

> we . . . in the very depths of historical relativity and our own insignificance are absolutes . . . and our choice of ourselves is an absolute . . . all the bonds of love and hate that unite us with each other and that exist only in so far as we feel them . . . this whole discordant and harmonious life combines to create a new absolute which I like to call *time*. This time is

intersubjectivity, the living absolute, the dialectical wrong side of history.[16]

This cannot be historical time, and, indeed, the use of addicts by Gelber clearly abstracts them from time as it threatens to divorce them from one another. It is an attenuated world. There is no confident selfhood, no relationship with others which is not threatened by self-created needs. But there are moments of consonance in which the ironies of this are momentarily annihilated and those moments, embodied in the harmonies and orchestrated dissonances of jazz, are crucial. As Julian Beck observed, 'Jazz is the hero, jazz which made an early break into actual improvisation' which was 'related to the automatic writing of surrealism'.[17]

If the theatre of the absurd entered the bloodstream of the American theatre through Gelber's *The Connection* and Albee's *The American Dream* and *The Zoo Story* it seems equally clear that the rigour of its vision is there subverted by another impulse. For it not only comes up against a persistent optimism but equally a resilient existentialism and, beyond that, a communitarian impulse which relates individual to group.

The Living Theatre was born out of a respect for language as transformed by the poetic sensibility. Indeed it set itself the task of providing a stage for the poet and began its life by producing Lorca, Stein, Eliot, Auden, William Carlos Williams, Goodman, and Rexroth. The bias towards modernism derived from Beck's conviction that this had constituted a formal commitment to expand the capacities of language in art and that the modernist experiments with language were intimately connected with a desire to transform perception and thereby to transform the real. Words were to be a revolutionary mechanism not through their prosaic literalness, their documentation of social truths, but through their transforming power, through their ability to bridge the spaces opened up by money, class, power or history itself. As he said in an essay which preceded the published version of *The Brig*, 'Storming the Barricades': 'The language is always good, like light. Language is the key. It opens the doors that keep us locked in, our confining chambers, the Holy of Holies, the instrument of unification, communication, and from communication let us derive the word community. The community is love, impossible without it, and the syllogism affirms then that love, as we humans may supremely create it, rises and falls with language.'[18] It was not an observation easily reconcilable with the scepticism of the modernists' stance, any more than was his belief that language is at its most honest in 'the grunts that rise from real feeling, satisfaction from food or with the body . . . those sounds wrenched from my groin upward and out of my throat'.[19] The authenticity of such flaccid assumptions was, after all, precisely the subject of debate. But his view of language was not entirely elemental or alimental. On the contrary, aware of its capacity for deception he nonetheless looked on it as a primary means to expose the truth: 'the spoken word must be the word we use when I speak to thee, not the language of deception, not the music of the word in order to dissemble, language that ultimately separates. The word must join us, else it is just another barricade. We kill one another when we do not speak the truth; it is the way to early death. But when you speak to me true I live, and you live a little longer. It is our joint struggle against death.'[20] This, in the words of Herbert Marcuse's book, was to be love against death.

It was a view which would come increasingly under pressure. Indeed two of the company's most successful productions, *The Connection* and *The Brig*, might have seemed directly to challenge his insistence on the authenticity and the liberating power of the word, but his tendency to accommodate both texts to a realistic norm reduced the pressure of the contradiction. Thus, he insisted that the work of both Gelber and Brown 'emerges on the distillation, extraction, re-presentation of exact words and actions of life as it is lived, honest, uncompromisingly honest', and that the audience is moved 'probably because being very near to life itself, we are moved . . . because it is close to life, shows us life itself, and that is always the encouraging thing'.[21] By 'life itself' he plainly did not mean simply a literal transcription. Indeed, he acknowledged an 'intimation of poetry' in both works. But the bias towards authenticity, established through setting and character and sustained through language, disguised the real force of plays whose power and originality lay elsewhere, most especially in their conscious retreat from the word, in their self-reflexive theatricality, in their reaction against a narrative drive, in a deconstructive logic established and resisted through deliberately non-verbal structures. It is as though Beck distrusted their metaphysical bias as in some sense inimical to his own anarchic and revolutionary convictions. Yet the verse plays with which the Living Theatre had struggled, with varying degrees of success, from 1951 onwards, had been nothing if not metaphysical in intent. Beck had learnt from these productions that precision of language and of rhythm was itself a primary mechanism, a necessary underpinning to analogical inference, but he seems to have been increasingly drawn to the social realism of the surface of both *The Connection* and *The Brig* and as a consequence to have deflected his attention from the metaphysical into the social. Of *The Connection* he has said that 'A resurgence of realism was needed: what had been passing for realism was not real . . . There had to be an end to sets with angled walls, the whole false perspective bit. There had to be real dirt not simulation. There had to be slovenly speech . . . there had to be real profanity.'[22]

Asked to provide a caption for a photograph of the Living Theatre staff in the early 1960s which would reflect their objectives, Beck suggested: ' *To increase conscious awareness, to stress the sacredness of life, to break down the walls.*'[23] It was offered as a summary of the three stages of the group up to that time – the period at the Cherry Lane Theatre from August 1951 to August 1952, which Beck characterised as their initial statements; the five years at One Hundredth Street, devoted, in his eyes, to the establishment of a theatrical institution; and the subsequent period, at Fourteenth Street and Sixth Avenue. But in fact it was a more accurate account of the last stage. Over the years the group had found themselves in increasing conflict with authority in its various guises. The Cherry Lane Theatre was closed by the Fire Department, the loft on One Hundredth Street by the Building Department and the theatre on Fourteenth Street by the Internal Revenue Service. As the 1960s advanced so the necessity to resist authority, to break through boundaries, became a chief preoccupation of their plays as well as a description of their methodology. And their desire to reach the audience, to disturb its equilibrium, took a more direct form. With Pirandello's *Tonight We Improvise*, as subsequently with William Carlos Williams's *Many Loves* (1959) and Gelber's *The Connection*, they produced a series of plays in which the audience's sense of the real was to be directly challenged, each employing the device of the play within the play. As Beck has said,

> We did not choose these plays because they contained these devices. It is true that our message, if you want to call it that, and our mission, was to involve or touch or engage the audience, not just show them something; but we did realize that these play-within-the-play devices arose out of a crying need on the part of the authors, and of us, to reach the audience, to awaken them from their passive slumber, to provoke them into attention, to shock them if necessary, and, this is also important, to involve the actors with what was happening in the audience.[24]

Unsurprisingly, since Joseph Chaikin was a member of the Living Theatre for a time, there is a striking similarity between Beck's invocation of the religious origins of theatre and that outlined by the Open Theatre's principal dramatist, Jean-Claude Van Itallie. He wished the audience to become again what once it had been, 'a congregation led by priests, a choral ecstasy of reading and response'. He sought to annihilate divisions by bringing into the theatre and mixing together spectator and performer, the intention being 'to equalize, unify, and bring everyone closer to life. Joining as opposed to separation'.[25] It is this that led Beck to be suspicious even of the theatrical mask. While acknowledging its power and its role in classical Greek drama and the *commedia*, he wished to expose the face, to stress the authenticity of the body. This stress on authenticity led him to be suspicious of their own simulated improvisations and to respond to what Paul Goodman called the pre-verbal element in his play *The Young Disciple* (1955).

The relationship between Goodman's own remarks in his preface to the play and the ideas of Artaud seems clear but the play was equally a natural development of the group's own concerns. As Goodman remarked, 'I have tried in this play to lay great emphasis on the pre-verbal elements of theatre, trembling, beating, breathing hard and tantrum. I am well aware that the actors we have are quite unable both by character and training to open their throats to such sounds or loosen their limbs to such motions.'[26] To Goodman this was to be a move towards abstraction which would make possible the renovation of the theatre. The articulation of pure sound was to be a means to facilitate a more complete poetic articulation. It was at this moment that Artaud's work itself became readily available for the first time. A pre-publication copy of the English translation was sent to Beck by the translator and, as he has said, from that moment 'the ghost of Artaud became our mentor'.[27]

The Artaud that they chose to embrace was an anarchist who rebelled against social structures in the name of spontaneous feeling; it was the man who invoked the id to break the power of the ego. The influence of chance, a submerged concern since their production of John Cage's *Music of Changes*, moved to the centre of their work, especially in a play like *The Marrying Maiden* (1960) by Jackson Maclow which had been specifically inspired by Cage, though this particular work proved remarkably unappealing to audiences. It even invaded their production of Brecht's *In the Jungle of the Cities*. There is little doubt, however, that the production that came closest to realising their enthusiasm for Artaud was *The Brig*, though Beck's remark that its subject was the same as Brecht's *Man is Man* suggested a slightly reductive version of that play.

Set in a Marine detention centre in Japan, it enacts the experiences of a group of prisoners whose daily life is determined by a detailed list of regulations. Since the whole function of the experience is to punish indiscipline and to enforce a rigid uniformity of behaviour involving a deliberate denial of individual identity, there is no attempt at psychological enquiry. Language is homogenised and reduced to the exchange of simple commands and acknowledgements of obedience. Orders are arbitrary and irrational, the action being generated less by character than by situation.

At one level the play is clearly designed to offer an image of America. The four guards are drawn from the east, west, south and midwest, while the prisoners, we are pointedly informed, 'make up a cross-section of American society'.[28] But, as Judith Malina, who directed it, noted, beyond that it is about any system, any structure which demands total obedience. If shrinking social, psychological and literal space had been the subject of much American drama from O'Neill to Miller, here it reached some kind of acme. The setting is a prison within a prison, a small area delineated by chicken wire within the punishment hut. A series of white lines painted on the floor further objectify the constraints within which they move. Each time a prisoner encounters a line he is required to come to attention and request permission to proceed. Even the simplest of actions may necessitate a number of such requests. The twin terrors are chaotic frenzy – represented by the 'field day' in which all prisoners clean out the building – and the anonymous discipline, which destroys the self.

There are traces of individuality. One prisoner breaks down and is taken away, another is provoked into tears, another is a new arrival fresh to the reductive process of the brig. However, the dominant impression is of a world in which survival and obedience are indissolubly wedded. For Beck, the play is a deliberate provocation, a didactic work designed to inspire a reactive revolt. The barricade of wire between audience and prisoner is designed to provoke a reaction against such barriers and in particular to 'break down the walls of all the prisons'.[29] But this is to ignore the real rigour of the play. A scene set outside the brig was deleted. We are allowed no glimpse of an alternative world, no sense of any environment beyond the prison except the suggestion of other, less literal prisons. The play exists as social commentary but also as a metaphysical conceit. Its inhabitants enter the world of the brig, sentenced without appeal. They learn the rules as quickly as they are able, enact the absurd rituals which an arbitrary authority insists upon, and then leave the world. They shape their fate but this scarcely mitigates their circumstances. Beck is clearly correct in suggesting that where Artaud chose to create his horrors out of the fantastic Brown chooses to derive his from the real, but this leads him to an over-literal reading of a play whose metaphysical implications are more chilling than the social. The continuous sound and movement which characterise the play imply neither purpose nor meaning. The sound and the fury add up only to an image of human activity undercut by absurdity. Beck and Malina were right to see in the play the realisation of certain of Artaud's theories, but the Artaud they sought to embrace was a social revolutionary. Artaud had, after all, insisted that it was no part of the function of theatre to resolve social or psychological conflicts or to serve as a battlefield for moral passions. He wished rather to reinstate theatre in its 'metaphysical aspect'.[30] Beck recognised in *The Brig* an exemplary text of the theatre of cruelty but chose to see in this a concern for social revolt. To Artaud, however, the theatre of cruelty was concerned with the more terrifying truth that 'We are not free. And the sky can still fall on our heads. And the theater has been created to teach us that first of all.'[31] The theatre of cruelty was not concerned with copying life but, through 'sounds, noises, cries' and 'violent and concentrated action',[32] Artaud wished to create a kind of lyricism. He proposed a theatre in which 'violent physical images crush and hypnotize the sensibility of the spectator seized by the theatre as by a whirlwind of higher forces'.[33] It would be hard to imagine a play which more fully realised such an objective than *The Brig*.

Judith Malina seized on Artaud's denial that any spectator who had seen such violent scenes as occurred in a theatre of cruelty could 'give himself up, once outside the theater, to ideas of war, riot, and blatant murder'[34] as support for her own pacifist convictions, but Artaud's interest was elsewhere. He was concerned with 'an energetic compression of the text', in a 'space thundering with images and crammed with sounds';[35] he wished to create a spectacle reminiscent of Hieronymus Bosch (as elsewhere he also invoked Bruegel and Goya), which would serve a 'real metaphysical inclination'.[36] Whether consciously or not Kenneth Brown had created just such a play whose force lies in a cruelty more metaphysical than social. And yet for Brown, as for Artaud, this cruelty serves the purpose of precipitating 'a state of deepened and keener perception'.[37] This was equally the objective of the absurdist. For, as Artaud insisted, 'If the theater, like dreams, is blood and inhuman, it is, more than just that, to manifest and unforgettably root within us the idea of a perpetual conflict, a spasm in which life is continually lacerated, in which everything in creation rises up and exerts itself against our appointed rank.' Julian Beck tries to make him a reformist, but he was never that and certainly the power of *The Brig* lies precisely in the 'spasm' that Artaud identified. It is not best regarded as having 'a second-hand psychological or moral function',[38] but as a powerful image of that 'perpetual conflict'. Artaud's definition of 'cruelty' was 'a kind of higher determinism, to which the executioner–tormenter himself is subjected . . . a kind of rigid control and submission to necessity' involving a full consciousness which gives it its 'cruel nuance'. Brown's play, in which the warden and guards are subject to the same constrictive ironies as the prisoners, displays precisely that cruel nuance. It is a play which, at its most significant, engages 'a cosmic rigor and implacable necessity . . . in the sense of that pain apart from whose ineluctable necessity life could not continue' but which thereby does battle with a 'sense of an appetite for life'[39] in a world in which 'evil is the permanent law, and what is good is an effort'.[40]

For Beck, *The Brig* was a crucial production in that Brown had written a play in which improvisation was essential. It was a lesson in the kind of acting that would express their sense of the real. Stanislavsky's reality had been a reconstructed emotional moment, a simulation rooted in analogy. Within the fixed limits established by Brown improvisation was not merely a necessary theatrical tactic, it was in Beck's words a way to 'Make it real, the real trip, physical, invented from moment to moment . . . reality which is always changing and creating itself, the need for reality (life) in this period of alienation; improvisation as the breath that made reality live on the stage.'[41] But if the prisoners were contained by the brig, Beck's actors were themselves trapped within Brown's fiction and the logic whereby the group now moved towards group authorship was clear. The objective now was free theatre and the first expression of this was a piece called *Mysteries*.

It was during the production of *The Brig* that the forces of authority moved in once more, the Internal Revenue Service closing the group down because of an alleged debt of $29,000. With special permission, however, they left for London where they were to perform *The Brig* at the Mermaid Theatre. This marked the beginning of four years of exile in Europe where they developed two of their best-known productions.

Mysteries was created in less than four weeks. It was a collaborative work with no specific director, though Beck and Malina were to retain their dominant position as directors in the company until 1966. It was a performance in which Beck insisted, more than a little naively, that 'we were no longer playing characters, but ourselves . . . *Mysteries* opened the door to a subversive technique: the courage not to be cast in a role.'[42] The theatre of character was over. In its place, however, Beck in effect offered a mythology of the self. He substituted one set of fictions for another as, increasingly, they enacted their myths of personal liberation in an increasingly formulaic manner and propounded the reality of revolutionary change in an ever more desperate way.

Mysteries was the Living Theatre's first communal creation and it is in part a celebration of communality. Beck has described the process as a natural outgrowth and consolidation of community feeling:

> A group comes together. There is no author to rest on who wrests the creative impulse from you. Destruction of the superstructure of the mind. Then reality comes. We sat around for months talking, absorbing, discarding, making an atmosphere in which we not only inspire each other but in which each one feels free to say whatever she or he wants to

say. Big swamp jungle, a landscape of concepts, souls, sounds, movements, theories, fronds of poetry, wildness, wilderness, wandering. Then
you gather and arrange. In the process a form will present itself. The
person who talks least may be the one who inspires the one who talks the
most. At the end no one knows who was really responsible for what, the
individual drifts into darkness, everyone has satisfaction, everyone has
greater personal satisfaction than the satisfaction of the lonely 'I'. Once
you feel this – the process of artistic creation in collectivity – return to the
old order seems like retrogression.

Collective creation is an example of Anarcho-Communist Autogestive
Process which is of more value to the people than a play. Collective
creation as secret weapon of the people.[43]

The potential for self-indulgence is plain enough, as is the regressive
impulse which can lie in the desire to restore a presumed unity of mind
and body or a lost cohesion of selves contained by common myths and
convictions. Judith Malina was well aware of the reactionary nature of
nostalgia but disinclined to see such qualities in their own work rather
than in the cultural politics of the art theatre.

The première of *Mysteries and Smaller Pieces* took place in 1964, though
the published text dates from 1969. The performance begins with a
deliberate subversion of the audience's space. The performers circulate
among the audience, wearing their own everyday clothes. There is no
curtain, and though there is a stage space the physical contacts between
audience and performers are designed to erode its significance as a
separate area of experience. Following a blackout, one of the company
stands motionless for at least six minutes until, in a manner reminiscent of
encounter groups and small group dynamics, the audience is provoked
into a response. The company then in effect re-enact a sequence from *The
Brig*, simultaneously an acknowledgement of the significance of that
work, a pivotal stage in their development, and an establishment of the
coercive fictions which *Mysteries* is designed to subvert. This blends
naturally into the next section in which the printed information on a
dollar bill becomes the only connection between the fragmented voices
of the performers, and in which a rigidity and military precision is
offered as a mockery both of their individuality and of that cohesiveness
which is a product of simple subservience to money and power, rather
than an expression of genuine community. The rest of the piece constitutes an alternative model, the slow construction of an organic unit.

It begins with 'The Raga', a woman's voice with guitar accompaniment which comes from the audience space. This is followed by 'The
Odiferie', in which the performers move through the audience with
incense sticks. Through a kind of phatic communion they set themselves
to relate to the audience through the senses and thus to become a part of

85

them. There follows a series of chants, calls and responses which call for the birth of freedom and the end of war, a ceremony into which the audience is drawn. Where previously the performers had infiltrated the audience space, now the audience is urged to join the performers on stage. Once there they walk in a circle before, clasping waist and shoulders, they close the circle as an image of the new community. The sounds die away into silence from which emerges 'The Chord', in which the new group begins to resonate a sound, a sound which is born out of the sonorities of breathing but which swells into a hum and then an open-throated note as the new organism senses its communal identity. The group then moves into the audience space. There follows a brief period in which the performers concentrate on the act of breathing, moving through this into a period of meditation. They then exchange sounds with the audience, enact a series of free-form tableaux, a product of improvisation, and then enact one of the Open Theatre's exercises in sound and movement by which sounds and movements initiated by one performer are received and modified by others. Eventually they all join together. As the text indicates, 'The piece is about communication. It unifies the community.'[44] The printed text ends with 'The Plague', a scene which is somewhat misleadingly described as 'After the conception of Artaud', and which dramatises a plague-ridden city. In the first production the concluding section was 'Free Theatre' but insecurity led to its abandonment until the June 1966 production in Milan. Free theatre, as Beck defined it, was improvised; it was a theatre in which 'anybody can do anything he wants to do'.[45] It was the basis for much of the work in the later *Paradise Now*, the work for which the group is perhaps best known.

When the play was performed in Berlin in 1965 they were attacked for using methods which were seen as close in spirit to those employed by the Nazis. Beck's response was somewhat gnomic: 'rituals have their own magic which is contained in their appeal to the psyche. The psyche hates and the psyche loves. And are we more prone to one than to the other? Ritual arouses feeling, and killing comes out of feeling that is non-feeling, and the new world will come out of feeling . . . In *Mysteries* we form a circle and invite the public to join us without making it a law . . . We appeal to free will . . . We arouse it.'[46] By 1969 the Living Theatre found itself under attack from left and right alike, the right throwing eggs, the left tomatoes (a somewhat inexplicable ideological response to vegetables), when it presented *Mysteries* in a theatre.

Mysteries was an effective piece. It did in fact examine the ambiguous nature of community, its power to coerce and to liberate. And since this ambiguity was precisely that which attached itself to the Living Theatre

– hectoring, bullying, dogmatising, but also, on occasion, dramatising a sense of lost community – it became doubly poignant. It abandoned plot and character as it did the simple contours of the social and the psychological, and it placed in their stead images of the feared and the desired. It sought to heal wounds which had opened up: the gulf between ego and id, the individual and the group, audience and performer. Having toyed with improvisation it attempted to give a freedom to the performer which could stand in paradigmatic relationship to the audience. Its images of constraint were designed to imply the necessity for freedom; its symbols of human solidarity were offered as evidence of that freedom shaped in obedience to a higher necessity. Its stress on the non-verbal was both evidence of a distrust of rationalism and an assertion of a truth which could operate directly on the sensibility. As its title implied, it was not designed to make itself available to conventional analysis. It aimed to enact experience which could only be drained of meaning when presented as didactic statement or simple narrative. Like *The Brig*, with which it clearly exists in dialectical relationship, it is aimed at speaking directly to those sensibilities engaged only at the level of sentimentality in conventional theatre. Its rituals are self-consciously presented as akin to those of religion.

Such methods are, of course, capable of concealing simple pieties, of distracting attention from banal metaphysics offered as revolutionary insights. And certainly the Living Theatre was prone to parading coy sentimentalities as spiritual truths and simple exercises in the projection of kinetic energy as vatic rites. The Berlin audience had its point precisely because disregard for intellectual structure led to facile assumptions about human nature and the logic of the liberated sensibility. A decade later at Jonestown in Guyana hundreds of people committed suicide with cyanide-laced Kool Aid precisely because they believed themselves to be united in a search for mystical realities which presumed the material world to be an enemy threatening death and apocalypse; they enacted a terrible communion ceremony which united them in a hideous death. *Mysteries* lacked precisely a rigorous intellectual component, a questioning mind not so easily seduced by the comfortable consummation of the orgasmic community.

At the same time, it is necessary to say that *Mysteries* did attempt not merely to rediscover the physical potential of the actor and to utilise this in a coherent ritual, but also to challenge assumptions about the nature of theatre. It accomplished what, in another sense, Richard Brautigan, John Hawkes or Robert Coover were doing for the novel. It, along with *The Brig*, attempted a redefinition of the theatrical event, abandoning those elements previously presumed to be definitional, and stressing instead those aspects of theatre which distinguish it from the other arts. The presence of the actor and the audience became not simply an incidental fact of the theatrical moment; it became the essence of it. Non-verbal elements reasserted their centrality. The symbiosis between individual actors, a *sine qua non* of theatre, became subject as well as method. The past is no longer invoked as explanation of the present. Character, plot and rational dialogue defer to an enactment of shared experience. The social and the psychological become aspects of the metaphysical. Form exists through the lines of force which connect seemingly disparate experiences. An exemplary text, *Mysteries* was, in effect, both a recapitulation of the development of the Living Theatre over more than a decade – bearing the marks of its concern with the formal images and compressed language of the early verse plays and the liberating improvisations of the more recent work – and an intimation of the direction which it would take with the rather more baroque arabesques of its next work, *Paradise Now*.

Beck's modest objective was to change the world through transforming the sensibilities of those who inhabit it. Unsurprisingly he looked back to the surrealists. He set himself to demystify the state through the subversion of language and the creation of a community of selves. *Paradise Now* (1968) was to be an instrument of this transformation. As Beck remarked, 'It would not be possible to do a play called *Paradise Now* and not (1) be free, (2) free anyone who might not be free. (To the point, alas, at which you draw the line or at which the line, alas, is drawn.)'[47] The latter remark, of course, identifies the source of a potentially disabling irony and raises the whole question of the power of the theatre to transform the world in which it functions. It was not, however, an irony which the Living Theatre were ready to engage, though it haunted their work.

To facilitate the freedom which they sought as method and objective they 'called into action mysterious forces, the influence of color, the wisdom of the *Book of Changes*, the physical–spiritual journey of Kundelini, the arousal of the energy which rests in the chakras, the holy world vision of the Chassidim, the high vision of the *Kabbala*'. With all that going for them how could they fail? As Beck explains, 'We energized the body segment by segment, and we devised rituals, movements, sounds, visions, and cadences that carried the actors (the guides) and the public into trance. In trance, in a spaced-out condition, maybe we could enter Free Theatre.' *Paradise Now*, he explained, 'was a voyage into freer forms, until, high, we walked into the street and re-entered the world prison'.[48] As if to stress the pressure of this world prison Beck and Malina managed to get themselves incarcerated in literal prisons in half a dozen different countries. The more unremitting the political system the freer seemed their theatre, the more accurate their analysis. But at moments Beck was able to recognise the degree to which their theatre was itself invaded by the values of the world. The situation in *Paradise Now* 'was hermetic, just because it was inside a theatre – with and without paid admission – the life of money threatened each one each second'.[49]

Paradise Now deliberately stresses non-rational elements. It relies on oracles, incantation, rituals, yoga. In particular it quotes from and incorporates into its structure the *I Ching, or Book of Changes, Ten Rungs: Hasidic Sayings* by Martin Buber and, less centrally, *The Politics of Experience* by R.D. Laing and *The Nature of the Universe* by Lucretius. The performance is divided into eight 'rungs' which constitute the ascending rungs of a ladder of experience and knowledge culminating in permanent non-violent revolution, a realisation of the self through the other. Each rung consists of a Rite, a Vision and an Action which express one aspect of the revolution which can be realised only when the elements combine. The rites are ceremonies, physical and spiritual; the visions, in Beck's words, generate images or dreams. These in turn precipitate the action. As Beck explains in the printed text, which described rather than preceded the production,

> The rites are enactments of political conditions performed by the spectators and the actors. These conditions are specified as taking place in a particular city but lead to a revolutionary action here and now. The Rites and Visions are performed by the actors, but the Actions are introduced by the actors and are performed by the public with the help of the actors. The actions are introduced by a text spoken by the actors themselves.[50]

The assumption of the performance is that change has to operate internally on the self and externally on society; that, indeed, these are two aspects of the same thing. This is the justification for a structure which tries to pull together the private and the public, the social and the personal, the physical and the spiritual. There is, indeed, an elaborate system of correspondences between the rung and its various components as there is between these components seen on a vertical scale. The central conceit of the rungs is derived from the Hasidim, who conceived of life as a passage up a ladder connecting earth with heaven. But, while movement up the ladder may mean movement towards God, each rung is itself suffused with God. Each rung is an assault on some aspect of experience which resists social change and spiritual transformation.

The performance begins with the 'Rite of Guerilla Theatre' in which each actor approaches members of the audience and complains of a restriction on his or her freedom ('I am not allowed to travel without a passport', 'I am not allowed to smoke marijuana'). The complaints build until the pressure of repression proves unbearable. Shouting 'I'm not allowed to take my clothes off' they tear at their clothes in a frenzy – thereby assaulting the culture which contains them and moving back towards a lost paradise. The 'vision' which corresponds to this is the destruction of the American Indian, the natural man. The corresponding 'action' is the reincarnation of the Indian as hippy, able to initiate the revolution: the accompanying text calls for the birth of a free theatre, the free man, liberated minorities. The first section, in other words, attacks the repressive nature of society and identifies other models of community in the form of the Indian tribe. It proposes a confrontation between the body, the naked self, and the system, through the medium of theatre.

The second rung begins with the rite of prayer in which the actors make physical contact with the audience, insisting on the holiness of all creation, on a spiritual unity once lost but now to be restored through revolution. The company spell out the words ANARCHIST and PARADISE with their bodies, thus expressing simultaneously their objectives and the means of realising that objective. Subsequent sections are concerned with teaching, with the exorcism of violence, the sexual revolution, redemption, love, the revolution of being and the permanent revolution. The coherence of the group and the increasing bond between performer and audience is set against the cruelties of the public world. Just as the Open Theatre seized on the Kennedy assassination as a powerful contemporary image so the Living Theatre utilises the shooting of a Viet Cong suspect by the Chief of Police in Saigon as another such moment. The scene of his shooting is repeated until the gesture is ritualised and overcome by the equally powerful rhythms of the sympathetic group. The physical bodies of the performers, and often of the audience, are combined in body piles which are designed to express the unity of the life force and the power of a love which can overcome the forces of repression. Radical divisions – between Jew and Christian, black and white – are freely enunciated and then overcome by pressing them to the point of absurdity and beyond, with false dualisms (short/tall etc.). When the audience begins to laugh, the performers give one final example – I/Thou – which now itself seems unreal and which the whole method of the production is designed to subvert.

The forces of reaction, as represented by a pentagon formed by the bodies of the actors, collapse. The actors anticipate a post-revolutionary world – here incautiously labelled Hanoi/Saigon – in which the state obligingly withers away and in which there is no longer any army, bureaucracy or money. Truly free at last the individual can 'fly' secure in his organic relationship to the group. This conviction is embodied in the form of an actor who launches into space only to be caught by his fellow actors – an extension of a familiar acting exercise into a social and metaphysical statement (Holden Caulfield, in *Catcher in the Rye*, had wished for no less). The play ends with a death neutralised by the new-found community of selves. The actors then quickly recapitulate the action of the play, encapsulating the new knowledge that they have experienced. Together with the audience they move out onto the streets – there, as often as not, to be obligingly arrested by the police who had failed to grasp their own revolutionary irrelevance and were glad only that revolutionary anarchist pacifists are easier to handle than the violent kind. To be arrested while shouting, 'The theatre is in the street. The street belongs to the people. Free the theatre. Free the street. Begin!'[51] may underscore the Living Theatre's analysis of present repression but it did little to demonstrate the power of their prescription. They set out to destabilise the theatrical frame only to discover that the police department had much the same respect for that frame as the conventional critic.

There is at least an iconographic parallel between those who had poured into the streets echoing the cry to 'Strike, Strike, Strike!' in the mid 1930s, following Clifford Odets's *Waiting for Lefty*, and those who spilled onto the sidewalks of New Haven more than thirty years later, seeking personal and public freedom. Not merely did each group encounter the implacable realities of the American political scene, as emotional solidarity broke against the tangible economic facts of life, but both occasions raised questions about the nature of the theatrical experience. Both plays were produced by groups with a strong sense of group solidarity. Both combined a concern with theatricality with clearly defined political convictions (though the Group Theatre was more concerned with transforming American theatre than American society). Certainly both paraded a series of pieties whose sentimental overtones were quickly exposed by the passage of time. Yet the naive politics which tied *Lefty* to an ideology whose practical corruptions were in process even then of being exposed, and the Living Theatre to a revolutionary post-war Vietnam at odds with the reality which followed, hardly invalidates their concern with enacting the sense of community which was the subject of both plays. *Waiting for Lefty* rested on melodrama, on the stereotype; the Living Theatre on the archetype. The former play relied on a conventionalised language which for the Living Theatre was an expression of the problem. The achievement of *Paradise Now* certainly did not lie in the banalities paraded as crucial insights but in the use it made of the physical presence of the actors, the resources of the human voice (released from its signifying function), the language of gesture, the energy to be liberated by penetrating the space reserved for the audience, by mobilising the creative power of those who could no longer behave as mere observers.

Yet the members of the Living Theatre were dependent on the nature of the public world to a degree which they were unwilling to admit. Although they deliberately intruded references to current events and to the cities in which they performed, the content of the play appeared increasingly conservative in a context in which the public world was itself in a state of turmoil. Despite the spaces left vacant for audience response this space was in fact carefully controlled and as the group repeated its performance across America so inevitably it became increasingly rigid in its structures. Though this is a familiar enough phenomenon in theatre it was likely to prove fatal to a production which identified itself as free theatre. The group was also destabilised when it encountered ideological acquiescence but personal revulsion. Hence at Bennington College a girl student legitimately observed: 'Don't scream at me, you fucking idiot! . . . I don't hate you because you're black. I hate you because you're spitting in my face!'[52] Physical contact degenerated too easily into assault. A woman was struck by one of the actors at a performance of *Mysteries* at the Brooklyn Academy of Music; Julian Beck tore a fur coat from a woman with whom he was in confrontation. Apart from subverting their own pacifist ethic, as they had done also through their participation in the riots at Avignon, this challenged the theatrical basis of their work. The erosion of the boundary between audience and performer, the insistence on 'being' rather than acting, on a direct physical engagement and even attack upon the audience, the dissolution, in short, of the frame, clearly raised questions about the nature of the theatrical event. Indeed in a sense it was designed so to do. Like Whitman's poetic warnings against the primacy of text over nature, they were concerned with advancing the claims of life over those of art. But in theatricalising experience they were in danger of turning life into formulaic art – though they would claim that this was precisely what it was already. The peremptory shapes of art were not synchronous with the flow of experience which they only allowed to infiltrate in carefully controlled ways. Indeed, with time that external world came to be resented. The result was a hermeticism, an arrogance which closed off the avenues they had ostensibly worked so hard to open up.

For Chaikin, their subsequent career, as they fragmented and went back to touring the world, was characterised by the opposite fault. As he observed in 1974, 'They have made a certain separation between themselves and their potential audience and they're playing for them, for the other, the outside other . . . they don't inhabit their work.'[53] Their rejection of the culture which they inhabited – pressed to the point of parody in their rejection of Mozart as a 'racist, classicist pig'[54] – placed them in a position which was crudely defined and which, in its Manichean simplicities, cast doubt on their eagerness to embrace all experience as holy. Chaikin dissolved his theatre when it showed signs of repeating its effects, of becoming unduly institutionalised. The Living Theatre made no such formal gesture, falling apart and then reforming like the multiple-celled creature which had once been their favourite image.

Their rhetoric, once briefly that of a sizeable percentage of the young people of America and Western Europe, was quickly outflanked by events and by other rhetorics. (It is preserved today only in the conversation of those wandering Americans who expatriated themselves in the 1960s.) Their communal ethic deferred in some respects to the concerns of the culture of narcissism. Their aesthetic experiments, which allied them with the artistic avant-garde of the 1960s, proved too vulnerable to the casual assumptions of a neo-romanticism. While seeking to broaden definitions of the real to include a sense of spiritual fulfilment and while trying to raise the physical being to full partnership with that spirituality, they never confronted the ontological or epistemological questions which they thereby implicitly raised. They set out to demystify, to defamiliarise, in the knowledge that these, too, are revolutionary acts but they underestimated their own power to mythicise themselves, to substitute the flaccid myths of natural innocence, physical purity and revolutionary optimism for the incorrigible evils of capitalism, racism and liberal individualism.

However, the Living Theatre did contribute to a revivification of the American theatre. Heavily influenced by Artaud, Julian Beck sought to assault the sensibility of the audience. In reaction against the cerebral, moralised theatre of O'Neill and Miller he set himself to expand the awareness of an audience whose responsiveness became the subject no less than the concomitant of performance. The language of the theatre for which he reached was not a wholly verbal one. Like Artaud he did not seek to deny the utility or value of words but to see them as only one means of communication. As he explained, 'We, the Living Theatre, are trying to reach towards some kind of communication of feeling and idea that push toward some other area that is beneath words or beyond words, or *in addition to words*. The object [he explained, was] not to destroy language [but] to deepen it and amplify it and to make the communication real rather than a series of lies.'[55] What the Living Theatre did create, firstly with *The Connection* and *The Brig* in obedience to Gelber's and Brown's texts, and subsequently in *Mysteries*, in

1.   The Living Theatre, *Frankenstein*, 1965. This production by Julian Beck and
     Judith Malina, 1968.

Frankenstein, *Antigone* and *Paradise Now*, was a series of powerful images, plays in which character no longer sustained its conventional form or moral force, in which the causalities implied by linear plot were abandoned in favour of emotional verities established through shared experience, in which the gesture, the modulated sound, the anguished posture communicated what once had been compressed into a language which could not bear such a burden.

It was not the first theatre to engage in such experiments (The Provincetown Theatre had staged O'Neill's *The Emperor Jones* which had concerned itself with the deconstruction of character and language. Thornton Wilder's *Our Town* had deliberately foregrounded technique while *The Skin of Our Teeth* had exploded linear plot; Tennessee Williams's *Camino Real* had sought to erode the audience's protective space) but, along with the Open Theatre, whose director had anyway begun with the Living Theatre, it was the group which dedicated itself most completely to challenging theatrical no less than social orthodoxy. Its emergence from behind the proscenium arch and into the auditorium and from thence to the street and, in its Brazilian experience, into the peasant community, involved a search for a new audience, as it did an attempt to define the parameters of the theatrical experience. There was nothing new about theatre taking to the streets. This, after all, had been a central strategy of post-revolutionary theatre in the Soviet Union not to mention the medieval miracle plays. But despite Julian Beck's anarchistic views the move to subvert the boundary between stage and auditorium derives less from a desire to enact political rituals than a wish to assert a model of community and an aesthetic rooted in physical relationship.

Its weakness, however, was precisely its unwillingness to submit basic assumptions to analysis. Repeated gestures are no longer spontaneous; a projected persona is no longer a naked self and even nudity can become a form of uniform. The performances relied, to a far greater extent than Beck and Malina would ever confess, on a tacit agreement with audiences who scarcely needed conversion to the new orthodoxy of revolt. When that agreement crumbled under the impact of the violent events of 1968 much of the force of the performance collapsed. The resistance was no longer there. They were outflanked. In 1961, when they were organising the General Strike for Peace, Beck and Malina wrote to Martin Buber soliciting his support. He replied that he dreaded 'the enormous despair that must be the consequence of the inevitable failure'.[56] The Living Theatre did not so much fail as become a purely theatrical force. Certainly the non-violent revolt has been deferred. The capitalist system survives. But the transformation which the group wrought in the face of the American theatre was real enough. The images of release, presented in works like *Paradise Now* and *Frankenstein*, in which man is dramatised as archetypal victim transformed by the realisation that violence is unproductive and yet resistance vital, came to represent a theatre similarly transformed. That such transformations were easily consumerised was predictable, that they did not usher in a golden age in the American theatre unsurprising, but they did identify a potential which had scarcely been recognised before. In a performance of *The Favella Project* (part of *The Legacy of Cain* series) in one Brazilian village, the Living Theatre performed a scene in which Death binds and gags all the actors. They relied on the villagers to release them. Since the performances were illegal the act of releasing the actors was inevitably an act of rebellion. According to Judith Malina, as one of the villagers released her he whispered, 'Tomorrow the favellados will free the people of the whole world.'[57] It seemed that they had found their natural audience. But they had already, perhaps, accomplished a more limited act of liberation within the less dangerous world of the American theatre.

3 The Open Theatre

The Open Theatre was formed early in 1963. It consisted at first of seventeen actors and four writers. Many of the actors had been pupils of Nola Chilton, an acting teacher who left America for Israel in 1962. One of their number, Catherine Mandas, approached Joseph Chaikin, himself a former pupil of Nola Chilton and a member of the Living Theatre Company since 1959 (when he had played a part in *The Connection*), with a view to creating a group which could concern itself primarily with the development of acting skills. It quickly became apparent that Chaikin was a central figure and, for all the group's emphasis on ensemble work, he remained the principal moving force.

Chaikin has described his own development as follows:

> My relationship to the theatre really changed while I was in Brecht's *Man is Man* at the Living Theatre. I had gotten involved with the Becks as an actor to whom they offered a part – not a very good part: I was a replacement in *Many Loves* – but I thought it would lead to better parts in that on-going theatre, which was the only one in New York at the time. Then I would be seen and would be able to get out of there and do what I really wanted, which was Broadway. Judith and Julian cast me in *The Cave at Machpelah, Tonight We Improvise, In the Jungle of the Cities*, and then, sometime later, had me take over the lead in *The Connection*. I wasn't very good in that part, although I did get better, but the Becks liked my performance, and they had me play it on the European tour in 1962. And I felt very swelled, like a minor star . . . While we were in Europe, the Becks asked me to do Galy Gay in *Man is Man* . . . And it sounds like a fairy story, but it was in the playing of Galy Gay that I began to change. There I was, night after night, giving all my attention to pleasing, seducing and getting applause from the audience, which is the very process whereby Galy Gay allows himself to be transformed from an innocent and good man into a thing, a machine – all because of flattery, one flattery after another. That's what really did it.[1]

As he explained, 'The Living Theatre was not really interested in acting at all, and hardly explored the actor's own powers or the ensemble experience . . . So I began working with writers and actors from Nola Chilton's class . . . When the Living Theatre went to Europe in 1963, I did not.'[2]

At first there was some doubt as to the objective of the new group –

whether, indeed, it should primarily be a communal group doing theatre or whether it should be a group of theatre professionals. The decision to call themselves the Open Theatre was regarded as an expression of their commitment to change and development. It was also, however, implicitly a decision that their concern was to be essentially theatrical and the Open Theatre never developed that communal dimension which was a mark of the Living Theatre, in which the group frequently lived as well as performed together. The other essential difference derived from their emphasis on the actor and the development of acting skills. At the heart of their work was a series of exercises specifically designed to facilitate a non-naturalistic style of acting able to respond adequately to a theatre which was itself involved in a process of transformation. The title was also a conscious declaration of independence from the conventional theatre. As he explained in his book, *The Presence of the Actor*, 'My intention is to make images into theatre events, beginning simply with those which have meaning for myself and my collaborators; and at the same time renouncing the theatre of critics, box office, real estate, and the conditioned public.'[3]

Nola Chilton had been a Method teacher but she had evolved a series of exercises designed to prepare the actor for performing in absurdist dramas where the usual techniques of psychological preparation seemed inappropriate. The exercises that Chaikin devised were in large degree an extension of this. His assumption was that 'Our training has been to be able to have access to the popular version of our sadness, hurt, anger, and pleasure. That's why our training has been so limited.'[4] The object of their training was therefore to avoid the stereotype, to investigate the way in which 'The stage performance informs the life performance and is informed by it.'[5] In particular they set about examining the nature of sound and movement.

All exercises, Chaikin remarked, must start from and return to the body in motion. Nor was this simply a theatrical observation. His stress on the body was to be found equally elsewhere in a culture for which the self in its various guises became a central icon. For an actor/director apt to quote Thoreau on the subject of individual freedom ('*The law will never make men free: it is the men who have got to make the law free. They are the lovers of law and order who observe the law when the government breaks it.*'[6]) the leap from practical skills to cultural observation and even metaphysical aphorism is scarcely surprising. 'What about the body of the character?' he asks. 'All of one's past – historical and evolutionary – is contained in the body. In America many people live in their bodies like in abandoned houses, haunted with memories of when they were occupied.'[7]

Reaction against the competitive ethos of Broadway expressed itself through an insistence on ensemble work and, in particular, through a series of exercises which were designed to emphasise the interdependence and mutuality of the actors. 'Ensemble asserts the way that people are alike. We live and die separate. But there is a point where we are completely interlocked, a point where we are brought together, all of us, by our participation in nature, where we are brought together two by two, or in threes or fours, by our participation in something larger than each of us.'[8] Hence, in an exercise called 'Trust in a Circle', an individual actor, standing in the middle of a circle of other actors, closes his eyes and allows himself to fall, trusting those around him to prevent his hitting the floor. In another exercise called 'The Chord' the actors close their eyes and listen to the breathing of those around them. This turns into a drone which they all take up, follow, intensify and diminish. The individual crucially contributes and yet exists in relation to the group. It is simultaneously a lesson in group dynamics and in the necessary connection between the actor's individual being and his participation in the collectivity.

Chaikin's theatre was to be open in respect to its approach to character, in its rejection of acting styles based on stereotype and reinforced by the kind of trade paper advertisements which called for 'young male lead', '*ingénue*', 'middle-aged character actor', etc. In contrast to established theatre, in which a group was assembled only for a single production and in which training was a form of grooming for the job market, the Open Theatre was to take chances, to break rules, to have the confidence to challenge assumptions of all kinds. In origin it was not set up as a production company. It began as a private laboratory. Such performances as it gave were an extension of that laboratory and were offered as unfinished pieces, their unfinished nature being another aspect of the group's openness. Then, with Megan Terry's *Viet Rock* (1966), they became a group performing a finished work which turned into a commercial venture. Much the same thing happened with Jean-Claude Van Itallie's *America Hurrah!* Although *Motel* (first produced at the Cafe La Mama in 1965), which formed one of the three components of that play, had already been written before he joined the group, the other elements were in some respects a response to what he saw of the exercises and the themes which the group was working on at the time. And the production was a normal commercial venture.

But in all this it is clear that, for Chaikin, there was an obvious parallel between their activity as actors and the need for transformation in the world beyond the theatre, although this had formed no part of their original objective. Indeed, while with the Living Theatre he had originally resisted the politicisation of the group's activities, feeling that this was extraneous to the real business of theatre, but subsequently he became a political activist, joining draft demonstrations and going to jail, and the connection between theatre and the political and cultural world was acknowledged. So that it is perhaps inevitable that he constantly makes the connection between the two worlds, the one existing less as a mirror of the other than as a microcosm. Thus, in addressing the actors in 1965, he insisted that:

> It would be good for certain boundaries, tacit as well as defined, to be broken. It would be good to have a tossing up of values and experiment with the comedy of sincerity, breaking down the structure that we work within, like a person whose habits in living have left him impaled in patterns of acting which anchor him. It would be good to change the relationships which we are frozen in: Theatre audiences', directors', and actors' relationships. Other kinds of recognition scenes must be played out.[9]

It was not, however, to be an open world in so far as the director's role was concerned. Here there remained an element of necessary tyranny, a degree of authority, indeed, which, very early in the group's history, led to the departure of a number of actors who were unhappy with the direction in which Chaikin was taking them.

Originally the Open Theatre was concerned with 'getting away from talking', a fact which in itself established a distance between themselves and a Method training which had taught them naturalistic delivery. This led to exercises and experiments in breathing rhythm and in voice, independent of words. It also led to a stress on physical movement. But it did not mean the abandonment of language – merely its re-evaluation. For Chaikin, as for Artaud, the need was 'to find how we can sing words and crush words . . . The spoken word is too often simply giving sound to the printed word. We should want to find how to speak words, not simply as data, but using the sounds which make up the word to create the universe of the word.'[10]

The Open Theatre first performed publicly in December 1963. At the urging of Gordon Rogoff, who had attended a number of their sessions, they hired the Sheridan Square Theatre for two performances. They presented a sound and movement exercise, some improvisations and short plays by Van Itallie and Megan Terry. The programme set out their conception of their work at this early stage:

> What you will see tonight is a phase of work of the Open Theatre. This group of actors, musicians, playwrights, and director has come together out of a dissatisfaction with the established trend of the contemporary

theatre. It is seeking a theatre for today. It is now exploring certain specific aspects of the stage, not as a production group, but as a group trying to find its own voice. Statable tenets of this workshop: (1) to create a situation in which the actors can play together with a sensitivity to one another required of an ensemble, (2) to explore the specific powers that only the live theatre possesses, (3) to concentrate on a theatre of abstraction and illusion (as opposed to a theatre of behavioral or psychological motivation) (4) to discover ways in which the artist can find his expression without money as the determining factor.[11]

At the urging of the reviewer and critic Richard Gilman the group began to perform regularly in public and to see their work more clearly in terms of that performance. Accordingly, in 1965, they gave regular performances at the Sheridan Square Theatre, performing improvisations but also ten plays, from Brecht's *Clown Play* and T.S. Eliot's *Sweeney Agonistes* to works by Van Itallie and Maria Irene Fornes. To Chaikin this was in some ways a threat to the workshop programme, for although it did indeed give them an opportunity to test themselves against an audience, it also tied them to a routine of rehearsal which threatened the more fundamental concerns of the group as he saw them. This was intensified when they agreed to appear regularly at Ellen Stewart's Cafe La Mama. The group showed signs of collapse, but they recovered with their production of Megan Terry's *Viet Rock* which was developed as a consequence of improvisatory work which centred around the Vietnam war. Though the script was written by Megan Terry this was a consequence of improvisations which she in part responded to and in part shaped. This did not prevent considerable bitterness as disagreements arose as to the correct tone for the production, Chaikin urging, according to Robert Pasolli, a more clearly angry tone, and Terry looking for irony. When the play transferred from La Mama, Chaikin withdrew. The play ran for six weeks Off-Broadway.

Viet Rock was developed in a series of workshops at the Open Theatre. It emerged from improvisation and from the incorporation of various acting exercises and techniques. It utilised and was built on media material about the Vietnam war. Megan Terry shaped this material and two weeks before its scheduled opening handed it over to Chaikin and Peter Feldman. As Terry explained, 'they finished it, clarifying the movement and line of action and working on individual acting problems. I sat back to take notes, rewrite, expand, edit, etc., at the same time making sure that the emotional imagery held firm.'[12] Though it grew out of the war the play was by no means a simple protest piece. It worked through parody, irony and humour. Its strategy was in part to propose physical intimacy as a counterpoint to the mechanical evils of the war.

101

The body was presented as a resource, an expression of authenticity. Indeed, Chaikin's theories of acting intersected with that emphasis on the physical being which Marcuse and others saw as the source of social and moral renewal and, at least on a symbolic level, as the essence of that rebellion against technology and materialism which he chose to see in the Vietnamese resistance to American involvement in South-east Asia.

The Open Theatre's emphasis was on sound and movement – the creation, initially, of 'pure' movement and sound and then the slow moulding of shapes and powerful images out of this material. This was the basis of several exercises which Chaikin developed but it was equally a central dramatic strategy, a compositional tool. The exercises were necessary stages in a process of deconditioning and sensitising. The basic premise is not merely that language has its own authoritarian impulse, that it is historically, socially and politically stained, but that the process of articulation has been impoverished – that the word offers only partial communication, that it is an imperfect way of encoding information whose complexities will not satisfactorily render down to merely linguistic functions. As Chaikin explained:

> One has to go through that first period of enthusiasm about unusual ways of using the body and the voice before you can draw from experience to speak through the voice and the body. This is very interesting to me. That an actor can be a messenger, can give testimony to what one otherwise might not find a way to transmit to each other. Because we know that the words we use have been taken out of our means. People now, today, in this period, trying to find a way to understand each other, have to go around the word and around the gesture to 'speak' in other ways.[13]

At the same time he admits that 'one has to know the conventional vocabulary pretty clearly as well'. In other words, Chaikin was especially interested in those qualities which distinguish theatre from its allied arts – the presence, in particular, of actors and audience, the fact of communication operating other than on a purely linguistic level. And for him, as for other theatre practitioners of the 1960s, the fact of performance became itself of central concern – theatrical performance operating as a parallel to, and in some senses, a paradigm of, social performance. Thus, he suggests that the actor

> has to study something about performance – about the fact that we perform for each other all the time by trying to make ourselves understood. So we're always performing, and sometimes one finds oneself all alone performing still to oneself. The nature of the social performance, which is a very slippery study, has to be one that the actor is willing to

undertake for my definition of an actor. Also this thing of presence – the actor has to be able to wake himself up out of this mesmerized state of being where he is unable to distinguish between a person and a picture of a person.[14]

But, for Chaikin, the essence of theatre resides in the fact that it is a controlled experience, that it must transcend privatism, and that the intuitive must remain subordinated to a central intelligence, this being provided by the writer and the director. The writer thus became an indispensable figure for Chaikin in a way that he or she did not for Julian Beck or Judith Malina. As he explained in an interview shortly before the group's final performance on 1 December 1973,

> I find that it is absolutely essential to work with a writer, that it isn't incidental at all, that the effectiveness of the piece depends on how effective the writer is. We can work as actors on trying to get through initial armor, and trying to get through the initial cliché ways of performing, and trying to find a way to use the voice in a very full way, to find an eloquence with the voice, not as a singer, but as actors who are speaking of other conditions. We can do these various things, but we need a form and words as well. Each of the pieces has words, but the words are much more like poetry than like the text of a play. They are very spare and they're very charged and they're very eventful.[15]

He equally set his face against the more direct forms of physical communication favoured by the Living Theatre. After an early experiment involving physical contact with the audience (in *Viet Rock*) the group never again resorted to the device. Chaikin recognised that such gestures easily become clichéd and sentimentalised. He also acknowledged what others involved in performance drama were less willing to concede, namely that such assaults were authoritarian in nature and potentially a substitute for theatricality. He was equally cautious about another favourite strategy of 1960s theatre – improvisation. Much that was valuable in Open Theatre productions came from the use of improvisation, which had its origin as much in the inventive cabarets of groups like Second City and the Premise as in Viola Spolin's more systematic ideas. But Chaikin, and his fellow director in *Viet Rock*, Peter Feldman, were all too aware that while improvisation may express a sense of spontaneity and shared experience, it is equally capable of prosaic reductiveness. As Feldman said, 'When I read words which have been spoken by actors in an improvisation, I realize again what banal and clichéd writers actors usually are.'[16] Artaud had made much the same point in *The Theatre and Its Double*. The essence of the director's role, therefore, was to retain the spontaneity, the spirit, and the sense of risk involved in improvisation, while clarifying the ideas and shaping the language. The essence of theatre, meanwhile, lay, above all, in the physical coexistence of the actor and the audience who begin by sharing the same moment and the same space but can be persuaded to share the same moral, social and spiritual world.

Thus, for Chaikin, the crucial distinguishing feature of theatre lies in the presence of the actor whose present must be made to coincide with the factitious present of his art. The process of acting is thus in part a celebration of that presence. 'The developed actor', he has insisted, 'is not practising in one moment what surprise he or she will do in the next. The action is not a reference to another action unplayed, but is itself.' The actor, Chaikin suggested, is working 'in a kind of third person present tense'.[17] And since, to his mind, the primary activity of mankind seems to be a denial of the present (the right giving iconic significance to the past; the left to the future), the theatre has a didactic force quite independent of the sentiments which it articulates. Hence the apparently formalist nature of his position is adroitly subsumed in, and paves the way for, a more overtly political stance. This was certainly in part the direction of Chaikin's own work.

The actor is charged with the responsibility of transforming idea into emotion, of giving physical form to texts – in other words uniting mind with body. And in that respect, too, the actor is proposed as a paradigm – a denial of dichotomy. When Chaikin remarks that 'In this age, we have too definitely divided the mind from the body and the visceral',[18] he is establishing a direct connection not merely with a contemporary desire for holistic experience but with a clear American tradition. Behind this statement lies Artaud but equally Marcuse, Norman O. Brown and an American line which would include Whitman. At the same time nothing marks him off quite so much as a product of his time as his persistent and natural leap from discussions of acting and theatre to assertions about public life and identity. If the social sciences had commandeered the language and processes of theatre as a central metaphor or even therapeutic device, then theatre had always offered itself in precisely this role. The difference now was that the language and strategies of theatre had so thoroughly infiltrated the culture that metaphor had deferred to synecdoche – theatre no longer standing for society, but presenting itself as microcosm.

For Chaikin it was axiomatic that 'the largest questions dealing with acting in the theatre also deal with acting in life'.[19] His concern, however, lay with transcending the limitations of what he called 'the psychological actor'. He felt the same dissatisfaction with Stanislavsky that dramatists had felt with naturalism. He was attracted to 'poets and artists who can reflect extreme conditions . . . unmediated by sympathy or conscience'.[20] The politics of a production lay less in its manifest content than in the nature of the relationship between artist and collaborators, between performers and audience, between theatre and its economic and social context. Liberation is thus to be less a subject than a theme expressed through relationship.

His analysis of social and metaphysical reality scarcely differed from that of the absurdist but his perspective was one which saw this absurdity as a product of denial, a self-created prison house. 'Whenever we are not in a time flow, waiting is what we do with our life . . . In the activity of waiting, a person is only partly present in what is taking place and is not even conscious that he or she is in the service of waiting.'[21] The theatre proposes a model of action and being; it is offered as inspiration. But it is a model which requires the shaping imagination of the writer no less than the perspective of the director.

The Open Theatre's principal writer was Jean-Claude Van Itallie. Born in Belgium in 1936 and raised on Long Island, he graduated from Harvard in 1958 and joined the Open Theatre in 1963. Though he wrote several plays before joining the group, including *Motel*, which was to form the third part of *America Hurrah!* with which he established his reputation, his relationship to the group was crucial both to him and them. In the improvisational work which the group engaged in Van Itallie would provide structures for the actors to work within. Two such were *The First Fool* and *Simple Simon*, which took as their premise the notion of total innocence, of continuously experiencing the world anew, while in *The Hunter and the Bird* that innocence is both accentuated, by contrast with civilised values, and made an ironic agent. A bird is wounded by a hunter. It represents pure innocence, receiving the wound as simple experience and loving the hunter as one more part of creation to be embraced, but at the end the bird shoots the hunter, having begun the process of learning. Once again, though more fully scripted, this play was designed primarily as a structure permitting the actors to develop their skills and explore their potential rather than as a script with its own authority and integrity. Indeed it was not until *America Hurrah!* that Van Itallie produced a text whose own visual and verbal density matched and extended the inventive complexity of Chaikin's actors.

In the Open Theatre's first public performance, at the Sheridan Square Theatre in December 1963, Van Itallie provided two scripts, *The Odets Kitchen* and *An Airplane: Its Passengers and Its Patent*. The former consisted of a brief scene written in the manner of Clifford Odets which the actors used as a basis for improvisation, undermining and penetrating the naturalistic surface. The latter began with the actors together forming the aircraft and then performing stereotypical roles before the plane is made to crash. It was based on various workshop concerns, identified by Robert Pasolli as 'machines, focus, transformation, catalyst, sound-and-movement',[22] just as his *Picnic in the Spring* (a short play in which young couples in a park switch from naturalism into a series of improvisations based on shifting emotional and ontological states) was rooted in the exercises called 'The Illusion Scene' in which various concentric circles of experience and mood are proposed, circles through which the actors move, adjusting their performances accordingly. It was to be with *America Hurrah!* (not, strictly speaking, an Open Theatre production but in part inspired by their exercises and staged by them) and later *The Serpent*, however, that the synthesis of actors and text was at its most impressive.

America Hurrah! is a triptych. Van Itallie has said of the first play, *Interview*, originally entitled *Pavane* (1965), that, 'Sometimes I work from an abstract place, almost like a musical form. I did that in my play *Interview*, where you could practically map it out: AB, ABC, ABCD, AABCD, AABBCD, AABBCCD etc.; it was more or less a fugal structure. I am turned on by that – I guess you could call it the "architectonic" approach.'[23] *Interview* also grew out of the Open Theatre actors' exercises. But, though written as an autonomous piece, it clearly stands as an integral part of a work which offers a satirical view of American values. A *pavane* is a stately dance, frequently performed with the *galliard*, a brisk dance with which it contrasts but which it complements. And plainly the musical analogy holds. Indeed the play is subtitled, 'A Fugue for Eight Actors', thus continuing this sense of contrastive complementarity, for a fugue is a contrapuntal piece for two or more instruments constructed around a theme stated first in the tonic, and then in the dominant key a response called the 'answer'. Other elements are then introduced as counterparts to the answer. Following the exposition other further elements in related keys are interposed, with 'episodes' contrasting with the central subject. In *Interview* the dominant subject is that of the interview itself, in which four applicants are confronted by four interviewers, their questions and 'answers' being formalised and delivered at times in the form of a musical round. The formulaic banality of the situation is accentuated and ironised by the reductive action of the characters who play leap-frog with one another and carry one another on their backs. Their language is interchangeable and drained of meaning, as are their characters. The various scenes flow into one another as a gymnastics class become passengers on a subway train, and as actors who have played interviewers and applicants imitate the breathing pattern of telephonists or the form of an operating table.

106

The language is so drained of content that it can effectively be substituted by nonsense syllables without the point being lost. Hence a psychiatrist can parrot the jargon of his trade, which can in turn blend into the Kyrie eleison of a church service:

Blah, blah, blah, blah, blah, blah, *hostile,*
Blah, blah, blah, blah, blah, blah, *penis,*
Blah, blah, blah, blah, blah, blah, *mother,*
Blah, blah, blah, blah, blah, blah, *money.*[24]

This gives way to the cynical banalities of a politician: 'I'm sorry about the war, I said. Nobody could be sorrier than I am. I said sorrowfully. But I'm afraid, I said gravely, that there are no easy answers. (*Smiles, pleased with himself.*) Good luck to you too, I said cheerfully, and turned my smile to the next one. (*The Politician topples from his box, beginning his speech all over again.*)'[25] The space between the politician and those who question him is the same as that between interviewer and candidate, minister and penitent, psychiatrist and patient. The world of *Interview* is a world of alienated individuals, of uncompleted actions and unrealised aspirations; a place where language serves no clear purpose.

But the play was equally structured around the exercises which Chaikin had developed, in this case called 'Inside–Outside' and 'Transformation', the former being concerned with locating and expressing the 'inside' of a naturalistic situation through the use of sound and movement, the latter being an exercise involving actors moving swiftly from one situation to another. 'Transformation' was designed in part to enable the actor to break with the Method's concern with psychological motivation, but inevitably it also encouraged a sense of the correspondence between apparently unrelated sets of experience and circumstances. *Interview* also made use of the exercise in which the actors worked together to form the parts of a machine, a collaboration with clear metaphorical overtones in a play stressing the anti-human and reductive world of the American present. They exist only as social roles. Like the figures in Albee's *The American Dream* they have compounded the absurdity of their position. The theme of the fugue is one of loss and alienation; the *pavane* is a formal dance of death. The society they inhabit consists of interchangeable parts; it is a closed system.

And this thought provides the epigraph for the second play, *TV*: 'The youth Narcissus mistook his own reflection in the water for another person . . . He was numb. He had adopted his extension of himself and had become a closed system.'[26] Taken from Marshall McLuhan's *Understanding Media*, this provides an apt introduction to a play set in a television viewing room in which reality and illusion are no longer clearly distinguishable.

George, Susan and Hal are three researchers charged with monitoring television programmes. They conduct conversations while the programmes are played by actors dressed in shades of grey, with their faces made up with horizontal lines to suggest the images of a television screen. They act stereotyped roles and as a consequence are allowed only stereotyped facial masks. In an early and crucial stage direction Van Itallie identifies the basic strategy of the play:

> As the play progresses the People on Television will use more and more of the stage. The impression should be that of a slow invasion of the viewing room. Hal, Susan and George will simply move around the People on Television when that becomes necessary. Ultimately, the control console itself will be taken over by television characters, so that the distinction between what is on television and what is occurring in the viewing room will be lost completely. The attention of the audience should be focussed not on a parody of television, but on the relationship of the life that appears on television to the life that goes on in the viewing room. All of the actors will need to be constantly aware of what is happening on all parts of the stage, in order to give and take the attention of the audience to and from each other, and also in order to demonstrate the influence of the style of certain television segments on the behavior of Hal, Susan and George.[27]

On one level the play offers a critique of a society for which the soap opera is less a reductive image than an accurate paradigm. The intercutting between the foregrounded action provided by the three central characters and the flow of programmes which they watch emphasises the continuity rather than the contrast between the two levels of experience. It also provides the opportunity for ironic commentary, and, in presenting the formal fictions of the scriptwriter alongside the images of the television commercial and the supposed realities of news reporting and feature interviews, emphasises the degree to which they are all homogenised to a stylistic and moral norm. But, beyond that, it enacts the human indifference and linguistic evasiveness out of which such alienation flows.

The structure of the play allows for a series of ironic juxtapositions, some of them minor and even somewhat trite (on the screen an amateur scientist conducts experiments so that 'If I succeed . . . nobody in the world will be hungry for love. Ever again',[28] while Susan discusses slimming), some of them directly engaging the issue of the Vietnam war (details of bombing raids are given as the trio of researchers enact tired seduction scenes). The juxtapositions operate on a number of levels. Hence, a war protester who tries to describe the violence which he has seen in Vietnam finds his protest easily absorbed by the style, language and assumptions of the chat show on which he appears ('I saw things that would make you sick. Heads broken, babies smashed against walls'; 'I *know* . . . War is horrible . . . Thank you, Ron. We've been talking this afternoon, Ladies, with Ron Campbell, war hero.'[29]). Descriptions of a bombing mission are invaded by cigarette commercials, the language of the latter clearly infiltrating the former. Accounts of public violence are intercut with the ritualised violence of the western and a parallel is established between the commercial and political world through the juxtaposition of references to the president of the company for which the trio work and the President of the United States.

In other words *TV* is structured around a series of extremely elaborate juxtapositions which operate on a number of levels. The ironies that are generated by the horizontal flow of television programmes and the developing story of the self-serving researchers are complemented by the vertical ironies which derive from the interference of these two elements. An underlying continuity is provided by the persistent lying which operates on both levels. Thus Hal asserts of his job that 'I love it more than my own life', while planning to leave it; George deceives his wife in the hope of an affair with Susan; and the advertising industry sells its death-dealing cigarettes with the same amoral plausibility as the President sells his lethal policies and the newscaster 'reports' official justifications – describing a peace march as 'A group of so-called peace-niks'. There is no evidence of human feeling. When George chokes on a chicken bone his two companions are too concerned with self-justifying arguments to help him, showing the same indifference with which they respond to events on the screen. When television characters change places with them (the television characters leave the screen and occupy the rest of the stage; the researchers deliver their lines to canned laughter), the exchange is no more than a logical extension of the rest of the play.

In *TV* the real has no status. It is fictionalised not primarily by the medium but by a language which grants no substance to event or person. The television programmes are less the source of corruption than an expression of it. The two-dimensional nature of experience is not a result of a reductiveness enforced by technology but of a world denatured by an aggressive egotism. Though Joseph Chaikin, in another context, has spoken of television becoming the origin of 'recommended personal fantasies to be shared by all' and creating a 'repertoire of fantasy and experience' which is the most effective way of 'manipulating the imagination through establishing a common premise and promoting a uniform inner life',[30] Van Itallie's point is perhaps different. It is that television is the perfect expression of a life without transcendent values, of a society in which role has replaced identity and a world in which language is a primary defence against the real and hence against a moral apprehension.

Nonetheless if society has, in a sense, become theatricalised it is plainly not in a vital and self-conscious way. It is simply that fiction has been substituted for experience. But neither Van Itallie nor Chaikin were interested in counterposing theatre to the real. On the contrary, *TV* dramatised the substitution of fantasy for reality, the essence of television being its power to denature and homogenise experience and in particular to eliminate the physical presence and potential community of theatre. Thus the very fact of the play's performance was already an identification of an antidote; in that the theatre implicitly offered an alternative model for personal and public relationships. And this gives theatre a moral responsibility and function. In an age of anxiety it becomes increasingly difficult to distinguish the authentic, and this places a special burden on an art which deals in roles and which proposes the shared present which is a condition of its own existence as a model of restored community. It thus becomes important for the actor to aim for truth rather than illusion. If film and television offer fiction then the theatre must offer authentic experience.

As Chaikin, possibly influenced by Grotowski, observed in *The Presence of the Actor*, 'social man is . . . the person as actor. Public figures, such as politicians and priests, are acting in their public role. Choosing clothes is picking costume. Actors, while they are acting, are recommending. Actors, through their acting, are validating a definition of identity and rendering other definitions invalid. Recommending a way to perform is working to sell a mode of being.'[31] As Chaikin asks,

> How does something become valid? If we can make our experience resemble the one in the movies, or if we can deceive ourselves into saying it resembles it, then the movies validate our real experience. We are intimidated by the fictional experience, not just because theirs is big and ours is little, but because theirs is authentic, ours is warped, out of gear, unintended. The more confused and chaotic the ear is, the more these icon personalities are taken as models.[32]

Van Itallie grants the force of this argument but tends to locate the incubus less in the power of the models (here presented as anything but overpowering in their richness) than in the willed retreat into banality. It was, after all, precisely this sleep of the spirit that the Open Theatre had set itself to terminate with its own vitality, its own attempt to proceed through the stereotype to the archetype.

The vision of his researchers watching television while consuming tranquillisers is offered as an adequate account of a retreat from the real as private and public worlds collapse towards a narcotised norm. The war is treated with indifference because all experience is seen as equivalent. The characters are in a sense living by proxy. The play ends with them sharing the same vacuous smile as the television characters who have usurped their imaginative independence. They wear, in effect, the grotesque mask of the role-player, a mask which becomes the basis for the final play of the trilogy, *Motel*.

This is presented as the logical extension of the pressure towards the inanimate and the non-human identified in the first two plays. It bears an epigraph from Yeats: '. . . after all our subtle colour and nervous rhythm, after the faint mixed tints of Conder, what more is possible? After us the Savage God.'[33] The play is described as a masque for three dolls and was inspired by Van Itallie's reading of Artaud.

The lights come up on the Motel-keeper, a huge doll with mirror eyes and a head three times the size of its body. Hair curlers on her head suggest electronic receivers. The décor is aggressively modern, dominated by bright colours and reflective plastic. The Motel-keeper's voice comes from a loudspeaker. It grows progressively harsher. The actor inside can only move the arms and the entire body. The doll represents not only the Motel-keeper but the motel room itself and beyond that other rooms and other spaces which have sheltered or precipitated violence. 'I am an old idea: the walls; that form from which it springs forth. I enclose the nothing, making then a place in which it happens. I am the room: a Roman theatre where cheers break loose the lion; a railroad carriage in the forest at Compiègne, in 1918, and in 1941.'[34]

A male and female doll enter, the woman immediately stripping off her dress. The two then systematically destroy the room and engage in a grotesque parody of sexual contact. A television set blasts out loud rock music and the two dolls scrawl obscene words and drawings over the walls. As they destroy the room so the Motel-keeper outlines her plans to create a motel secure against nuclear attack. The rock music gets louder; a civil defence siren wails. The two dolls finally dismember the Motel-keeper as her language begins to disintegrate. The two then leave the shattered motel room and walk down the aisle as doors at the back of the stage open, the headlights of a car shine into the eyes of the audience, fans blow from the stage into the auditorium, and, after an excruciatingly loud noise, there is a blackout followed by silence.

Jean-Claude Van Itallie has said:

> Years ago I wrote the play *Motel*. I started with a feeling of great anger. I was really angry that nobody had been liking my three-act conventional plays that were trying to please everybody. Along with an image of the tearing apart of a room, there was an almost sexual energy going. All of

2. Jean-Claude Van Itallie, *Motel*, 1966. Production by the Open Theatre, New York, 1968.

me was involved in wanting to tear down, wanting to break through, wanting to show those feelings. I had an image of a gross motel room with gross people tearing it apart, and I proceeded from there. I also heard a woman's voice in my mind, going from soft to sharp, and I put the image and the voice together without trying to be too literally logical.[35]

But beyond this the play is plainly offered as a parable. The mechanistic figures, the brutalism of the environment, the surge towards apocalypse provide a logical climax to the alienation of *Interview* and *TV*. The link between the railway carriage at Compiègne and the motel room suggests a continuous menace, a potential compounded by a failure of cultural purpose. The two grotesque dolls do not acknowledge the existence of the Motel-keeper; they emanate destruction and relate to one another only as the objects which they have indeed become.

The influence of Artaud seems clear. Artaud had looked, among other things, for the use of 'Manikins, enormous masks, objects of strong proportions' which would 'appear with the same sanction as verbal images . . . with the corollary that all objects requiring a stereotyped physical representation will be discarded or disguised'.[36] Where what he called 'digestive' theatre relinquished its power to affect the senses and the sensibility of the audience, the theatre of cruelty was to be a theatre of dissonances, relying on 'intensities of colors, lights, or sounds, which utilize vibration, tremors, repetition' which were designed to overwhelm the audience. The set, meanwhile, was to 'consist of the characters themselves, enlarged to the stature of gigantic manikins and of landscapes of moving lights playing on objects and masks in perpetual interchange'.[37]

And if Van Itallie shared Artaud's approach, creating his own theatre of dissonance, it is perhaps because he shared, too, Artaud's apprehension of the world. The distortions of American society, under the pressure of materialism, a disengagement from the real and the moral dislocations consequent upon the Vietnam war, offered some kind of parallel for that sense of crisis which Artaud had felt in late 1930s Europe. Artaud had observed then that 'We are living through a period probably unique in the history of the world, when the world, passed through a sieve, sees its old values crumble. Our calcined life is dissolving at its base, and on the moral and social level this is expressed by a monstrous unleashing of appetites, a liberation of the basest instincts, a crackling of burnt lives prematurely exposed to the flame.'[38] Van Itallie clearly seems to have sensed something similar in his own time and reaches for an image of this failure of morale and morality which is close in spirit and in form to that which Artaud had identified. He, too, created a theatre in which 'all movements will obey a rhythm' and each character be merely 'a type'; a

113

'theatre in space' in which the force derives from a 'dissonance', a 'dispersion of timbres, and the dialectic discontinuity of expression'.[39]

In his next major work with the Open Theatre he created a play which, in its mythic pretension, was his and their attempt to approximate to that imaginative theatre for which Artaud had looked when he said that,

> the theatre must make itself the equal of life – not an individual life, that individual aspect of life in which CHARACTERS triumph, but the sort of liberated life which sweeps away human individuality and in which man is only a reflection. [For, the] true purpose of the theatre is to create Myths, to express life in its immense, universal aspect, and from that life to extract images in which we can find pleasure in discovering ourselves. And by so doing to arrive at a kind of general resemblance, so powerful that it produces its effect instantaneously. May it free us [he observed] in a Myth in which we have sacrificed our little human individuality, like Personages out of the Past, with Powers discovered in the Past.[40]

And it was to the past that the Open Theatre turned, as it was to the past that the Performance Group and the Living Theatre also turned. What they sought was renewal. The danger was that in seeking to invoke the past against the present they would relax into simple nostalgia, that myth would devolve into a callow mysticism. The protection against this was to come from a professional rigour and from the coherence of the text which, once developed, was not available for subversion. The workshop met for four hours a day for four days a week, its enthusiasm boosted by the visit of Jerzy Grotowski and his group, since Grotowski's belief in the need for physical discipline, combined with an investigation of the nature of sound and movement, was close to their own. Indeed, the Open Theatre was the only one that Grotowski was willing to endorse, doubtless because its emphasis was on the actor, and its distrust of the substitution of a physical for a spiritual, emotional or intellectual contact with its audience was one to which he responded.

The Serpent (1968) was to be a revolt against rational theatre, against linearity as a structural device and causal assumption, and against the liberal theatre of individual angst. It was to be part of a theatre of images, of archetypes, whose effects were to be achieved by appeal to popular myth and whose form was to be constructed around familiar models. It was, as its subtitle implied, to be 'a ceremony', a shared ritual which provided an occasion and an environment for performers and audience to come together. As Van Itallie remarked, the essence of theatre lay in the live presence of those two elements in a single space: 'This is the theatre's uniquely important advantage and function, its original religious function to bring people together in a community ceremony where the actors are in some sense priests or celebrants, and the audience is drawn to participate with the actors in a kind of eucharist.'[41]

The play itself relates the biblical story of the Fall of Man and the murder of Abel by Cain to the assassination of President Kennedy, not simply from a thematic concern with life and death and the question of moral responsibility, but because they represent a source of shared images and myths – the details of the assassination still being remarkably clear to a generation for which it had been the most traumatising of public events.

The decision to use the Genesis narrative as a structuring mechanism did not involve an acceptance of its assumptions. Indeed, for Joseph Chaikin the text was a repudiation of those assumptions and hence created an internal dialectic. While relying on myth, the objective was in some degree to demythologise. The premise of the play, as he saw it, was the belief that 'Man made God in his own image, and held up this God to determine his own, Man's, limits.'[42] Mythic past and mythic present are brought together in order to force a confrontation, in order to measure distance travelled and to locate the moment when the ability to choose was apparently abandoned. Most of the play focusses on that past, but the essential concern is with the present, the present which is celebrated in the mere notion of a ceremony and in the fact of the theatrical performance. It is, in some degree, a play about shared responsibility no less than shared images.

The play begins with the actors performing individual warm-up exercises. In other words they are seen first outside the roles they are to play. The theatricality of the occasion is thus exposed as is the professionalism of the company who, in revealing something of the physical strenuousness of their preparations, reveal, too, the manner in which, and the fact that, they have to prepare themselves for what is to follow. The ceremony thus demands induction. For both the actors and the audience the induction into the communality of the play lies through the play itself.

This begins with a procession in which the actors produce percussive sounds by striking their arms, chests, and so on. It is described in the text as resembling a parade of medieval mummers and this is clearly the remnant of what was once to have been one of the play's central structural devices. As the procession moves around the theatre so the action is frozen on three occasions, the actors portraying various of the play's dominant images. The play then continues with a ritualised autopsy which is carried out by a doctor, following the sound of a gunshot. The victim is a woman but the scene merges naturally into the next, which is entitled 'Kennedy–King Assassination'. Since the assassination was one of the few contemporary events which had been shared by large numbers of people and since, thanks to the television coverage, its iconography had registered deeply on the sensibility of people who had perhaps shared little else, it was offered both as evidence in a debate about the moral sensibility and as the closest the contemporary world was likely to come to generating a set of images which required no verbal articulation.

The scene itself re-enacts the moment of Kennedy's assassination, with his wife first cradling his head and then starting to climb over the back of the car. The assassination is broken down into twelve segments, like cinematic sequences, and these are played slowly in normal and reverse order. The crowd watching these events then move forward, each section of it shouting his or her justification for non-involvement: 'I was not involved. I am a small person. I hold no opinion. I stay alive.'[43] The statements are themselves broken into fragments, like the action itself. The individuals are, in other words, all presented as accomplices who through their desire to remain innocent paradoxically articulate their responsibility for the corruption and destruction of their world.

The scene blends into Martin Luther King's 'I have a dream' speech in which he looks towards a shared future of mutual commitment, a speech potentially threatened by the audience's knowledge of his own assassination. The continued miming of the Kennedy assassination behind him also plainly undercuts this as does the continued disavowal of responsibility by the crowd, now joined by the assassin himself. Like Arthur Miller's characters, they already live after the Fall and the play now turns back to the Genesis account of that Fall, which is presented as the symbolic if not actual moment in which innocence was wilfully abandoned and in which the process of rationalising human behaviour had its beginning. The point is less that man became irremediably guilty than that he conspired to justify his own surrender of a moral self; that by inventing a mythic world in which good and evil competed on a metaphysical plane he could relieve himself of responsibility for his actions in the world of reality. Thus the serpent is represented by five actors, members of the chorus speak for Eve, and the voice of God is resonated through those who invoke and invent him. When Adam bites the apple further apples are distributed to the audience, thus implicating them in the action. A fatal dualism has entered the world: 'Now shall come a separation / Between the dreams inside your head / And the two shall war within you.'[44] The play ends with the re-telling of the story of Cain and Abel, a recital of genealogy from the Bible and a re-enactment of conception, birth and death. Drained of purpose, the people who have wilfully placed limits on their own potential, succumb to entropy.

116

The Serpent is predominantly a play about loss, on the level of the individual, the group and the race. Built into the process of mortality, it is compounded, Van Itallie implies, by a surrender of freedom and a denial of that relationship with the natural world and one's fellow man which could prove redemptive. In that sense the form of the play, the communal method, the incorporation of contributions by playwright, actors and director, is offered as a model of restored consonance. The first play to be fully constructed as a collaborative work within and by the Open Theatre, it was in effect offered as a justification of their method and a defence of the convictions behind much of their work. In placing such stress on physical movement and elemental sounds, in emphasising the importance of communal work, in stressing ritualised performance in their exercises, they had in effect predicated their work on precisely that sense of universalised experience which was the essential subject of *The Serpent*, and, which, incidentally, Artaud had also looked for.

It is, perhaps, not hard to see why Ronnie Davis, of the San Francisco Mime Troupe, should have consigned Chaikin to the radical right. Certainly, despite his hostility to the Vietnam war, he was proposing a model of alienation which owed nothing to Marx, and invoking a sense of community which was more spiritual than material; and, though *The Serpent* is hostile to a nostalgia which is merely an expression of impotence in the face of time and events, his concern is with the restoration of a sense of unity which is not without its atavistic and even sentimental overtones. Chaikin's direction is rigorous, his vision less so. And though responsibility for the text must rest with Van Itallie the production-values play such an important part that it is impossible to discuss it as though it were a unique product of his sensibility. Indeed, this is, of course, in part the point of the production. The body broken in the first scene and presented as a simple cadaver has to be restored as a primary force and not merely as the means to perpetuate a continuing existence. While experience is perceived in fragmented form, *The Serpent* insists on an underlying structure of belief and action which must remain a piety if the force of the theatre as paradigm is not accepted. That is the risk that Chaikin and his group ran.

The power of *The Serpent* does not lie in the text and in a sense it was never meant to. The language is almost wholly one of defeat, corruption, self-deceit and self-justification. The power lies in the physical fact of ensemble acting, in the muscular reality of co-operation which works against an admitted sentimentality. It lies in a language literally shared out among the actors, each contributing syllables, words, phrases and sentences to the whole. It lies in the trust which was an essential element in Chaikin's exercises and which became a part of both method and theme in *The Serpent*. It lies in the relationship between performers and audience. The passing of apples to the audience, a feature of the play, was designed to involve equally a passing of responsibility and mutual strength. As Joseph Chaikin explained, the significance of this relationship was crucial, perhaps most obviously in this moment in which limited improvisation was possible.

> The confrontation is with that delicate but powerful pulse of people assembled in the same room. For this reason it is the rhythm and dynamic responses, rather than the confrontation of attitudes between the actor and the audience, which are important. This special task is possible in the particular context of the *anonymous intimacy* between players and audience, and through it the main theme which is the confrontation of our mortality.[45]

Indeed it is significant that the play began not with the script but with a series of improvisational exercises based on Genesis. It was, as Van Itallie admitted, a script after the fact; though, if anything, this increased the problems for the eventual author, it suggests the degree to which the methods of the group shaped the material which they performed.

For the Open Theatre improvisation was a part of the process of creation rather than a basic strategy of performance. Thus, in the production of *The Serpent* the text was developed by Jean-Claude Van Itallie partly on the basis of ideas and images explored by the company, but while some space was left for limited improvisation this did not include the freedom to develop new dialogue. Indeed, Van Itallie was anxious to insist that 'Actors are not poets', and that 'Their concentration had better not be on the invention of words while they are performing. If it is then the words are at very best trite, and the performances suffer.'[46] There is a difference in emphasis in this respect between Chaikin and Van Itallie. While Chaikin speaks of the text as giving 'a structure for the playing out of the story', and includes places for the company to improvise, Van Itallie asserted that 'The two ensemble companies that I know and most respect – the Polish Lab and the Open Theater – never "improvise" during a performance of a play (except in the sense that every good actor and every good company is always improvising). In fact contrary to what is sometimes believed about them by some who haven't seen them, the success of their performances is due in large part to an extreme discipline, albeit one of their own devising.'[47] Indeed, writing in 1977, he said,

> There's a mistaken belief, in the contemporary theatre – one that I hope is getting less prevalent – that a group of actors can create a piece by themselves, which to me is like having a body without a head. It's

impossible. You have to have a strong writer and a strong director, or a strong writer–director. Someone has to function as the leader of the work. A non-hierarchized group will produce only chaos. I don't think it's going on so much any more, but people used to try to do pseudo-Grotowski work or pseudo-Open Theatre work, thinking that they would come together and make 'something', a group effort. But unless there is an acknowledged head to a group, a writer and a director, it won't work.[48]

Jean-Claude Van Itallie (whose subsequent work included *A Fable* (1974) and *Bag Lady* (1979)) was not the only writer associated with the Open Theatre, though he was the most accomplished. For a subsequent play, called *Terminal* (1969), they turned to Susan Yankovitz. This was to be concerned with the subject of dying or death.

Though the play was written by Susan Yankovitz, it, too, was developed as a result of collective work, an investigation by the actors into the nature and processes of death. The directors and performers all read David Cooper's book, *Death in the Family*, and the prison letters of George Jackson. They enquired into the processes involved in embalming and brought to their workshop sessions information, ideas and images which formed the basis of their improvisations. Those were then shaped by Yankovitz. It begins with the summoning of the dead, the actors joining in an incantation in which the meaning lies as much in the sound of calling as in the words. As the grace of the language collapses into cacophony, and then into a single syllable and then silence, so the actors subsequently enact the decay of mind and body. The processes of embalming are then described and enacted in gesture and mime. The dead then possess the dying. The play is a series of images, the minimal words being counterparted by actions which highlight equally the fact of decay and the living presence of the actor. The emphasis is on process, on ritualised movement, on repetition. Nor is the reduction of life to death presented as a simple consequence of time. In a section called 'The Interview' an individual is persuaded to embrace the pain inflicted on him by another as a necessary function of existence. In 'The Executed Man and the Song' a man asserts the freedom which comes with the knowledge of death. The play begins with that moment of absurdist realisation of which Camus spoke. Indeed, in 'The Judgements' we are offered what is in effect a paraphrase of Camus's own description of the awareness of routine which lies at the heart of the absurdist experience: 'You moved from the house to the office, from the office to the house; from sleep to waking and from waking to sleep; you moved from yesterday to today, from today to tomorrow – and you will repeat that movement for eternity . . . the judgement of your life is your life.'[49] During this speech actors seek out an objective correlative, acting out the reductive world described by the speaker, but the point seems to be that the absurd is less a metaphysical condition than a product of a collapse of will. 'There is a space between what was done and what could have been done', observes a voice at the end of the play. And the antidote is implicit in the process of the play itself which has been precisely concerned with linking body and mind, and with creating meaning communally by means of gestures, music (partly composed by Sam Shepard) and movements which have in effect been a denial both of simple literalism and of alienation. It is in that sense that the notes insist that 'Everything is part of the theatrical world and derives its functions from the needs of the world.'[50] It is for that reason, too, that the actors are always present, either in a central space or in a peripheral area where they remain visible. As ever with the Open Theatre the presence of the actor is of central significance.

Terminal received its first performance in Europe when the group was on a tour which included Germany, France and Switzerland. When they returned to America there was radical disagreement within the group as to the direction in which they should move. In a cultural environment radicalised by the war and by major civil disturbances they debated whether their primary allegiance should be to theatrical or social experiment. So fundamental were the arguments that the group was actually disbanded and re-formed by Chaikin a few months later. In a sense it was a false dichotomy for, though it was apparently resolved in favour of theatrical experiment, in fact for Chaikin theatre was so implicated in the social process and so potent as a paradigm of individual and collective behaviour that it could never disinherit itself of its synecdochal role. *Terminal*, with which the group resumed, was primary evidence for that fact.

And the war did itself penetrate the text. In one scene, called 'The Dance on the Graves of the Dead', one of the 'dead' – a soldier – speaks through the mouth of an actor: 'Dead because I said "Yes".' This is that acquiescence against which the play argues. Thus at the end a Judgement is offered as those on the stage are accused of having created their own fate: 'The judgement of your life is your life . . . You neither faced your death nor participated in your life . . . The judgement of your life is your life.'[51]

In their penultimate production, *The Mutation Show* (1971), the language is more attenuated. The printed text consists of a mere five pages. Action predominates. Actors identify themselves, even displaying photographs of themselves, while performing rites of suppression and liberation. The play was a product of a series of workshops in which the actors had studied the rites of passage celebrated in different cultures.

Like Peter Handke they were especially fascinated with the case of Kaspar Hauser, confined to a cellar for the first sixteen years of his life. Rescued from isolation, he is brought into society but is destroyed in the process. Mutation comes to stand for the process of adaptation and accommodation whereby the self is lost in the process of socialisation and the process whereby people modify themselves in the course of their lives. This touched precisely on the rationale of the Open Theatre which was founded so that the actor could understand and accomplish the transformations required in theatre without accommodating to the moral and aesthetic standards of art as business, and which was designed to engage the question of identity on a social and dramatic level. In a sense the play also expressed a growing fear on the part of Chaikin that accommodations had been made, that public performance, once secondary, was becoming primary and that the demythologising of the actors had not proved an adequate protection against hubris. The risk was that they were beginning to fall into a rut, to repeat effects and to succumb to pressures which had nothing to do with their original objective. Chaikin thus decided to conclude the experiment, though not before one more play, *Nightwalk*, produced in 1973.

The absurdist element, evident in their earlier plays, exists equally in this last work as God is indicted for his absence and the consequent sense of absurdity is compounded by the materialism and sexual role-playing of society. But the play is part satire, part celebration. The same characters who enact the grotesques of the social world also perform the physical arabesques which imply a level of lyric potential. There is a struggle for supremacy, resolved in the direction of wholeness. Even language reasserts itself. Sections are acknowledged as the work of Jean-Claude Van Itallie, Sam Shepard and Megan Terry. The balance between movement and language shows signs of re-establishing itself. The move seems to be in the direction of celebration. But the play was incomplete – a work in progress which was never further refined because of the disbandment of the group.

Chaikin shared both Meyerhold's belief in the need to work from the physical fact of the actor's presence on stage and his conviction that this meant exploring the mechanics of physical movement, but, more than that, he saw in the presence of the actor a statement about the power of human intervention. As Meyerhold has said, 'Since the art of the actor is the art of plastic forms in space, he must study the mechanics of his body. This is essential because any manifestation of a force (including the living organism) is subject to constant laws of mechanics and obviously the creation by the actor of plastic forms in the space of the stage is a manifestation of the force of the human organism.'[52] And it was that force, the power of the individual and the group to intervene in their own fate, which lay at the heart of his work. In 1969 Jan Kott observed that 'In the theatre the basic icon is the body and voice of the actor.'[53] This was equally Chaikin's position, but for him physical presence had more than an iconographic significance: it implied a faith in the centrality of the human figure not merely in terms of the processes of theatre, or, indeed, the mechanisms of society, but in relation to existence itself. In exploring the full potential of the actor he was seeking simultaneously to assert the infinite capacities of man; in stressing not only the physical accomplishment of the actors and their ability to communicate across a wide range of emotions and through a wide variety of channels, but also their intellectual involvement in the creation of the drama which they perform, he was also offering a model of the integrated sensibility, a self restored to its own lost unity. When the group chose to perform *Terminal* and *The Mutation Show* in a number of prisons across America they were seeking to liberate themselves (feeling that they had become stale) and entertain the prisoners. But their visits also had a symbolic significance for they were also concerned with liberation in its psychological, social and even metaphysical sense. That had been the basic theme of all of the plays which they had developed. It was the implication of their exercises, exercises which emphasised a freedom born of trust. It was, in fact, the fundamental objective of the group. The Open Theatre was dedicated to the opening of horizons as it was to the release of energies, but beyond this it was concerned with liberation in a sense so basic as to make nonsense of their own earlier debates.

At one point in *The Mutation Show* the actors, displaying photographs of themselves, give details of their personal lives, thereby making clear those radical transformations in their experiences and identities which have brought them onto the stage as members of the Open Theatre. In a decade for which such transformations were a central article of faith this was offered as evidence of the possibility and reality of change. Other groups sought their transformations elsewhere. The theatre was merely a convenience of the moment, a platform for a self whose liberation was presumed to be a matter of political action or social revolt. For Chaikin there was a prior revolution to be won, a transformation, moreover, which could begin in the theatre precisely because it was there that the distinction between identity and role, enactment and re-enactment, presence and absence was a matter of critical concern. When he declared the Open Theatre closed it was scarcely because he thought those issues resolved. It was simply because he felt that that particular group had taken the issue as far as it could and, rather than watch it slowly disintegrate, betray its principles and squander its energy, he and the others moved on, leaving behind one of the most interesting and accomplished theatre groups in the history of post-war American theatre.

4 The Performance Group

In an interview published in 1969 Jerzy Grotowski offered what was in effect a criticism of American performance art, and in particular of its assumptions that theatre was 'an act of life'. He noted the temptation to 'devalue certain socio-political attitudes by reducing them to simple generic and verbal affirmations', and to substitute improvisation for work. Placing himself momentarily in the position of a member of such a group, he observed that:

> Thanks to the 'working atmosphere' I would already feel as though I were immersed in the warm waters of family relations with the other members of the group – delivered of all responsibility. It is the group that creates instead of me. I would find myself interesting. It would suffice me to be who I am. Whatever I might do – walk, howl, shout – I would feel absolved by the group. If I wished to show myself human, I would seek contact: touch the hands of my partners, look them straight in the eyes. I'd see nothing at all there, but no matter, the essential thing is to be human and do improvisations; it is not difficult, so I would do it. To demonstrate that I am also an animal, I would crawl on four feet and utter inarticulate cries. That is biological, that is spontaneous.[1]

It was a parody but not entirely so. For Grotowski, a product of a collectivist society, a naive faith in the virtues of the group was by no means self-evident; for those in revolt against a fierce individualism the group seemed a source of alternative values.

Against what he saw as the flaccid aesthetic of American performance theatre Grotowski proposed precision. Having attended a workshop with Grotowski, Richard Schechner aimed at just such a precision but hardly purged his work of sentimentalism. As Grotowski said, 'If I boast of questing for a reconciliation with myself, and of seeking a totality which would put an end to my division into body and soul, sex and intellect, it amounts to saying that I refuse any longer to feel apart from my own body, my own instincts, my own unconscious, that is, from my own spontaneity. The trouble is that spontaneity could end in a lying spectacle.'[2] He also reminded his interviewer of a central truth too often lost sight of in the American theatre of the 1960s, 'Experience proves that by putting a distance between the actors and the spectators in space, one often rediscovers a [psychical] proximity between them; and, inversely, the best means of creating a sort of abyss between them is to have them mingle in space.' Indeed, he went so far as to say that he had never seen direct participation by an audience, that it had become 'a new myth, a miraculous solution'[3] in an American theatre which, to his embarrassment, had enthusiastically embraced his ideas without fully understanding them, as they had those of Stanislavsky before him. While exonerating Chaikin, he attacked others who had seized on him as a cultural icon, as they had on yoga, group sensitivity and the rest of the panoply brought to bear by the Living Theatre and the Performance Group. To his mind yoga, which his company had once tried, led to subjectivism, while obsession with the group was likely to result in an unregulated approach to experience and to theatre.

Richard Schechner was perhaps the most erudite of those who exemplified the new performance-oriented theatre. An editor of the *Tulane Drama Review* from 1962, and a founder of the Free Southern Theatre, he welcomed the transformations wrought by Chaikin, and the nexus between social and theatrical change that Beck embraced. Moreover, he was better placed than most to see these in the context of the history of dramatic theory and theatrical practice. His involvement with the New Orleans Group, of which he was a founder director, exposed him early to the problem of creating a new theatrical environment, while his creation of the Free Southern Theatre, of which he was also a founder director, was a sign of his liberal commitment and in part an expression of his concern with the European avant-garde whose plays, somewhat curiously, constituted the mainstay of their repertoire as they set out to take theatre to the deprived blacks of the South.

But when the *Tulane Drama Review* moved to New York, where it was renamed *The Drama Review*, he was attracted by other, more radical, changes in the theatre. *The Drama Review* itself brought news of European developments, printing information about Grotowski's and Brook's experiments, and certainly the influence of such theoreticians/ exponents was clear on the work which he did when, in November 1967, he formed the Performance Group.

Schechner gathered a number of people together and for three nights a week they met and engaged in a series of exercises that Schechner had developed when working with the New Orleans Group or learned directly from a four week workshop which Grotowski and his principal actor, Ryszard Cieslak, ran at New York University in that same November. Like Chaikin's this group was not formed primarily for the purpose of developing a production but rather to explore theatrical and personal possibilities. As ever with such groups, the welding of some kind of group solidarity perhaps inevitably mimicked the procedures of group therapy as these mimicked those of theatre. Hence Schechner described the fact that they 'exchanged touches, places, ideas, anxieties, words, gestures, hostilities, rages, smells, glances, sounds, loves'.[4] The risk, as ever, of course, was that this would breed a sense of solidarity achieved, in part at least, in contradistinction to the world beyond the confines of the performing space, a sense of exclusiveness, a condescension with respect to the experience of those outside the magic circle who could be alternately wooed and patronised. It was at least a danger.

Work began on *Dionysus in 69* when the group moved into a garage on Wooster Street which they converted into a performing space, painting it white out of a desire to foreground rather than conceal the structure of that space. Two large wooden towers were constructed and, together with various levels, and the open space at the centre, this constituted the playing area. The audience, when they were allowed in for 'rehearsals' (in May 1968), were invited to find their own places. The performance opened to the public in June.

The Performance Group set itself the task of responding to *The Bacchae* of Euripides 'as if it were part of an oral tradition'. As Schechner explained in an essay on 'The Politics of Ecstasy' published in 1968, only parts of Euripides' text were to be used (itself a reflection of Grotowski's influence) and those were to be joined to and set against fragments of other texts. The event was to be 'a dance, an ecstasy',[5] in which the audience would in part join. If it was to be an engagement with a specific text it was also to be an encounter with the self and with the Dionysian elements which seemed, to Schechner, to characterise the youth culture of America in the late 1960s.

The audience was allowed into the performance one at a time, a rite of initiation designed to charge the event with a personal significance subsequently to be subsumed in a communal response. Such a procedure was not without its destabilising effect. The actors began with various exercises derived directly from Grotowski and which were designed to 'relate the body to the mind in such a way that the two apparently separate systems are one'.[6] These exercises were incorporated in the performance to some degree but when Grotowski himself visited the production in November he urged the confinement of the exercises to the workshop, as he also criticised their naive assumption of a direct correlation between physical and psychic contact.

Schechner chose to make the chorus the matrix of the play, the scenes being generated from it and dissolving back into it. His decision to rotate the roles was thus a logical extension of this central device as, more pragmatically, it was a way to handle an extended run without slipping too easily into formula.

The play was not performed as in the text, which becomes a kind of

126

3.   The Performance Group, *Dionysus in 69*, New York. Production by Richard Schechner. The birth ritual.

pretext to be fragmented, ignored or built upon. Language itself was attenuated or amplified, split into single syllables or elongated into pure sound, sonorities, wails. Actions were shaped into rituals, one of them adapted directly from an authentic ritual performed by the Asmet tribe in Western New Guinea and which Schechner had found described in a book on *Headhunters of Papua* by Tony Soulnier. The original ritual had been a ceremony concerned with the adoption of a couple from one tribe into another; here it is offered as a ritual of rebirth in the most literal way, as the women, naked, pass the men through a tunnel created by their open legs. The actors are born first as themselves, announcing their actual identities and giving a brief description of themselves (much as the Open Theatre's actors were to do in *The Mutation Show*), before moving into the characters they are to play – a foregrounding of the actual process of creating drama and a consolidation of the group, underlining their physical and spiritual unity.

Dionysus in 69 used nearly 600 of the 1300 lines in Arrowsmith's translation of *The Bacchae*, and a few lines from Elizabeth Wycoff's translation of *Antigone* and David Greene's translation of *Hippolytus*. But Schechner was insistent that the text had its own formal construction. It was not improvised. His claim was that as a result of this process a text was generated which incorporated 'conceptual as well as affective diversity', which reflected 'the complicated internal dynamics of the Group' and did 'justice to the implications of Euripides' genius'.[7] It is hard to know what he meant by almost any of these terms. What, after all, are the virtues of conceptual diversity and what are the 'implications' of genius? Why should reflecting the complicated internal dynamics of the group be thought an advantage in dramatic terms? The virtues of affective compromise between the various objectives are confused with dramatic effect, and this psychodramatic dimension of the performance was underlined by a 'mortification scene' in which the performers questioned one another, probing levels of real experience until the actor playing Pentheus was unable to answer. It was a procedure which once continued for more than an hour and was finally, in later performances, abandoned in favour of the 'transformation circle' – in which a description of an event or action was passed around a circle with each individual transforming the message in some respect before passing it on. The objective of this was to isolate the figure of Pentheus by leaving him stranded in his theatricality while the other performers allowed their private lives to subvert this with the reality of their identities. The contrast, however, turns on an unexamined difference between the performed character and the performed self. On one occasion the actor playing Pentheus was 'rescued' from his isolation by a woman from the audience. Released from the play he walked out and the play stopped abruptly. Where for the Becks such a release would have been the objective of the play and stood as a clear model for social action, here it was by no means clear what the release meant. On another occasion Pentheus was kidnapped and taken from the theatre. Schechner's response was to intervene and call for a volunteer to continue the play. The release for which the Becks had worked so hard was thus voided by Schechner whose commitment, paradoxically, was to the continuance of the play within which Pentheus was supposedly trapped.

The crucial speech of the play is that delivered by a Messenger who defines clearly the ambiguous roles of both Dionysus and Pentheus, the struggle between the id and the ego, the battle between freedom and authority:

> Yes, it's a death struggle. Dionysus versus Pentheus. The organism versus the law . . . I could tell you how Dionysus led Pentheus into a trap on a mountain called Cithaeron. How he tantalized hundreds of women with frenzy, released their energies so they could kill a man for their sport. For a god's sport. What I can't tell you is the reason why anyone, god or candidate, can promise a man joy, freedom, ecstasy. And then make him settle for a bloodbath. Then Dionysus and Pentheus will rise from the pit, we'll get on with the action, and you can have a mute catharsis. But there is chance to be considered. Each of you is chance. And most of you are

passive. Night after night you go along with Dionysus, just as we do. And night after night you confirm the need for a Pentheus. Look, if Dionysus could lead you into the promised land, Dionysus or someone else could lead you right out again. Dig? Most of us have a pretty cheap fantasy of self-liberation. So before I open the pit door and set your catharsis in motion, consider this. It's harder to be a man than to be a god.[8]

It is a critical observation and plainly goes to the heart of the contemporary dilemma which Schechner wished to address, as it touches on a theme in Euripides' play. But it is an insight to some degree invalidated by the group's own methodology. The mere exposing of a coercive fictionality does not liberate. And though Schechner was plainly alive to the dangers of an anarchy of the senses their own methods were Dionysian. The physical caress, part of the performance, was not offered as a corrupt gesture but a genuine act of contact. The ambiguity about the power of physical presence, about non-verbal communication and an instinctive sense of community, is expressed in terms of the play's content; it is not, for the most part, acknowledged in terms of the group's dramatic strategy, its practices or its philosophy. Its exercises are built on the possibility of reaching for a level of personal truth behind the mask of the performed self. The play, indeed, is built around the possibility of such a release, but when one of the actresses tried to realise this possibility by refusing to 'kill' Pentheus and thus asserting her own freedom, she found that she 'could not shed the actor, that no matter how you try to escape the bounds of the theatrical you find yourself inside one or another succession of symbolic acts'.[9] The escape onto the streets at the end of the play becomes a parody, an ironic announcement of freedom, and yet this was precisely the freedom that Schechner had unambiguously claimed in his development of 'guerilla theatre', which was a deliberate attempt to intervene in daily life with theatrical gestures designed to make political points.

The actors in the play not merely enacted the roles in Euripides' play but also themselves. Dionysus was both a character and the actor who played his part, and as such he was addressed by name. The nudity, which was a feature of the play, was in part similarly designed to penetrate beyond mask as was the resort to a form of psychotherapy. The members of the group eventually all attended weekly therapeutic encounter meetings designed, as Schechner insisted, to 'expose our feelings, to reveal ourselves, to be open, receptive, vulnerable'. Their basic assumption was that excellence in art is 'a function of wholeness as a human being'.[10] The play tends to show the impossibility of this, even the dangerously deceptive nature of such assumptions; the performance implies the opposite. The 'whole human being' was a favourite piety of the 1960s and certainly Schechner offers no evidence for his assumption that artistic and personal wholeness have any relationship. Indeed one might suspect that the opposite might be closer to the truth. Certainly incompletion was an important part of the aesthetic and the ethic of *Dionysus in 69* which ends in mid sentence. On one level Schechner was fully alive to those contradictions. Indeed, they were incorporated within the play. On another level he was their victim, his own authoritarian position leaving him ambiguously placed in relation to a play which offers to enact and debate a conflict between anarchic freedom and a repressive authority. However, *Dionysus in 69* is undoubtedly one of those productions that addressed an issue implicit in the social no less than the cultural politics of the 1960s, while its efforts to incorporate the audience, its own collective method no less than its use of nudity, its attempt to forge a contemporary ritual and its commitment to exploring and expanding the language of the theatre made it a paradigm of performance theatre.

Following their production of *Makbeth*, Schechner's restructuring of the Shakespeare play to address the subject of fascism in America, the Performance Group created their next performance from a wide range of material, including contemporary accounts of the Manson killings and the My Lai massacre in Vietnam. *Commune* was a product of ten months' work. The text was assembled from work by Shakespeare, Marlowe, the Bible, Melville and Thoreau as well as from newspapers. It was developed through improvisation and exercises in verbal association.

Commune (1970) was allegedly born out of fears that the Performance Group was in danger of breaking up. The project thus grew out of an interest in community as such. As a consequence Schechner and others read a large number of books about communes of various kinds from Fourier and Engels through to Hawthorne and the more recent fringe groups of California. The objective which slowly emerged was, as Schechner wrote in his notebook for 23 June 1970,

> No longer a theatre of telling a story – or even doing a story. But doing/showing something here and now. The audience as partner–participant. Most impassioned speeches not dialogue but addresses to audience. Ritual *vis-à-vis* audience. Not to search for story but for themes and gestures, for sounds and dances *vis-à-vis* audience and with ourselves. To be at once absolutely personal and absolutely collective – communal.

The theme, somewhat stunning in its intellectual naivety, was to be 'The existential crime of being born in America, the rich land; of being born white, the oppressor class/race? . . . American history = killing of Sharon Tate.'[11]

4.   The Performance Group, *Commune*, 1972

The suspicion grows that this is a theatre generated every bit as much by liberal guilt as that of Arthur Miller; and at base it offers the same pieties, the same longing for a lost community, expressed equally in *Death of a Salesman* and *After the Fall*. The difference is that Schechner was concerned with demonstrating that sense of community through the communal playing of the group, yet he was also aware not merely that there is a history of the failure of communitarian projects but, more threateningly, that there is a dark side to group action. And so at the heart of *Commune* is placed the Sharon Tate murder, in which Charles Manson's manic 'family' murdered Roman Polanski's wife; and the My Lai massacre, in which an army unit destroyed the inhabitants of a Vietnamese village. The two are seen by Schechner as 'rather identical incidents of national policy'.[12] What never emerges from the play is the mechanism which distorts the group experience in the direction of violence or the legitimacy of presenting such moments of apocalyptic cruelty as an image of a specifically American experience. It never, in other words, seems to get far beyond its sources. Despite the slow process of its gestation it seems to have begun with its conclusions which, according to the methodology of the group, are to be demonstrated and enacted rather than argued. The result is a series of individually powerful images which never seem to cohere into a convincing form. And it is precisely the intellectual deficiencies of the piece which are so striking. It builds its effects through collage, through juxtaposition, an ironic use of music and quotation, a physical intervention in the logic of history, a cathartic recitation of crimes designed to release performer and audience from a destructive set of mythologies and fictions. But the strategies of performance theatre have their own coercions. They, too, rest on a series of unquestioned assumptions about the self, the group, the existence and therapeutic power of communality, the value of the senses, which are tested, if at all, only at the level of theme.

Commune and *Dionysus in 69* acknowledge a certain critical danger in a pure anarchy of the senses, in an id unregulated by ego, but since their own stance is one of profound scepticism with regard to rationalism, this concern, which exists on a thematic level, never really invades their own aesthetic. A critical element of doubt is deflected onto the surface. In *Commune* they are not even dealt with there; they are simply exposed. And a fundamental problem of performance theatre, namely the middle-class nature of its personnel but more significantly of its audience, was simply sidestepped. What, after all, is the nature of the communality proposed as a model? Is it class bound? Certainly blacks had no need of the models proposed by Schechner. He responded to a sense of the collapse of shared values and feelings which was plainly not felt by those who could speak out of a very precisely apprehended set of experiences and convictions. And though performance theatre was in revolt against Broadway, its audience was arguably similar homogenised. It was at any rate a risk which potentially left the group separated from those they wished to engage, a group which could create a priesthood but perhaps not finally a congregation. The audience is induced to collaborate in *Commune* by surrendering their shoes to be used later in the performance and giving small paper items up to be burnt as a camp fire, but the line between coercion and persuasion is not easily sustained and perhaps required more sophisticated analysis.

On the other hand these were the risks which all too few theatres were willing to take. The essence and the achievement of groups such as Schechner's was precisely that they were willing to transgress boundaries and to press their efforts beyond normal limits. Perhaps, in order to rebuild a sense of community, it may be necessary to deploy a coercive methodology just as it may be necessary to release the sensual being in order to redress a balance disturbed by a dangerously rationalist society. Certainly, for any theatre so deeply implicated in the processes of performance any text-based work must be regarded as deeply suspect.

Commune was followed by Sam Shepard's *The Tooth of Crime* (1972), *Mother Courage and her Children* (1974), and the *Marilyn Project* (1975). These, in turn, were followed by *Oedipus* (1977), Ted Hughes's version of the Seneca play, *Cops* (1978), and Genet's *The Balcony* (1979). Perhaps inevitably, internal pressures began to emerge which eventually led to Schechner's withdrawal and to a series of experiments which took the reformed group in rather a different direction. But then, as Schechner has said, 'starting in 1975 new circumstances arose. People who were in their '20s when the Group started reached ages where they wanted to do their own work independent from me. Stephan Borst did his own version of *The Beard* and later ran a workshop for gay performers. [Spalding] Gray and [Elizabeth] LeCompte began working on *Sakonnet Point*, the first of the Rhode Island plays. Libby Howes joined the Group, more in tune with LeCompte than with me.'[13] From 1977 onwards, the Group began to split up. In 1978 two performers – Joan MacIntosh and Leeny Sack – left and Spalding Gray began to perform independently. No new pieces involving the entire Group were developed after *Mother Courage*, which opened in 1975, was taken to India, and restaged by Schechner on his return. In January 1980, Schechner ceased working at the Garage with the Group, though, renamed the Wooster Group, it continued to operate in his absence under the direction of LeCompte.

Looking back over the history of the Performance Group, Schechner feels that they failed because they 'were not able to make a group that integrated a repertory of performances into a larger scheme including teaching, research of new kinds of performance modes, and the relationship between performing in America to performing in other cultures'.[14] In all honesty few can have attempted more in this direction outside of Grotowski and Brook. And Schechner has admitted to the concealed authoritarianism of performance theatre:

> throughout the sixties and into the seventies directors argued that performers should have direct creative access to audiences, and that part of the relationship between audiences and performers should be about the performers' actual private experiences. But I think that at least at the start of the period we directors were dishonest. We spoke on behalf of the performers – we instructed performers in how to 'be themselves' even while playing at 'being another' – but what we were really doing was carving out a domain for ourselves: overthrowing the writers.[15]

But if 'My generation effectively destroyed the idea that the playwright is the only, or main, originator of a theatrical event; the generation after me did the same for the director.'[16] He was thinking of such people as Spalding Gray, who had begun his career as an actor at the Alley Theatre in Houston and joined the Performance Group in 1969. While Schechner

5.　The Performance Group, *Mother Courage*, 1975.

was rehearsing *Cops* in 1978, Gray, working with Elizabeth LeCompte, began working on what were to become the Rhode Island plays (*Rumstick Road, Nayatt School* and *Point Judith*) which drew heavily on autobiographical material. From this the step to monologue (*A Personal History of the American Theatre, Seven Scenes from a Family Album, Forty-Seven Beds*) was both logical and perhaps inevitable. And it was paralleled elsewhere in the American theatre, the group work of the 1960s and early 1970s giving way to drama which Schechner saw as private and increasingly privatist. Now director, writer and performer were contained within the same sensibility and he saw the consequence as an exclusion of content or at least of a content with the power to speak to other people or to address the public issues of the day. There was much that he could find to praise in their work but in some fundamental sense he saw it as a betrayal – a betrayal of that humanist dream which he rightly saw as lying at the heart of performance theatre. Because, as he said of the attempt to create a theatre group, what was at stake was not just the construction of a theatre but also the creation of a putative society. As he observed, 'Once you make a whole out of many parts you've constructed a social model; intentionally or not you've constructed an alternative City.'[17] Thus the decay, the closure or the radical change in the various groups was not just the exhaustion of a particular line of theatrical enquiry; it was the end or the deferment of a particular model of social action. His alarm was thus not that a privatist art was being created but that it had acquired a central position, for the risk is that with this 'personalism comes a passivity, an acceptance of the City, the outer world, the world of social relations, economics and politics as it is. I worry about the passivity', he said, 'because the City is changing. If artists do not participate in the changes, do not make them more humane, artists will end up either among the victims or, like [Robert] Wilson, as pets of the rich.'[18]

Unsurprisingly, Elizabeth LeCompte of the Wooster Group saw things rather differently. For her, 'The most radical development in theatre was the combining of the playwright, director and designer in one person. The result', she suggested, 'was a wedding of text, theatre space and movements of the performers where nothing modified anything else.'[19] It was an observation which underlined the logic that led from group composition to the solo work of people like Jack Smith, Leeny Sack, Bob Carroll, Stuart Sherman and Spalding Gray or the monologues of Jane Martin. It is tempting to see this, as Schechner did, as primary evidence of that elevation of the self which characterised so much of the 1970s and indeed in many ways it plainly is. The artist assumes a significance to his or her own experience, a paradigmatic quality which is by no means self-evident. When Lee Breuer claims for Spalding Gray's performance in *Rumstick Road* (not itself a monologue but identifying his drive in that direction since it consisted in part of autobiographical material gathered by Gray) that his implied statement reads: 'I'm my own material on all fronts – visually, vocally, historically, spiritually, psychologically, intellectually and emotionally. I am myself',[20] and claims that as 'the third idea about acting in this century' after Stanislavsky and Brecht, we are plainly edging towards a view of drama which potentially leaves us little more than spectators to a personal psychotherapy. But Gray has argued otherwise. For him an apparent retreat to the personal was in fact merely a route to a renewed sense of community, a Thoreau-like withdrawal to refocus energy and attention. As he has said,

> For me there is nothing larger than the personal when it is communicated well. The very act of communication takes it into a 'larger vein' and brings it back to the community. The personal confessional, stripped of its grand theatrical metaphors, is what matters to me now. I am trying to redefine what is significant for me . . . This personal exploration has made me more politically aware because now I've come to myself as authority I

have found that I still feel repressed and because of this feeling of repression I am forced to look further into the outside world for its source.[21]

When he left the Performance Group, because it was 'an artificial "polis"', he discovered what had been apparent to others for some time, namely that those in downtown New York with whom he felt the need to relate were struggling 'to survive in a corrupt world that contained a corrupt country that contained a corrupt "City" that was controlled by the rich and I realized that all of us, not just Robert Wilson, but all of us in the "arts", are pets of the rich'.[22]

He seems to imply a concern which would link him with those individuals for whom radical change or cultural redefinition was crucial, those who sought to force society to the point of recognising their identity (as blacks, women, Chicanos, and so on) and hence transforming its values, but it is hard to see such people responding to his essentially personal work, and recently even Elizabeth LeCompte has said that 'Experimental theatre has not only lost a large part of its audience – it has also lost critics who now write about political science, film or philosophy', adding, depressingly, that 'Bright, intelligent people don't go into theatre and don't write about it.'[23]

But looking at the developments of these years from the perspective of 1983 Schechner could still see both a residue of experiment and an image of possible future change. He might lament the ending of a particular phase of work but he was by no means ready to despair of a theatre in which he had himself played a by no means undistinguished role:

> Clearly the experimenters of the past few decades have expanded the range of what we accept as theatricality . . . Having freed themselves both from playwrights and directors, they've made new connections to dancers, musicians, visual artists, novelists, and nonfiction writers . . . Out of these active negotiations – not around a table but in performing spaces – comes a different basis for making theatre. That all this conceptual, outreaching labor has till now mostly brought forth only a narcissistic mouse is not so awful.
>
> For soon, I think, this re-thought and expanded aesthetics is to be joined to several social purposes. Theatre doesn't 'do' politics, any more than it does ordinary life or ritual. All of these processes – ritual, ordinary life, politics – stand side by side with the theatrical process. And one of the truly fine things to come out of the period now ended is the recognition that theatricality is a primary human activity. Theatricality doesn't imitate or derive from other human social behavior but is side-by-side with them in a weave. It doesn't do politics as Beck and Malina think; it doesn't do ordinary behavior as Stanislavski thought; it doesn't do ritual as Grotowski believed in his 'holiday' phase. Theatricality is a process that is braided into these other processes.[24]

The statement stands as Schechner's obituary for a decade and more of experiment and if the achievements of the decade seem to have shrunk to the size of mice, narcissistic or not, his claims for its significance have scarcely diminished. Offering himself as the obstetrician of the new he looks for the developments which will offer the work of the 1960s and 70s a retrospective grace as precursor.

The central assumption behind performance theatre was that the division between art and life was as unreal as were those other dualisms under attack (mind and body, performer and observer). The argument was that ordinary life also had its rituals – and not merely those associated with birth, marriage and death – since all human interactions are shaped by conventions which provide a kind of hidden notation, and it scarcely took Erving Goffman to tell us that social behaviour rests on a multiplicity of roles and an awareness that we 'perform' the kaleidoscope of selves which we choose to homogenise into a fiction called identity. And yet the distinction between theatre and 'life' remains crucial. Indeed, for Grotowski, 'The forms of common "natural" behavior obscure the truth . . . A sign, not a common gesture, is the elementary integer of expression for us . . . we compose a role as a system of signs which demonstrate what is behind the mask of common vision.'[25] Thus, while attempting to demythologise actors (exposing acting exercises to view and identifying them by their 'real' names), these groups did not release their grasp on fiction. In fact, a striking number of the productions staged by performance groups were based on classical dramas or were the enactment of myths. They virtually all foregrounded a ceremonial or ritualistic element. And this was by no means fortuitous. But, where O'Neill had turned to the *Oresteia* to give resonance to his melodrama *Mourning Becomes Electra*, these works were concerned with fracturing the illusionistic surface, with enacting the rites and capturing the rhythms of forms which were engaged in their pure state.

The turn to myth may have been in response to the decay of religious belief, the declining faith in both religious and secular rituals, art being made to assume more completely a role which it had originally played in subservience to formal faiths – hence references to 'holy' theatre. But there were a number of other reasons. For a theatre anxious to stress communitarian values, and thereby to deny the assumptions behind an assertive individualism, myth constituted an expression of shared perceptions in which these communal apprehensions existed equally on a horizontal and vertical axis (across classes and races and through time). There was no authoritative author because the self was forced to see itself in relation to archetypal experiences. As Grotowski observed, 'While

137

retaining our private experiences, we can attempt to incorporate myth, putting on its ill-fitting skin to perceive the relativity of our problems, their connection to the "roots" and the relativity of the "roots" in the light of today's experience.'[26] Myth becomes a bridge. This, Grotowski implies, is why James Joyce had turned to *Ulysses* and Thomas Mann to *Dr Faustus*. But the essence of such works lay in the confrontation of the myth by the sensibility which transforms and even deforms it. So, too, he argued, must the actor and the director confront themselves through the historic work which they restage. Hence, to some degree, individualism is smuggled back in as that confrontation becomes the basis for a personal and group transformation. The theatre becomes a means for audience and performers to confront both themselves and one another. And in the 1960s there were those who treasured the notion that theirs was a special generation and their work the culmination of historic process no less than a sudden and revelatory consonance in the arts – a true epiphany.

There was plainly a profound sentimentalism and a familiar arrogance in the assumption that the present age is in some senses pivotal, crucial to human development. There are few ages which have not had this conviction about themselves. Richard Schechner's observation in his essay, 'Negotiating with Environment', that 'the ritual undercurrents of our lives are now more tangible than they have been in centuries',[27] is surely a manifest nonsense, a piece of cultural and temporal chauvinism. His rhetoric is suffused with nostalgia for what is presumed to be a lost organicism, an art which was an extension of life, a golden age preceding the fatal dualisms bred by scientism. He (like Julian Beck and to some extent Peter Brook and Jerzy Grotowski) looks to primitive societies not simply to locate models of ritualistic theatre but beyond that to identify paradigms of communal life threatened by the modern – paradigms which are presented at the level of symbol or theatrical model but which are never submitted to the social and economic realities of post-industrial America. He was plainly not merely in reaction against an exhausted and utilitarian theatre but against *Gemeinschaft* become *Gesellschaft*. It is true that he laments that 'We are not "primitive" and cannot hope to regain the superb elegance of the Orokolo by merely "being ourselves".'[28] But, while he asserts that 'Experience is neither universal nor personal' being 'social, arising out of culture patterns peculiar to a society and reflected in each individual', the social does not occupy a central position in his work. His notion, expressed in 'Public Events for the Radical Theatre', that 'There is a special beauty in an art whose extraordinary complexity precludes a uniquely personal creativity',[29] is an ideological statement without referent or justification; more especially if the distinction between art and communal ceremony is not clearly maintained.

138

(And how could it be when the erosion of that distinction was an essential element of his thought?) His assertion that our 'models should be the civic celebrations of Athens, the processional pageants of the Middle Ages, the tumultuous simultaneity of Elizabethan life, the embracing rituals of many nonliterate peoples'[30] fails precisely to acknowledge the nature of the social world which generated such art (a world encompassing slavery, feudalism, and a rigid social hierarchy which provided the primary motivating force for a controlled breaking of boundaries, and a substitution of magic and ceremonial for free enquiry). His rejection of the 'self-consciously aesthetic', presupposes an absence of that dimension in, for example, the processional pageants of the Middle Ages, for which there is no evidence or for which no evidence is supplied. But in order to tap the roots of myth and examine the nature of ceremony Schechner, like others, sought to locate authentic rituals. As he observed, 'The birth ritual of *Dionysus in 69* was adapted from the Asnot of West Irian; several sequences in the Living Theatre's *Mysteries* and *Paradise Now* were taken from yoga and Indian theatre; Philip Glass's music draws on garnelan and Indian raga'[31] while Eugenio Barba, a colleague of Grotowski, brought Kathakali exercises to Poland. The Performance Group itself went to India in 1976. He was, to be sure, aware that while 'Any ritual can be lifted from its original setting and performed as theatre – just as any everyday event can be . . . the rituals created were unstable because they were not attached to actual social structures outside theatre.'[32] Though this was a crucial understanding it was not one which was always evident in the work of these groups. Nor was this the only paradox. Thus the spontaneous and even erotic validation of human solidarity is in fact carefully sculpted and advertised as a product in the cultural exchange market, while the decentering of the author places the director/creator in a more powerful position, as Meyerhold had observed it would.

Since language is an expression of a social bond, distrust of language is likely to precipitate a sense of social crisis, more particularly in a predominantly Anglo-Saxon culture in which phatic communion, a dense structure of proxemic and gestural meaning are minimised. Performance art was in part a response to this. Its shock effect (necessarily short-lived and the source of a quickly exhausted sense of innovatory pressure) relied precisely on the fact of a suspicion of physical proximity, of non-verbal or minimally verbal experience, of the non-rational, of the apparent denial of social authority in the name of an assumed transcendental unity. However, in doing so it tended to make certain assumptions about the cultural orthodoxies of contemporary society which were not always examined for their accuracy but which nonetheless provided its own justification and constituted the basis of what it presumed to be its dialectical relationship with that society.

The retreat from psychologically derived character and the suspicion of illusionist theatre created a pressure for the physical, the immediate, the present, the tangible, but required that this become simultaneously mythicised, translated into a kind of supra-realism. The body became an icon which contained its own transcendence. Yet this was also a theatre that wished to question surfaces as themselves the origin of deception – language, in particular, being a mechanism for this deceit. The unclothing of the members of the Living Theatre in *Paradise Now* was less enactment than re-enactment, despite their claims to the contrary. It was Lear's stripping of himself to the truth of the body, to remove the illusion that had blinded him and thus open up a world undeceived by the surface. It was, in short, metaphor and not pure experience – but its heart was squarely in the right place. The deconstruction of character in performance theatre is not an antihumanist gesture but a stage in the recuperation of meaning through myth or through an acknowledgement of the ultimate significance of the group. It is not hard to see, therefore, how what began as an aesthetic could end up as a political process. Or yet why it came to challenge a contemporary alienation by a resort to social models derived from the past.

The response was in part the anarchism of Julian Beck and Judith Malina, the romanticism of Richard Schechner and in part the radicalism of those groups who paraded as new models what in truth owed their authority precisely to the past. Beginning with a concern with regenerating the American theatre they found themselves, by what increasingly came to seem to them to be an ineluctable logic, seeking the regeneration of America. And it was this that established the link between their work and that of those other groups who sought the reconstruction of American institutions and the revivification of American values (the San Francisco Mime Troupe, the Bread and Puppet Theatre, El Teatro Campesino and the increasing number of black, women's and Chicano theatre groups), just as it was their concern with the physical texture of experience and the need for a heightened consciousness on the part of their audience which connected them with the theatre of Robert Wilson, Richard Foreman and Lee Breuer.

The 1930s saw the development of an avowedly political theatre in America. The Communist Party in particular was active in stimulating the creation of small theatre groups on the model of the Blue Blouses in Russia and Germany. Black Americans took a tentative step towards the use of theatre as weapon in their own political and cultural emancipation. Major organisations such as the Group Theatre and the Federal Theatre mobilised political discontent and challenged the values and direction of American society. Though not particularly innovative as far as theatre was concerned they generated a broad interest in drama among those who had shown little interest in it before.

Though this experience helped shape the work of Williams and Miller and gave their work its undertone of social concern, often refracted through individual psychosis, the political edge disappeared from the American theatre until the latter half of the 1960s when the civil rights movement, Vietnam, and subsequently concern for the role of women, Indians and Chicanos precipitated the emergence of new groups or the radicalisation of existing ones. Since this coincided with a re-examination of the theatrical experience, prompted in part by the publication of the first English translation of Antonin Artaud's *The Theatre and Its Double*, and in part by a renewed sense of experiment in allied arts and a concern with examining the boundary between theatre and therapy, acting and social role-playing, the consequence was the development of a number of groups who blended theatrical and social radicalism in different quantities. They were, for the most part, united in their reaction against American materialism and the adventure in Vietnam as they were in their belief that theatre was to be a celebration of life. They joined, too, in the value that they ascribed to the theatre group as model community. Where they differed was in the relative value which they placed on theatrical and political innovation, in the degree to which they were concerned with a radical reconstruction of society, in the priority to be established between the transformation of consciousness and the transformation of the world. Nor did such groups remain static. Aesthetic experiment was apt to give way to political commitment (The San Francisco Mime Troupe) or vice-versa (El Teatro Campesino). For Ronnie Davis, founder of the Mime Troupe, there was a distinction to be made between the radical left and the radical right, between, that is, the Bread and Puppet Theatre, the San Francisco Mime Troupe and El Teatro Campesino, on the one hand, and the Open Theatre, the Living Theatre and the Performance Group on the other. The former groups are concerned with prompting or supporting movements for change in the community. They are in revolt against the very idea of the privileged space which is the theatre. They are concerned with locating an audience beyond the conventional middle-class intellectual fold. Their style is a product of a desire to communicate directly, to discover a form which combines clarity with significance. The radical right is more likely to be concerned with prompting a transformation in lifestyle or consciousness. It is more likely to deal in generalities, to show a greater respect for the theatre building, to appeal to an intellectual audience, to be concerned with the craft of acting, to insist, indeed, on the special qualities of the actor even while ostensibly seeking to demythologise his role.

For Davis, the Living Theatre was concerned with offering catharsis to the middle class:

> They disputed bourgeois conventions in the protective atmosphere of the theatre, where the bourgeoisie had historically demanded that their stage first portray the good life of the rising middle class, and then, when the contradictions between surplus value and religious morality were too great, they demanded that the stage (not the church) punish them . . . The Living Theatre both hates and works over the middle class, not to change them, only to exorcise the original sin.

More directly, he has accused them of spewing out 'their pseudo-religious, guilt-ridden, despicable, metaphysical, anarchist, elitist rap'.[33] But the radical left, as he identified it, was also powerfully attracted by metaphysics, by a sense of the religious, the transcendent. Both El Teatro Campesino and Bread and Puppet were increasingly drawn towards myth and archetypal experience. Beginning with a direct engagement with specific issues, they had, by the time of Davis's assault on the radical right, in 1975, both moved towards a more generalised concern with a human nature whose constancy was in effect a denial of radical left assumptions. Only the Mime Troupe, which Davis had left partly because it seemed to him to have become too doctrinaire, remained politically committed in an ideological way. For Davis, Schechner was concerned with 'trying to find some perfect virgin theatrical group that could espouse causes that were so pure that no one would touch them'. While the Becks were 'truly searching for T.S. Eliot's ant hill of martyrdom', Schechner had approached 'creation in the theatre from a purely hop-skip-and-consumer sense', and Chaikin had tried 'to invent one's world by hiding from it'.[34] The bitterness is perhaps that of the left-wing radical out-manœuvred by a more radical left and anxious to establish his bona fides. Certainly the distinctions he tries to make between left and right have dissolved with time if they ever really applied. His animus against the Becks and Schechner is not without some basis. Certainly the distinction between bourgeois society and their own art was never as clear as they would have wished, their art being too easily accommodated as consumer product. But the drive to re-examine social and aesthetic assumptions was real enough. That self-indulgence was a constant temptation (too often acceded to), that these groups often preached freedom through authoritarian forms and with an immodesty at odds with their declared objectives, that they feared the very spaces they worked so hard to open up, did not deny the importance of the task they set themselves, which was simply to ask questions which the American theatre had not been prone to ask itself in the past. At the same time it is too reductive a view of groups such as Bread and Puppet and El Teatro Campesino to say, as Davis does of them, that they are concerned to 'sort out the garbage and transform rotting elements into social insights'.[35] Their political commitments were real, though they were, perhaps necessarily so, modified with time. But they, too, were dedicated to rediscovering the resources of theatre and, like the groups so casually assigned by Davis to the radical right, they turned to the past as a means of discovering a way forward. In that they were very much a product of their time.

Nor was this concern limited to America. In the 1968 book, *The Empty Space*, Peter Brook observed that 'Group creation can be infinitely richer, if the group is rich [a crucial proviso not made by Richard Schechner in his similar remark], than the product of weak individualism.'[36] In that statement can be seen how political ideologue and theatrical innovator could find their paths crossing. On one level Brook's observation is a simple truism. The theatre is a collaborative art or it is nothing. But he is clearly concerned with something more than the simple process of technical collaboration. Like so many other people in other spheres, particularly in the 1960s and early 70s, he was stirred by a conviction not merely that theatre worked by shared presumptions, values, icons – a shared space and time – but that it was itself primary evidence for a universal language reflecting a universal set of experiences. Accordingly, he, like Schechner, set out to explore other cultures (travelling to Africa and elsewhere), to develop that universal theatrical language for which Artaud had looked. At first, like Artaud, he tried to generate a literal language, having Ted Hughes create one for *Orghast*. But at base he distrusted language as much as Artaud had and as much as did several key American groups in the late 1960s. As he had remarked in 1961,

> I believe in the word in classical drama, because the word was their tool. I do not believe in the word much today, because it has outlived its purpose. Words do not communicate, they do not express much, and most of the time they fail abysmally to define. There have been great theatres in the history of the world with a concrete language of their own that is not the language of the streets nor the language of books – all great theatre is religious . . . I want to see outer realism as something in endless flux with barriers and boundaries that come and go . . . I want to sense what truly binds us, what truly separates us.[37]

His experiments began with a season in which he worked with the expatriate American Charles Marowitz. As Marowitz explained, in an article published in the influential *Tulane Drama Review* in 1966:

we insinuated the idea that the voice could produce sounds other than grammatical combinations of the alphabet, and that the body, set free, could begin to enunciate a language which went beyond text, beyond sub-text, beyond psychological implication . . . Sounds were created which had the resonance of wounded animals . . . Movements became stark and unpredictable. Actors began to use the chairs and tables as sculptural objects instead of functional furniture. Facial expressions, under the pressure of extended sounds, began to resemble Japanese masks and Zen sculpture.[38]

In Poland Jerzy Grotowski worked along very similar lines, asking, in *Towards a Poor Theatre*, 'Why are we concerned with art?', and answering, 'To cross our frontiers, exceed our limitations . . . to give ourselves nakedly to something which is impossible to define but which contains Eros and Caritas.'[39] He, too, reached out to myth as an expression of a common human truth; he, too, was concerned with developing the physical skills of the actor, with stressing sound and movement. And when Brook, Grotowski and Chaikin met in London for the Royal Shakespeare Company's production of *US* in 1966 a crucial nexus was established. The production involved a large dummy, representing a Marine commando, just as had Brook's production of Genet's *Les Paravents*, and just as did Chaikin's production, also in 1966, of Jean-Claude Van Itallie's *America Hurrah!* which in turn was brought to Britain. In 1968 Brook began work in Paris with an international group of actors and three other directors. One of these was Joseph Chaikin. When the student rebellion broke out in May 1968 the Théâtre des Nations season, under whose auspices they were working, was cancelled and the group moved to London. It would be impossible to imagine a politically oriented group passing up such an opportunity and the gulf between those motivated primarily by theatrical concerns and those having more directly political objectives was aptly symbolised by the fact that the Living Theatre, which also happened to be in Paris, threw themselves with enthusiasm into the occupation of the Odéon Theatre, Beck, not untypically, regarding the occupation as 'the most beautiful thing I have ever seen in the theatre'. It was this, indeed, which gave him the dangerous illusion that he and his group were in the forefront of revolution, a conviction of which he was swiftly disabused later that same year on the group's visit to Berkeley.

Brook's subsequent work, in which his company tried to develop 'on the one hand a very simple, moving popular theatre work, and on the other a very intense, cool, hieratic theatre work',[40] could be paralleled by some of the experiments of Beck, Schechner and Chaikin but none, I suspect, had his ascetic spirit or the kind of controlled commitment which he brings to everything he does. Perhaps Chaikin comes closest but he lacked the energy, and, indeed, the physical well-being, to sustain this over time. But, arguably, Brook has come no closer to solving the problem of the audience than have Beck, Chaikin or Schechner. His performances in Africa seem to have communicated most fully when simplified to a degree which perhaps undermines some of their value. His performances in Paris and London tended to be viewed by a coterie audience. The experiments continue but where once they could appear to reflect a genuine sense of cultural crisis, a revolt against authority in all guises, a society in search of a language and an iconography commensurate with a sense of spiritual need, by the late 1970s this resonance was largely missing and the experiments of the previous decade threatened to become simple mannerism.

As in many revolutions, the discoveries of the American theatre of the 1960s were in part re-rediscoveries. Though the theatre of the absurd had a limited impact in its pure form it did unsettle a theatre steeped in realism, with a penchant for melodrama and a preference for the psychological and the social over the metaphysical. Its primary acting mode, encouraged by the Method, was one which reached out for a realism authenticated by experience or re-created by a process of analogical reconstruction. The theatre of the absurd did at least challenge this and was in part responsible for a new concentration on the craft and, indeed, the metaphysics of actor training. The work of Viola Spolin assumed greater importance and subsequently that of the Becks, of Chaikin and even of Schechner. It is, perhaps, therefore, not surprising that a work like Artaud's *The Theatre and Its Double* should assume such significance, or, later, Grotowski's *Towards a Poor Theatre*. But, in truth, Artaud, for all his eccentric brilliance, was himself reinforcing the values and in some senses the methods of other theatre practitioners. Thus, it is not difficult to find in Meyerhold that emphasis on physical movement, admittedly in the service of a form of psychological truth, which one finds in Artaud, and that same desire to subordinate speech which is such a feature of *The Theatre and Its Double*: 'The *truth* of human relationships is established by gestures, poses, glances and silences. Words alone cannot say everything. Hence there must be a *pattern of movement* to transform the spectator into a vigilant observer . . . The difference between the old theatre and the new is that in the new theatre speech and plasticity are each subordinated to their own particular rhythms and the two do not necessarily coincide.'[41] It was Meyerhold, rather than Artaud, who stressed the importance of improvisation, the significance of abrupt changes of mood and personality, the value of disrupting illusion, all of which were features of Chaikin's theatre. It was Meyerhold who discovered these elements in the *commedia dell'arte* tradition, as Ronnie Davis of the San Francisco Mime Troupe was to do.

American performance art could have taken Meyerhold's 1913 statement about the nature of theatre as its own motto: 'A theatre which presents plays saturated in "psychologism" with the motivation of every single event underlined, or which forces the spectator to rack his brains over the solution of all manner of social and psychological problems – such a theatre destroys its own theatricality . . . The stage is a world of marvels and enchantment; it is breathless joy and strange music.'[42] It was Meyerhold, too, who abolished the proscenium arch. In his *Mystery-Bouffe* he had his actors invade the auditorium and at the end the audience were invited onto the stage. It is not simply that there is nothing new under the sun but that a large part of the new theatre in America in the 1960s was concerned with identifying ancestors who could be claimed with pride, while necessarily representing their activities as new, as an expression of a generalised revolt particular to their own generation. There is, perhaps, something specifically American about the need to locate a pedigree for revolt, to seek validation beyond the confines of American cultural history.

And the next development also had its roots in the past, more especially in modernism. In a sense Schechner could have looked back to T.S. Eliot for a justification for his own interest in ritual. It was, after all, Eliot who had said:

> The realism of the ordinary stage is something to which we can no longer respond, because to us it is no longer realistic. We know now that the gesture of daily existence is inadequate for the stage; instead of pretending that the stage gesture is a copy of reality, let us adopt a literal untruth, a thorough-going convention, a ritual. For the stage – not only in its remote origins, but always – is a ritual, and the failure of the contemporary stage to satisfy the craving for ritual is one of the reasons why it is not a living art.[43]

But theatre practitioners like Robert Wilson, Richard Foreman and Lee Breuer could also have invoked a modernist support for their own experiments which were to command the attention of the avant-garde in the 1970s, finding in Nietzsche's observation, that 'Art is not an imitation of nature but its metaphysical supplement, raised up beside it in order to overcome it',[44] a central statement of their own convictions, and in William Carlos Williams's remark, that 'the principal movement in imaginative writing today [is] that away from the word as symbol to the word as reality',[45] a description of their theatrical strategy.

PART III

The theatre of images: art, theatre and the real

INTRODUCTION

> You may think that every picture you see is a true history of the way things used to be or the way things are. While you're ridin' in your radio or walking through the late late show, ain't it a drag to know you just don't know you just don't know. So here's another illusion to add to your confusion of the way things are.
>
> Sam Shepard, *The Tooth of Crime*

A number of American playwrights were recently asked to comment on the direction being taken by avant-garde theatre. Their replies take us in the direction of art history rather than theatre history. The writer Megan Terry, herself trained as a sculptor, replied that: 'Painters and sculptors who are also theatre people are now leading the avant-garde in New York, emphasising "look", "style" and "form"',[1] while Sam Shepard remarked that the 'single most important idea is the idea of consciousness . . . For some time now it's become generally accepted that the other art forms are dealing with this idea to one degree or another. That the subject of painting is seeing. That the subject of music is hearing. That the subject of sculpture is space.'[2] And this is, indeed, reminiscent of a statement by the photorealist painter Ralph Goings who has said: 'My attitude is that the subject of realism is subject matter – not painting about painting but painting about looking.'[3] As Shepard explained, 'I'm interested in exploring the writing of plays through attitudes derived from other forms such as music, painting, sculpture.'[4] Or, as Robert Wilson remarked, 'People are just beginning to return again to discerning visual significance as a primary mode.'[5] Certainly, any account of the American theatre of the 1970s would have to begin with a description of developments in art and in particular with the rise of photorealism. What follows is an attempt to do just that, particularly in relation to three figures whose names became synonymous with the theatrical avant-garde from the late 1960s through to the 1980s and whose work the critic Bonnie Marranca has collectively described as the theatre of images: Robert Wilson, Richard Foreman and Lee Breuer.

The connection between art and theatre is obvious enough and of long standing. For Wagner, the arts not merely had a symbiotic relationship but were deeply implicated in one another's gestures, forms and structures. The *mise-en-scène*, of course, once actually incorporated a painted backcloth, while the framing of the stage, the proscenium arch, significantly also known as the 'picture frame stage', was used very self-consciously as a painterly gesture encouraging the use of tableaux, imitations of realist art, and lighting effects derived from artistic models. The Diaghilev ballets actually drew on the talents of painters such as Bakst, Benois and Picasso, the latter designing the costumes for *Parade* (described at the time as a 'ballet réaliste' precisely because, in our contemporary sense, of its resistance to a narrative drive, because of its emphasis on the physical reality of the body and its movements in space). Picasso, indeed, no less than Cocteau, actually generated stage texts.

In the American context, the stage set for Mike Gold's *Hoboken Blues* was described by him specifically as a 'futurist composition'; the scenes were to 'overlap slightly' so that there was 'an effect of simultaneous planes of action – as in some futurist paintings'.[6] O'Neill's set for *The Emperor Jones* was in effect an expressionist painting given a third dimension, as was that for Susan Glaspell's *The Verge*.

But in the 1960s, with happenings, the logic of art history development seemed to move very much in the direction of theatre, as later the logic of theatre development would move in the direction of art. The flat plane of the picture expanded to collage and environment. As the sculptor George Segal remarked, 'If I was prevented from making the illusion of going into the canvas space, I felt the only place I could go was forward from the wall. Logically that demanded sculpture . . . it demanded that the sculpture occupy my own space, that there be no pedestal, that there be no psychological distance. It implied environmental art.'[7] The space of the gallery, transformed by the artist, or simply redefined by the objects with which he or she chose to fill it, became as important as the objects themselves. And sculpture is potentially a highly theatricalised form; at least, for Segal, there was a kind of logic in the multiple-planed surface of sculpture which reached back to cubism and forward to theatre. Thus Segal, who had himself participated in Allan Kaprow's happenings, has described an experiment which he conducted in which the starting-point was an etching by Picasso:

> I became intrigued with his idea of cubism. I was attracted to an etching as a blueprint from which I could build a genuine cubist sculpture. I cut out a piece of plywood and that was the wall, except that it was standing in pure space. I added one element on top of and in front of the back plane, another element in front of that; it also had a plane that went backwards.

> Picasso, that thundering genius, had made a quick drawing and the sculpture stood up on its own legs. It needed no other help from me. I discovered something extraordinary after I finished doing it. Using the pure Cubist technique to make an absolutely orthodox cubist work, I had replicated a proscenium stage and the precise method of seeing perspective in planes in receding space.[8]

Interestingly enough, one feature of the American theatre in the last decade has been the rediscovery of the proscenium stage, and less for purely theatrical than for art-historical reasons, while in art and sculpture we have witnessed a renewed interest in the tableau and in what look to some degree like stage sets merely awaiting the appearance of actors – the work of the photorealists.

Appollinaire once wrote that the true poetry of our age is to be found in the window of the barber shop thereby emphasising the power, the authority, the mystery, even, of the real. As Max Beckman said of his own painting in 1938, 'It may sound paradoxical but it is, in fact, reality which forms the mystery of our existence.'[9] Or, as Clement Greenberg half predicted in 1954, 'The connoisseurs of the future may be more sensitive than we to the imaginative dimension and overtones of the literal.'[10] It may not have been the barber shop but for the photorealists of the 1960s and 70s it was the butcher shop, the drug store and the diner.

Certainly the emergence of photorealism in painting, and of forms in sculpture which at first located rough-cast figures in a familiar environment and then, through the use of plastics, mimicked the texture and substance of the human body, seemed to justify the prediction, as had the earlier 1962 exhibition of the 'New Realism' and the 1968 exhibition at the Museum of Modern Art called 'The Art of the Real'.

Unsurprisingly, this development was seen as a revolt against abstract expressionism and certainly George Segal for one has described his sense of the insufficiency as well as the dogmatic power of that movement. But it is equally possible to see these developments as extensions of some of the concerns of abstract expressionism – particularly their emphasis on process, on a reflexive dimension, on an exultance in colour and texture. Certainly, in terms of those painters and sculptors variously referred to as photorealists, super-realists, etc., the real is perceived precisely in terms of planes, colours, fragments, discontinuous gestures, reflections, refractions, reductions, redactions. For George Segal, speaking of his construction *The Diner*, 'the white figure, the waitress, is against the pure intense red of a wall: the bottom half of the seated man is against the dark, black/green linoleum of the counter. And they are austere, abstract, dark, light, vivid . . . I like the counter's surface, I like the associations of the pure rectangular shape.'[11] It is an observation echoed in another context by the theatre practitioner Robert Wilson who has said that he likes straight lines, 'Like a rectangle which is the frame of the stage', and whose own use of the human figure is not detached from his own art-historical background.

There is, however, a danger of accommodating these developments in the 1960s and 70s to a featureless norm. The use of the word 'realism' for the works shown in the 1962 and 1968 exhibitions and the appropriation of the term for painters like Richard Estes, Ralph Goings, Robert Cottingham or sculptors like George Segal, Robert de Andrea and Duane Hanson is plainly misleading. 'The Art of the Real' exhibition had consisted mostly of minimalist art – that is to say mostly non-illusionist works which drew attention to the physical qualities of objects, the nature of materials and so on. In the 1970s the emphasis tended to be on the manner in which those properties were rendered, the way in which objects were perceived, on consciousness itself. Indeed the word realism is especially suspect since in some ways such work consti-tuted precisely an attack on realism in that the implicit accusation was that realism had in some sense devalued reality in so far as it concerned itself with revealing a supposedly latent meaning inherent in context or character and not with the thing itself or the means whereby it was apprehended, mediated and rendered.

If you hear echoes of Robbe-Grillet here you would not be wrong. Ralph Goings has actually acknowledged Robbe-Grillet's *Le Voyeur* as a factor in his own development towards photorealism, recalling in particular that moment in which the protagonist, remembering the sight of a seagull on a window ledge, realises that he can recall nothing of the emotional overtones of the moment but only the physical details of feathers, colour and texture.

In an essay, Robbe-Grillet observed that

> cultural fringes, bits of psychology, ethics, metaphysics, etc., are all the time being attached to things and making them seem less strange, more comprehensible, more reassuring. Sometimes the camouflage is com-plete: a gesture is effaced from our minds and its place taken by the emotions that are supposed to have given rise to it; we remember a landscape as being 'austere' or 'calm' without being able to describe a single line of it, or any of its principal elements . . . And so we should try to construct a more solid, more immediate world to take the place of this universe of 'meanings' . . . so that the first impact of objects and gestures should be that of their *presence* . . . the world is neither meaningful nor absurd. It quite simply *is*.[12]

Translated into theatrical terms this implies a shift from Stanislavsky illusionism, whereby an object or gesture provokes an affective memory

6.   Harold Gregor, *Steve's Café*, 1972.

7.   Detail from *Steve's Café*.

– precisely prompting an emotional recall – towards the stance of Richard Foreman who has said of his theatre, 'everybody should wake up. Begin to "see", "listen", "touch", "taste", "smell" but in such a way that it is "THINKING" and not passive acceptance . . . The world of signs is to be replaced by a world of perceptions.'[13] Certainly presence was significant in both the theatre and art, but Robbe-Grillet, of course, was not concerned with mere presence because, as he said, 'matter itself is at the same time solid and unstable, at the same time present and dreamed of, foreign to man and yet perpetually in the process of being invented by man's mind'.[14] In the 1970s it was this process which moved to the real centre of attention.

The term 'photorealism' is misleading in a number of respects. Take, for example, Harold Gregor's *Illinois Barn* series and particularly *Steve's Café*, 1972. At first sight this looks much like a photograph by Walker Evans. Its power seems to come from a precise delineation and from the simple framing. But to inspect the surrounding grass is to find that no attempt is made to make this realistic. It remains as a kind of quotation from a more painterly tradition. Or, consider Richard Estes' *Helene's Florist* – a picture of a florist's shop. Here certain aspects have been reproduced as though they were a photograph. But the flowers themselves come out of a wholly different aesthetic. Even more striking and interesting from my point of view is Richard Estes' *Cafeteria*. Here, once again, the neon sign is reproduced with an apparently photographic realism, as are the signs in the window. But the figures inside are not so reproduced, while the whole picture is framed in a way which can only be called theatrical. That is, the two pillars which frame the front window of the cafeteria are reproduced as though they were the painted pillars of a stage set, while the scene is even complete with theatrical curtains. No attempt has been made to make these realistic.

In other paintings the deformations are of a different kind. What we see in particular is an emphasis on fragments, on magnification (which is itself, incidentally, a form of abstraction), and most significantly, on reflection. The works tend to stress metallic colours (acra red, dioxazine purple) and to emphasise reflective surfaces through the use of reflective materials (acrylics, polyesters, polychromed fibre glass and liquitex). The unreality of the gloss is apparent when it is carried over into the wrecking yard, and it is in Don Eddy's *Wrecking Yard* sequence. We see less with the cold eye of the camera, which critics have invoked, than the warm eye of the commercial artist creating painterly folds of cloth, rustless crumples in automobiles, and an air-brushed serenity which is disturbing precisely because of its artifice rather than its naturalness.

In terms of sculpture there is a distinction to be drawn between the

8. Richard Estes, *Helene's Florist*, 1974.

9. Detail from *Helene's Florist*.

10.   Richard Estes, *Cafeteria*

work of George Segal, who, until the late 1960s, tended to leave his figures rough cast, and that of Duane Hanson and Robert de Andrea, whose figures were simultaneously disturbingly real and alarmingly dead, physically present and spiritually absent. Photorealism begins with the fact of physical presence – the very titles of the paintings and sculptures underlining this (*Man Leaning and Woman, Some Shoes, Two Women, The Diner*, etc.) – but its real concern is with the problematics of the real, with the process whereby that presence is rendered and hence with the nature of perception and consciousness. And this was also essentially the development within the work of Robert Wilson and Richard Foreman, the metonymic and synecdochal method of photorealism being equally observable in their theatre.

The incapacity of art to create an unproblematic realism becomes in some sense the subject. The destabilising both of art and of the 'real' is achieved, paradoxically, by the very precision with which it is rendered. The movie in which the research department has filled the screen with the minutiae of life in, say, the 1920s may actually threaten not only its own illusionism but in some ways even the supposed reality of the 1920s which is now revealed as a kaleidoscope of artifacts, gestures, fashions and social habits which must now seem no more than a series of ironised conventions – exemplary forms. Thus the 'reality' is not merely fictionalised in the sense of being captured in a fiction but equally in the

154

11.   Detail from *Cafeteria.*

155

sense of being revealed for what it is – a series of conventionalised exemplary fictions. Thus, too, the computer-enhanced laser photographs, so popular on American campuses in the early 1980s, through the very minuteness of their details, which capture every glistening drop of water in the curling spray of a wave, undermine not only their own realism but also that of the frozen moment itself. As Robbe-Grillet said of the photograph: 'It is as if the conventions of photography . . . all help to liberate us from our own conventions. The slightly unusual appearance of this reproduction world reveals to us, at the same time, the *unusual* character of the world around us; it, too, is unusual in so far as it refuses to submit to our habitual ways of understanding and to our notion of order.'[15] Or, as he said of Raymond Roussel's work – incidentally drawing his imagery both from the world of painting and theatre: 'The greater the accumulation of minutiae, of details of form and dimensions, the more the object loses its depth. So this is an opacity without mystery, just as there is nothing behind the surface of a backcloth, no inside, no secret, no ulterior motive.'[16] It is not hard to see how this applies to photorealist painting. But opacity without mystery was equally the objective of theatre practitioners such as Robert Wilson and Richard Foreman. Ionesco once said that there has never been a play without a detective. Wilson and Foreman set out to expel the detective.

One of the more striking characteristics of photorealism, I think, is its reversal of role between object and person. The human form is deliberately drained of spirit while the environment, which has no spirit to lose, becomes charged with nostalgia. Hence, what Peter Conradi has called the pathetic fallacy of the *nouveau roman*[17] might be extended to this art. The human figure is frozen into a disturbing stasis, disturbing precisely because it denies its animate identity. The stasis of the object, however, is familiar and acceptable and though these works have been described as supercool, in fact, by an act of displacement, the objects have perhaps been invested with a spirit expelled from the human body. There is a kind of transubstantiation of souls and, as Michel Butor has pointed out, given the nature of planned obsolescence, even a three-year-old car in America accretes a nostalgic aura. Though both the objects and the persons are presented as generic (either, as with Segal, with no distinguishing feature or, as with Hanson, simply accommodated to cliché), it is the objects rather than the human figures that invite empathy. Character is, as it were, frozen whole – itself an ironic rendering of the presumptions of realism – and realism is not so much embraced by these works as mocked by them. There is an opposition between self and the world but this is rendered less by stressing the coldness of the world than by draining the human form of its animation and breathing warmth into the setting, or at least charging it with the force of nostalgia.

In a sense the object, in the work of the photorealists or super-realists, is fetishised in both a Marxist and a Freudian sense. Krafft Ebbing commented on the fetishistic significance of the shoe, which he regarded as a consequence of the custom in the middle ages of drinking from the shoe of a beautiful woman, and the shoe interestingly enough crops up in a number of paintings by the photorealists! And certainly objects in these paintings tend to be drained of their utility. They do, indeed, possess some of the qualities of a fetish. The paintings and sculptures tend to emphasise the exchange rather than the use value of the objects which they portray. It is not coincidental that so many photorealists concentrate on the advertising sign, the façade, on consumption – and in that context the prevalence, in such works, of restaurants, diners, cutlery, condiments, and food is plainly a deliberate pun. And the central figure of such paintings tends to be the automobile – perhaps the central figure of consumer society, the principal symbol of exchange value. They are shown outside of a use context, driverless, stationary. More often than not they are dazzling new, with unreal reflections. Even if old they are new – a kind of simonised art. In other words they are showroom cars, paradigms. Time is frozen, as in the advertisement whose aesthetic principles these paintings seem to borrow. There is indeed a place where neither moth nor rust doth corrupt and it's called Madison Avenue. As Alfred Sohn-Rethel has observed, in *Intellectual and Manual Labour*:

> in the market place and shop windows, things stand still. They are under the spell of one activity only; to change owners. They stand there waiting to be sold. While they are there they are not there for use. A commodity marked at a definite price, for instance, is looked at as being frozen to absolute immutability through the time during which its price remains unaltered. And the spell does not only bind the doings of man. Even nature herself is supposed to abstain from any ravages in the body of this commodity and to hold her breath, as it were, for the sake of the social business of man.[18]

For Madison Avenue, the means of production and the means of reproduction have always been intimately related, the qualities of the sexual object being accommodated to those of the manufactured object. And this nexus is preserved, for example, in the work of John Kacere where the sexual component of that fetishism is clear in his pictures of the lower female anatomy but equally in the smooth lines and gentle folds of the cars which he was painting at the same time. It is not hard to see why he has described his own work as 'the return of the repressed'. The framing of automotive parts or human parts not merely dislocates the part from the whole but in a sense stresses the dysfunction of the part. It removes it from its use value. These are signs with no signifieds, like the

157

neon signs which are so often decentred so that the 'meaning' is subordinated to their physical qualities and the means whereby they have been reproduced.

It is not difficult, then, to see an element of implied social criticism in the work of the photorealists or the sculpture of Segal, Hanson and De Andrea, though we are so often told by critics of the completeness of their detachment. As Hanson has said, 'I am not satisfied with the world. Not that I think you can change it, but I just want to express my feelings of dissatisfaction.'[19] De Andrea, from a rather different perspective, contrasts the world of his art to that beyond it: 'I set up my own world', he has said, 'and it is a very peaceful world – at least my sculptures are.'[20]

The photorealism or hyper-realism of American art of the 1970s tended to concentrate on the texture of the urban environment. The human subject tends to be displaced or more usually completely re-moved. Instead we are presented with urban landscapes (the store fronts of Richard Estes, the neon signs of Robert Cottingham, the empty gas station, store and deserted parking lots of Ralph Goings) or with the stylised grace of the motor cycle (David Parish and Tom Blackwell) or the motor car (Don Eddy and Ron Kleeman). Subway cars tend to be empty, streets filled with vehicles but devoid of people. Where people do appear they tend to be drastically reduced in scale (as in Paul Staiger's *El Segundo* (1972) or *Santa Monica* (1972) in which the simple geometry of a beach scene subordinates the human form to design) or, as in the case of the three-dimensional figures of Duane Hanson, they are forms which startle by their detailed realism but which have the effect of rendering that realism as cliché, as in *Florida Shopper* (1973) or *Tourists* (1970) which offer the individual as type, as object. Like the holographic portraits of the 1980s these have the effect not merely of foregrounding technique but of emphasising the processes of perception, thereby undermining the very realism which seems and only seems their objective. Above all they stress absence, the absence of the human figure, the absence of the animate.

If the loss of the human subject reaches some kind of apogee in what seems to be contemporary realist art with the work of the photorealists in the 1970s much the same could be said of the theatre. In Mamet's work the characters are little more than animate De Andrea figures; in Sam Shepard's work, no less than in Lee Breuer's, they owe something to the comic strip, the published version of Breuer's *Red Horse Animation* being available in what is literally a comic-strip version, while Shepard's *La Turista* is not remote from Duane Hanson's *Tourists*, Shepard incor-porating the aesthetic principles of the media, and, in *The Tooth of Crime*, creating a play in which character, plot and language are all rendered in terms of style. In Jean-Claude Van Itallie's *Motel*, and in the work of the Snake Theatre in California, puppet figures replace actors. In Paul Foster's play, *Balls* and Albee's *Box* there are no characters at all, while in the work of Robert Wilson and Richard Foreman the human form is apt to become an object among other objects, the voice, for example, being electronically detached from the figure who produces it. In Lee Breuer's work, the human figure is substituted by animal masks or a puppet.

The connection between the disturbing figures created by Segal, Hanson and De Andrea and some of the creations of 1970s theatre seems clear but not always direct. I am less concerned here with influence than with parallels. Plainly the surrealists made use of manikins, though not in the same way as Segal, although Marcel Duchamps inscribed a catalogue of Segal's 1965 exhibition. And the use of puppet figures by the Bread and Puppet Theatre, for example, owes as much to Oskar Schlemmer and the Bauhaus Group, to Kurt Schwitters and the Japanese Bunraku theatre as to the super-realists. But when we turn to Jean-Claude Van Itallie's *Motel* the link with the contemporary art world is less tenuous (though Antonin Artaud clearly lurks in the wings), the grotesque figures for this production being designed and constructed by someone deeply involved in the art world, a man who had created an environmental art project in the unlikely locale of Grailville – Robert Wilson. It is less tenuous, too, when one considers the Performance Group's *Cops*, very deliberately staged to recreate the style of photorealist paintings, the work of Adele Shank in San Francisco, or the figures created by the Snake Theatre. For though the founder of the last, Christopher Hardman, had worked with Bread and Puppet, both he and his co-founder, Laura Farabough, had trained in the visual arts and set out specifically to create a visual theatre with live performers used as moving sculpture. Wilson and Foreman used performers in the same way, while David Mamet created a theatrical correlative to Duane Hanson's figures in plays like *American Buffalo, Sexual Perversity in Chicago, The Water Engine*, and so on.

Mamet's figures in *Sexual Perversity in Chicago* are generic figures. Their language, their assumptions, their form is both shaped by and an expression of the media. Like the photorealists, to some degree he derives his aesthetics from the same source as his ostensible subject matter, thereby making those aesthetics, those methods of perceiving and rendering experience, the actual focus of the work. In effect *Sexual Perversity* dramatises a vacuum. His characters have no existence outside the rhythms of their speech, beyond the white noise of their parallel monologues. The human subject disappears to be replaced by the body as object. Commodity value, exchange value, alone seem to survive. Much

159

12. T.C. Fox, *Cops*, 1978. Direction by Richard Schechner. The cops are Tim Shelton and Stephen Borst, the hostage is Ted Hoffman and the killer Will Patton.

the same could be said of *A Life in the Theatre* which not merely parodies a series of realist plays but also mocks the audience's obsession with locating meaning, depth, and hidden significance by incorporating this obsession within the text. The two characters in the play exist only as a succession of roles, generic figures. The essence of *American Buffalo*, whose set is in effect a parody of the *mise-en-scène* of a realist play, similarly resists the assumptions of that realism. The central thrust of the play lies in the felt vacuity of characters who have all the insubstantial precision of Duane Hanson figures or those figures created by George Segal who said, for example, of his construction *Don't Walk*: 'People moving around seem to be in some kind of hypnotic dream state. They seem to be programmed. I wondered how it would be to see a group of people waiting on a street corner for a light to change.'[21] The figures in *American Buffalo* are just such people. It is a play voided of plot and character, a play in which language consists of a series of fragments, recycled words, incomplete gestures. Detail is rendered precisely not out of any sense of respect for the power of that environment or out of a conviction that context and self interact but because the more faithfully that detailed surface is rendered the more the felt absences become apparent. The proscenium arch, filled with the clutter of mock realism, is empty.

Foreman and to some extent Wilson and Breuer have reclaimed the proscenium stage, as have Mamet and Shepard precisely because of its ironic resemblance to and derivation from the picture frame. Both Wilson and Foreman perceive their work primarily in visual terms. They are prone to use the words 'picture' and 'tableau'. For Foreman and Wilson the tableau is as central a strategy as it was for the photorealists. And where the latter very often began their work with a very precise geometric division of the canvas or an exact placement of elements in a sculptural composition, so Wilson does likewise, while Foreman actually uses elastic strips to stretch across the stage, focussing the action much as an artist directs attention through a use of angles, perspectives, the lines of a figure or scene, or as an art historian may quarter the canvas to identify sight lines and focus. In conventional plays the 'blocking', the 'placement' of actors and objects, tends to come last, to be subordinate to other factors, to be a facilitating mechanism. For Wilson and Foreman it is central. These are theatre practitioners who begin, like Shepard, with images – not language, not a moral conviction, not a sense of character, not a conflict, not a plot. They build their productions much as an artist will fill his or her canvas. They are concerned with perspective. They are drawn towards stasis and, particularly in their early works, came close to achieving it. They deliberately slowed the action down, freezing time, seeking to defamiliarise, as Robbe-Grillet had insisted that the photograph does. And if they kept vestigial elements of a more familiar dramatic strategy, in the sense of a highly tenuous narrative gesture, for example, this was rather like the painterly quotation in the photorealist's work.

Wilson's aesthetic principles are directly related to the visual arts. He is primarily concerned with the relationships between objects, with scale, perspective, presence and absence, plenitude and paucity rather than conflict, character, or narrative. Just as the photorealists will deform the real by intensifying it, by magnifying fragments, exaggerating reflections or the clarity of outline, so Wilson, like John Cage, does it by amplifying normal sounds or by slowing the action down so that it has an unusual intensity. The emphasis on the banal transformed by perception, on detail, on the real made irreal by exaggeration or juxtaposition, is central to his work. Indeed, he even goes so far as deliberately to try to induce a quasi-trance condition in his audience by repetitive gestures and sounds and by the physical stress which his work induces as each action is prolonged. There is a precise visual geometry to his work which is again reminiscent of the photorealists but it is a geometry which for the most part he will not allow to be subordinated to thematic or psychological explanation. Much the same could be said of the work of Suzanne Hellmuth and Jack Reynolds, himself a sculptor, and of Richard Foreman.

As the title of Foreman's theatre suggests (The Ontological Hysteric Theatre) his concern is less with the elaboration of fictions or the creation of systems of meaning than with exploring the intense reality of individual moments. His work falls into two periods. Up to 1975 he was primarily concerned, as he explained, with putting an object on stage 'and finding different ways of looking at it – the object was there in isolation bracketed from the rest of the world'. He insisted that art should be 'a field for noticing'.[22] He wished, he said, 'to retree the tree'. Later, however, he became more interested in detailing the development of his own consciousness rather than exposing the qualities of a supposed reality. Frequently objects and figures were duplicated in a kind of equivalent of the reflections of the photorealists. He, too, amplified voices and slowed action down (though more recently he has taken to speeding it up into a swift succession of visual images). He no longer wishes to retree the tree: now he wishes to detree the tree.

Robert Wilson's is plainly not a political art. Though he uses figures such as Stalin, Freud and Einstein in his work, these are simply accommodated as objects drained of ideological force. They are less historical markers than formal structures, simple features in a world which offers to incorporate all aspects of existence without raising questions as to social or moral provenance, or public meaning. Perhaps it is possible to see him in this respect as a product of the 1970s, an example of a displacement of concern from the political into the aesthetic sphere. This is certainly how Susan Sontag chose to see him. But the loss of the subject in his work is less an observation about the collapse of public and private form than a device which forces the audience back upon itself, enforcing a thickening consciousness, a stimulation and expansion of the imagination and the mind. The best description of his plays, and perhaps those of Foreman, is that given, in a wholly different context, by Donald Barthelme in 'Robert Kennedy Saved from Drowning', in which Kennedy discusses the Marivaudian being: 'The Marivaudian being is a pastless, futureless man, born anew at each instant. The instants are points which organise themselves into a line. But what is important is the instant, not the line . . . In consequence he exists in a certain freshness which seems, if I may say so, very desirable.'[23] Or, as one of Sam Shepard's characters says in *The Tooth of Crime*: 'Just look at the road. Don't worry about where it's going.'[24]

Introduction

In 1977 Susan Sontag expressed doubts about an art which concerned itself primarily with consciousness, precisely to the degree that this is an asocial activity – a modernist recoil from the public world, a denial of the 'notion that some intentions are more valid than others'. To her mind it was

> hardly surprising that so many modernist artists have been fascinated by the disease of consciousness – that an art committed to solipsism would recapitulate the gestures of the *pathology* of solipsism. If you start from an asocial notion of perception of consciousness, you must inevitably end up with the poetry of mental illness and mental deficiency. With autistic silence. With the autistic's use of language: compulsive repetition and variation. With an obsession with circles. With an abstract or distended notion of time.[25]

It was a direct attack on the work of Wilson who of course had used a brain-damaged boy in his performance, but also of Foreman and behind him of Gertrude Stein. It implied a suspicion of photorealism.

The thrust of Susan Sontag's argument seems to imply an element of betrayal, a failure on the part of artists or theatre practitioners to see that consciousness has a structure, a thematics, a history; a failure to make a human engagement. But, again, perhaps the best response to this is that offered by Robbe-Grillet who observed of his own novels, and those of his contemporaries, that the absence of characters, the absence of human engagement, did not imply the absence of man.

> Man [he insisted] is present on every page, in every line, in every word. Even if you find many objects in them, and objects which are described in minute detail, you will always, and in pride of place, find the eye that sees them, the thought that considers them, and the passion that deforms them. The objects of our novels never have any presence outside human percep-tions, whether real or imaginary . . . Far from neglecting [the reader or the spectator] the contemporary author proclaims his absolute need of his co-operation, an active, conscious, *creative* co-operation. What he is being asked to do is no longer to accept a ready-made, completed world, a solid world, shut in on itself, but on the contrary to participate in an act of creation, in the invention of the work – and the world – and in this way to learn to invent his own life.[26]

Foreman himself has said essentially the same, even laying claim to the moral values which Susan Sontag saw as evacuated from such work, asserting that 'Good (moral) art and (yes, I dare refer to those categories) [is that] in which – to make it be for himself – the spectator must use active, intentional perceptive modes which might then, someday, enter life itself . . . and transform it.'[27] The absent figure thus becomes the crucial one.

In Beckett's *Endgame* Hamm remarks, 'Absent always. It all happened without me.'[28] That absence is a primary fact of the world presented by the photorealists, of the figures created by George Segal, Robert de Andrea and Duane Hanson, and of the holographic portrait. It is equally a dominant fact in the theatre of Kenneth Brown's *The Brig*, of late Albee and of Mamet, and, in a different sense, in that of Wilson and Foreman. Mamet, in particular, along with Shepard, offers a series of plays in which style becomes subject and the human figure is hollowed out, pressed towards stereotype, in which the components of a realist drama are established precisely in order to destabilise them. The absences which he creates, however, clearly invite an active response. But then I suspect that much the same might be said of the work of some at least of the photorealists whose empty gas stations, vacant car lots, deserted beaches, abandoned automobiles, and unpeopled buildings seem to demand peopling; or of the dead eyes of the holographic portrait, or the blank, sightless stare of the automata of contemporary sculpture, which require, if not the breath of God, then at least the breath of man. The compulsion to see Galatea descend is all but irresistible. As Fumio Yashimura has said of his own work, 'I'm not really producing the thing. I'm producing a ghost.'[29] Or as George Segal remarked, 'The hunt is not for verisimilitude, not for naturalistic reproduction. It's a hunt for the spirit.'[30] Or, finally, as Robert de Andrea has somewhat forlornly lamented of his own figures: 'I want them to breathe.'[31]

5 Robert Wilson

Robert Wilson was born with a speech impediment. In overcoming it in his teens, with the assistance of a dance-instructor, he not only cleared an occluded artery of communication but came to feel that speech is itself only one imperfect mechanism for that communication. Born in Waco, Texas, he studied at the University of Texas but withdrew just before graduating. While there, however, he became involved in working with children's theatre, work which he continued at Baylor and Trinity Universities. In 1962 he studied painting with George McNeill in Paris and in 1963 returned to America where he studied architecture at the Pratt Institute in Brooklyn, graduating in 1965 at the age of twenty-four. But at the same time he continued his work with children, though now, as Stefan Brecht has pointed out, working especially with those suffering from brain damage. Perhaps putting into practice his experience in resolving his own speech defect, he placed considerable stress on physical activity, feeling that in many ways this was the key to unlocking mental activity. Indeed, he has described participating in a programme to help a brain-damaged five year old which required constant physical stimulation.

On the face of it there seem to be connections with the body mysticism popular in the 1960s but, when he insists that 'the body is a resource, and the body can become conscious and that . . . it is possible to . . . activate brain cells by working with the body',[1] it is plain that he is not simply interested in neo-Freudian notions of a resurrected and dominant pleasure principle. The emphasis on physicality is not just an assertion of the primacy of instincts or the suspect nature of rationality. It is the assertion of clinical theory, the suggestion that rational processes may be restored through a deliberate programme of physical stimulation. The body redeems the mind by quite literal and physical means; it is not an article of spiritual faith. Thus, he suggested,

> we took children that were having difficulty reading, children who were in difficulty . . . in learning language . . . in catching a ball . . . or repeating a rhythm . . . or awkward in getting their hand on the . . . doorknob . . . and we went back through [a] series of exercises . . . over a six week, six month period . . . in almost every case where the child was having trouble with hearing a sound, repeating a sound, he improved.[2]

165

Wilson was concerned with release, with the discharging of tension, but the purpose was therapeutic in a much more narrowly defined sense than that proposed by the proponents of performance theatre (although, at the same time, he did express an interest in performance art). This was the basis for a classic misunderstanding between Robert Wilson and Osia Trilling. When Wilson asserted that 'the body doesn't lie . . . we can trust the body',[3] he was not simply parroting the cant of 1960s liberationist rhetoric; he was referring to empirical data about the communication of meaning through non-verbal channels — a subject that became of increasing interest to him as a tool of the therapist, a strategy of the teacher and a natural concern of the theatre.

And Wilson was deeply involved in theatre. In 1963 he designed and constructed the huge dolls used in the *Motel* section of Jean-Claude Van Itallie's *America Hurrah!*. In the same year he made two films (one for National Educational Television), and before graduating had staged a number of theatrical presentations, including one called *Clorox* which reportedly involved a combination of actors and objects, a familiar tactic of happenings. He gradually abandoned his ambitions to be a painter and, following what seems to have been a severe mental breakdown, concentrated more and more on theatre. He refused an attractive offer to join a firm of architects and accepted a number of teaching assignments.

Wilson has suggested that his own style was to some degree formed by a performance which he gave in San Antonio, Texas, in 1964 and 1965. Charged to produce a brief play he lost confidence in the work and instead of performing it he and his two fellow actors merely entered the set, sat down and performed 'small activities' before leaving the stage thirty minutes later. Unsurprisingly the San Antonio audience was less than enthralled by this but Wilson himself detected a shift in audience reaction over the two-week run which he could only attribute to his own changing response to the event. 'I learned that part of it was that as a performer somehow if I could relax to begin with . . . if I could release the tension in myself . . . then the situation would be better, because then the exchange of energy between me and the audience . . . was an even flow and it wasn't blocked. And that . . . helped with the other performers. And then I started going back to my body.'[4] On one level, of course, this is a banality, a truism learned by all actors and an essential component of most actor training, but, at least as retrospectively described in 1970, the performance was a conscious attempt to divest the theatrical moment of its conventional components, to ask, 'Is it necessary to have a story, is it necessary to have characters, is it necessary to have . . . symbolism?'[5] The emphasis was simply to be on the fact of the exchange between actor and audience, not on its content, its context or its quality. It was thus in effect a kind of happening, in which events, movements and sounds were drained of metaphoric content. It is also, inevitably, reminiscent of John Hawkes's parallel enquiry as to the necessity of the same components in the novel, or of Alain Robbe-Grillet's much earlier assault on character in fiction. In 1965 Hawkes had observed, 'I began to write fiction on the assumption that the true enemies of the novel were plot, character, setting and theme, and having once abandoned these familiar ways of thinking about fiction, totality of vision or structure was really all that remained.'[6] This was not offered as a deliberately provocative manifesto. It was a response to a sense of some profound caesura in moral history no less than in the history of art. Robbe-Grillet had called for the abandonment of a stable notion of character, and, by implication plot and language, because they implied 'a stable universe, coherent, continuous, univocal, and wholly decipherable',[7] which he could not reconcile with the reality of his experience in the immediate post-war period in France. It will be recalled that Julian Beck had likewise chosen to regard fiction as a parenthesis in the history of art, looking for some other quality in theatre beyond its story-telling function. But where a writer like Beckett responded with a traumatised minimalism Beck turned to celebratory revels and to a native strain which saw the surrender of self in the group as an organic law, rather as had Steinbeck. In Wilson's case Hawkes's concern with 'vision' became central.

According to Stefan Brecht, in 1966–7 Wilson became involved in 'psychosomatic therapy work' with adults while at the same time designing an environmental sculpture called 'Poles' (consisting of 600 telephone poles in a field in the somewhat incredibly named Grailville, Ohio), and staging the first of a series of 'performance pieces' called *Baby*, followed by *Theatre Activity*, *Byrdwoman* (1968) and a 'pyramid piece'. Then, in 1968, he became the artistic director of the Byrd Hoffman Foundation, whose principal purpose was to conduct workshops in dance movement, theatre and related arts, and to produce public performances. In the same year he began work on *The King of Spain* (1969) which is perhaps the first of the performances which brought him national attention. The performers came from the awareness classes which he was running – classes designed to make their members more fully aware of themselves and their circumstances. And, though the actions they were required to perform were defined by Wilson himself, they were told to 'be themselves' and to perform them in their own way. The link with the various performance groups of the late 1960s is clear.

Wilson's own description of the origins of *The King of Spain* makes it plain that it was conceived in terms of a visual imagery assembled like a mental collage from aspects of his literal and fantasy life. While the methodology of the surrealists plainly hovers in the background, he seems to have developed his images through a process of random association. It is not simply that the images are juxtaposed and allowed to generate their own assonances but that the links are already forged in his imagination. Though there had been a certain consonance of imagery in the earlier minimalist works, this had tended to rely simply on a repeated use of a specific gesture or prop. Now he tended to assemble the elements of his performance rather as an artist gradually fills the canvas. Indeed, this image was clearly in his own mind when he attempted to describe the event itself. Thus he identifies a group of people playing at a game table as in a sense an image of the whole play, a synecdoche suggesting that they constitute 'a tiny sort of capsule of what was happening . . . in the larger stage picture'.[8] The subsequent actions are then introduced as part of 'an additive process [as] you begin to fill these layers, these horizontal layers *around* that are on the stage . . . so that . . . the next sort of picture happened in front of that'.[9] Unlike the performance pieces of the Living Theatre or the Performance Group, Wilson's 'plays' tended to slow action down in order to encourage concentration and to enable an audience to drain it of its significance (though Chaikin had used a similar device in the Kennedy assassination sequence of *The Serpent*). Though they clearly had a density which went beyond the banalities of Warhol's tedious exercises in boredom, they perhaps owed something to his concern with the interaction of time and space. If time is slowed down space assumes a new density and visual nuances become apparent. As Wilson explained, except on the relatively rare occasions he 'couldn't focus on everything that was happening'; he 'was being bombarded with so many . . . things . . . at one time' that he 'could only hear the surface of it'. He therefore set himself to get 'more beneath the surface' by creating a series of 'moving pictures' so that the audience could 'get inside' each successive picture, and 'once you could register or have experience of that material then the picture would change – so that you could experience the next picture – see the next picture, see the inside of it'.[10]

In *The Life and Times of Sigmund Freud* the event had grown to four hours and *The King of Spain* had been swallowed to re-emerge as the second act. Wilson's own account of the play is instructively confusing. Indeed he is deeply suspicious of the very act of trying to translate images into words. He seems to feel that it is rather like dredging up deep–water fish only to see them burst and putrify once they have reached the surface. He is equally suspicious of attempts rationally to analyse images whose authenticity and authority can only be recognised instinctively – another link he has with the surrealists. Wilson's aesthetic principle seems to be that of the artist whose compositional sense has to do with relationship, scale, colour and texture rather than 'meaning'. He is concerned with the simultaneous presence of elements which must nonetheless be perceived individually. A sequential narrative hence inevitably betrays something of the effect, just as it must when applied to a painting. Looking for a means to describe shifts in intensity or rhythm, therefore, he turns not to dramatic models of development (Aristotelian or other) but to the dynamics of collage. It is an aesthetic precise in execution but not in origin. The interactions on the stage are calculated; that is, they are not arbitrary. However, the logic they obey is intuitive, associational, and the effect they generate is designed to be available to a similar response. This does not mean a pure relativism. The images on stage, whether they be of Sigmund Freud, a white man dressed up as a black woman, or a lion, have clear associations which are culturally derived and knowingly manipulated. But the combination, though suggestive in its image clusters of certain themes, nonetheless is intended to generate new realities rather than reflect existing ones. It is plainly not mimetic in intent. The absence of a coherent plot is not fortuitous but an observation about the processes of perception and the misleading linearities of thought. The capacity for this to degenerate into the sheerest nonsense, however, is obviously considerable and the intensely private origins of his images are no guarantee of their theatrical effectiveness. Though his own inadequate descriptions of the purpose and processes of his images can be explained by reference to his desire not to make lucid what works precisely by retaining an element of its opacity this is not always totally convincing as an explanation. But the problem is at least in part one of vocabulary, of finding a language adequate to experiments that were exploring territory beyond that which could be contained by the conventional language of dramatic criticism.

The theatrical group, for Wilson, does not have the mystical or sociological overtones which it had for the Living Theatre, though he has expressed an admiration for the unity exemplified by that group. Indeed, the essence of the heterogeneous elements of his work resides, for him, in the degree to which they generate a certain homogeneity. Inevitably the pieces are open not merely to his own fantasies and images but to those of his fellow performers. The very gnomic quality of the productions focusses the energy of all those present and requires an active involvement by audience and performer. He has no desire to enforce his own interpretations beyond the shaping influence which goes into the detailed juxtapositions and overlapping images which constitute the performance. But this common activity enforces a sense of shared experience if not shared perception. The inevitable failure to arrive at a definitive model of the action and the resistance to any act of simple decoding which is built into the aesthetic is itself an assertion. It validates an openness to experience; it denies the authenticity of singular translations of events; it refuses validity to versions of truth which depend on sustaining rigid and definitional boundaries. Such boundaries, after all, are constantly violated in works in which men 'play' women, whites play blacks, people play animals. The content of the work lies less in a recitation of its events than in its processes. Such works also incorporate their own defences against criticism. They are, after all, not about experience; they are experience. Neither can they easily be discussed in terms of the constituents of their images. Even boredom is, perhaps, not a legitimate test since the slowness of the action and the degree to which it turns the observer back on him or herself is a crucial component of their aesthetic. And yet, such a stance seems to provoke and justify the most pragmatic of all critical responses. If such a work fails to stimulate a response from the individual who is asked to experience it, if the image clusters conjure nothing, if it offers little but a series of isolated gestures, then the individual seems justified in rejecting it as hermetic, as a failure of composition or imagination. But this implies a detachment which is likely to prove difficult to sustain. Its repetitive physical gestures, its reiterated sounds, its protracted time-scale which introduces the possibility of physical and mental exhaustion, in fact create the classic potential for trance. And it seems likely that Wilson is operating on the boundary of therapy and hypnosis. On occasion, indeed, people have actually hallucinated at his performances (as who would not in productions lasting several days?) while, in preparing *Deafman Glance* (1971), his performers consciously developed the power of repetitive actions precisely in order to induce a trance-like state.

In describing these performances himself Wilson tends to talk in terms of fullness and depletion, repetition and variation, shapes and juxtapositions, intensity and relaxation. The images at this stage in his career were deeply personal and validated intuitively while requiring the active participation of the audience (on an intuitive and intellectual level) for their completion. His reference point is always visual art, though the pieces do contain some element of dialogue and sound. Like John Cage he was prone to wire chairs and other objects for sound, placing microphones on them and amplifying the results so as to deform the apparent realism by intensifying it, thereby creating a sense of irrealism not merely in the total effect but in the component elements. He insisted, in interviews, that he worked to no clear formula but that, as he explained of *The Life and Times of Sigmund Freud*, he thought 'of the whole piece, all three acts . . . like . . . different pictures – they were moving pictures or a collage of moving pictures'.[11] The structure, however, is clear enough, though it relates neither to conventional notions of character nor to plot. It is not best described in linear terms. It has no 'subject' that is separable from its process. The best description would seem to be that given in the speech which introduces the play and which, though it devolves into illogical reverie after a precise and rational opening section, does represent Wilson's own view of his work. Describing the performance as 'a three-act dance play', the speaker explains that:

> The structure of each act is very similar. And the people, characters, materials, activities and sounds parallel and repeat throughout the entire play. Each has a full register. This means that at any one point an element may be in full focus with all its parts together and later less or more of the parts are together. Like Chinese Checkers with all the marbles in pegs some of the time, other times, less or more. There are two main levels of reality that we are attempting to maintain throughout the play. They are obvious and opposed in nature and throughout the three acts they change until in the final scene they are seen to have completely reversed themselves. Perhaps it's more like making an 'X' in that one level starts low and the other high; the other the opposite, that's thinking of it though in graphic terms. If you think of it in terms of color one starts out black and ends up white and the other starts out white and ends up being black. Most of each act is very self-contained, or stripped down until the end, which is very open, rich and (purposely) theatrical. But the end of each act, which in itself is very short in time, balances the preceding time – or 'contained duration'. Compare it to a long line with a block at one end, and the block (necessary for) balancing the line. The same basic quasi-structure is repeated throughout each act though that happening may not (upon first viewing) be apparent. And that same hidden structural skeleton is latently apparent for all three acts taken together. All three acts are contained (unto themselves) compared to the ending which is the biggest opening – in the sense of release (and relief).[12]

The connection with Freud is not purely arbitrary. He is one of the figures in the play. But Wilson has little concern with the intellectual side of the man. As he went on to explain:

> This piece . . . as a kind of hybrid 'dance play' doesn't deal with any big ideas – it just pays inordinate attention to small *detail* [sic] things. Although we do see him plotting and making charts, notes, undoubtedly the most moving event in his life was when his prized grandchild, Heinerlie, died . . . A very simple emotional experience. A death. And suddenly all of his ideas about living and theorizing about feeling were suspended, rendered meaningless . . . Freud is plotting and scheming up these charts and yet what we *see* happening – the stage activity, is very human-like –

someone running and someone sitting, another making small talk, someone pouring a drink, someone dancing, people doing ritualistic exercises.
The activities are just very mundane and thus in that way pointedly
human.

Another thing that happens is that the stage is divided into zones –
stratified zones are behind another that extends from one side of the stage
horizontally to the other. And in each of these zones there's a different
'reality' – a different activity defining the space so that from the audience's
point of view one sees through these different layers and as each occurs it
appears as if there's no realization that anything other than itself is
happening outside that particularly designated area. People might associate this with Freud and the layers of consciousness – different levels of
understanding but that kind of obvious intention has been erased or
eradicated from this production. I see it more simply as a collage of
different realities occurring simultaneous[ly] like being aware of several
visual factors and how they combine into a picture before your eyes at any
given moment. Awareness in that way occurs mostly through the course
of experience of each layer rendering the others transparent. And this
might, at first, confuse some people, because we are so being [sic] used to
going to the theater and having the play explicitly narrated to us in verbal
direct(ed)ness. Like Shakespeare. Like Shaw. Like Tennessee Williams.
Those kinds of plays are primarily constructed *with* words, although other
elements are included. On the other hand in dance people as diverse as
Jerome Robbins, Merce Cunningham and Yvonne Rainer focus the
intention of their work on the formal presentation of movement. The
focus here is neither verbal nor concerned with specifying the physicality
of people in virtual space. It's simply more visual. And people are just
beginning to return again to discerning visual significances as a primary
mode – or method – of communicating in a context where more than one
form, or 'level' exists. In that sense of overlays of visual correspondences
we can speak of multi-dimensional realities.[13]

The parallel with ballet cannot be pressed too hard in so far as Wilson
reacted against its closed aesthetic which, at least in conventional work,
requires little input from the audience. But the emphasis on detail, on the
banal transformed by perception, on the real made irreal by exaggeration
or juxtaposition, is central to his work.

Trace elements of Zen, pop art, happenings, photorealism, and the
new music of Cage coalesce. He is, he insists, 'not particularly interested
in literary ideas' because

having a focus that encompasses in a panoramic visual glance all the
hidden slices ongoing that appear in a clear awareness as encoded fragments seems to indicate theater has so much more to do than be concerned
with words in a dried out, flat, one-dimensional literary structure. I mean
The Modern World has forced us to outgrow that *mode* of seeing. We're

interested in *another* thing – another *kind* of experience that happens when
encoded fragments and hidden detail become without words suddenly
transparent.[14]

It is not hard to find similar if somewhat less elliptical statements in the
other arts. Robert Coover and John Hawkes have spoken in much the
same terms of new modes of perceiving and consequently of writing. It is
in this context that Wilson's work with brain-damaged or handicapped
children becomes important to him as a model and a method, for their
perceptions are likely to be different, just as their own means of
communication is likely to be unique to themselves. Thus, in teaching a
young girl with a speech impediment to sing, he simply encouraged her
to develop her own means of forming and performing sounds to the
point at which, when the girl found a schoolfriend mimicking pop
music, she urged her to 'sing your own way'. The private nature of
Wilson's images is thus offered as his own songs sung in his own way.
The man who marches to a different drummer does not necessarily invite
others to march to the same beat; he merely indicates that they should
understand the possibility and the value of an alternative rhythm.

The aesthetic principle of Wilson's work, as Richard Foreman has
suggested, was the need to avoid manipulation. He created, to borrow
Wilson's own borrowing from sociology, a field situation in which the
spectator could respond individually, discovering not so much the total
meaning of the piece as the internal dynamics of movement, colour and
rhythm in relation to precisely designated actions. To Foreman, indeed,
the subject of the play was in effect the sensibility of the individual who
perceives it. The private vision is not offered as a hieroglyph to be
translated or as an icon to be respected. Its coherences are not fundamentally rational. They are the expression of conjunctions which materialise
not only or even primarily in the mind of the artist–writer–performer
but in the sensibilities of those who see the assemblages with their own
eyes and from their own perspectives. Wilson is a composer, a designer.
His 'actors' are usually not professional actors. They are not, indeed,
even quite performing a text. They are elements in a series of tableaux;
they are imagistic markers. Some, in a sense, play themselves, in a
recognisable gesture from performance theatre; some play fantasy creatures or animals; some become brush strokes in a larger scene whose
patterns do or do not assemble for those who observe.

While Wilson resists the notion of meaning – rejects the idea of an a
priori content, preferring to say that his work, above all, is an architec-
tural arrangement – this is not to say that such work is without coherence
or that at some level he does not betray himself into metaphor. The point
is that, for Wilson, meaning is generated by interaction, and the artist is as

interested in those interactions, deformations, efflorescences, as he is in the qualities of the component elements.

The surrealists were fascinated by madness, by drugs, by dreams, by any means through which the real could be made to render up its hidden charge. Wilson works in precisely this tradition, though without citing it as the origin of his methods. Thus in his next performance, *Deafman Glance* (1971), he turned not to the mad but to a deaf child called Raymond who, because he was incapable of hearing or speaking, had been forced back to other less direct means of communication. The symbols of speech were exchanged for visual images. Wilson responded to the boy both as someone needing help and human contact and as someone whose intense and desperate gestures offered a way of tapping into a different system of signs, a system which could be utilised in a theatrical context to suggest elements of non-verbal communication and to undermine the otherwise inescapable coerciveness of Wilson's own imagination. As he explained, 'it's amazing the wealth of knowledge that he has . . . He developed another sense of seeing–hearing . . . that's very amazing – his association with color or light with people is – just amazing . . . if he wants to tell me about someone . . . he can draw some symbol . . . [so] that you know who that person is . . . he's got . . . a great knowledge of a mystical [kind].'[15] The play thus consists in part of 'images that he's had', and while these are patently shaped by Wilson he felt that he had achieved a sense of freedom and perspective that he had not had before. He was drawn to the boy because of his necessary emphasis on visual communication. Wilson's contribution lay in structuring those images and figures because, as he explained in a statement which could equally have been made by André Breton or Luis Aragon, 'I'm very interested in the way things fit together . . . what they seem like next to each other or against each other or with each other.'[16] Interestingly enough, Aragon himself wrote an open letter to André Breton following the Paris production of *Deafman Glance* which underlines the connection, if such were needed. In excessive terms, which themselves characterise a movement attracted by excess, he praised the production as uniquely beautiful and moving.

The essence of Wilson's concerns is expressed in a quotation from Isadora Duncan which appeared in the programme notes for the first production of *Deafman Glance*. Here he stressed, most crucially, the ultimate aim of freeing the body and the sensibility, the desire to offer method without insisting on content or the authority of paradigm. And, typically, he did so by referring not to the theatre but to an allied form in which movement, tableaux vivants and sound were the primary mechanisms – dance. Thus Duncan had described a school which she wished to establish,

174

WHERE A HUNDRED LITTLE GIRLS SHALL BE TRAINED IN MY ART, WHICH THEY IN TURN WILL BETTER. IN THIS SCHOOL I SHALL NOT TEACH THE CHILDREN TO IMITATE MY MOVEMENTS, BUT SHALL TEACH THEM TO MAKE THEIR OWN . . . I SHALL HELP THEM TO DEVELOP THOSE MOVEMENTS WHICH ARE NATURAL TO THEM. AND SO I SAY IT IS THE DUTY OF THE DANCE OF THE FUTURE TO GIVE FIRST TO THE YOUNG ARTISTS WHO COME TO ITS DOOR FOR INSTRUCTION FREER AND (MORE) BEAUTIFUL BODIES — AND TO INSTRUCT THEM IN MOVEMENTS THAT ARE IN FULL HARMONY WITH NATURE . . . THE DANCER OF THE FUTURE WILL BE ONE WHOSE BODY AND SOUL HAVE GROWN SO HARMONIOUSLY TOGETHER THAT THE NATURAL LANGUAGE OF THAT SOUL WILL HAVE BECOME THE MOVEMENT OF THE BODY . . . HER DANCE WILL BELONG TO NO NATIONALITY BUT TO ALL HUMANITY.[17]

Time and space become key concepts. The stage fills and empties, with every part of the playing surface being utilised to create a density or a willed absence. As his work developed so the plays became longer, the material having a critical temporal as well as spatial dimension. The space between his characters and figures becomes as important as the figures themselves, while the speed with which they move or the length of time they remain in view in some degree moulds the response of the audience. Thus, in the first half-hour of *Deafman Glance* there is no movement whatsoever while in the succeeding half-hour a mother slowly pours a glass of milk for a boy, tucks him into his bed and then stabs him. The images are, at times, hermetic to the degree that they had originated in the sensibility of an individual whose vision was private and not necessarily available for translation. But the formal arrangement of the component elements of these images, the presentation on stage of the fantasy or dream images, is not designed to recreate the mood or the state of mind which generated those images. It is in part an assertion of their 'reality', their independence, their mutual coexistence, their ontological co-regnum with other more familiar aspects of existence. Again, the statement is not contained within the work; it is the work; it is implicit in the methodology. The work thus becomes an assertion of the rights of the imagination and the significance of channels of communication beyond those endorsed by society and confirmed by the traditional theatre.

The human subject seems excluded as is the conventional notion of character. There is no protagonist, no plot, no coherent dialogue, no allegorical or metaphorical thrust, although there are apparent gestures in this direction. He seems to create a world of signifiers with no signifieds. Some elements of the performance overlap. They happen at the same time or are partially or wholly concealed from the audience or from parts of the audience, as though the private origin of these images were being acknowledged in the fact that they are reabsorbed before they can even impinge on the sensibility of those who are watching. The spoken word is for the most part distorted and electronically separated from the speaker, language existing quite separately from those who appear to generate it. Empathy is impossible. In any conventional sense this is anti-theatre in that it self-consciously abjures or parodies the normal resources of theatre. Indeed the obvious objection is that, like happenings, Wilson's work is perhaps not best seen in terms of theatre at all. Its roots in art are so strong, its conscious resistance to the conventional resources of drama so apparent, that it is more reasonable to see it as a form of kinetic art in which the real is deformed by presenting it as a series of planes, shapes, movements, energies, rhythmic pulses. Its shifting facets should be responded to more as aspects of a painter's design or as projected fantasies by a man whose thesis at the Pratt Institute was indeed concerned with designing an imaginary cathedral or a future city. The loss of the human subject, after all, is a familiar enough mark of architects' models, which are usually bereft of all but the most stylised of figures and whose concern with size, shape and texture all too frequently take precedence over human scale and comfort.

There is certainly an irony in the fact that Wilson's compassionate concern for physically disabled children translates itself into images in which such concern has been carefully evacuated. He may choose to celebrate physicality and the power and the rights of the imagination, but there is, perhaps, an element of emptiness in his serenities and a vacancy in his plenitude. Moreover, I suspect that the above account is likely to inspire a deep scepticism on the part of readers not exposed to his performances. It is a scepticism which in part I share. The problem, of course, is that it is a 'theatre' which refuses the legitimacy of analysis and resists the idea of definition. And, perhaps, matters of definition are hardly central. Indeed the mere act of calling his works theatre is a refusal of such definitions. As a character in Ishmael Reed's *Yellow Back Radio Broke Down* observes of the novel, 'What if I write circuses? No one says a novel has to be one thing. It can be anything it wants to be, a vaudeville show, the six o'clock news, the mumblings of wild men saddled by demons.'[18] The absence of psychological or sociological concern, the failure to develop character, to allow figures to inter-relate, to develop a narrative or move towards a recognisable sense of peripeteia plainly sets it at odds with our usual sense of theatre. However, the process of defamiliarising potentially recuperates precisely that human dimension most rigorously excluded because now the collaboration of performer and audience becomes critical. Potentially, the question is how real that collaboration becomes.

The real worry, I think, is not one of definition. It is that the air of ritual and ceremony, which is in part a consequence of his deliberate slowing of movements and in part a product of the stylised figures, may be in the service of nothing beyond a sensitised awareness of physical being (though that in itself is not, of course, without value). It is that a bias against the mind, so evident in some aspects of performance theatre, is being perpetuated. Wilson's own incoherences in interview, his admission of the closed nature of some of the experiences which he offers and the gnomic quality of some of the images which he presents, images which are unclear, if he is to be believed, even to himself, imply a deliberate degree of mystification and a wilful refusal of the imaginative complicity which it otherwise seems to invite. It is a familiar romantic tactic, of course, to grant special insight to those on the borderline of madness. It was equally a basic element of surrealist thought no less than a fundamental tenet of that challenge to normative values made by R.D. Laing in the field of psychology. But, if fantasy may liberate, it may also constrain. The oblique insights and sharpened sensibility of the mentally or physically damaged individual may strike sparks but it may also close off avenues of perception. The chief defence against such criticisms lies in the fact that Wilson's is an aesthetic of excess and that he provided for this in the structure of his performances. Increasingly he built into them the opportunity to withdraw from the event into another space so that although the performances became longer, rigorous attention was not necessarily required. The individual thus, in a sense, invented his or her own performance, juxtaposing his or her experience of the theatrical performance with what was in some ways the equally theatrical experience of the alternative space. The coercive power of performance was thus eased and the audience's involvement in the process of creation facilitated. In a sense, however, it could be argued that this merely formalised a basic fact of audience behaviour, differing only in so far as a physical space was made to perform the role of the private mental space into which individual members of the audience have always been able to retreat, thereby creating their own collages out of the experience of theatre.

In *Overture for Ka Mountain and Gardinia Terrace, a story about a family and some people changing* (1972) he attempted to do with language what he had previously done with images. A number of members of Wilson's family participated in a performance which centred around an eight-foot high wooden pyramid. The dance critic and poet William Demby read aloud from a number of works, including Nijinsky's autobiography; Wilson recited a text which he had himself devised. At another moment Wilson's grandmother spoke about her own family life. These texts were juxtaposed, much as the visual images had been in his earlier work, while Wilson's own monologue itself deconstructed language into elements, fragments of sound, rhythms, harmonies. At some moments it seems close to re-assembling into coherent phrases, rational sequences of words; at others it is a kind of music or an assemblage of sound. Hence:

THE OVER REVERBERATIONS THE BODY
JESTICULATE A LAYERING A RING, A LING
A DING THE OVERREVERBATIONS
THE BODY OVERREVERBERATIONS A ZATION
REVERBALIZATION A NATION REVERBARAT
ING A RATIONING OF ALL NATIONS

or

PARTS PARTICULAR THE MAN SLICING
THE ONION AS THEY DO AS DO
THEY DO AN ARTIST PAINTING A
PICTURE A MONSTER WORLD
TRANSMIGRATES AS THE BODY JESTICKLE
YOU LATES A LAYERING A RING
THE BODY JESTICKLE YOU LATES
ERUPTING ENTERING REERUPTING
THE ABSENCES OF SELF IN EVERYTHING[19]

The language is deployed in part as a kind of jazz scat or a form of mantra. He uses language against itself. On the one hand he relies on a certain associative power while on the other he reveals a distrust of the rational and constrictive force of that associative power. He wishes to press his model of simultaneous experience into the realm of language while at the same time wanting to dis-assemble it. In retreat from a means of communication which has been allowed to fragment, the audience is forced to pick its clues up elsewhere. But once again the chant is not voided of meaning; as with the images the meaning lies more in the process than in the content. The free rhythms, the refusal to subordinate lexis to the constraints of grammar or even semantic coherence, are offered as an act of release. Like the young deaf child who 'sang' in a way which seemed incoherent to others but which released her own energies and communicated the fact of her own conquest of silence, Wilson is attempting to wrest language free from its formal containments. Thus, these recitations/incantations/songs are designed both to contain scepticism about language and to assert a potential for the re-assemblage of its constituents. They seem close to the nonsense poetry of the dadaists whose subversive drive was omnivorous, and there is a relationship with their work. But Wilson's drive is never purely destructive. He is defamiliarising, breaking language down into its constituents as he did movement, and that parallel is enforced by the balletic components of the piece, moments of movement which are not examined for their metaphoric or analogic force.

In Paris the performance lasted for twenty-four hours while the production of *Ka Mountain* in Iran lasted for 168 hours. It incorporated *Deafman's Glance* and was preceded by *Overture*. By definition it was of course impossible for anyone to follow the entire performance. The mere fact of length was in a sense also an announcement of an aesthetic. It was not a closed logical structure where to lose one element is to disrupt one's perception of the whole. The assembled fragments as perceived by any one individual merely mimicked the assembled fragments which were the content. Thus various constructions were erected, some apparently mimetic in intent (as with a suburban American landscape) and others not so. Animals were interspersed with human figures. The problem of language was resolved through the subordination of lexical meaning to rhythm, tone, sound and volume. When Peter Brook went to Iran he had commissioned the poet Ted Hughes to generate a text for *Orghast* entirely in an invented language. Wilson's strategy was similar except that in his case it has always been an element of his work and was centrally related to his aesthetic. Visual references to western and eastern myths created a context for work which could no more be reconstructed in summary than it could be in performance. But the wish for coherence was not wholly ironised. The need for community at any rate had always been an implicit theme in Wilson's work and the occasion of an international gathering strengthened that component. However, it was clear that over a period of 168 hours and given the extent of the space over which the event took place any sense of a shared experience was likely to be attenuated and problematised. It is a paradox which seems to fascinate him.

Wilson's is, in part, a theatre born out of a concern for developing therapeutic methods. He claims that his use of radically slowed speech derived from attempts to control his own stammer and was prompted by the use of a tape-recorder whose batteries were running low. The effect was to stretch words to the point at which he perceived the complexity of their construction. This is perhaps a clue to his wider concerns and in particular to an approach which demands a degree of concentration on sound, movement, and the physical characteristics of phenomena. His conviction that the problems of communication from which his autistic and brain-damaged children suffered concealed active minds and imaginations, merely waiting for the right stimulus or operating strategy to release them, is generalised to incorporate those who constitute his audience, and who are themselves brain-damaged to the degree that their thought processes are conditioned.

His methods are various. In *Ka Mountain* he utilises visual icons, ancient and contemporary myths, sounds, and stylised movements. Even the move from large stage to a setting which includes a literal mountain and its surroundings is expressive of his desire to generalise out of the theatrical environment. On the whole, however, his images do not seem to be the product of an intellectual experience. They are not in the service of ideas; the ideas follow the images. Even the performers are expressive shapes rather than characters. If Freud is put on stage it is not as a psychologically dense and interactive personality but as a two-dimensional figure drained of all but a certain associative quality. History enters his work in the form of Freud, Stalin, Alexander Graham Bell and others but they are deliberately decontextualised, used as shapes or patterns. They are employed for certain resonances which are required for the harmonics of the performance, much as Roy Lichtenstein employed the image of Marilyn Monroe; his repetitions, indeed, in a sense constitute a pictorial equivalent of Wilson's slow-motion device.

Ka Mountain was followed in December 1973 by *The Life and Times of Joseph Stalin*. The performance consisted of seven acts and lasted for twelve hours and, as Frontisek Deak has observed,[20] that fact required a certain adjustment of lifestyle on the part of the audience which thus had already begun the process of transformation which was Wilson's objective. Once again the performance incorporated elements from his previous work. The stage was divided into 'seven layers of zoned activity' and the play was structured around a series of repetitions or parallels. It required almost a hundred performers and, true to his usual tactics, consisted largely of amateur actors whose movements he choreographed (though literal dance sequences were the responsibility of Andrew de Groat). The choice of non-professionals derives in part from his belief that they have in a sense not been trained to formalise their behaviour in the direction of pretence, and in part from an almost opposite conviction that they are more likely to be repressed in certain ways which may produce oblique bursts of energy once that repression is circumvented (by analogy with his work with autistic children and as an extension of his work on personal awareness with adults). Finally, the gesture of turning to non-professionals is in a sense an assertion of the relevance of performance to those in the audience who are no longer separated from the performers by the mystique of specialised skills and knowledge.

For Stefan Brecht the production of *A Letter for Queen Victoria* (1974–5) marked a new direction in Wilson's work. It seems to have been an attempt to accommodate itself in some respect to more conventional models of theatre, while at the same time subverting them with the use of a language whose incompleteness and deceptions would thereby be exposed. It was also the first performance in which he drew on the special talents of Christopher Knowles. Knowles was a brain-damaged boy and Wilson plainly seems to have wished to set up some kind of opposition between an apparently naturalistic dialogue and the oblique, non-rational communication which the actors were to learn from Knowles. As Wilson remarked, 'You have got to get past the lines – the most important thing is your awareness of where you are in space – you must master the space – the dialogue is *supported* dialogue – the lines should be delivered . . . as something secondary . . . by act IV, the play should have been dissolved, you should be beyond it, into something else.'[21] Where in previous plays he had subverted language by subordinating it to visual images, now he chose another path, hollowing it out, establishing a series of disjunctions – between word and act, word and context, word and gesture. Movement was designed to be independent of speech while the dialogue was distributed to characters in a seemingly arbitrary way, subject to a schema independent of notions of character or meaning. It did simulate the formal structure of social interchange but this, according to Stefan Brecht, was subverted by these studied disjunctions. Where his earlier work had shared something of the surrealists' aesthetic, stressing a certain sense of wonder, seeking to expand avenues of communication, *Letter* seems to have been closer to a dadaist attack on a suspect rationality and the primary mechanism of that rationalism – language.

His next production, *The $ Value of Man* (1975) was in many ways a more conventional performance centred on the theme of money. Inspired by an article in *The New York Times* which had concerned itself with a philosophical debate about the dollar value of human life, it incorporated images and parodic references to movies, television and theatre. It included familiar aspects of his work, including the 'whirling' of De Groat and the use of non-professional performers who were not formally part of his group, but the result, according to Brecht, was unimpressive, though it was followed in 1976 by a further attempt at innovation, *Spaceman*, employing videotapes for the first time. Indeed eight videotapes were played through twenty monitors. The performance took place within a tunnel of translucent plastic containing various objects and people, including a 'spaceman' immobilised on a board, a green monster composed of several members of the company, and Christopher Knowles, who sat at a typewriter and produced copy which appeared directly on the television screens. The event seems to have been in part a throwback to the earlier days of happenings, though its apparent comment on a kind of menacing aphasia, the subordination of the human to sheer technics and the natural progression from a limited and dehumanising language to a language which is simply informational input suggests a conscious metaphoric intent. The event was brief by Wilson's standards – a mere hour and a half – and seemed a retreat from the sheer scale and imagistic variety of his earlier work. But it represented an interlude rather than a change of direction in his work in that it was followed, in 1976, by one of his best-known works, *Einstein on the Beach*, which received its world première at the Festival d'Avignon.

This was another large-scale production marked by the increased importance which he gave to music, which continued throughout. And though the play centres on the figure of Einstein, as earlier ones had focussed on Freud or Stalin, the imagery is not merely generated by the fact of this figure and the implied connotations of his work, but also by Wilson's own eclectic imagination. Thus a judge's bench and a jury make their appearance, according to Wilson, not because of any sense of judgement but because of the then-current interest generated by the trial of Patty Hearst and the performatic power of John Dean in the Watergate case. Where the connection with Einstein is real it is often of an oblique kind – his supposed interest in sailing and music – though clearly the image of a clock is intended to relate directly to the theory of relativity. Wilson even had a clock especially constructed which would go backwards one hour in a period of twenty minutes. As he remarked, 'I think Einstein would have liked clocks that go backwards!'[22] The relativity of time is also reinforced by a gyroscope which slowly progresses down a wire, thereby marking off periods of time. Travel is represented by a nineteenth-century locomotive as well as by a spaceship, a progression which also underlines the move from youth to old age as the Einstein figure himself ages. So, past is juxtaposed to future, both in effect occupying the same space. Projections of the working of an atomic bomb are shown and number sequences voiced. A young boy, presumably the young Einstein, is juxtaposed to the old, a confrontation which once again recalls the consequences of Einstein's theories. Hints of apocalypse are offered in the form of a glowing column of light which divides the stage, perhaps as the Einsteinian world is divided from the non-Einsteinian. A tower suddenly lurches at an angle.

For a person such as Wilson, intensely concerned with redefining space and time in theatrical terms, Einstein provided a natural focus. Perhaps this accounts for an increasing coherence in his images. They are clearly no longer quite so arbitrary as they had been in his earlier work. When the locomotive juts onto the stage it inevitably suggests a surrealist image but in fact it is directly related to, and a development of, his thematic concerns. Similarly, the obsession with note-taking and with numbers is no longer simply a gesture to redirect us in the direction of physical experience. It serves what can now be called a plot. The slow-motion sequences are abandoned. The image clusters construct a coherent model, though ironically that coherent world is one in which the real is disassembled; and the coherence is by no means total. Elements of earlier productions survive, particularly in the dance scenes, but in interview Wilson tended to relate the components to his central theme. Thus, he explained that, 'You see two characters lying on plexiglass tables: they are supposed to be floating in water.' This, however, is no arbitrary image. It is included because 'In 1900, there was a 25-foot diameter barrel of water that had mercury in it. They shot two beams of light through this to measure the speed of light.'[23]

Though some of the elements seem totally arbitrary – Wilson himself remarked of the trial and prison sections that 'I just thought about the dramas of our time: courtroom dramas, Watergate, people even in Brazil rushing home to watch their TVs in an effort to follow these dramas'[24] – they are perhaps not quite as arbitrary as they seem. The connection between Einstein's theories, the bomb, and images of trials and imprisonment are not difficult to elaborate. And as he moves towards a coherent theme, so he seems to drift back towards a more familiar theatrical model. However, the performance is still dominated by a precise visual geometry, straight lines and diagonals providing a structural coherence overriding apparent contingency. Philip Glass's music was itself composed in relation to a series of drawings that Wilson made rather than to the rehearsed material or a prepared script. Its reiterative phrases, its insistent rhythms, its incremental variations both reinforce the method of the text and constitute the content rather than the form of the work. The same could be said of Andy de Groat's choreography. The precision of music and movement are reminiscent of those to be found in Indian temple music and the effect is perhaps somewhat similar.

Wilson has suggested that the titles of his plays are in effect substitutes for a missing narrative dimension. Since the histories of the individuals with whom he deals are already known, it becomes unnecessary to recount them. *Einstein on the Beach* does not recount the history of Einstein; it compacts it into images. To Wilson, he represents not the intellectual but the dreamer so that the image becomes an appropriate mechanism for unlocking his meaning. The composer of the music, Philip Glass, made a similar point. 'Einstein was also a scientist involved in all the imagery of modern science that we are accustomed to. My music is something that I subjectively associate to modern machinery, engines and motors and that kind of thing.'[25]

13. The trial scene from Robert Wilson's *Einstein on the Beach*, 1976.

The debt accumulated by *Einstein on the Beach* – it cost around one million dollars to tour through Europe – reportedly led Wilson to attempt a more directly commercial venture in the form of his next work, *I was sitting on my patio this guy appeared I thought I was hallucinating* (1977) produced at the Cherry Lane Theatre. Ostensibly it moved Wilson further in the direction of conventional theatre. It had a recognisable, though spare, set. It had only two characters, each of whom, in sequence, performs the same text. They are precisely dressed as though to suggest distinctive roles. The text they speak seems to constitute one side of a dialogue, whose shifts imply different relationships and events. But the lighting, the stylised sets and the disruptive text (apparently composed of fragments drawn from the media as well as from material derived from snatches of conversation overheard by Wilson) work against the density of character and event. In other words, where his early work had been concerned with stressing the wide range of available channels for communication beyond language, this work seems to have been more committed to exposing the inadequacy of language and the incorrigible desire to project deceptive models of the real from fragments. Character, language and plot are reinstated precisely in order to ironise them.

Theodore Shanks has observed that Lucinda Childs, who performed

184

the piece with Wilson, saw her work on the production as involving the same kind of exploration as her earlier post-modern dance experiments as a member of the Judson Dance Theatre. That group had also disassembled the elements of movement, images and words so that it was the spectator's job 'to make sense out of what he sees and to decide if it's chaos or order, formed or formless, or if that matters'.[26]

In recent years, and in common with other American theatre groups, Wilson has increasingly turned to Europe where he has become something of a fixture in the cultural scene. When *The Golden Windows* opened in Munich in 1982 Madame Pompidou flew in for the première giving Wilson the seal of retrospective approval. The title of *The Golden Windows* is borrowed from the title story of an American book of fairy-tales. As described by Michael Wachsmann, the dramaturg of the Munich Kammerspiele Schauspielhaus, all that remains of the tale is:

> The picture of a house on a mountain, differently viewed at different times of the day. That congealed into quite a precise optical concept that Robert Wilson carried in his luggage: on top of a triangular black slope the narrow black house which in the course of the three parts a, b and c will change its position wandering from the right/evening over half right/midnight to left/early morning. From 'The Beggar's Opera' there was the haunting tune 'Over the hills and far away', there was 'The Cabinet of Doctor Caligari', there were the face and the gestures of Louise Brooks in 'Lulu', the silent movie.[27]

This was the concept which Wilson brought to Munich and which he developed there. The play is not devoid of language: there are a series of fractured monologues and even a number of hesitant and occluded dialogues; certain images, references, and phrases recur; implications of violence, violation and danger coexist with sentimental remarks, suggestions of relationship and domestic encounters. But his concern remains in part with the spatial organisation of the stage. The printed text is accompanied by small drawings which detail the precise positions and movements of the characters, each drawing constituting a sketch of the tableau he wishes to form. In a sense, the language also forms itself into a tableau of sound. Coherence exists moment by moment. Sometimes the unit is a paragraph of logical prose. Sometimes the unit is a sentence, a phrase or a fragmented word. Sometimes he presents a collage of words unrelated except in their proximity to one another. Sometimes we have a fragmentary plot. The urge to reconstruct a complete, logical and coherent narrative is all but irresistible, but there is no model of truth to be unravelled except in its individual moments and the patterns which form, dissolve and reform. Sound effects, shapes, choreographed movements, frozen moments, modulated voices, images combine less as predetermined fragments of a predestined whole than as sensory stimuli, provocations, implied harmonies and tentative gestures. The incompletions are deliberately designed to leave space for the audience. The images are suggestive rather than precise in order to provoke an active response. The vague references to violence, to affection, to fear and to memory invite translation in terms of private experience. Their sharpness, their definitional shape is a product of the mind and sensibility of the observer who becomes thereby more a collaborator than an observer.

It is not easy to assess the importance of Wilson's work. In one sense it is obviously rooted in the aesthetic values of the 1960s. His own background in art, architecture and music led to a concern with form, shape and rhythm, and to a disruption of models of theatre which depended on character, language and plot. This he plainly shared with the creators of happenings. The human form was a shape to be moulded; movement was something to be choreographed. At the same time his therapeutic work led him to place considerable weight on the body's power to communicate in a non-verbal way and this, together with his expressed conviction that the body told truths which the mind would deny, seemed to locate him firmly in the context defined by Marcuse and Norman O. Brown on the one hand, and Julian Beck on the other. His desire to generate images through juxtaposition and to liberate the marvellous from the prosaic was a familiar tactic of the new surrealism of the 1960s. His use of non-professionals was even a natural extension of that desire to destroy the barriers between actors and audience, theatre and life, which was a basic tenet of performance theatre. However, the sheer length and complexity of his major works implied an acceptance of the relativity of perception and the multi-faceted nature of reality which was rather more a mark of 1970s fiction and theatre. His 'operas' were not celebrations of human community, as performance theatre tended to be. Indeed, the human figures which he choreographed seldom engaged one another or their audience directly. On one level, then, his work offered precisely that kind of formalism against which Susan Sontag had inveighed. It was a retreat on almost all levels from the public art of the previous decade. His work was private in origin and effect, and offered little in terms of shared experience. Certainly the potential for wilful obfuscation and privatism in his work is considerable. And yet, operating, as he does, on the boundary between art, dance, design, theatre and opera he persists in posing questions about the nature of aesthetic experience which have seldom been asked in America. The rigour of his theatre lies in its individual moments which cannot be experienced as printed texts (though of necessity those not able to experience them directly are forced into an act of imaginative reconstruction on the basis of published materials, texts, interviews, descriptions). Presence is in some degree a prerequisite for their effect and to this extent they exemplify that dimension of theatre which Beck chose to press in the direction of secular ceremony but which Wilson is content to leave demythologised. For him, experience is a value in itself. His art, like his therapeutic sessions with children and his awareness exercises with adults, is designed to sensitise sensibilities blunted by what he seems to feel is an oppressive rationalism, to open paths of communication to the self and to the other which may lead beyond the word, the page and the stage to a sense of receptivity and personal creativeness which a previous generation had sought in drugs or pseudo-mysticism. He is unconcerned with whether or not other people choose to call this theatre.

He is, then, more than a simple aggregate of 1960s concerns. His commitment to a theatre of images is different in kind and content from the carefully contrived metaphors of the Performance Group and the Living Theatre, nor is he inclined to structure his work around ancient or modern myth, though the figures which he has used on stage have frequently themselves been mythicised. The scale of his major works has been considerable, as has their duration, so much so that they tend to be called 'operas', with music playing an important part. They do not lend themselves to conventional criticism, in part, at least, because they seek actively to deconstruct recognisable tenets of drama, and it was, perhaps, this element of his work, a scepticism about precisely those components of drama (character, plot and language) then being challenged in the novel, which made his concerns seem so significant in the 1970s. His concern with the authenticity of madness or with the physically or mentally damaged individual had its counterparts in the theories of R.D. Laing as it did in the insights of Artaud. His concern with tonalities and with electronically amplified sound was reminiscent of Cage's work, though where Cage increasingly sought to eliminate himself from his works Wilson tended to offer intensely personal images, to build structures of sound and vision which stemmed from his own subconscious. His implicit emphasis on the need to observe a sometimes banal phenomenon closely and over a period was reminiscent of Warhol. And, like Warhol's, his model is not of an undisclosed truth locked away beneath a deceptive surface. But where Warhol's is largely an art of pure surface for Wilson meaning is inter-actional and plural. It is generated by juxtaposition and by an attentiveness which moves in the direction of trance. His world is mystical only in so far as the route to its mysteries lies through a self transformed by its own efforts. In the words of one of John Barth's fictions, the key to the treasure is the treasure. Wilson offers not a series of artifacts, frozen images summoned up from his subconscious to redeem the world of the senses, but a method (rather like Whitman in *Leaves of Grass*). His eclecticism is his subject. His work is in a sense an equivalent of Whitman's celebratory lists. In the sheer variety, the expansive pleasure of propinquity, lies both a strategy and a subject. All experience, all senses, all areas of life are drawn into the poem or the play because that very profusion and the infinite combinations which result from it is both the cause and the theme. For both men fragments exist not in relation to a priori wholes but as potential elements for a constantly changing kaleidoscope of new forms. There is, however, a reifying dimension to Wilson's work which is lacking in Whitman's. For though the nineteenth-century poet also preferred experience to language and life to art, Wilson's suspicions of language are so intense that on occasion he seems more committed to dislocating lexis, grammar and structure for its own sake than out of any desire to generate new combinations and forms. Nonetheless, the central impulse behind his work is Whitmanesque.

The disjunctions that he presents, the discontinuities, the absences, are not offered as evidence of alienation but as areas charged with potential and, though in some moods he seems to mock the impulse to fill these ostensible voids, the overwhelming aesthetic compulsion is to permit a discharge of energy across the spaces, to generate the potential for change, at least on the level of the imagination. He tends to see things as held together by lines of force rather than as dialectically counterposed or simply as random components in a system of power. The apparently reductive image of character is not an assertion of social alienation but an attempt to coerce the audience into an active response on the level of the mind and the imagination. This is the closest he comes to implying a political stance. His use, in a number of performances, of a black mammy costume is, not untypically, an attempt on his part both to accept a stereotyped model and to detach it from the referents which give it its meaning and which enforce its stereotypical nature in the first place; it is an act of subversion which is not without its naivety. But the gesture is central to his method.

Wilson's art is intended to disconcert. But, in contrast to the work of, say, Joe Orton, his performances are not in the service of an anarchic impulse. Behind them there lies a romantic conviction about continuity, a touching faith about the possibility of communication and the essentially holistic nature of experience. He is supremely an optimist and not simply in the sense that anyone offering a play lasting seven days would have to be. It is not just that he has a symbolist's conviction of a fundamental correspondence between the senses and the arts but that his implicit model of experience is one in which everything can ultimately be connected through the imagination. He was certainly the American figure who commanded the greatest interest internationally among theatre practitioners in the 1970s. That this was so perhaps says more about the concerns of a decade obsessively concerned with consciousness and with the self than it does about the final significance of a man whose work was intensely private in origin and disturbingly gnomic in its effects. Indeed, in so far as it challenged conventional notions of the dramatic, it inspired both a certain fascination and a deep sense of anxiety.

6 Richard Foreman

Harold Rosenberg once remarked that 'at a certain moment the canvas began to appear to one American painter after another as an arena in which to act – rather than as a space in which to reproduce, design, analyse, or "express" an object, actual or imagined. What was to go on the canvas was not a picture but an event.'[1] The observation might almost be reversed with respect to Richard Foreman. He was certainly concerned with the theatricalised environment but it was as a picture, a space in which an object might be exposed and a design elaborated, that he responded to the stage. Though very precisely controlled from moment to moment – the placing of figures, the performance of actors being closely designated – the total effect was impressionistic. Pierre Bailey has said of his own musical composition *Structures la* (1982) that it exhibits an excess of order which is equivalent to disorder. Much the same effect results from some of Foreman's work. What is clear is the structure. No longer serving the cause of 'meaning', his performances foreground process and the centrality and necessity of the audience's imaginative contribution. Just as Robbe-Grillet had remarked that 'All my work is precisely engaged in the attempt to bring its own structures to light',[2] so Foreman exposed the mechanics of his productions. Just as Robbe-Grillet insisted that 'invention and imagination . . . finally become the subject of the book',[3] so they became the subject of Foreman's theatrical pieces.

Like Robert Wilson, Richard Foreman also began his work in the 1960s, founding the Ontological Hysteric Theatre in 1968. Identifying Gertrude Stein as a central influence, he insisted that he 'wanted a theatre that did the opposite of "flow"' – a theatre that was true to his own mental experiences, which saw 'the world as being pieces of things, awkwardly present for a moment and then either re-presented by consciousness or dropped in favor of some other momentary presentation'.[4]

For Stein, life involved a series of repetitions shaped by the mind into a form of ritual. Her plays tended to consist of a series of individual gestures, plotless moments. In a sense her subject was artistic consciousness and the mind was the principal focus for her as it was for Foreman. Her book, *The Geographical History of America*, was actually subtitled *Or the Relation of Human Nature to the Human Mind*. To her, the process of

190

knowing was crucial and the human mind was capable of engaging an infinity of objects: 'To understand a thing means to be in contact with that thing and the human mind can be in contact with anything.'[5] She accordingly had little interest in the logical unfolding of narrative. Indeed, she asserted that the notion of a beginning, middle and end was a redundancy in a world of perception and action in which, she insisted, 'Moving is in every direction.' This statement I take to lie behind Foreman's sketches – in which arrows shoot out from a centre (the mind?) in all directions – and his productions, which try to do likewise. Stein resisted the conventionalised language of the theatre in the name of a freedom from determinism, aesthetic, social and moral. Something of the same logic obtains for Foreman.

Like Wilson, he reacted against the conventions of plot, character and language but, where Wilson was concerned with presenting a series of images and free-floating forms and with opening up new channels of communication, Foreman was more centrally interested in the mental processes involved in the act of imagining. As he has said, 'The scripts themselves read like notations of my own process of imagining a theatre piece.'[6] In that sense at least his is a metadramatic gesture. The process of the plays reflects and enacts the process of their invention. But at the same time there are links with Wilson's work. The characters which he creates are deliberately decontextualised, while the moments of experience are consciously atomised. His work shows the same desire to alter the consciousness of his audience and, unsurprisingly, he is as prone to quote surrealists as models as he is Gertrude Stein. His plays also rely on a series of tableaux, and combine a disruptive dialogue with apparently arbitrary sound effects and visual stimuli – an approach designed to deny empathy and to enforce an acknowledgement of simultaneity while encouraging concentration on the detailed components of experience. As with Wilson's works they have no clear meaning. Their intention, as the strange title of his theatre suggests, lies less in the elaboration of fictions, the creation of artificial systems of meaning, than in enforcing the intense reality of individual moments. The irony is that the atomisation is invoked in the name of some supposedly ontologically secure reality – the 'foundations' of the individual being.

As suggested earlier, his work seems to fall into two periods. Until about 1975 he was primarily interested in a process of recuperating the real through a systematic defamiliarisation. In other words, by slowing the action down or by creating a series of unlikely juxtapositions, he invited the audience to consider afresh objects and gestures that had lost their impact and in a sense their reality through familiarity. Later he became concerned with detailing his own shifting obsessions, presenting a series of fragments, each displacing one another at speed. The processes of consciousness rather than the supposed qualities of the real moved to the centre of his concern rather as in art there was a shift from minimalism to photorealism. The interest was no longer in the objects themselves, but in the process whereby the human mind in a sense summons them into being by observing them and then generates meaning by relating them to other objects or events.

Like Wilson, Foreman also tends to offer explanations for his work which, though accurate enough, are somewhat gnomic and parodistic in effect: 'Ontological-Hysteric Theatre', he has explained, 'is a form of "concrete theatre" in which the moment-to-moment resistance and impenetrability of the materials worked on stage are framed and re-framed so that the spectator's attention is redistributed and exhilaration slowly invades his consciousness as a result of the continuous presentation and re-presentation of the atomic units of each experienced moment.'[7] The purpose of his work is in some way to retrain the sensibility of the audience in that he wishes to force the audience to pay attention to individual moments, rhythms and constructions, those qualities which 'saturate the givens (objects, words and actions) of any particular play', and thereby to ensure that 'the spectator is made available (as I am, when writing) to those most desirable energies which secretly connect him (through a kind of resonance) with the foundations of his being'.[8] The language is dense but the meaning is reasonably clear. He is intent on reinvesting the physical world with a freshness dulled by habit thereby restoring not only the world to itself but also the mind which observes to a sense of its own participation in that world. Foreman, too, is not that remote from Walt Whitman and his leaf of grass.

Richard Foreman, who writes, directs, designs and produces his own plays, has issued a series of manifestos, a significant act in an American context in which the manifesto has not been the familiar device which it has in other countries. The three collected in *Plays and Manifestos* were issued between 1972 and 1975. They consist of charts, drawings, aphorisms and statements, the first manifesto offering hints of his methodology. Hence: 'Theatre in the past has used language to build: What follows / We use language not to destroy, but to undercut pinnings of *there*. / Art = make *there* assert self, not turn into project that absorbs there.'[9] In other words, language is not to be the agent of a narrative that pulls attention away from each moment by subordinating that moment or that word to the flow of a causal development. The moments and the words have an authority and a quality of their own which is threatened by the pull of narrative. In a sense this is an equivalent to demands that the individual should perceive himself in terms of being and not becoming, that individual meaning is best seen not as an endlessly deferred project but as something experienced moment by moment. As the manifesto implies, all acts radiate. They are not subsumed in an already-existent meaning or in one which will manifest itself only when all the components have been assembled – an idea which anyway depends on a notion of completeness as a goal and a possibility. This is the essence of a statement which he presents in two different ways – a formula and a design. The drawings do not merely explain his rationale; in effect they exemplify it:

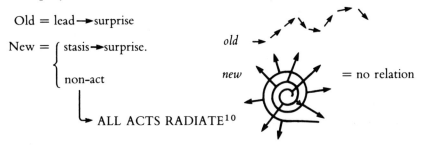

Old $=$ lead $\longrightarrow$ surprise

New $=$ $\left\{\begin{array}{l} \text{stasis} \longrightarrow \text{surprise.} \\ \\ \text{non-act} \end{array}\right.$

    $\longrightarrow$ ALL ACTS RADIATE[10]

old $\rightarrow$

new $=$ no relation

His theatre consists of a series of careful acts of subversion. He seeks to 'destroy' the stage through 'delicate maneuvers', deliberate distortions. Again, as he explains in his first manifesto:

> Distortions: (1) logic – as in realism, which we reject because the mind already 'knows' the next move and so is not alive to the next move.
>   (2) chance & accident and the arbitrary – which we reject because within too short a time each choice so determined becomes equally predictable as 'item produced by change, accident, etc.'
>   (3) the new possibility (what distorts with its weight) – a subtle insertion between logic and accident, which keeps the mind alive as it evades over-quick integration into the mental system. CHOOSE THIS ALWAYS!
>   The field of the play is distorted by the objects within the play, so that each object distorts each other object and the mental pre-set is excluded.[11]

The opaque prose is not mere linguistic incapacity. It is a product of his distrust of translating images into words. Thus, in trying to define his objective he retreats to an instructive imprecision. He wanted, he explained, a 'resonance between the head and the object'. At first interested in the qualities of an object or event, he became more concerned with the process of invention within the mind which the playwright/performer merely mimics.

In 1967 he had perversely reacted against Peter Brook's production of *A Midsummer Night's Dream*, rejecting what he saw as the absurdity of its orchestrated speech and activity, its emphasis on counterpart and relationship. Out, too, went Chaikin and Grotowski because of what he saw, again somewhat perversely, as the emotional commitment which they forced. The problem, as he saw it, was how to 'create a stage performance in which the spectator experiences the danger of art not as involvement or risk or excitement, not as something that reaches out to vulnerable areas of his person, but rather the danger as a possible *decision* he (spectator) may make upon the occasion of confronting the work of art. The work of art as a *contest* between object (or process) and viewer.'[12] This does not imply a conflict model of theatre, which he would equally reject. The dynamism of his work is to derive not from a struggle between discrete persons or forces, or between being and the threat of non-being (existential or absurd drama), but from the activity of the mind coerced into activity by the theatre artist. In other words, and perhaps paradoxically, after the Artaud-influenced theatre of the 1960s he was proposing a return to cerebral theatre, and though he used the word 'ecstasy' this was in the context of an equation which defines it in terms of a 'total action of all forces – a "stasis"'[13] (a definition which would appear to underline his apoliticism). The aim for Foreman, as for Wilson and Beck, is harmony. Though he was precise enough about the moment in which a shift of direction became necessary – 'In 1968, the theatre became hopeless'[14] – the year seems chosen not for any political significance, in the way, for example, that it did indeed mark a shift of emphasis in the English theatre (which between 1968 and 1975 generated a large number of socialist writers and theatre groups). Indeed, Foreman's response was quite otherwise. He wished to abandon an art generated by the nature of the relationship 'between a changing world (events march in) and a posited ego which VIEWS events and in so doing EXTRACTS art from the flux of the world'. In its place he wished to see a 'repeating mechanism' and the 'scanning mechanism superimposed on the repeating mechanism'.[15] Beneath the jargon he was interested in creating a theatre which concerned itself with consciousness. He was not interested in staging completed gestures or events to which an audience would merely respond. He wished to co-opt the audience as co-creators. For him the brain is a mechanism not an ego; the world does not change, it recurs. Art is not mimetic; it is, he insists, 'a parallel phenomenon to life itself'. Thus art is not a product offered to a passive brain; it is the invention of that brain just as is the self which does not pre-exist but comes into being as it invents the world which it inhabits.

However, this does not eliminate the artist whose responsibility it is to bring to bear a certain rigour and clarity in terms of each discrete moment. It might seem the more surprising, therefore, that his own descriptions of his work are themselves so vague, but the precision relates to the events, the objects and the gestures which provoke the mind, not to what the mind may make of them. Thus he rejects an art which is fuelled by the audience's need for consolation or self-regard but seeks to replace that with something he finds difficult to define: 'Nervous energy? Basic hum of life? Vibration?'[16] The self-doubt implicit in the question marks is not apparent in his diagrams of the system he seeks to replace but it does reflect his own method which is to work against his own certainties, to guard against the power of his own assertions. His image is of the explosive co-presence of matter and anti-matter. In a scrawled note to himself he insists, 'Don't sustain anything.'[17]

In his second manifesto, dated July 1974, he stresses the significance of the individual moments in his work and experience, insisting (as Richard Brautigan was implicitly doing in the novel) that it is the brick which determines the architecture of a building and that to understand the work it is necessary to understand the individual cell which generates that work. Indeed, he constantly turns to biology and physics for his images. One consequence of this is to reinforce his apoliticism. While rejecting the surrealists as true models it seems clear that the only revolution in which he can believe is a revolution of consciousness. Otherwise his art seems an art of adjustment:

> A solution to the problem of what is
> doesn't imply a utopian vision – how
> to fix the world – but how to BE
> so that
> One can respond to the world-as-it-is
> instead of
> responding to a dream world, or inherited
> world in which institutions and training
> hypnotize us to see THEIR version of reality.[18]

His objection to realism and romanticism (in which latter category he rightly places surrealism) is that it 'puts man to sleep – returning him to animal nature or deluding him that his dreams are objectively real'.[19] His various aleatory devices are thus designed precisely to disrupt all forms of illusionism and even 'image making'. Art emerges, he suggests, from a tension between the concrete object, the body, and the mind's yearning for abstraction. It follows that he rejects an art of resolution or a drama with a 'message' which subordinates all elements to idea. The image on its own becomes a mere icon as does art as masterpiece: 'Idols. Dead things. Hamlet'. For such drama, he insists, is 'based on inertia, entropy, deadness as conflict works out to resolution – i.e. object, end, death, sizeable "meaning"'.[20] To live as a human being, he insists, is consciously to live the tension between wish and reality. His is a theatre which aims to 'show the mind at work, moment by moment',[21] a process which he regards as a true realism. His is a theatre which works by increments, small variations and displacements which generate energy. His repetitions are never simply that. Minor changes are offered as paradigms of other critical disjunctions, '[dream and resistance of world] / [mental image and unexpected data]',[22] just as minor similarities become disturbing and crucial events. He rejects the gross contrasts (army of ferocious Indians and pure maiden) that he associates with the conflict model of theatre. In its place he calls for a new sensitivity such as had been demanded by the creators of happenings, an art which should be full of 'noticing'. And once the supposedly gross effects have been dispensed with the individual member of the audience is free 'to go "visiting" / to "reconnoiter" / to "wake up and explore" the world before him'.[23] Since the work itself offers minimal help, the viewer is forced to fill the apparent void and create out of the few fragmentary gestures. Perceptual effort is offered as a necessary path to conceptual reward. Beauty is not presented; it is created in the mind of the observer.

This is the key to his device of incorporating his own comments on the unfolding action and on occasion his own literal presence within his plays. To see and to see yourself seeing is to establish a model of human existence (the inner and the outer, body and spirit) and to create an alienating device which inhibits that empathy which he associates with mere passive acceptance. It is an image of the creative tension for which he reaches – the necessity to sustain a clear notion of your own existence apart from the stimuli to which you respond. Without this constant awareness of your own perceptual distinctiveness, he insists, you are merely hypnotised. This process, which he calls 'intentional perception', becomes a device which he claims exposes the inadequacy and the shallowness of conventional theatre. Thus he employs various means of inhibiting empathy. The performance is speeded up or slowed down. Elastic cords are extended to an object thereby both focussing attention on it and disrupting perceptual patterns. Members of the audience find themselves the sudden object of attention thus making them aware of their own role and the significance of their consciousness.

Accusations of formalism are not entirely gratuitous. He has himself described the degree to which the formalists' concern with defamiliarising, with precipitating, through conscious deformation, a fresh response to experience, influenced his early work. Accordingly at first he set out to 're-tree' the tree. But later he came to feel that the real objective should be to 'de-tree' the tree, that is to see it in relation to the process whereby the human mind summons it into being and utilises it to open up other abstract realities such as hope or memory. His theatre is to be concerned with processes rather than completions. This is to say that the absences are crucial. Thus, he suggests, 'dissonances, dissociation, discontinuity, dehumanization / and GAPS remind one of what is true; that man is always shipwrecked / That his conscious resources are never equal to his dilemma / That he will never WIN / (Which is different from saying that he cannot / PLAY magnificently and joyously – in which / case not-winning is hardly a cause for sadness.)'.[24] Suddenly he seems to be hinting at the humanism which paradoxically he sees himself as recuperating, for in a theatre which seems to exclude the human he wishes to claim a central role for the mind and the imagination for which, he could claim, the conventional theatre can find no place.

The third manifesto, dated June 1975, takes up the analogy with physics once again to press the notion of critical absences. He invokes, in particular, Paul Dirac's 1931 theory in which he had predicted the discovery of a short-lived anti-electron, summoned into being by a sudden space in the invisible world of sub-atomic particles, energised by a burst of energy derived from cosmic rays. For Foreman, the creative moment itself produces a spark (gesture) of anti-matter which has the power to neutralise matter, this being the clutter of received ideas and behaviour patterns which might themselves be the detritus of earlier pulses of creative energy. But, like the anti-electron, it exists only briefly before being re-absorbed. That moment is the crucial one and it is an event, an isolable process, not an object. The reality of a play is not its subject matter; it is its moment-by-moment existence. Foreman suggests that while the author of an anti-war play offers the suggestion that war is a product of greed and militarism he does so by inviting the audience to accept that his fictions should be treated as real; but there is another reality, namely the author's concern with creating the play moment by moment. 'And that real part', Foreman suggests, 'is where the audience / Could possibly discover something / evidently true / not just postu-latedly true.'[25] It is only by concentrating on the act of making the thing which we are looking at that it is possible to avoid 'the built-in deadness of the language in which it articulates itself'.

Language thus becomes in a sense the subject of Foreman's work – the language of vision and gesture as well as of the word. And in this respect he is close kin not merely to certain post-modern novelists but to a shift of emphasis equally evident in post-structuralist criticism. Language, he insists, 'doesn't have to be something "refers to" / since it is DIFFERENT from what it refers to / but tries to EVOKE it but only spins out itself – web-like – as its own evidence of what it is, in collision / with what one would make (a play with perhaps / an ostensible "other" subject)'.[26] On the evidence of that statement one might suspect that his bias against language as meaning was a piece of special pleading by a man seemingly incapable of lucidity but since he is concerned with dislocating narrative flow there is a logic even in his own incoherences. It is not, however, a logic which can be pressed too far.

Foreman's manifestos, if gnomic, are cogent. But it is hard to grant his published texts the subtlety of his theoretical writings. The first production of the Ontological Theatre took place in April 1968. *Angelface* consists of a number of figures (rather than characters) some of whom are 'doubled', splitting into two versions of the same person. Their speeches are rarely longer than a single sentence. The comments contained in his manifestos notwithstanding, there is a fragile narrative development. The dialogue has its dissonances but these are contained in what seems to be a slightly odd conversation which is not without its coherences. Slowly, however, the odd, though rational, language, comes under increasing strain. The figures seem to acknowledge one another's existence, but their actions are increasingly stylised. A mock marriage gives way, apparently, to an action in which a woman is forced into a closet; another figure appears with wooden wings; a man is tied to a rope suspended from the ceiling; a rock comes through the window. Though it is difficult to reconstruct event from text the script offers little to substantiate the claims of theory. The narrative pressure remains and though character is made abstract its configuration remains an important element. As we shall see later, Foreman was fully aware of this problem, recognizing the final impossibility of breaking loose from the assertive power of 'meaning'.

Total Recall (Sophia = (Wisdom): Part 2) begins with a more disturbing image than any in that first play as a woman is revealed apparently holding a lamp. She subsequently disappears but the lamp remains in space. However, such visual distortions are not left to work for themselves, being underscored by a language which makes verbally explicit what is already visually apparent. Thus the character called Ben, stepping through a window-frame, announces that 'Standing out here is a revelation. (*Pause*) When I have a revelation I can't move and I find everything very unusual. (*Pause*) I feel like I'm standing in the ocean with the water halfway up to my waist. (*Pause. Cabinet opens. SOPHIA there*) I can imagine there are lots of things happening I can't see. Some of them are behind my back and some of them are in the centre of the light.'[27] But, again, the striking fact is that the play has a clear narrative drive, a plot, characters, who, if liable to behave strangely and assume double personalities, are nonetheless clearly delineated, and a language which is fully transitive. However, the rational dialogue is set against sudden disruptions. At one stage a duplicate set of furniture is introduced, thereby transforming both physical context and action. At another moment the stage crew enters and throws one of the characters, together with his table and chair, out of the room. The world of Foreman's plays is not as remote from that of Ionesco as his own accounts would suggest, except that rather than projecting a model of existence as subject to the pull of the inanimate he is concerned with generating energy through simple acts of displacement, disconcerting games involving repetition and moments of self-conscious intervention which draw attention to those processes of invention which in fact constitute his central interest. Thus at one stage a character asks the whereabouts of a dog only to be told that 'that dog was in the first part of the play'.

Hotel China (1971–2) more clearly exemplifies his model of theatrical activity. Into a scene in which a man has a rock placed on himself, he intrudes a film which consists of shots of rocks being placed in different positions, in different rooms. This is followed by what he punningly describes as a 'rock ballet' in which a number of stones are placed on the stage furniture and the floor while a romantic passage from Mahler is played, disrupted at regular intervals by discordant notes on a piano. Various surreal images are presented. One figure enters, balancing a tray on his head; a woman sleeps with her head resting on a table set for a meal but, when she rises, the cloth clings to her face and all the objects which are on it remain adhered to it; a tray is suddenly turned into a vertical position but the objects remain in place. Again, characters are doubled. A woman splashes herself with water in front of a projected film of waves; angels appear; strings representing lines of force are attached to rocks, rather as in the diagrams to be found in his theoretical writings in which meaning is shown as spilling out of objects made to render up their energy through being momentarily charged with significance. Though each image, each defamiliarised gesture, is not without its naivety, it is aimed at a constant undercutting of conventional responses. The work is never in a state of rest. Any empathetic response is obviated not only by the disappearance of the subject and the intervention of filmed material but also by Brechtian slogans which underline the theatricality by announcing impending action or identifying the stage of the play. A recorded voice instructs the actors to repeat their actions and they in turn debate whether or not they should comply. The play concludes with a description of the action as it unfolds and with a summary presented in the form of a legend. 'NOW YOU REALIZE THAT IT WAS THE LAST ACTION OF HOTEL CHINA, PART TWO. THERE WERE MANY OTHER ACTIONS THAT PRECED-ED THE LAST ACTION. THEY WERE ALL INTER-RELATED AND YET THEY WERE ALL BEAUTIFUL AND COULD BE SEEN FROM DIFFERENT POINTS OF VIEW. YOU

ONLY REMEMBER SOME OF THEM. CAN YOU REMEMBER THE NAMES OF ALL THE CHARACTERS?'[28] A similar device is employed in *(Sophia = (Wisdom): Part 2)* (written 1971; performed 1972–3) in which the audience is repeatedly invited to reconsider what it has seen and is urged to limit its response to the assertive power of the moment.

Foreman's work is in essence close in spirit to that of Robbe-Grillet in the novel. His intention is to free objects, and the human forms which he dramatises, of their cultural overlay – the conventions of seeing – in part because this reveals their qualities and in part because this forces the brain into active collusion. And, indeed, beyond the object is the human brain and, where Ralph Waldo Emerson observed that 'Every object rightly seen, unlocks a / new faculty of the soul',[29] Foreman would simply substitute the word 'mind' for 'soul'. The photorealism of the painter or the presentational aesthetic of Foreman and Wilson is predicated on the failure of realism – on its insistence on the primacy of meaning and hence the subordination of the object. As E.H. Gombrich has observed, 'We had thought to control it [the world around us] by assigning it a meaning . . . But this was merely an illusory simplification; and far from becoming clearer and closer because of it, the world has only little by little, lost all its life. . . .'[30] Wilson and Foreman, and painters like Richard Estes and Ralph Goings are concerned, first and foremost, with presence, the incontestible existence of the event, the moment, the object. They are also concerned with the problem of perception. The question of meaning is secondary and is inevitably the source of a certain irony.

The same characters appear in virtually all of Foreman's plays but we learn little or nothing about them. It is as if he were creating a hermetic world in which the human form and inanimate objects move on the same plane and are equally capable of generating or prompting responses. These responses are only partly controlled by Foreman. A naked woman, even in the artificial environment in which he chooses to place her, has an associative power which is difficult to deny; and despite the precision of the moves, it is hard to determine the precise response to a rock placed on a piece of cloth. The plays, then, are a combination of the determined and the free. Since his real interest lies not in notions of structured meaning but in the process whereby each instant is mobilised and reconstructed by the brain, the idea of subordinating language, action or character to a dominant image is irrelevant. While the desire to assemble fragments into wholes is understandable and the process where-by this desire seeks to realise itself through acts of mental incorporation fascinating, there is no totality which Foreman sees his art as serving. As a consequence it constantly teeters on the brink of absurdity. It smacks of pretension. Its occasional jokes suggest a sense of irony which is not sustained. Thus, when a voice asks the audience to consider the proposition that people are more interesting than props and, following the appearance of a naked girl, invites them to 'THINK HARDER', the joke foregrounds one of the problems of his approach without suggesting an ironic stance. The audience is in effect invited to make what they will of the apparent jumble of actions, objects, figures, projections and statements provided only that they concentrate on the processes whereby they seek to formulate meaning and become aware of the power of these things, simply and in combination, to generate an energy which does not necessarily bear any relationship to their intrinsic qualities. In aestheticising the environment (his plays are apt to use natural scenes ironised by their new context) he is asserting the degree to which it is already aestheticised, subordinated to conventional models of beauty, utility and meaning. But it is difficult to perceive any real development in his work, beyond an intensified use of certain devices, beyond the shift from simple awareness to a concern for the processes of thought. To an extent he relies on a certain accumulative power but it is hard to feel, at least in terms of his published texts, that he has much more to do than repeat the same point so that his works do in effect become a single play.

In terms of theatre, Richard Foreman's work, which once seemed to have a valuable disruptive power by working against the grain of conventional forms, has itself become conventionalised – always the principal risk of an approach such as his. The combinations of images are limitless as are the radiating paths of their imaginative projections, but the necessity to reconstruct our perceptive powers and to become fully conscious of the processes of thought, once stated and enforced, gains little from elaboration unless, like converts to religion, it is necessary to meet together at regular intervals in order to renew our faith.

Foreman's suggestion that his productions 'write themselves' implies more than a fortuitous link with the theoretical writings of Robbe-Grillet and Roland Barthes though several of his own observations seem little more than restatements of Robbe-Grillet's position as spelled out in his essays of the late 1950s and early 1960s. He too had been fascinated with the physical properties of a world summoned into existence by the collaborative power of writer and reader who conspired to create a fictive but nonetheless substantial present (a concern which equally came to typify the world of art, sculpture and theatre). He, too, had reacted against the tyranny of meaning, stressing the importance of the present moment, prolonged if need be by a narrative precision. Like Robbe-Grillet, Foreman began by wishing to reinstate the qualities of the objects and shapes which he presented. The world of signs was to be replaced by 'a world of perceptions' just as Robbe-Grillet had seen 'the universe of meanings being replaced by the physical presence of objects and gestures'. And, like Robbe-Grillet, Foreman wished to free objects and human forms of their cultural overlay. The coherences of his theatre are thus not those of the conventional realist theatre, but coherences there are. His decision to use professional and semi-professional actors, as in *Penguin Touquet* (1981), for example, in which he deployed not only the talents of his increasingly professional colleague Kate Manheim but also performers from the Open Theatre, was surely likely to diminish the freshness and directness of his early work. Inevitably his performances became more predictable, even in their unpredictableness. But there is no end to the process of de-treeing the tree and Foreman's commitment to that process has scarcely slackened.

It also has to be admitted that the audience for Foreman's plays does not consist of a number of individuals whose sensibilities, imaginations and minds are unshaped by the cultural assumptions of their society. The universe of meanings exists not merely in the work but in the cultural presumptions of those who view it. Modes of perception have their own historiography. The completion of patterns is not a function only of the brain but equally of the society whose models may be seductive rather than coercive. Foreman's scattered fragments do not fall on a naive mind; they are liable to filter down through a grid which collates with an efficiency scarcely impaired by its unconscious nature. The lust for meaning may be curtailed in the artist; it is more difficult by far to effect the same control in the mind of the recipient/collaborator. And his own disruptive gestures have become cruder. Invited to produce a Strauss opera in Paris in 1983 he caused a scandal by, somewhat pointlessly, substituting a number of striptease artists for the expected ballet dancers. Also, as this production suggests, like Robert Wilson he has in some degree been co-opted by the theatre which he set out to resist.

In his description of the preparation of *Café Amérique*, which took place from May to July 1981, Foreman offers a further account of his own aesthetic principles. 'The task', he suggests, consists 'of the elaboration of a new world (within the play) in which each moment of experience is intended not to further some linear development, but rather to provide a "unit of experience" with the (repeated) opportunity to present itself to consciousness, to allow the latter to cover the full scope of that experience, and meet its limits. It is, therefore, the presentation of a moment.'[31] But this is merely the first stage, for, as he explains,

> the next step, rather than a direct response to such a presentation, consists of an attempt to describe an oscillation (with as wide an angle as possible)

triggered by the invisible field of gravity of the moment 'being presented'. The characters then stand swinging in a diabolical, furious way, spurred on by this 'presented' moment (or sentence) and, in the midst of their suffering, they try to convince themselves, through this deliberate fidgeting, that what is being presented has less weight than 'real life.'[32]

But the paradox which plainly delights him lies in the thought that the value of the 'real' lies in the possibilities which it contains for its own transcendence. It is justified by its power to trigger the aesthetic moment. The aesthetic world thus becomes the justification of human life.

> Let us assume that each moment in life has only one real, usable object; that it conceals within itself its secret treasure, some sort of 'key' which would enable me to awaken from it. Life, reality, are only there as the offer of a possibility of getting away from them. As we keep missing the chance, we simply contribute to making life more complex, adding more and more nooks and corners which provide in their turn as many secret exits for whoever might discover them and know how to use them. There are, indeed, within my plays . . . some desperate and enlightened creatures who do use reality as a way of escaping from it. So life really does . . . exist in order to end up in a book (or play) (or whatever may act as its negation).[33]

His characters 'hurl themselves, are hurled again and again against the walls that define the imaginable, thus provoking that muffled noise, the vibrations of which suggest what lies beyond, what is, for us, really unimaginable'.[34]

But this escape is impossible; it is a kind of absurd struggle to achieve a transcendence denied by the very conditions of existence. The unimaginable is just that. It is a territory whose existence is inferred from images, momentary visions and dissolving realities, but it cannot be grasped. In the same way his own work is in a sense doomed to failure. Setting out to create 'plays' which will not be pulled down to earth by the prosaic weight of 'meaning' he acknowledges that it is an objective which cannot succeed. The desire to seek meaning, to endeavour to decode experience, is inescapable. It is the essence of the absurd. But such an absurdity is, perhaps, not without its victories.

7 Lee Breuer

The third of this trio of writer/performer/directors is Lee Breuer. His involvement in the American theatre has brought him into contact with a wide range of different styles and approaches. In the early 1960s he was a director at the San Francisco Actors' Workshop under Herbert Blau and Jules Irving and also worked with Ann Halprin's Dancers' Workshop and the San Francisco Mime Troupe. In Europe he concerned himself with the Berliner Ensemble and Grotowski's Polish Laboratory Theatre. He directed Brecht and Beckett, his interest in the latter leading to the foundation of the Mabou Mines Company.

Lee Breuer also bridges the supposed gulf between art and theatre. The 'animations' which he wrote and produced for Mabou Mines from 1968 onwards were first shown in an art gallery before being staged in the theatre (at the La Mama Theatre Club in the case of *The Red Horse Animation* and *The B Beaver Animation*; and the New York Festival in the case of *The Shaggy Dog Animation*). If they reveal something of the quality of poems, his fables, which are confessedly influenced by those of Kafka as well as by the animated figures of cartoons, also reveal an aesthetic kinship with developments in art from pop art to super-realism. Indeed a number of artists have played important collaborative roles in Mabou Mines productions.

Mabou Mines, a theatre collective, had its origin in the early 1960s when Breuer worked with Ruth Maleczech, Joanne Akalaitis and a group of artists in San Francisco. The group then worked in Europe from 1966–9, though joined now by the actor David Warrilow and the composer Philip Glass. In 1969 they assumed the name Mabou Mines, after a mining town in Nova Scotia and the following year became the resident company at La Mama ETC. By the beginning of the 1980s they were a resident company at the New York Shakespeare Festival. Mabou Mines creates both original works and their own versions of modern classic plays.

Breuer's plays have tended to feature animals as their main characters. These are seen in part as offering analogues for human behaviour patterns. In the 'Outline' segment of *The Red Horse Animation* the link is made explicit as the voice observes, 'WHY PRETEND I CAN DESCRIBE MYSELF. I SEE MYSELF IN EVERYTHING THAT WALKS AND TALKS AND CRAWLS ON ITS BELLY. OR JUST LIES THERE. WHY NOT PRETEND MY LIFE HAS COLOR. I LIKE RED.'[1]

Lee Breuer

14.   Mabou Mines, *The Red Horse Animation*, 1972.

The Red Horse Animation, first performed at the Guggenheim
Museum in New York City in 1970 and later, in a revised and expanded
version, at the Whitney Museum in 1972, begins with a tape-recorded
prologue. The three actors perform lying on the floor and jointly enact
the consciousness and being of the horse as it struggles into a conscious
possession of its surroundings. The acting area is space rather than place.
It is an area in which the consciousness of the animal expands. The play
itself is constructed around three separate components which are described as the 'Outline', the 'Lifeline' and the 'Story Line'. At first these
are separate though interactive. But eventually they merge. The 'Outline' is literally concerned with shape, an actor joining dots to form the
configuration of a horse. The 'Lifeline' expresses a growing consciousness of qualities of being, of distinguishing characteristics. The 'Story
Line' component reflects what appears to be an autobiographical fragment, the writer expressing his own involvement in the act of creation.
The constitution of the text thus becomes a model of the constitution of a
self and of reality. In the published version photographs of the production are deliberately presented in single-framed compartments like a strip
cartoon or the still frames of a movie film. The figures move either
against the blank canvas of the floor or the wooden slats of a barn. In
another published version it is presented in the form of a literal comic
strip.

The next play in what Breuer has called a trilogy, *The B Beaver Animation*, was performed at the Museum of Modern Art in New York as part of a programme called 'A Valentine for Marcel Duchamp' and at the Theatre for the New City in New York in 1974. This is a cautionary tale about the struggle for existence in which the beaver faces the possibility of extinction, like the man to whom he is compared and into whom he seems to change. The beaver tells the story of his own daily struggle and of the more fundamental struggle which lies behind this and of which it is an image. As he observes in his poetic monologue, 'A SPECIES IN EXTREMITIES. AT ODDS WITH ITS ENVIRONMENT. A CLASSIC CASE. MUTATE. OR FACE YOUR FATE.'[2] Meanwhile, parallel to this text, we are offered interventions or 'Takes' which seem to be the author's own comments. So, here, the 'takes' voice observes:

> READ THAT ANY GIVEN SPECIES REDUCED BY MORE THAN HALF. REDUCED TO PEERING INTO EXTINCTION. STARTS TO MUTATE. SAY EACH MUTATION IS A NEW IDEA ABOUT COMING TO GRIPS. MOST OF THEM ARE RATHER REDUNDANT LIKE TWO TAILS OR A THIRD BALL. BUT THEY REPRESENT A CERTAIN EFFORT. AT THIS POINT A GIVEN SPECIES BLOWS ITS CREATIVE WAD . . . AND THERE IS THAT BEAVER THAT KNOWS IT'S ALL OVER BUT THE SHOUTING. THIS DUDE IS A HEAVYWEIGHT. THE RAT WHO STANDS PAT WHILE THEY PLAY NEARER MY GOD TO THEE. AND THEN GOES DOWN. VERY RARE. HE IS ROMMEL RETREATING ACROSS AFRICA. HE IS VON STROHEIM SHOOTING GREED.'[3]

It is not hard to see in this an artist's defence of his own activities – a claim for the moral force of the imagination and for the power of a certain formalism.

Decline may be best opposed by creating shapes and other necessities. The act of resistance, of desperate invention, may itself be the origin of whatever redemption is available. And the very lyricism of much of the language in the piece is itself offered as a value, a way of teasing harmony out of the disharmonious. But it is not a harmony which can be sustained. The Beaver is required to stutter. His eloquence is not a perfect defence any more than the dam which he builds can sustain its perfect geometry against the forces which oppose it. His mate apparently dies, plunging to the muddy bottom, clutching a stone. He struggles on, though Breuer undercuts the sentimentality with an ending which parodies the Hollywood cliché.

For Bonnie Marranca, editor of an edition of his plays, the fable is concerned with the artist's struggle to express himself. It is in effect about writer's block and the stuttering delivery of the Beaver, ironically referred to in the title, is his struggle to articulate himself, to break down the dam which is an obstacle to his creativity. And certainly the 'takes' advise us that 'B Beaver is a stutterer. He's a small commuter train of split personalities all reading for his part. Out of sync.'[4] But the process of artistic creation seems secondary to his ironic, comically reductive, struggle to make sense out of an existence whose absurdities repeatedly strike him. He attempts to explain and control experience by discussing it in terms of science, mathematics and even language – much, presumably, as do those people whom he represents. But collapse is inevitable: 'DAM COLLAPSES. CURTAINS FALL. YIKES. EXPLODES. ACROSS THE FRAME. THE PIECE. THE ANIMATION.'[5] The existence which the text reduces to the simple formula, 'EAT. CRAP. SCREW. CROAK', a Beckettian minimalism, exerts its inexorable power – 'NOTHING STOPS. IT.'[6] The full stops constantly inhibit even the continuities of grammatical structure.

The influence of Beckett seems clear in the combination of perception and ironic vision, contradictory actions and simple lyricism. Thus the voice of the Text observes: 'WAKE UP WITH JOY IN MY HEART. I COME ALIVE NO MATTER WHAT I DO. ITS KILLING ME. RIGHT. WRITE. BEING OF SOUND. STOP.'[7] There are passages of sustained comic lyricism in which the pointless battle aspires to a certain dignity but even these are ironised by the context.

In the early 1960s Philip Roth observed that as 'reality' became daily more bizarre so it challenged the status and creative resources of art. The response of such figures as Wilson and Foreman was to reconstitute the real by means of the unreal. And if society threatened to turn the individual into a simple object then, like the photorealist artist, they responded in kind. Thus Duane Hanson's and De Andrea's frozen figures suggested a crucial and definitional absence of being while Wilson and Foreman, through a choreography of the body and its environment, redirected the attention to consciousness as a critical dimension. Breuer's strategy was somewhat different. He works through parody, ironic allegory and a subversive pop art humour.

The Shaggy Dog Animation received its première at the New York Shakespeare Festival Public Theatre in 1978. Much longer than the other two parts of the trilogy (as a shaggy dog story should be) it is a sustained comic account of love, turned ironic by transposition into the love of a dog for its master. Rose, the dog, plots against her master's wife – an ageing actress whose appearances are limited to small parts in Bromo Seltzer advertisements and playing the Wicked Witch of the West in *The Wizard of Oz*. The story is a kind of pastiche of Hollywood schmaltz and the hip novel. The story of the love-affair, mythicised in song as well as celebrated in the imagination of the animal, becomes an account of need and loss and entropy which, despite the humour, is offered as a comment on human relationships. It is also a patent send-up of the Marin County sensibility: 'WHAT CAN I DO. I GO INTO MYSELF. I BECOME SELF

INVOLVED. I TRY TO BE SELF EFFACING. BUT THAT'S SELF DEFEATING. I INDULGE IN SELF RECRIMINATION. BUT ALL THAT DOES IS MAKE ME MORE SELF CENTRED. I LONG TO BE SELF TRANSCENDING. BUT THIS BECOMES TOO SELF DELUDING. WHICH BRINGS US TO THE BRINK OF SELF DESTRUCTION. WHICH BECOMES A SUBJECT OF SELF CONCERN. AM I BEING SELF INDULGENT.'[8] Later this speech surfaces as a part of *A Prelude to Death in Venice* where it occurs in the context of a character in the process of mental breakdown.

The Shaggy Dog Animation is that rarity in modern American theatre – an extraordinarily funny comedy. It parodies genre movies, radio, popular music and the sentimentalities of a society hyped on self-fulfilment. It is a collage of incidents and forms and is presented with all the showbiz verve and brittle performatics which are equally its subject. Its production values – its use of stereo-sound, of pop groups, of a high-gloss presentation – are those of the world which it sets out to capture and satirise. Thus Breuer is reported to have remarked that, 'You can't say "I love you" anymore without an echo chamber . . . [it] has captured the myth of the expression more clearly than the human voice.'[9] Experience comes to us, he seems to suggest, precisely through the refractions of the media – a point equally made by Mamet in *Sexual Perversity in Chicago* which also deliberately mimics and parodies the forms of popular myth and the techniques of the popular arts. And the transposition of human behaviour onto animals need not be traced back to the beast fables, the stories of Kafka or even the allegory of George Orwell's *Animal Farm*. It is already embedded in the national (and indeed the international) psyche in the form of the film and television cartoon: LeeBreuer's Shaggy Dog is perhaps no more than a version of Charles Schultz's Snoopy who has stumbled into the adult world of tranquillisers, kinky sex, downtown language and uptown morals. He is close kin to the quasi-pornographic 1970s version of Fritz the Cat. The two previous elements of the trilogy seem reticent by comparison. In *The Shaggy Dog Animation* he utilises music, singers, puppets and a set which includes a giant radio dial and multiple microphones. The use of puppets, indeed, implies a comment on the degree to which perceptions and emotions are manipulated – most especially sex which is by turns sentimentalised and rendered in porno-graphic terms as part of a process of conscious and cynical manipulation. To this end the performance is scattered with references to the names of consumer products, television programmes and commercials.

To Bonnie Marranca, the play is a feminist work expressing the plight of women who are seen as the primary victims of such reductiveness. It is 'a mature feminist statement of remarkable metaphoric and philosophi-cal richness. It demonstrates the awakening of consciousness.'[10] If this is so, all that Rose, the dog, learns is her incapacity to escape the need which

love expresses: 'WE GO. ON. MISSING. THE POINT. BABY. ONE MORE TIME.
LEARNING TO LOVE. NOT LEARNING. TO LOVE LOSING. BABY. OH YEAH.
LEARNING. TO TRANSMUTE. LOSS TO GAIN. BABY.'[11] But there is perhaps
evidence of some resistance, an understanding that love of a kind can
mean the obliteration of identity: 'WE ARE THE SECRET SPOUSES OF
MANKIND. WE ARE AN IMAGE PERCEIVED ONLY IN THE MIRROR OF A MASTER'S
EYE. WE ARE A SELF. IDENTIFIED ONLY BY SELFLESSNESS. WE ARE THE LAWFUL
WEDDED SPECIES OF THE RARE. FOR WE ARE NOTHING. BUT A SPECIES OF
DEVOTION. AND DEVOTION TO ANOTHER ANIMAL IS THE TEMPTATION OF THE
FLESH TO KILL THE SOUL. GOING TO THE DOGS IS CHOOSING PAIN FOREVER.'[12]
As in so much of Breuer's work, the pun and the cliché are seen as
offering instructive truths. Love becomes an escape from truth: 'SOME-
THING'S WRONG WITH US. YOU SEE. I DON'T THINK OUR EYES ARE MADE TO
SEE THE LIGHT, YOU SEE. NOT ONE OF US BELIEVES WE'LL DIE ALONE. BY
DITCH. BY SIDE OF ROAD. ALONE. TONGUE OUT. NOT FOR A LAST DRINK. FOR A
LAST KISS. DEAR. JOHN. EYES WIDE OPEN. NOT TO SEE TRUTH. BUT TO SEE YOU.
JOHN. DEAR. NOT ONE OF US BELIEVES WE'LL DIE LIKE DOGS.'[13]

So if pop culture forms and images suggest a level at which we are
manipulated, they also hint at a potential for truth never quite evacuated
from the cliché, the sentimental gesture or the euphemism. Thus Rose
accuses herself of being doomed to see only the surface, like the media
world to which she is drawn, but the very moment of that perception
gives birth to a sudden awareness of an alternative possibility. By
presenting a two-dimensional, strip-cartoon world Breuer ironically
makes the absence of that third dimension more palpable. The brilliance
of Breuer's animations lies not only in their comic appearance and
fundamental seriousness, but in a profound ambivalence, honestly and
lyrically expressed, about the means whereby we choose to conceal from
ourselves the nature of our suffering – means which may both exacerbate
that situation and offer some final consolation. In that sense the theatre is
for him a moral instrument.

As Breuer has said,

> Being an artist is a real thing. Loving, being afraid of dying is a real thing.
> But I think there are very few real things that I really understand. What I
> understand very well are the clothes that they hide in, the coats and hats,
> the illusions and the covers: this is the theatre of the world, this is the
> illusion of the world, and my part as a craftsman is to understand illusion,
> to be able to create illusion. In a way, I feel that in world terms my job is to
> be a magician, in an attempt to perceive truth.[14]

And in a sense his next work, *A Prelude to Death in Venice*, was precisely concerned with this, exploring the processes whereby the real is constructed,
by the artist or by a self increasingly vulnerable and increasingly alarmed.

15.   Bill Raymond with 'John', puppet by Linda Hartinian in the Mabou Mines
production of *A Prelude to Death in Venice*. Written and directed by Lee Breuer.

A Prelude to Death in Venice grew out of the third part of *The Shaggy
Dog Animation*. It was first performed in New York and then at the Mark
Taper Forum in 1979. Further revised, it finally arrived at the Public
Theatre in 1980. It won an Obie for Breuer as writer and for Bill
Raymond as actor. It consists of a 'dialogue' between John Greed, a

puppet, and a character called Bill, as they stand between two pay phones on a New York street. In an elaborate Playwright's Note Breuer explained how he saw the production working:

> In the production by Mabou Mines the performer Bill Raymond attempted to show the character Bill's fragmented personality by abrupt vocal changes that bordered on completely different characterizations. For the puppet, John Greed, there were basically three personae: In speaking to 'Johns Anonymous' and Bill, John was a 'little junkie' – a bit of a parody of the New York method style of film acting from Marlon Brando to Peter Falk to John Cassavetes. Vocal range was high, anxious and cloudy. In speaking to his girl friends and their tape machines, John used a macho bedside 'come-on'. In speaking to his mother, John was a campy little number – arch, petulant with the trace of a Ronald Colman affectation. For Bill, Bill Raymond basically used himself as should any actor doing the role. His Bill Morris was a contemporary film agent – flat, underplayed. This reading always walked the line between straight and a put on. Bill Raymond built the concluding monologue around the idea of a schizophrenia becoming progressively more overt. The speech touched upon the previous characterizations and contained a level of vulnerability that was almost infantile.[15]

The puppet was loosely based on Japanese Bunraku figures but, as manipulated by Bill Raymond, became an extension of his personality. Indeed for Breuer, 'Performer and puppet were in fact aspects of a single person', so that aside from 'this "Doppelgänger" effect the image became a study of manipulation which had its textual reverberations'. Thus Raymond 'made a visual pun out of "I'm beside myself" by leaning over to put his head beside John's'.[16]

The production's main metaphor was to be that of film-making – with the title being an allusion both to the film version of Thomas Mann's novel and perhaps a reference to Venice, California. Sound amplification was, he explained, to be 'overt' so that it would resemble a film soundtrack. In other words a basic strategy of the play was to expose the way in which 'reality' is created and, as Breuer underlined, this 'idea of "producing" reality was demonstrated by the animating and de-animating of John'. The effect, he suggested, was 'related to Brechtian "distancing"'.[17] By the same token the set was deliberately distorted, the wheel of a police car suddenly appearing as a huge object dominating Bill and his puppet. Again the reference was to the distortions created in the cinema by the use of wide-angled lenses. Beyond that it operated as an expressionistic device extending Bill's fragmenting psyche and his paranoid fears onto the *mise-en-scène*.

A brilliant *tour de force* by Bill Raymond, the play is extremely funny. And if it is offered as an account of a fragmenting psyche it also stands as

Breuer's account of the process of artistic creation. As he insisted in an interview, 'you are never one thing . . . you are constantly giving off energy the way an atom would radiate. All of this energy is characters.'[18] In a play partly concerned with the process of manipulation he seems simultaneously to emphasise the degree to which the writer/director creates his own reality and is himself the voice of influences beyond his control. The wilful distortion of perspective underlines the extent to which the real evades the observer. As he has said of his own career, 'The way I've chosen, I think, is the *via negativa*. Through my "Animation" plays (the trilogy consisting of *Red Horse*, 1970; *B Beaver*, 1974; and *Shaggy Dog*, 1978) I have eliminated as not true the Horse, the Beaver, the Dog and in *Prelude*, John, so far. This has taken twelve years. What I now find is that at least the truth is that it is not that.' The theatre thus becomes 'a way of saving the self . . . It is an offering and a hope that there will be a response.'[19]

Breuer's achievement in the theatre lies in the success with which his essentially simple conceits are made to express a range of subtle thought. A series of modern comic myths, they address the contemporary sensibility with considerable humour and energy, both being apparent in his more recent work with doo-wop capella groups (black close harmony groups) as in *Sister Suzy's Cinema*. His puns, his parodies, his openness to the full range of the popular arts, fuse to create powerful metaphors which tap into central fears and aspirations. In part the effect of transposing those anxieties and hopes onto an animal plane is to expose their fatuity, their mannered and pretentious nature, but these are not unsympathetic works and the humour is by no means evasive. They are in a sense concerned with the degree to which we manufacture our own pain, our own fictional models of existence – a fact underlined by the author's own intrusions into the text. The prevailing tone is perhaps that of pathos, the posturing of the human animal being undercut precisely by the simple device of taking that animality literally. But the sympathy is real enough and, paradoxically, humanism retained its hold on the American theatre of the 1970s precisely through these inventive fables, monologues which nonetheless contrive to compress a whole range of human experiences and cultural realities into a form which eschews the conventional context for that humanism. Character is detached from voice, as in Wilson's work (frequently a number of actors and actresses will voice a single speech). Past and present are not held apart by narrative tension. No conventional notion of morality is advanced, no social responsibility claimed. At the same time Breuer's works are celebrations of variousness and of a poetic sensibility which transcends circumstance. They propose the existence of a resistant self, under pressure but committed to the business of self-invention. He is a romantic set loose in a world of technology. He is a social satirist who is nonetheless drawn to the very things which he chooses to satirise. His use of popular culture is not wholly ironic. Even its banalities express something which he is not inclined to reject. If his are knowing nursery stories then that combination of knowledge and innocence is offered as essential and is certainly definitional of his work. They are self-conscious works and foreground that self-consciousness as a crucial element of their aesthetic and moral perspective. They strip off the romantic veils. But they also incorporate a certain naivety, a directness of effect, as an equally crucial element of their aesthetic and as an assertion of the virtue of imaginative transcendence and a childlike openness to the world. Their weakness, however, lies in the same area. The form denies him access to the complexities which so often freeze Miller's characters into inaction while the simplifications offer a vividness and a clarity which has difficulty making room for ambiguity.

Performance theatre in the 1970s seems to have turned far more towards private visions than did that of the 1960s. Collaborative texts designed to operate on the sensibility of an audience perceived as a community have given way to private texts designed to trigger individual responses in individual members of the audience. The emotional has been superseded by the cerebral. The iconographic significance of presence, seen in the 1960s as the root of authenticity because of its reinforcement of shared experience, has now become important to the degree that the personal perception of events consisting of discrete moments becomes the subject. Coherences only form in the mind of the observer. There is no a priori meaning. The private myths/obsessions of Wilson, Foreman and Breuer are offered to the audience as means of triggering personal moments of self-discovery through an openness to the reality of their surroundings or through momentary images which spark activity in the brain.

Modernism tended to involve the imposition of form on a threatening chaos. This work is liable to see experience as inherently discontinuous, to celebrate the moment and to retreat from a model of art as controlling mechanism. It deals with fragmentation not, as the modernists were prone to do, by imposing a structure of myth or by seeing language as providing a kind of tensile strength to a potentially dislocating reality, but by proposing the self as the only synthesising force, and in this respect the links back to romanticism, via surrealism, seem clear. For while ostensibly isolating moments or objects and while celebrating the power of the individual mind to invent a series of separate worlds, there is a sense in which this vision implies a fundamental harmony, a total environment in which the self's concern with its own procedures transcends its apparent privatism. Which is to say that there is a risk that liberalism may have been exchanged for mysticism. The narrative thrust of realism, with its implications of historicism, of rational progress, of character as a product of environment or an assertive will struggling to define itself against the deconstructive nature of biological process or the power of material fact, defers to a fundamentally different model. The question of self-definition becomes internal and secondary. Though the art of Wilson, Foreman and Breuer is fiercely autobiographical, it emerges less from a confident self than from a storehouse of images and visions which that self has absorbed and now spills out in an attempt to define its own qualities. Like the sub-atomic particle which only has a momentary existence when struck by other such particles, this self exists only in the light of its own collisions with the external world. The images become the evidence of singularity but, gone in an instant, they have to be constantly renewed. This is equally true of the process of Wilson's plays, or of those of Foreman or Breuer.

Which is not to say that this strategy has nothing to tell us of the world. It is, after all, a strategy into which such writers and performers have been manœuvred by an experience of art and theatre which has left them dissatisfied. Personal style is always the contract negotiated between the individual and the world in response to those other contracts which seem to have been invalidated by experience. At the same time, perhaps, as we speed up in our rush towards the end of the twentieth century, we can detect a certain *fin-de-siècle* mood – a desire to aestheticise experience as finally the only way to rescue it from itself and since this was the logic which had led to modernism perhaps a certain circle is in process of closing.

Such figures as these can be accused of recoiling from history, taking a private voyage through times inimical to man. And their route to truth or truths plainly takes the inward path. The public world which had engaged much American theatre in the 1960s is excluded. There is no suggestion, I think, in the work of any of these writers/producers that America was meanwhile slipping into the chaos of Vietnam or struggling with the revelations of Watergate (except, perhaps, in Lee Breuer's sense of experience as fiction). The bewilderment that many felt about a lost America, and which surfaces in the work of Van Itallie, Shepard and Mamet, no less than Albee, Miller and Williams, fails to penetrate the carapace of art which proposes an unproblematic relationship between the self and its environment. They were products of the culture of narcissism not because they were hucksters for inner truth or the superior reality of macrobiotics, yoga or the Moonies but because the presumptive authority of the individual mind and imagination went unchallenged. It is an art without tension. Precise and rigorous in execution, demanding in the concentration which it requires, it is nonetheless flaccid in the degree to which all objects, all experiences, all actions are drained of any meaning not given to them by the questing mind.

They are accommodated not to normative values but to a simple plan of existence in which crucial distinctions are liable to be lost. Transformations of consciousness may of course effect transformation of experience, though the surrealists knew that it was necessary to put an occasional thumb on the scale of history. And there is no reason why the theatre any more than art should be concerned with anything other than its own processes, with texture, tone, configuration. In Foreman's case, at least, however, there are hints of an objective beyond this which is never realised. Wilson speaks falteringly about his own aims and the source of his own images – a stuttering attempt at explanation which offers itself as a primary justification of this approach. Foreman speaks confusingly about his objectives, though still more lucidly than he does through some of his plays. But both men choose as their target less a world which has the power to warp and destroy than those cultural assumptions which coerce us into receiving experience in the way we do. Their work is more an attack on the conventions of art which have trained us to see objects, events and experiences in a certain way than a sceptical account of a reality presumed to be independent of the mind which perceives it. In that sense, perhaps, it is anti-theatre. Certainly Susan Sontag was to argue as much. Indeterminacy of meaning becomes one more defence against authority in all guises. If no one can be trusted then the only legitimacy lies in anarchy – seen not as chaos but as a rigorous individualism – a hint, maybe, of a certain nostalgia for American values. Perhaps this is the true defence against those who see such writers and performers as wholly apolitical. The authority respected was the self. No other could be accepted and hence they rebel against what it became fashionable to regard as the terrorism of meaning.

But for Lee Breuer, as for Wilson and Foreman, the alliance between event and observer is if anything more crucial than it had been for Julian Beck or Richard Schechner, for they wished to claim the individual members of their audience as co-authors of their texts and in that they assumed a relationship which could triumph over fragmentation and alienation. The language of theatre, the coherence of the image, could, it seems, still imply the possibility of contact. Thus when Lee Breuer asked himself, 'Why a script? What kind of speech act is a theatre text?', his answer was 'Asking for love. That's the precise answer . . . It is an offering and a hope that there will be a response.'[20] Beneath the surface, then, beyond the atomised moments of experience and the opaque images there still lurks a familiar American piety. Once more, with feeling, it is Love, Love, Love.

What are we to make of some of these developments in theatre? In a sense they rest on a premise which is not dissimilar to that implicit in Walt Whitman's work; that is, the self (or versions of the self) is moved to the centre of attention while that self's authority over the reader/viewer is denied. The poem/the play becomes a means to an end – that end being the liberation of the mind and imagination of the reader/viewer. The strategy seems to be to deconstruct the principal elements of theatre in order to create a pressure for reconstruction on the part of the audience. Thus dramatic character is disassembled and linguistic coherence consciously dislocated in favour of what seems at times a literal aphasia (literal, certainly, in the case of Christopher Knowles made a crucial figure by Robert Wilson). Conflict, assumed to be definitional by the textbooks, is discarded. The social, the psychological and the political are for the most part displaced. The physical presence of the actor is not eliminated but the full potential of that presence is vitiated. Dialogue defers to monologue (sometimes, admittedly, distributed among different players). Illusionism is abandoned; in a sense in some of these works the 'actors' are neither seeming nor being, in that they neither play specific roles nor incorporate their off-stage personalities simply transferred to the public arena (a central tactic of the performance theatre of the 1960s). In other words we are confronted with a series of absences, refusals, denials and incompletions.

However, these are not the vacancies of more conventional, if interesting, work, such as Arthur Kopit's *Wings*, Mark Medoff's *Children of a Lesser God* or Michael Cristofer's *The Shadow Box*, in which spaces begin to open up in the fabric of existence because of the natural processes of mortality (here, specifically, the characters suffer from a stroke, from deafness and from cancer) – wounds which are ultimately healed by the grace of the writer's attention. Certainly Kopit courageously attempts to reproduce the terrible gulf between consciousness and expression which is a literal fact of those suffering from cerebral haemorrhage and thereby touches on the ironies of communication itself (ironies underlined by Roland Barthes). But that gulf is acknowledged only to be bridged by the playwright and the actor. Such plays exist to confront and still the terror. They may, as in Kopit's case, have been born out of personal experience but the personal origin becomes incidental. For Wilson, in particular, but also in some degree for Foreman, the personal does not only function as stimulus. Since their work is in some degree an interrogation of the self, a public presentation and hence to some extent a validation of private images, that privileged experience is deliberately deployed for inspection. In the work of Spalding Gray, Meredith Monk and other monologists this is more acutely so. But the spaces in these performances are not merely designed to mimic mental process; they invite the individual members of the audience into the work on the level of the mind as, in the 1960s, they had been incorporated on the level of the body and the emotions. In that sense they doubly reinforce an individualism seen as profoundly suspect by the performance artists of an earlier decade. An anarchy of the senses gives way in this work to an anarchy of the mind whereby, despite its origin in a public event, meaning ultimately becomes the hegemony of the self. And, indeed, it is not hard to see this as an intensely conservative impulse, aesthetically radical but socially reactionary. But this is beside the point. The recovery at which such works aim is not a primal unity nor yet a set of social values but a presumptive right to shape experience and to become aware of the processes whereby that shaping occurs, and, if pressed, Foreman, certainly, but I suspect also Wilson and Breuer, would see this as a necessary prerequisite for social change. Thus what seems like an authoritarian form – the imposition of private images and ideas – is offered as a key to a certain freedom. That, at any rate, seems in part the objective.

Neither are these performances quite as solemn as this perhaps suggests. Foreman's sense of fun and even erotic exuberance is clear and, if it were not, then Kate Manheim, his principal actress, would tend to enforce it. Certainly his somewhat subversive approach to *Die Fledermaus* makes this apparent. Likewise, Lee Breuer's work has never been offered as simply a privatist account. Energy, invention and humour have always been key elements in his theatre, apparent not only in his *Animations* but also in his more recent work with the doo-wop capella group in *Sister Suzy's Cinema*. And, as Herbert Blau has pointed out, in *Blooded Thought: Occasions of Theatre, A Prelude to Death in Venice* freely acknowledges the potentially destructive side of a solipsism which does not always offer itself for incorporation and transformation by the audience. But it is not a self-doubt which has proved disabling and indeed all of these theatre practitioners have moved in the direction of plenitude, placing music at the centre of their work and being increasingly tempted by spectacle as something more than an ironic gesture. Like the brilliant Serapian theatre group in Vienna they have worked to fuse private and public images in such a way as to create a field of meaning to be specifically validated or denied by the individual observer. Plainly the work is uneven, while Wilson and Foreman in particular have been all too readily absorbed by an international cultural elite anxious to sustain its status. Schechner accuses them of formalism, as does Theodore Shank in his study of American alternative theatre and it is not hard to see what they mean, but, as Alain Robbe-Grillet remarks in his essay on 'Some

Outdated Notions', this is a term which can easily be inverted. Thus he suggests that,

> the word 'formalism' . . . in its pejorative sense . . . should, in fact – as Nathalie Sarraute has pointed out – only be applied to novelists who pay too much attention to their 'content', who, in order to make it easier to understand, purposely reject every sophistication of style in their writing that might possibly offend or surprise: to those, in fact, who adopt a form – a mould – which has stood the test of time, but which has lost all its strength and all its life. They are formalists because they have accepted a ready-made, rigid form which is no more than a formula, and because they cling to this fleshless carcass.

Formalism, in other words, is, at least in part, a matter of perspective. And this is a useful reminder. Thus it is that Robbe-Grillet recalls a Russian cartoon in which, on seeing a zebra, one hippopotamus remarks to another, 'Look, that's formalism!'

Whether Wilson, Foreman and Breuer are zebras or hippopotamuses, they were, for more than a decade, what passed for avant-garde theatre in an America which itself grew increasingly detached from the public issues of the 1960s and the shared intimacies which had then been proposed as a route to private transcendence and social regeneration. The 1970s tried another track, another version of the romantic dream. Having tried the dissolution of boundaries, the unleashing of the libido and the celebration of community, now the self was reinvented, the swirl of movement stilled and the human mind once more made the creator of its own universe. As ever, theatre, sensitive to shifts in cultural pressure, both responded to this change and participated in it. The result can only be characterised as formalism if the process of creation is felt to be inherently inferior to the fictions thereby created, or if the ideographs of this theatre are designed to resist the mind invited to resolve them. And even then mystery (though not, perhaps, mystification) has its presumptive rights.

PART IV

The playwright

INTRODUCTION

Despite the reaction against the writer which for a time typified some branches of the theatrical avant-garde in America, the period since 1940 has seen the emergence of a number of remarkable talents. Indeed, the figure rejected in favour of communally generated works was quickly reinstated even if in the process a healthy demystification of his role of writer had taken place. The careers of Tennessee Williams, Arthur Miller and Edward Albee are dealt with in another volume. Here, writers are, for the most part, examined in relation to the groups with which they collaborated or the movements to which they acknowledged their affinity. What follows in this section, however, is a consideration of two of the most significant and powerful voices of the 1970s and 80s – Sam Shepard and David Mamet. By the very nature of a study of this kind there is regrettably no space to offer a similar analysis of other figures, no less worthy of attention, writers such as John Guare, Lanford Wilson and Terence McNally, or emerging talents such as Wallace Shawn, Christopher Durang and others, but their achievement is equally manifest.

In many ways the sharp distinctions which once existed between Broadway, Off and Off-Off Broadway and regional theatre have blurred in the last twenty-five years. Lanford Wilson, whose career began Off-Off Broadway, has emerged as a figure whose elegies for a lost America have an appeal across a wide range of audiences. Terence McNally, likewise, has moved from an anti-war play like *Next* (1967) to Broadway farce, in the form of *The Ritz* (1975). The awards that have gone to both Shepard and Mamet show the extent to which they, too, have moved with relative ease between the avant-garde and the mainstream. In a sense that fluidity is a primary inheritance of the changes wrought in the institutional structure and aesthetic presumptions of the American theatre. The accomplishment of such writers as Shepard and Mamet is considerable. Though the influence of Tennessee Williams and

Edward Albee, of Beckett and Pinter, is clear in their work, the fact is that their voices are very obviously their own, both men incorporating qualities to be found in the allied arts of music and painting, and creating thereby a language of the theatre at times lyrical and at times disturbingly fragmented but always powerful and original. They are, without doubt, two of the finest playwrights of their generation and that not merely in the context of the American theatre.

8 Sam Shepard

Sam Shepard is very much a product of the Off-Off Broadway movement. His first plays to be performed – *Cowboys* and *The Rock Garden* –
were staged at Theatre Genesis, in October 1964, while his work was
subsequently performed at La Mama, Caffe Cino and the Judson Poets'
Theatre, before securing production by the Performance Group, Yale
Repertory and even Joe Papp. He has received Obie awards, scripted
Antonioni's *Zabriskie Point*, turned movie actor and, in 1979, won the
Pulitzer Prize. He is, in short, probably Off-Off Broadway's most
successful writer, a status achieved during the 1960s and 70s, the latter of
which he characterised as a time in which 'you could hear the sound of
America cracking open and crashing into the sea'.[1] Convinced that
'Everybody's caught up in a fractured world that they can't even see',[2]
he has seemingly set himself both to expose those fragments as the
components of a potential apocalypse and to close the gaps which breed
alienation. He tackles the new chiliastic myths, combining them with
other myths scrambled together from the media and his own array of
personal images. As his introductory note to *The Unseen Hand* indicates,
for those caught up in the 'fractured world . . . What's happening to
them is unfathomable but they have a suspicion. Something unseen is
working on them. Using them. They have no power and all the time
they believe they're controlling the situation.'[3] His work both explores
and validates this paranoia as, at times, it seeks to find ways to transcend
it. He has the 1960s desire to make fragments cohere and the 1970s belief
that truth may ultimately lie in those fragments.

Sam Shepard is an intuitive writer. His plays are inspired by, and
elaborate on, animating images. These images begin beyond words but
words prove the primary refracting device through which they can be
perceived. The images are not static. The world he dramatises is protean;
it changes its shape. It is typified by a dynamism or perhaps an entropy
that he sets himself to capture. His work seems dominated by a sense of
loss but equally by a desire to identify and even urge a return to
consonance.

He began writing in his late teens, with little experience of theatre. In
California he had written a pseudo-Tennessee Williams play 'about
some girl who got raped in a barn and her father getting mad at her or

221

something',[4] but it was the coincidence of arriving in New York at a time when the Off-Broadway movement was starting that created a climate in which he could work. He had read few plays, *Waiting for Godot* being an exception, and as a consequence 'didn't have any idea about how to shape an action into what is seen'.[5] Somewhat disingenuously he has suggested that 'the so-called originality of the early work just comes from ignorance'.[6] It is, to be sure, characterised by a willingness to submit to images provoked by drugs or illness, and he resisted reshaping or subordinating these images to a rational structuring. But it was less a case of ignorance than of a faith, perhaps an undue faith, in the authenticity and authority of the spontaneous vision. This was the source of the sometimes startling freshness of his work but also of a certain wilful hermeticism.

Working as a waiter at the Village Gate, a night-club, he met Ralph Cook, then the head-waiter but shortly thereafter artistic director of Theatre Genesis, a playwrights' workshop theatre sponsored by St Mark's-in-the-Bowerie. When one of his plays was favourably reviewed by Michael Smith of the *Village Voice* his career was launched, Smith himself directing the first production of *Icarus's Mother* at the Caffe Cino in November 1965. Smith's description of Shepard's early work as 'a gestalt theatre which evokes the existence behind behavior'[7] is gnomic but not without relevance in so far as he does seem to concern himself with dramatising images which spring from the individual and group subconscious and which are reconstructed as popular myth. He tends to plunder the world of popular music and film because they generate virtually the only common fund of images and because they embody that substitution of style for substance, of surface for depth, which seems both an evasive strategy and a possible source of energy. In a sense he wishes to reconstitute an inner world by deploying those gestures, images and forms which only seem detached from the anxieties which generate them.

Shepard's early plays tend to elaborate single images or image clusters. *Chicago*, which he wrote in one day, is a kind of reverie in which the central figure, who for much of the play occupies a bath, invents a world of incidents, using language to pull them together into a coherent if barely rational whole. There are echoes of popular music and suggestions of clichéd figures; and in the apparent separation of the two main characters a sense of loss and collapse. But the play never resolves itself into metaphor. The fragments are held in a kind of tension. Indeed, Shepard's early plays, in many ways imperfect, make a virtue of the indefinite. He is interested in resonances that cannot be wholly controlled. As he explained later, if his was indeed a theatre of images then when you talk about images, an image can be seen without looking at anything – you can see something in your head, or you can see something on stage, or you can see things that don't appear on stage. You know. The fantastic thing about theatre is that it can make something be seen that's invisible, and that's where my interest in theatre is – that you can be watching this thing happening with actors and costumes and light and set and language, and even plot, and something emerges from beyond that, and that's the image part that I'm looking for, that's the sort of added dimension.[8]

He was interested in particular in the inner life of the individual, the suppressed world of desires, images, myths; he was concerned with a poetic sensibility turned into prose by the process of daily experience and with the expression of that experience through a language drained of symbolic content and inadequate to the task. The experience that he sought to express bore the imprint of his upbringing in South Pasadena, California: as he explained, the images 'come from all kinds of things, they come from the country, they come from that particular sort of temporary society that you find in Southern California, where nothing is permanent, where everything could be knocked down and it wouldn't be missed, and the feel of impermanence that comes from that – that you don't belong to any particular culture'.[9] So *Chicago* begins, apparently incongruously, with a recitation of the Gettysburg Address, introduced by a policeman, which constitutes an ironic commentary on what follows. Experience comes in fragments. If they threaten to cohere it is by an incremental or associative process. Shards of experience overlap and create patterns whose suggestive force is generated by their interaction. Not even past and present are held reassuringly apart. Dreams, visions, fears and memories have a status scarcely subordinate to that of the supposed realism of the sets. It is a world in some sense not remote from that of another Californian writer, Nathanael West in *The Day of the Locust* and not merely in the sense that he too was concerned with the incongruous juxtaposition of levels and kinds of experience and fascinated with a culture which subsisted on style, role and insubstantial but powerful images. For Shepard also shares West's apocalypticism.

In *Icarus's Mother* the dominant image is of nuclear destruction. A group of people hold a barbecue in a public park as they await a firework display. High overhead a jet plane traces arabesques in the sky. Slowly the separate images coalesce. The plane, the fireworks, and the barbecue, fuse into a threat of destructive fire. Despite its apparent naturalistic setting, the play is concerned with potential, with a fear that lurks just below the surface of routine, so that when one of the characters describes the firework display his language simultaneously contains a reference to the apocalypse of which the display is itself merely an image:

> And the whole sky is lit. The sirens come and the screaming starts . . . And
> the tide breaks open and the waves go up! . . . The water goes up to fifteen
> hundred feet and smashes the trees, and the firemen come. The beach sinks
> below the surface. The seagulls drown in flocks of ten thousand . . . And
> the pilot bobbing in the very centre of a ring of fire that's closing in . . .
> His hand reaching for his other hand and the fire moves in and covers him
> up and the line of two hundred bow their heads and moon together with
> the light in the faces.[10]

It is an effect that Albee had equally reached for in *Quotations from
Chairman Mao Tse-Tung*. The image coheres in the mind of the observer
rather than the iconography of the stage. It relies on the reality of an
anxiety which transcends the apparently insignificant nature of the
action. Shepard becomes almost a painter, in the sense that West's Todd
Hacket was also a painter, constructing a canvas which is threatened by
its own logic.

Nor is reality singular in Shepard's work. Rather like the novelist
Robert Coover in *Pricksongs and Descants* he presents a series of alternative fictions which are not simply different perspectives on a single event
but different possibilities which coexist. Hence, for one character the
plane has written the formula $E = MC^2$ across the sky, while for another it
has exploded and crashed into the lake. Clearly there is an underlying
assonance, a unifying sense of terror and imminent destruction; there is,
in other words, an emotional consonance and it is that emotional,
intuitive realm which interested him. His plays are realistic on this
plane. He is concerned with the level on which people respond instinctively to their environment. That is not to say that he is looking
for the psychological motivations as a means of explaining their behaviour. This is one of the reasons that American actors and directors have
reportedly had such difficulty with his work. He is concerned with the
way in which private and public myths interact at a pre-conscious level.
Thus he has described the origin of this play as lying in a Fourth of July
celebration in which fireworks were exploding in the sky, 'And then
you've got this emotional thing that goes a long way back, which creates
a certain kind of chaos, a kind of terror.'[11] Asked whether *Icarus's Mother*
was not in effect a political play, he responded by attempting to relate it
to what he called 'the emotional context' in which people moved,
explaining that 'people in New York are cutting themselves down every
day of the week – from the inside, you know, but the conditions come
from the outside. Junk, heroin and all that stuff is a social condition and
it's also an emotional response to the society they're living in'.[12]

Structurally, his plays owe something to his interest in music.

Shepard's father was a musician and he himself plays guitar, piano and drums. He has written scores for his own works and regularly plays jazz, which exists as image and structural principle in a number of his plays, as well as constituting a literal feature. The plays improvise around a central image as a musician will around a basic theme. The language is at times deliberately lyrical and mellifluous, at others consciously discordant. The characters exist primarily as voices, modulated tones. His stage directions tend to stress the manner of delivery, sound effects, volume, lighting levels and simple actions rather than psychological or even descriptive information about character. And the voices are orchestrated with an ear to mood and emotional pitch rather than to naturalistic models of character or conflicting psychological stances. Sometimes individual voices dominate; sometimes he is interested in the harmonics of the group, as visions cohere momentarily in agreed fictions or drift apart into contrapuntal tension.

Indeed, in works like *Melodrama Play*, *Mad Dog Blues* and *The Tooth of Crime* music plays an important role as an emotional trigger. As he has explained, 'I think music's really important, especially in plays and theatre – it adds a whole different kind of perspective, it immediately brings the audience to terms with an emotional reality. Because nothing communicates emotions better than music.'[13]

In a play like *Fourteen Hundred Thousand* the tensions exist equally on a stylistic level, as he juxtaposes a naturalistic scene (about the construction of bookshelves) with a deliberately non-naturalistic, heavily scored section (in which the virtues of a linear city are extolled in a language whose constrictive regularities offer an ironic commentary on its subject matter). But again the subject is, in a sense, subordinated to the pleasure he takes in controlling not merely language but sound (as the book-shelves are hammered into place or collapse to the ground) and light (precisely prescribed lighting changes take place). Indeed, he offers an oblique defence of his strategy in the form of a brief speech by one of the characters who sees the pleasure of collecting books precisely in terms of their size, shape and colour rather than their contents, 'With various sizes and shapes and groups together. Without concern for what they're about or what they mean to me and who wrote them when. Just in terms of size and shape and colour.'[14] The aesthetic is close to that of the minimalist artist, concerned with colour field, texture and form rather than narra-tive content or expressive symbol. To some degree he also seems to be suggesting that the pleasure lies in the process itself. He has the abstract expressionist's delight in the action of creation. Thus he has said of his work that it 'is not written in granite. It's like playing a piece of music. It goes out in the air and dissolves forever.'[15]

Shepard's plays, particularly the early ones, are by no means easy to follow. They work by an association of ideas. They hint at a satirical intent which is rarely sustained. Indeed, in his notes on *Melodrama Play* he insists that he is more interested in shifts in theatrical style than he is in its potential for social parody: 'A production of this play should not be aimed towards making it strictly satirical but more towards discovering how it changes from the mechanism of melodrama to something more sincere.'[16] So, too, in *La Turista*, in which a satirical account of American incapacity when confronted with Third World realities defers to a fascination with shifting styles, parodic gestures and myths which generate both action and character. To be sure, as in *Icarus's Mother*, there is a moment in which one character's description of sunburn begins to imply a more apocalyptic dimension:

> Everything burns and everything you touch is as hot as the sun . . . You stand in mid-air with space all around you. The ground is on fire. The breeze feels like boiling-hot water. The moon is just like the sun. You become a flame and dance in mid-air. The bottom is blue. The middle is yellow and changes to green. The top is red and changes to orange. The breeze dances with you. The flame reaches up and then shrinks and bursts into sparks. The ground bursts into flames and circles the breeze.[17]

The central image of sickness also has clear political implications, as does the transformation of the principal figure into a kind of monster. However, the play's central concern is with exploding the naturalistic surface which it presents in its opening minutes. What Shepard provides is a kaleidoscope of fictions, shifting identities, mythic roles and masks. Nothing is fixed. Characters change skin colour as readily as their clothes, rather as did the actors in the Open Theatre whose transformation exercises Shepard saw when he worked with that group. Time and space prove plastic. Theatrical assumptions about the reality of stage props are deliberately exposed as fraudulent and then reinstated as functional. The audience is directly addressed and the play ends with a comic-strip cartoon cliché as the central figure dives through the scenery (rather as in Jim Dine's happening) leaving a cut-out silhouette of his body in the wall – not so much escaping myth as being wholly absorbed by it.

Clearly these are plays, then, which operate principally on a non-rational, associative level and are not best approached through rational textual analysis. Indeed, as with happenings, they are in a sense designed to resist precisely such an approach. The characters do not exist in any conventional sense. They are confessedly theatrical figures, fictions. The plot is not of central importance. The language operates obliquely. It was, you will recall, John Hawkes who said, 'I began to write fiction on the assumption that the true enemies of the novel were plot, character, setting and theme, and having once abandoned these familiar ways of thinking about fiction, totality of vision or structure was really all that remained. And structure – verbal and psychological coherence – is still my largest concern as a writer.'[18] Much the same could be said of Sam Shepard's work in the theatre. Indeed, it would be surprising if the theatre proved resistant to the kind of pressures which Hawkes acknowledged. And Shepard was interested to some degree in texture, style, abstract form, much as contemporary musicians and artists were, remarking that 'I'm interested in exploring the writing of plays through attitudes derived from other forms such as music, painting, sculpture.'[19]

In her essay Susan Sontag had declared herself 'Against Interpretation', as Robbe-Grillet had resisted the literary speleologists who wished to propose a 'depth' to his work which was a denial of the surface. In a sense this is manifestly true of Shepard's early work. He, too, is interested in surface planes. Like Robbe-Grillet, in excluding conventional notions of character he may be reacting against the excesses of an arrogant humanism but he is simultaneously placing greater emphasis on the aesthetic collaboration of his audience. He is, indeed, concerned precisely with the processes of consciousness – his own, in so far as the plays are the product of images rooted in his own conscious and subconscious experience – and those of the individual members of the audience whose own efforts to impose form on the performance are themselves in some degree his subject. Their collaboration becomes a form of corroborative evidence. Thus even his deliberately simple stage sets are expressive of an aesthetic which relies on a subjective response from his audience, on their participation in a world of contemporary myth which is a modern equivalent of the mythological literateness of the ancient world. Shepard is fascinated by the world of the comic book, the movies, television, popular music. His images derive from this world and depend on it. The audience, to which his characters frequently appeal directly, is presumed by him to share a common stock of images, but while he depends on that shared knowledge he is not concerned with radically changing the nature of the relationship between performer and audience. In this regard, at least, he remains conventional and resistant to the more extreme attempts to create an environmental theatre, caricaturing their methods and insisting that

> An audience can sit in chairs and be watching something in front of them, and can be actively participating in the thing that's confronting them . . . And it doesn't necessarily mean that if an audience walks into the building and people are swinging from the rafters and spaghetti's thrown all over

them, or whatever the environment might be that they're participating the play is going to be any closer. In fact it might very well be less so, because of the defences that are put up as soon as that happens.[20]

To his mind the audience participation at which he aims is less facile, more intuitive and spontaneous. The opacity of some of his work is in large part a product of the circumstance of its creation; nor can he be absolved of a certain arrogant mystification, but beyond that there is also a desire to preserve a necessary mystery which resists that kind of analysis which would threaten to dissolve the self. Meaning, in his world, is not a given, not an a priori assumption on the part of the playwright. It is a construction of writer, performer and audience, and implicit in that assumption is an active collusion which insists on the pre-eminence of the imagination. The gnomic becomes in some sense a defence against a destructive rationalism which may threaten to dissolve art as, on a more immediate, practical level, in the form of political and moral hubris, it may one day threaten to dissolve all our realities. And that risk haunts his work.

Shepard's satirical intent strengthened with *Operation Sidewinder* (1970), which received its first performance at the Repertory Theatre of Lincoln Center, itself a sign of Shepard's arrival on the dramatic scene. It marks a clear change in his work as the vaguely perceived sense of menace becomes objectified and an implicit need to intervene, at the level of myth or reality, is proposed. It was, however, an intensification of his satirical impulse which did not prevent black students demanding its withdrawal from production at Yale. The play concerns an advanced computer in the shape of a giant sidewinder snake. Designed to identify and track UFOs, it is developed by the Air Force and then released by a Dr Strangelove-like creator to range at will in the nearby desert, absorbing information and creating its own selfhood. Unfortunately, when provoked by passing tourists it wraps itself around the voluptuous but simple-minded wife. The distraught husband is then shot dead by a member of a conspiracy which is seeking to drive the Air Force from the desert by putting drugs in a local reservoir. But the agents of this conspiracy, a group of Indians employed to facilitate the plan by a gang of militant urban blacks, though first dismembering the sidewinder, eventually take it to their retreat where it is incorporated into a ritual. The Spider Lady, a wizened old Indian shaman, has previously outlined the details of a myth according to which the material and spiritual needs of man had once been held in some kind of balance – the eventual disruption of this being marked by a struggle for possession of a giant spirit snake. The division of the snake – re-enacted in the play – had opened up a gulf from which sprang pain and an ignorance of that original primary unity. Now a Third World War is prophesied in which 'only materialistic people' need 'to make shelters. Those who are at peace in their own hearts already are in the great shelter of life. There is no shelter for evil. Those who take no part in the making of world division are ready to resume life in another world. They are all one – brothers. The war will be a spiritual conflict with material things. Material matters will be destroyed by spiritual beings who will remain to create one world and one nation under one power, that of the Creator.'[21] The play ends with the pure in spirit apparently taken up into a UFO and the military left presumably to confront their fate.

It is very much a play of its times. The fact of Vietnam, the contemporary stress on the body, on spiritual realisation, on the special insight of the primitive, on the compelling power of myth, on the ritualistic dimension of theatre, all find expression in one of the most powerful and consistent of Shepard's plays. Like Jean-Claude Van Itallie's *The Serpent*, this is a modern version of the creation myth, with the snake representing here a perverted form of knowledge but also a classic image of eternity and completion. The division of God from man stands as a paradigm of the division of man from man. But Shepard is more concerned with forging a contemporary myth in which the Fall is a consequence of banality rather than evil. The Young Man in the play who is presented as a ruthless killer had been turned into this by the steady erosion of hopes. Indeed, he himself describes the process which had led to an alienation which can apparently only be cured by violence or by drugs – in short through flirtation with the apocalypse. The speech is, in what is Shepard's most political play to date, an aria, a lament for a decade, for an America losing itself. It explains and enacts a return to identity and consonance accomplished on the level of myth as perhaps it could not be on the level of the real: ·

> It was like all that oppression from the month before had suddenly cracked open and left me in space. The election oppression: Nixon, Wallace, Humphrey. The headline oppression. And every other advertisement with their names and faces and voices and haircuts and suits and collars and ties and lies. And I was all set to watch 'Mission: Impossible' when Humphrey's flabby face shows up for another hour's alienation session. Oh please say something to us, something soft, something human, something different, something real, something – so we can believe again. His squirmy little voice answers me 'You can't always have everything your way.' And the expression of my fellow students becoming depressed. Depressed. Despaired. Running out of gas. 'We're not going to win.' There's nothing we can do to win. This is how it begins, I see. We become so depressed we don't fight any more. We're only losing a little,

we say. It could be so much worse. The soldiers are dying, the Blacks are dying, the children are dying. It could be so much worse. Everything must be considered in the light of the political situation. No getting around it. It could be so much worse . . . Let's not do anything at all. It can only get worse. Let's give up. And then I walked through the crowd of smiling people. They were loving and happy, alive and free. You can't win all the time. You can't always have everything your own way. You'll be arrested. You'll be arrested, accosted, molested, tested and retested. You'll be beaten, you'll be jailed, you'll be thrown out of school. You'll be spanked, you'll be whipped and chained. But I am whipped. I am chained. I am prisoner to all your oppression. I am depressed, deranged, decapitated, dehumanized, defoliated, demented and damned! I can't get out. You can get out. You smile and laugh and kiss and cry. I am! I am! I am! I am! I am! I am! Tonight. In this desert. In this space. I am.[22]

The play is the story of the regeneration of the Young Man and of his country – the principal agent of that regeneration apparently being a renewed sense of mystery, a determination to resist constriction. Even the snake computer could not bear to be contained by the laboratory. The music, which runs throughout the play, changes from ironic jingle or rhythmic comment on the action to the Hopi chants of the final scene. For Shepard, as for Marcuse, spiritual progress lay through a necessary reversion to older models, through the body as moral agent, through mystery, through a restoration of the individual to the natural world, to a sense of selfhood and a community of other selves.

The play draws its images from science fiction films, from westerns and from crime movies. It rests on a mythic structure which is part ancient and part derived from the fast-congealing myths of black liberation and the idea of spiritual renewal through a reversion to the primitive. But these images and these myths are not free-floating. They have their own history; they are themselves responses to cultural anxieties. They are acts of displacement and Shepard relies on this, on the seven-eighths of the iceberg below the surface, for the play's moral, psychological and political power. And Shepard is a moral playwright, though critics have seldom responded to this dimension of his work. If at times he has shown something of the surrealists' fascination with juxtaposing images and experiences for their own sake, more often he has also deliberately brought together images whose origins in guilt and fear (both private and public) have made them conscious and potent elements in a moral drama. But the mere act of invention carries a similar charge.

Shepard's works are mythic *Bildungsroman*, picaresque accounts of the search for meaning and value. Thus, *Mad Dog Blues* (1971) is aptly subtitled, 'A Two Act Adventure Story'. But this adventure takes place less in a real world than in a psychic terrain. The characters are drawn from popular myth – Marlene Dietrich, Mae West, Captain Kidd, Paul Bunyan and Jesse James. They exist only in terms of their fictional selves and their significance lies rather less in the play's ironic commentary on materialism than in the energy which is generated by bringing these figures into confrontation. It is Shepard's *Camino Real*. But where Williams subordinates character to plot and mythic roles to thematic concern, Shepard allows his characters to create their own meaning and sees the juxtaposition of mythic figures as itself a liberating mechanism. As he has said:

> In my experience the character is visualized, he appears out of nowhere in three dimensions and speaks . . . He speaks to something or someone else, or even to himself, or even to no one. I'm talking now about an open-ended structure where anything could happen as opposed to a carefully planned and regurgitated event which, for me, has always been as painful as pissing nickels. There are writers who work this way successfully, and I admire them and all that, but I don't see the point exactly. The reason I began writing plays was the hope of extending the sensation of *play* (as in 'kid') on into adult life . . . ideas emerge from plays – not the other way around.[23]

This is the essence of both the weakness and strength of Shepard's work. In fact he is at his best when there is a dominating idea – as in *Operation Sidewinder* – even if this began as a simple image. In his early plays he resisted rewriting his first drafts, regarding this as in some sense inauthentic. The result was a dense quality, an insistence on the authenticity of the act and the truth of a guiding subconscious. For all his ironic view of happenings, their influence seems clear. Events, words, characters, actions exist in their own right, liberated by the imagination but not subordinated to plot or narrative coherence. They exist to resensitise the imagination. References to popular myth underline the arbitrary and fictive nature of the structures; they resist a view of art as simple intellectual meaning encysted in form and style. For although myth has its own rigorous structure it operates on levels other than the purely rational. Shepard has insisted that he is interested in the 'world behind the form'. He rejects the notion that a playwright deals with 'ideas', turning to myth precisely because it 'speaks to everything at once, especially the emotions', insisting, however, that by myth he means 'a sense of mystery and not necessarily a traditional formula'.[24] One consequence of this, however, is that at times the freedom which he grants himself becomes merely repetitive. Suspicious of a dominating thematic drive he allows his plays, as in *Mad Dog Blues*, to become too static. Not all juxtapositions generate energy while his dramatisation of figures from popular culture purely within the terms of their mythic roles raises questions about the possibility of transformation which he fails to acknowledge. And clearly at times the mythic figures have a meaning for Shepard which is not necessarily that which his audience would recognise or respond to. This, too, may be one of the reasons why directors find so much difficulty with his work.

But *Mad Dog Blues* says something about Shepard's own ambivalent stance with respect to the myths which he generates. For the figures from the movies derive their mythic power precisely from the lack of a more rooted mythical structure to the society. They may express common fears and anxieties but they do not imply a common faith. People who share their guilt and terror and nothing else remain in some fundamental sense alone. The world which he dramatises is fragmenting. It flirts with apocalypse. On a public and private level it lacks cohesion. If he shares with Kerouac and Tennessee Williams a faith in rootlessness as a defensive tactic he equally shares with them a sense of the insufficiency of such a solution. All three writers are drawn to the simplicities of a world – indefinitely located in time and space – in which the relationship between individuals and between the self and its environment is clear and fulfilling, but such a world has disappeared. Myth is now a product of the very forces which created the need which it thereby satisfies and the instability of character becomes a final though inadequate protection. Most of the figures he invokes are dead – some by suicide, some by accidents which are a product of playing the mythic role too completely. Style is not finally an adequate response. The nostalgia with which Shepard, at times, no less than his audience, is apt to invest the figures from popular culture who spill into his plays is actually a conscious acknowledgement of the desire to retreat from the anxious world of the present. It seems to stand for a simplified world in which causality is abated, an adolescent world without consequences, an existence immune to mortality, a world with a clear plot, with definable characters and a reassuring sense of completion. In fact, it represents a security, a style and an emotional, social and spiritual consonance which has disappeared. Now, it seems, only music and the power of the imagination, expressed through words and images, can hold a dislocating world together.

And yet, for all his emphasis on the visual quality of his work, for all his concern with using music and myth to provoke an emotional response, Shepard is centrally concerned with language, with words 'as tools of imagery in motion'.[25] He responds to the incantatory power of language, its rhythmic associations, its power to provoke the imagination, 'to evoke visions in the eye of the audience'.[26] He has explained that 'American Indian poetry (in its simplest translation) is a prime example.

The roots of this poetry stem from a religious belief in the word itself. Like "crow", like "hawk". Words as living incantations and not as symbols. Taken in this way, the organization of living, breathing words as they hit the air between the actor and the audience actually possess the power to change our chemistry.'[27] Acknowledging that 'words, at best, can only give a partial glimpse into the total world of sensate experience', he nonetheless insists that 'Language . . . seems to be the only ingredient . . . that retains the potential of making leaps into the unknown.'[28] Other elements are important but more limited. 'Change the costume, add a new character, change the light, bring in objects, shift the set, but language is always hovering right in there, ready to move faster and more effectively than all the rest of it put together . . . Language can explode from the tiniest impulse . . . In these lightning–like eruptions words are not thought, they're felt. They cut through space and make perfect sense without having to hesitate for the "meaning".'[29] At times he practised what Jack Kerouac had called 'jazz-sketching with words', a kind of free-associative writing, which perhaps owes something to the surrealists' automatic writing. The conviction is clearly that improvisation places the individual in touch with a level of experience and being of a kind inhibited by strict form and rational process. Some of his early plays show evidence of this approach. But as he acknowledged, the 'structure of any art form immediately implies limitation . . . narrowing down my field of vision . . . agreeing to work within certain boundaries',[30] and, indeed, the problem of some of his work lies precisely in the identification of those boundaries and in his acceptance of the need for a strict framing of his visions. Thus *Mad Dog Blues* is self-indulgent. It lacks, in particular, the taut linguistic control of *The Tooth of Crime*, also a product of 1972, in which, despite his own account of the process of composition, he creates a powerful image in which the elaboration of style is in part the subject as well as the central strategy of the play.

Shepard's own description of the play emphasises the genesis of the image and offers a somewhat disingenuous account for what amounts to an elaborate metaphor of social and moral collapse, a play not unrelated to Gelber's *The Connection* or even Beckett's *Waiting for Godot*. According to Shepard,

> The character of Crow in *The Tooth of Crime* came from a yearning toward violence. A totally lethal human with no way or reason for tracing how he got that way. He just appeared. He spit words that became his weapons. He doesn't 'mean' anything. He's simply following his most savage instincts. He speaks in an unheard-of tongue. He needed a victim so I gave him one. He devoured him just like he was supposed to. When

233

16. A production of Sam Shepard's *The Tooth of Crime* at the University of
California, Davis; John Vickery as Hoss, Tony Bruskas as Crow.

you're writing inside of a character like this, you aren't pausing every ten seconds to figure out what it all means.[31]

The play is introduced by a song called 'The Way Things Are' in which Hoss, apparently a hired killer increasingly uncertain of his status and powers, offers what is in effect a defence of the play itself and of the oblique vision of the dramatist:

> You may think every picture you see is a true history
> of the way things used to be or the way things are
> While you're ridin' in your radio or walkin' through
> the late late show ain't it a drag to know
> you just don't know you just don't know
> So here's another illusion to add to your confusion
> of the way things are[32]

He is a man who owes his position but also his vulnerability to the fact that he has been 'moulded and shaped', that he works within a 'code'. It is the code which gives meaning to his actions – 'Without a code it's just crime. No art involved. No technique, finesse. No sense of mastery.' But he now lives in a time when 'the code's going down the tube',[33] and true individuality has disappeared. When Hoss asks, 'What about the country? Ain't there any farmers left, ranches, cowboys, open space? Nobody just livin' their life?', the answer is that 'That's old time boogie. The only way to be an individual is in the game.'[34] He is defeated by someone who is outside the game but who represents pure anarchy rather than individuality; a direct descendant of Melville's confidence man or Ralph Ellison's Rinehart, his chief weapon is his plasticity, his ability to change stylistic form. Meanwhile, like Gelber's or Beckett's characters, he spends his time waiting. 'Alone. That's me. Alone. That's us. All fucking alone. All of us.'[35] Neither he nor any of those who surround him, have 'a self . . . Something to fall back on in a moment of doubt or terror.'[36] He is caught in just such a moment of existential doubt, trying to convince himself that 'It's good to change. Good to feel your blood pump', only to ask himself, 'But where to? Where am I going?'[37] He finally falls back on the conviction that 'It don't matter. The mood's what counts. Just look at the road. Don't worry about where it's goin'.'[38]

In his contest with Crow he is disoriented by his sudden realisation that 'we're just ignored? Nobody's payin' attention . . . We're playing in a vacuum? All these years and no one's watching . . . The Outside is the Inside now.'[39] Given what amounts to a lament over existential abandonment (familiar both from *Waiting for Godot* and Stoppard's *Rosencrantz and Guildenstern Are Dead*), style assumes an authority which it would otherwise have lacked. And style becomes the chosen weapon and battlefield for the fight between Hoss and Crow. In the words of 'Crow's Song':

> What he doesn't know – the four winds blow
> Just the same for him as me
> We're clutchin's at the straw and no one knows the law
> That keeps us lost at sea
>
> But I believe in my mask – The man I made up is me
> And I believe in my dance – And my destiny . . .
>
> The killer time – will leave us on the line
> Before the cards are dealt
> It's a blindman's bluff – without the stuff
> To reason or to tell[40]

Style and language are means and end, and when Hoss is defeated he has nowhere to go and nothing to do but commit suicide or become like his vanquisher, 'Plunged into fear and come out the other side. Died a million deaths. Tortured and pampered. Holds no grudge. No blame. No guilt. Laughs with his whole being. Passed beyond tears. Beyond ache for the world. Pitiless. Indifferent and riding a state of grace.'[41] This is that ironic absurdist triumph, that desperate and self-negating strategy, to be found equally in Camus's *Caligula* and Beckett's *Endgame*. But Hoss commits the only definitional and original gesture that he can. He shoots himself, a gesture which denies the identification of face and mask and which resists co-option by the other. It is the only existential action of which he is capable.

It was easily Shepard's most accomplished work to date. The language battles are finely tuned, the contrapuntal rhythms carefully sustained, the rhetoric of popular culture raised to poetic significance. The songs are not simple commentaries on action; they are an integral component of the play. They, like the play itself, are a model of the attempt to impose structure on experience, of the conscious display of style as substance, the attempt to make poetry out of alienation. Unlike the earlier plays it was very carefully constructed. As he wrote to Richard Schechner when the Performance Group was to perform the play, 'This play for *me* is very preconceived. I got exact diagrams and pictures in my head about how it should be done . . . This play is built like *High Noon*, like a machine Western.'[42] Crow's language is bizarrely esoteric but nonetheless communicative through its rhythms and images which are drawn from contemporary sub-culture but turned into clear and even lyrical exchanges.

The theme is extended in *Geography of a Horse Dreamer* (1974), written during a three-year stay in England where he had gone partly because he admired the musical scene and partly because 'everything seemed to be sort of shattering'[43] in a New York in which he was high on drugs and driven back on himself by a threatening environment. The play, described in a subtitle as 'A Mystery in Two Acts', is concerned with Cody, kidnapped, presumably, from the town of the same name in Wyoming, by gangsters who wish to capitalise on his talent for dreaming the winners of horse races. Now, with his powers failing, he is reduced to prophesying the winners of greyhound races in England. Menaced by the Doc, who wishes surgically to remove a bone which contains traces of this magic, he is rescued by his two cowboy brothers who kill everyone but Fingers, the gang leader. The characters' names are by no means fortuitous. Cody is clearly named for Buffalo Bill Cody and the Doc for Doc Holliday, but beneath the deliberate mythic resonances is a familiar homily about alienation and lost powers. Fingers is a kind of Godot/God. At first he is simply an absent force: 'We're like his mirror. We never see him but we're always in touch.'[44] The petty gangsters simply follow instructions, live out determined lives, trapped in their own myths: 'It's like a snake bitin' its own tail. We keep infecting each other . . . The pressure's there. It comes from the outside. Somewhere out there. We wind up with the effects.'[45] As the Doc himself insists, in a passage which could equally well have come from the Tennessee Williams whose plays Shepard had started by imitating: 'We're each on our own territory right now. Each of us paralyzed within certain boundaries. We'd do anything to cross the border, but we're stuck. Quite stuck . . . There's no way for any of us to be in any place but the one we're in right now. Each of us. Quite separate from each other and yet connected. It's quite extraordinary, isn't it.'[46] The magic which exists within the individual is deflected, destroyed. *Geography of a Horse Dreamer*, like *The Tooth of Crime*, is a threnody, a lament for a lost dream. Cody's dream of the Midwest is forced to defer to a simple mechanism for making money. For Shepard, much the same process has typified America, and, since he now locates his play in England – a country in which gambling is described as a national pastime ('The government has hooks directly into the bookmakers. There's protection on every level except for the bums. The police are paid off by high syndicates. For the rich it's a sport. For the poor it's a disease.'[47]) – this is offered as simply a modern condition. Though rescued by his brothers, Cody, pure at heart but destroyed in spirit, cannot recapture the world he has lost.

For Ross Wetzsteon, Cody is Shepard himself, the writer who 'dreamed' a succession of plays and was then 'kidnapped' by the cultural entrepreneurs. He, like Cody, longs to be rescued and the text is full of references to the artistic nature of Cody's dreams. But if the play is indeed an expression of Shepard's sense of the betrayal implicit in the act of sharing one's dreams, the apparently inescapable diminution involved in the fact of art being absorbed by the system, it is not a comment restricted to his own dilemma as an artist. Corruption, the decay of natural powers, the substitution of the consciously crafted for the instinctively felt, is a fact of life, and the last-minute rescue an ironic gesture, a blatant piece of wish-fulfilment which can be sustained only at the level of myth and imagination. The redemption, such as it is, lies only in this level of self-consciousness. Those who wish to operate on Cody to remove the source of his magic are perhaps the critics who wish to isolate out the essence of his skill but his final magic is to effect his own disappearance at the very moment he seems willing to surrender a simple meaning. His obscurities, like Shepard's, are not accidental. There are privacies in his work which are designed for protection. The moralist, always present in Sam Shepard even when he was pursuing pure abstraction, has increasingly moved to the centre of his work. Though he grants a fundamental absurdity in the human situation he, like Albee, also sees this as wilfully compounded by materialism and a failure of human relationship.

The same conviction is expressed in *Action* (1976), a post-apocalyptic play in which the very word 'community' has lost all meaning and in which prison seems an adequate analogy for a life in which there is 'No escape. For a second'.[48] It is a play which expresses the same sense of disorientation and in which the characters are in some way psychically scarred. They hardly exist as characters in a conventional sense but together they create a sense of alienation. And this was, indeed, how he saw character. As he explained in a lengthy note to *Angel City*, also first produced in 1976:

> The term 'character' could be thought of in a different way when working on this play. Instead of the idea of a 'whole character' with logical motives behind his behaviour which the victor submerges himself into, he should consider instead a fractured whole with bits and pieces of character flying off the central theme. In other words, more in terms of collage construction or jazz improvisation. This is not the same thing as one actor playing many different roles, each one distinct from the other (or 'doubling up' as they call it), but more that he's mixing many different underlying elements and connecting them through his intuition and senses to make a kind of music or pattern in space without having to feel the need to completely answer intellectually for the character's behaviour.[49]

Angel City, as its name implies, is set in Los Angeles, or at least a mythicised version of a part of that city – Hollywood. For Shepard, the group of people who sit in a Hollywood office, desperately trying to invent an idea for a disaster movie powerful enough to stimulate the jaded sensibilities of the public and to distract them from the man-made urban catastrophes which they inhabit, stands as an image of a society of lonely people for whom such movies provide a grotesque parody of shared experience. It is a society in which genuine individuality is denied. When a saxophone player appears he is attacked for 'trying to reverberate us into the past with that solo crap',[50] and it is indeed this musician who expresses the principal mood of the play. As Shepard tells us, 'The dominant theme for the saxophone is the kind of lyrical loneliness of Lester Young's playing, occasionally exploding into Charlie Parker and Ornette Coleman.' His playing 'remains aloof and above the chaos for the most part',[51] and the chaos is born out of the Spenglarian conviction expressed by one of the characters that 'Money equals power' – equally the conviction behind Tennessee Williams's parables.

On one level the play is Shepard's version of *The Day of the Locust* in which individuals, terrified of their mortality and of the stark indifference of the world, act out their desperate fictions. It is this which breeds, 'The ambition to transform valleys into cities. To transform the unknown into the known without really knowing. To make things safe. To beat death. To be victorious in the face of absolute devastation.'[52] It is, in a sense, both another absurdist account of existence and a warning of the hubris that threatens to destroy us from within and without. The positivist dream slowly compacts the self into an ever smaller space, generating a logic which eventually will have no room for mystery, the imagination or, eventually, in the final day of technological triumph, man himself. Thus Wheeler, who slowly turns into a green monster, observes that 'Creation's a disease . . . We're dying here. Right now',[53] an observation which would scarcely have been out of place in a Beckett play. Hollywood, the west coast, is the ultimate boundary – the leading edge of American myth. It is the end of space. Movement is no longer possible. In terms of the Indian ritual which one of the characters invokes, it is the 'Looks-Within' place. But the consequence of this desperate search for the self on some inner plane spawns the same green slime which slowly engulfs two of the characters. *Angel City* ends with an insistence that the play itself hardly differs from the movie which they have supposedly been creating. It ends, that is to say, in parody, in a meta-theatrical gesture which decreates the text just established. *The Day of the Locust* had done no less. Both writers found themselves poised between the absurd and social satire and both recognised with a sense of horror their own unavoidable complicity in the process which they described.

Curse of the Starving Classes (1976) marks what is possibly a further change of direction in Shepard's work. It is a realistic play, albeit charged with qualities which strain that realism in the direction of metaphor. Like so much else in his work it is about a lost lyricism, the collapse of dreams and hopes, and the decay of relationships. The family at its centre are the victims of gangsters and confidence tricksters. There is an air of desperation. They have allowed their farm to deteriorate, the father turning to drink, the mother to the false promises of a land agent. They are locked into a destructive cycle in which their dreams are finally the source of their destruction. This indeed is an implication of the story, which the father, Weston, tells, of an eagle which carries a cat into the sky. The cat tears at the eagle but dare not let go. The two crash to earth and die together.

Gambling on the future, Weston gets deeper in debt. The family collapses, reaching out for things which they hardly need, oblivious to the human demands of those around them. It is a rural *Death of a Salesman*. However, Shepard is, as he has said, less interested in the delineation of a character's social circumstances than in his 'capacity to evoke visions in the eye of the audience'.[54] Indeed, as the father comments in this play, 'The family wasn't just a social thing. It was an animal thing.'[55] Shepard's own imagery tends to be drawn from the natural world. His attraction to the American Indian, cited in his interviews and infiltrated into the language of his plays, derives from a conviction that they had achieved an organicism, a view of the world which incorporated mystery and accommodated the spirit to the daily realities of the natural world. Almost invariably, however, that view is shown as being placed under pressure by the material world, by the corrupting and prosaic world of money and power and the myths which that world generates. The central fact is loneliness. The spiritual dimension is dead. His characters are isolated. And in *Curse of the Starving Classes* there is no release.

In *Seduced*, staged by the American Place Theatre, this process reaches some kind of apogee as he creates a Howard Hughes character, Henry, who sees human relationships as contaminating, listens to Randy Newman's song, 'Lonely at the Top' and asks, 'There's no one over my head somewhere? Somewhere lurking?'[56] His misanthropy is a constant temptation and a logical enough conclusion to visions which are always tinged with violence and haunted by criminals. 'My vision', says Henry Hackamore,

> It's the same thing I saw in Texas when I was a boy. The same thing I've always seen. I saw myself. Alone. Standing in open country. Primitive. Screaming with hostility toward men. Towards us. Toward me. As though men didn't belong there. As though men were a joke in the face of it . . . And far off, invisible little men were huddled against it in cities. In tiny towns. In organizations. Protected. I saw the whole world of men as

pathetic. Sad, demented little morons moving in circles. Always in the same circles. Always away from the truth. Getting smaller and smaller until they finally disappeared.[57]

He is the new god, the epitome of the material society. As his assistant shoots him, so he announces, 'I'm the demon they invented! Everything they ever aspired to. The nightmare of the nation.'[58] It is a vision relieved only by a certain lyricism which is the source of still further irony. For him, it seems, life consists of a desperate attempt to locate, define or create order. The irony, however, is that this is the essence no less of music than of art. This is the sense in which Shepard's doubts have increasingly extended to his own work, and is perhaps why he is drawn to the contingent, to an art which spills spontaneously from the mind and imagination. But the absurd is a constant threat which has its purest description in *Suicide in B♭* (1978), when a character is given an extended account of the absurdist position:

> You struggle to the window. You hold yourself up by both elbows and stare down at the street, looking for your life. But all you see down there is yourself looking back up at you. You jump back from the window. You fall. You lay there gaping at the ceiling. You're pounding all over. You crawl back for another look. You can't resist. You pull yourself up to the window sill and peer down again. There you are, still standing down there on the street. Still looking straight back up at yourself. Your terror drops for a second. Long enough to start getting curious. You look hard at yourself on the street. You check out all the details. You examine yourself in a way you never have before. Not to resolve any conflicts but only to make an absolute identification. You check the face, the hands, the eyes, the turns in the mouth. You look for any sign that might give him away to you as an imposter. A man in disguise. But then you see him signalling to you from the street. He's pointing to his head, to his own head, then pointing back to you. He keeps repeating this over and over as though it's very important. As though it's something you should have understood a long, long time ago but never did. You pick up the gesture from him and start repeating it back to him. Pointing at your head first then pointing down to him on the street. He starts to nod his head and smiles as though you've finally got the message. But you're still not clear what he means. You pry open the window with the last strength you've got and the shock of cold air almost kills you on the spot. 'If only I don't die before I find out what he means!' You say, 'Just let me live five minutes longer.' Then you see him more clearly than before. You see for sure that he is you. That he's not pretending. He yells up to you in a voice you can't mistake. He yells at you so the whole street can hear him. 'YOU'RE IN MY HEAD! YOU'RE ONLY IN MY HEAD!' Then he turns and walks away. You watch him go until you can't see him any more. Then you make a clean jump all the way to the bottom. And your life goes dancing out of the window.[59]

The play, a parodic detective story in which one of the detectives screams out the archetypal absurdist lament, 'WHY ARE WE BEING SYSTEM-ATICALLY BUMPED OFF BY AN UNSEEN ENEMY! IT'S NOT FAIR!',[60] is itself an ironic commentary on the quest for meaning in life and art. As one of the characters asks, 'Are you waiting for the truth to roll out and lap your faces like a Bloodhound's tongue? Are you diving to the bottom of it? Getting to the core of the mystery?'[61] It is an ironic extension of John Barth's observation that the key to the treasure is the treasure. As in Kafka's work, the reader, or the audience, is forced to re-enact the process which is the subject of the play. The ironic search for meaning is indeed in some respects the subject of Shepard's work.

Shepard's characters are thrown into a world which they can barely understand. The plot of their lives consists of their attempt to understand the plot of the story in which they are contained. They are confronted with mysteries, with a past which they presume will explain the present if they can only recover it. But for the most part the past is merely a mirror of the present. In that respect his work has moved closer to that of Pinter in recent years, though the edge of social criticism is always paradoxically present; that is, an irreducible absurdity is compounded by the elaboration of equally destructive social myths. The glimpse of a lyrical and spiritual alternative, clear in *Operation Sidewinder*, has now all but disappeared. His Pulitzer Prize-winning play, *Buried Child* (1978), like much of his work in the 1970s first produced at the Magic Theatre, San Francisco, carries an epigraph from Pablo Neruda which is, for the most part, ironic: 'While the rain of your fingertips falls, / while the rain of your bones falls, / and your laughter and marrow fall down, / you come flying.'[62] There is little evidence of flying.

An old man called Dodge lies apparently dying, while his wife, Halie, abuses him. Their two sons, Bradley, a menacing amputee, and Tilden, an infantilised man, exhibit the same sense of personal indifference. Into this curious world come Tilden's son, Vince, and his girlfriend, Shelly. At first, nobody recognises Vince, and Shelly is terrified by their hostility and aggression. But, by degrees, Vince is infected. He begins to exhibit the same cruelty as the rest of the family. Only Shelly resists, running from the house. The play ends as Tilden enters with the decomposed body of his baby brother, killed long before by his father but washed to the surface of the garden, where he had been buried, by continuous rain. The allegorical action implies the implacability of human nature, evidence for which is constantly coming to the surface. For the most part Halie's observation that 'We can't not believe in something. We can't stop believing. We just end up dying if we stop. Just end up dead'[63] is ironical, given the play's action. The only possible hope lies in the person who escapes the squalid determinism of the family – Shelly. But her prosaic good will is no match for the oppressive cruelty of those around her. As Dodge remarks, 'you're all alike you hopers. If it's not God then it's a man. If it's not a man then it's a woman. If it's not a woman then it's the land or the future of some kind. Some kind of future.'[64] Yet, of course, it is the future to which Shelly flies which constitutes the only glimpse of light in the play.

Robert Woodruff, who directed *Buried Child*, has remarked that when rehearsals began the play had a rather different third act. 'It was much more of a mystery play, with the murderer being unveiled.'[65] The 'contradictions' implicit in the present version he sees as a consequence of the fact that 'much of the third act was rewritten seven months after the first two acts, and there were no major changes made in them. But it played. It played incredibly well, because the idea of contradictions was built into the play from the beginning. As a result we have different people's perspectives on the same ideas.'[66] The effect, however, is not wholly convincing. The contradictions are essential. They are presumably what keeps Shepard writing. The persistence of hope is indeed a fundamental condition and definitional quality of the absurd. But it is equally a basic premise of art. It is, as Beckett and Camus have implied, entirely possible to neutralise the absurd by rendering one's humanity inoperative: 'Pray your God to harden you to stone. It's the happiness He has assigned himself',[67] says Camus's character in *No Exit*. But this is to destroy the absurd by succumbing to it. It is also to make the writer mute since to speak is already to begin the ironic task of shaping chaos into order. Silence offers an ironic victory which finally neither Beckett nor Shepard will accept. Living with the irony is the only alternative. It was not for nothing that for Camus Sisyphus became the paradigm. *Buried Child* taunts us with our capacity for concealing truth and for the fragility of the structures which we build out of personal relationships and the apparent coherences of art. But Shepard continues to speak. He continues to assume that at some level word and image carry a code and that the unlocking of that code, as much as the content of the message, is itself the source of meaning, but there is no denying the power of the absurd or the degree to which he sees us as accelerating its ultimate ironic triumph in a fratricidal cataclysm. Such a conclusion, at any rate, was the subject of another of his allegories of human self-destructiveness – *True West*.

Shepard's *True West* is close in spirit to Tennessee Williams's *The Red Devil Battery Sign* – that is, it offers an image of apocalypse, a desert world voided of human content in which the scavengers gather. Set in a Southern California suburb forty miles east of Los Angeles, it begins as a realistic account of the conflict between two brothers: one, Austin, a scriptwriter, is about to close a deal on a new film; the other, Lee, is a drifter and petty thief. In his opening stage direction Shepard also insists on the realism of the set, but this surface is quickly disturbed, disrupted by a plot whose very improbabilities place that realism under pressure. The drifter brother, whose menacing presence is reminiscent of Pinter's characters, proposes a banal idea for a modern western which is, surprisingly, immediately accepted by Saul Kimmer, the Hollywood producer, at the expense of the other brother's project. Thus the play, set in the West, centres on a script about the West. Both end in a battle to the death as script and play dissolve into one another. The real, it seems, is wholly problematic, the myth-makers themselves proving the victims of myth.

As the play develops so it becomes apparent that character is no less contingent in the world inhabited by Austin and Lee than it is in the world of the figures whom they mutually invent. Indeed in the course of the play they seem to exchange roles so as to give a literal truth to Austin's observation that the producer thinks 'we're the same person'.[68] Thus Austin begins to steal as his brother had done, and to long for a life in the desert, while his brother struggles to write the script of a story which he insists is concerned with 'the real West'. Yet if the reality of this West is deliberately subverted on one level by Shepard's metadramatic strategy (he writes a play about a man writing a play about a mythic West), there is another sense in which he does indeed seem to offer the play as an accurate account of an America slipping into a chaos of which the fratricidal final scene is an image. Indeed, the process of the play seems to be precisely a shift from a realism drained of effective truth to a symbolism whose authenticity remains unquestioned. The final image is not remote, in fact, from that which concludes *Zabriskie Point*. Having wrecked their mother's house, the two brothers fight one another as the lights fade. They appear to be caught 'in a vast desert-like landscape' just as, earlier, Lee had described the conclusion of his planned film, thereby simultaneously hinting at an apocalypse which would run down the curtain on the American dream:

> So they take off after each other straight into an endless black prairie. The sun is just coming down and they can feel the night air on their backs. What they don't know is that each of 'em is afraid, see. Each one separately thinks that he's the only one that's afraid. And they keep ridin' like that straight into the night. Not knowing. And the one who's chasing doesn't know where the other one is taking him. And the one who's being chased doesn't know where he's going.[69]

The stage direction at the end of the first act indicates that the lights go '*to black, typing stops in the dark, crickets fade*'.[70] At the end of the second act we are told that the '*lights go slowly to black as the after-image of the brothers pulses in the dark, coyote fades*'.[71] The two moments are in a sense the same moment, as the two brothers are in effect the same person in battle with himself while, on the level of history, there is another, more lethal, battle which threatens to destroy the West – that foreshadowed more than a decade earlier in *Icarcus's Mother*.

Apocalypse has haunted Shepard's work from the beginning. In *True West* it is enacted not merely at the level of myth, but, in so far as the play concerns an author who fails to find the words to express his vision, through the very processes of a play which disassembles character and deploys a language which defers to the visual tableau. It is a play which hints at the irony of creating myths as a means of communicating truth – an irony which leads Shepard in the direction of parody. It is not, I think, that, as Richard Gilman suggests, Austin represents imagination and Lee realism. Their roles are never secure enough for that and the real is too shot through with destabilising myths. It is rather that both men are trapped within myths, are, indeed, the products of myths which draw them towards apocalypse and which lead them to destroy the world they inhabit. For William Kleb, Austin represents objectivity, self-control and self-discipline, and Lee anarchy, intuition and imagination while the play becomes a metaphor for the creative act, a kind of *Sense and Sensibility* of the theatre. Creativity requires both elements. Some such image does seem to be implied but no sense of balance is projected, merely a self-annihilating and mutually destructive battle. Shepard is apt to distrust even the coherences which he creates in so far as they imply a sense of order to which he is drawn but for which he sees little evidence.

The characters in *True West*, like those in many other Shepard plays, are not coherent and consistent creations. In the case of the producer and the mother he leans toward stereotype. In the case of the two brothers he creates what are less clearly differentiated figures than shifting attitudes and assumptions. Thus the description of the voices in the 'Piece for Voice and Percussion', *Tongues* (1978), which he developed with Joseph Chaikin, could in some ways stand for those in *True West* and most of Shepard's other works: 'The various voices are not so much intended to be caricatures as they are attitudes or impulses, constantly shifting and sliding into each other, sometimes abruptly, sometimes slowly, seemingly out of nowhere.'[72] Which is to say that in some senses they are abstractions, conscious creations whose perimeters are accepted as being arbitrary. But in *True West* he is less celebrating variety than dramatising narcissism. His implicit image is the mirror. The man whose neck you crush with your hands is less your brother than yourself, while the fact that both brothers are writers in thrall to an industry that requires the subordination of creative energy to the needs of business perhaps hints at a kind of self-accusation. For Shepard is not unaware that even his warnings of impending apocalypse are appropriated by a system which in other ways is precipitating that apocalypse.

On the other hand, *True West* is extremely funny. Its improbabilities, its characters and its humour owe something to vaudeville and situation comedy, while the mayhem which develops, as one brother savages a typewriter with a golf club and the other lines up a score of stolen toasters and feeds them with sliced bread, is an ironic rendering of the chaos which threatens throughout his work, transposed, now, into the style of a silent comedy. The comic may not redeem absurdity but it does provide much of the energy of his work and the vitality of his characters.

There is, however, an area of authenticity which Shepard seems willing to acknowledge, an area, even, of sentimentality which establishes a further connection with Tennessee Williams – namely the force and reality which he is willing to grant to love. Indeed, in *Savage/Love* (1981), again working with Chaikin, he produced an encomium to love which makes overt what exists elsewhere in his work as a significant absence, a need implied by the bleakness of the world which he otherwise dramatises through his anti-myths. In *True West* that capacity is so thoroughly evacuated as to press individual and society beyond the possibility of redemption. In *Tongues* and *Savage/Love* that space is filled.

The two collaborations with Chaikin suggest something of what draws Shepard to theatre and the degree to which redemption lies less in the thematics, the characters or the plot than in the act of collaboration, that blend of self and community of which jazz was a primary image and for which the theatre itself is a paradigm. As Chaikin explains of their composition of *Tongues*, 'We would sit there and make something up. I'd sometimes make up a line, he'd follow it; he'd make up a line, I'd follow it. Or sometimes he would write something and read it back to me, and I would say why I didn't want to go in that direction or – you know how I like everything to be distilled, how I can't stand anything that spreads – I'd say why it would be better like that.'[73]

Tongues is in part a contemplation of language, its inadequacies and its potential. The concern with death (distressingly relevant for Chaikin who had long suffered from a heart condition and actually underwent open-heart surgery on his return from San Francisco to New York) recurs but the principal structuring device is less dramatic logic than musical coherence. As Chaikin observed, 'One of the things which we share, Sam and me, is our intense involvement with music. We're never looking for the dramatic structure. We're looking for [a] . . . shape that's

17.   Joseph Chaikin and Sam Shepard in *Tongues* at the Magic Theatre, San Francisco, 1978.

musically tenable.'[74] The performance was also accompanied by percussive music produced by Shepard who remained on stage behind the dominating figure of Chaikin.

Savage/Love was scarcely less ambiguous. Love is seen in all its guises – its betrayals no less than its victories. Again music was both a component and a model. 'As we were writing', Shepard explained, 'we were really trying to think in terms of being economical enough with the words so that it left space where music could really make the environment for it', while 'Both these collaborations are an attempt to find an equal expression between music and the actor.'[75] Both productions were produced at the Public Theatre, New York in 1979 to enthusiastic reviews.

A further play, *Fool for Love* (1983), presses the theme still further. Again set on the edge of the Mojave desert – a kind of no-man's land between the social world and a natural world indifferent to human concerns – it seems to concern the love of a half brother and sister, Eddie and May. It is a love which, for all its betrayals, is nevertheless the key to whatever meaning their lives possess. He is a rodeo cowboy; she is a short-order cook. Plainly, the only reality their lives possess derives from the feelings they hold for one another, feelings which alternately attract and repel. The word 'reality', however, is a problematic one for despite the apparent realism of the set – the action takes place in a run-down

247

motel – that realism is under pressure. The sound of slamming doors is amplified by concealed microphones; when the headlights of a car sweep across the stage Shepard is careful to specify that they should not appear to be realistic. One character, who sits at the side of the stage, may be no more than a memory, the projection of guilt or the product of a persistent anxiety. He is their father, himself a victim of love and the cause of suffering to those who gave their love to him.

Emotions and actions are as amplified as the sound, as the characters beat their fists against the wall as though that were the unyielding substance of their feelings. Outside the window a vindictive lover shoots up Eddie's truck, setting it on fire; inside, the double story of the father's two lives and Eddie and May's passion is unfolded. In neither case can we be sure of truth. As the old man remarks: 'I thought you were supposed to be a fantasist, right? Isn't that basically the deal with you? You dream things up.' The play has the quality of myth. Again not without its humour (May's date – a farmboy called Martin – wanders uncomprehendingly through the action), it is a celebration of a passion which has little to do with the rational world. As its epigraph observes, 'The proper response to love is to accept it. There is nothing to do.'

The sense of threat is nearly always present in Shepard's plays. As here, a fire frequently flickers outside the window; violence is always possible; experience leads towards disaster. But, within that logic there is another. The imagination resists. It breathes life into myths; it animates those spun off to the periphery of society. More important still, it pulls together into a compelling mutuality those whose experience is fragmentary.

In a West which is part real, part fantasy, he stages the contradictions of a love which is drained of sentimentality and which, at times, is still capable of shaping the world, of deforming and transforming it until the desert momentarily blooms. The threat never wholly retreats; the victory is never final or complete. It is, simply, the way things are. As the screenplay which he wrote for Wim Wenders's *Paris, Texas* (1984) makes clear, to Shepard love may be the source of pain and absurdity but it is also the path to transcendence.

Shepard resists critical co-option. His work ranges from startling and private images to carefully constructed and elaborate allegories. He is musician, poet, playwright, and a highly accomplished actor (even showing signs of giving up writing for a career in films). It is almost as if this itself were a strategy to avoid being pinned down, defined, fixed. Joseph Chaikin thinks of him as one of the Open Theatre's writers but Shepard himself has said, 'I never knew my place in the Open Theater, you know? I didn't have a place in the Open Theater. I was hanging out

248

with different people, and I would come by. I felt a kinship with Joe. But I didn't know how to function as a writer there at all.'[76] He is apt to disavow any awareness of complexity in his work, to play the role of naive artist, and, to be honest, something of his power as a writer does indeed come from the force of images which are not the product of rational process. But such elaborate defences against critical engagement should not disguise the power and achievement of a writer whose plays express the anxieties and, at times, the naive hopes of a society for whom the myths of popular culture are simultaneously paradigm and ironic commentary. For Shepard, the discontinuities, the absences, the incompletions of personal and public existence are a primary fact but so is the music whose freedoms and structural integrities imply a world to be reached for if only momentarily grasped. Like the *Savage/Love* which he analyses, celebrates and expresses, it, too, reinforces a sense of loss but also hints at consolation. And the process of making a play, the fact of integrating image, sound and movement, at least suggests the possibility of that sense of completion for which his characters and plays reach.

The enemy for Shepard is essentially the same as that identified by Kierkegaard – it is a passionless existence, a positivism which has no time or space for pure energy. Kierkegaard had remarked that 'By comparison with a passionate age an age without passion *gains in scope what it loses in intensity*.'[77] Shepard's images are designed in themselves as antidotes to a banal rationalism, operating on another level from the intellect alone. They are offered as the source of visions, of a new vitality, an animism which can be tapped. Everyday experiences or objects are charged with significance. At base he is accusing the whole culture of bad faith. He is a natural companion to those other instinctive existentialists, the Beats, who sought to breathe life into America by detecting a secret underground life in which experience radiates meaning, a neo-romantic conviction that life can be transformed by simply changing the way in which it is viewed. Shepard offers a prism through which to view a reality which seems banal because of the false values which make it impossible to recognise the brilliant variegations of experience, the spectrum of life concealed by a monocular vision. But the intensity of that vision has dimmed in his work; the power of entropy and the absurd has become increasingly dominant.

Shepard's conviction that 'language is a veil hiding demons and angels'[78] links him in a sense with Pinter and Beckett, no less than Freud, but, in some moods, he still wishes to close the gap, to restore a symmetry. The quest of his characters 'is the same as ours in life – to find these forces, to meet them face to face and end the mysteries'.[79] In other moods, however, not merely does he feel that the desire to penetrate mysteries is the essence of the absurd but, more fundamentally, he feels the need to protect those mysteries, for were that absurdity ever rendered null the consequence might not only be a transcendental unity; it might equally be an insufferable banality. Perhaps this is why he has confessed to being 'pulled toward images that shine in the middle of junk'.[80] We are perhaps redeemed precisely by our capacity for wonder, by our struggle to shape chaos into order and by our unexplained and ultimately unexplainable response to a startling moment which reveals nothing but its own capacity to move us. In *Paris, Texas* the same love which breeds vulnerability and betrayal, which narrows the world to a single point of suffering, can also inspire a moment of selflessness. Finally, perhaps, the dark is light enough.

9 David Mamet

With the apparent decline of Edward Albee and the disappearance or attenuation of the various groups that had enlivened the American theatre in the late 1960s and early 1970s, American drama seemed at a low ebb. Certainly in terms of major figures there were no dominant names. Miller, Williams and Albee produced a series of major failures throughout the 1970s. Such figures as did emerge were not products of Broadway. They were graduates of Off-Broadway or of the regional theatre. Indeed, perhaps the most impressive – David Mamet – was born in November 1947, on the South Side of Chicago, and was fully alive to this shift away from a New York dominated theatre. He looked for a new decentralised national theatre constituted by the new non-profit theatres of the country, and acknowledged an expanded professional community not tied to any specific theatre or city but moving between them, but at the same time his own imagination was shaped by, and his plays concentrate on, his experience of Chicago.

Mamet's father was an attorney and an 'amateur semanticist', and Mamet later suggested that his own subtle use of language derived from him. He studied literature and theatre at Goddard College, in Plainfield, Vermont, and wrote his first play, a revue called *Camel*, as part of the graduate programme there. In the middle of graduate work, he took an eighteen-month leave of absence to study acting at the Neighborhood Playhouse in New York, and while there he worked as the lighting man and then the house manager for the Off-Broadway musical, *The Fantasticks*.

Following completion of his degree in 1969, he worked briefly as an actor and then became a teacher at Marlboro College in Vermont. Here, despite his own somewhat limited experience, he unashamedly taught acting and wrote a play, *Lakeboat*, which he had listed on his curriculum vitae when applying for the job but which did not then actually exist. The appointment lasted only a brief while and was followed by the usual succession of odd jobs which seems to constitute the necessary training for American writers (he worked as a cab driver, a factory worker, a short-order cook and a telephone salesman). But in 1971 he returned to Goddard as an instructor and, once there, began writing short plays to use in his acting classes.

He formed a small acting group called the St Nicholas Company,

251

which performed not only his own plays but also O'Neill's *Anna Christie* among several others. Later he was to direct a production of *Beyond the Horizon* and the connection between O'Neill's early sea plays and *Lakeboat* seems close enough to suggest an influence. Certainly he, like O'Neill, was less concerned with generating a theatre of action than with creating dramatic tone poems. Returning to Chicago in 1972, Mamet secured productions of a number of his plays. *Duck Variations* was staged by an experimental group called the Body Politic while *Mackinac*, a children's play, was performed by the Centre Youth Theatre of the Bernard Horwich Jewish Community Centre. The same group produced *Marranos*, which is set in Lisbon during the time of the Inquisition. Success was finally secured when *Sexual Perversity in Chicago* won the award as best new Chicago play for 1974.

In the same year he re-established the St Nicholas Company, renaming it the St Nicholas Players and, as well as directing the poorly received *Beyond the Horizon*, saw the production of two more of his plays – *Squirrels*, about the problems of a writing partnership, and *The Poet and the Rent*, a comedy.

It was thus in Chicago that his reputation was established and he is essentially a Chicago writer. It is this city which provides the setting for *American Buffalo*, as for the later *The Water Engine*. New York showed remarkably little interest in his work, Joe Papp being only one of the producers who rejected his scripts. It was not until 1975, indeed, that a double bill by Mamet (*Duck Variations* and *Sexual Perversity*) reached New York where it played Off-Off Broadway at the St Clements Theatre. But the production was an immediate success. It won an Obie for the best new play of the year and this led to a transfer to the Cherry Lane Theatre Off-Broadway and to his Broadway début with *American Buffalo*. This opened in February 1977 and received the New York Drama Critics' Circle Award for best play of the year. In the following year Mamet strengthened his Chicago connection becoming the associate artistic director of the Goodman Theatre in Chicago. By now he had established himself as a major new voice in American drama.

Mamet's gifts to the theatre are akin to those of Edward Albee. He is concerned with language as poetry. As he remarked in 1976, 'If it's not poetic on the stage, forget it. If it's solely serving the interest of the plot, I'm not interested. As a consequence, I go overboard the other way.'[1] Plot is subordinated not so much to character as to the harmonics and dissonances of language. His concern is with orchestrating human voices and as such he is as reminiscent of O'Neill as he is of Albee.

Like Albee, Mamet is a poet of loss. The world he creates is one drained of transcendence, one in which individuals no longer communicate because they share nothing but their situation. They are role-players deprived of an audience, entropic figures struggling to come to terms with their own depleting energy. The friction of violence and a hermetic sexuality become a substitute for human contact. The central mood is one of aimlessness. His characters are liable to be marginal, deprived of purpose, vacant: two old men staring into a duck pond, actors in an empty theatre, a group of men who can barely articulate their indefinite longings. And yet there is a kind of poetry to be found in that inarticulateness. The disjunctions of their speech, though accurate enough as a rendering of the real language of the streets, gain power less as a simple strategy of naturalism than as an analogue of their social and psychological incompletions and the disintegration of that dream of upward mobility, personal completion, spiritual fulfilment and national achievement which is the special promise and animating myth of their society. Which is to say that there is a level at which Mamet's work, like Albee's, is an examination of the failure of the American dream, the decay of American revolutionary principles and American spiritual pieties. It is offered as an elegy for a world in a state of decay. Hence the fusion of lyricism and a linguistic brutalism. But where Albee began his career in the Kennedy years, and in his early work insisted on the persistence of values, the possibility of deflecting society from its simple materialism and its surrender of the spirit, Mamet began his career in the 1970s. His work contains fewer direct encomiums to moral principles presumed to operate in a not too distant past, fewer direct injunctions to human contact and the necessity to engage the real (of the kind to be found in *The Zoo Story, Who's Afraid of Virginia Woolf?* and *Tiny Alice*). Such convictions are, however, implied in the very stress on the fact of loss and in the need for companionship felt by characters who cannot articulate it for fear of the vulnerability which this will suggest. They are implied, too, perhaps, in the harmonies which Mamet generates from the stuttering and apparently unrelated monologues of his characters. What Albee states in his early works and suggests through absence in the later ones, Mamet implies through tone, image and rhythm.

Duck Variations, first produced at Goddard College, Vermont, in 1972, obviously owes something to Edward Albee. The action, like that of *The Zoo Story*, involves two characters sitting on a park bench, discussing, among other things, a zoo. It is concerned in part with abortive attempts at communication and its rhythms are as carefully calculated and as consciously derived from a musical analogy as those of Albee. Indeed the play consists of a series of fourteen 'variations' in which the intervening intervals are 'analogous to the space between movements in a musical presentation'.[2] The two characters sit in a park on 'the edge of a Big City on a Lake' on an Easter afternoon, the capital letters of Mamet's description implying the special and ironic resonance which he ascribes to this setting and this season.

For those aware of Beckett, Pinter, Stoppard or Albee, this is scarcely an unfamiliar situation: two marginal characters in a marginal setting pass the time and try to reassemble experience into coherent forms. Equally recognisable is the concern with the process of invention whereby those characters create scenarios which invest them with a meaning apparently absent from their own lives. Thus Mamet's two old men in effect create a series of dramas, animating their static world much as does the playwright himself. So, a glimpse of a passing duck leads them to reconstruct the life cycle of the species as a simple drama, but it is a dubious consolation since their own logic leads them to recognise both the inevitability of death and the absurdity implicit in an endlessly replicated biological process. The consolation which they had sought in the patterns of their own invention, in their own dramatisations, becomes all too apt an image of their own absurdity. And so, in their mini-drama, the leader of the ducks is born, lives and dies, only to be replaced by another. As Emil remarks, 'It's boring just to think about it.'[3] The duck spends its life in battle with its hereditary enemy, the Blue Heron:

> EMIL: So why do they continue to fight?
> GEORGE: Survival of the fittest. The never-ending struggle between heredity and environment. The urge to combat. Old as the oceans. Instilled in us all. Who can say to what purpose.
> EMIL: Who?
> GEORGE: We do not know.[4]

Their account of pointless struggle, of an endless cycle of birth and death, implies no such purpose, but rather than face this they retreat into the conviction that 'Everything has got a purpose . . . Ducks . . . Sweat glands . . . The very fact that you are sitting here right now on this bench.'[5]

Such convictions prove fragile enough, however. Turning to the duck as a contrast to a violent and polluted world – 'A self-destructive world . . . A cruel world . . . A dirty world [which] Almost makes a feller want to stop trying'[6] – they once again find themselves trapped in a logic which moves them from celebrating its simple life to acknowledging that it 'too, is doomed to death'. The supportive rhythms underlying these exchanges break down as the subject of death forces its way back into the conversation:

David Mamet

EMIL:	Who asked you to talk?
GEORGE:	Why are you getting upset?
EMIL:	You upset me.
GEORGE:	Yeah?
EMIL:	With your talk of nature and the duck and death. Morbid useless talk. You know, it's a good thing to be perceptive, but you shouldn't let it get in the way.[7]

The breakdown is immediately neutralised with a litany of words, an encomium to friendship and companionship, to that shared experience which is finally the only consolation. The rhythms are re-established.

GEORGE:	It's good to be a friend.
EMIL:	It's good to have a friend to talk to.
GEORGE:	It's good to talk to a friend.
EMIL:	To complain to a friend . . .
GEORGE:	It's good to listen . . .
EMIL:	Is good.
GEORGE:	To a friend.
EMIL:	To make life a little less full of pain . . .[8]

And though a minor disagreement over the ability of cactus or even ducks to survive alone introduces a dissonant note, the seventh variation ends with Emil looking at his companion and insisting that 'Nothing that lives can live alone.'

The park, the lake and the zoo are apparently their only refuge beyond the bare fact of their shared condition. They stand as a contrast to an apartment which is 'Joyless. Cold concrete . . . Stuff. Linoleum. Imitation'.[9] But the lake is full of pollutants and the park is depressing because 'At the park the only place I have to go is home', while at home at least 'I can come to the park.' The consolation thus becomes a part of the problem while thought of the zoo leads them back to an awareness of a dying world, suffocating on oil spills and garbage: 'The surface of the sea is solid dying wildlife.'[10] The consequence, in the eleventh variation, is an almost complete breakdown of communication as the two men generate brief spasms of language, dislocated phrases, incoherent monologues, insults, misinformation, which fill the silence which they fear; but better these simulated exchanges, they assume, this almost random talk, these parallel utterances only occasionally intersecting, than the nothingness to which they repeatedly aver. It is at least a resistance of sorts – a resistance to death and the thought of death. Thus, when once again their fantasies about the life cycle of the duck, their consolatory dramatisations, lead them back towards the same dangerous subject, it is tenaciously resisted.

GEORGE: Some must die so others can live.
   EMIL: But they must die, too.
GEORGE: So some must die so others can live a little longer. That's
       implied.
   EMIL: And then *they* die.
GEORGE: Of course. So that others can live. It makes sense if you
       think about it.[11]

And so the duck becomes a primary image for the two old men and
beyond that for man who has apparently lost whatever freedoms he
might once have had and whose physical environment simply exacerbates that essential absurdity which is a product of mortality. Thus, the
duck is liable to be shot at any time, the hunter having contrived the
shooting season so that 'the only time it's not legal to shoot 'em is when
they *ain't here*'.[12] As George remarks, in the most lyrical of the play's
'variations', death is 'The Law of Life'.[13]

George and Emil are like the Ancient Greeks whom they like to
imagine but of whose obvious relevance to their own situation they are
largely oblivious. They are 'Old men. Incapable of working. Of no use
to their society', representatives of 'A crumbling civilization'. They sit in
the park and contemplate the birds on a polluted lake, the futility of their
lives underlined not merely by the specious dignity with which they try
to invest their existence but by the linguistic bathos of the play's
concluding sentence: 'Watching each other. Each with something to
contribute. That the world might turn another day. A fitting end. To
some very noble creatures of the sky. And a lotta Greeks.'[14] The
reductive ending is all too appropriate an epitaph for two individuals
and, by implication, a whole society in a state of decay. Entropy rules.
The Easter setting is purely ironic. The redemptive confidence of *The
Zoo Story*, whose symbolism had been derived precisely from the
iconography of Easter, defers here to an absurdist image, or, at best, an
elegy for a botched civilisation gone in the teeth, for a life whose
determinisms cannot be neutralised by language, by the imagination or
even by a companionship which is more an expression of need than of
real consolation. Mamet's duet is for two voices seeking to create
harmony out of dissonance but only occasionally achieving a momentary consonance.

The play is not merely a series of variations on the subject of absurdity
or human need; it is also, to the degree that its characters compulsively
stage their own dramatisations of their plight, a comment on the fragility
of art and the degree to which it, also, compounds the forces it would
resist, bringing us back to the one subject we would ignore. All stories,
said Hemingway, if continued long enough, end in death. It is a central

truth which not only George and Emil set themselves to deny.

Mamet clearly runs the same risk of sentimentality as Albee had done. The assumption that marginality is normative is not merely logically problematic, it is also a familiar piety. That his work largely escapes such an accusation is a consequence of the fact that his figures are not the willed deviants and social outcasts of Steinbeck, nor yet the self-aware figures admired by Mailer. Like Beckett's or Pinter's characters they simply find themselves in a world without evident purpose, blessed with a language which cannot fully articulate their meanings, aware only of some sense of incompletion which can never be defined or resolved.

Like the plays of Albee, Pinter and Beckett, Mamet's are extremely funny. On occasion this is a product of conscious wit on the part of characters who deploy humour as self-protection. More often it emerges from the space which opens up between the character's consciousness and the audience's awareness of the total context of the play. It is, in other words, in large part an ironic humour. But the urban myths and realities which he sets out to capture in *Sexual Perversity in Chicago* and *American Buffalo* do also generate a protective humour which is a crucial element in his own position, for it implies that the individual is not wholly the victim of the language which he deploys and thus perhaps not wholly the product of the system in which he finds himself. At the same time a play like *Sexual Perversity in Chicago* does set out to dramatise what he sees as the emotional and spiritual vacuum at the heart of contemporary experience. Beneath the insistent rhythms of the speeches and the white noise of the parallel monologues is a silence which his characters try to neutralise. The urban aggression which typifies the encounters in the play drives the characters ever further back into privatism. The mask not merely conceals the self; it substitutes for it. The subject disappears to be replaced by the body as object. Loneliness, pain, simple human need, are implied only through the rigour with which they are expelled from a world in which pace, ironic humour and a brittle energy are substituted for anything more solid. *Sexual Perversity* is a kind of disco *Dance of Death* in which reified sexual relationships are offered as an image of the collapse of all shared values. Commodity value alone seems to survive – sexual voyeurism, sexual fantasies and sexual possession being offered as correlatives of a vapid materialism. And yet the energy of the play is not without its seductiveness, the sardonic humour not without its attractions. Even the fragmented nature of the construction, the rapid, almost cinematic, cutting from scene to scene, creates a dynamism which seems to imply vitality. In a sense, then, the very form of the play enacts its theme. The refusal of social and psychological depth, which is in part the subject of the play, becomes equally its method, and its frenetic compulsions equally those of the world which it describes. The audience is thus in part made an accessory at least to the degree that it finds itself responding to the images, the pace, and the reductive humour of a play whose satirical thrust is not untouched by an element of celebration.

Mamet's earliest experience of theatre was watching the improvisations of Second City in Chicago and his first play, written at Goddard College, was a satirical review. The influence of this was evident in the structure of a number of his plays, more especially in *Sexual Perversity in Chicago* and *Lakeboat*. Indeed, the former actually began as a series of revue sketches. First produced in Chicago by the Organic Theatre Company in the summer of 1974, it is a fast-paced, episodic work which explores sexual stereotypes and the pathos of urban life. The principal characters are Dan Shapiro, described by Mamet as 'an urban male in his late twenties', and his older friend, Bernard Letke. The latter plays the role of the ostensibly confident and accomplished sexual performer; the former his eager pupil. But the line between reality and fantasy is blurred as they substitute the orgasmic rhythms of their own quick-fire dialogue for the violent and vivid experience which they feel to be the necessary gauge of their own worth. What Mamet offers is a blend of knowing street talk and stand-up comic routines in which the necessary lies of two vulnerable people, intent, at all costs, on concealing that vulnerability, are simultaneously exposed to view and rendered momentarily null by the sheer pace and energy of their delivery. Hence, in the opening scene, Bernie describes the girl he had picked up the night before in terms of fantasy clichés but is torn between two tantalising images, that of a young inexperienced girl and that of an experienced woman. He settles for both, bridging the contradiction with the authenticity of a rhythm which communicates virtually independently of lexical meaning.

DANNY:	So how'd you do last night?
BERNIE:	Are you kidding me?
DANNY:	Yeah?
BERNIE:	Are you kidding me?
DANNY:	Yeah?
BERNIE:	Are you pulling my leg?
DANNY:	So?
BERNIE:	So tits out to here so.
DANNY:	Yeah?
BERNIE:	Twenty, a couple years old.
DANNY:	You gotta be fooling.
BERNIE:	Nope.
DANNY:	You devil.
BERNIE:	You think she hadn't been around?
DANNY:	Yeah?
BERNIE:	She hadn't gone the route?

DANNY: She knew the route, huh?
BERNIE: Are you fucking kidding me?
DANNY: Yeah?
BERNIE: She wrote the route.
DANNY: No shit, around twenty, huh?
BERNIE: Nineteen, twenty.
DANNY: You're talking about a girl.
BERNIE: Damn right.
DANNY: You're telling me about some underage stuff.
BERNIE: She don't gotta be but eighteen.
DANNY: Was she?
BERNIE: Shit yes.
DANNY: Then okay.
BERNIE: She made eighteen easy.
DANNY: Well, then.
BERNIE: Had to punch in at twenty, twenty-five easy.[15]

The play consists of a series of episodes, images of human relations in the urban America of the 1970s. As Bernie objects when a woman resists his heavy-handed charm, 'You don't want to get come on to, go enroll in a convent . . . You're living in a city in 1976 . . . I mean, what the fuck do you think society is, just a bunch of rules strung together for your personal pleasure.'[16] The girls they meet are quite likely to turn out to be lesbians ('As a physical preference, or from political beliefs?' asks Danny); the television which they watch to combine piety and pornography. They all steadfastly lie about their jobs, their sexual identities, their experience. Everything centres on a sexuality which becomes the principal medium of exchange between people. Moments of self-perception are aborted, undercut by fear of loss. Thus, Joan laments:

> It's a puzzle. Our efforts at coming to grips with ourselves . . . in an attempt to become 'more human' (which, in itself is an interesting concept). It has to do with an increased ability to recognize *clues* . . . and the central energy in the form of *lust* . . . and *desire* . . . (and also in the form of hope). But a *finite* puzzle. Whose true solution lies, perhaps, in transcending the rules themselves . . . and pounding of the fucking pieces into place where they DO NOT FIT AT ALL . . . Some things persist. 'Loss' is always possible.[17]

Then the lament is simply interrupted by the ringing of a telephone. No insight can be sustained. The urban rhythm is simply too relentless.

There is no evidence of real feeling and no language adequate to its expression. Male and female images are presented in a wholly reductive way, and yet there is a curious innocence as though this reductiveness concealed a fear of vulnerability. Nearly all the incidents and the fantasies with which they regale one another are bathetic.

The dominant image is one of impotence. The lesbian couple is balanced by an implied homosexuality underlying the macho hysteria of the two men. Sexuality rarely gets beyond voyeurism or fantasy, so the idea of masturbation recurs as an image of the hermeticism which is at the heart of their experiences. Despite the cynical pose the characters are in effect terrified of experience and even of the words which they choose to substitute for that experience.

Their world is one in which young boys are molested in movie houses and kindergarten teachers are raped. It is a world of sexual aggression – of singles bars, militant lesbianism and predatory males – in which the social value placed on innovation, conspicuous consumption and style has been displaced from the social into the sexual sphere, as the notion of freedom (of speech and action) has been displaced from the political. Sex, as reality and fantasy, becomes a central image. Mamet simply takes the subtext of Madison Avenue and Hollywood – the pursuit of wealth and sexual satisfaction – and makes it the text. Yet perhaps the problem is not so clear cut. Deborah tells a story about her youth which raises precisely this question. 'I was about four. I said, "Mommy, can I have a cookie?", and she for some reason misunderstood or misheard me, and thought that I said that I wanted a "hug" so she gave me a "hug", and I said "Thank you, Mommy. I didn't want a cookie after all." You see? What is a sublimation of what? What signifies what?'[18] But whether sex is a sublimation of the emotional and the spiritual or the other way round the nexus is crucial to Mamet's strategy, as is the contrast which this speech implies between the child's natural affection and the stereotyped roles which his characters so painfully enact.

Indeed, at times he is tempted to press the absurdities still further, seeing in the impotence, the frustrations and the violence which he drama- tises an image of a more radical disjunction in experience. As Joan suggests,

> Of course, there exists the very real possibility that the whole thing is nothing more than a mistake of *rather* large magnitude, and that it never *was* supposed to work out. . . . Look at your divorce rate. Look at the incidence of homosexuality . . . the number of violent, sex-connected crimes . . . all the anti-social behaviour that chooses sex as its form of expression . . . Physical and mental mutilations we perpetrate on each other, day in, day out . . . trying to fit ourselves to a pattern we can neither *understand* (although we pretend to) nor truly afford to *investigate* (although we pretend to) . . . It's a dirty joke . . . the whole godforsaken business.[19]

The speech, though undercut by its context, is to be taken wholly seriously and is an apt description of the action of the play. In a literally godforsaken world they are, indeed, trying to adjust to models that they cannot understand. The contradictions of the social world (in which children at the kindergarten are told by their lesbian teacher that playing 'Doctor' is perfectly natural but are punished for doing so) is extended to a metaphysical world in which the failure of aspiration to breed fulfilment is perhaps no less than an indication of total contingency. Their life is indeed a dirty joke.

The figures whom he dramatises in *Sexual Perversity* are terrified of genuine feeling. It is an undiscovered country. They choose to deal with it by rendering all experience into clichés, by denying the unknowable. Other people are transformed into objects because it is as objects that they can be dealt with, that they become predictable, safe. And language is the principal weapon in this process of control. The language of pornography only seems to be concerned with the process of exposure; in fact it is a primary act of concealment. It is a denial of depth and complexity, of a threatening opacity. It is an act of evasion which seeks to deny the disturbing and at times menacing facts of emotional life. Just as the theme of pornography is the self's total command of the other, so its language is designed to facilitate that command. It is a world necessarily drained of feeling because feeling implies an openness to experience which threatens the self. As Mamet himself has remarked, 'Voltaire said words were invented to hide feelings. That's what the play is about, how what we say influences what we think.'[20] So what begins as a defensive strategy ends by influencing the way his characters perceive and hence shape and deform the real. The loneliness dominating not only this but most of Mamet's plays is in large part self-inflicted. His characters, like Albee's, opt for a world of unreality out of simple fear of the demands made upon the psyche by the natural flux of experience. They are adolescents who wish to deny any substance to a life which may involve failure, pain, a knowledge of death – all those things, in short, so assiduously denied by a culture for which the euphemism is a primary resource. They are, like George and Martha in *Who's Afraid of Virginia Woolf?*, 'sad children' substituting language for action, and fantasy for the reality which they fear but which nonetheless defines the parameters of their existence. The apparent vitality of the exchanges, the pace of the speeches, the confident and even arrogant nature of the conversations are all illusory. Like George and Martha's verbal battles they are no more than spasms of misdirected energy and elaborate strategies designed to conceal a need which they dare not, and perhaps cannot, articulate. Written and first performed in Chicago, home of Hugh Heffner's *Playboy* empire, the play offers a comment on the curious *mélange* of reductive sexuality and macho adolescence to which that magazine so successfully caters.

In the play men and women are in some sense antagonists, defending themselves against one another, asserting their rights, defending their territory. Even when they do come together the loneliness is total, since they cannot even enact the myths that they have come to accept as a total explanation of the real. The play ends as the two men lie on the beach and simply admire the physical attractions of the passing women whom they are incapable of perceiving or engaging as people.

American Buffalo captures a similar world. It is a savage satire on the collapse of American values, on the process whereby American liberal principles have been accommodated to a rapacious self-interest. It enacts the disintegration of community and the failure equally of language and morality. Like the American buffalo itself, such things have fallen victim to greed, to a confusion between price and value. Mamet regarded the play as in part an attack on American business principles. As he explained in an interview, 'We excuse all sorts of great and small betrayals and ethical compromises [in the name of] business . . . Part of the difference between the lumpenproletariat and stockbrokers or corporate lawyers who are the lackeys of business. Part of the American myth is that a difference exists, that at a certain point vicious behaviour becomes laudable.'[21] The characters repeatedly justify their actions by reference to the necessities of 'business' which becomes little more than a self-justifying mechanism. Albee offered *Who's Afraid of Virginia Woolf?* as an examination of American revolutionary principles recast as a personal drama of illusion and reality. Mamet's play is hardly less. His characters also inhabit a world of unreality. They, too, retain the vocabulary of a world which has slipped away from them. In both plays simple human need is a central fact concealed behind the desperate rhetoric of an American dream deflected from the spiritual into the material world and hence drained of its transcendental power.

American Buffalo is set in a junk store amidst the gathered detritus of American society. Here Don, the owner, dispenses a streetwise version of cracker-barrel philosophy, offering his own version of native American virtues suitably adjusted to the realities of petty criminality. Hence larceny becomes business, which he, in turn, defines as 'people taking care of themselves'.[22] And this 'business' requires all the virtues of perseverance, self-reliance and integrity of purpose more normally associated with the classic model of the American dream. Thus Teach, described as his friend and associate, about to embark on a burglary, defines free enterprise as 'The freedom . . . of the *individual* . . . To embark on Any Fucking Course that he sees fit . . . In order to secure his honest chance to make a profit'.[23] This becomes a contemporary urban version of the Constitution. Indeed, in a parody of revolutionary rhetoric he insists that 'The country's *founded* on this . . . Without this we're just savage shitheads in the wilderness . . . Sitting around some vicious campfire.' This yoking of violence and criminality to familiar American pieties is characteristic of Teach's rhetoric. Thus, in defending his own ability to break into someone's house he objects, 'What the fuck they live in Fort Knox? (Get in.) You break in a *window*, worse comes to worse you kick the fucking *back door* in. (What do you think this is, the Middle Ages?)'[24] Like Don, he elevates friendship into a central principle, thus justifying their predatory response to all those not so defined. But the distinction is a fragile one. When Teach feels insulted by one such friend, he characterises her as 'a Southern bulldyke asshole ingrate of a vicious nowhere cunt', and suggests that 'The only way to teach these people is to kill them.'[25] Nor was this inversion of values, this attachment of familiar virtues (friendship, teamwork, self-improvement) to criminal activities, without its relevance to a world in which the Mafia had appropriated the American iconography of the family, the brutalities of Vietnam were defended in terms of recognisable American virtues and in a language whose deep ironies were apparently lost on those who uttered them, and the American President deployed the language of statesman, team leader and patriot to justify his abrogation of the oath of office and his disregard for the law. *American Buffalo* is persuasive as an account of the amorality of an American subculture but it is offered as much more than this. The ethics of Don and Teach hardly differ from those of ITT or of a society then in process of defoliating and bombing South Vietnam in the name of freedom.

Beyond the domestic scene there is perhaps a wider implication as Mamet projects the logic of this collapse of values onto an international scale. Thus Teach carries a gun as 'deterrent', although it is his possession of the weapon that creates the danger of violence. Preaching the virtues of peace and friendship he prepares himself lest 'something inevitable occurs', and the play ends in a paroxysm of violence as Teach beats a young junkie friend of Don, and Don, in turn, beats Teach before Teach sets out to destroy the store, using an instrument which, we are told, had originally been designed to drain the blood from dead pigs. In the midst of this apocalyptic scene Teach recites a litany of the collapse of values of which he is both principal and agent. 'The Whole Entire World. / There Is No Law. / There Is No Right and Wrong. / The World Is Lies. / There Is No Friendship. / Every Fucking Thing. / Every God-Forsaken Thing . . . We all live like the cavemen . . . I'm out there every day. There's nothing out there . . . I fuck myself.'[26] Though the play ends with a sentimental gesture this can hardly neutralise the brutality of what precedes it. The outcasts cling together in the wreckage of their lives and their world simply because there is nothing else. The apocalypse never

18.   David Mamet, *American Buffalo*, 1976.

seems far away on the contemporary American stage (see Williams's *The Red Devil Battery Sign*, Albee's *Box*, Shepard's *Icarus's Mother*, Wilson's *Einstein on the Beach*).

The world of *American Buffalo* is charged with violence. The characters can barely articulate their baffled rage or their sense of impotence. Their stuttered insults, their incoherences, the disproportion between words and objects underline the incompletions of their lives – the gap between their experience and their articulation of that experience. The bathos implicit in Don's response to Teach's sustained and brutal invective – 'You're probably just upset' – is a natural counterpart to the hyperbolic speech itself. The *non sequiturs*, the contradictions ('I am calm. I'm just upset.)'.[27] underscore the discontinuities of their experience. The characters deplore the violence and the decay of values for which they are the principal evidence and in which they are prime movers. Moral values are still invoked but they are simply inverted. To Teach, arming himself for the robbery, the weapon is a necessary protection against 'some crazed lunatic' of a householder who may irrationally see the assault on his property 'as an invasion of his personal domain' since 'Guys go nuts . . . Public *officials* . . . *Axe* murderers.' Paradoxically, therefore, he admires the police since they at least have the wit to go 'Armed to the hilt. Sticks,

264

mace, knives'. As he piously observes, while loading his revolver and preparing to break into a house, and if necessary murder the inhabitant, 'Social customs break down, next thing *everybody's* lying in the gutter.'[28] It is an irony carried a stage further when their accomplice is mugged on the way to the rendez-vous.

The plot is slender. A coin dealer has paid Don $95 for a buffalo-head nickel, and Don now plans to rob him and sell his coins to another dealer, not simply because this will be to his profit but because he suspects that the dealer has taken advantage of him in some way. The play is ostensibly concerned with the planned robbery. In fact this never takes place due to the incompetence and cowardice of the men. It is, it seems, simply a way to pass the time for three desperate people, the plot of whose lives is no more substantial than that of the play in which they appear.

American Buffalo, though winning an Obie for the best American play in 1976, as well as the New York Drama Critics' Circle Award for the following year, was not received with unanimous praise. For Brendan Gill in *The New Yorker*, it was 'a curiously offensive piece of writing less because of the language of which it is composed' than because it 'provides only the most meagre crumbs of nourishment for our minds'. The play, which featured 'characters of low intelligence and alley-cat morals', conveyed 'the message that life, rotten as it is, is all we have', while the characters themselves 'appear to know no more about their squalid means of survival . . . than we in the audience have long since learned from reading the papers and watching TV'.[29] To Gordon Rogoff, in the *Saturday Review* (2 April 1977), Mamet is concerned only with bringing us the news that 'Americans living on the dark underside of small business and petty crookery speak of macho frustrations almost entirely in four letter words.'[30] The play, he found, was weak on plot and destructive of language. However, the play's revival in 1983, with Al Pacino playing the part of Teach, provoked a reappraisal which at last acknowledged its significance as a classic of the modern theatre.

The misunderstandings are instructive. For both critics the play is simple naturalism, poorly plotted, and with inarticulate characters whose perceptions fail to transcend their circumstances. These characters merely indulge in 'tiresome small talk for a couple of hours' (Gill) in a play in which nothing happens. It is as though Beckett had never written, but then Beckett's plays tend to take place in some spatial and temporal void where Mamet's are clearly locatable in an American setting and, in the case of *American Buffalo*, present a stage as densely filled with naturalistic detail as any Belasco production, as charged with the kinetic energy of realism as Arthur Miller's *The Price* (in which, also, the assembled impedimenta of life become a central image as well as an authenticating mechanism). And realism plainly matters to Mamet. He has, after all, said that 'I'd like to write a really good play sometime. Like O'Neill, Odets, Chekhov, something the way it really is, capture the action of the way things really go on.'[31] But his is a renovated realism, fully informed by absurdist assumptions about the pressures which offer to dissolve character, aware of the displacement of the subject, the deceptions of language and the cogency of entropy as image and fact. *American Buffalo* is not plotless through inadvertence or incompetence. The lives which Mamet dramatises are themselves without plot, without direction, purpose, transcendence. His plays do not so much employ symbols, as did Tennessee Williams or Arthur Miller; they are symbolic enactments of their own themes. The language which his characters use is plainly closer to the rhythms of actual speech than is Albee's, for example. Grammar and syntax are fractured; conversations are characterised by disjunctions familiar enough from actual speech. But it is not transcribed speech nor is the attempt simply naturalistic. The paranoid assertions, advanced and then withdrawn, the contradictions, the incomplete sentences, the aborted dialogues, the words delivered more to the self than to the other, the shifting perspectives (indicated as such in the text by the use of brackets), the pressure of the unexpressed and the inexpressible, are not offered as naturalistic detail, but as evidence of the collapse of character, language and structure. Unable to act, to commit themselves to the causalities of a moral existence, the characters allow their impulses to be deflected into language which must then carry the weight of their blunted aspirations. However, this language, which must discharge an energy which has lost its outlet into action or into the interaction of personal relationships (except for the final frenzied assault), cannot sustain the burden. The power of naturalistic language lies in what it reveals; the force of the language that Mamet's characters speak lies in what it attempts to conceal.

Teach's aggressive language is designed to cover his paranoid fears, but on either level it proves inoperative and this aphasia suggests something of his inability to shape experience into meaning. He regards those who beat him at cards as cheats by definition; those who eat with him are laughing at him for his generosity or deriding him for his parsimony. No act can be innocent; each one is designed to defraud him of some experience, some possession, some knowledge to which he has presumptive rights. He arms himself to guard against a hostility generated in part by his own delusions and his seemingly instinctive distrust of human responses. His companion, Don, is apparently more compassionate, dispensing advice to enable his companions to survive the urban jungle which he underwrites, but when a customer willingly pays several hundred times the face value for an old coin his only response is bitterness as he plans to steal it back from the buyer. His redeeming virtue lies in the care he takes of a young junkie. But even this can be laid aside when it conflicts with his interests and he watches coldly as the boy is beaten by Teach. This boy, Bobby, is apparently the only innocent character in the play, but his innocence is a product of ignorance, a naivety which makes him a threat to others and a natural victim.

The model of human relations is familiar enough from Pinter's work, where a similarly deceptive naturalism is to be found. For Mamet and Pinter alike, human relations seem to be typified by a struggle for dominance, an attempt to establish the authority of one model of reality in preference to another. Pinter, too, has an acute ear for the rhythms of speech and for the inarticulateness that frequently communicates far more than fluent speech, and while his dialogue also comes closer to the actual structure and nuances of spoken language than does the supposed realism of a writer like John Osborne, it would make no more sense to regard him as a naturalist than it does so to regard Mamet. The junk that fills the room in Pinter's *The Caretaker* plays much the same role as the junk in *American Buffalo*. It does indeed represent the past, as it does to be sure in Miller's *The Price* – a past, moreover, which resists sentimental-ism. In Miller's play a fencing foil recalls the psychological battles of youth; in Pinter's play the electrical consumer goods, the electro-convulsive treatment of Aston; in Mamet's play a metal knick-knack turns out to be an implement for draining blood from dead pigs. In Pinter's or Mamet's work these are not presented as a means of defining character through establishing environment or through locating the origin of past traumas. For both writers these objects exude a sense of menace; they offer a striking correlative of the dissolution of character, the move from subject to object. The obscure implement for bleeding pigs anticipates all too clearly the bloodletting that will leave Bobby bleeding at the end of the play. The assembled junk all too accurately mirrors a world in which people (the social and moral world) seem drained of their meaning, inert; in which, deprived of their function, they derive value only from the price that they command.

The humour of the play derives from the gap between their solemn moralising and the amorality of their behaviour, from the disproportion between stimulus and response. Thus Teach's response to heavy irony is to threaten murder; his reaction to what he takes to be the success of others is to wish to rape their wives. In other words it is a reductive humour stressing impotence, undercutting assurance and denying con-sonance. Their hopeless incompetence, as they plan a robbery with no idea as to how they will break into the apartment, open the safe or select the valuables to steal, underlines the degree to which they lack control over their lives, lack, indeed, any real perception of their circumstances and yet persist in their fantasies. Which is to say that *American Buffalo* is not remote from the world of Beckett's *Waiting for Godot*, as socially marginal figures struggle to give meaning to their lives with activities that are never capable of moving from thought to action. The stasis objected to by Rogoff is the essence of the play as it is of the lives of the characters and of the society which they inhabit. When Brendan Gill observes that the characters 'appear to know no more about their squalid means of survival – burglary, cheating at cards, and the like – than we in the audience have long since learned from reading the papers and watching TV', he offers this as a criticism of Mamet's imagination; but in fact this is precisely Mamet's point. For these characters do, indeed, inhabit fantasies shaped in part by the media. They try to live mythologically and end up hardly living at all. For myths they substitute fantasies. Myths unify; fantasies isolate. Mamet's characters inhabit a world constructed for them by fantasy and sustained by the language with which they distance themselves from one another. There is perhaps some hope in the simple and virtually monosyllabic conclusion. Rather as in *Who's Afraid of Virginia Woolf?* it is the moment when language ceases, when the protective noise stills, that some residual humanity asserts itself. It is a fragile hope but it is not quite the absurdist irony which implies that only through silence and immobility can absurdity be transcended. For Mamet as for Albee absurdity may exert a gravitational pull but it is in part at least a product of human fear, a terror of vulnerability. In Mamet's words *American Buffalo* is about 'comporting oneself in a capitalist society', and as such implies the persistence of other values, other means of comporting oneself, other contexts which do not result in the same collapse of character and purpose.

For Mamet, *American Buffalo* was an attack on the business ethos. As he explained,

> The play is about the American ethic of business . . . About how we excuse all sorts of great and small betrayals and ethical compromises called business. I felt angry about business when I wrote the play. I used to stand at the back of the theatre and watch the audience as they left. Women had a much easier time with the play. Businessmen left it muttering vehemently about its inadequacies and pointlessness. But they weren't really mad because the play was pointless – no one can be forced to sit through an hour-and-a-half of meaningless dialogue – they were angry because the play was about *them*.[32]

Mamet's next play, *Reunion* (1976), continues his thematic concern with the collapse of community. It is a word picture of a society of strangers. A 24-year-old woman comes to see her father after years of separation. There is no spontaneous outburst of affection but, as the play proceeds, and as they tell one another about their lives, so a portrait of loneliness and pain begins to come into focus. Mamet's pointillism gradually assembles the details of a world of broken relationships and desperate lives. Both Bernie and his daughter have divorced and remarried, as has his ex-wife and her new husband. Indeed Bernie's second wife, Ruth, has now been displaced by another woman, Leslie, who is also divorced, while he has lost contact with his son by that marriage. When asked by his daughter why he is thinking of marrying again he replies, 'Companionship'.[33] In that word are compressed all the needs, the pains and the ironies of personal and social experience. Though hardly unique to America, divorce and remarriage are indeed a recognisable American phenomenon. Few societies can have so adroitly accommodated the sentimentalities of romantic love to the pragmatics of divorce, a frantic search for happiness whose victims are not only the children whose initiation into human relationships is marked by litigation and separation. It is a recurrent theme of Mamet's work. His indignation at the models of human relationships purveyed by the media, his sense of the loneliness and desperation which people seek to annihilate through a love which is simultaneously required to carry the weight of personal fulfilment and metaphysical consolation while satisfying expectations scarcely different from those applied to consumer durables in a world of planned obsolescence, is apparent from *Sexual Perversity* to *The Woods*.

The ironically named *Reunion* is a duet in a minor key in which the nature of human relationships is exposed. Thus, Bernie embraces the very pragmatism and materialism he seems to be rejecting:

> married.
> Living well . . .
> The rest is not very important.
> It's for the weaklings . . .
> Take a chance.
> You got to take your chance for happiness.
> You got to grab it.
> You got to know it and you got to want it.
> And you got to *take* it.
> Because all the possessions in the world can't take it from you.
> Do you know what I'm talking about? . . .
> It's a fucking jungle out there. And you got to learn
> the rules because *nobody's* going to learn them for you.[34]

By degrees the insufficiency of both characters' lives is exposed. Bernie comes to admit that 'The only two worthwhile things I ever did in my . life were work for the Phone Company and fire a machine gun, and I can't do either of them anymore',[35] while his daughter confesses to the inadequacy of her marriage. After twenty years she searches out her father because, as she says, 'I feel lonely.'[36] In a world in which 'a Broken Home [is] the most important institution in America' she longs for contact, even if it is with an ex-alcoholic father whom she has not seen for twenty years. But it is impossible to rebuild what she has lost, while Bernie's conviction that 'I am what I am and that's what happiness comes from . . . being just that . . . you've gotta be where you are . . . While you're there. Or you're nowhere',[37] does nothing to solve her problem or to address her sense of need. It is too close to the empty rhetoric of self-fulfilment groups. The play ends with nothing resolved.

Mamet is especially aware of the ambiguity which emerges from the image of consonance offered by the theatre even when it is dealing with the subject of alienation and disharmony. In *Dark Pony*, a simple play in which a father recounts a familiar story to a child, a story in which loneliness and fear are invoked only in order to be dispelled, he offers an image of the power of fictions to console. To dramatise dislocation and the collapse of order is already to neutralise their power as realities. It is a central tension from which much of Mamet's work emerges. His plays enact their central theme. They are, inevitably, moments of consonance, of ostensibly shared experience. The ironic ending thus becomes a crucial device to deconstruct the apparent assurance of the form. For the most part his plays seem to end reassuringly, relationships seem restored, fears have apparently been suppressed; but the physical contiguity of the concluding moment has been drained of its significance. The simple gesture of consolation or shared experience is simply not powerful enough to neutralise the fears, the incompletions and the isolation exposed by the motion of the play. So the final act is ironised and the dissonances are seen as more important than the deceptive harmonies. Thus, in *Reunion* there is no actual reunion, while in *Dark Pony* the lies told to children are merely the first of many lies which are offered as an adequate account of the real. And art is deeply implicated in such deceptions.

Mamet's metadramatic concern is intensified in his next play, *A Life in the Theatre* (1977). He has said that the question which imposed itself on his imagination while writing the play, was 'How does one train oneself to live in the moment – to make the moment (every moment) on stage so beautiful, so full, so *unbelievably* affective and true that one is *forced* to proceed to the next moment?'[38] However, it is not merely a play about

Shatford Library
Pasadena City College

Material Due Date

- ❖ Maximize use of the PCC Shatford Library Collection!
- ❖ Return materials promptly.
- ❖ See reverse for Fines & Replacement Policy.

Date Due:

NOV 1 2 2003	
NOV 1 1 2003	
NOV 2 6 2003	
DEC 0 1 2003	

Fines and Replacement Policy

A fine of **10 cents per day** is assessed for material not returned by the due date.

Exceptions:

❖ Videocassettes: $1.00 per day

❖ Equipment or Treasure Room item: 25 cents per day

❖ Math or Telecourse Videocassettes: 50 cents per hour.

❖ Reserve Material: 50 cents per hour.

The maximum overdue fine per item is $60.00.

No check-outs if your account has more than $5.00 in fines.

If material is lost or damaged beyond repair, the library's cost for the item plus a $10.00 service charge will be fined.

For renewals or circulation information
Please call the Circulation Desk at
(626) 585-7174

Visit our web site at
http://www.paccd.cc.ca.us/library

David Mamet

19.   Mamet, *A Life in the Theatre*, 1977

living intensely for if he is fascinated by the processes of invention he is
also concerned with the elaboration of the lie. We are thus presented with
a double image as we overhear a backstage conversation between two
actors intercut with brief excerpts from the plays in which they perform
together. On the one hand, the apparently banal discussion slowly
reveals the tensions, the fears and the sense of inadequacy of the actors; on
the other, it raises questions about the nature of theatricality and the
appropriateness of the theatre as an image of the world beyond the stage.
Thus, many of the comments about acting are plainly equally applicable
to the struggle to impose order and style on a recalcitrant experience, on
the necessity to enact fictions as though they were realities, to play out
roles in the social arena or even before the eyes of a distant deity. This is
surely in part the ambiguous thrust of the epigraph from Kipling which
Mamet employs: 'We counterfeited once for your disport / Men's joy
and sorrow; but our day has passed. We pray you pardon all where we
fall short − / Seeing we were your servants to the last.'[39]
    Robert is an older actor. He speaks pontifically; he seems confident.
But he needs reassurance from his younger colleague and desperately
wants his company while announcing his independence. Released from

271

his stage role, he is vulnerable and even pathetic. The jealousies and the egotism bubble to the surface and eventually the roles are reversed as he defers to the arrogant confidence of his junior. The ages of man are compressed into a single relationship. The techniques of upstaging one's colleagues are effortlessly employed off stage as well as on, as they work, consciously or unconsciously, to reinforce their own self-images. The make-up table is littered with the materials from which they construct their stage masks, but they deploy an equal sufficiency of roles in their relationship with one another.

The series of excerpts that they enact provide Mamet with ample scope for parody. He offers only a slightly distorted version of *What Price Glory?*, a modern drama of sexual tensions, a vapid piece of mock-Chekhov, a bombastic historical play, a melodrama of survival at sea (reminiscent of Steinbeck's *Lifeboat*) which they struggle to invest with metaphysical subplot, and a hospital soap opera in which they both forget their lines. In other words their serious discussions about their art and their dedication to the craft of the theatre are undercut by a reality which is almost wholly reductive. The older actor's homilies are rendered hollow by the fact that he is reduced to performing in what is patently a provincial repertory, while the young man's ambitions are at least suspect given the context. Their desperate efforts to detect 'another level of meaning' in the banal plays which they perform is an attempt to give significance to their roles and hence to their lives (as well as a deserved dig at critics). This nexus between their life in the theatre and their life beyond it is crucial, for beyond the comedy of a play which has ample scope for visual as well as verbal humour there is an elaboration of the familiar metaphoric significance of the theatre – a significance spelled out a little too clearly at times. Hence, Robert suggests that the process of life is 'A little like a play'. He remarks that the history of acting 'goes back as far as man's' and that 'our aspirations in the Theatre are much the same as man's',[40] that 'We *are* society.' He elsewhere elaborates:

> The Theatre's a closed society. Constantly abutting thoughts, the feelings, the emotions of our colleagues. Sensibilities (*pause*) bodies . . . *forms* evolve. An etiquette, eh? In our personal relations with each other . . . One generation sows the seeds. It instructs the preceding . . . that is to say, the *following* generation . . . from the quality of its actions. Not from the discourse, John, no, but organically . . . What is 'life on stage' but attitudes? . . . Damn little . . . One must speak of these things, John, or we will go the way of all society . . . Take too much for granted, fall away and die. On the boards, or in society at large. There must be law, there must be a reason, there must be tradition.[41]

The portentous tone is undercut not merely by his difficulty over the word 'preceding' and the reductive effect of his claim for the virtues of keeping your mouth shut but also by his evident failure to rise to his own level of solemn morality. Thus, objecting to an actress destroying one of his scenes by 'mugging' at the audience, he accuses her of lacking 'humanism' and 'fellow-feeling' and suggests that he would like to 'kill the cunt', because she lacks a 'sense of right and wrong'.[42]

If his tone of self-righteousness is mocked, the image itself is given authority and the rapid switching between role-playing and a supposed authenticity (which is simply a more sophisticated example of that role-playing which is the central strategy of the play) is offered as an accurate account of social behaviour. All the world is indeed a stage and all the men and women merely players. Life, it is implied, is equally compounded of melodrama, sub-Chekhovian ennui and sexual adventuring. It has something of the quality of soap opera. Where in the 1960s the theatre group (united by shared values, alive to one another's sheer physical presence and speaking lines in which they invested their own psychic beings) was presented not merely as an analogue of society but as a paradigm of authentic being, Mamet chooses to stress the ironies, the selfishness and the cruel irrelevancies of theatre and life alike. Actors inhabit roles already created for them. They project formularised emotional responses and speak words that they inherit. They derive their sense of personal worth from the value that others are prepared to concede them. They must suppress evidence of spontaneity and suggestions of fallibility. If theatre is, indeed, not merely, as Robert claims, '*part of life*',[43] but an image of that life, it is more than touched with absurdity. Like Tom Stoppard's *Rosencrantz and Guildenstern Are Dead*, or Williams's *Out Cry*, the epitome of that absurdity is realised in the image of the actor addressing an empty theatre – a life suddenly drained of function not by any transformation in the life of the individual but by the removal of the audience: 'Sweet poison of the actor, rehearsing in an empty theatre upon an empty stage.'[44] The irony of the actor's benediction at the end of the play to a supposedly absent audience, but in fact to the actual audience, is a gesture of incorporation which should not leave that audience as assured of its own role as the gentle banalities imply. 'The lights dim. Each to his own home. Goodnight. Goodnight. Goodnight.'[45] The repetition of the words, 'Ephemeris. Ephemeris',[46] a few moments before, is sufficiently destabilising to curdle the convention. The audience now cease to play their roles as an audience and assume a myriad of other roles. They go, presumably, to play out their personal melodramas, to lapse back into their Chekhovian stasis, to resume their parts in a drama whose denouement they know but of whose lines they are uncertain. Which is to say that the play rests on a cliché – perhaps the central cliché of theatre – (that art imitates life) and certainly on a basic conviction of the late 1960s and early 1970s (that life imitates art). It is, finally, however, too fragile a play to press these concerns so far. The humour is rather too gentle. The pain is present, the sense of abandonment plain, but it stops short of the kind of ontological enquiry which concerned Pirandello or, indeed, the metadramatic complexity of Stoppard.

Mamet's work is a conscious attempt to dramatise a contemporary sensibility. As he has said, 'In the theater today we're beginning to recognize ourselves as Americans. In the sixties we rejected pride in being American. In the seventies the theater is saying that being American is nothing to be ashamed of. But we have to learn how to deal with it. We need to take a look at certain taboo aspects in ourselves.' That is, indeed, the task which he has set himself as he has probed American values, sexual assumptions, pathological evasions. And to Mamet the theatre is precisely designed to accomplish such a function: 'Theater people tell us about our national unconscious . . . Their true responsibility is to make our dreams clear.' The theatre also offers something of a paradigm of the human psyche. It constitutes a sustained tension between the desire for order and the need for an inventive freedom. Indeed, *A Life in the Theatre* was precisely designed to dramatise two aspects of the artistic consciousness which are equally two aspects of the human consciousness. As he has explained, 'Robert, the older actor, is trying to codify and prolong what's happened to him. The younger actor is trying to achieve, explore and enjoy.'[47] He has also said that he was drawn to the theatre because 'I saw those people who operated on their intuitions rather than by reference to a set code. Their ad hoc universe functioned not in reference to any universal laws but in reference only to the needs of the play they were doing.' But if this stresses that aspect of Mamet's work which is autotelic, which is fascinated by language and form in its own right, it also points back to the same tension implied in *A Life in the Theatre*. For while the actor plays the moment, the line, the action, the emotion, he does so in terms of a totality which these moments are required to constitute.

Simplicity has always been the keynote of Mamet's work. He has confessed to reading fairy-tales because 'They get me in touch with drama as a primordial instinct rather than an instinctual exercise. Good drama is not perceived at a conscious level.'[48] Indeed, as he has suggested, his plays 'are getting more spare as I go along. Success has made it possible for me to work and produce as much or as little as I want. In the past I felt compelled to write. Now I'm trying to force myself to relax. My writing is coming at a more leisurely pace. "The Woods", for example, was written in a more *legato* mood.'[49]

Although he has said that 'In this country we only understand plays as dope, whose purpose is anaesthetic, meant to blot out consciousness', this is an attack on the anodyne nature of Broadway rather than a suggestion that his plays are designed to work primarily through conscious channels. Indeed, the simplicity of his work is deceptive. If it has something of the quality of the folktale, like that folktale its simple outline conceals a level on which it addresses fundamental anxieties and hopes. Mamet's achievement is to forge a series of plays which, in remarkably different ways, respond to this need while avoiding the casual resolution and reassurance of a theatre which has too often seen its principal function as to 'sooth or reinforce certain preconceived notions in an audience'.[50]

Mamet's concern with probing American myth and reality, with charting the collapse of value and the anguished facts of personal despair, continued with *The Water Engine*, written for 'Earplay', the curious title for a series of radio plays co-produced by the BBC and National Public Radio. This, once again, probes behind the bland and confident surface of the American dream, though perhaps less out of a moralist's desire to expose the gulf between appearance and reality than out of a wish to examine the nature of fictions, the impulse which leads the imagination to invent and people the world it would inhabit. It is a theme which pulls together his moral and aesthetic concerns, for, on the one hand, he sets out to penetrate the fiction which is America, and, on the other hand, he begins to inspect with greater rigour his own fictions, his own implication in the processes which he observes. *The Water Engine* is about the invention of America and the inventions of art. Subtitled 'An American Fable' and first produced for the stage in May 1977, it ostensibly offers an account of the hounding and eventual destruction of an inventor who creates an engine which can run on distilled water rather than gasoline. The patents lawyer to whom he takes his device is in fact in league with those industrial forces who stand to benefit by its suppression. When bribery and intimidation fail to secure their objective, they resort to simple violence, seizing his sister and torturing both until they should reveal the whereabouts of the plans. When they fail to co-operate they are killed, the plans having already been mailed to an energetic young man who will presumably carry on the battle.

However, behind the simple outlines of this melodrama is a more complex play, for this homily of capitalist greed and the betrayal of trust is in fact presented as a radio programme – appropriately enough given its intended audience. The result is that social drama becomes metaphysical game, that text and character are deconstructed. As Mamet himself observed of the stage productions, 'In Steven Schachter's productions, in Chicago and New York, many scenes were played on mike, as actors presenting a radio drama, and many scenes were played off mike as in a traditional, realist play. The result was a third reality, a scenic truth, which dealt with radio not as an electronic convenience, but as an expression of our need to create and to communicate and to explain.'[51] In the Earplay version the complexities were compounded, the different levels of reality depending on the foregrounding of style, an approximation of the style of radio in 1934.

The play, indeed, is set at the time of the 'Century of Progress' at the Chicago World Fair (which in fact had run from May to November 1933). Mamet does not for the most part comment on the more obvious ironies which were generated by the celebration of a century of progress in the midst of the Depression (though he does have a character identify these clearly enough), but he does imply an ironised account of history even while confessing to the degree to which the clichés of social myth are attacked through the clichés of art.

The story of the inventor is presented as a dramatised account of the fate of a man referred to in a chain letter (the kind which invites recipients to send a dollar to the next person on a list of attached names and thus establish an unbroken chain of people each of whom is thereby promised wealth but each of whom is also threatened with disaster should he choose to break the chain). We are to presume that the inventor, Charles Lang, is this man and the voice of the Chainletter punctuates the unfolding story, outlining his seemingly inevitable move towards death. Thus, yet another level of 'reality' is established, another layer of fictionality which resists the apparent realism of plot and character. And the play inevitably becomes less concerned with exposing the mechanisms of an amoral social system than with revealing the mechanisms of fiction, the desire to plot utopian dreams, to invent our own past and future, to use the imagination as an instrument of communication and a means of explanation. But if the story-telling of the radio play is one such fiction then the myths of industrial and scientific progress are others. As the voice of the Chainletter observes, 'We are characters within a dream of industry. Within a dream of toil',[52] while a Soapbox Speaker at Bughouse Square insists that the honeyed myths of patriotism simply 'support the torture of the ages. The Great War, the pogroms, the Crusades, the Inquisition . . . The power of the torturers comes from the love of Patriotic Songs.' When urged to 'Go back to Russia', he replies, 'Russia is a fiction, friend. She is a bugaboo inventor [sic] to distract you from your troubles. There is no Russia. Russia is the bear beneath your bed.'[53] The real question, as he observes, is 'When will we learn to choose between the quality of our impressions?'[54] The Chainletter, as Mamet observes in his prefatory note, is an expression of our need to create, to communicate and explain. As its threats make plain, however, it is also an instrument of coercion. The drive for scientific advance, the pursuit of technological efficiency, the development of the spaceship, a central icon of the Chicago exposition, are equally ambiguous, subject to and expressions of a fallible human nature whose imaginative and creative impulses are seemingly ineluctably wedded to a destructive self-concern. As a Barker at the World Fair remarks, in a speech whose rhetorical flourishes do not negate its truth, science is 'Our thoughts, our dreams, our aspirations rendered into practical and useful forms. Our science is our self. What are our tools, but wishes?'[55] And the writer is scarcely irrelevant to such considerations. *The Water Engine* is about inventions and the need that fires those inventions, and as such it could scarcely be more central to the question of artistic creation which is inspired by its own psychic and social necessities and is at least ambiguously related to the political and cultural realities which it may choose to resist but which can successfully accommodate it. The Soapbox Speaker denounces the contradictions of his society much as Mamet has done and is for the most part listened to politely, his comments being seen simply as a 'performance', a show which is actually produced by a Moderator. It is the classic dilemma of the writer as, perhaps, is the feeling that to move one's private inventions into the public world is to invite their destruction, to lose them.

This metadramatic dimension of the play is reinforced by a staging which foregrounds the process of production. The play, as Mamet observed, generated 'a third reality' as the actors on stage played actors performing a play. While this scarcely destroys illusionism, in a sense simply raising the stakes of realism, the shifts of convention inevitably expose the mechanics required for this double game – a simulation of emotional truth and social coherence which can scarcely be detached from the subject of the play which they perform, in which deceit and betrayal of social and moral contracts are at the heart of personal and public experience. Deceit is the essence of the artistic process. In a sense it relies on the reality of one of the Chainletter's claims, namely that 'All civilization stands on trust. All people are connected',[56] even while dramatising the falsity of such claims; just as, contrariwise, a journalist in the play writes a eulogy to trust and mutual respect, glad only that he will not have to sign his name to sentiments in which he has no faith.

The supreme fiction is perhaps America itself. As the Speaker in Bughouse Square asks, 'Whatever happened to this nation? Or did it ever exist? ... did it ever exist with its freedoms and slogans ... the buntings, the goldheaded standards, the songs? With Equality, Liberty . . . In the West they plow under wheat. Where is America? I say it does not exist. And I say that it never existed. It was all but a myth. A great dream of avarice . . . The dream of a Gentleman Farmer.' Living, as he insists, 'in the Final Time . . . With want in the midst of abundance',[57] he challenges the substance of the dream, just as the voice of the Barker, at the end of the play, observes that 'Technological and Ethical masterpieces decay into folktales' and asks 'Who knows what is truth?'[58] Truth is problematic, more especially in a play in which fiction enfolds fiction. And if in a sense the claim equally of the Barker and the voice of the Chainletter that 'All people are connected' must be true to the degree that communication operates at all, the nature of that connection, the play implies, is as likely to be a commitment to shared illusions as to manifest realities and those illusions may contain a corrosive element which will destroy what is plainly at best a tenuous link.

When *The Water Engine* was produced on Broadway Mamet wrote a brief companion-piece – *Mr Happiness*. This, too, takes place in a radio station in 1934 and consists of an extended monologue by a Miss Lonelyhearts figure. His function is to respond to the cries for help by people bewildered by their lives and seeking some kind of absolution for the acts of betrayal which they plan or the hopes which they are unable to realise. A woman wishes to remarry and abandon her old mother; a man wants to leave his wife; a young boy with a twisted spine is frightened to ask a girl to a dance. In reply Mr Happiness offers a mixture of pieties, popular philosophy and cant mixed in with common sense. But the essence of the play lies less in the figure of Mr Happiness than in the orchestrated cries of suffering, the sense of incompletion, loss, and pain, the desperation that lies behind the letters. With a kind of pointillist effect Mamet builds up an image of the society outside the studio and of the degree to which those writing to the radio station are prepared to surrender control over their lives, to defer to modes of morality defined for them by the media, becoming, like Mr Happiness himself, a source of entertainment and distraction.

In *Reunion* one of the characters observes that 'People always talk about going out to the country or getting back to nature and all the time I say, "Yeah, yeah," and what does it mean? I see the logic of it, but it means nothing to me. Because my entire life I'm looking for a way around.'[59] The retreat to nature, a popular panacea of the late 1960s and early 70s, is likened to the character's alcoholism or his multiple marriages. It is an attempt to tackle a problem which is internal by external means. The move out of the city is an act of displacement which may offer a sense of perspective but which does little else. In *The Woods*

Mamet examines the strategy, locating his characters in a setting whose mythic and historical overtones merely serve to underscore their sense of insufficiency and alarm.

The Woods reads like a parody of Edward Albee's work. Its mannered language, its mock precisions, its stylised relationships and even direct quotations ('Who knows what's real?' is an echo of *Listening*) are not merely reminiscent of Albee; they establish a direct relationship with his work. Thematically *The Woods* picks over the ground left by the older writer. Like *Who's Afraid of Virginia Woolf?* and *A Delicate Balance*, indeed like virtually all of his work, it is concerned with the simultaneous failure of and desperate need for love; it addresses the bleak realities of personal relationships. Like Albee in his later plays Mamet isolates his characters from the asocial world of urban America, implying rather than describing its corrosive effects. It is in fact a play which works through a series of absences – the pressure of which defines the nature of the characters' lives. Those absences range from a lost relationship with a natural world, to the spontaneous love for which they yearn but which they can no longer feel or express. The two characters, Nick and Ruth (both names inevitably recalling figures from Albee's work), seek out of time what they can apparently no longer find in time – a consolatory relationship which will fill the vacuum of their lives, which will restore poetry to an existence rendered prosaic by egotism and the alienation of modernity. As Mamet has said, it is a play 'about heterosexual love', one which raises the question, 'Why don't men and women get along?' It is 'about the yearning to commit yourself, to become less deracinated – or more racinated'.[60]

The play is set on the porch of a summerhouse in the fall. Appropriately enough, therefore, it deals with the decay of a love affair. The young couple have come to the woods and to the isolated house in order to be alone together but also in a sense to find their roots, to re-establish a sense of identity. They tell one another stories about their own families – stories whose themes, however, are about danger and loss as well as relationship. Their love for one another is an assumed fact; but the cracks in the structure of their relationship are already apparent, both in the dark underside of the past which they invoke and in the over-fastidious way in which they correct one another's usage and question one another's memory. There is a tension which strains their language. Ruth, in particular, reaches out for a form of poetic utterance. Some of her speeches are actually written in verse whereas Nick's are in prose. In a sense this tends to reinforce the sexual roles. Nick's is a direct, prosaic, and even brutal approach; Ruth's is an expression of a poetic desire to sentimentalise their relationship. But this stylistic dissonance also exposes the different needs and expectations of the two people. The mannered conversation also suggests a tension which strains the language. As in Hemingway's 'Big Two-Hearted River' the very over-concern with detail, the obsession with precision seem to imply some trauma, some sense of emptiness and apprehension which has to be concealed with words. It is not quite that the first scene is concerned with the euphoria of love which will turn to disenchantment in the following scene, as Richard Elder implied in *The New York Times Magazine*, but that there is a barely suppressed sense of hysteria apparent from the very beginning. The careless spilling of language by Ruth is an attempt to stave off what later seems an inevitably entropic pattern:

> You could live right out in the country.
> I slept so good yesterday.
> All the crickets, you know?
> With the rhythm.
> You wait.
> And you hear it.
> Chirp.
> Chirp chirp
> Not 'chirping'.
> *Pause*
> Not '*chirping*', really.
> *Birds* chirp.
> Birds chirp, don't they, Nick?
> Birds? . . .
> . . . Who knows what's happening?
> Down by the lake there is a rotten boat.
> A big green rowboat.
> It might be from here to here.
> It's rotten and the back is gone, but I'll bet it was pretty big.
> I sat in it.
> Inside the front was painted up. It smelled real dry.
> I mooshed around and this is how it sounded on the sand.
> Swssshh. Chhhrssssh. Swwwssshhhh.
> Very dry.
> You know. I think I would of liked to go to sea.
> Girls couldn't go to sea.
> As cabin boys or something . . .[61]

The short sentences, the abrupt change of subject, the continuous flow of language, the curious signalling of the onomatopoeia, all suggest something other than a confident relationship and a serene mind. As in so much of Mamet's work the meaning exists less in the words themselves than in the tone, the manner of delivery, the simple fact of speech when silence would serve better; it resides in the acts of concealment implied by a language deliberately opaque, distracting and hermetic. In *The Woods*, rather as in Hemingway's 'Hills Like White Elephants', Nick and Ruth discuss the Vikings, crickets, racoons, bears and family history as a means of not addressing their real concerns. The further irony is that they do not even share their fears. Each tells a story about his or her family past. Ruth's story is about being lost, abandoned in the forest; Nick's is about being trapped. And these are precise analogues of their own sense of alarm at their relationship. Ruth is afraid of being abandoned, laid aside as being without value (hence her invoking of the Viking's supposed habit of destroying female children and her assertion that women were invariably left behind by warriors). She invokes natural beauty and the natural order as validating the status quo: 'It all is only things the way they are. That is all there ever was.'[62] Nick, who has been careful never to declare his love for her (as he later claims), struggles to retain his freedom. She suggests that they should wear rings, bracelets, necklaces 'Wrapped around. / To show that we are lovers',[63] and gives him such a bracelet inscribed with an announcement of her love; he, later, throws it away, afraid of such proprietary claims. Ruth fears the temporary: 'Nothing lasts. This is what I thought down on the rowboat. It had rolled. It had gone back to the earth. We all go. / That is why the Earth is good for us. / When we look for things that don't go back, we become sick. That is when we hurt each other. / I thought about you and me.' The statement is an appeal which undercuts the apparent assurance lying behind her celebration of 'the things we do. / To each other. The night things.'[64] The attraction of the woods lies in the fact that here 'all things have stopped'.[65] The pressure of history and of change is relaxed. It was a place 'To be still . . . be content'.[66] She wishes to stay. But he insists that 'Things change.'[67] And in the second scene they do precisely this as their relationship fragments.

In some degree their positions are reversed in the second scene, with Nick recalling his dreams of a settled life, of security and of the reassuring nature of a continuing relationship, while Ruth justifies the implied imperfections of their relationship: 'sometimes things are different than the way you thought they'd be when you set out on them. This doesn't mean that, you know, that they aren't . . . Things can be unexpected and be beautiful if we will let them. And not be frightened by them . . . You don't have to be nervous when a thing is new.'[68] His method for dealing with the tensions between them is more direct. He settles for sexual assault. But the loveless advance is easily deflected by a sense of disgust which he displaces onto the mildewed rainwear that she has put on. The moment betrays the distance between them, the alienation which they have tried to neutralise first with conversation and then with what she, at least, has chosen to call love. The more she insists on his commitment, the more he withdraws. Her desperation is apparent in her argument: 'When you come up here that means you are committed . . . Because I am your guest.'[69] Her anguished cry, 'I thought that we were both in this together',[70] is the truth not merely of their relationship but of virtually all of the relationships in Mamet's plays. His characters share their situation but little else. Like figures from a Tennessee Williams play they seem sentenced to solitary confinement inside their own skins for life, though in the case of Mamet's characters this is a result of fear. It is fear which drives them together but it is also fear which intervenes even in their intimacy to keep them solitary beings. Thus Ruth outlines the natural logic which draws her to Nick, a logic as implacable as natural law. Observing the seagulls she says:

> They either eat the fish or insects (*Pause*)
> We eat fish. The fish eat seaweed.
> It all dies, the things turn into shells.
> *Pause.*
> Or deposits. They wash up. As coral.
> Maybe they make sand, or special beaches.
> They decay and wash away.
> *Pause.*
> Then they form the islands.
> *Pause.*
> Nothing lasts forever.
> *Pause.*
> Don't make me go home.
> *Pause.*
> I want to live with you.[71]

By the same token her act, her self-consciousness, her very femaleness, reminds Nick of this logic and makes him withdraw into a protective solitude. The sex with which he tries to drive out thoughts of death in some way incorporates those thoughts.

In the final scene the relationship dissolves. The exchanged intimacies, the memories, are forged into weapons. They fight, striking out at one another. Ruth, rightly, identifies the terror which drives him: 'Fuck me. I don't want to die. Nobody wants to die.'[72] Nick confesses that he had longed for someone who would justify his life to him but 'What is the point? If one is like the other?'[73] Mutual incomprehension and fear can solve nothing. He cries out in pain, 'What are we *doing* here? What are we *doing* here? (*Pause.*) What will *happen* to us? *We* can't know ourselves . . . How can we *know* ourselves?'[74] The play ends with the two of them together, with their arms around one another, as Ruth repeats the story of the two children lost in the woods.

The play is clearly offered as an account of human relationships and of the ambiguous pressures which lie behind the supposed intimacies of men and women. The house in which the action takes place is built over a cave (reminiscent of Tennessee Williams's *Period of Adjustment*) which is a patent correlative of that void which inspires such terror in both Nick and Ruth (as it had in Albee's Harry and Edna in *A Delicate Balance*). Clinging together, like the lost children in the story, they try to neutralise their terror through simple propinquity.

Though extravagantly praised, particularly by Richard Elder, for whom it was 'simple, profound, and intense', it is reminiscent of late Albee not merely in its foregrounding of language and in its attention to the rhythms of speech and of human relationships but in its mannered metaphysics. However, what may seem coy simplifications and pretentious dialogue are for the most part the product of character under pressure, though the truth of the relationship and of its broader implications is spelled out rather too clearly. The characters themselves are more manifestly literary creations than those in the earlier plays. The careful sculpting of verse and prose is functional and not without subtlety but the rhetoric is not always generated by character. Mamet has said that *The Woods* marked his movement towards 'a faith in something or other'.[75] It is hard to see what that faith might be except a conviction as to the need for a human contact which is equally the source of pain and irony and which has been the theme of virtually all of his work.

Mamet's characters are damaged. They are incomplete and, more painfully, are vaguely aware of that incompletion. They struggle to fill the spaces in their lives with fantasies, with a barely coherent language and with a hesitant and unsuccessful attempt to forge personal relationships. Indeed his plays seem obsessively concerned with such relationships; they are almost invariably structured around pairs of characters. Even where the cast is more various the scenes themselves tend to isolate two figures at a time as though to permit any more to intrude would be to create a threatening critical mass. In fact, social experience is disturbing to his characters. Society is perceived by them only vaguely. For the most part it is seen as threatening. Rather like O'Neill's characters, who also have a tendency to forge shifting alliances of two and who retreat from a menacing externality, they fear social interaction. As a consequence they are, more often than not, frozen into inaction, shaped and defined by the physical and mental constrictions which they too readily embrace. They are unwilling to resist, to press back against the experience which alarms them or to transcend the model of existence which they have too willingly accepted as a protection against the unknown, the flux of life. The reductive image of men and women which they embrace, the authority which they grant to media inventions, the simplistic models of human behaviour which they endorse, are all expressions of their need to feel some control over experience. His characters wish to open themselves to other people. They offer confidences, recall or invent moments from the past. But the intimacy is never sustained.

The connection with O'Neill is perhaps strongest in *Lakeboat*, which in some senses is reminiscent of that writer's early sea plays. Written at the beginning of his career, this was first performed by the Theatre Workshop at Marlboro College in Vermont in 1970, but, following his success, it was rediscovered, revised and produced in its published format by the Milwaukee Repertory Theatre in 1980. In a note on the staging Mamet actually recommends a realistic set and the play is, on one level, an attempt to recreate life on board a merchant marine ship on the Great Lakes. In a series of twenty-eight scenes he builds up a picture of the daily routine, the vacuous conversations, the memories and ambitions of those who form an asocial society of individuals, held together only by virtue of sharing the same situation and participating in the same voyage. The metaphysical implications are obvious and are not articulated directly, but the aggregation of isolated moments – the sum total of their delusions and fears – offers a picture of a society and an existence drained of transcendence. The figures on board the lakeboat *T Harrison* scarcely differ from those who inhabit the junk store in *American Buffalo*. Both works are equally plotless. In the latter play the characters plan a robbery which will never take place; in the former they describe a robbery which may never have taken place or one which if it did take place has already gathered about it the kind of fictional accretions which are their substitutes for meaning. The victim of the supposed mugging is described by one of the sailors as being young and inexperienced and as having been robbed by a prostitute, while to another he was a gambling degenerate attacked by the Mafia and beaten insensible. To a third he was armed with a Colt revolver and was set up by the FBI. By the end of the play they have convinced themselves that he had been killed, but when they are told that he had probably missed the boat through over-sleeping they have no difficulty in adjusting. They simply abandon one fantasy drama for another. With no real excitement, no sense of progress in their lives (they constantly repeat the same voyage and for the most part are still minor functionaries in their mid 40s) they live in their imagination and, in effect, create the worlds in which they live. The reiterated story of the supposed mugging recurs like a series of variations on a theme. The triviality of their daily lives – one man watches two gangs for four hours at a stretch, another makes sandwiches – is relieved by brief spasms of soul-less sex and extended bouts of drinking whenever they reach port or by conversations, the banality of which merely emphasises their need for some kind of human contact. Their only other recourse is a sense of irony. Thus Fred, an Able-Bodied Seaman in his thirties or forties, informs a young student doing vacation work on board that 'the main thing about the boats, other than their primary importance to the Steel Industry, is that you don't get any pussy'.[76] Their ironic detachment is a central strategy but it is also a symptom of their own literal and symbolic situation. Sailing the lakes they only touch shore occasionally and then only to anaesthetise themselves with alcohol and sex before sailing again. Only the young student seems to stand aside from this, to have a chance of escaping. Yet the evidence of his other plays, of *The Water Engine*, *The Woods* and *Reunion*, does not suggest that the questions which Mamet addresses are the product of class. The sense of anguish, of indirection and isolation are not the result of social position. The marginality of his characters, their sense of missing the point of their lives, of failing to achieve either happiness or a sense of selfhood, is not presented as a special consequence of economic circumstances but as a central fact of existence. *Lakeboat* does nothing to indicate the source of any transcendence.

With *Edmond* (1982) Mamet dramatises the experiences of a man who sets out in search of transcendence but finds its reverse. Having convinced himself that he is superior to what he takes to be his fate – his marriage, for example, has decayed into routine and his spiritual life become attenuated – he attempts to liberate himself through sensual fulfilment. But his odyssey through the underworld of American life reveals nothing but his vulnerability, that and the exploitative nature of human relationships when reduced to simple exchange value. He is systematically defrauded, cheated of his money and denied the satisfaction which he imagines himself to be seeking. Though he deploys the rhetoric of liberation his experience suggests the extent to which his freedom is circumscribed. Though Mamet has hinted that he sees it as a play about life, it is perhaps more accurately seen as concerned with death – spiritual and emotional death. Indeed, Edmond himself reveals a prejudice and even a callous brutality which Mamet seems to imply is the underside of middle-class values. He becomes the thing he would once have feared. He is the spectre of dark violence which had once doubtless haunted his own imagination. The play ends with Edmond imprisoned for murder, literally deprived of the freedom he had sought. In that sense an image always present in Mamet's work here becomes literal in so far as his imprisonment is merely a concrete form of that deprivation which is a mark of virtually all his characters.

A similar literalness is apparent in *Glengarry, Glen Ross* (1983), which pursues the implications of *American Buffalo* to a logical conclusion. The play is concerned with a group of real-estate salesmen who find themselves involved in a make-or-break sales campaign. Those who succeed will be rewarded with prizes (including a Cadillac car); those who fail will be fired. In other words we are offered the capitalist system in microcosm. Mamet, though, is less concerned with the drama of their competition than with its impact on their characters. Exploited themselves, they become exploiters. The customers become 'marks' who are to be pursued, deceived and, in effect, defrauded. Their colleagues are merely obstacles to their success. No other values obtrude and when for a brief moment they seem to, as one of the salesmen apparently offers us a personal philosophy which turns on the need to seize one's power of action, this is quickly and ironically exposed as a sales pitch. The values of business are applied directly to personal relationships. And if *American Buffalo* implied that business and crime are mutually allied, in *Glengarry, Glen Ross* that crime is actually enacted as two salesmen, down on their luck, contrive to steal the list of potential clients. Since their action hardly differs in intent or form from the deceptions practised as a necessary part of their trade, the moral criminality and corrupting power of commercial life is asserted as literal fact.

Once again the force of the play, however, has less to do with propositions about capitalism than with Mamet's power to imply the spaces left vacant by human need and filled only with the brutalising jargon of exploitation. Behind the obscenities, the incoherent sounds, the relentless platitudes of the salesmen's chatter and the neurotic and overlapping monologues which pass for communication is a vacancy, a world whose existence can only be implied from the consistency with which it is ignored. That world – a world of genuine emotion, of human need and of spiritual aspiration – finds no solace, no articulation, no correlative in a public world defined only by completions which bear no relationship to the necessities of a private life or a moral existence. Those absences become crucial. They are what give the play its special force. The language of his characters may indeed accurately reflect realistic speech – which is composed of just such incoherences and incomplete linguistic gestures – but that is only the beginning of Mamet's accomplishments. His supreme skill, like Pinter's, lies in his ability to create a sense of what never reaches the level of language, a need which can barely be apprehended let alone expressed. The real betrayals are less commercial and social than they are moral and spiritual. What alarms him is the denial of fundamental human needs, a retreat into a language which is perverted precisely because it is a denial of a basic desire for communication. There are moments in this play when that desire becomes apparent. Characters reach out for the contact which their world seems to deny them, ultimately having to settle for the consolations contained in their own fictions. But, offered the chance to betray one another not all of them succumb and that is the basis of a tenuous hope.

Mamet builds his plays from fragments, from details which exist independently of naturalist function. He has the artist's skill at creating effects with overlapping layers and with small individual gestures which cohere. He has the musician's concern for rhythm. But his roots are in theatre. He was trained as an actor and his imagination was in part shaped by those writers whose work has most clearly shaped the nature of the contemporary theatre – playwrights, moreover, whose own use of language could also be more sensibly related to a concern for musical structure than for naturalistic detail. Like Beckett, he is concerned with dramatising a largely plotless world in which nuance and gesture become of central significance. Like Pinter, he tends to locate his plays in an ostensibly realist environment only to deconstruct the assumptions of realism as they relate to plot, character and language. Indeed, in speaking of the influences on his own career he has said, 'Pinter was probably the most influential when I was young and malleable . . . "The Homecoming", "The Basement", especially his revue sketches. I felt a huge freedom because of Pinter's sketches – to deal in depth and on their own merit with such minutiae. Beckett and Pinter – of course I'm influenced by them. If you're in modern dance, how could you not be influenced by Martha Graham?'[77]

Peter Conradi has argued for a pastoral impulse in realism in that the assumptions behind its technical means depended on nostalgic simplification, wantonly faking an easy continuity with the past. In a sense Mamet's work is less realistic than concerned with the problematics of realism. The surface tension of his realism is such that it sustains a world which could so easily be sent plunging into its own depths if that surface is once punctured. So long as critics praise the realism, the elaborate structure of detail and fact which his characters equally struggle to sustain, he becomes not merely a faithful servant of mimesis but a mordant poet of modernity. But the power of his work surely lies elsewhere. It comes into existence in those moments when language becomes attenuated and when the surface realism is stretched to the point of translucency. It materialises in the terrifying blank which lies behind the surface clutter and the silence which lies behind the hysterical flood of words. His characters may seek to impose a simple realism on events, resisting disturbing notions of character or event which fail to correspond to this model, but it is not a realism which he is willing to endorse. They are people who are falling through space, desperately trying to imagine a world of substance and opacity which can arrest that fall. It is not, however, a strategy which he offers to validate.

Mamet's work presents a myth of decline. His own use of verse formalises but does not resist the collapse of language which parallels the collapse of other forms. His characters fear life almost as much as death. Coerced by public myths they try to enact them in the supposed privacy of their own lives; but that privacy has been infiltrated. The imagination itself has been deformed, inhabited by the very forces which it would resist. Spontaneous feelings defer to formulae which are not even seen as such.

Realism encodes a version of the real; historicist, positivist, open equally to the formal logics of Freud or Marx. Mamet's version of the real is somewhat different – charged with an energy which owes little to personal psychology or class. His characters may be drawn largely though not exclusively from an underclass. They may be marked by specific traumas. But the anxiety is more vague. Mamet's texts resist their own potential for nostalgia and in doing so expose equally the coercive power of the real and the authority which we grant that real. Mamet is not simply a satirist deploring a destructive urbanism. He is a moralist regretting our desire to create alibis for our own inadequacies, our failure of moral courage.

Mamet's world is a world of collapse. Relationships are attenuated. There are no transcendencies, secular or religious. Myths exist but they have been hollowed out. Language no longer works to bind people into a common world. Fantasy is the only force which retains its power – fantasy in the form of a nostalgia drained of human content or of ambitions which can only be entertained so long as they are not enacted. It is a world not unlike that of O'Neill's *The Iceman Cometh*. His characters live provisionally, enacting uncertainly the models offered to them by the media. They are drawn together by need but held apart by suspicion and fear. Deeply vulnerable, they struggle to conceal that vulnerability. Innocence has to be fervently denied. The essence of living is to allow no one to take advantage of you, never to reveal weakness, never to voice the need which is the dominant fact of lives which have no purpose beyond mere survival. His characters pay lip service to civilities. They like to believe that language can bridge gaps in experience and link people held apart by self-interest and fear. The impulse is there. It is simply blunted, turned back on itself. It falls victim to anger, frustration, despair and the public clichés of emotion. It is as though someone had already lived their lives for them. Mamet's humanistic drive derives from the vestigial will-to-contact which his characters retain; his meta-dramatic leanings are an expression of the ease with which they substitute performance for being – the theatre becoming an appropriate model for human behaviour less because of its imaginative economy than because he sees the insecure self as rushing desperately into roles which seem to protect even as they suffocate. A poet of urban brittleness, he is unwilling to retreat into deceptive pastoralism or a nostalgia which could never conceal the fact that betrayal is not simply a product of a contemporary brutalism. Yet wherever he looks, if he sees cruelty and despair, he also sees moments of consonance and mutuality. And though they disappear, the space they leave has its own compulsions.

The past rests heavily on the present. The two old men in *Duck Variations* stare blankly over lost years. The store in *American Buffalo* is full of the material detritus of American life. And at the intersecting point of a solid material past and a future composed of fantasies generated by anxiety are his characters, self-obsessed, nervous, like threatened animals, doomed creatures. For the most part they are unwilling to risk themselves outside the small worlds which they develop as a protection against the natural processes of life – sexuality, age, change, mortality. For the most part there is no central character, no one with sufficient grasp of selfhood, no one in clear-cut battle with his situation. His figures come together aware of their incompletions but unwilling or unable to make the sacrifices or offer the gestures necessary to heal their wounds.

But their incoherences, their stuttering apprehensions, are contained within a redemptive rhythm which is the product of the writer. Below the level of banal conversation and self-pitying laments there is a lyricism which is created by Mamet's synthesising imagination. Starting at the level of language he implies the possibility of form and grace which his characters deny; he reaches out for a harmony which they glimpse only as memory. What cannot be resolved in the action of the plays or the person of the characters is in a sense resolved by the gesture of the playwright who proposes a consonance to which his characters aspire but which they cannot realise. In other words something of the modernist impulse remains in Mamet along with the liberal humanist's responsibility simultaneously to dramatise the alienations of contemporary life and to imply a possible route to a moral existence, in art if not in life, in imagination if not in fact, and hence to transform life and fact through art and the imagination. The poetry of the work is the promise. The collapsing city is balanced by the power of the mind to contain that collapse and turn disorder into order – which may be a source of irony but is equally a mark of humanity. The accumulated objects in the junk store in *American Buffalo*, drained of their function, are at once an appropriate image of the men who are similarly bereft of function, and of the society which they inhabit where energies are directed to the proliferation of such objects, to reaching out for possessions whose value derives only from their price and not from intrinsic beauty or utility. They conspire to steal a nickel. The only thing which gives it a value is the market economy. So, too, with the people who inhabit the world of things, carrying guns to protect themselves from the robbers who are themselves. Mamet may hesitate to say that property is theft but he does seem to imply that to value that inanimate world is to rob oneself of a necessary human quality, to become inanimate. However, if the world is unintelligible to his characters, then redemption lies in the fact that it is not unintelligible to the sensibility which observes it. But the irony lies in the fact that he seems to be arguing for the necessity of a humanism for which he cannot always find space within the plays.

PART V

The theatre of commitment

INTRODUCTION

The resurgence of the American theatre in the early 1960s coincided with an increasing politicisation of the culture. If the 1950s were never quite as bland as they seem in retrospect – the assaults of the House Un-American Activities Committee inspiring an admittedly somewhat ineffectual liberal response and the civil rights movement growing in strength and confidence – the 1960s witnessed political revolt across a broad spectrum. The emergence and consolidation of the black movement was followed by and in part inspired the women's movement, and the revolt by Chicanos and Indians. The dilemma of a minority in a democracy generated a reliance on direct intervention. Physical presence became a mark of authenticity and committed drama its corollary and occasion.

But what do we mean by commitment? In his essay 'On Some Outdated Notions', published in 1957, Alain Robbe-Grillet argued that 'the moment the writer starts worrying about conveying some meaning (exterior to the work of art), literature starts to retreat, to disappear'. It was not, as Sartre feared, that a moral literature would become a moralistic literature and hence deprive readers or audiences of the very freedom which they were being invited to embrace but that this freedom must be factitious if it does not address the constricting power of language itself; if it does not recognise the coercions of literature. Thus he suggested,

> Let us restore to the idea of commitment, then, the only meaning it can have for us. Rather than being of a political nature, commitment, for the writer, means to be fully aware of the current problems of his own language, convinced of their extreme importance, and desirous of solving them from within. Therein lies his sole possibility of remaining an artist, and also, no doubt, by means of some obscure and distant consequence, of maybe one day being of some use – maybe even to the revolution.[1]

Or as he said in his later essay 'New Novel, New Man' (1961):

We no longer believe in fixed and ready-made meanings, which gave man first the old divine order, and then the eighteenth-century rationalist order, but it is in man himself that we place all our hopes; it is the forms he creates that give meaning to the world.

Consequently, it is not reasonable to aspire to serve a political cause in our novels, not even a cause we consider just, and not even if it is one for which we militate in our political life. In our political life we are all the time obliged to assume known meanings: social meanings, historical meanings and moral meanings. Art is more modest . . . To believe that the novelist has 'something to say', and that he then tries to discover how to say it, is the gravest misconception. For it is precisely this 'how', this way of saying things, that constitutes the whole, obscure project of the writer, and that later becomes the dubious content of his book. And in the final analysis it may well be this dubious content of an obscure project that best serves the cause of freedom.

However, in a final sentence he posed precisely the question which eventually forced the black writer beyond a commitment to freedom generated by imagination alone, for he concluded this passage by asking 'But how long will we have to wait?'[2]

The urgencies of the moment would, it seemed, precisely not permit this more metaphysical view of freedom to prevail. There is indeed a kind of freedom in writing as there is in the act of reading, which itself preserves the idea of imaginative and hence, perhaps, social transcendence – an imaginative possession of experience, a power to invent the world one inhabits. But there is an irony too apparent to be ignored, a need too apparent for the black writer to be content to articulate a freedom for which no social, political or economic correlative can be found. The struggle with language was real enough and not drained of metaphoric significance, but other struggles were more immediately pressing. Robbe-Grillet may rightly point out that 'the work of art contains nothing, in the strict sense of the term (in the same way as a box, for instance, may or may not enclose within itself some foreign body). Art is not a more or less highly-coloured envelope whose function is to decorate the author's message, the bit of gold paper round the biscuit packet',[3] but the pressure of events, the necessity to articulate the suffering and anguish of those rendered voiceless by social fiat or political dictat, militates against a revolt which is too oblique, too fully shaped by the imagination. What seems to be required is that social experience should be transmitted as intact as possible, processed by the mind but not the imagination which can too easily turn reality into fiction and pain into art.

The fact is that the American theatre from the late 1960s onwards was characterised by an energy generated in part at least by the urgencies of political, social and moral revolt. There were those for whom theatrical experiment was primarily a question of aesthetics, but increasingly there were others for whom the principal impulse was social and the distinction between aesthetics and ethics untenable. The theatre became an arena, a crucible, a public forum. It became a place where the shared components of experience could be identified and translated, at least at the level of imagination, into the beginnings of communal action. And if the theatre, which had its own traditions and its own constricting social assumptions, proved incapable of accommodating a new spirit of enquiry and revolt then there was always the street.

The problem is that theatre has historically been the domain of the bourgeoisie. It was a part of the very economic and cultural system against which the new committed playwrights were in ostensible revolt. It thus became necessary to identify a new audience, to redefine conventional assumptions about the theatrical moment. In part this was done, and the various minority and special interest groups who turned to the theatre did at times address an audience defined precisely in terms of its racial, political or sexual identity. However, there is another impulse at work. For though immediate injustice frequently provides the rationale for such work and while the distinctiveness of the black, the Indian or the Chicano experience provides a focus for the theatrical event, this frequently coexists with another impulse of equal power and conviction – a desire to see behind the social surface a sense of shared anguish. It is thus often simultaneously a theatre of revolt and reconciliation. At the level of language the pressure is towards fragmentation; at the level of theme towards a proffered grace. Often, therefore, what appears at first as an irreconcilable tension fuelling a necessary sense of distinctiveness defers to a desire to deny the absolute nature of that distinctiveness. Thus the political frequently shades into the moral or the metaphysical, and the committed theatre comes to meet and share assumptions with that drama which it imagined itself to be rejecting.

This was especially true at the level of language. In a fundamental sense these playwrights were in revolt against the word. They saw themselves as representing and addressing those whose marginality was assumed at a linguistic no less than a social level. The language which they were forced to use in order to communicate was historically stained. It was more than a symbol of the coercive power of society; it was a primary agent of that power. The demeaning language of the racist, the sexist and the politically dominant had already infected the nature of daily discourse. The battle, therefore, had to be waged first at this level before the power which it masked and facilitated could be actively engaged. And here, too, the concerns of the committed writer coincided with those of the playwright (Gelber, Albee, Kopit) or the director–creator (Wilson, Foreman, Breuer) for whom the deconstruction of language was intimately related to the reconstruction of meaning. The committed writer and the politically engaged group wished to claim the right to speak for and to those excluded as effectively on a linguistic as on a political and cultural level, to reinvent a self which existed outside social and lexical definition. But this was no less true of the writer or director who saw dialogue, narrative and plot as theatrical conventions with the power to coerce actor and audience alike. It is in this sense that Theodore Adorno regarded Kafka and Beckett as profound revolutionaries; it is on this level, too, that political commitment repeatedly led to aesthetic experiment. The structures of society could scarcely be smashed while leaving the structures of art intact. And so commitment in the American theatre moved quickly from the social realism of *A Raisin in the Sun* (1959) to the conscious manipulation of stereotype in the black revolutionary and Chicano theatre. The self trapped in the constraints of a naturalistic environment quickly deferred to a self liberated through challenging its own density, its own social, moral and metaphysical fixity. An assumed solidity of identity was exploded, the social components of that identity being exposed through a conscious use of caricatures, a resort to puppets and masks or even a deliberate theatricalising of relationships. Words were constantly tested against the authenticity of experience. Plainly there is a space between those for whom the theatre is a means rather than an end and those whose commitment is to form rather than function, but there are few writers, actors or directors who would wish to claim either objective as a full and satisfactory account of their work. For the fact is that in turning to theatre they accept a distinction between discipline and constraint and acknowledge a double loyalty to the world which they would transform and the imagination with which they would transform it.

The committed decade (which ran, as far as the theatre was concerned, approximately from 1964 to 1975) was, interestingly, introduced by a play which simultaneously offered an analysis of American imperialism and contemplated the dangers of resisting power with violence. It combined the energy of moral revolt with a poet's concern for language. It was a play which reached back into the past in an effort to trace the origins of a corruption which stemmed from a displaced sense of the ideal. In that sense Robert Lowell's *The Old Glory* was a document for the times, a work of genuine integrity in which, with Vietnam beginning to edge towards the centre of national consciousness, he inspected both the arrogance of power and the betrayals awaiting those who would resist that power; and as such, before turning to a consideration of the impact on the theatre of Vietnam, the struggle for women's rights, minority rights and so on, it is worth contemplating one of Off-Off Broadway's most impressive plays of the 1960s.

It was not a committed play, in the sense that many of those which followed it were. But it was a political work to the degree that it was a contemplation of history in which Lowell identified a plot whose narrative energy had disturbing implications for the present; and it was a moral work in that he called America to book for the betrayal of its own ideals, for the destructive power of its myths, and for the pragmatism which seemed to have been born out of its liberal impulse. It was a play which, on the threshold of an era, identified the issues that were to preoccupy a generation: American violence, an imperial pretension, racial discrimination and that growing gulf between experience and the language in which that experience is rendered.

I offer an extended analysis of this play both because it can stand as a representative of those many plays generated by Off-Off Broadway and whose achievement far transcended the size of their audience (though aware that there is no such thing as a typical Off-Off Broadway production), and because it is a work of genuine subtlety and accomplishment, a play that ushered in a decade in which the moral health and political fate of America was debated on the nation's stages as it was on its embattled streets.

Challenged by Dürrenmatt to explain how the bleakness of the modern world could be enacted on the stage, Brecht replied by asserting a revolutionary faith in the possibility of change; a reified present is justified by hope of an expansive future. Accepting this logic, Beckett's minimal world can be regarded as simply a social construct – the product of economic and political forces – rather than as evidence of metaphysical desolation, of a nerveless and self-destructive human nature. However, for those less willing to renew their faith in human perfectibility, for the liberal empiricist acutely aware of the failure of cherished illusions, the revelations of recent history are more likely to resolve themselves into nothing more constructive than the traditional synthesis of liberal faith and failure – public and private guilt. Neither radical reconstruction nor fashionable despair offer a credible alternative. The only option, in the novel as in drama, seems to be the confessional. Camus's *La Chute* and Miller's *After the Fall* are two aptly named works.

But a second strategy is available, a strategy which, in the guise of documentary realism, set out to detail the harrowing lessons of the concentration camp and the bomb while at the same time retaining a style which implies the survival both of genuine values and a convincing structure to life. Weiss's and Hochhuth's verse plays mediate between the liberal's twin needs for truth and hope without capitulating to the logic of either; Lowell's *The Old Glory* pursues this liberal anguish to its origin in the paradoxes of history and human nature alike. However, where Weiss and Hochhuth turn to historical documents in order to trace the severe contours of human imperfection, Lowell seeks in fiction the mythical dimension behind the face of history and the mask of progress. Where Weiss and Hochhuth itemise the data of betrayal and inhumanity, Lowell probes the paradox whereby evil is born of goodness and the redeemer stained with other blood than his own. Here is the modern world seen neither as absurdist wasteland nor Marxist model but as the product of a history forged from frustrated hopes and blunted idealism – a present endlessly repeating the errors of the past while fighting to avoid a soulless capitulation.

The Investigation, far from constituting a simple documentary comment, is, as Weiss himself has explained, 'shaped as a piece of art. I've called it "oratorian"', he added 'to make clear that it's not meant to be realistic court atmosphere but rather reminds us of antique tragedy. It's devised into eleven songs – so called songs – and this puts it onto another level from the real trial atmosphere.'[4] Weiss consciously avoids a realistic setting and uses verse to frame the action in a ritualistic structure. In this form the play becomes less a comment on a particular historical event than an attempt to penetrate to the essence of human nature. In the *Marat–Sade* he had utilised a more varied verse form but with a similar rationale. Indeed, Peter Brook, while stressing the influence of Artaud and Brecht on Weiss's work, also emphasises the significance of his use of verse. Speaking of Shakespeare, but with direct relevance to Weiss, he explains that 'The possibilities of free verse on an open stage enabled him to cut the inessential detail and the irrelevant realistic action, in their place he could cram sounds and ideas, thoughts and images which make each instant into a stunning mobile.'[5]

The same is essentially true of Hochhuth's *The Representative*. Recognising the difficulty and even the impossibility of dramatising certain aspects of man's moral history he comes to the conclusion that 'Documentary naturalism is no longer any sort of stylistic principle.' At the same time he is equally suspicious of resort to metaphor, saying that 'however great the power of suggestion emerging from word and sound, metaphors conceal the infernal cynicism of the real thing'.[6] Thus Hochhuth turns to poetry both to avoid a prosaic morality, which substitutes cold statistics for an anguished reality, and to give form to an otherwise uncontrolled mass of documentary material. He quotes Schiller as saying that the playwright 'can use no single element of reality as he finds it, that his work in all its aspects must be a work of the Idea, if it is to possess reality as a whole'. He accepts Schiller's call for an 'open and honourable war upon Naturalism in Art', and asserts with both Schiller and Brecht that the theatre remains true only so long as 'it destroys the illusion which it has itself created'.[7]

Just twenty months after the first performance of *The Representative* and a few months prior to the first production of *The Investigation* Robert Lowell's *The Old Glory* received its première in New York. While this was not a detailed documentation of human depravity on the scale of these other works it did have a great deal in common with them. It was in essence a compassionate recognition of the fact that, as one of his characters says in an early draft of the play, 'men are twisted'.[8] Set in a historical America *The Old Glory* is no less concerned with the moral arabesques of national and private conscience than Weiss's and Hochhuth's accounts of Auschwitz. The difference is finally one of emphasis, for Lowell insists, perhaps with a Catholic fervour, on discovering in life itself the justification for continued existence. For, as one of his characters remarks, 'bearing with diseases is the body's business'. Nevertheless there is a direct line between Lowell's play and Weiss's *Marat–Sade*, for example. Both attempt to analyse the nature of revolution as a political act while probing for the human impulse which provides history with its momentum. All three of these playwrights in fact tie the private and public world together and attempt an evaluation of human nature from the bleak vantage point of the 1960s. But where Weiss and Hochhuth are drawn inevitably to Hitler and the concentration camp, Lowell chooses a different route which takes him into the American past. The Europeans analyse the brutal meaning of European imperial fantasies: Lowell expresses alarm at America's imperial posture. The difference, however, is not merely geographical. It also indicates a differing conception of the value of history as a moral force. As one of Hochhuth's characters says in *Soldiers*:

> The theatre isn't a museum.
> History only ceases to be academic
> when it can illustrate for *us* and *now*
> man's inhumanity to man . . .

Yet this same character then continues in a way which makes clear the basis of the divergence between Hochhuth and Lowell, for Hochhuth rejects:

> . . . the historical cliché.
> Richard Coeur de Lion – just a handsome suit of armour,
> no longer alive and no longer dangerous,
> but what we and the Germans did twenty years ago,

has become the A.B.C. of the airmen of *today*.
Korea, Vietnam: the murdered civilians there –
that is *our* teaching, the Anglo-Saxon precedent![9]

For Lowell, however, the more distant past is very much alive and holds the key to our modern dilemmas as truly as does more recent history. He knows, as clearly as Hochhuth, that the bombing of Dresden, though a response to the inhumanity of fascism, was itself cruel and callous. Indeed, it was this knowledge which made him register as a conscientious objector in the Second World War. Yet this is a lesson which, to Lowell, was implicit in the whole fabric of history and his play sets out to document this in a purely American context.

In his volume of poetry, *Near the Ocean*, Lowell places side by side poems drawn from his native surroundings and poems which concern themselves with Rome. In a note he explains that 'The theme that connects my translations is Rome, the greatness and horror of her Empire . . . How one jumps from Rome to the America of my own poems is something of a mystery for me.'[10] *The Old Glory* explains that mystery, for it is, at base, a dramatisation of Lowell's version of Juvenal's Tenth Satire entitled, 'The Vanity of Human Wishes'. It is a comment on empire; a lament over man's talent for self-destruction. In the words of the final stanza of 'Walking Early Sunday Morning', the first poem in the collection:

> Pity the planet, all joy gone
> from this sweet volcanic core;
> peace to our children when they fall
> in small war on the heels of small
> war – until the end of time
> to police the earth, a ghost
> orbiting forever lost
> in our monotonous sublime.[11]

The Old Glory is, at least in part, an analysis of the state of the union. As Jonathan Miller, the play's producer, has explained, 'Refracted through the work of Hawthorne and Melville, Lowell has caught a piercing Yankee insight into the character of his own country.'[12] *The Old Glory* consists of three plays based on short stories by Hawthorne and Melville and drawing on Thomas Morton's *New Canaan*. It is a triptych whose unifying theme is human fallibility and whose central image is that of the flag – not simply the American flag but, finally, any of the thousand banners which men have flown, behind which they have united and in whose name they have sallied forth to defend freedom, overthrow tyrants and protect economic hegemony. For his play is not merely an examination of the American character at three stages in its history: it is also an analysis of the nature of power, the inevitability of corruption and the danger of an innocence which is no more than ignorance and self-deception. *The Old Glory* details not only the betrayal of the American dream but also the failure of an older and more honoured illusion – that of man's innate purity and compassion. Lowell denies none of the insights which political disillusionment and inhuman brutality have offered us but attempts to uncover the reality of failure in the hope of discovering a genuine basis for hope.

The first play, *Endecott and the Red Cross*, which was dropped from the original production, is set in colonial days and examines the nature of the American conscience at the beginning of the 'great experiment'. The action takes place on a Mayday in the 1630s. King Charles, afraid lest the colonies should begin to slip away from his control, has sent Mr Blackstone, an episcopal minister, to reassert his authority and that of the Church of England. As an ecclesiastical scholar, Blackstone feels out of place in the frontier colony of Merry Mount, which is controlled by the obsequious and pragmatic Mr Morton. Nevertheless, Blackstone and Morton both officiate at the Mayday celebrations in which the local people masquerade as animals and dance around the maypole.

At the height of these festivities a detachment of soldiers from the nearby Puritan settlement of Salem arrives with the avowed purpose of suppressing the colony's trade with the Indians. When Morton is accused, he retaliates by revealing the King's plans for appointing a governor to political leadership of the colonies. The Puritan Governor, Endecott, recognises the threat to their independence which is implied by this move and is stung into fomenting a rebellion which he knows will prove fruitless and into becoming precisely the kind of demagogue he has always despised. He cuts down the English flag and orders the settlement of Merry Mount to be destroyed.

This particular play is based on two of Hawthorne's short stories: 'The Maypole of Merry Mount' and 'Endicott and the Red Cross'. To Hawthorne, Merry Mount is an innocent community but one whose innocence stems from an immature concept of reality. Its inhabitants, he explains, 'would not venture among the sober truths of life not even to be truly blest'.[13] The destruction of the settlement, even by the relatively unyielding Endicott, is thus a step towards maturity. The loss of innocence, as so often with Hawthorne, becomes synonymous with the achievement of full humanity, and nostalgia finally has to bow to necessity, however painful that process may be.

In Lowell's play this ambivalence still functions but it is clear that a different kind of political and commercial corruption has already begun to erode Merry Mount from within. As the innocent and gullible citizens dance around the maypole they are blind to the intrigue being planned by their leaders. Endicott's action at least has the virtue of facing them with their real situation. Man, it seems, to both Hawthorne and Lowell, has nothing to gain by closing his eyes to the reality of the human situation or the truth of human nature.

'Endicott and the Red Cross' is Hawthorne's sketch of a Puritan community, stark, sombre and with the instruments of torture and humiliation openly displayed. It spells out the inhumanity of a society convinced of the superiority of its own ethical and political system. Here, the differences between Hawthorne's and Lowell's version become especially significant. Hawthorne's Endicott is a hard man, blind to his own intolerance and reacting to the threat from England with a blunt and unsophisticated anger. He lacks the introspective strength of Lowell's character, who recognises the falsity of his own moral stance and the flaw in his own position. Conversely Lowell replaces the calm humanity of the heretical Roger Williams, used by Hawthorne, to point up Endicott's brutality, with the studied insolence of Elder Palfrey. The effect of these changes is to transform the nature of Endicott's rebellion and to transfer our attention and sympathy from the man who observes power to the man who wields power. Hawthorne's story is a comment on the nature of Puritanism; Lowell's play is a comment on the nature of political commitment, the origin of power and the human price of national or sectional ambition.

In Lowell's play it soon becomes apparent that the different ideologies, the opposing systems of morality, the conflict between the colonies and England is rooted in finance. Mr Blackstone, a trained cleric, is not so much a spokesman for spiritual salvation as an ambassador for economic expansion. Religion, indeed, becomes a cloak for usury and brutality while both sides justify their violence by invoking God's name – a fact which leaves both Blackstone and the Reverend Palfrey unmoved. When a soldier insists that

> . . . we are talking too much about the numbers of our soldiers.
> God is a host.
> Here in America, we are in Israel[14]

he is silenced and told that the future lies with the Bible and the gun. In a century in which a Pope can bless Italian troops as they leave to slaughter the Abyssinians or German troops set up the apparatus of tyranny under the banner, 'Gott Mit Uns', this tendency to mask corruption and brutality in the guise of innocence holds a persuasive relevance.

Endicott himself comes to recognise the true nature of this masquerade whereby every dogma, every crumbling regime, feels obliged to justify itself by condemning others. Each sect raises its particular banner and refuses to accept the possibility of moral neutrality. You are either with us or against us. This is the essence of the Puritan division into the 'elect' and the 'damned'. Man's imagination, it seems, is manichean by nature. As Endicott points out, 'Rome, Geneva, London, and now America . . . Flags of a hundred colors . . . all made of cloth'[15] The image of the flag is introduced, therefore, as a symbol of divisiveness. In its name reality is distorted and ultimately inhumanity perpetrated.

Endicott recognises that the world is not susceptible to the kind of schematic divisions which are represented by King Charles's autocratic designs or Palfrey's simplistic religion. Human complexity and the sheer diversity of intellectual development make a mockery of dogmatism. As he perceives, a fierce allegiance, which is not open to logic or reason, leads ultimately to the *auto-da-fé*. Indeed he has a vision, later partially translated into reality, in which he sees himself, in the guise of Palfrey, sentencing other men to death until in an orgy of self-justification his own soldiers drag one another to the stake, leaving him as the only man alive in the world. This apocalyptic vision gives Endicott the kind of insight into the nature of power and the consequence of arrogant factionalism which was to lead Lowell himself to say of the concept of sovereign nations, 'despite their feverish last minute existence' they 'are really obsolete. They imperil the lives they were created to protect.'[16]

Not even Endicott is exempt from this divisive chauvinism which he has identified as underlying human cruelty. In fact he admits that. He succumbs to precisely the kind of cynical statecraft which he had himself condemned. He gains the support of his soldiers by means of a carefully planned speech, which, as he confesses, is little more than a 'hollow, dishonest harangue / half truth, half bombast',[17] while his call for 'Bible, blood and iron'[18] is itself an ironical comment on the nature of the justice which he invokes.

Endicott's new insight is gained at the cost of guilt and responsibility. He gains freedom but in doing so destroys beauty and his own vision of personal innocence. His revolution succeeds in eliminating the opportunist Mr Morton but it also destroys the 'beautiful woman' and 'fine young man', Edith and Edward, who had played May King and Queen, together with the Indians whose only crime had been racial fraternisation. With the immolation of Merry Mount, therefore, we witness the loss of simple-minded naivety but also the death of vitality and beauty. At the end of the play the revellers dance their last masque, to seal the passing of an age. But now they perform 'pathetically' and 'wiltingly', with Edith and Edward dressed in Puritan gray. The English flag lies in the dust and Endicott has won a temporary victory at the expense of his own compassion and humanity.

What we witness in 'Endicott and the Red Cross', as in many of Hawthorne's short stories and novels, is ultimately a re-enactment of the Fall of Man. Endicott and his soldiers take upon themselves the responsibility for their own fate. They sunder the links between themselves and England and seal this act with the ritual killing of the Indians and the destruction of Merry Mount. They thus claim their freedom at the cost of a sense of guilt. In Hawthorne's short story it is made plain that when Endicott cuts down the red cross of England he is rejecting not merely the symbol of English power but also the image of the Christian God. In Lowell's play the action is pointedly declared to be 'blasphemous'. The rebel, whether his revolt be social or metaphysical, inevitably loses his innocence but as a result he gains perhaps a new insight into the realities of human affairs.

To Baruch Hochman, in an article in the *Tulane Drama Review*,[19] these three plays demonstrate Lowell's anguished conservatism. For all the stringency of his analysis he could scarcely have been further from the point. The anguish that Lowell faces is one known to every liberal who at some time in his career has been asked to come to terms with violence as a necessary means of achieving desirable ends. It was a question which confronted, and in some cases destroyed, the liberal of the 1930s – a question which in the 1960s was in danger of freezing him into inaction. In terms of *Endecott and the Red Cross* Lowell's sympathy lies with the tortured Endicott rather than with the conservative Blackstone. For the anguish of the conservative lies in an entirely different direction. It emerges from the threat to old values and institutions. While he recognises the value of existing conditions, as does the intelligent liberal, he feels no desire to change things and has no difficulty in condemning violence, except that which is necessary in order to defend the status quo. Accordingly he tends to regard liberal vacillation with the contempt which perhaps it deserves. Endicott is wracked with doubts. For men like Blackstone and Palfrey the issues are plain.

In the second play, *My Kinsman, Major Molyneux*, we have moved on to the period of the American Revolution. Two boys, Robin and his brother, arrive in Boston hoping to find their cousin, Major Molyneux, who they believe will help them to make their fortune. Instead they find the city in a state of turmoil and are themselves abused whenever they mention Molyneux's name. The city is on the verge of revolution. The young brothers' first encounter is with the ferryman whose dress 'although eighteenth century half suggests that he is Charon'. Appropriately, therefore, the 'hell' of Boston stretches out before them, distorted houses providing an expressionistic analogue for their twisted inhabitants. In rapid succession they are exposed to all the main characters in the drama; to the tavern-keeper and the barber whose humorous banter is backed with a ready violence, the clergyman who believes the church should be a rock only in so far as it should be similarly blind, the prostitute who provides an apt image of a mercenary society, and the periwigged aristocrat whose effeminate temporising successfully survives the revolution.

There is a bizarre, almost Alice-in-Wonderland quality about this Boston which is peopled with such grotesque caricatures. Hypocrisy and deceit are commonplace so that Robin cries desperately, in the words of Carroll's Alice, for people to 'Say what you mean; mean what you say.'[20] Indeed, Jonathan Miller, in staging the play, has said that Gilray (the eighteenth-century political cartoonist) and Lewis Carroll were the dominant influences. 'The costume designer, Willa Kim, and I worked on the basic idea of the eighteenth-century political cartoon which dramatised the violent fervour of the times and gave it an almost surrealist nightmare sting . . . The controlling image for all this was Alice-in-Wonderland – as if the flesh and blood Deerfield boys had wandered into a dream world of sloganeering playing cards.'[21] Reduced to these terms the 'glorious revolution' is seen in an entirely different perspective, with the new regime represented by a homosexual who struts around in a periwig and tries to prove his manhood with a prostitute – an image, perhaps, of the politician anxious to prove the orthodoxy of his views. As the barber comments,

> Once to every man and nation
> comes the time a gentleman
> wants to clear his reputation[22]

Even the hero of the revolution, Colonel Greenough, is depicted as a grotesquely masked figure who sympathises with the forces he is to replace. During the play his mask changes from gray to red, a mutation which reflects the changing mood of the citizens of Boston and which suggests that the revolution itself is little more than a change in the complexion of power. For if Greenough can list the instruments of their oppression, 'whipping-posts, gibbets, bastinadoes and the rack',[23] the first act of the revolutionaries themselves is murder. The revolution in other words has achieved no fundamental change; only an inversion of the old order. As Greenough points out, not without a sense of irony, 'the last shall be first'. If this is taken as a comment on the rise and fall of empire then this is particularly apt. As the ferryman points out, again with a strong note of irony, 'The French are finished. The British are the only Frenchmen left.'[24] There is almost a note of biblical inevitability about this process. In the words of Revelations, 'He that killeth with the sword shall be killed by the sword.'

Revelations is in fact an obvious source for much of the play's imagery. Boston itself, which Jonathan Miller peoples not only with revolutionaries but also with a corpse in a winding sheet, is reminiscent of the 'great city' in Revelations where the corpses lie in the street. When the clergyman invokes precisely this apocalyptic imagery to describe the revolution, therefore, it serves to underline the ambiguous nature of the rebellion. On the one hand it is presented as the final victory of justice, while on the other it stands as a warning of the inexorable movement towards dissolution. Deriving his images directly from Revelations he demands:

> How long, how long now, men of Boston!
> You've faced the furious tyrant's trident,
> you've borne the blandishments of Sodom.
> The Day of Judgement is at hand,
> now we'll strip the scarlet whore.
> King George shall swim in scarlet blood,
> Now Nebuchadnezzar shall eat grass and die[25]

Against this imagery of a disintegrating society there stands only the figure of Colonel Greenough, who embodies this same sense of ambiguity. Half saviour and half corruptor he represents the dilemma of the radical reformer. He is said by Robin to talk like Christ and reminds one of the figure in Revelations, 'just in judgement, just in war', who (like Colonel Greenough) has eyes which flash with fire. Thus, when he announces, somewhat bewilderingly, that 'I am the man on horseback . . . I am a King',[26] the reference is to this same figure, who rides on a white horse and strikes the kings of earth with a sharp sword. He it is who kills those who bear the mark of the beast (note that Molyneux has a white scar on his face). But Greenough is not merely 'someone out of "Revelations"',[27] as Robin shrewdly realises; he is also the embodiment of the society he is helping to create. He wears a blue coat and white trousers, which we are told are 'like General Washington's'.[28] He also shares another characteristic with the revolutionary leader. He 'tends to speak the truth'.[29]

For all his virtues, however, he too is trapped by the dilemma of liberal and revolutionary alike. To take violent action against an oppressor is to become corrupt oneself. In spite of this perception that 'wars leave us where they find us',[30] therefore, it is he who first plunges his sword into the fallen tyrant. Lowell underlines the doubtful morality of this action

304

by referring indirectly to the regicides of both Julius Caesar and Hamlet's father. For as the revolutionaries look at the fallen Major one observes, in Hamlet's words, 'Take him all in all, he was a man',[31] while the Major himself protests, on seeing his young cousins in the mob, 'Et tu, Brute!'[32] The overthrow of one tyranny may merely presage the development of another.

Even here, at a time when issues seem clear enough: justice versus injustice, freedom versus colonial dependence, Lowell notes with a weary cynicism the seeds of corruption that seem to lie at the heart of every revolution. The symbols of office which are thrown aside so contemptuously are quickly retrieved and soon grace those who had formerly set their faces against authority. Those who tear down one flag merely raise another in its place. The revolutionaries themselves are presented as a gang of drunks, homosexuals and simpletons, aided and abetted by a church which defends an expedient morality rather than a firm faith. The momentum of revolution is such, indeed, that even Robin and his brother are swept forward by it, instinctively responding to the cries for violence. Here, at the beginning of the Republic, as earlier in Puritan New England, the Bible and the gun are placed side by side as the instruments of change. And here too, as in the earlier play, those who seem most conscious of the violence which is being done to humanity are themselves persuaded and become agents of that violence.

As the revolutionaries take up the trappings of power there is a clear indication that the course of empire is to continue under a new banner. As the historian, R.W. Van Alstyne, has emphasised, the United States was 'conceived as an Empire'.[33] So that Lowell seems to be making essentially the same incautious suggestion that Washington Irving had made in 'Rip Van Winkle', namely that the exchange of one system for another may finally be little more than a matter of appearance. The newly awakened Rip, on returning to his old village after a twenty-year sleep during which the Revolution has taken place, notices the inn sign which has undergone a subtle change. As Irving explains, 'he recognised on the sign . . . the ruby face of King George . . . but even this was singularly metamorphosed. The red coat was changed for one of blue and buff, a sword was held in the hand instead of a sceptre, the head was decorated with a cocked hat, and underneath was painted in large letters, General Washington.'[34] With the aid of the sword, power has changed hands. The nature of power itself remains unchanged. As Milovan Djilas once noted, 'Revolution only changes the form of power and property, but not the nation itself.'[35] This is not the comment of an embittered conservative. Djilas, like Lowell, is a revolutionary, facing, with brutal honesty, one of the central truths of revolution.

My Kinsman, Major Molyneux ends ominously with the young boy sighting along a flintlock and announcing that the weapon represents the real cause of his visit to Boston and thus by implication the real cause of a revolution whose aim was likewise the seizing of the instruments of power. In an interview in *Encounter* Lowell once recalled that Frost had said of poetry and power, 'We should have more of both.' In disagreeing, Lowell insisted that 'it is our curse that we can't disentangle these two things', for, as he points out, 'Violence and idealism have some occult connection' made particularly evident by America's obsession with weaponry. As he remarks, 'I remember reading Henry Adams's *History of Jefferson and Madison* . . . I noticed the strange pride that Adams takes in American gunnery – it's almost wild-western.'[36] The young boy's fascination with the flintlock is thus the embodiment of what Lowell sees as the ambiguous relationship between idealism and violence, pride and arrogance. It is an image of lost innocence.

In *Benito Cereno*, the last of the three plays, we are shown the consequences of this quest for power. Indeed the protagonist, Captain Delano, could almost be the young boy, seen now some thirty years later, after his initiation, or even a natural descendant of the masked man who had guided the ambiguous forces of revolt.

With the final play of the series Lowell turns his attention to the early years of the republic. The play is set 'about the year 1800' and concerns the encounter of a New England captain, Amasa Delano, with a Spanish ship, the *San Domingo*. As the American ship, a sealer, is at anchor off the coast of Trinidad so a Spanish vessel appears, sailed clumsily by a motley crew of Spaniards and Negro slaves. Anxious to offer help, Captain Delano boards the *San Domingo* and greets Benito Cereno, her captain. He is plainly sick and ill at ease while his ship is in a decrepit state. Unaware that Cereno is merely a hostage of the Negroes, who have rebelled and now control the ship, Delano naively accepts the lies with which he is fed. When the pretence is finally dropped he escapes with his life thanks to the prompt, if brutal, action of his own sailors who discharge their muskets into the menacing Negroes. The rebellion is defeated but not before Lowell has emphasised something of the changing nature of the new republic and presented a persuasive analogue of the most acute of America's contemporary problems.

That he should choose a short story by Melville as the basis for his play is itself appropriate enough for there can be little doubt of Melville's own attitude to the Negro question. In *Mardi* he created a biting satire of America's racial problem. On landing in Vivenza, Melville's soubriquet for America, a group of strangers observe a huge statue which has been inscribed with the words, 'In-this-republi-can-land-all-men-are-born-

free-and-equal.' Beneath this, however, there is an Orwellian amendment which reads, 'Except-the-tribe-of-Hamo'. As one of the strangers
observes, 'That nullifies everything.'[37]

Benito Cereno is a more subdued but ultimately more disturbing
picture of Negro/white relations than LeRoi Jones's *The Slave*. Both
plays are concerned with a Negro rebellion but to Lowell the problem is
less the antipathy which grows out of race than the plight of a nation
which closes its eyes to reality. Delano's smug self-satisfaction covers an
ignorance and a blindness which literally kills.

Delano's denial of reality is in part political and in part metaphysical.
Politically, he is unable to grant the possibility of a threat to the system:
spiritually, he refuses to acknowledge anything inimical to his vision of
human nature. He maintains these illusions even in the face of various
signs of the huge gulf that exists between appearance and reality. When
Benito Cereno warns him that 'if we only see with our eyes / sometimes
we cannot see at all'.[38] Delano accepts this as a simple platitude rather
than as a comment on his own lack of insight.

Delano is the victim of his own prejudices. To him the Negro is a
primitive animal, physically strong but intellectually deficient. Because
it is impossible to reconcile this stereotype with the idea of guile and
deceit he is totally incapable of appreciating the reality of his situation.
When he does suspect treachery he ascribes it to the enfeebled Benito
Cereno. Melville himself had been at pains to emphasise the fatuous
nature of Delano's assumptions. In fact in his description of the final
capture of the rebel leader by the bewildered New England captain he
deliberately reverses the stereotypes. 'As for the black, whose brain, not
body, had schemed and led the revolt . . . his slight frame, inadequate to
that which it held, had at once yielded to the superior muscular strength
of his captor.'[39]

For the Melville who wrote that 'All men who say yes, lie', and that
the greatest need is to pronounce 'No! in thunder',[40] Babu's rebellion
has a certain attraction. In a real sense he becomes a black Ahab, inhuman
perhaps, but great by virtue of his challenge to the basic terms of his
existence. It is this challenge, in fact, which creates the sense of metaphysical unease that dominates Captain Delano. For an ordered society
suggests the possibility of metaphysical order and purpose. Thus Delano
feels especially uncomfortable on board the *San Domingo* precisely
because of the disorder which seems to dominate its every aspect. On his
own ship everything is in its place. Function and purpose are allied and
this in turn suggests a cosmic order. On Cereno's ship nothing is certain;
order has been challenged and subverted and the precarious nature of
reality exposed. When Delano grasps the ship's rail, it crumbles to dust

under his hands. The New England captain thus feels himself threatened but is unwilling to concede that there is anything to fear since his life is predicated on the principle that 'God is good',[41] and that evil, if it exists, has only a subordinate role to play. And yet as Melville had insisted in *Moby Dick*, 'That mortal man who hath more of joy than sorrow in him, that mortal man cannot be true.' To him 'the truest of all men was the Man of Sorrows',[42] and the only response to life, a challenge. As Ahab points out, if we obey God, we must disobey ourselves.

When Delano shoots Babu, therefore, it is in a desperate attempt to uphold his vision of an innocent world. Like Ahab he projects his vision of evil onto a single object and sets out to destroy it. Ahab thrusts the harpoon into Moby Dick; Captain Delano empties his revolver into Babu. Both are trying to restructure the universe to their own pattern. However, where Ahab's is a wild and heroic gesture of defiance in the face of the gods, Delano's is a desperate attempt to maintain the status quo. He is rejecting the logic of history. When Babu points out that 'The future is with us', Delano replies with the gun. Thus, Cereno's despairing shout, 'My God how little these people understand!',[43] becomes an apt comment on the American's determined myopia.

Benito Cereno can be seen as part of the continuing debate between innocence and depravity which has been waged by American writers from Cooper to Mailer. Melville's conviction that the world is dominated by darkness finds an echo in Lowell's anguished historical analysis. The desperate inevitability of oppression is spelled out with a weary precision. The revolutionists of the former play become the new imperialists. The masked man, leader of the revolutionists, is transmuted into the figure of Captain Delano of Duxbury, Massachusetts. The captain first appears dressed in the same blue coat and white trousers, with the self-assurance of his forebear having hardened into the arrogant chauvinism of the second generation. 'America', as he points out to his subordinate, 'is wherever her flag flies.'[44] The America of *Benito Cereno* has clearly picked up the baubles of imperial power. Having freed itself from the dominance of the British Empire it has by this time begun to trace its own particular version of manifest destiny, while digesting the fact of its newly discovered power. Already, in 1800, America was flirting with the idea of war while President Adams, entranced by what R. W. Van Alstyne has called an 'avid dream of a dazzling commercial empire',[45] had begun to build America's navy and insist on the kind of respect for the American flag which the British had formerly demanded for the Union Jack. It is no accident, therefore, that Lowell chooses to change the name of Delano's ship from *Bachelor's Delight* to the *President Adams*.

The name of Cereno's ship offers a similar comment on the wider significance of these events. The action on the *San Domingo* clearly parallels that in Santo Domingo itself, which at this time was experiencing the Negro rebellion that finally brought Toussaint L'Ouverture briefly to power. To reinforce the parallel Lowell transfers the action from South America, where it had been set in Melville's account, to the coast of the West Indies.

On the prow of the ship the figurehead has been replaced by the dry white bones of a Spanish aristocrat, complete with an inscription which reads, 'Follow Your Leader'. The implication is clear enough. For this acts both as a warning to the Spanish sailors and perhaps also as a reminder that the Negroes themselves are part of a continuing process of repression and rebellion.

When Babu leads his revolt and resorts to violence he is merely acting on the precedent set by the Spanish themselves and powerfully detailed in the previous two plays. The oppressed revolt and in turn become the oppressors. Babu places a crown on his head and holds a silver sceptre, representing the earth, just as Major Molyneux had 'seemed to hold the world like a gold ball in the palm of his hand'.[46] As Babu points out the logic is irrefutable:

> When Don Aranda was out of temper
> he used to snap pieces of flesh off us with it.
> Now I hold the whip.
> When I snap it, Don Benito jumps![47]

As William Faulkner once said, 'No tyrant is more ruthless than he who was only yesterday the oppressed, the slave.'[48]

Babu's rebellion, like Ahab's, ends in death. Both men, however, demonstrate not only their superiority over those who surround them but the very possibility of challenging the terms of their own existence. If Lowell chooses to emphasise the callous inhumanity which accompanies this revolt he finally acknowledges that the rebel, be it Endicott, Colonel Greenough, or Babu, has a firmer grasp on reality than those he supplants. Both Endicott and the masked man regret the cruel necessities of rebellion. The former admits that he has no stomach for the dishonesty and brutality that go hand in hand with revolt while the latter confesses that 'wars leave us where they find us'.[49] Even Babu recognises the painful logic of the process in which he is involved. When Delano taunts him with the easy brutality which he plans, his reply is both an expression of his agreement and a justification of his action. 'That's what we thought when Don Aranda held the whip.'[50] Like his earlier co-conspirators, however, he has a clearer perception of reality than those he seeks to overthrow. As Cereno says, 'For some men the whole world is a mystery; they cannot believe their senses.'[51] This is not true of the rebels. These men are acutely aware of the implications of their actions but, seeing the inevitable consequences, they stubbornly maintain their resolve, thus contributing to the momentum of history, and the corruption which seems to inevitably haunt the source of power.

Throughout the three plays Lowell scatters references to the British, Spanish and French empires. He presents a series of vignettes of these empires at the beginning of their decline. The implication for the nascent American empire seems obvious, so that *The Old Glory* becomes a powerful political image – a regret that beneath the honest exterior of just rebellion there lies future oppression just as beneath the palsied appearance of the Negro slaves are eventually discovered the powerful leaders of the insurrection.

What we see in the final play, therefore, is in essence a ritual of sin and expiation, with Benito Cereno suffering not only for his national imperial posture but for man's instinct for oppression. At the end of the play he is forced to kneel and ask for pardon 'for having enslaved my fellow man'. But the American captain, strengthened by pride, refuses this opportunity for expiation and, rather than admit to guilt, levels his pistol at the rebels, thus initiating a withering fire. National pride and national innocence have been preserved. In the words of Arthur Miller's *After the Fall*, 'innocence, . . . To get that back you kill most easily.'[52] It is entirely appropriate that this event should take place on Independence Day, exactly twenty-four years after Adams had placed his signature on a declaration propounding the equality of all men and outlining their inalienable rights.

In an interview, Lowell once spelt out the nature of his fears as far as America was concerned and it is fascinating to note how precisely *The Old Glory* embodies those fears.

> We were founded on a Declaration, on the Constitution, on Principles, and we've always had the ideal of 'saving the world'. And that comes close to perhaps destroying the world. Suddenly it is as though this really terrible nightmare has come true, that we are suddenly in a position to destroy the world, and that is very closely allied to saving it . . . I suppose this is too apocalyptic to put it this way, but it is the Ahab story of having to murder evil: and you may murder all the good with it if it gets desperate enough to struggle.[53]

Not only is this an accurate summary of the thematic content of *The Old Glory* but it also serves to underline how closely allied Lowell is to Peter Weiss and Rolf Hochhuth. But, while racial conflict, the agony of Vietnam, the breathtaking brutality of the concentration camp and the ever present possibility of nuclear annihilation are seen as in part a product of national aggrandisement and the determined pursuit of national goals, more significantly all three writers recognise the apocalyptic implications inherent in the substance of history and through an examination of the past attempt to emphasise, if not resolve, the fundamental paradox of man's ambivalent nature. It is this paradox, revealed most clearly by the complicated moral dilemmas of revolution, which Lowell sees as the key to an understanding not only of America but of man's troubled history.

In *The Old Glory* Lowell responded to the increasing internal and external pressures being exerted equally on the American political system and the ideals to which it wished to lay claim. Those pressures were shortly to prove almost insupportable with black revolt breaking out in America's cities and an increasing number of American citizens becoming disaffected with their government's foreign policy to the point of massive civil disobedience. The apocalypticism which Lowell had seen as implicit in American messianism proved, for nearly a decade, to be a reality too great to be borne. And though this was a period of very considerable social and cultural change there was one issue above all others which seemed to focus questions of national purpose and moral being – Vietnam.

VIETNAM

In 1983, the English dramatist David Edgar was reported to have expressed surprise and some indignation that, ten years on, the Vietnam war no longer provoked much theatrical interest. It was the comment of a committed writer for whom the theatre was specifically designed to expose the social lie, to deconstruct national myths and to reveal the betrayals implicit in public policy. But, though it may have proved a memory quickly suppressed, in fact Vietnam entered the artistic bloodstream quickly and its effects were considerable. Not merely have there been a large number of plays which have attempted to deal with the war but the destabilising effect of the conflict was such that it influenced the concept of character, the nature of language, and the structural coherences of plays and performances across a wide range. It radicalised companies formerly concerned with aesthetic experimentation and it contributed to that sense of a problematic reality which invaded the work of a number of writers, not excluding Arthur Miller (*The Archbishop's Ceiling*), Tennessee Williams (*The Two Character Play*) and Edward Albee (*Box* and *Quotations from Chairman Mao Tse-Tung*).

In his brilliant book, *Take Up the Bodies: Theater at the Vanishing Point*, Herbert Blau charts the impact of the war on his own sensibility. He was nobody's radical except in aesthetic terms. He resisted the intrusive demands of the war, attempting to shore up his artistic life against the moral demands of the day ('I wrote letters and read much and dreamed up equivocations, with some remorse of conscience, as the Vietnam war dragged on. The war on certain days seemed less senseless than other natural disasters in the deranged ecological cycle'[54]). His commitment was to exploring theatre and, on a more fundamental level, perhaps, securing his own solitude against exposure. But solitude, privacy, and the right to moral and psychological neutrality were among the victims of the war. A public offence required a public response. The irony in his own case was that what critics took to be the beginnings of commitment was largely a result of a misunderstanding. His decision to stage *Danton's Death* at Lincoln Center, and even more the programme notes that he wrote for the production, were seen as a deliberate assault on national policy. In his view this constituted both a failure to penetrate his own motives and a misconstruction of the play, but the point is that commitment is not wholly a matter of choice. A play is a public event whose meaning is liable to be transformed by the context in which it is presented. To see *Hamlet* in Britain during the Falklands war was to feel with special force the curious mixture of honour and futility in Fortinbras's war to regain a border territory of no value. This hardly transformed *Hamlet* into an anti-war play but it did underline the degree to which it is inevitably reconstructed by the pressure of the moment, enrolled by the imagination in a debate which may be private and psychological or may be public and social. As the Polish theatre discovered amidst the crushed hopes of 1982, even the gesture of coming together to experience a shared event at a time when public gatherings were banned may breed a solidarity which itself makes the link between a life of art and the art of life. Few plays exist which cannot be made to glow with a sympathetic light when performed in such circumstances.

In the case of Blau, the resistance continued. He was drawn to the private and the introspective. Theatre for him was about a mystery which should be approached but never fully revealed. His own subsequent experiments with his group Kraken suggest how true that was, the Kraken being a sea creature which would die the moment it reached the surface. But, for all that, Vietnam and the political corruption which logically, if farcically, followed it, led him to confess:

> That other kind of theater may have had better motives. I increasingly believe that if one has the choice, and one does, it's better to think in terms of purpose, mission, action, task, service to others than in terms of identity, alienation, otherness, division, being-in-itself-for-itself *ad nauseam*, not values but default of value. It is a matter of preferring the

illusion of objective cause to the self-destruct mechanisms of a vain intro-
version. I say this, however, knowingly against the grain.[55]

Danton's Death had, in his view, been a warning against the cruelties
which spill out of idealism and there was, of course, plenty of evidence
for the damage to be done by those so confident of their own rightness
and the justice of their cause that any action seemed justified. In a sense
even America's involvement in Vietnam could be seen in the same light.
But inevitably he was drawn closer to the vortex. Indeed, he acknowledged the paradox implicit in the fact that even the solitude of the
privileged realm of art and the freedom to work beyond the fact of social
and economic relations were in some degree shaped by a world whose
own definitions he could resist but not deny. Whether he was working
with his group in San Francisco, negotiating with the New York
businessmen who bankrolled Lincoln Center, operating at an institution
of higher education (Oberlin College) or fighting (at the California
Institute for the Arts) a rearguard action with the Disney brothers, he was
in the world from which he could only play at abstracting himself. Only
play? Well, of course, since play was the objective that tension was in fact
vital but it implied demands which at least on one occasion he felt obliged
to respond to.

When President Nixon decided to escalate the bombing of North
Vietnam, the man who had once told a group of actors who had wished
to leave rehearsals to take part in a demonstration, 'I don't care if a bomb
drops next door. We work, then go out after and clean up the rubble',[56]
himself organised a demonstration. The event was called 'Invitation to a
Burning' and involved a carefully choreographed march on the centre of
Oberlin where people were to burn personal belongings on funeral pyres
to symbolise the destruction of the communities of Vietnam, Am Lok
being approximately the same size as Oberlin itself. The demonstration
included giant puppets and masks, and culminated in the mock deaths of
many of those present who lay down on the ground at a sign from Blau.
However, having initiated the events and prompted the mock deaths,
Blau was appalled precisely because it was scripted, because it was a
calculated attempt to orchestrate public feelings:

> Even in the communal sympathy spanning continents, art and politics
> conflicted. There it was again, the easy vulnerability of collective senti-
> ment, and the manipulability of any crowd. A true emotion on a false
> premise – nothing but theater again – and what does one make morally of
> that? After the first wave of directorial omnipotence, I thought the bodies
> were disgusting. I couldn't wait to get back to the laboratory.[57]

A scruple too refined for belief? What Blau reacted against was that the

313

war had in a sense co-opted him into its own values. It had provided the images, the visual language, the tactics and the metaphors which dominated the moment and shaped even the nature of revolt. It had enrolled art itself, demanding its attention, the subordination of its own coherences and dissonances, to those of a cause. And what appalled him above all was the legitimacy of the demand, for in any debate between the necessities of art and those of a public world in which people suffer and die art can ostensibly do nothing but surrender its space to other urgencies. Art, in its essence, is not a genie to be summoned forth at will, but its right to ultimate seclusion cannot easily be defended, more especially in the case of the theatre where the recreation of at least a provisional community is the prerequisite of its existence. Art claims an exemption which at moments of stress tends to be summarily revoked. For innocence can breed not merely an illusion but also a reality of guilt. History also has its prescriptive rights and during the Vietnam war those rights were asserted. It was, of course, perfectly possible to resist its blandishments but suddenly such a stance was seen precisely as resistance and not a simple choice to explore form, celebrate presence, generate humour or stage the private self. The political activist reached out for a stage, deliberately theatricalising his or her actions. The theatre practitioner felt the sudden thrill of a personal art which reverberated on a public level. And judgement, suspended at the behest of aesthetic experimenters for whom it implied a divided consciousness, was now assaulted in the name of relevance. Art was a means and not an end. It was a tactic in which discussions of adequacy of form or performance were considered irrelevant or even wilful distractions. Vietnam theatricalised the streets. Like the civil rights movement before it, it required presence. The body, turned into icon by the experimental theatre, was now the ultimate test of authenticity. To be there – at the White House, the Pentagon, in the streets of New Haven or Berkeley, on the campus and in the town centre of Oberlin – was to be an actor in the central drama of the moment. The writer, the director and the actor felt this as acutely as anyone else, the more especially since the theatre was the source of the imagery and the strategies employed in daily conflicts with authority; the more especially since the drama enacted on the streets was about more than national policy. It was about the relationship between the self and society, about the plot of history and about the power of language and gesture to command attention and carry meaning and this was a point at which aesthetics and ethics fused.

The Vietnam war prompted a very considerable literature, from novelists such as John M. Del Vecchio, Tim O'Brien, George Cain, James Webb, Donald Pfarrer and Tom McCloy through to those dramatists for whom it was the central event of late 1960s and early 1970s life. Its effects seemed to echo down the following decade. For the most part the dramatists made no attempt to recreate the world of the battlefield directly. That was the domain of the novel (Donald Pfarrer's *Neverlight* and John Oliver Killens's *Captain Blackman*) and the film (*The Deer Hunter* and *Apocalypse Now*). What they chose to do was to examine the extent to which the horrors of that war had dislocated America's values, undermined its myths, disturbed its moral equilibrium and eroded its language. The effects are shown in terms of the shattered psyches of those who had suffered; but in some ways the principal subject of most of these plays is America itself, scarred with guilt, disturbed at the ease with which its idealism had succumbed to a moral anarchy which was assumed to be the product of other times and other places.

Military defeat, in the end, was easier to accept than a self-image which now had to expand to include the wilful slaughter of peasants, the arrogance of power and the destruction – subtle and not so subtle – of that model of personal integrity and moral action which was assumed to be the basis of American enterprise. Vietnam held a mirror up to the American people in which they saw an image irreconcilable with public myths and private values.

In two hundred years of independence the United States has lost only one war (provided that, like most Americans, you are prepared to forget the war of 1812). Though each foreign involvement had had its critics no conflict so divided the country or precipitated such self-doubt as did American involvement in Vietnam. US imperial pretensions in the Mexican–American War (to which Thoreau took such exception) had been easily accommodated to myths of national independence, as in the Spanish–American War. Not so with Vietnam. Accustomed to casting itself in the role of defender of democracy, America found itself involved in a political morass which refused to resolve itself in the simple manichean terms that had proved adequate in the Second World War and even in Korea where, by a fluke of diplomacy, it found itself acting as the agent of the United Nations. Vietnam, in which American high technology took on the low technology of a guerilla army and in which even friendly villagers were coralled into reservations (known as pro-tected hamlets), stirred memories of an earlier conflict in which the pragmatic needs of a predominantly white society had been satisfied at the price of non-white natives – that against the American Indian. It was a parallel not lost on those whose unease grew throughout the 1960s as the deceits, the cruelties, the confusions and the betrayals of a distant war were brought nightly to the television screens. Certainly there were a number of writers who chose to press home the connection.

The Vietnam war, of course, stretched over some thirty years. But in terms of the direct involvement of American troops it was largely an affair of the 1960s and 70s. US military presence grew from 900 in 1960 to 3,200 the following year. When President Kennedy died there were nearly 17,000 American troops there, and America sanctioned the murder of President Diem. Air strikes against Vietnam were approved in December 1964, following the Tonkin Gulf Resolution (which itself followed the carefully provoked North Vietnamese attacks on American destroyers). Under President Johnson the number of troops expanded rapidly to 389,000 in December 1966, and, under President Nixon to 541,000 in 1969.

Opposition to the war began early. The first mass demonstration took place in the autumn of 1965 when two Americans, in imitation of a number of Buddhist priests in Vietnam itself, burned themselves to death as a protest. In 1967 demonstrations in New York and San Francisco attracted over 100,000 protesters, but the critical year, in this as in so much else, proved to be 1968. Optimistic government accounts of the war were suddenly exposed by the Tet (Lunar New Year) offensive of the Viet Cong in which the fighting penetrated not only into Saigon but even into the US Embassy compound. In the same year Lieutenant Calley and his company massacred men, women and children in the small village of My Lai, and in the presidential election campaign Senator Eugene McCarthy, running as an anti-war candidate, attracted such support that Robert Kennedy announced that he, too, would join the race. Under considerable pressure, and to the surprise of most people, President Johnson announced that he would neither seek nor accept nomination as his party's candidate. At the end of the year peace talks in Paris were agreed between all interested parties but, despite troop withdrawals, large-scale public demonstrations continued in both 1969 and 1970, President Nixon ordering the invasion of Cambodia (Kampuchea) in April of that year. In 1972 the United States broke off the Paris peace talks, alleging that the negotiations were fraudulent. The North Vietnamese then began a major offensive. In June, American combat involvement was terminated though, as the North Vietnamese advance continued, bombing of the North was resumed. In January 1973, a cease-fire was finally signed in Paris. Following President Nixon's resignation as a result of the squalid revelations of Watergate, further attacks were launched on the South and in April President Thieu resigned, the remaining American citizens being withdrawn by helicopter. In May 1973, a Communist government was established in South Vietnam.

The Vietnam war was the longest conflict in American military history; it devastated a generation. Fighting for a cause in which diminishing numbers of Americans believed, American troops found themselves hooked on drugs, psychologically disturbed, maimed and largely ignored. When they returned to America it was not to any welcoming parades. America wanted to forget not merely a military débâcle but, more significantly, a failure of morality and morale at odds with national myths of sturdy self-sufficiency and secure material and spiritual values. More Americans died in Vietnam than in any other foreign war (with the exception of the two World Wars). The country whose security they had supposedly fought to preserve was in ruins. One-and-a-half-million Indo-Chinese were dead; one-third of all forest land in South Vietnam had been destroyed by defoliants and 6.7 million tons of bombs had turned one of South-east Asia's most beautiful countries into a wasteland.

The writer responded early. In 1963 Alan Ginsberg went to Cambodia and Vietnam, admittedly on an odyssey of his own, but in the process came to regard the American presence as corrupting. By 1968 he was more precise in his accusations, seeing the war not merely as destructive of individuals but as dislocating language and as a threat to communication on all levels:

> Flesh soft as a Kansas girl's
>   ripped open by metal explosion
> three five zero zero on the other side of the planet
>   caught in barbed wire, fire ball
>   bullet shock, bayonet electricity
> bomb blast terrific in skull and belly, shrapnelled
>   throbbing meat
> while this American nation argues war:
>   conflicting language, language.[58]

In a sense Ginsberg's war poems are a natural extension of his other work which had always rejected the positivist, the materialist, the mechanical, and which had pitched the body against the body politic. But for Denise Levertov the war was more of a disruption. In *Sorrow Dance* (1967) a series of war poems are gathered at the end of a book of poems on other subjects. The war itself is seen as a threat to the poetic both in its reality and in its corrosive effect on the imagination. When she tries to address it, as in 'Life at War', the result is a horrified recoil, a psycho-sexual spasm, as she describes

> . . . the scheduled breaking open of breasts whose milk
> runs out over the entrails of still-alive babies,
> transformations of witnessing eyes to pulp-fragments,
> implosion of skinned penises into carcass-gulleys.[59]

317

For Robert Bly the war was yet further evidence of a materialism intent on subordinating the merely human. It was, in a sense, a logical consequence of that shift of emphasis from the person to the object which he regards as a corollary of capitalism. Such a diversion of energy is a form of death and hence the literal deaths of Vietnam, sold to the country like consumer products, are simply natural extensions of a desire for extinction.

The threat of the war is clear but for the writer the fear is that its disruptions extend to language itself. Thus, for Robert Bly, the state begins to offer its own shaping authority to experience, a process which becomes a parody of art itself:

> (Johnson now, no inspired poet but making it badly,
>   amassing his own history in murder and sacrifice
>   without talent)
> . . . irreplaceable irrevocable in whose name?
>   a hatred the maimed and bereft must hold
> against the bloody verse America writes over Asia.[60]

James F. Mersmann's admirable book, *Out of the Vietnam Vortex*, identifies the extent to which it was, indeed, at the level of language that the poet responded since this was crucial both to understanding and expression. In a world in which 'annihilation' could be rendered as 'pacification', 'area bombing' as 'limited duration protective strikes' and a defoliant with severe biochemical effects be described familiarly as 'agent orange', there was clearly a problem in finding a language not wholly corrupted and drained of meaning. In *Authors Take Sides on Vietnam* Robert Creeley chose to phrase his own rejection of American involvement precisely in terms of language, suggesting that 'The intervention of the United States in Vietnam stands to perpetuate a locked "vocabulary" at a time when the public consciousness of this country is admitting a most significant change. I am against the intervention, simply that it commits the United States to a policy of public falsehood . . .'[61] In one of her books on the war Mary McCarthy was to devote a whole chapter to language and its coercive power.

There were indeed very few American writers who did not oppose the war. Some, like S.N. Behrman and Arthur Miller were quietly disapproving; others, like Robert Lowell, made their protests as publicly as possible, Lowell refusing to attend a White House function. Mary McCarthy argued strenuously against American intervention in *Vietnam* (1967) and *Hanoi* (1968) while Norman Mailer celebrated the anti-war movement directly, in *Armies of the Night*, and explored the corrosive effects of its violence indirectly in *Why Are We in Vietnam?*

Much the same story was true in the movies. There were, of course, the conventional attempts to boost sagging morale with a film such as *The Green Berets* but rather more sophisticated versions of the war and its effects quickly became available. Indeed the radicalisation of the cinema was in effect the subject of Haskell Wexler's *Medium Cool* (1969). Brian DePalma's *Greetings* (1968) and *Hi, Mom!* (1970) examined the before and after of the war while Martin Scorsese, in *Taxi Driver* (1976), created a film in which Vietnam is seen in terms of its corruscating effect on a returned veteran, as had Elia Kazan in *The Visitors* (1972). A gentler version was apparent in Hal Ashby's *Coming Home* (1978) which seemed to offer a therapeutic gesture.

There then followed a series of films which addressed the war rather more directly – films which made its moral ambiguities their subject. *Go Tell the Spartans* (1978), set in 1964, implies the defeat which lies ahead, even while celebrating the qualities of the professional soldier whose expertise enables him to detect the Viet Cong sympathies of women and children, gunning them down as they are about to betray his troops. *The Deer Hunter* (1978) was a deeply ambiguous questioning and yet celebration of American values. A central character, like America itself, is corrupted and, as in Joseph Conrad's *Heart of Darkness*, embraces the evil in which he finds himself. But the final gesture of the film, as a returned veteran sings 'God Bless America', hints at a recovery which may survive even the ironies implicit in the gesture itself. *Heart of Darkness* plays an even more central role in Francis Ford Coppola's *Apocalypse Now* (1979), self-indulgent, sometimes bewildering, but capturing the surrealism and the moral confusions of the war which was itself partly squalid adventure, partly television spectacular, and partly a reminder of a flaw in American idealism.

At a poetry reading in Lawrence, Kansas, in 1969 Robert Bly observed: 'I think the Vietnam war has something to do with the fact that we murdered the Indians. The Vietnamese are our Indians. We don't want to end this war! We didn't want to quit killing the Indians but we ran out of Indians, and they were all on reservations.'[62] The parallel may have been put into his mind by the fact that he was in Lawrence, the site of an Indian college, and certainly his psychological justifications for his theory were tenuous in the extreme, but it seems likely that some such idea was in Arthur Kopit's mind when he wrote *Indians*, as it was in Sam Shepard's when he created *Operation Sidewinder* (1968) in which an Indian tribe transforms a lethal Air Force computer into a mystical totem which may have the force to restore some human value to a world dying of its own empty myths and destructive rationalism.

For Bly, speaking in 1968, Andrew Jackson had been the 'Westmoreland of yesterday [the commanding general in Vietnam] . . . recommending murder of a race as a prudent policy, requiring stamina'.[63]

Ironically, Michael Wayne, the producer of *The Green Berets* which starred his father, made essentially the same point when he confessed to an interviewer from *Variety* that 'Maybe we shouldn't have destroyed all those Indians, but when you are making a picture, the Indians are the bad guys.'[64] Indeed, two westerns of the time – *Soldier Blue* and *Little Big Man* (1970) – were seen by many as conscious comments on the Vietnam war simply transposed to the American past in order to identify a historical continuity, while in *Apocalypse Now* Kilgore, a psychopathic commander, wears a US Cavalry stetson and leads his helicopter assault on a Vietnamese village like a cavalry attack on an Indian village. And this was very much the point. For a number of poets, novelists, playwrights and film-makers, Vietnam was not best understood as an aberration but as part of a historical logic. The challenge to American moral values was seen as of a piece with other such challenges. What was at stake was not merely America's sense of itself as a defender of democratic freedoms but, beyond that, a model of human nature which proposed cruelty and callous violence as aberrant. It was in part that which Robert Lowell had chosen to examine in *The Old Glory*, which had documented an emerging American imperialism, and which he also chose to address, albeit indirectly, in his version of Aeschylus' *Prometheus Bound*, produced by the Yale Drama School in 1967.

As he confessed, 'I think my own concerns and worries and those of the times seep in', though he insisted that 'Most of what may be found perplexed or too vehement in my Zeus and Prometheus is also to be found explicitly or hazily in Aeschylus.'[65] Thus, the figure of Zeus becomes the 'laws of nature . . . or even a stage in Greek political evolution'.[66] And by extension he becomes 'Tiberius, or Trujillo', Lowell making a connection between the classical and modern world familiar from his poetry. It is a play which, like *The Old Glory*, touches on the ambiguity of revolt. For, as he suggests, Prometheus can be seen as 'justly fighting for intelligence and justice, or justly fighting against necessity, or . . . *un*justly fighting, because he is fighting necessity, what is'.[67] But, while noting that such 'confusions and insights' are as evident in Aeschylus as in Milton, he insists that they are 'irreconcilable with reason only if one wants to translate the old myth into marching orders'.[68] That, one suspects, is exactly what he felt to be happening in the public world of his own day. For while at first sight this is apparently a play less concerned with immediate and identifiable issues – the fast-developing crisis in Vietnam, for example – than with metaphysics, man in rebellion against the gods rather than temporal powers ('miserable, dying, though equal to the gods in thought' and offered the drug of hope), in fact the pressure of the contemporary is palpable. In the image of 'the River of violence [which] now runs across this land like a scar',[69] in Prometheus's prophecy of a 'people, who are more gaily industrious and disciplined than their neighbors, people who have forced every land and water to be a highway for their daring, who imagine they have left imperishable monuments for good or evil behind them . . . men who hold electrons and know how to obey . . . soldiers, but more like a broken herd than a healthy army',[70] he seems to offer a prophetic apocalypticism not without its relevance to the contemporary world. Indeed, Prometheus' prophecy of Io's child being born, its eyes 'already hurt by the light of the sun breaking across the muddy shallows of that dismal little Asian backwater',[71] is difficult to separate from the unwinding history of American involvement in Vietnam, particularly as the image dissolves into apocalypse, a world 'sighing and dying, the black droppage of the leaves falling on your back and splotching like flies. You will run out into the putrifying sun. You will stand on the edge of a blazing river.'[72] His observation that 'The suspicions of tyrants create the usurpers they fear'[73] is hardly without its relevance to the situation as it then was in Vietnam or to the wider conflict in which the American assumption of the satanism of communism itself provoked the conspiracies which it feared. Prometheus, burning in his own fire, could not easily be detached from the flames which were even then blooming in Vietnam or from those which wrapped the bodies of protesting Buddhist priests.

The Vietnam war sparked an immediate response in the theatre, coincidentally focussing for a while around the Yale Drama School, now under its new director, Robert Brustein. Looking for a replacement for *Little Murders*, withdrawn by its author Jules Feiffer for a Broadway production, Brustein recalled an Open Theatre work-in-progress by Megan Terry called *Viet Rock*, the first play to address the question of the war. This was duly staged in 1966 and followed by Lowell's *Prometheus Bound*, the production attracting a $25,000 grant from the National Endowment for the Arts which was almost cancelled as a result of President Johnson's anger. In the same year Brustein brought Barbara Garson's *MacBird* to the campus. This over-praised skit placed Lyndon Johnson in the role of Macbeth and John F. Kennedy in that of Duncan. It was over-praised in so far as its undergraduate humour and facile assumptions were excused because of relevance to an issue of increasing concern not only to those who opposed the war on principle but also to those who stood in some risk of being drafted. As Brustein later explained:

> Many found the play to be infantile and libellous, and my endorsement of it brought rebukes from friends and enemies alike. I knew that *MacBird* was irresponsible, particularly in its blithe assumption that Johnson had arranged for President Kennedy's assassination, but I believed the play to

be valuable less as a historical tract than as an emotional cathartic for our unrelieved feelings of frustration over the current political situation. Johnson was single-handedly conducting an illegal war in Southeast Asia, and he was justifying his usurpation of Congress's war-making powers through the fraudulent machinery of the Tonkin Gulf Resolution.[74]

As he quickly discovered, however, political expediency is a poor basis for dramatic criticism and the swift radicalisation of Yale very quickly left him vainly trying to negotiate between the competing demands of a professional training programme and a student body committed to political action. Indeed the fact of the war became not merely a central fact with which the theatre had perforce to deal but a destabilising factor in cultural politics itself. It was not only Brustein's drama school that found its aesthetic objectives under pressure from the real; for a time that disruption became an article of faith for theatrical groups such as the Living Theatre. Back from Europe, with illusions as to its revolutionary centrality, this group staged *Antigone*, which celebrated the confrontation between youthful idealism and a repressive system. And then, in 1968, Brustein invited them to Yale to perform *Paradise Now*.

Brustein regarded himself as something of a radical. During 1967 he attended a number of anti-war marches. He also believed in 'the central obligation of the theatre to soak up the pressing concerns of the time, confronting audiences with their own fears, hopes, and anxieties'. Even so, already he was disturbed at the effect which the protest movement was having on a personal and public level, and at its impact on theatre itself: 'The more inflamed the antiwar movement grew, the less it was willing to countenance complexity. Life became a melodrama, a battleground of moral extremes.'[75] This concern was heightened by the visit of the San Francisco Mime Troupe in the 1967–8 season. They performed a Goldoni play but after it was finished 'Ronnie Davis informed the spectators applauding the curtain call that if they wanted to end the war, they would have to take to the streets with guns.'[76] As Brustein observed, 'This was my first encounter with the more violent side of the Vietnam protest, and I was shaken. How could we criticize the violence of our government if we advocated violence ourselves?'[77]

Joseph Heller's *We Bombed in New Haven* raised no such problems but its anti-war position was seen as insufficiently radical by the Yale Draft Refusal Committee who planned to disrupt the performance until talked out of it by Brustein and Jules Feiffer. Much the same was true of a projected performance of Sam Shepard's *Operation Sidewinder* which, though satirising the American military, fell foul of black radicals for what they took to be its reductive portraits of a group of black revolutionaries.

However, the real problem, from Brustein's point of view, came with the arrival of the Living Theatre. *Paradise Now*, intended as an encomium to love and a protest against authoritarianism, struck him as anti-intellectual, repressive, amateurish and resonant with hatred. Its provocations to the audience to express their freedom by wandering the streets of New Haven stripped of their clothes led to a series of arrests by bemused policemen and a polarisation in the Yale community which did nothing for the anti-war cause or the needs of students concerned with the nature of theatrical experience. In part his response was a factor of his distress at being manœuvred into political and moral positions which at other times and in other circumstances he would wish to have repudiated; but in part it was alarm at a growing conviction in the theatre that right thinking was a satisfactory substitute for the subtlety and control of the playwright, the discipline of the actor and the orchestrating intelligence of the director. In other words he learned the unwisdom of his own response to *MacBird*.

Nor was the radical period in Yale's history over. The following year 50,000 people attended a Moratorium Against the War on New Haven Green, while following the My Lai massacre the company staged *The War Show*, the proceeds going to the children of Vietnam. But this did, in effect, mark the end of a period in which theatrical and political necessities seemed in a permanent state of tension.

And Yale was not the only institution radicalised by the war. The Open Theatre (*Viet Rock*), the Living Theatre (*Antigone*), El Teatro Campesino (*Vietnam Campesino*), the San Francisco Mime Troupe (*The Dragon Lady's Revenge*), the Bread and Puppet Theatre (*A Man Says Goodbye to His Mother*, 1968) and even the Performance Group (*Commune*, 1970) responded to this major foreign and domestic issue. During the summer and autumn of 1966 a group of New York artists created a loose organisation called 'Angry Artists Against Vietnam' which the Open Theatre joined. Besides its production of *Viet Rock* in 1967, it created a programme of anti-war material. In 1967 also, Luis Valdéz said of El Teatro Campesino, 'When it became clear to us that the United Farm Workers Organizing Committee would succeed and continue to grow, we felt it was time for us to begin speaking about things beyond *La Huelga*.'[78] The first thing he listed was Vietnam. Few large-scale demonstrations took place without the Bread and Puppet's mournful figures, or without agit-prop sketches. Schechner's guerilla theatre even penetrated the staid world of Broadway, while his Performance Group cancelled a production of *Mother Courage* in May 1976 in order to stage *The Thirty Years' War*, a dramatisation of aspects of the war in Indo-China. The performance in 1975 of *XA: A Vietnam Primer* by the Provisional Theatre of Los Angeles was just one of many such productions. Bread and Puppet's Vietnam pieces included *Fire and Burning*

Towns or *Johnny Comes Marching Home Again* as well as pageants and parades such as *Gas for Vietnam* (1965) and *The Shark Plane* performed in the Fifth Avenue Parade of 1966. The demonstrators at such parades tended to see themselves as a form of theatre; indeed, since they were in effect performing for the television cameras, they were. The attempt to levitate the Pentagon was itself an odd mixture of the comic, the farcical, the absurd and the tragic.

But while the Vietnam war left a clear mark on the American theatre few dramatists created anything more than the occasional play. The major figures of the period seemed to ignore it as fact while responding to it as destabilising idea. But for one writer – David Rabe – the war and its effects lay at the heart of most of his major works.

Rabe completed a draft of his first play, *The Basic Training of Pavlo Hummel*, in the autumn of 1968 and immediately began work on *Sticks and Bones*. The following year he sent both scripts to the Public Theatre. Both were rejected, though the former was eventually produced there in 1971. *Sticks and Bones* had meanwhile been produced at Villanova but, in a revised form, it, too, was produced by Joe Papp at the Public Theatre before transferring to Broadway.

Rabe himself served in Vietnam but found it virtually impossible to deal with the experience in fictive terms while still a part of it. All he could manage was to keep a diary in which he recorded the bare facts. But when he returned he reshaped that experience into a series of plays which he forbore to call protest or anti-war plays. As he explained:

> an 'antiwar' play is one that expects, by the very fabric of its executed conception, to have a political effect. I anticipated no such consequences from my plays, nor did I conceive them in the hope that they would have such consequences. I have written them to diagnose, as best I can, certain phenomena that went on in and around me. It seems presumptuous and pointless to call them 'antiwar' plays. First of all, I believe that to think a play can have immediate, large-scale political effect is to overestimate vastly the power that plays have. In addition, if there is (as I deeply hope there is) more content in these plays than the thin line of political tract, then to categorize them as such is to diminish them. A play in which young people seem not the most perfect of beings is not called an 'antinecine' play. I think these labels do exist because family, marriage, youth and crime are all viewed as phenomena permanently a part of the eternal human pageant.[79]

In effect the play takes place within the mind of the bewildered and dying Pavlo Hummel. It opens in Vietnam with Pavlo severely wounded by a fragmentation grenade thrown, as we later discover, not by the enemy but by a fellow soldier aggrieved by an argument over a prostitute – that irony, that sense of a world in which values are inverted and action arbitrary, is the keynote of the play. Pavlo himself is naive, anxious to be thought streetwise, and yet for all his increasing cynicism and physical resilience he never understands the lessons which are offered to him. The title, therefore, is itself ironic. Pavlo undergoes his basic military training but the other lessons which he is offered are lost on him. Indeed, as Rabe indicates in a note, 'he will learn only that he is lost, not how, why, or even where',[80] and in this he is clearly presented as an image of a society equally confused and uncertain. He is taught the mechanics of soldiering, methods of killing, and even, as a medical orderly, of saving life, but he is never taught why and is never unduly concerned. He admires those who can function though is himself inept and lazy for much of the play. He is also a thief and a liar, and even slightly insane. In the madness of Vietnam, however, these qualities no longer seem particularly aberrant. Indeed, there is a degree to which the soldiers' contempt for him is ironic given their own dedication to killing.

The play is not realistic. Pavlo is accompanied in many scenes by a black soldier, Ardell, who acts as a kind of chorus, commenting on the action, but never intervening. Pavlo's move towards death generates no insight. His various initiations (his military training and his sexual exploits becoming confused and intermingled) leave him untouched. When wounded he volunteers to go back to the war. When he finally wishes to opt out he finds himself returned to his unit, the victim of the regulations which provide the only structure to his world. As an orderly he treats the shattered bodies of those destroyed by the war but seems incapable of linking their experiences to his own. The enemy is, for the most part, perceived only vaguely. When he lies dying he is asked by Ardell, 'You tell it to me. What do you think of the cause? What do you think a gettin' your ass blown clean off a freedom's frontier?' He can only reply, 'Sheeeeee . . . ittttt'.[81] And in a sense the question is irrelevant. Thus his reply to Ardell's subsequent question is the same: 'What you think a all the "folks back home" sayin' you a victim . . . you a animal . . . you a fool?'[82] For Hummel, the war is not an ideological gesture, a political necessity, a cause or a betrayal of values. It simply exists as a kind of chaos which he is unequipped to understand. He recalls an incident from his youth in which he had dived into the Hudson River and, twisted by the current, lost all sense of direction, desperately swimming downwards, scrabbling repeatedly at the sand, and, despite the insistence on order and direction which he encounters in the army (he is repeatedly told how to locate the North Star), he and those who surround him are indeed caught in a world that exhibits neither.

The Basic Training of Pavlo Hummel is less a denunciation of the

Vietnam war than a portrait of a society whose governing ideas, whose simple models of action and whose social rules do nothing to explain the chaotic world in which its citizens find themselves functioning. Hummel's lies are finally scarcely different from those of the public world. His model of himself as tough, self-sufficient and independent is ultimately no different from that of the society itself and the glimpses which we are given of the civilian world suggest that Rabe's target is not merely the moral and literal anarchy of war but equally that of the culture which wages it. If Pavlo Hummel's single talent is for 'leaping into the fire', this was a talent which, to many people, seemed to typify the American political system.

Rabe's first play opened in May 1971. His second, which in a different form had already been produced at Villanova University in 1969, opened in New York in November 1971, and transferred to Broadway in March 1972. *Sticks and Bones* ran at Joe Papp's Festival Theatre for 225 performances. Its losses averaged a thousand dollars a performance but Papp insisted that 'it was the best investment I ever made'.[83]

In a sense once again the play is not so much concerned with Vietnam as with the desperate attempt of its characters to deal with a radical disjunction in their lives. By a series of accommodations they have adjusted to the disappointments of their existence; they have settled for a bland contentment which they take for happiness. They have become a kind of soap opera family, and, indeed, the characters are based on one of the most popular of post-war situation comedies on radio and television – 'The Adventures of Ozzie and Harriet'. The series, which ran for some twenty years, concerned a middle-class American family – Ozzie, Harriet and their two sons Rick and Dave. A sentimental celebration of American values, the series excluded all evidence of anxiety and pain. Rabe's characters similarly seem to inhabit a world evacuated of political tensions, devoid of pain and death and drained of real anxiety, and it is into this world that Rabe intrudes Dave, a son returned from Vietnam, blinded, profoundly guilty and disoriented. Their attempts to accommodate him to their own banality and to refuse the implications of his experience become an image of a denial of reality which transcends Vietnam and of which Vietnam is merely an example. Dave's return has to be acted out in clichés which derive from the media. His blindness and his fragile mental state are ignored because their own myths, no less than those of their society, cannot acknowledge such disruptions. And this posed certain problems for the actors. In a note Rabe outlined the approach he was after:

> everything is being communicated. Often a full, long speech is used in this play where in another, more 'realistic' play there would be only a silence

during which something was communicated between two people. Here the communication is obvious, because it is directly spoken. Consequently the ignoring of that which is communicated must be equally obvious. David throws a yelling, screaming tantrum over his feelings of isolation and Harriet [his mother] confidently, cheerfully offers Ezy Sleep sleeping pills in full faith that they will solve his problem. The actors must try to look at what they are ignoring. They must not physically ignore things – turn their backs, avert their eyes, be busy with something else. The point is not that they do not physically see or hear, but that they psychologically ignore. Though they look right at things, though they listen closely, they do not see or hear. The harder they physically focus and concentrate on an event, the clearer their psychological state and the point and nature of the play will be, when in their next moments and speeches they verbally and emotionally ignore or miss what they have clearly looked at.[84]

At the beginning of the play the characters seem close to those in Albee's *The American Dream*. Ozzie, the father, remembers the exploits of his youth and spends his time watching television. His wife Harriet divides her time between reminiscing about her children's upbringing, uttering platitudes and pressing food on everyone. Her other son, Rick, does no more than play the guitar, go on dates and drink innumerable sodas. This placid equanimity is disrupted by the arrival of a sergeant-major who delivers their now blind son, David, like a package; and this disruption is mirrored by a stylistic shift that punctures the apparent naturalistic surface. Though they respond to him with all the clichés appropriate to the return of a son from the wars, he is in fact a threat which they attempt at first to ignore and later to exorcise and finally kill. The price of acknowledging the relevance of his experience and the fact of his disfigurement is too high. Their definition of reality and hence also their grasp on sanity is at risk. When they do acknowledge that something is wrong it is to accuse one another, to preserve their own self-image and ultimately their sense of their own innocence.

David did not return alone. He brings with him his memories of Vietnam, which take the form of a girl called Zung – a fantasy, an illusion of the girl he had loved and left and an image of the corruption of which he accuses himself and his country. And the play is, indeed, full not simply of the casual cruelties of the war, recalled by Dave as he struggles to come to terms with himself and his sense of guilt, but also of a racism which offers some clue as to how such cruelties came about. While the family can adjust to the fact of David having resorted to prostitutes, what they cannot face is the fact of his having had a serious relationship with 'A yellow whore'. For them, no less than for their son, the acknowledgement of such a person as something more than an object of contempt disturbs their sense of themselves and incidentally of the self-evident justice of the war. The racism implicit in the father's language – 'You screwed it. A yellow whore. Some yellow ass. You put in your prick and humped your ass. You screwed some yellow fucking whore!' – is presented as intimately related to violence and stands in sharp contrast to David's poetic language – 'They are the color of the earth', while 'what is white but winter and the earth under it like a suicide'.[85]

Ozzie, the father, is equally capable of such language: when he remembers his youth he reveals a complexity which he has wilfully rejected in the name of a protective banality. Thus he objects, 'They don't know how I feel . . . I lived in a time beyond anything they can ever know – a time beyond and separate, and I was nobody's goddam father and nobody's goddam husband! I was myself.'[86] The frustrations of his subsequent life, his loss of freedom, his failure to realise aspirations, have resulted in a will to violence contained only by the numbing vacancy of his existence ('How I'd like to beat Ricky with my fists till his face is ugly! How I'd like to banish David to the street . . . How I'd like to cut her tongue from her mouth!'[87]). It is a portrait which is not without its social correlative for a country waging a distant war whose cruelties are concealed behind a language of euphemism and for whom the gap between ideal and actuality is the source of a profound anxiety.

At one stage David shows a film of the torture of Vietnamese peasants but nothing appears on the screen but a flicker of green light. He who is blind sees the scene because he has experienced it. For those around him it is nothing but a flicker of light – just as the war was itself reduced to just such a flicker of coloured light on television screens, turning it into another and terrible kind of nightly soap opera.

On the most literal level, of course, the fate of the Vietnam veterans has been almost exactly that which Rabe predicted in *Sticks and Bones*. They did, indeed, return to a country that wished to know nothing about the war. They were required to become invisible, not to disturb the myths of American military and moral superiority and the play ends with David's suicide (assisted by his family) just as the lives of many Vietnam veterans were to end in similar fashion. His dreams, profoundly disturbing and destabilising, were those equally of thousands of others who found themselves undergoing psychiatric treatment. The rapidly restored equanimity of David's family was swiftly matched by that of a society in which other issues quickly displaced those of a war whose corruptions were too profound to be closely inspected. When Harriet objects that 'we've had a little trouble . . . no more yelling. Just be happy', David replies, 'You mean take some old man to a ditch of water, shove his head under, talk of cars and money till his feeble pawing stops, and then head on home to go in and out of doors and drive cars and sing sometimes.'[88] The point is not merely a political one. For he is struck for the first time by what seems to him to be a fundamental truth: 'We are hoboes . . . We make signs in the dark. You know yours. I understand my own. We share coffee.'[89] This is not offered as an expression of his cynicism but of his recognition that violence, betrayal, contempt – the whole panoply of responses manifest in war – are equally a fact of everyday life. War expresses a total contempt for human opacity, for the individual mystery of people's lives, but so does an existence in which role-playing is substituted for being and in which appearance becomes more important than reality.

Rick wanders around taking photographs but, like the projected slides which start and conclude the play, they offer no insight either into the lives of individuals or the nature of events. Indeed the slides are misread by those who comment on them. Perhaps, too, this is a comment on the inadequacy of a pure dramatic naturalism (which O'Neill called holding the family Kodak up to ill nature). And when the play was moved to Broadway Rabe responded with enthusiasm, observing that 'With the audience further away, the actors were freed from the need to "behave" which the intimacy of the Anspracher had forced upon them. Because the play lives in a middle ground between what is thought of in theatre terms as "realism" and "fantasy", precise stylization is a crucial production factor, and now this ingredient was more possible. Though it is set in a living room, the play is primarily taking place in theatrical space.'[90] The family's protective room is invaded; their strategies for evading the real are exposed. But they reassert their roles, move back into the soap opera of their lives. It is in this sense that Rabe sought for a comic element in the play and looked for a stylisation that would inhibit pretension. As he has said:

> The forms referred to during the time of writing *Sticks and Bones* were farce, horror, movie, TV situation comedy. These should have their effect, though it must be remembered that they are where form was sought, not content. What is poetic in the writing must not be reinforced by deep feeling on the part of the actors, or the writing will hollow into pretension. In a more 'realistic' play, where language is thinner, subtext must be supplied or there is no weight. Such deep support of *Sticks and Bones* will make the play ponderous . . . A major premise of the play is that stubbing your own big toe is a more disturbing event than hearing of a stranger's suicide.[91]

Sticks and Bones was clearly concerned with more than Vietnam. At its heart is the family – a central icon of American life. But as the play progresses it becomes clear that its members share very little but the myth of their own communality. Behind the façade are the fears, frustrations

329

and cruelties which are obscured but not neutralised by rhetoric and the formularised gestures of concern. It is less a play about war than about loneliness and self-betrayal; less an account of political perfidy than of the failure of private morality. The characters collude in their own insignificance. They become accomplices to those forces, natural and social, which turn their lives into a history of decline.

And much the same could be said of a later play, *Streamers*, voted best play of 1976. First produced at the Long Wharf Theatre in January 1976, it moved to the Mitzi Newhouse Theatre, Lincoln Center, in April under the aegis of Joe Papp. Set in an army barracks during the early years of the Vietnam war, it dramatises the tensions in a group of soldiers under threat of being sent to a war of which they know very little. Vietnam exists as a threat but in a sense it becomes a dramatic device – the source of the pressures which precipitate self-revelation. Richie is a wealthy homosexual, insecure and vulnerable; Billy is an intellectual and Roger a black from the ghetto who has now put space between himself and that experience of violence and deprivation. The only thing they share is the war, or the threat of the war.

The various tensions erupt into violence when Carlyle, a black soldier from another unit, intrudes. For all his streetwise stance he is profoundly insecure to the point of being psychotic – 'I got thoughts, man, in my head; alla time, burnin', burnin' thoughts a understandin'.'[92] Despite his macho stance he makes homosexual approaches to Richie. But most of the characters are similarly disturbed. Roger has been under psychiatric care, Billy recalls a criminal past on the fringes of the homosexual community, Richie is homosexual but uncertain in his commitment to it. Two sergeants appear, both on the verge of breakdowns, one having just returned from Vietnam and the other about to go there. The play ends in a spasm of violence as Carlyle kills first Billy and then one of the sergeants. They are all men at the end of their tether, having lost whatever values, whatever structures, support their lives. This is the origin of the play's title which refers to a parachute which fails to open and by extension to those who plunge to earth as a result. They have all lost this support. They are enlisted in an army whose purpose baffles them and whose daily rituals they suspect to be pointless, but the play is not simply a critique of army life. As with *Sticks and Bones* it is a portrait of a desperately uncommunal world in which human relationships are simply an expression of private need, and in which nothing is really shared but pain and a certain bafflement. But to some degree the situation is so implacable, the characters so manifestly deformed by their experiences, that their utility as images of a wider society is suspect. The pressure is certainly at least as much internal as it is an expression of the imminent war. They are all adrift before the specific events of the play. The war simply serves as a focus for their profound uncertainties. Rabe is, in effect, not best seen simply as a Vietnam playwright though in *The Orphan* even his version of *The Oresteia* is infiltrated by references to My Lai. In many ways what appears political is more strictly psychological; what seems social is more clearly metaphysical. Perhaps this is what Vietnam did for the writer, as for the average American: it destabilised his sense of the real; it challenged assured notions of character, language, moral value and national purpose; it made relations problematic, not only between the generations but between the individual and that society whose demands had ultimately proved insupportable. It had come to stand for the implacable and the contingent, and it exposed a profound level of self-doubt at the heart of the individual and the nation alike. And the parallels with the past – in many ways simplistic and misleading – nonetheless established a direct relationship with a history which could no longer be seen as morally stable.

This is very much the feeling behind Tom Cole's *Medal of Honor Rag* (1975), first presented by the Theatre Company of Boston. This takes the form of an extended interview between a white psychiatrist and a black medal of honour winner called DJ who has been traumatised by the war. The doctor's area of specialisation is 'impacted grief'. He defines the soldier's problem thus:

> This man was sent by his country to fight in a war. A war unlike any war he might have imagined. Brutal, without glory, without meaning, without good wishes for those who were sent to fight and without gratitude for those who returned. He was trained to kill people of another world in their own homes, in order to help them. How this could help them we do not really know.[93]

The play ends with an epilogue in which the doctor explains that after the interview the soldier had gone AWOL and staged a robbery, apparently to raise money for his wife's hospitalisation but in reality, it is hinted, in order to join his dead comrades and thus in some sense neutralise the absurdity both of his own survival and of the whole war of which he was an ironic hero. Not without a certain humour, the play is an indictment not only of the war but of a country which struggles to forget the war by metaphorically, and often literally, burying its survivors by sheer neglect or by forcing them to play the requisite role in a national myth of heroism. What dies, in other words, is not a simple soldier but a whole myth about American virtue and metaphysical purpose.

Nor was the writer wholly inclined to absolve himself of the charge of turning pain into art, for the process of transmuting social experience into drama was inevitably a betrayal both of the immediate reality of the war and of its sheer contingency. Thus in *How I Got That Story* (1979) Amlin Gray chooses to offer an ironic account of the war through the eyes of a naive reporter slowly made aware of the falsification involved in the act of writing. When a guerilla accuses him of a failure to intervene in history he objects:

> REPORTER: . . . I don't make them die. They're dying anyway.
> GUERILLA: You just watch.
> REPORTER: That's right.
> GUERILLA: Your standpoint is aesthetic.
> REPORTER: Yes.[94]

In the course of this non-naturalistic play he is slowly exposed to the reality of the war, degrading, physically and mentally debilitating, and destructive of human relationships no less than of coherent meaning. The form of the play – a series of isolated events – and the collapse of character, plot and dialogue is offered as a patent parallel to the social action.

By the end of the 1970s the war and its effects tended to be seen in terms of an anxious and ironic comedy. The wounds opened up by that conflict are not so much cauterised by this humour as highlighted by it. In *Lone Star* (1979), by James McLure, one of the characters is suffering from a physical wound; in *Pvt Wars* (1979), by the same author, his figures are mentally as well as physically maimed. Thus McLure recreates the war not by invoking its details but by deploying its victims. Both plays are extremely funny but the humour is a product of trauma. In *Pvt Wars*, set in a mental hospital, the characters are fragile. Hysteria is a constant potential, as is violence. They suffer from a kind of aphasia ('The thing about the world is . . . the thing about the world is . . . the world is . . . you see what I'm trying to say?'[95]). The humour is an unconscious product of their condition rather than a willed defence against their memories. They talk about release from the hospital but this is never a real possibility. Their lives are a blend of fantasy and memory. They have negotiated the only kind of existence which they can tolerate and sustain. At least in the hospital the clichés of reassurance are self-evidently ironic. When one of the inmates objects that he is 'a fucking psychotic with his pecker blown off' he is told 'Things could be worse . . . it could rain.'[96] It is a black humour which slowly strips away the protective tissue from their lives. One turns to poetry, reciting *Hiawatha*, another to the consolation of constructing a radio (by stealing parts from other already functioning radios), but it is a therapy that contains the very neurosis against which it is deployed. And in a sense in the hospital, with its shattered patients struggling to make sense out of lives suddenly drained of meaning, deploying a language devalued by experience and reaching for myths that no longer sustain, we have the image of a post-war America trying to adjust to the fact of national trauma. A decade on, David Edgar may regret the paucity and weakness of plays addressing the war directly but in a sense virtually all of American theatre bears the marks of that war. The result has been a highly self-conscious drama for which almost all aspects of theatre have been problematised.

10 The San Francisco Mime Troupe

The radicalisation of the American theatre which occurred in the 1960s found expression in a number of ways: a new-found fascination with the stage as an agent of social change by racial and special interest groups, the creation of new theatres and the appearance of new writers, directors and actors whose primary allegiance was to political transformation rather than aesthetic experiment. In some cases existing groups were transformed by the impact of events; in others, they were summoned into existence by the pressure of the public world. From the many such groups, I have chosen to look in some detail at three – the San Francisco Mime Troupe, the Bread and Puppet Theatre and El Teatro Campesino. Very different from one another, they nonetheless proved influential and durable, and can stand for the many companies which have chosen to see the theatre as potentially at the heart of a changing social and moral world.

The Mime Troupe was founded by R.G. Davis in 1959. Inspired by a visit to the José Limon dance company, he had studied modern dance at the universities of Ohio and New Mexico, as well as Connecticut College and at various professional studios in New York. But he became disenchanted with the possibilities of dance and, inspired by Marcel Marceau, decided to train as a mime artist, working firstly with Paul Curtis's American Mime Theatre in New York and then, in 1957, with Etienne Decroux in Paris. Decroux had been a member of the Charles Dullin Theatre during the war and had worked with Jean-Louis Barrault. On his return to America, Davis performed for a while on his own but then joined the Actors' Workshop, run by Jules Irving and Herbert Blau, then a teacher at San Francisco State College. And it was while working with this company that Davis gathered together a small group called the R.G. Davis Mime Troupe. Their first performance, 'Games – 3 Sets' took place on 29 October 1959 at the San Francisco Art Institute. Subsequent performances were given under the aegis of the Actors' Workshop, anxious to justify itself to the Ford Foundation which had just begun to fund it in the 1960–1 season (to the extent of $56,000).

The programme for the '11th Hour Mime Show', so called because it began at 11 pm, was something of a manifesto and made plain both the tradition in which they saw themselves operating and their central emphasis on craft:

> When Jacques Copeau, one of the great innovators of the modern theatre resigned from the Comédie Française, he went literally to the country, to go back to the soil of his art. He formed a young troupe, trained in all the instruments of the art of acting, among them Mime. The art of Mime might even be considered the soil of the art of acting. It is made of muscle, and gesture, and rhythm and motion, and may give birth by the devious route of internal action to the unexpected Word.
>
> Mime has not yet found its way in any significant fashion into modern American drama. But we trust it will in time. As practised by the R.G. Davis Mime Troupe it retains, even when well-formed, a connection with its spontaneous and improvisatory sources. It is young in spirit, and truly experimental.[1]

The programme note was signed by Blau and Irving, hence, perhaps, the stress on experimentalism. The talents of the group were, anyway, employed by the Workshop through their work on Beckett, more especially Beckett's mime plays. Nor were these mimes devoid of dialogue, though the main emphasis was on the elaboration of images.

Then, in 1962, the group began to perform outside the context of the Workshop, with Davis borrowing certain movements from Joe Chaikin's Open Theatre exercises, and discovering the *commedia dell'arte* as a principal vehicle for their talents (it was to remain such for seven years). *Commedia dell'arte* was a form of improvised comedy popular in Italy and throughout Europe from the sixteenth to the eighteenth century. The entertainment was improvised around stock characters, situations and speeches. There was considerable emphasis on visual jokes and the half-mask was used for the first time in a theatrical context. The effect of this latter was to place greater emphasis on gesture and the body and to underscore the mime element of drama (indeed the *commedia* became a principal influence on the British pantomime). That the Mime Troupe should have been drawn to this form is therefore scarcely surprising.

The year 1962 also saw their first outdoor performance, the broad gestures of the *commedia* being precisely designed for such a setting. It was a style of acting which the group retained, proving especially appropriate as it became radicalised in the 1960s and found itself increasingly performing broadly political homilies before large crowds. The move to the city parks which started in 1962 met with opposition from city officials who wished to deny them a permit – a fact which played its part in the politicisation of the group – but a court case in 1965 resulted in a ruling that efforts to prevent their performances were unconstitutional attempts at censorship.

At first the plays were far less significant for their content than for their performance potential; less important for their political implications or linguistic subtleties than for the opportunities which they offered for mime. But this began to change. As Davis himself commented,

> Directors in academic theatre usually emphasize the literary style of their productions. Since I have not spent years and years being impressed by the grandness of language, I viewed the text as only material for mime. I had always approached the actual performance as more relevant than the text. The existential reality of a performer in front of an audience required that something happen – even if the text could not do it. In 1964 we put our trust in content.[2]

The show which marked this transformation was *Tartuffe*, the first half of which ended with a song which Davis regarded as illustrating 'our multiple-image style and our new political consciousness'.[3] But in truth the performance of *Ubu King* the previous year had suggested something of this new direction. Their adaptations of Molière and Goldoni were not usually attempts to translate the original author's intentions. They were not acts of homage. As a programme note pointed out, they did not offer themselves as antiquarians. They were concerned with using what they found useful and discarding the rest.

At this time Davis's name was dropped and the group was renamed the San Francisco Mime Troupe. As he explained, 'I couldn't see my name on a banner above the *commedia* stage. Mime stayed in the title because it was closer to the dance troupes yet apart from the regional theatres. We were to travel light and move around – thus, Troupe. San Francisco, naturally.'[4] The group now took as its motto, 'Engagement, Commitment and Fresh Air' and its radicalisation reflected the changing mood of America in the 1960s. The Free Speech Movement began in Berkeley in 1964 while the civil rights movement was gathering force. In 1965 the Vietnam Day Committee began work in Berkeley, eventually seeking to stop troop trains from passing through. At the same time the Mime Troupe moved from performing Brecht to creating what they called *A Minstrel Show or Civil Rights in a Cracker Barrel*. Increasingly they found themselves at odds with city and state officials as they performed in public places without the requisite licences.

In 1967 they began to work on *L'Amant Militaire*, by Goldoni, adapted as an anti-war play and seen by Davis as equally an anti-pacifist play. In the original version the Spanish army is fighting a war in Italy. Pantalone, the Spanish mayor, is in league with a general to their mutual profit and he wishes to cement the relationship by marrying his daughter

20.   San Francisco Mime Troupe, *L'Amant Militaire*, 1967.

to the old man. But she prefers a young lieutenant who dresses up as a woman in order to avoid serving in the army. The parallel with the situation in Vietnam appealed to Davis and to Joan Holden who adapted the play. According to Holden 'The heroine debunks pacifism as an answer. She says that you have to fight war with war. It called for a revolution, but it didn't say who the revolutionaries should be.'[5] The original text was rewritten and additional material was added. 'The process', Davis suggested,

> was fluid for we were cross-examining our own views on the war. Our liberal pacifism came to the stage and was punched around by some radical thoughts. More interested in telling the audience what to do or 'where it's at' than delineating the process within antiwar positions, we wanted to deliver a heavier punch than we had previously with the commedia structure.[6]

Accordingly they introduced a puppet outside the play, indeed off the stage, who spoke directly to the audience. This became the voice of radicalism and enabled them to establish some kind of dialectic in the play. *L'Amant Militaire* was eventually taken to New York where it was favourably contrasted by the London *Times* to the Yale production of Joseph Heller's *We Bombed in New Haven*. The puppets, renamed Gutter

Puppets, were retained and became a standard part of the repertoire after 1969, in works like *Meter Maid* (1970), which offered advice on how to beat or sabotage parking meters, and *Ripping Off Ma Bell* (1970), which advised on how to defraud the telephone company.

However, the group became increasingly dissatisfied with relying on the *commedias* which were not always easily adaptable to their purposes and which anyway grew out of an experience that was not their own. As such they did not wholly lend themselves to the group's increasing concern with engaging the nature of American reality in the present. The solution was itself in part a compromise. In 1970 Joan Holden wrote *The Independent Female, or A Man Has His Pride*. As she has explained,

> For several years, we had been dissatisfied with commedia because it was foreign, and we had been talking about what would be an American equivalent. We liked commedia because the characters were so clear, it had a broad comic style, it was funny, it was highly stylized, and it was really good for us to work in. We didn't know what could work as well. We sort of stumbled on it when we did a melodrama, *The Independent Female*. We didn't know then that we were replacing commedia with melodrama, but that is basically what we have done. We found American stereotypes that can be used the same way as the commedia stereotypes — the capitalist, the young naive man, the strong woman.[7]

The play itself concerned a young woman, Gloria Pennybank, who is engaged to marry an equally young executive. The price to be paid is that she must give up her own career and become a supportive wife, but she is dissuaded by a militant feminist, Sarah Bullitt, and together they lead a campaign for women's rights. After various complications the putative husband shoots Sarah. The play in its original form was then to have ended in the convention of nineteenth-century melodrama with Gloria's return to her husband, but a group of feminists insisted that this should be changed and as a result of discussions the new ending was substituted. Faced with choosing between the logic of their self-imposed form and their intensifying political convictions, they chose the latter.

Davis himself became increasingly concerned with what he called 'the heavy Maoist dogmatism' which had begun to infiltrate the rhetoric of American radicalism. He was also disturbed by the tensions within the group between those who saw themselves as professional theatre practitioners and those who placed a premium on an authenticity which they associated with a kind of amateurism. The Mime Troupe, like so many other groups born in the 1960s, reflected the virtues and vices of that decade. Questions of authenticity and ideological correctness became of central importance, while, in a self-consciously theatricalised environment, a touch of megalomania in theatrical groups was perhaps not surprising. As Davis himself observed:

> The society around our theatrical enclave became more and more theatrical. The Mime Troupe had revived the emphasis on the single performer from 1960 to 1965 and made the skilled performer a probability. From 1965 to 1970 the lid was lifted off the big box. The hippies unleashed a surge of incompetence from below and the lumpen middle class wanted to express itself by being . . . Associated as we were with political factions, we often came under the same false thinking that has permeated American political organizations . . . When the amateurs had as much say, as much right to speak up at meetings (and who dare say 'no'), we lived in a daily burning of passions. Irrationality rose until the fires were too hot and people left. It turned out that both extremes split – the professionals and the politically confused theatrical amateurs. The professionals, the ones with talent and skill, could not take the lack of structure. We saw the dissolution of the dialectic between expertise and participation, between improvisation and training, between a script (written by a talented philosopher) and the actor's freedom to invent.[8]

Davis's own authority declined after the production of Brecht's *Congress of the Whitewashers*. It proved an unsatisfactory experience for many in the company who felt that his right to a central position in the group derived from a claim to superior insight of a kind which he was no longer exhibiting and which anyway was mystifying a theatre that wished to associate itself with, rather than distinguish itself from, the people. In fact he was a victim of a growing sense of radicalism and group confidence. Two years before, he had dismissed most of the group and started again. Now it was no longer possible because authority in all guises was being questioned and by no means solely in a theatrical context. The feminist reaction against male authority, the black rejection of white authority, the denial of moral or political authority to a government waging war against peasants could not be insulated from questions of authority within the arts.

Davis left the company in March 1970. Thereafter they became a more clearly Marxist theatrical group, inserting the word 'collective' in their title. In a statement dated autumn 1971, the Troupe described themselves as a 'small theater collective dedicated to the principle that all art is political', and asserted with Brecht that 'the artist who considers himself above history has merely taken the side of the ruling class'. They worked in a collective 'rather than the individualistic fashion to create a theater that is relevant to the lives of the masses of people in our country'. Their commitment, they declared, was 'to change, not art'.[9]

The Dragon Lady's Revenge, a product of that year, was thus not the work of a single writer or director. It was the product of five writers and the result of lengthy discussions, each individual writing assigned scenes. Set in a small country in South-east Asia, it was concerned with a supposed link between the CIA and the drug traffic. A blend of the *commedia*, melodrama and comic-book stereotypes, it was offered as an ironic commentary on events in Vietnam, though not all the naiveties of the production were conscious and deliberate. As Joan Holden remarked, 'We were looking for a play to do against the war, against imperialism, but we didn't know what line to take. Somebody heard that *Ramparts* was going to come out with an article that linked the CIA to the drug traffic. So somebody had the idea that that would be a good subject.'[10] A company wishing to subordinate aesthetic to political convictions might have been expected to be somewhat more rigorous in its politics and perhaps less proud of the Obie award which it won.

The San Francisco Mime Troupe moved from its early concern with craft, through the *commedia dell'arte* morality plays, to specific issues of direct relevance to the community which it increasingly saw less as a passive audience and more as a human resource to mobilise against war, racism, industrialism or simple conformity. They developed styles commensurate with a public role which was to take them into the streets, into public parks and to local communities. Their over-solemn commitment to their own political education and to that of others did not prevent an emphasis on broad humour in their work which remains a distinguishing characteristic of a company now a quarter of a century old. In the 1980s the political commitment of its actors and the plays they perform remains the central issue, the broad style of acting successfully accommodating those whose professionalism is less than total. They have broadened their skills to include certain circus techniques, including juggling. Music is an important part of their performances. They frequently do work addressing local issues (*High Rise*, 1972, *San Fran Scandals*, 1973) even straying into territory which El Teatro Campesino had once made its own (*Los Siete*, 1970; *Frijoles, or Beans to You*, 1975). It has set itself to demythologise theatre and to blur the distinction between audience and performer not as a consequence of aesthetic theory but because they see themselves as a natural extension of the community, as fellow workers involved in a dialogue.

The Mime Troupe played its part in liberating theatre in America from its role as simple entertainment or civic facility. Its conception of guerilla theatre emphasised the subversive qualities of an art which had been all too often easily assimilated by a system adept at transforming protest into entertainment and radical disaffection into cultural object. It is a group whose published texts do no more than hint at the energy and resilience which are in effect the real resources which it mobilises against

340

the reductivism of contemporary life. And there is indeed a sense in which the values the Troupe celebrate have rather less to do with Marx than with Whitman, in which they express less a desire for a transformed future than a restored past. On the other hand, despite its continued solid work, the Troupe owes something of its reputation to the events of the 1960s which placed political groups at the centre of attention and which saw in theatricality a powerful image of self-consciousness and of that sense of community so frequently invoked as an antidote to contemporary alienation.

Writing from the perspective of 1975, Davis observed that,

> When we were moving from the avant-garde to a radical political stance, we retained the progressive spirit of the avant-garde. The Troupe, collectivizing like many other groups in 1970, experimented with leaderless production and domination by the women's liberation point of view, called itself a voice of the movement, and tried like many to extricate itself from its history – denying its past, rewriting its records, proclaiming its instant self.[11]

To his mind, the effect of this was likely to be ambiguous on a political no less than an aesthetic level. For he doubted whether a collective could have the skill and the ideological energy to create a play – 'No great examples exist, whereas we do have plays that cut beneath the surface of current events and can be improved and delineated by a collective group' – while 'collectivization has, in many groups, tended to deny the expertise of the writer and director and, for that matter, secretaries and other technicians'.[12] In reply, Joan Holden observed that 'The main charge Ronny lays against us now is that we have lost our artistic integrity by participating in the radical movement.' But why, she asked, 'is remaining on the sidelines more artistic than jumping into the fight? A left-wing artist who is jealous of his independence risks crossing into that "exempt" status for which artists trade away a noble role in history.'[13]

Arthur Holden has explained succinctly the philosophy of those in the group. 'We make theatre', he explained,

> for one main purpose: to dramatize a way of looking at the world. And we do that because in our experience it is an effective way of engaging people in important questions. I'm not interested in the theatre except as a device for raising questions, for confronting people with the issues, and making them palatable, interesting, fun, entertaining. I'm not an artist in the sense that I think art is somehow separate from what's going on politically. I think what's going on politically is the most important thing, and if you are an artist you should relate to that in order to make your art meaningful.[14]

The San Francisco Mime Troupe has survived into its second decade without receiving any support either from private foundations or state or federal governments, with the exception of grants in the late 1970s from the California Arts Council. It has survived on its own income, paying salaries of between $25 and $40 a month. It follows that while its auditions are conducted on a professional basis and are concerned with identifying those with genuine theatrical abilities it is only likely to be the politically committed who are prepared to stay with the company for long. Their new premises in San Francisco provide extensive rehearsal and storage space as well as a flexible performance area but it remains in essence a poor theatre, reflecting in its own style and in the lifestyle of its members the lives of those to whom it wishes primarily to address itself. Over the years its racial composition has changed so that, as Theodore Shank reports, by 1980 the Company consisted of seven white, five Latin, and three black performers enabling it to address a variety of audiences with genuine understanding and confidence. Indeed, in 1980 they became the first American theatre group to tour Cuba since the revolution. But its main audience remains domestic and it sets itself the task of dramatising social inequity and thereby attempting to transform American society. As Joan Holden has said, 'The basic theme of all our plays is the same: there is a class system in this country that is not run in your interest. It is run in the interest of rich people and they fool you about your interest.'[15] Their survival, a quarter of a century after their founding, is thus a testimony to their own resilience, their continued struggle with the kind of financial problems which are perhaps a consequence of the system which they identify. It is also, however, a sign of the strength and the resilience of the system itself and perhaps of the relative ineffectualness of an assault launched by a dozen or so performers who offer energy, insight and entertainment against an economic and political power which has proved implacable. Even this account, in accommodating them to a history of twentieth-century American drama, is at risk of shifting them from the political into the purely aesthetic realm.

11 Bread and Puppet

Antonin Artaud was not the only one who was struck by the reductive impact of illusionistic theatre on the audience. Bertolt Brecht also rejected what he called 'Aristotelian' drama, observing that 'looking around one discovers more or less motionless bodies in a curious state – they seem to be contracting their muscles in a strong physical effort, or else to have relaxed them after violent strain . . . they have their eyes open, but they don't look, they stare . . . they stare at the stage as if *spellbound*, which is an expression from the Middle Ages, an age of witches and obscurantists'.[1] The theatre seemed to offer the opportunity for vicarious living. But for Brecht theatre should be less concerned with catharsis, which discharges energy harmlessly, than with didacticism. He attacked what he called 'culinary' theatre, which was wholly digested in the process of production and consumption, and advocated a theatre which left a crucial residue of commitment. Empathy with individual characters was likely to lead to an unquestioning acceptance of their views; without a clear understanding of the issues the critical space between character and audience is annihilated by illusionism. The solution was to foreground technique, to stress the theatrical nature of the event, to liberate the audience from passivity, to force them to locate themselves in a historical context, to remove them from the factitious present of the stage and situate themselves and the events which they observe in terms of the social and economic forces which determine them. This led him to an emphasis on epic theatre, a theatre in which history became a crucial subject; and it led him to advocate a theatre in which a deliberate space was to be maintained between the audience and the action which they observed.

Brecht's art was non-tragic. It denied inevitability as it resisted the notion of an unyielding human nature. Fundamental to his political beliefs was a conviction that change was possible; basic to his theatrical strategy was the conviction that the audience should not be allowed to surrender its own freedom and judgmental abilities to an illusionist aesthetic. And all elements of a production were to be mobilised to facilitate this. The *mise-en-scène* was released from its simple role of compounding illusion. It could now be seen in a dialectical relationship to the action, commenting on it, undercutting it with irony or establishing a larger context which made that action merely paradigmatic. The actor, similarly, was encouraged to create a space between himself and his role, to resist the vortex of mimesis. The acting was thus to be deliberately drained of realism. There was to be a clear distinction between the mask and the man. It is that distinction which makes critical judgements possible. As Brecht remarked, the actor must be able to suggest 'apart from what he does something else . . . he does *not* do: i.e. he acts in such a manner that one can see the alternative course of action, so that the acting allows the audience to detect the other possibilities, so that any given action can be seen as only one among a number of variants.'[2] And the emphasis tends to be on externals. His theatre was not concerned with the internal emotional realities of his characters but with the external forces that exert pressure on a self which is now seen as primarily a product of those forces. It follows that his interest in projecting stylised expressions of social behaviour leads to a degree of stylisation in performance and production. The use of giant puppets in Brechtian productions was thus an entirely logical development, and that logic was also recognised by others alive also to the long history of the puppet.

It was Peter Schumann, a sculptor and choreographer, who observed that 'alienation is automatic with puppets. It's not that our characters are less complete, they are just more explicit.'[3] Schumann moved from Germany to the United States in 1961. In the following year he established the Bread and Puppet Theatre in New York, in the belief that 'the theatre should be as basic as bread'. Though based in New York and subsequently at Goddard College in Plainfield, Vermont, Bread and Puppet travelled widely and reached a wide variety of different audiences. Unlike El Teatro Campesino it had no precisely defined constituency, though the political dimension intensified and quickly became a distinguishing characteristic.

For Schumann, 'Masks are older than actors, faces of wood and stone are older than mimes. Masked dancers and the effigies they carry are certainly at the origin of theater.'[4] He conceded, however, that, in the modern theatre, puppetry had been relegated to a minor role, that it was seen as technologically inferior and as too simple in its effects and its intent. And yet Schumann, a true product of the decade, wished to make a case for the simple, for an art of the surface relying on physical skills and a direct and even naive relationship between performer and audience. Though his theatre became increasingly interventionist, addressing itself to the major issues of the day, he also looked to a new world, purged of commercialism and militarism alike, in which the naive art of puppetry could operate without risking collaboration with the values which it imagined itself to be challenging. Thus he warned of the folk-singer and puppeteer whose 'harmless contribution of good throat and skilful

21.   Bread and Puppet Theatre. An anti-war parade in Washington, 24 April 1971.

fingers' enables marines to be sent around the world and lipstick sold to grandmothers. But he insisted that,

> assuming the good old world succeeds against McNamara and his like, then the simpletons and demons of puppetry are also going to win against show business . . . the Heartbeat Movement will set out with lots of music and puppets to beat hearts and to move heartbeats, and we will all be able to work together, puppeteers, folksingers, poets, painters, housewives, everybody, because we are all tired, oh tired of books . . . we are tired of spray guns and machine guns, we want fiddle bows and love instead.[5]

Bread and Puppet, like El Teatro Campesino, does not rely on trained actors. The use of a narrator means that those manipulating the puppets are not usually required to perform. The action is unmediated by actors, or rather, as Schumann himself insisted, the puppets are the actors. It does mean, however, that the emphasis is placed on movement, on choreography.

Despite the group's increasing politicisation as a result of the Vietnam war, speaking in 1968 Schumann explained that he rejected the idea of Bread and Puppet as simple protest theatre: 'We are all sick of Vietnam. But the theatre must do more than protest . . . most of our stuff is more general. We are not very interested in ideology.'[6] Like the San Francisco

Mime Troupe, he was not concerned with shocking the audience or with imposing an aesthetic; he wished to return to traditional theatrical values, behind which, I suspect, he believed lay traditional moral values. Like Marcuse, he was asserting the need to progress through reversion to older models. And like Davis, he invoked the *commedia*: 'We don't necessarily have to revolutionize theatre. It may be that the best theatre – if it comes – will develop from the most traditional forms. A theatre is good when it makes sense to people. A small theatre that tries simply to do that does not exist in this country. We do not yet have our own version of the *commedia dell'arte*.'[7] However, he wished to resist the temptation of becoming simply a professional protest group and on those grounds was suspicious of El Teatro Campesino, particularly when it performed not to Chicanos but before an audience in Newport, Rhode Island, for whom their performance became part moral catharsis and part a pain anaesthetised by aesthetics.

Bread and Puppet is quintessentially a street theatre. Their mere presence theatricalises the environment; it is a statement in itself. And the fact of performing before an audience which has not paid or selected itself in the customary way implies the need to develop a simplicity and clarity which might be suspect in a theatre. Indeed Schumann has said that unless a performance is clear to a five year old it will be ineffective. But energy and intensity are too easily discharged in a situation in which the environment is not specifically designed to focus on the theatrical event. This fact necessitates a clarity of line and a concentration of effect which is designed specifically to have an emotional appeal. Bread and Puppet make a virtue of the limitations within which they work. Their plays are, as Schumann himself has admitted, raw and rough, without scenic subtlety. They work with puppets of all sizes: 'the very small puppets are best in comedy. The really large ones – the eighteen foot ones – are also at their best when they are buffoons. The medium sized puppets are very good for drama.'[8] Clearly for street demonstrations and marches the largest are the most effective and it was these which began to appear in the various public demonstrations of the late 1960s. The plays, which were developed through improvisation, sometimes contained dialogue, but more often, especially when the large puppets were in use, employed a narrator. They were sometimes, in effect, agit-prop sketches and sometimes allegories.

One of the most frequently performed at this time was *A Man Says Goodbye to His Mother* (1968), a play about Vietnam and beyond that about all war, Schumann being a pacifist. Set in an Asian village, it tells not only of the destruction of the countryside by war but also of the collapse of all moral and social form. The narrator, who wears a skull mask and carries a sack, describes a son's farewell to his mother. He leaves for a distant country but is shot and wounded in the arm. The mother is now transformed, through exchanging her mask, into the women of the village in the land to which her son has gone. The son is now equipped with a gun, a gas mask, and a plane. With the latter he poisons the plants and burns the villager's houses. Finally he kills a child and is killed in turn by the women of the village, played, of course, by the same figure who had played his own mother. The body is carried off by the narrator and the woman, both wearing death masks.

Ernst Bloch has said that 'The Mask has always had a denaturalizing effect but it made whatever it represented unrecognizable in order that it might be known.'[9] This is the primary strategy of Bread and Puppet. Despite the real grace and beauty of many of the puppets, one primary effect is to prefer the type to the individual, to suggest levels at which experience is shared or actions are archetypal. When the mother of the killer is transformed into the mother of the victim, Schumann is engaging the ironic vulnerabilities of motherhood and behind that the betrayals of mother earth rather than the psychological dilemma of individual characters. The grotesque puppets find their equivalent in a public world whose distortions of the human are presented by their perpetrators as necessary policy. He does not imply, with O'Neill, that the mask is an act of concealment, but rather, with Oscar Wilde, that it contains an essential truth. It is not a mimetic theatre; its concern is not with imitating an action but with suggesting a level on which those actions are rooted in an archetypal pattern, on which primitive notions of good and evil, basic ritual, conflicts and ceremonies still suggest a truth disregarded by a society focussed on rationalism and materialism. As Meyerhold remarked of the mask, referring less to the *commedia* half-mask than to a style of acting, 'The mask enables the spectator to see not only the actual Arlecchino [Harlequin] before him but all the Arlecchinos who live in his memory. Through the mask the spectator sees every person who bears the merest resemblance to the character.'[10] And the fact that Bread and Puppet is a 'poor theatre', literally, in terms of its refusal to charge for open-air performances and in its eschewal of technical complexities, but also in terms of its denials of subtlety, of the supposed sophistications of contemporary production values, suggests something of the vision which it chooses to present. It offers itself as a model of the world which it implicitly invokes, a world which exists outside the material demands of rational society.

There is an element of retreat in Bread and Puppet. Their move from New York City to the countryside – in 1970, Schumann, his family and some puppeteers moved to Goddard College in Plainfield, Vermont, living and working at Cote Farm, before moving to another farm near Glower, Vermont in 1974 – was a pragmatic rejection of the filth of the city but it was also, arguably, an escape from modernity and from the complex. The other side to a willed simplification is a naive simplification. And often Schumann's reductions run the risk of reductiveness. His preference for the elemental can at times run the risk of ahistoricism as his presentation, and, in part, celebration, of human fallibility implies a determinism not entirely neutralised by his respect for those who pitch themselves against the drift of their own times.

This is perhaps true of *The Cry of the People for Meat* (1969), which begins with a prologue rooted in the Greek myth of creation and which continues with a biblical account. As the play progresses, various incidents and parables from the Bible are dramatised. But sheer process carries a logic of its own, a logic which resists too simple a location of evil as an objectified force. By the same token the acknowledgement of it as a potent force and constant temptation potentially reduces the political to the metaphysical or biological. It is a conflict and an ambiguity which perhaps explains Schumann's resistance to the notion of protest. Though fervently opposed to the Vietnam war, his work always seems to suggest his awareness of the immediate conflict as an image of a more primal battle within the human sensibility and the unnerving constancy of human nature, the disturbing fallibility of the race. War is not a special circumstance; it is the distinguishing characteristic of man. It is an image of his internal self as it is a description of his social life over time. The Vietnam war thus becomes not primarily a product of immediate geo-political decisions made in a specific socio-economic context; it becomes an image of that tragic contradiction which came into being with man's appearance. Schumann's puppets seem out of place, grotesque, disproportioned, unable to move with ease. Man's fundamental condition, he seems to imply, is one of alienation. Thus his present circumstance is merely one feature of a fundamental condition. But if violence is presented as inherent then so, too, is the impulse to resist. If the individual and the race seem born to deny the possibility of transcendence, then they are presented as equally determined to feed the spirit. Indeed, the Bread and Puppet Theatre offers itself as evidence of this and frequently distributes bread to its audience as a symbol of the communion towards which they reach, a communion which is an attempt on a literal and symbolic level to restore a lost unity. Their opposition to war thus derives not merely from their acknowledgement that it is a denial of life but also from the fact that it is an objectification of that gulf between the life and the death instinct which is the origin of tragedy.

The predominating tone suggested by the features of Schumann's puppets is one of sadness, a sense of loss. At the root of this is a wilfulness expressed in the title of *The Cry of the People for Meat*, a reference to the Israelites' desire for meat and for physical pleasures even while they were on their journey across the desert, a journey of the spirit. This is the fundamental conflict which lies at the heart of many of Schumann's plays. Thus, in the context of Vietnam, *Fire* dramatised equally man's capacity for violence and for genuine sacrifice. A woman slowly tears red tape into strips representing flames (as the Buddhist priests had immolated themselves to protest the war). She sticks these to her clothes until she is covered with paper fire and collapses. A bell rings. There is silence. The lights go out. But such consonance comes only with death. And there is a sense in which the distorted features of his puppets derive from the imperfections of life, from a primal failure re-enacted from generation to generation, of which any one conflict is merely a special case.

But the grotesque also functions in another way in Schumann's work. It projects tendencies to extremes; it suggests the pressure of the unseen; it draws attention to form and shape; it implies a moralised surface. As Meyerhold, who was similarly drawn to the work of the *commedia* and to mask, remarked in an article which he published in 1912, 'The grotesque does not recognise the *purely* debased or the *purely* exalted. The grotesque mixes opposites, consciously creating harsh incongruity, playing entirely on its own originality . . . The grotesque deepens life's outward appearance to the point where it ceases to appear merely natural . . . The basis of the grotesque is the artist's constant desire to switch the spectator from the plane he has just reached to another which is totally unforeseen.' And herein, of course, lies a spiritual dimension, a possible springboard into religious enquiry. As Meyerhold observed, 'Beneath what we see of life there are vast unfathomed depths. In its search for the supernatural, the grotesque synthesises opposites, creates a picture of the incredible, and encourages the spectator to try to solve the riddle of the inscrutable.' As Alexander Mashin wrote, 'It became clear that for Meyerhold the grotesque was not merely a means of expression, a way of heightening colours, it was no less than the content of that reality, that dislocated world in which he found himself and which formed the subject of his art.'[11] Much the same could be said of Schumann whose art was born out of a sense of loss which he sought to neutralise by invoking a world which lay not so much beyond the mask as in it; in it and the language of gesture which suggested a world beyond simple action. Walter Brown suggested of the Epic Theatre that it 'is gestural. Strictly speaking the gesture is the material and epic theatre its practical utilization.'[12] Much the same could be said of Bread and Puppet, which at moments, perhaps, could be said to have achieved that theatrical language drained of its illusionist

349

function for which Artaud had looked, 'a language of signs, gestures and attitudes having an ideographic value as they exist in certain unperverted pantomimes'.[13]

There is a powerful Christian drive in the work of Bread and Puppet. Certainly the iconography of Old and New Testament recurs, partly as an image of a promise proffered but still resisted, partly as a reminder of man's crucifixion not only of Christ but of his own capacity for transcendence. As in the 1930s Christ recrucified had been a potent image of man's denial of man so it is here. But where the 1930s offered a new sacrament of man born out of Marx and made flesh in Lenin, Schumann offers a call to spiritual renewal. Confronted by puppets whose expressions remain unresponsive the audience are forced back on themselves, offered archetypes which have to be translated into individual experience; they are parables to be decoded only in terms of personal perceptions. The implications of the action are not debated in the plays, nor are they offered for intellectual consideration. If they are to work at all then they must be felt on the pulse; they work by appeal to a stored fund of images, by a reticence seemingly at odds with the grossness of the figures which the group employs. The co-option of these works as simple protest did less than justice to them. The fact that the group frequently allied itself to public protests and that one of its central puppets, Uncle Fatso, was taken to be a deliberate caricature of President Johnson, gave it the appearance of a theatre group committed primarily to political change. However, the transformations it sought were of a subtler kind, its concern with life over death part of a more elaborate interpretation of man and his fate. And in that context, for Schumann, it seems, women represent the life force; men the greed, the aggressiveness which threaten that life (indeed in their 1972 production, *The Stations of the Cross*, Christ was played as a woman). But the puppets, though sexually differentiated, unavoidably seem to imply an androgynous mean, a reconciliation, albeit one that can only be realised at the cost of full humanity. Thus, just as the productions themselves are left deliberately rough and unfinished, so the space between different aspects of the human sensibility are productive of creative energy as well as irony.

In *The Presence of the Actor*, Joseph Chaikin acknowledges the importance of Schumann and the Bread and Puppet Theatre to his own work. It was, he suggested, 'the company that impresses me the most of all of New York. Peter creates his creatures of wood and cloth and moves them about in moral and theatrical terms much as a priest uses parables in a sermon. He has discovered a special form, and creates things with it that have not existed before.'[14] But this is not, of course, to suggest that Schumann's theatre had no forebears. He himself has acknowledged the importance of both the Bauhaus and Kurt Schwitters, while behind Uncle Fatso lurks the shadow of George Gross whose grotesque dummies had been a feature of *The Good Soldier Schweik*. For Oskar Schlemmer and the Bauhaus group the mask and the marionette were basic tools of theatre and, as Schumann acknowledged in an interview with Françoise Kourilsky, he 'had some wishful thinking about popular entertainment. He made definitions of what could be done on the stage, and popular entertainment played a part in his system.'[15] Kurt Schwitters's visionary Merz stage was to incorporate all elements of the production process and to employ everyday materials, transforming them in the process of absorbing them into an anti-rationalist art. But such influences were blended with that of circus (though he has pointed out that his actors never attempt anything more daring than a somersault). In particular he has spoken of the way in which circus exists outside the conventions of everyday life: 'The circus was a way of life that, compared to the life of the bourgeoisie, was almost as outside the civilized world as the world of the Gypsies – and it was a complete other world. That was the attraction of the circus.'[16]

Schumann's plays begin with pure music and movement ideas, and slowly develop towards communicable form. In a sense that process mirrors his own development as an artist. In Germany in the mid 1950s he ran a New Dance Group, which, on occasion, made use of large figures, and it was attending a John Cage concert in Germany in 1960 which led to his leaving for America. Once there he gravitated to Merce Cunningham's studio. But he was already reacting against the formalism of their stance and that of the creators of happenings. As he explained to Kourilsky, 'Their work is a work of intensity, and for me there is a difference between a work like theirs that constantly intensifies itself *in* itself, and a work that deliberately gives up that intensity for the sake of a communal act, for the sake of doing it *with* others *for* others.'[17] He seeks to reinstate narrative, to reach for clarity (emotional if not intellectual clarity), and to develop a language of myth which will enable an audience to relate the specific to the general, event to archetype. At the same time the narrative is developed from disparate elements braided together, choreographed with a view both to the underlying theme and to the integrity of individual elements as well as the unexpected confluence of those elements. This was something which Schumann found in Japanese puppet theatre (Bunraku), in which 'incredibly contrasted, completely unmarried ideas . . . are put forward to create the communication'. In particular, he was impressed by 'the interference of narration and musician with what happens visually, the order of separateness and coming together of these different stages', because 'It creates such a

351

broad spectrum.' As he admitted, 'That same kind of ambition is very much in the Bread and Puppet Theatre: to try to use the most possible unmarried and uncombined means – any garbage can, any music, anything we can find, any smallness or bigness – and get a communication out of it, not by creating atmosphere and moods and dialogues and tales, but by leaving these things as pure as they can be and eventually touching them together, bringing them really together.'[18] In a sense the Bread and Puppet brought together the aesthetic and political avant-garde, the two principal elements of 1960s theatre in America. Schumann's sensibility had itself been forged by those two traditions. In America he created from them one of the more impressive groups of the post-war American theatre – a group which took theatre onto the street without, for the most part, succumbing to a temptation to substitute one set of radically simplified convictions for another, without merely offering a view of theatre as pragmatic tool. The revolt against a materialistic theatre and society was a commonplace of the period. A genuine attempt to combine moral commitment and a concern with opening theatre to a broader public (both as audience and performer) and a fascination with exploring both the formal and metaphysical potential of theatre, was much rarer. And this was the nature of Schumann's achievement.

Edward Gordon Craig, in what was admittedly a heavily ironic essay, 'The Actor and the Uber-Marionette', observed of the puppet that though regarded today as 'rather a superior doll' it is in fact 'a descendant of the stone images of the old temples'. Though now 'a rather degenerate form of a god . . . There is', nonetheless, he insisted, 'something more than a flash of genius in the marionette, and there is something in him more than the flashiness of displayed personality. The marionette appears to me to be the last echo of some noble and beautiful art of a post civilisation.'[19] He called for a return to the 'noble artificiality' of classical theatre, observing 'who knows whether the puppet shall not once again become the faithful medium for the beautiful thoughts of the artist. May we not look forward with hope to that day which shall bring back to us once more the cunning of the artist, so that we can gain once more the "noble artificiality".'[20] Though these remarks were offered in the context of a critique of melodramatic acting styles it is tempting to see in Schumann's work a realisation of the hopes offered by Craig as a rhetorical gesture.

His mute figures, his puppets frozen into expressions of pain or sadness, horror or happiness, contain a meaning; they are not simply substitutes for a set of conventionalised responses, nor do they exist as reductive images of the real. Speaking of art and music, which he

352

describes as non-signifying arts, Sartre makes a distinction which I suspect is directly applicable to the work of Bread and Puppet at its best:

> I have always really distinguished meaning from significance. It seems to me, an object signifies when an allusion to another object is made through it. In this case, the mind ignores the sign itself; it reaches beyond to the thing signified; often it so happens that this last remains present when we have long since forgotten the words which caused us to conceive of it. The meaning, on the contrary, is not distinct from the object itself and is all the more manifest inasmuch as we are more attentive to the thing which it inhabits. I would say that an object has meaning when it incarnates a reality which transcends it but which cannot be apprehended outside of it and which its infiniteness does not allow to be expressed adequately by any system of signs: it is always a matter of a totality, totality of a person, milieu, time or human condition. I would say that the Mona Lisa's smile does not 'mean' anything, but that it has a meaning. Through it, that strange fusion of mysticism and naturalism, evidence and mystery which characterize the Renaissance is materialized . . . Thus does music seem to me, a beautiful mute with eyes full of meaning.[21]

So it is with Peter Schumann's puppets. Since 1974 the group has not existed as a permanent company, though from time to time a group is formed for a specific project, and each year past members of the original company gather at the Vermont farm for *The Domestic Resurrection Circus*, a performance whose religious overtones underscore the celebratory and even redemptive role which Schumann believes art can have in a world which has lost its other animating faiths. But, as he insisted, 'Art is no longer a decorator for religion. Art is by now what religion used to be. It is the design for the line of thought, the form for the communal event, the shape of the celebrations that we might have with each other.'[22]

Other groups are invited to join in these events, which sometimes retain a political element, attacking those divisions between people which are the source of conflict. The ultimate objective is the healing of division. Thus, in 1976, bicentennial year, Schumann chose to celebrate the American Indian, not only because of the ironies apparent in a year which celebrated independence but because he saw in their traditions something of that unity of thought and experience, man and nature, for which he, too, reached:

> The idea for this *Circus* was to have an Indian Pageant to telescope, in the midst of the bicentennial celebrations, what the Indian mind and philosophy is. Their thought and philosophy has been completely neglected by the American people. So the idea was to do a piece of landscape in order to carry that Indian thought – what Schweitzer called *Erfurch vor dem Leben* –

the respect for life. It's a philosophy of equalizing humans with ants and leaves of trees. To make that thought strong and powerful – for us that was the idea of the Bicentennial *Circus*.[23]

If the Bread and Puppet Theatre now seems very much a product of its time (despite the fact that in June 1982 it called upon people to join a giant puppet parade, to be held in Manhattan, and to be directed against nuclear war), it remains true that for more than a decade it was one of the more fascinating and influential of America's theatrical groups, contained neither by a theatre building nor a restrictive ideology. Its huge puppets are fixed forever as part of the iconography of radical protest but it was always more than this, as Schumann and his collaborators explored the world of gesture and ceremony and presented their doleful figures, beautiful, mute and 'with eyes full of meaning'.

12 El Teatro Campesino

El Teatro Campesino was founded in 1965 to support the strike of Filipino and Chicano migrant workers against the grape growers in Delano, California. In other words, from the beginning the primary function was to be political rather than aesthetic. The title of the first production, *The Conscience of a Scab*, underlined its significance as an arm of a revolt which began as a struggle for economic justice and ended as an assertion of cultural identity.

The group's founder, Luis Valdéz, had majored in drama at San José State College but it was on a trip to Cuba that he first came to appreciate the social power of theatre. In 1965 he joined the San Francisco Mime Troupe. He was impressed by its ability to infiltrate contemporary material into its playing of classic texts, in particular *Tartuffe*. But within months of his joining, the *huelga* (strike) broke out and he took his newly learned ideas of theatre to the *campesino* (fields).

As he explained in *The Drama Review* in 1967,

> There's a dramatic theory – we used to talk about it in the Mime Troupe. I think we've put a different use to it in the Teatro just out of necessity, but it is that your dramatic situation, the thing you're trying to portray on the stage, must be close to the reality that is *on* the stage. You take the figure of Di Giogregio standing on the backs of two farm workers. The response of the audience is to a very real situation of one human being standing on two others. That type of fakery is not imitation. It is a theatrical reality which will hold up on the flatbed of a truck.[1]

Performers and audience alike were farm workers. They shared a perception of the real. Theatre was a deformation of the real only in the sense that it isolated nodal experiences, thereby giving them synecdochic force, the single image or act representing the whole. It resisted co-option as a metaphor. As he explained in 1970,

> The actos were born quite matter of factly in Delano. Nacieron hambrientos de la realidad. Anything and everything that pertained to the daily life, la vida cotidiana, of the huelguistas became food for thought, material for actos. The reality of campesinos on strike had become dramatic (and theatrical as reflected by newspapers, TV newscasts, films, etc.) and so the actos merely reflected the reality. Huelguistas portrayed huelguistas, drawing their improvised dialogue from real words they exchanged with the esquiroles (scabs) in the field every day.[2]

The *acto* was a short dramatic piece which obviously owed a great deal to agit-prop sketches. Its purpose, as he defined it, was to 'Inspire the audience to social action. Illuminate specific points about social problems. Satirize the opposition. Show or hint at a solution. Express what people are feeling.'[3] They were not written but created collectively through improvisation by the group. As a result, Valdéz claimed, the reality reflected in an *acto* is a 'social reality' while the figures which were developed were not pathological forms but group archetypes. In this respect there are clear parallels between the Chicano and the black theatre. And as the Chicano theatre developed so its goals broadened and the archetypes came to play a central role in the process of cultural no less than economic and political liberation. Viewed by an outsider the archetype and the stereotype may seem too close for comfort; viewed from within the community it is an intensification of social reality. It follows that audience participation, practised as aesthetic tool, theoretical device or paradigm of a desired but not yet realised sense of community by East Coast theatre groups, was a central premise of Chicano theatre. There existed no clear barrier between art and life. As Valdéz observed, 'The characters and life situations emerging from our little teatros are too real, too full of sudor, sangre, and body smells to be boxed in.' Audience participation was 'no cute production trick' but 'a pre-established, pre-assumed privilege'.[4] And, like black theatre, Chicano drama was in some senses a declaration of hegemony over experience, a means of countering economic and social power with a sense of unity of spirit and purpose of which the *acto* is an expression rather than a justification.

In *La Quinta Temporada* (1966) a farm labour contractor, Don Coyote, is satirised. He is the middle man between grower and picker and is presented as a primary exploiter. Like the weather, which is objectified as a series of characters representing the seasons, he is an implacable force systematically destroying the workers. The only hope which they have is the United Farmworkers Organizing Committee. It is this which effectively turns the seasons from being the enemy of the worker to being the enemy of the owner as summer passes without his crops being picked. With the assistance of the church, which also comes to the aid of the workers, winter is transformed into a fifth season – social justice. The form is a familiar one; the code is deliberately transparent.

Born as a pragmatic device of the strike movement, El Teatro Campesino quickly broadened into an agency of cultural liberation. As Valdéz asserted,

> Beyond the mass struggle of La Raza [the race] in the fields and barrios of America, there is an internal struggle in the heart of our people. That struggle too calls for revolutionary change. Our belief in God, the Church, the social role of women – these must be subject to examination

and redefining on some kind of public platform. And that again means teatro. Not simply a teatro composed of actos or agit-prop, but a teatro of ritual, of music, of beauty and spiritual sensitivity. A teatro of legends and myths. A teatro of religious strength.[5]

Writing in 1937, Richard Wright had said of the black writers of his generation that 'They are being called upon to do no less than create values by which their race is to struggle, live and die. They are being called upon to furnish moral sanctions for action.'[6] Something of the same kind could be said of the creators of Chicano theatre. They were concerned not merely with challenging the system which chose to accord them a marginal economic and social role, but with re-examining their own system of values. More especially, they were concerned with moving from a theatre which addressed itself to immediate local issues to one which celebrated a sense of national identity. For Valdéz the Ballet Folklorico of Mexico was a model, at least with regard to its skill and prestige. The Ballet successfully integrates folk legends and rituals into workable theatrical form; that is, it is both a repository of folkloric tradition and evidence of a contemporary possession of that experience, its translation into a usable present. And in this sense, too, it was an obvious model. Certainly Chicano theatre did develop in the direction of reinforcing a sense of cultural consciousness, in particular by developing the *corrido* (ballad) and the *mito* (myth).

The *corrido* is structured around songs, usually familiar ballads. The *mito* is a deliberate attempt to bridge past and present, to find a form that will fuse the cultural and the political, and act as a focus for a positive sense of group identity rather than simple pragmatic protest. As Valdéz remarked in an article in the first edition of *Chicano Theatre* in the Spring of 1973:

> The FORM of our mitos is evolving from something-resembling-a-play to something-that-feels-like-ritual. At the centre of our mitos so far (as opposed to the actos) is a story. A parable (parabula) that unravels like a flower Indio-fashion to reveal the total significance of a certain event. And that vision of totality is what truly defines a mito. In other words, the CONTENT of a mito is the Indio Vision of the Universe. And that vision is religious, as well as political, cultural, social, personal, etc. It is total.[7]

The two forms represent different kinds of resistance but both propose a positive version of Chicano identity.

The original strike which had led to the emergence of El Teatro Campesino was a moderate success, and what had begun as a local venture quickly spread, with Campesino travelling widely and performing in a variety of venues, including productions in the open air and in local halls, and other groups emerging. Then, planning to build a theatre, in 1970 Valdéz established El Centro Campesino Cultural, firstly in Del Rey and subsequently in San Juan Bautista, California, where he purchased forty acres of land which they now work as a collective.

In a sense the Mexican-American shares a cultural dilemma with the black American. He has a double identity, a double consciousness. Pushed to the periphery of the American political, economic and cultural system he has found himself asserting his rights to be included in the very society whose hostility had led to his exclusion. In a privileged position to see both the strengths and weaknesses of American society, he finds himself asserting simultaneously both his independence and his desire to be acknowledged as a full-fledged citizen. In 1926 the black American W.E.B. Dubois had asked a crucial question, 'What do we want? What is the thing we are after?' The answer, apparently, was that 'We want to be Americans, full-fledged Americans, with all the rights of other American citizens.' But the question remained, 'Is that all? Do we want simply to be Americans?' For the problem was that 'Once in a while through all of us there flashes some clairvoyance, some clear idea, of what America really is. We who are dark can see America in a way that white Americans cannot.'[8] Much the same could be said of the Mexican-American for whom the dualism is not simply an identity compounded of a Mexican and American experience but also a heritage with roots in Mexican and Indian myth. 'The duality of life is a reality', Valdéz has said. 'As Chicanos, we are Mexicans, we descend from the Indians. Mexico means Quetzalcoatl; it means the sun and the shadow, life and death, the bird and the serpent, the material and the spiritual.'[9]

Plainly the Chicano sense of identity is rooted in the Spanish language, the colonial ironies of that fact being sufficiently distant no longer to be the source of immediate concern. At the same time the claim to be regarded as fully functioning American citizens is in turn related to mastery of the English language. And language is clearly not simply a communicative tool. It is potentially an act of aggression, a fact clear enough in the derogatory terms applied to Mexican–Americans by whites, themselves in turn being contemptuously referred to as Anglos. Even the pronunciation of Spanish words becomes a clue to cultural identity and political conviction. In an early *acto, Los Vendidos* (1967), a Chicano secretary from Governor Reagan's office visits Honest Sancho's Used Mexican Lot in order to acquire 'a Mexican type' for the front office. She is greeted in Spanish by Sancho but insists on replying in English. Likewise she rejects the Spanish pronunciation of her own name, insisting on JIM-enez. Offered a reconditioned Mexican, with a special feature of returning to Mexico automatically at the end of the season, she rejects him because he does not speak English. What she is after, she explains, is a Mexican model made in America. In the end she settles for Sancho, a middle-class Mexican–American, who speaks perfect English, sings 'God Bless America!' and lives on apple pie. The play ends with him malfunctioning and beginning to call for Chicano Power while the others share out the proceeds, having profited from the fact that they are regarded as no more than puppets, work-horses, by white America.

The play clearly draws on the classic folk tradition of the victory of the underdog. It is a Mexican-American version of Brer Rabbit. And yet there is an irony which is not examined, which the form itself, indeed, does not really allow to be examined. A clear distinction is drawn between the assimilationist secretary, proud of her command of English, and the Mexican farm worker who speaks only Spanish, but the play's denouement makes it plain that it is in effect the ability of a character such as the Mexican–American (at one moment apparently subservient at the next militant) to operate in both languages which enables him to take advantage of the whites and the Mexican imitators. The *actos* themselves, indeed, are frequently written in what is known ironically as Spanglish, a mixture of the two languages. And the cultural implications of this fact are no more examined than are the linguistic ambiguities of the characters in *Los Vendidos*. The flow from English to Spanish and back, not only in the *actos* themselves but also in the manifestos of this theatre (the Tenaz Manifesto of 1973, for example, asserts that 'Los Trabajadores esl Teatro Nacional de Aztlan are committed to a way of Life/Struggle aydandole a la gente a entender el porque de sus problemas sociales individuales and to search for solutions'[10]), is not without its implication for the cultural meaning of the Mexican–American.

The central problem is to locate, define and assert a cultural autonomy. And, as ever, the source of that identity has to be sought in the past. Relegated to a footnote in American history, the Chicano has to identify a history beyond that defined by white America and identify a territory – Aztlan – which is the real or symbolic home to be contrasted with the America in which they are seen as merely strangers. As Valdéz observed:

> We have to rediscover ourselves. There are years and years of discoveries we have to make of our people. People ask me: What is Mexican history in the United States? There is no textbook of the history of La Raza. Yet the history of the Mexican in this country is four hundred years old. We know we predate the landing of the Pilgrims and the American Revolution. But, beyond that? What really happened? No one can tell you. Our history has been lost. Lost! . . . Our generation says, Wait! Stop! Let's reconsider our roots![11]

This was to be the primary function of the *mitos*. And yet, while asserting

22.   El Teatro Campesino, *Vietnam Campesino*, 1970.

that 'We want to become Ungavachados (de-Anglicized) down to the last hair', the Chicano is ineluctably a part of the society against which he seeks to define himself. Indeed Valdéz's assumption that the process of entering into one's identity lies through a process of being de-Anglicised concedes the power of the dominant culture and the degree to which definition results from a process of elimination.

Certainly, in many respects the problems of the Mexican–Americans are coterminous with those of the society of which they are a part but with which they have had such an ambiguous relationship. It was scarcely surprising, therefore, that the *acto* should address itself to the question of Vietnam as well as tackling the issue of exploitation. Indeed, in *Vietnam Campesino* (1970) a direct connection is established between the exploitation of the fruit picker and that of the Vietnamese peasant. Each is seen as a victim of American capitalism, the military, and the agricultural businessman working in a harmony marked not only by shared objectives but also by common methods. Thus both are shown as using chemical sprays to destroy their enemies (an issue concerning the pickers at the time being the indiscriminate use of crop-spraying with no regard for the effects on those actually working in the field). Accordingly, Butt Anglo, landowner, and General Defence, find themselves in a natural alliance, the army purchasing crops which are the subject of an organised boycott and conspiring to see that minority groups rather than Anglos are drafted for service in Vietnam, where, it is implied, they will simply be killing people like themselves:

> GENERAL (*points at Vietnamese*): Farm workers just like them farm workers. (*points at campesinos, then back at Vietnamese*)
> Campesinos just like them campesinos. (*points again*) Poor people just like them poor people. (*points again*) And we've been killing them for ten years.
> BUTT: Ten years?
> GENERAL: It's been open season over there.
> BUTT: A regular gook shoot.
> GENERAL: Exactly – gooks! They aren't people, they're gooks. (*goes over to campesinos*) And these are greasers, spics, chili-ass taco benders. They deserve to die.
> BUTT: Hold on, General. I don't think the public will go for that.
> GENERAL: Of course they won't, at first. You gotta build it up. And the first step is to attack the leadership.[12]

But the plays are not simply designed to ridicule and expose the values of white society. More importantly, like much black drama, they are fundamentally concerned with alerting the Chicanos themselves to the dangers of an unquestioning acceptance of the morals and mores of a society in process of denying that morality. The play ends with that kind of call for unity and that iconography of raised fists which had typified the committed theatre of the 1930s.

Not all the productions of Campesino are easily assignable to a particular genre. *Mundo*, developed over a period of years, and performed in one of its versions on the Mexican Day of the Dead in 1975, is in part a *mito* and perhaps in part a *corrido*. A Chicano who dies of a drug overdose becomes a kind of Orpheus travelling through the underworld of the *barrio* (the Chicano community/ghetto), a world cut off from the realities of world power and national concerns. He returns to life, transformed through music, in touch with the community and a cultural history which transcends the American experience.

Plainly the Teatro has moved a long way from the simple political homilies of the original *actos*. Plainly, too, the theatrical dimension has assumed a greater importance as value is placed less on stimulating or supporting political and economic action than in a declaration of cultural hegemony. Theatre moves to the forefront as itself an assertion of national identity and cultural confidence. It was, perhaps, this confidence which enabled Valdéz to accept a commission to write a play for Los Angeles's Mark Taper Forum.

Zoot Suit received its première in 1978. It focusses on an incident which occurred in 1943 when soldiers were employed to control riots in the Mexican quarter of Los Angeles which led to sentences of life imprisonment for a number of those involved. In part a protest against the injustices perpetrated against the Chicano people, it is also a celebration of the life of the *barrio* and beyond that of life itself. And that is the essence of this theatre. It is not concerned with creating a pathology of the ghetto. As Valdéz insisted, Chicano theatre is 'theater as beautiful, rasquachi, human, cosmic, broad, deep, tragic, comic, as the life of La Raza itself... Chicano theater... is first a re-affirmation of LIFE.'[13] What had begun as protest has ended as celebration. What had started with a concern for changing the physical conditions of life has ended by concerning itself with a transformation of consciousness. El Teatro Campesino pursued an interest in myth which had an immediacy and force lacking in the experiments of East Coast groups precisely because it had the force of a cultural reality behind it, because the sense of community between audience and performer could be assumed where for the Performance Group or the Living Theatre it had to be self-consciously forged, sometimes out of hard-won rituals of physical and psychological consonance, but sometimes out of patent sentimentalities, mere wilful assertions. The question was, could El Teatro Campesino carry its own *actos* and *mitos* beyond the *barrio*? Indeed, would it want to try? At the Mark Taper it succeeded: on Broadway it did not, closing after fifty-eight performances at a loss of $825,000. The question is why it was ever felt possible to reconcile the special qualities of Chicano theatre with what Valdéz had once referred to as 'the limp, superficial, productions in the "professional" American theater'?[14] But the shift from a racially specific and theatrically parochial drama group to the rewarding world of Broadway is familiar enough to cause neither surprise nor undue disillusionment. It is an experience which each generation and each group has to undergo for itself and Valdéz seems to have learned the lesson quickly, choosing thereafter to consolidate his own foundations in the Chicano community and to reach back into the past in search of an experience not available for mediation for the benefit of those seeking a blend of entertainment and social relevance at $20 a ticket. And in that regard the development of El Centro Campesino Cultural has signified a change of direction for Valdéz and his group. Part Yaqui Indian himself, he has become increasingly interested in examining the Indian as well as the Spanish element of Mexican culture. Those living at the Centre learn the Nahuatl language and re-enact Indian rituals, as well as farming the land and developing a cultural resource centre. It is in effect a commune and, most significantly for the development of Campesino, it is a religious commune. According to the 'Creed' of the Centre: 'We are a family composed of families of married and single people, children and adults, *compadres* and *comadres*, uncles and aunts, brothers and sisters, who live communally. We are all brothers and sisters because we have a Common Father . . . He who created us, He who uplifted us, Our Father of the Astros, GOD THE FATHER.'[15]

The change of direction has alienated many of their former supporters. It was a move towards spiritual renewal and religious revival which many others, including former radicals, such as Eldridge Cleaver, and Watergate villains, such as Charles Colson, were to take in the 1970s. Certainly, when Valdéz announced that 'We'll be getting deeper and deeper into ourselves . . . because the sixties was a time of outward explosion, while the seventies is a time of inward explosion',[16] he anticipated a rhetoric which did, indeed, increasingly come to typify a decade, later christened the 'me decade' by Tom Wolfe, and identified as part of a developing 'culture of narcissism' by Christopher Lasch.

For Valdéz and his group the political has now given way to the cultural and the mystical. The actors are now less likely to be speaking out of their immediate experience and more likely to be seeking a state of mind in which they can enact ceremonies which contain a clue to their own identities and to the historical/cultural experience of their audience. But, paradoxically, it seems likely that to that extent, too, their work thereby becomes less available to those they had originally set out to serve. The turn to myth could be seen as a retreat from the political, an acknowledgement of the impracticability of challenging a system which is no less implacable in its policy of neglect than it had been in its hostility. Viewed in this way the turn to myth is less a path to identity than an evasion, an acknowledgement of impotence in the economic and political realm. In fact Valdéz was never an ideologue. He responded originally to immediate issues but he related those less to an ideological analysis than to a history of oppression rooted in racial contempt.

Writing in 1977, Valdéz defined the artistic aims of El Teatro as being 'to replace the lingering negative stereotype of the Mexican in the United States with a new positive image created through Chicano art, and to continue to dramatize the social despair of Chicanos living in an Anglo-dominated society'.[17] Those aims extended to include the need to 'express Chicano reality to other Americans' and 'the inspiration and development of actors, actresses, directors and playwrights, giving them the opportunity to work locally, nationally, and internationally in television, motion pictures and professional theatre'.[18] But, beneath the new note of pragmatism, there has remained a commitment to recovering lost roots, through the annual performance of a *Pastorela* (shepherds' plays of Mexico brought from Europe by Spanish Franciscan missionaries in the sixteenth century) and a miracle play, and through the performance, on 24 June each year, of *The Dance of the Giants*, a recreation of a thousand-year-old ceremony of the Chorti Indians of the Yucatán peninsula. Based on the mythology of a Mayan sacred book which dramatises the creation of the world, it represents Valdéz's continued concern with exploring the spiritual and literal history of the Chicano, while his adaptations of traditional plays of early Californian history represent his acknowledgement of the significance of the American experience. In the 1980s the double consciousness remains the key to Chicano identity.

13 American Indian theatre

Whatever its content, the mere fact of theatre works against alienation. It is the public gesture of private people, an endorsement of imaginative freedom and an exercise in communality. The audience is addressed not only as an aggregation of individual sensibilities but also as a group, sensitive to the responses of those around them. There is in effect no closet drama. It is an act which affirms the existence of shared assumptions, the possibility of creating meanings through a co-operative act. And the conscious creation of selves on a stage can hardly help but imply the possibility of similar acts of self-creation on the part of those who watch and for whom the theatre is not merely a mimetic gesture but a paradigm of personal and communal self-invention.

It is no wonder that those feeling alienated from a social world which offers them only highly determined and even demeaning models of identity and imaginative possibility should have turned to the theatre. Not merely does the public stage appear to operate as the political platform which, iconographically, it resembles, but it offers a model of group strength, of imaginative purpose and of a confident identity. The characters' command of the playing space has implications for those whose own psychological and social space is intimately connected with a sense of alienation. The vertiginous excitements of theatre – which can never be replicated on television or film – the sense of genuine risk, is liable to be closer to the experience of a threatened group than is the aesthetic closure of the film which is about the process of being rather than becoming.

Drama requires the active intervention of an audience as the film does not. It requires a physical presence. For the black American, the Chicano, the Indian as also for women it is the necessity to intervene (in historical and social processes; in the reconstruction of an autonomous self and group identity) which is the essence of their struggle (an intervention whose authenticity is underlined by physical presence – on the picket line, at the lunch counter, in the courtroom). Theatre therefore offers the most compelling and relevant experience. Theatre is about process. It is volatile. Once a film is completed, fully edited and dubbed it is a finished product. It exists as an artifact. Obviously responses differ from audience to audience, from situation to situation. A film may become a crucial aspect of the events which it documents (as with Wajda's films about contemporary Poland). But though audiences respond, the film does not. It is unyielding, completed. Theatre is never completed. It is always being made. And for those oppressed by the unwillingness of the public world to allow them to 'make' themselves, by the insistence on the part of society that they accept stereotypes, finished and unyielding models of their own being, there is something compelling not only about theatre's power to present that process of making as subject matter but about the fact that it itself exemplifies that process. The private experience is revealed as a shared experience – shared over time but also shared in the present, across classes, tribes and communities. And if, on the one hand, the American theatre of the 1960s and 70s was typified by a somewhat soft version of sensual metaphysics, in the form of performance theatre – which also talked of authenticity but in the context of a pre-existent self to be discovered, unlocked, perhaps, by drugs or simply by the warm propinquity of Dionysian rites – on the other hand it also generated a committed theatre, by no means always typified by strident protest, which was concerned with seeing theatre as a means of confronting people with their own possibilities. There were those, in the black community in particular, who chose to counter stereotype with stereotype, who simply wished to substitute one hermetic self for another. But, for the most part, the stereotype was invoked by black writers, by Chicanos, Indians and women as a means of escaping the false assumption that they were fully knowable and hence fully controllable. In writing about their own lives, perceptions and sensibilities they were, in Gramsci's sense, reasserting their hegemony over their own experience. They were speaking with their own voice and by that very act denying territory if not to the enemy then at least to those who compounded social neglect with aesthetic arrogance. The risk, of course, as ever for committed theatre, was that they would deflect ethics into aesthetics, that the pressure of social truth would be trans-muted into art and judged more for aesthetic reasons than for its power as a transforming mechanism. The fear is that dynamic experience may be converted into inert text. But the choice of theatre, or any other art, implies this tension; indeed the risk of aestheticising experience is perhaps just as real outside the realm of art as within it.

To say that this theatre has probably produced little of lasting value is to ignore the purpose of much, though not all, of this work. In so far as the moment of performance was crucial – not merely in the sense in which this must always, in some degree, be true of theatre, but because the very shared nature of perceptions not usually expressed or acknowl-edged was its essence – its continued existence as text or production may in a sense be irrelevant and, in some cases, illogical. For in so far as some of the works were designed as consciousness-raising gestures they had their

366

own obsolescence built in. If they were effective they would, by definition, cease to be regarded as crucial or even adequate explanations of experience, except in a strictly historical and limited sense. The most obvious example of this is the agit-prop black theatre of the 1960s and some of the early work of El Teatro Campesino. It may also prove true of the latest minority drama, that of the American Indian.

The American Indian was and is, to say the least, equivocally placed in relation to the American nation. His very identity as an Indian, rather than as a member of a series of autonomous nations, derives from white geographical and cultural myopia. And it was not until 1924 that all Indians were declared to be citizens of the United States and of the states in which they lived – a status, however, which conflicted with the autonomy implied by a series of treaties with which the whites had defined their relationship to the tribes. And the systematic abrogation of those treaties, when it served the interests of American expansionism or when those treaties came into conflict with primary American myths (the capitalist ethos, individualism, the American dream of personal and national advance), itself stood as an indictment of the values in whose name such acts were perpetrated.

Plainly the civil rights movement of the 1960s was likely to prove appealing in many ways to a group which had been so consistently denied their rights. Yet, at the same time, in so far as this seemed at first a move out of a separate cultural identity and into a homogenised Americanism, it was likely to inspire a deep scepticism, and few Indians joined the March on Washington in 1963. But the mood of militancy did have an effect and in 1966 the Secretary of the Interior was forced to change his plans to 'terminate' a small tribe in eastern Washington state (that is, the forced dissolution of tribal organisations and the breaking up of tribal assets) when the National Congress of American Indians arranged for representatives of sixty tribes to converge on Sante Fe. In 1968 over a hundred Indians joined the Poor People's March on Washington, some of them holding a sit-in in the office of Stewart Udall, Secretary of the Interior.

At the same time the American Indian Movement was established in the Midwest. This was in part created to prevent police harassment of Indians. Though in origin a small group centred in Minnesota, it had something of the same effect as the Black Power Movement had among blacks. And in 1969 a small group of Indian students from San Francisco State and Berkeley landed on Alcatraz, followed, a few weeks later, by several hundred others who established an occupation of the island. It was a symbolic act of repossession which inspired hope, in a number of Indian tribes, that they might similarly one day reclaim their own lands. And a certain amount of land was restored to tribes in the following years as the result of legal action. But in the early 1970s the confrontation between Indians and American officials and police agencies began to be more violent. A number of individual Indians were murdered and in 1972 Richard Oakes, who had led the invasion of Alcatraz, was shot dead by a guard at a California prison camp. One consequence was a decision to stage what was called the Trail of Broken Treaties which was to go from the West Coast to Washington during the concluding stages of the 1972 presidential campaign. When they arrived they occupied the Bureau of Indian Affairs.

But the most dramatic event occurred in South Dakota. Following the murder of an Oglala Sioux named Bad Heart Bull, and the indictment of his killer for the lesser crime of manslaughter, Indians from a number of tribes converged on the area. Although this, and a subsequent incident in Rapid City, was settled peaceably a confused conflict within the Indian movement led to the occupation of Wounded Knee, site of the 1890 massacre of Big Foot's Oglala Sioux by soldiers of the Seventh Cavalry, and shortly before this the subject of Dee Brown's hugely successful *Bury My Heart at Wounded Knee*. The historic significance of the spot prompted considerable media coverage, and the group occupying Wounded Knee began to demand a reconsideration of the rights guaranteed them under the Fort Laramie Treaty of 1868. Indeed, it was announced that the Oglala Sioux Nation had been formed and that it was independent of the United States, with borders as defined by the 1868 treaty. In the 72-day occupation two Indians were shot dead and a federal marshal partly paralysed by gunfire. Considerable damage was done as each side fired at the other. The occupation finally ended with a government promise of negotiation.

The event was of considerable psychological importance not merely in so far as it constituted a public act of armed resistance by Indians presumed to be cowed by their dependent relationship to federal agencies, but because it challenged the whole legal status of the Indian. It was an assertion of independence and a restoration of pride.

The federal government had not been wholly delinquent in its approach to Indian affairs. President Johnson's special message to Congress in March 1968 had at least recognised the plight of the Indian and the necessity for action, while the Civil Rights Act of 1968 contained provisions of importance. President Nixon's special message on Indian affairs had frankly acknowledged the historic injustices which the Indian had suffered and continued to suffer:

> The first Americans – the Indians – are the most deprived and most isolated minority group in our nation. On virtually every scale of measurement – employment, income, education, health – the condition of the Indian people ranks at the bottom. This condition is the heritage of

centuries of injustice. From the time of their first contact with European settlers, the American Indians have been oppressed and brutalized, deprived of their ancestral lands and denied the opportunity to control their own destiny . . . But the story of the Indian in America is something more than the record of the white man's frequent aggression, broken agreements, intermittent remorse and prolonged failure. It is a record of enormous contributions to this country – to its art and culture, to its strength and spirit, to its sense of history and its sense of purpose.[1]

The rhetoric was impressive; the action less so. But it was this cultural tradition and an emerging sense of purpose which was a key to the identity and purposive action of various individuals and groups in the 1970s. Over the years acculturation had diminished the significance of old rituals. American culture, through movies and television, had become increasingly dominant, though in the case of some tribes (the Hopi among others) separate cultural traditions had been maintained. The number of Indian languages had declined. In 1965 only one per cent of Indian children in elementary schools were taught by Indian teachers. The conditions in which many Indians lived continued to be appalling. The income of Indians living on reservations in 1970 was about a quarter that of whites; that of off-reservation Indians approximately a half. Literacy was about 15 per cent. But the events of the early 1970s sparked a change in various directions. As Vine Deloria Jr, a Standing Rock Sioux and spokesman for the Indians, observed in 1974: 'It has been only within the last decade that Indians have taken a critical look at their history, their conditions and the answers that American society have given them to explain their fall·from prosperity . . . More and more Indians are questioning both their knowledge of the tribe and their understanding of how the tribes have been split into a quarrelling, scattered conglomerate of people.'[2]

Though the Indian tradition was an oral one it was Indian poetry, the novel, and, finally, the drama which played its part in this questioning, in this critical evaluation of past and present. And though there is no tradition of formal drama, the public ceremony which western theatre worked so hard in the 1960s to foreground, filling the void of modern urban existence with a communality invented for that purpose, has always been an essential element of Indian life and a vital expression of individual, tribal and racial identity. Though there is as yet only a single collection of plays by an Indian author, it seems likely that the theatre may yet become an important element in Indian life, complementing but never replacing those ceremonies which relate more directly to the Indian past and to tribal identity.

Performance, in the sense of ritual, ceremony, dance and music, is an aspect of Indian life placed under pressure by the realities of reservation life. Indeed *Body Indian*, the first play by Hanay Geiogamah, the principal Indian playwright and himself a Kiowa, which was produced by the La Mama Experimental Theatre Club in October 1972, was a frank account of degradation, drunkenness and despair. Though Geiogamah insists that 'It is important that the acting nowhere is conducive to the mistaken idea that this play is primarily a study of the problem of Indian alcoholism'[3] this clearly provides the central action of a play which finds some surviving, if ironised, sense of community even in the despair and the alcoholism of a present drained of dignity. Set in a one-room apartment, the play focusses on Bobby Lee, a crippled alcoholic in his middle thirties. He has just leased his land allotment to a white man and has saved money to take the cure at a rehabilitation centre. Meanwhile, he joins his friends and relatives in drinking cheap wine. Befuddled, he is robbed of the money which he keeps in his artificial leg. When they have taken all his money they steal the leg to raise money for more wine.

The play slowly builds to the climactic moment in which Bobby Lee loses his leg on a railroad track. The sound of the approaching train penetrates the action, growing louder each time it intrudes. It is both a past and a future action. The maiming of one Indian is clearly presented as the maiming of many. Indeed those gathered in the dingy room are themselves drawn from a number of different tribes. The wound which Bobby Lee bears is both a past fact and a future possibility. It is both a consequence of white indifference and exploitation and a self-inflicted wound. The communal efforts of those individuals who come together to steal Bobby Lee's money parody the communality of the tribe. They combine only in the process of degradation. And the final irony is that the young, high on drugs and drawn to white popular culture, are as humiliated as their elders.

It is not a play which primarily concerns itself with indicting the white world, but, though this scarcely intrudes, it is clear that it is this world which has defined the nature of Indian life and has established its parameters. The power of the play lies in the extent to which the characters compound the absurdity of their situation, sacrificing their freedom of action and turning on one another with a casual indifference which is the real source of Geiogamah's lament. And though Jeffrey Huntsman, in an introduction to this work, suggests that a comparison with the black theatre of the 1960s would not be appropriate, there is something of Ed Bullins's honesty of approach about a play which manages to delineate the diminished world of possibility while at the same time hinting at resources misdirected into internecine strife.

Foghorn, first presented at the Theater Im Reichskabarett in West Berlin in 1973, is an exuberant work which engages history both on a

370

literal and a literary level. As the author himself notes, 'Almost all the characters in this play are stereotypes pushed to the point of absurdity. The satire proceeds by playful mockery rather than bitter denunciation.'[4] The stage set is required to reflect the prison yard at Alcatraz and the countryside at Wounded Knee, while the action involves incidents from white popular culture (the Wild West Show, Pocahontas and the Lone Ranger) as well as scenes in a contemporary schoolhouse. Music plays a central role. At the beginning, the text calls for a background of progressive electronic music designed to evoke a journey through time and space to parallel action which suggests a forced journey, a kind of compound of the forced marches of American Indian history. The play, indeed, begins ironically with the misnaming of the native inhabitants by a Spanish sailor under the impression that they have landed in India: 'Los indios! Los indios!'[5] Thus, from the very start, the Indian's identity and historic reality is established by whites.

The arrogant presumptions of whites are balanced against a new sense of pride and assertiveness on the part of the Indians. White nuns and teachers seek to control, civilise and discipline the native Americans but these scenes all end with the Indians attacking their oppressors. A list of broken treaties is read out by an actor wearing a bull's head, to the accompaniment of a 1940s song, 'Pass That Peace Pipe'. A Wild West show culminates in the Wounded Knee massacre, which is related to the 1973 Siege of Wounded Knee in which those protesting were arrested. The play ends as the Indians from various tribes lift their handcuffed hands and the voice of the Spanish sailor once again announces 'Los indios! Los indios!', while the narrator declares his innocence. A simple agit-prop play, *Foghorn* (named after the foghorns sounded by the whites to discomfort the Indians occupying Alcatraz) is designed to sound a warning note, to demythologise the relationship between white and Indian and to imply the threat of Indian action.

49, performed by the Native American Theatre Ensemble at Oklahoma University in January 1975, also unites past and present. A 49 is a celebration consisting of singing and dancing in which, as Geiogamah says, 'Young Indians are in an extremely heightened state of awareness of their "Indianness"',[6] and a sense of intertribal group conviviality is created. The play takes place on a ceremonial ground in the year 1885 and in the present. The two periods are united by the figure of the Night Walker, who can move through time, and by the rhythmic beat of drums. The Night Walker is part prophet, part commentator. He is, in some sense, the spirit of the Indian, surviving, losing ground, but still resisting by merit of the strength of tradition. As Geiogamah explains, 'More than anything else I wanted the young people to be affirmative in

371

the face of despair and unreasoning force. I had an instinct to minimize the negative and sought to do this even though much of the action is essentially negative. Let that be, I said, and let the principal focus fall on the young people's spirit, the sinews of strength that hold all of them together, that keep them going, that provide their energy.'[7]

The play blends non-naturalistic elements – stylised movements, ritual gestures – with intercut naturalistic scenes. The young Indians gather for the 49, watched over by police patrols who gradually close in on them. The music, the ballad, the dancing, bring the Indians together, and if this is in a sense a parody of a former instinctive tribal unity it is nonetheless real. In a scene set in the past, Night Walker prophesies a time when the singing will stop and the stories be forgotten. In the background is a field littered with the skeletons of buffalo – images which blend in with the young people as though they, too, are doomed to extinction. But this is offered more as warning than prophecy. For though the signs of disintegration are strong – a car crash offering an image of this – the Night Walker tells a story of the restoration of lost children which seems to be offered as an account of a recovered sense of identity. The play ends as the Indians group together under the threat of the advancing police and Night Walker offers his invocation to their new sense of solidarity.

> Go!
> Go forward!
> The tribe needs you.
> I go with you.
> I am always with you.
> We are a tribe!
> Of singers.
> Of dancers who move with the grace of the bird.
> Of people who know color.
> Of weavers.
> Of good hunters.
> We pray.
> We are a tribe!
> Of people with strong hearts.
> Who respect fear
> As we make our way.
> Who will never kill
> Another man's way of life.[8]

The young people go off together. As Geiogamah says,

> The self-realization comes about largely through non-verbal means. Instead of using the kind of abuse ('Pigs!') that accomplishes nothing, they move smoothly to form the human barricade in the final scene as if by a shared and positive instinct. Their defiance is strong, but calm and totally

controlled. They feel and know what they should do, and the power of this understanding is expressed in the body formation that is the 'beautiful bird' that Night Walker sees flying.[9]

In so far as the theatre offers a similar experience of consonance, of shared experience, the play can perhaps be seen as a defence of the theatre itself as an agent of change, as offering precisely that moment of shared consciousness which is a prerequisite for cultural and personal identity. As far as American Indians are concerned, theatre, in a conventional form, remains something of a novelty. Indeed, in so far as the old ceremonies and traditions survive, it is likely to seem marginal to the quest for a revivified sense of tribal and group identity. But it is not wholly without significance that they too should have begun to see in drama a resource which may yet play its role in the process of cultural and political renaissance.

And so each racial group in turn has established its own theatres and created its own drama in part, at least, as a means to escape the reductive images offered over the years by a society which invited the world's poor and needy and then consigned them to the periphery of social and cultural life. To escape the stereotype it became necessary to create a counter-image and the theatre was deeply implicated in resisting images which had themselves often originated in the theatre or cinema. As the Chinese-American author David Henry Hwang objected, 'producers and directors who consider Asian American actors only to play coolies, foreigners, and "ethnic" roles deny the reality of our world. We live in a multi-ethnic society, and it is a measure of producers' reactionary tendencies that this mix is rarely reflected on our mainstream stages and screens.' But, by the same token, he resisted the idea of a ghetto theatre: 'In America, the term "ethnic theatre" is ultimately a misnomer. There are simply the ethnics that have had access to an audience and those that have not. As Asian American theatre artists, we are claiming our audience.'[10]

The Chinese-Americans were by no means the only ones to stake such a claim but if they were concerned with exploring their own experiences then those experiences, like those of all the other minority groups, were themselves deeply ambiguous. As Hwang, the author of *The Dance and the Railroad* and *Family Devotions*, both of which ran successfully at the New York Shakespeare Festival, observed of his own play, *FOB* (1980):

> The roots of FOB are thoroughly American. The play began when a sketch I was writing about a limousine trip through Westwood, California, was invaded by two figures from American literature: Fu MuLan, the girl who takes her father's place in battle, from Maxine Hong Kingston's

novel *The Women Warriors*, and Gwang Gung, the adopted god of early Chinese Americans, from Frank Chin's play *Gee, Pop!*

FOB's sources testify to the existence of an Asian American literary and theatrical tradition. Chinese operas, many featuring Gwang Gung, have long been performed in Chinatowns. Theatres such as Los Angeles' East West Players, San Francisco's Asian American Theatre Company, New York's Pan-Asian Repertory, and Seattle's Asian Exclusion Act, have established themselves as centers for a body of new and exciting dramatic work.[11]

The essence of this 'minority' theatre of the last twenty-five years is precisely that it acknowledged the multi-ethnic nature of American society, as mainstream theatre had not and that in doing so it not only expanded the subject matter and range of American drama but potentially moved drama closer to the centre of the lives of those for whom it had seemed both an irrelevance and, at times, an affront. The black, the Indian, the Chicano, the Chinese and, in another area, the homosexual, had found their own lives reflected, if at all, only as stereotype, as comic caricature or simple villain. They were effectively excluded from national myths which turned on white supremacy. In the central plot of American history – that of the invention of a nation – they had been presented as either mere observers or dangerous impediments. The culture hero was on the whole Anglo-Saxon and male and his self-invention and the construction of a national identity were seen as coterminous. In claiming the country he defined it, and out of that sprang a mythology which made the mastery of circumstance and the acquisition of property a moral virtue. And if the physical and social mobility, which both facilitated this process and was primary evidence of it, was threatened, then the removal of that threat was justified just as was any use which might be made of those whose labour could ensure a substance to that freedom. It was in this context that the new ethnic theatre created new myths, deployed its own style and forged its own values. For the first time the stage offered back to them an image of themselves to which they could respond. Suddenly they were at the centre of dramatic if not political attention.

14 Black theatre

If the question of personal identity and the nature of the relationship between the self and society was a central item on the agenda of the American theatre there was one area where this was an issue of immediate social and political concern. The black American has spent the whole of this century, as of the preceding two, struggling precisely to determine the terms of his relationship to American society and the values it claims to embody, as he has struggled equally to establish and assert the nature of his own racial and cultural identity. It is an irony that it should have been a white dramatist, Eugene O'Neill, who produced the most original and powerful account of this double struggle. But the black American turned early to the stage for a self-image which he could respect just as he, under commercial pressures, was also encouraged to act out the caricatures with which white Americans had sought to justify their injustices. The nigger minstrel was harmless and acceptable to the white public precisely because he was de-sexed, trapped in a role which combined self-mockery with an endearing musicality. When he appeared, as he did in O'Neill's *Emperor Jones*, as an astute confidence trickster, markedly superior to his white companion, or, in *All God's Chillun Got Wings*, as an intellectual married to a white woman and destroyed by a self-hatred engendered by American racism, he was wholly otherwise. The sheer brutality of Langston Hughes's *Mulatto* (1935), which surprisingly ran successfully on Broadway, similarly staked out new territory. Despite the renewed exoticism of the Federal Theatre's *Macbeth* and the *Swing Mikado* it, too, tackled the problem head on, its Negro units producing, among much else, Theodore Ward's *Big White Fog*.

And a number of attempts were made to create black theatre groups throughout the early decades of the century. The most significant in this period, however, was the American Negro Theatre (ANT). The ANT was founded by Abram Hill and Frederick O'Neal. Following the collapse of the Federal Theatre in 1939 they set out to establish a new group, based in Harlem. Hill was born in Atlanta in 1914 and became interested in theatre at Lincoln University. He worked as a drama director for the Temporary Relief Association on Long Island and in 1938 studied drama under John Gassner at the New School for Social Research. He joined the Federal Theatre as a play reader and was commissioned to prepare a history of black life for the Living Newspaper Unit. His play *On Strivers' Row* was accepted by the Rose McClendon Players in Harlem and performed in 1939. In 1940 he joined with others, including Langston Hughes and Theodore Ward, to found the Negro Playwrights' Company but left shortly afterwards because he came to feel that they were primarily interested in propaganda. Frederick O'Neal had been a member of the cast of *On Striver's Row*. He, too, had been born in the South – in Mississippi – and in the 1920s had organised the Ira Aldridge Players, a black group in St Louis. Once in New York he enrolled in the New Theatre School and studied privately with Komisarjevsky. In June 1940 he and Hill, together with others, formed the ANT. They operated from the same 135th Street Library Theatre as had been used earlier by other black groups such as the Kwigwa Players, Langston Hughes's Harlem Suitcase Theatre and the Rose McClendon Players. Their objective was 'to break down the barriers of Black participation in the theatre, to portray Negro life as they honestly saw it; to fill in the gap of a Black theatre which did not exist'.[1] As Ethel Walker has pointed out, it was not a wholly black theatre, though situated in Harlem. It hired both white actors and technicians. It claimed later to have trained over 200 people and given 325 performances to an audience of 50,000. In the nine years of its existence the company produced nineteen plays, twelve of which were original, four of these productions transferring to the commercial theatre.

But if the objectives of the company seemed clear enough in one regard – providing work for black theatre workers – it was less clear in another. In its bid to the Rockefeller Foundation it had said that it was 'calling for plays which furnish commentary, interpretation, illumination and criticism of our common lives during contemporary times, located in the Harlem section of New York City, with its theatre, workshop and affiliated with Negro theatre groups throughout the country, and acting as parent body to such affiliates'.[2] And yet, after 1945, all of its plays were by white writers. The ANT's own drama school, of which both Harry Belafonte and Sidney Poitier are products, produced plays like *Our Town* and Kaufman and Ferber's *Stage Door*. Clearly the existence of original and viable black drama was the key to a theatre which wished really to address the realities of the black community and to examine the nature of the black sensibility, if such there was. For Hill there was also a central and irreconcilable conflict between playwrights who drew on and sought to address the black community, and actors, whose careers almost necessarily lay outside the black world, on Broadway and elsewhere. The ANT ran into increasingly severe financial trouble. By the end of 1947 its Rockefeller grant had run out and it had already had to leave its rent-free accommodation at 135th street. It ended its life producing variety shows, having by then lost much of its direction and purpose. It was, however, one of the most sustained and successful attempts to create a black drama group in America and as such was influential both as model and as warning.

The American Negro Theatre defined itself as 'a permanent co-operative acting company co-ordinating and perfecting the related arts of the theater, eventually deriving its own theater craft and acting style by combining all standard forms and putting to artful use the fluency and rhythm that lies in the Negro's special gifts'.[3] It was an ambiguous statement and seems to have reflected an ambiguity in the stance of its members. Thus, though it was formed as a separate black theatre, one of its founders, Frank Fields, has reportedly said that ' *The people in the ANT didn't really believe in Negro theater.*'[4] Like many such groups it was torn between celebrating an ethnic identity and providing a pathway into the theatre at large. Its two most successful productions were Abram Hill's satire on middle-class Negroes, *On Striver's Row* and Philip Yordan's *Anna Lucasta*. The latter, by a white playwright, was originally concerned with a working-class Polish family in a Pennsylvania city but was adapted by Hill for a black cast. It was immediately successful, transferring to Broadway where it ran for nearly a thousand performances, thereby inspiring other plays with Negro protagonists by white authors, such as *Deep Are the Roots* by Arnaud d'Usseau and James Gow, staged by Elia Kazan, and *Jeb* by Robert Ardrey.

The very success of *Anna ·Lucasta*, however, was ironic. It owed nothing to the supposed 'fluency and rhythm' of Negro life. Indeed the mere fact of its adaptation implied that the plight of the Negro was merely one aspect of poverty in America, thereby denying the distinctiveness which was part of the *raison d'être* of the ANT. Meanwhile, the transfer to Broadway stretched the resources of a company which struggled for survival in its 135th Street Library Theatre in Harlem, despite the financial assistance which it received from the Rockefeller Foundation. In the words of Abram Hill, writing in the 1970s, ' *Anna* was a history-making event. It put the organization on the map and ironically it planted the seeds of its own destruction. For, from that point on the organization was going downhill. People came into it after that trying to get to Broadway. The ANT became a showcase instead of an experimental theatre.'[5] For all its success – it spawned two films and many more productions – the ANT received only $1\frac{1}{4}$ per cent on the Broadway production of *Anna Lucasta*.

The departure of actress Ruby Dee to appear in the Broadway production of *Jeb* in 1946 was merely one more blow, though her observation in 1952, several years after the collapse of the ANT, that 'I think the next few years will see us develop a great theatre because the Negro people are at that point in their history which inevitably produces real works of art . . . I think the vital theater in America will come from the Negro people'[6] proved prophetic. The question was what form this would take. On the one hand the black writer Ossie Davis has observed that the 'functioning cadre of ANT joined the march into the theatrical mainstream because the suction, the sweeping undercurrent, flowing toward Broadway, only a subway ride away, was irresistible',[7] while on the other hand few plays about Negro life appeared on Broadway and, according to an article written by the President of Actors' Equity, Frederick O'Neal (himself a Negro actor), as late as the season 1964–5 only seventy-four black actors were employed on Broadway and thirty-two in Off-Broadway shows. Broadway may have played its role in undermining the ANT by siphoning off its best talent but it hardly constituted a threat to black theatre as a whole. The reality was that the Great White Way all too seldom found room for material which dramatised the plight of the black American, even when, in the late 1950s and early 1960s, this was the principal subject of moral and legislative concern in the country. But plays about the black situation did reach Broadway.

Theodore Ward's *Our Lan'*, written in 1941 but first produced Off-Broadway at the Henry Street Playhouse in 1946, eventually appeared on Broadway in a revised version while Louis Peterson's sensitive account of the initiation of a young black boy into the realities of racism and personal betrayal, *Take a Giant Step*, was staged on Broadway in the 1953–4 season.

Theodore Ward came from the South but was educated at the University of Utah, where he won the Zona Gale Fellowship for Creative Writing, and at the University of Wisconsin. His *Big White Fog* was one of the best plays to have come out of the Federal Theatre in the 1930s. He was also one of the founders of the Negro Playwrights' Company, whose announced objective was 'to foster the spirit of unity between the races, provide an outlet for the creative talents of Negro artists . . . and supply the community with . . . theatre reflecting the historical reality of the life of the Negro people'.[8]

Our Lan' is set in post-bellum America as newly freed slaves prepare to receive the promised benefits of Emancipation. Believing General Sherman's promise of forty acres and a mule they assert their rights to a plantation on an island off the coast of Georgia. Betrayed by President Johnson, who vetoes the bill as a gesture of conciliation to the South, they find themselves in conflict with the army which once played a part in liberating them but now destroys their fragile hopes. For Ward, the principal character, Joshua Tain, is the epitome of the resistant spirit, forging the group of slaves into a community:

> One senses his sincerity and warm-heartedness which seem to bind him to the others in deep, sympathetic accord. Indeed, he is an expression or symbol, if you will, of the best traits of his people. There is a sure sense of dignity about him and his very physical strength bespeaks something of the relentlessness and courage which characterizes the bulk of the vilified black men of the period – a people conditioned by the terrors of ruthless oppression who communicated their spirit from generation to generation; not by precept but by example – now graphic, now more or less obscure; not passive, nor insurrectionary, but always passed on: the son emulating the inarticulate father; the daughter fashioning her life on the pattern offered by her mute but undaunted mother. In a word, one senses that here is a man.[9]

In that stage direction it is not difficult to see Ward's concern with presenting a model for action in the present. Ostensibly a historical drama, it is, in effect, an assertion of the rights of the black American and an insistence on the need to struggle for those rights. As a slave, Joshua had planned to revolt against his slave master; as an emancipated black man, he prepares to challenge the forces of the United States itself. The debate which rages between his values and those of the accommodationists who are anxious only to protect their own status within the black community clearly reflects something of the similar debate over objectives and strategies in the post-bellum world of the 1940s and the succeeding decades.

The play blends an articulate debate over black rights with consciously crafted elements of folk drama. Negro spirituals are presented as political statements as well as sentimental expressions of group pride. Indeed, the emphasis on dialect may have contributed to the play's failure on Broadway, as, of course, may its uncomfortable subject matter. It is, in effect, a melodrama with little ambiguity in its charcterisations and no equivocation in its moral logic, though it ends apparently without a resolution of the issues, with the slaves united as they face inevitable defeat at the hands of the army. The play was in no way innovatory in technique. What it does offer is a subtle blend of folk elements and simple realism in the service of a racial assertiveness which is ahead of its time.

Louis Peterson's *Take a Giant Step* was a different matter. In the vein of Robert Anderson's *Tea and Sympathy* or Salinger's *Catcher in the Rye*, it was a sympathetic account of a young boy's initiation into the realities of adult life. Peterson himself had been born in Hartford, Connecticut, returning to study at Yale after receiving a bachelor's degree in Atlanta.

He then completed a master's degree at New York University, studied playwriting with Clifford Odets and acted professionally.

Take a Giant Step is set in a middle-class white community in which the protagonist is the only black boy. In a sense it starts where the later *A Raisin in the Sun* leaves off. The very presence of the black family in the white neighbourhood is a mark of their achievement, but their misplaced pride merely blinds them to the pain of their son who comes into possession of his sexual and racial self in a context in which both are deeply prejudiced by his situation. His innocence enables the playwright and his audience to re-experience the realities of racism. The notion that a young black boy could have reached the age of seventeen in ignorance of the corrosive effects of racism would have been sceptically received a few years later, but, in a sense, part of the effect of the play lies in Peterson's refusal to present that racism in its most extreme and obvious form. For his concern is not primarily with the public realities, with the overt battles for justice; it is with registering the more subtle and spiritually destructive aspects of racial exclusion.

The young boy and his white friends are slowly infected with the virus of racial prejudice. At the school dance he finds himself without a partner. His friends begin to desert him, less because of any desire on their part than because they are anxious not to challenge the values of their community, not to find themselves outsiders. Rather than see himself betrayed, the young boy, Spence, himself withdraws. His sexual insecurity is resolved with the help of a young black widow, but there is no one who can heal the wounds opened up by racism. His grandmother, a friend in distress, dies. His parents, anxious to avoid trouble and to remain inconspicuous, are unsympathetic. The play ends not with the confident and somewhat false optimism of *A Raisin in the Sun* but with a kind of baffled and self-defeating resignation. If its setting was atypical its refusal to succumb to the simple pieties of revolt was the source of real strength. *A Raisin in the Sun* did little to question the world into which its characters wished to move. Louis Peterson does probe that world and the moral vacuum at its core. Racism, as he dramatises it, is not a matter of evil or of willed brutality. It subsists, rather, in the coercive power of the majority, in betrayals which operate on a private rather than a public level, and which make the individual an accomplice of the system that threatens to destroy him less through social action than through the slow destruction of self-esteem. In many ways Peterson's play, a straightforward naturalistic drama, is more subtle and affecting than Lorraine Hansberry's much praised play.

The black American writer has always been ambiguously placed. The question of which audience he should legitimately address has always been the subject of debate. It is an issue which goes to the heart of a doubleness of vision which W.E.B. Dubois had seen as offering a privileged viewpoint but which was equally the root of a profound anguish. This had been a crucial issue for the novelist and poet, constrained by the exigencies of publishing economics. For the playwright it was, if anything, a more immediate and pressing problem. For Lorraine Hansberry and James Baldwin this dilemma was to be resolved in the direction of Broadway. Moved by the urge to protest they sought out the audience whose moral conscience they wished to touch. But, increasingly in the 1960s, with writers like LeRoi Jones and Ed Bullins, the emphasis changed. The theatre was no longer an agent and expression of a nervous liberalism but a means of engaging the black community by confronting it with an image of its own acquiescence or by elaborating myths of a heroic past or a revolutionary future. Either way, it acknowledged a responsibility to engage the political, social and cultural realities and myths of a period in which race was seen as the area in which American principles were to be tested and the familiar American concern for identity and the limits of social action examined.

Following the Second World War the civil rights movement gained new impetus. In 1957 federal troops returned to the South for the first time since the Civil War, ordered in by President Eisenhower to secure enforcement of the Supreme Court's 1954 school de-segregation decision. Two years later, a young black woman, Lorraine Hansberry, saw her first play, *A Raisin in the Sun*, appear on Broadway. It was very much a product of its times. A simple naturalistic play, it takes as its subject the decision by a black family, the recipients of a fortuitous insurance policy, to move into a white area. Its theme is the need to recognise that personal pride and identity lie in a refusal to allow one's own possibilities to be determined by others. It is less concerned with debating the virtues of integration, which are simply assumed, than with examining the moral and psychological effects of refusing to accept responsibility for one's actions. It bears the marks, in other words, of Sartrean existentialism, to which she later expressed her debt, and of Arthur Miller's anguished account of the individual's desperate struggle to value himself above the price determined by society (again a debt which she later acknowledged, relating *A Raisin in the Sun* to *Death of a Salesman*).

The play is set in the South Side of Chicago. Like Richard Wright's 1940 novel *Native Son*, its action begins with the ringing of an alarm clock, which figuratively echoes throughout the rest of the work. It is indeed time to wake up and the play is in effect concerned with the awakening consciousness of one black family as they come to realise the

23. Lorraine Hansberry's *A Raisin in the Sun*, produced on Broadway in 1959.

effects on their own sensibilities and identities of internalising the values of their society. The inheritance enables them to think for the first time of challenging the rules, written and unwritten, which leave them locked in a ghetto, with their hopes doomed to remain unrealised; and this forces them to confront the reality of boundaries which they had always known to exist but which they had not been obliged to acknowledge. The moment of decision is forced upon them. A central weakness of the play, however, is precisely the artificial nature of this moment. It is only the fact of the insurance money – a device which seems to have been lifted directly from Clifford Odets's *Awake and Sing* – that enables them to challenge the white world and hence arrive at a crucial level of self-knowledge. But, that accepted, the play precisely captures the mood of the civil rights movement as it then was, dramatising the various evasive strategies which the characters adopt as they struggle to make sense of their lives in a world made alien by their own crucial failure of nerve as much as by the more massive and definitional cruelties of the society which denies them access to its dreams no less than to its realities. It does, however, beg an important question. Though the acquisition of the house is, in one sense, merely a dramatic tactic for putting pressure on her

382

characters, there is a tendency to accept the value of the dreams to which they now lay claim. Hansberry analyses with clinical precision some of their more romantic delusions but the house in the suburbs seems legitimised by the play's structure which makes the claiming of this house both the objective and the vindication of the family. This is the more surprising given the influence of *Death of a Salesman* in which it is precisely the assumption that possession of property is a value in itself, providing a link into American myth, which is questioned. Linda Loman is baffled by Willy's death because they have just finished paying off the mortgage on the house. The fact is that such a thing becomes an irrelevance to Willy who simply wishes to evaluate himself highly. This is a central theme equally in Hansberry's play but the chimerical nature of the world to which they aspire cannot be submitted to critical scrutiny precisely because it was at the time a central article of civil rights faith to regard such aspirations unambiguously. Such an objective had to be accorded value in order to validate their policy.

But in a sense the existence of the money and even the decision to move out of the ghetto merely provides the occasion for the play. The main emphasis is on the black family itself. Only one white character appears, a man who tries to bribe them to stay out of his neighbourhood. In a way the virtual absence of white characters constituted part of the interest of the play. It was, after all, something of a novelty for a serious play with black actors to run successfully on Broadway. Indeed the play itself became a liberal cause, to be supported not only in its own right but also as a public symbol of the moral battle then still in its opening stages. It was theatrically unadventurous and its characters were perilously close to cliché (a shiftless black man who rediscovers his identity, a gallantly enduring black grandmother, an aspiring young woman drawn to the glories of an emergent Africa). Its middle-class thrust was even, arguably, only marginally relevant to the immediate fight for de-segregation which, at the time, was focussed on the South. In that respect it mirrored Lorraine Hansberry's own middle-class origins. It was, in short, finely calculated for a Broadway audience. But the fact remains that it tackled an issue which had not been seen on Broadway for some considerable time. It constituted a breakthrough for the black writer. Given the times, it was, inevitably, both a cultural and political fact. And it was not a didactic play. Beneath the immediate issues was a concern for personal dignity, for the necessity for the individual to construct his or her own identity out of choices made. The moral world was not inherited; it was to be reconstituted out of the self's encounter with the other. The weakness of the play lies in the extent to which she is seduced by her own myths. The young girl Beneatha, who wishes to be a doctor, is drawn to the cultural style and exotic politics of an Africa which seems to have restored national pride and identity through rebellion. There is a hint of reproval in Lorraine Hansberry's suggestion that her enthusiasms are naive and shallow but the power of the African model is allowed to stand untested and unexamined. The weight which is placed on the move into the white suburb is itself deeply suspect, as is the dramatic emphasis on the sudden redemption of the Younger family. There is little in the play to substantiate the clear suggestion that the move will change either their circumstances or their characters. The quixotic gesture, indeed, has earlier been presented by her as a family characteristic and as evidence of a failure of sustained will. However, the myth commands not only the action of the play but also, I suspect, the moral imagination of the writer. Its resolution will sustain neither political reality nor dramatic conviction.

In a sense none of these observations begin to explain the significance of the play to the American theatre or indeed to the black community. For Lorraine Hansberry had little need to plunder theatre history for the origins of her play. It was rooted in her own experience. When she was just eight years old her family moved into a racially restricted area near the University of Chicago in order to test the restrictive covenants which effectively excluded blacks from buying such houses. The response was constant harassment and they were eventually evicted, though in 1940 her father won a resultant case on appeal to the United States Supreme Court. This found against such covenants, though the decision had little effect. In other words Lorraine Hansberry can have had very little illusion as to the significance of the move into the white area. Indeed, an early draft of the play reportedly ended with the Younger family sitting inside their new house and waiting for the whites to attack. That we never see them submitted to such a test leaves their commitment at the level of rhetoric, but, in fact, by 1959 there were more than enough black families who were prepared to risk their lives for a sense of dignity to ensure that the play was charged with a moral power which was not always apparent from what seemed little more than a naturalistic account of character and event. The fact is that the play meant a great deal to a large number of people and if the individual characters tended to be weak and apparently unequal to the battle except at the level of language then audiences were all too aware of the nature of the pressures which they struggled in a baffled sense to resist. And that external reality was the prism through which the play was viewed. It was a reality which scarcely needed to be incorporated within the play since it was an implacable fact of daily life and experience. *A Raisin in the Sun* was the first play by a woman or a black writer to win the New York Drama Critics' Circle

Award. It was a play about survival, and its characters' struggle for dignity was too close to that being fought daily by millions of black Americans not to be thought a central text and a major event.

Her second play, *The Sign in Sidney Brustein's Window* (1964) has only a single black character and he is guilty of an act of profound personal betrayal. The commitment of the family in *A Raisin in the Sun* had been inadvertent. They had stumbled into public confrontation through private need. Now Lorraine Hansberry chooses to probe the nature of commitment more thoroughly as she examines the degree to which involvement in a public cause may be a flight from responsibility rather than an expression of it. Sidney Brustein is a romantic idealist wandering from cause to cause. He supports a reform politician only to discover that he has been deeply betrayed. But he and those around him are guilty of what are, perhaps, more fundamental betrayals in that they fail to acknowledge or engage the human complexity and private needs of those they meet. In so far as the play could be said to relate to the civil rights movement it was as a lament that the individual runs the risk of being lost in the cause, that abstractions were being invoked precisely as a justification for not dealing with the reality of individual human beings. But her attention is not focussed primarily on the issue of race. It is a play about values, about responsibility, and about the individual's struggle to be evaluated by standards other than those that appear to predominate in a society in which an actress is required to sell commercial products, a politician to sell his personality and his soul, a woman to sell her body (Sidney Brustein's sister is a call girl) and a black man his simple humanity (his imagination can leap racial barriers but not deal with the private desperations of the woman he wishes to marry). It is a lament for human imperfection by a woman who was herself dying of leukaemia and who, indeed, did die during the run of the play. But it is equally a call for a constant fight against that imperfection.

The Sign in Sidney Brustein's Window is a lucid melodrama. The betrayals are carefully calculated and interrelated. The tone of near hysteria and compulsive, though seldom honest, self-examination is presented as an essential part of the culture of this particular Greenwich Village scene. The play is about articulate people who readily discharge their feelings and fears in language. And to that degree language itself becomes its subject. Words are a retreat for Sidney and his actress wife. As in Albee's *Who's Afraid of Virginia Woolf?* language is an excuse for failing to act, a means of papering over the cracks in experience, of denying the real terrors of experience. The up-beat ending, like that of Albee's play or Miller's *After the Fall*, also a product of 1964, was perhaps the expression of a cultural and political mood. Certainly, it is difficult to credit the gesture of faith and redemption with which it concludes. We have learned too much to have confidence in new beginnings. But such beginnings, perhaps endlessly renewed, constitute her essential theme. Theatrically, the play represented a slight advance over her first work. There is a gesture towards dismantling the naturalistic structure. A dream sequence suggests a level of human communication which exists quite outside the arena of language. But it is not allowed to disturb the re-establishment of the play's naturalistic drive, any more than it is to deflect Sidney from his retreat from private to public world. At the end the play rests on a simple piety – people should love one another and endlessly forgive their faults. The problem, once again, is that the characters which she creates do not seem able to bear the weight which she would place on them, while the contrivances of the plot threaten to vitiate the play's assertion that the real is in essence a product of the moral imagination and the free will.

Lorraine Hansberry was acutely aware of what she saw as the moral responsibility of the writer, more especially of the black writer whose function it was to articulate the experiences of those denied access to the institutions and myths of American life. She rejected an absurdist stance which she saw as simply compounding metaphysical and social cruelty and included such a playwright as one of the characters in *The Sign in Sidney Brustein's Window* precisely in order to chastise him for elevating self-pity to moral precept. These were not academic matters to her. She was, after all, dying at the age of thirty-four and had seen enough in her own life to understand all too clearly the degree to which social fiat could drain life of dignity and purpose. But at the same time she was uncomfortable, as a liberal writer, with the stridency and moral equivocation of those who chose to counter racism with violence, with, that is, a suppression of the very human values in whose name they chose to revolt. And in her last play, *Les Blancs*, not performed in her lifetime, she dramatises this issue, opting, uncomfortably, for revolution, but with a sense of unease and self-doubt which is not purged by the momentum of the plot. Set in the Africa she had invoked as image in *A Raisin in the Sun*, it concerns not merely the revolt of a colonial people and the seemingly inevitable conflict between differing sets of values, but also the dilemma of the writer who observes historical process without intervening, who requires a certain detachment in order to operate but for whom that detachment may be the source of ultimate guilt. It was a dilemma openly confessed by other black writers, not least by James Baldwin, but it located Lorraine Hansberry's own position precisely. Her mind conceded that necessity for action which her heart could never wholly endorse. The logic of her first and last plays leads to a conflict she believes to be inevitable but one which her own sensibility would have found difficult to negotiate.

Her plays express a middle-class black sensibility. Her anguished debates over the moral implications of commitment set her apart in some large degree from many black Americans for whom such ethical considerations were at best a luxury. After her first play the pressure of the real relaxed in her work. Her eyes, perhaps unsurprisingly, began to focus beyond the immediate realities of daily existence. *The Sign in Sidney Brustein's Window* struggled somewhat for an audience, being sustained by the financial help of well-wishers. *Les Blancs*, in part a response to Jean Genet's *Les Noirs*, was not produced until 1970. Yet there is no denying the significance of her life and her career. Her first play, for all its derivative elements, for all its conventionalities, not merely intruded the racial problem on the Great White Way but also offered the black American a self-image which he or she could recognise and to some degree identify with. It made possible the emergence of other politically and theatrically innovative work while its cast contained a number of actors who would constitute the backbone of black theatre in the 1960s and 70s. One may, as I have, choose to quibble with aspects of her work but there is no doubting the importance of a woman whose personal courage no less than her plays made her, for a few brief years, a central figure in America's cultural, political and moral life.

Like the writer in *Les Blancs*, James Baldwin was equivocally placed: he wished simultaneously to claim a certain moral and intellectual space between himself and the world which he observed while at the same time asserting his involvement in the struggle. At a time when physical presence was dramatised as a necessary badge of authenticity (this was equally the strategy behind civil rights sit-ins and Vietnam protests) he had a record of evasion. He had fled to France in 1948 rather than confront the brutal realities of a racist society. He distanced himself from those who protested Patrice Lumumba's death in a demonstration at the United Nations, as he later failed to join Marlon Brando when he went to San Francisco to support the Black Panthers gunned down by the police. He retreated, unavoidably perhaps, into words, offering himself in some way as an interpreter of the black psyche, writing, again perhaps unavoidably, for a white audience. His anger and indignation were real enough and certainly grew out of personal experience, but they were carefully shaped and sculpted and composed in a lucid and articulate style which inevitably implied a gulf between himself and those whose daily realities he chose to render into balanced sentences and finely wrought paragraphs. LeRoi Jones was later to warn his fellow blacks against the temptation to become 'fluent in the jargon of power'. Baldwin acquired such a fluency early, at a time when the ambiguity of inhabiting a language so thoroughly stained with history was not yet so apparent. He claimed an incorporation into America on a linguistic level which he denied on the level of subject matter.

Yet the bitterness was there and it came spilling through in an unregulated way in a novel like *Another Country*. And that was a primary difference between his novels and his essays for in the former he is obliged to let other voices than his own enter his linguistic space. A cool rhetorical strategy has to make way for the incoherences of action and the emotional realities of characters caught in the process of responding to public contempt and private betrayal. His essays offer an image of containment, of rational control, which is reflected on the level of style and which, particularly to the white audiences with whom in the early 1960s they were incredibly popular, thereby seemed to imply the possibility of debate, with both sides inhabiting the same linguistic and perhaps therefore social and moral world. Thus, while he might threaten the fire next time, his pose of detachment and his tightly controlled style suggested otherwise. Not so with the novels – particularly a work like *Another Country*. In a sense it was simply a mess, with the author failing to control its straggling plot lines or contain characters whose outbursts seemed to send shock-waves through the book's structure, disrupting its narrative voice and disturbing its plot structure. But this was also its strength. As soon as Baldwin ceased to speak with his own voice, other voices asserted their rights – voices which could not lay claim to his articulateness, voices for whom contained emotion would have been in conflict with character. As a result, the novel is contrived in its laboured construction but authentic in its sudden release of energy, an energy which he had previously been inclined to contain within the language of reasonable debate. It seemed likely, therefore, that the theatre might be a principal mechanism for releasing this side of Baldwin's creative powers. It would be in the theatre that these other voices would be freed to some degree from his rhetorical control.

His first play, *Amen Corner*, written as early as 1952, was not produced until 1965. Set in a black community church and concerned with a private struggle for meaning and identity, it seemed largely irrelevant to the battles of the mid 1960s. Its strategy of displacing the question of identity from a racial to a sexual sphere, of deflecting social bitterness into psychological trauma, mirrors that which he employed in *Go Tell it on the Mountain*, which was a product of the same time. But his 1964 play, *Blues for Mister Charlie*, produced by the Actors' Studio amidst considerable rancour and controversy between Baldwin and the

Company, did release an unregulated energy which brought him, for a moment, closer to those other figures in the black movement – LeRoi Jones and Eldridge Cleaver – who otherwise regarded him with the greatest suspicion.

The play was inspired by his anger at the killing of civil rights worker Medgar Evers. Set in the South, it dramatises the murder of a young black man, Richard Henry. The civil rights movement provides the background but not the subject for the play which opens and closes with a protest march. Between the two marches Baldwin tries to dramatise the powerful racial myths which trap black and white alike. Richard returns from the North bitter and violent. Like Rufus Scott in *Another Country*, he is destroyed by an anger forged out of constant humiliation. His relationships with white women in the North, which he flaunts on his return, are unsubtle attempts at revenge. The love that he needs requires a willed vulnerability which he cannot permit himself. He defends himself from injury by hardening himself to the point at which he becomes virtually unreachable, turning, in the process, into a baffled rebel, determined to confront the white world and wring some recognition of his humanity from it. But in the process he surrenders that very humanity to hatred – the more profound because it has grown into self-contempt.

The problem is that there seems no middle ground. His father's name, significantly, is Meridian, but his temporising (he failed even to revenge or secure justice for his wife's probable murder) makes him a dubious value in the play. A white liberal, Parnell James, fails to support the black community when faced with the stark choice at the trial and anyway is presented as having been motivated in his liberalism by sexual obsession with blacks. The two communities are clearly separated. They live apart but more importantly are held distinct from one another by a mythology which is no less powerful than social custom or personal bigotry. Baldwin dramatises this in the trial scene by dividing the stage on racial lines into blacktown and whitetown. In such a situation ambiguity seems to have no place.

And yet, as always with Baldwin, his Old Testament conscience, intent on preaching the fire next time, on warning of judgement and the necessity to condemn the guilty, does war with a New Testament sensibility, intent on offering grace and identifying the power of love to neutralise hatred and reconcile the apparently irreconcilable. And, again typically, the redemptive love is rendered in sexual terms. Richard is tempted to lay aside the gun which he carries in favour of Juanita, a young black girl who offers him both the love which he has sought and a possible way of avoiding the confrontation towards which he is otherwise heading. But it is a path that history, myth, and Baldwin's stern Calvinist conscience will not allow him to take. Richard lays aside his gun but not his bitterness and when he insults a woman her white husband is as bound to kill him as Richard is to refuse to retract the gesture. He dies, unarmed, an ironic fact for which Baldwin does not take full responsibility in that this action casts doubt on the validity of the love which disarmed him but which the author also plainly offers as a possible means of transcendence. So, too, the line which divides the two communities is simultaneously presented as implacable and historically rooted – immune to the moral appeal of the civil rights workers, as it is to the well-meaning but ineffectual Christianity of Meridian and the deeply compromised liberalism of Parnell – and paradoxically capable of moral and imaginative transcendence.

Baldwin has pointed out that the play is less a lament for a black man killed on the intersecting point of public and private myths than a blues played for the white man – for Mister Charlie – whose life is no less circumscribed by such myths and who, ironically, condemns himself to an identity effectively defined by those he most fears and affects to despise. This is true enough and there are, indeed, moments of satirical comedy in the play which stress the pathos of the whites, in particular a carefully observed and rendered social meeting of whites whose affected banter scarcely conceals a profound anxiety. But for the most part it is a simple melodrama which at times comes perilously close to embracing the stereotypes it seems intent on denying. Juanita is what she is described as being – a black girl apparently willing to dispense her sexual favours with some abandon. The white liberal is profoundly compromised by the motives with which Baldwin chooses to invest him. And though Lyle Britten, the white murderer, is dramatised with some subtlety, the other members of the white community are allowed no substance.

The play is an uneasy blend of naturalism and expressionism, a stylistic tension which reflects accurately enough his own divided sensibility. It has a double and essentially contradictory progression. The action moves towards the murder, which is the culmination of historical process and personal psychology. But this movement is contained within another logic which makes Parnell seek to walk alongside the black people he has betrayed and which forces Juanita to concede a place to him which he has plainly forfeited. Baldwin seeks to pay his debt to Medgar Evers by indicting the system which destroyed him while simultaneously celebrating the civil rights strategy which he had embraced. It proved an impossible task. When the play was published Baldwin suggested that it was one man's attempt to bear witness to the reality and power of light in a terrible darkness. But it is hard to see that it identifies the source or reality of such a light beyond its final gesture which, lacking any dramatic logic, becomes little more than a piety.

Baldwin's play was not merely, in his view, *about* whites, it was directed *at* them and as such did reflect the civil rights movement which, at this time, was largely an alliance of white liberals and black activists. Indeed, when the play was threatened with closure after a single month's run it was precisely these white liberals who came to its rescue, sustaining it for a further two months as a result of their intervention. But it was a support which was not without its irony, given the play's portrait of liberal equivocation. It was a support which also placed Baldwin himself in an ambiguous position as the black movement shifted its emphasis, looking for its audience in the black community. The difficulty which the play had in finding an audience perhaps suggested the degree to which that audience was splintering but it was also perhaps evidence of its own weaknesses – its suspect rhetoric, melodramatic simplifications and fundamental ambiguities. The relationship between Baldwin and the Actors' Studio was not a happy one and the play, cut down from an original five hours running time, was never really subjected to the rigorous attention which it needed. Yet Baldwin's conflicts, the conflicts which survive in the play, were equally those of the black community. The urge to indict white racism did in fact coexist with the need to believe in its possible transcendence, and for a while those contradictory elements seemed to inhabit the same space. But under the pressure of the murder of civil rights workers and the assassination of President Kennedy they split apart, with the integrationist ethos increasingly deferring to a militant separatism on the political front, and to a black cultural nationalism on the artistic.

A principal problem for the black writer in America has always been the nature of the audience. For a long while the simple facts of literacy, the economics of publishing, the realities of the theatre business ensured that the audience would be predominantly white. As a consequence, the black writer was required to make certain adjustments, accommodations. It was not that the white ego had necessarily to be flattered but that certain forms, styles, treatments and characters had a life sanctioned as much by literary and dramatic tradition as by social reality. However, problems of literacy could clearly be circumvented by performance and anyway dwindled in significance as the century progressed. Performance, in a broad sense, had always been an important element in the black community – from the communal experiences of the store-front churches through to the dance halls. If there was no tradition of theatre-going there was a strong sense of community (partly because of the external pressure of discrimination) which the writer and the black drama group could appeal to. For Lorraine Hansberry in her first play the solution for the black family was to leave the ghetto. Increasingly, however, as the 1960s progressed, so this response tended to be seen as demeaning by a number of black activists and artists who ceased to direct their attention to the white world or to validate the dreams of those who wished, in effect, to enter it, and sought instead to address the black community directly (albeit a black community which tended, for ideological reasons, to exclude the bourgeoisie even while they constituted a vital component of that community). Writers like LeRoi Jones and Ed Bullins tended to see their works as consciousness-raising gestures, as elements in a political struggle which was to begin with the restoration of pride to those whose self-image had been demeaned by centuries of oppression, and to end with a vaguely perceived revolution – a revolution of consciousness which tended, confusingly, to be rendered as actual revolt. So that sometimes the plays tended to deal with literal revolution; sometimes they were concerned with dramatising a consolidated ghetto which would be the equivalent of a separate black state; sometimes they seemed to see present action as a prelude to participation in the American body politic. But whatever the ultimate objective the audience was initially to be primarily a black one. This was at its most obvious in the work of LeRoi Jones and his imitators, or in the plays of Ed Bullins, who started his career by writing brutal agit-prop plays and then produced a series of powerful and lyrical works about the ghetto. But it was equally clear in the movement to found the Negro Ensemble Company and in the changing role of the Free Southern Theatre.

In August 1966, Douglas Turner Ward, who earlier had written *Day of Absence*, a gentle comedy set in the South suddenly made aware of its need for its black citizens, wrote an article in *The New York Times* in which he stated that 'If any hope, outside of chance individual fortune, exists for Negro playwrights as a group – or, for that matter, Negro actors and other theatre craftsmen – the most immediate, pressing, practical, absolutely minimally essential first step is the development of a permanent Negro repertory company.'[10] It was essentially the statement of an individual devoted to theatre as such rather than concerned with theatre as an agent, or extension, of political conviction. As he observed when, remarkably, this manifesto was translated into the reality of the Negro Ensemble Company, located not in Harlem but the Lower East Side,

> In the first place, we designed a project which was not a community theatre project. People interested in community theatre would have to locate in the midst of that community – in Harlem or Bedford-Stuyvesant. Our project was designed for the entire metropolitan area.

> Therefore we wanted a central location that would be easy reach from all
> the outlying Black communities . . . It was not designed as a cultural arm
> of the community.[11]

In the early days the audience was predominantly white, the organisation
was supported by the Ford Foundation and some of its plays were by
white authors (its first production being the *Song of the Lusitanian Bogey*
by the European writer Peter Weiss). This gradually changed until it
became more clearly a black theatre, though its plays were for the most
part politically and even theatrically unadventurous. But at a time when
the American theatre offered few opportunities for black actors, directors, technicians or writers it performed a vital purpose. The Negro
Ensemble Company is now one of the more impressive theatre companies
in America and has adopted a more adventurous policy.

Meanwhile, in the South, another group, the Free Southern Theatre,
was founded. This was a product of the civil rights movement and set
itself consciously to achieve precisely what the Negro Ensemble Company eschewed. Founded in September 1963 by two black actor–
directors – John O'Neal and Gilbert Moses – and one white – Richard
Schechner – it staged its first season the following year. Moses was a
product of Oberlin College and the Sorbonne. He had appeared Off-
Broadway in *The Good Soldier Schweik* and at the black Karamu
Playhouse in Cleveland. John O'Neal was a graduate of Southern Illinois
University and an executive member of the Student Nonviolent Co-
ordinating Committee (SNCC). Schechner was the editor of the *Tulane
Drama Review* and owner-director of the East End Players in
Provincetown, Massachusetts. In fact several of the group's actors and
directors were graduates and most came from the North. But this was to
be a specifically Southern theatre, based in New Orleans and travelling to
small black communities, many of whom had never seen theatre before.
Indeed its motto was 'Theatre for people who have no theatre'. In the
words of *The Free Southern Theatre Newsletter* for December 1964,

> The FST tour is unique in American theatre history. Never before has a
> professional theatre with a repertory of plays gone to small towns such as
> many of these are; never has an area had the opportunity to see live theatre
> without travelling to large population centers. If the concept of 'popular
> theatre' still has meaning, it is embodied in the FST tour. One aspect of
> segregation, ironically enough, works for the FST: in most places
> Negroes are still denied access to movie houses or are forced to accept
> segregated seating. Therefore, the FST is not competing against the
> movies. Although we would welcome such 'competition', the fact
> remains that the FST is, in many places, the *only theatrical entertainment*
> available to large portions of the community.[12]

A representative of the group was quoted in the *Christian Science Monitor* of 16 April 1965, as saying that the FST was 'unique in that it seeks to present socially relevant drama which reflects life honestly while maintaining high artistic and theatrical standards. The three directors see theatre as a communal experience, an event in which the audience as well as the actors participate.'[13]

The group made no charge for their performances, simply collecting a small donation of about 25 cents a head. They survived initially on gifts until, in 1966, they received a large grant from the Rockefeller Foundation ($62,500). The first production was Martin Duberman's *In White America*, a collage of documentary material about the black situation in America throughout history. It was well-calculated to appeal to their audience, bridging the gap between fact and fiction. But subsequent productions caused rather more debate. The second season consisted of Ossie Davis's *Purlie Victorious*, a comedy relying to some extent on racial stereotypes, and Beckett's *Waiting for Godot*. The latter choice was justified by the fact that it 'speaks in universal and yet concrete terms about the situation of *human beings* (not simply racial beings)', while the successful production of the play in San Quentin convinced them that 'the play would be readily understood and welcomed in that larger prison, Mississippi' because, underneath its anguish, '*Godot* is a play about freedom and its difficult demands on the human consciousness.'[14] By the same logic later productions included work by O'Casey and Brecht, which had the added advantage of requiring low royalty payments. But the principal problem lay in the dearth of available material by black writers. *Purlie Victorious* was seized on despite what the company felt to be its serious flaws. More surprisingly a similar complaint was still being voiced in 1968, by which time a considerable body of material by black writers was available, most of it, admittedly, being rooted in an urban setting.

As a creation of the civil rights movement the Free Southern Theatre naturally reflected changes in that movement, slowly becoming a largely black company and, in common with many cultural and political organisations of the period, expending much of its energy in internal arguments as to its proper nature and function. It was, however, an important venture in an American tradition of populist theatre which would include the Federal Theatre of the 1930s. Unlike some of the black groups in the North, however, and unlike the Chicano theatre of California, it was not a spontaneous product of the local community. It was a professional group of middle-class origins which aimed to create a regional theatre.

The main thrust of the theatre in the 1960s, however, lay elsewhere, just as the emphasis of the civil rights movement itself shifted northwards. It lay in the emergence of a theatre which sought to address directly the realities and myths of black life. It lay in a racially conscious, racially derived and racially directed theatre which, for a time at least, saw itself as the cultural arm of the black power movement. It was urban in setting and tone, didactic in intent and self-consciously concerned with elaborating a pantheon of black heroes and villains. Its principal and most talented voice was that of a man whose own transformations over a period of not much more than a decade were evidence of transformations wrought in the black community itself and whose own shifting persona suggested the degree to which a principal item on the cultural and political agenda was the construction and assertion of a private and public identity. LeRoi Jones, who became Amiri Baraka, moved from being a promising poet, whose work was related to that of the Beats (whose poems and prose he published as editor of a Greenwich Village journal), to being the principal exponent and spokesman for a militant cultural nationalism. Then, in the second half of the 1970s, he changed direction yet again becoming a Marxist-Leninist, indeed virtually a Stalinist, whose works could easily have appeared in the 1930s. He went, also, from being an experimental writer, whose powerful images and carefully constructed fables explored new dramatic no less than social territory, to being a third-rate party hack, pathetically seeking to make American reality correspond to ideological theory, the greatest waste of artistic talent in post-war America.

As a poet in the 1950s, he regarded himself as in the modernist tradition but admired the Beats because of their respect for the physical world and for the socially marginal figure whom they recast as romantic hero. Behind a writer such as Alan Ginsberg, of course, there lay Walt Whitman whose inclusiveness appealed to Jones who had a personal investment in eclecticism. It was this which pulled him equally towards the work of people like Hubert Selby Jr and John Rechy, who celebrated deviancy while locating it against the harrowing reality of its setting, who combined a romantic eye with a modernist's concern for stylistic innovation. Married to a white Jewish-American, Jones was likely to prove responsive to the easy bohemianism of Greenwich Village and to a literature which celebrated heterogeneity and the synthesising self. But the pressure of social reality was not easily denied. If the sending of federal marshals to Little Rock, Arkansas, in 1957, had brought a guilty James Baldwin briefly back to America, the increasing violence which accompanied the civil rights movement – the assassination of President Kennedy, the bombing of black children in a Birmingham, Alabama, Sunday school and the burning of Watts – made it increasingly difficult to inhabit or even believe in the possibility of a comfortable no man's land for the artist or the black man in America. Nor was Jones unaware of developments on the international scene. In 1962 he was among the crowd at the Union Nations protesting at the murder of Patrice Lumumba of the Congo. On a visit to Cuba he was struck by the possibility of revolution, the fact that sudden change was possible. Increasingly the rhetoric of the civil rights movement seemed to him inadequate to the task of transforming America. He drifted towards the Black Muslims, taking instruction from them though never actually joining their organisation. Then he divorced his white wife and moved to Harlem, using money from Johnson's poverty programme to found and finance the Black Arts Repertory Theatre, a small Harlem theatre from which he excluded white audiences – a not unreasonable gesture given the size of the theatre and the history of white patronage of Harlem nightspots in the 1920s. This eventually proved a model for similar projects in other American cities. Though the same two plays which he staged here, *Dutchman* and *The Slave*, had been well received when performed at the Cherry Lane Theatre, their simple transfer to Harlem and an all-black audience gave them the appearance of revolutionary tracts and secured the withdrawal of OEO (Office of Economic Opportunity) money.

Later Baraka, as he was now called, moved to Newark, New Jersey, where he founded Spirit House, developing an interest in Africa which began to influence his poetry. Following an incident in a riot in the late 1960s he found himself charged with assault. Though no conviction resulted this did nothing to harm his reputation in the black community. He became a central figure, mediating between various black groups who were frequently as hostile to one another as to whites, and then involving himself in the battle to secure the election of a black mayor. When the problems of the city proved less tractable than hoped and when it became apparent that a simple change in the complexion of the city's leading official, unaccompanied by a radical political and economic restructuring of the system, was likely to prove futile, he deeply regretted his involvement in what he now came contemptuously to regard as reform politics. Accordingly he moved to a Marxist-Leninist stance and, as a result, also moved into that particular cultural void which was constituted by the American Communist Party in the 1970s. As a result, one of the most promising talents in the American theatre and one of the finest black writers has chosen to turn his back on the society which he had once challenged so articulately and whose public symbols he sought to neutralise with the powerful myths of black nationalism. His most recent plays have been simple formula works all too familiar from fifty years of Party art. The man who once stunned the American theatre and whose wit and corrosive language once disturbed that theatre's equanimity now stands at the gates of factories distributing tracts to workers whose concern for the benefits of a materialist society are only matched by their hostility to an ideology which they regard as threatening their very existence.

His first play, *A Good Girl is Hard to Find*, had been produced as early as 1958, in Montclair, New Jersey and in 1964 *The 8th Ditch*, part of his novel *The System of Dante's Hell*, and *The Baptism* were performed, as, later, was *The Toilet*. This last, set in a men's urinal, was a curious blend of violence and sentimentality, ending with the suggestion of an inter-racial relationship forged out of sexual need, a kind of Baldwin-like conclusion which he later came to regret. But it was the production of *Dutchman*, at the Cherry Lane Theatre, which really established his reputation. This play, like its companion piece *The Slave*, had two lives, the shift to a Harlem location changing equally the cultural meaning and political force of works which were transformed from deeply ambiguous metaphors into literal models of social action.

Dutchman, so named because its continuous action invoked the myth of the Flying Dutchman condemned to sail for ever with his crew of the living dead, is set in a subway car in the 'flying underbelly of the city', a world which, he reminds us, is rich in myth. It concerns the encounter of a young white woman, Lula, and a buttoned-down black man, Clay. It is itself a mythic encounter not merely to the extent that they are required to act out an Edenic myth, with Lula performing as temptress eating an apple and luring Clay to his death, but because the encounter of black man and white woman in American society involves the clash of two symbolic systems, because it is itself defined in terms of social myth.

To a degree the play is something of a self-portrait and the autobiographical component is strong in Jones's early work. Clay is trapped in his own articulateness. His mastery of language, which has apparently given him access to the white world whose style he mimics, is, paradoxically, a sign of his subservience. His natural anger and his assertive identity have been deflected into words which have redefined him as effectively as his bourgeois appearance. When Lula goads him, alternating racial abuse and sexual precocity, he tries to tune into her bantering tone, to accept the abuse and the sexual role which she seems to wish to project onto him, rather than resisting which would oblige him to throw off his disguise. Her role seems to be a double one. She is to test the extent of his subservience and to provoke the violence which she both desires and must punish. They are, in a sense, one another's invention. Locked together, historically and mythically, they are fated to define themselves

397

by reference to one another. Simultaneously thrown together and thrust apart by a myth which proposes a sexual attraction which must nonetheless be punished, they are one another's hell.

And so Lula taunts Clay with his assimilationist desires, mocks his appearance and provokes him, finally, into action. He beats a white drunkard to the floor and momentarily dominates Lula and the other whites in the compartment. But he relapses into language, slips back into his disguise and discards the brutal sanity of violence. A black intellectual, like Jones himself, he recognises clearly enough the simple logic of revolt, recognises, too, that what confronts him is evil rather than a simple lack of style; but, by the same token, he wishes to lapse back into the safety of words and the indirections of art: 'But who needs it? I'd rather be a fool. Insane. Safe with my words, and no deaths, and clean, hard thoughts, urging me to new conquests.'[15] The relevance of this to a black playwright himself balanced between a successful career as a writer and political necessities which require that the word defer to the act is not hard to see. The very articulateness which enabled him to write the play itself constitutes a temptation to substitute aesthetics for action. It pulled him not only towards the safety of art but also towards the 'jargon of power'. Only a few months before, on the death of President Kennedy, he had pasted a new poem into the winter edition of *Kulchur* magazine, a poem which seemed to assert the implacable nature of history and the impossibility of transforming the world with language:

> From now on we will sit in nightclubs with jewish
> millionaires listening to the maudlin political verse
> of a money narcissist.
>
> And this will be the payback for our desires.
> For history, like the ringing coin
>
> that will not bend
> When we bite it.[16]

Clay is knifed by Lula and his body is thrown off the train by the unspeaking white passengers. The play ends as another young black enters the compartment. Clearly the same ritual is about to be re-enacted. The mere understanding and articulation of black suffering is insufficient. And so it proved for Baraka.

The point seems clear enough. The only way to break out of the cycle is to tackle history and myth head on, to abandon efforts to appease those who destroy the black man just as effectively by persuading him to embrace their values as by the violence with which, historically, they had responded to black attempts to lay claim to American principles. And yet the play also acknowledges that revolt itself can be said to be determined by those who provoke it. *Dutchman* is an honest play by a man literally poised at a moment of choice. Its power derives precisely from the integrity with which he renders a dilemma which was not his alone. Just as the civil rights movement itself was reaching a point at which it splintered into different opposing camps, so the debate about the role of the black writer was reaching a critical point. And Baraka, too, was confronted by a painful choice equally reflected in *The Slave*.

Dutchman is a ritual. The two principal characters act out social roles which are also racial and sexual roles. The stereotype is granted substance as a social fact but is tested against language and action. However, Jones is also concerned with probing the ambiguities expressed by that language and through those actions. He attempts to compress the history of black/white sexual, cultural and social relations into a single 'plot' – a conspiracy and a narrative alike. And since it is a plot which touches so closely on his own situation the consequence is a profound ambiguity which exposes the dangerously vulnerable position of the black writer just as it does the morally insecure and even ontologically ambivalent state of a society at war with itself. His doubts about language extend to the work itself in which action tells a truth which the words would conceal. His doubts about his own position as a writer, warning against the deceptions of language, pose questions which not only address the special circumstances of the committed artist but also acknowledge the unreliability of language itself. In other words the insecurities that he confronts go beyond simple acts of racial prejudice, just as the real betrayal that he addresses is the betrayal of the self rather than the other. Clay is condemned to death and Lula to her everlasting task because, like the Flying Dutchman, they have in a sense blasphemed against the natural order. They have betrayed themselves.

A similar dilemma is at the centre of *The Slave*, which is set at the moment of a literal revolt. The title is ironic, for while the play is concerned with a revolution the leader of that rebellion remains in essence a slave – a slave to the values and ideas of the white world which he otherwise wishes to destroy, and a slave to the language which shapes his thought. The play begins with an old slave who delivers a knowing prologue. He then in effect becomes the rebel leader. And, if it is true that it is white society which, by its prejudice, or, at best, its liberal temporising, has transformed the shambling slave of the nineteenth century into the articulate and violent rebel of the twentieth, then the rebel seems no less determined by white society than that slave had been. Instead of leading his black troops to victory – itself, of course, something of a fantasy in a country nine-tenths white – the leader slips into the city to confront his white ex-wife and her white university professor husband. It is a scene of self-justification which the true revolutionary would have found redundant but which Jones, in process of leaving his white wife, seems to have felt compelled to address.

The prologue is in a sense a paradigm of the play. The shambling slave speaks a twentieth-century language and in doing so confesses to a self-doubt which penetrates the action of the play no less than its characters and dialogue. For the speech acknowledges the power of selfishness which makes all actions suspect, and the ease with which the individual seeks protection behind 'whatever thing we feel is too righteous to question, too deeply felt to deny'.[17] Opinion, he suggests, too easily becomes a means of self-protection so that it is possible that just because ideas are 'beautiful and brilliant . . . just because they're *right* . . . doesn't mean anything. The very rightness stinks a lotta times.'[18] Thus a poem, a play, music may become nothing more than a diversion, a distortion, a form of wish-fulfilment. So Jones prefaces what he calls his 'fable' with a warning of his own ambiguous motives in creating the work as he simultaneously warns of the complex of motives which will lead his audience to recreate it. He is, he confesses, aware of the need for a meta-language which can bypass cultural confusions and is aware of the need to annihilate racial distinctions and announce the triumph of love, much as Baldwin might do, but finds himself instead, 'Discovering racially the funds of the universe. Discovering the last image of the thing. As the sky when the moon is broken.'[19] And so the play ends balanced between these two possibilities, as was Jones himself, with the action moving towards apocalypse but with the gesture which is the play being offered as a redemptive act. It is an articulate play by a man deeply suspicious of the implications of his own articulateness; an ambiguous play by a man increasingly doubtful of the legitimacy of such ambivalence and the relevance of art at a moment of political and cultural crisis. If Walker Vessels, the leader of the revolt, should be at the head of his troops rather than offering self-justifications to middle-class whites, then Jones was inclined to make much the same point about himself, producing plays for the Cherry Lane Theatre and receiving an Obie from the *Village Voice*, as he did for *Dutchman*.

The play is an act of exorcism, imperfect but fully willed. Walker, himself a poet, struggles to escape other people's language – 'I learned so many words for what I've wanted to say. They all come down on me at once. But almost none of them are mine.'[20] His side-journey to his ex-wife's apartment is really the essence of his rebellion. It is his attempt to lay the ghosts of his past life, to find a voice and an identity which is wholly his own. How else to rebel in spirit as well as in deed? But it is perhaps an impossible task, even though the sacrifice is a real one. There is a prophetic nature to the accusation levelled at Walker Vessels by Bradford Easley, the white university professor, when he suggests that he has decided to write 'inept formless poetry . . . A flashy doggerel for inducing all those unfortunate troops of yours to spill their blood in your behalf . . . Ritual drama, we used to call it at the university.'[21] This was, after all, in essence, the art which Jones opted for after 1964, not inept but direct, simple, even simplistic agit-prop sketches aimed at motivating those who wished to transform their society. Placing doubt on one side he produced a drama absolute in its images and in its language – unworried by the subtle fears and self-doubts which had marked and distinguished his earlier work.

In the context of Jones's own dilemma, *The Slave* is a remarkably honest play. When Grace remarks of Walker that 'You're split in so many ways . . . your feelings are cut up into skinny horrible strips . . . like umbrella struts . . . holding up whatever bizarre black cloth you're using this performance as your self's image. I don't even think you know who you are any more . . . you never even found out who you were until you sold the last of your loves and emotions down the river . . . until you killed your last old friend . . . and found out *what* you were',[22] this is an accurate account of Jones's own real and painful dilemma, just as Walker's reply, 'I know what I can use . . . I move now trying to be certain of that',[23] seems a faithful enough description of a process of self-invention which requires the stripping of old selves, the elimination of other definitional elements, until what remains must be the usable identity. Walker's movement from a belief that the black man alone could restore the idealism of rational liberalism to western culture, towards a faith in the authority of revolt was in essence a reflection of Jones's own shift, as was the deep regret expressed by Walker that he was turning his back on a world which in part he respected (a world of literate debate and aesthetic value) for one which he did not (a world in part of culturally de-sensitised individuals, willing collaborators in their own demise). Certainly Jones did no less and this is in part the achievement of a play whose dramatic tensions are rooted in the sensibility of a writer genuinely alive to the social reality of the ambiguities which he presents with such power and articulateness. The violence which erupts is a logical development of action and character alike, as Walker, in killing Easley, kills also that part of his own sensibility which he values.

Dutchman and *The Slave* are remarkable plays. To be sure they derived a certain *frisson* from the context in which they were presented, a context of racial tension. But Jones's modern myths were rooted in more ancient and no less potent myths. The interplay of sexual and racial elements

401

charged both works with a power contained by his precise control of rhetoric and rhythm. It was the last time that he would exercise such control, the last time he would leave his work open to ambiguity. Thereafter he relied precisely on that 'ritual drama' which Bradford Easley dies condemning. He increasingly worked for a directness of effect, assumed the unambiguous pressure of history, and generated a series of melodramas, simple myths of dispossession, revolt and racial identity. Drama became less an anxious debate with the self and with the community, against which that self defined itself, than a series of public pronouncements; less a tentative shaping of experience than an assured statement of an unambiguous reality. The 'revolutionary' plays which followed were designed to raise consciousness and inspire a transformation in the style and context of black experience. Brief agit-prop performances, they set themselves to offer an analysis of social experience which identified heroes and villains, developed a conscious myth of the black past and proposed a simple model of the black future. The sacrifices which were discussed in *The Slave* were enacted in his subsequent work. Their virtue lay precisely in their directness of effect. Designed for a purely black popular audience, they had to appeal to those unused to the indirections of art. Their weakness lay in precisely the same area. Politically, they underestimated the enemy, dramatising him only in his most obvious and hence most easily resisted form. Aesthetically, they could afford to leave no space for the audience imaginatively to enter. They were works which began with their conclusions. The only role for the audience was to translate them whole into their daily experience. But given the absence of any acknowledgement of the complex economic, social and political nature of that experience they could do little to effect those objectives.

And Jones, now renamed Amiri Baraka, became increasingly aware of this. Following his disillusioning experience with reform politics, he moved towards a Marxist-Leninist stance, rejecting all of his former work as 'ideologically incorrect'. The emphasis on a purely black experience in the late 1960s now seemed a distraction from the central issue, a piece of blatant bourgeois nationalism. The real problem lay deeper, in the class system and in the country's economic organisation. His response was to write two plays – S–1 and *The Motion of History*. The former was aimed at an actual piece of proposed legislation which threatened a number of constitutional rights. The latter was a historical drama, an attempt to reclaim the past as a prelude to seizing the present and determining the future. Both plays are aesthetically regressive, pieces of Party literature which only very occasionally offer glimpses of Baraka's dramatic originality.

Baraka's is a sensibility that apparently craves submission to ideology. Confronted with the ambiguities that are the birthright of the black American and the natural inheritance of the writer who wishes to transform the world which he inhabits by reinventing it, he has always been tempted to resolve this by opting for a single interpretation, by being drawn to one pole of experience. It remains true, however, that his most impressive and honest work remains that which he wrote when poised in hesitation, when he could still acknowledge not merely the strength but also the legitimacy of the competing demands on his mind and imagination (*Slaveship* was one such, as were *Dutchman* and *The Slave*). He has chosen to sacrifice his talents to other battles, to recognise other urgencies than those demanded by art. In the 1960s he had an undeniable impact on the world into which he threw himself with such energy. In the process, however, he laid aside a talent which might have made him one of America's leading writers and which had already established his command of theatrical form and idiom – the influence of Albee, though real enough, being a minor facet of his work. He believes himself to have moved from a theatre expressing simple rage to one which offers an analysis of the components of that rage, but as a consequence he has replaced metaphor with statement, ambiguity with simple assertion, character with role and a painful attempt to sift an authentic language from inherited forms with mere rhetoric and party slogans. He is fully aware of the difficulties involved in devising a form and a language commensurate with his self-imposed task; he is aware, also, that thus far he has achieved this, if at all, only imperfectly. But where once he was content to find his audience among the intelligentsia and then among a community which was self-selecting on a principle of race, he has now set himself the more difficult task of inventing an audience whose class homogeneity has more to do with ideological fictions than with the reality of American society.

For Ed Bullins, LeRoi Jones was a dominant influence and 'one of the most important, most significant figures in American theatre . . . He created me as a playwright and created many other young Black playwrights.'[24] Bullins has explained his own move into theatre as deriving from a desire to reach a black audience uninterested in the novel. 'Black literature', he explained in 1969,

> has been available for years, but it has been circulating in a closed circle – the Black Arts circle and the colleges. It hasn't been getting down to the people. But now in the theatre, we can go right into the Black community and have a literature for the people . . . for the great masses of Black people. I think this is the reason that more Black plays are being written

> and seen, and the reason that more Black theatres are springing up. Through the efforts of certain Black artists, people are beginning to realize the importance of Black theatre. LeRoi began this movement through his Black Arts project in Harlem and now with the Spirit House in Newark which takes his plays across the country. Other groups such as the old Black Arts/West on the Coast which we had a hand in, the Aldridge Players/West also on the Coast, the Free Southern Theatre, Concept East in Detroit, and now the New Lafayette in Harlem [founded in 1967, closed in 1974] have tried to continue what LeRoi began. As a result of these efforts, theatre is becoming more acceptable to Black people on the whole.[25]

Bullins's optimism was plainly justified by what was indeed a sudden explosion of black creativity. Black Arts theatres had sprung up in a number of cities across America, with Bullins launching his career in San Francisco. But any movement whose genesis is directly related to political mood is likely to be vulnerable to shifts in that mood and if the fortunes of black theatre changed radically in the five years from 1964 to 1969 then they suffered a comparable decline in the following five years. Certain institutions did consolidate themselves (in particular the Negro Ensemble Company and the New Lafayette, in Harlem, along with Barbara Ann Tear's National Black Theatre, founded in 1968); others disappeared entirely.

Bullins's first two plays, *How Do You Do* and *Dialect Determinism*, were written in 1965 but at first he could find no one willing to produce them. As a result they were staged by the San Francisco Drama Circle, a company founded by Bullins and a colleague called Buck Hartman, at the Firehouse Repertory Theatre in San Francisco, together with a third play, *Clara's Ole Man*. Bullins subsequently founded Black Arts/West. He has described seeing a production of Jones's *The Toilet* and *Dutchman* shortly after writing his first plays and before they had been staged. As he explained subsequently, 'A whole new world opened up to me. Until I saw THE TOILET, I didn't realize how right I was in what I had done in CLARA'S OLE MAN. I know CLARA was a radical departure from the work of those Black playwrights I had read. It was radical in its depiction of Black people, but I didn't realize how right it was in a deep and profound revolutionary sense, until I saw THE TOILET.'[26]

How Do You Do is a slight work about a stereotypical black assimilationist (obligingly called Roger Stereotype) and a black whore with a predilection for white men. The third character is a young black man who urges them and the black audience not to submit to the white man but to 'Kill him in the mind' because 'the age of the body is done . . . Become a guerilla warrior of ideas.'[27] It is in effect the new

404

black dramatist's defence of his own strategy. For, as the first words of his first play indicate, 'I must make music today, poet music. I've sat here too long making nothing, and I know I've been born to make song . . . How shall I begin? Should I find the words first, or the melody? Should I suggest a theme?'[28] He is, he announces, an image maker. And his first images are of a subversive black art. The satiric thrust of *How Do You Do* runs through much of his later work as does his association of jargon and cant with the forces of reaction, and, in *Dialect Determinist*, with those of the reactionary left.

But while Bullins was clear as to his desire to address the black community, he did not wish his work to become a simple product of ideology. If his first play seemed to share something with LeRoi Jones's black revolutionary works, in its deliberate contrast between assimilationist blacks and a young man in possession of a clear sense of black identity, this was not designed to serve a vague myth of black cultural separatism or ethnic superiority. Far from working to mythicise black experience he wished to strip it of its pretence and to expose the daily tensions of black life, while his central character, even in that first play, advocated education, cunning and intellectual rigour rather than violence as a central strategy. For a time he did produce a number of plays which seemed to conform to the pattern laid down by Jones (*The Gentleman Caller* and *A Short Play for a Small Theatre* being two obvious examples) but even these are shot through with irony. Indeed, in 1973 he objected that his own early works had been 'swept away in the Black revolutionary emotionalism and resulting fratricide of the '60s'.[29] He endorsed attempts to heighten the black community's awareness of its potential as he did the need to reproduce the reality of its circumstances, but he treated with suspicion those who sought to reduce that potential to a simplistic programme for cultural or political change. 'If all around us are losing their heads', he remarked, 'it may be provident for the black artist to attempt to hold onto his, which is a conservative impulse, true, but radical in terms of heretical viewpoints. Political theorists of the Black Arts . . . are confused and disappointing . . . The dogs may bark but the caravan passes on.'[30]

Bullins's world is in fact composed of a series of numbing determinisms. His bleak urban landscapes are peopled by grotesques, by people warped in their hopes and their lives by the pressures exerted upon them. *Clara's Ole Man* is subtitled *A Play of Lost Innocence*, a phrase which could be applied to most of his work. Set in the 1950s in a slum kitchen in Philadelphia, it is a drama of stunted lives, frustrated dreams and distorted characters. It dramatises a hermetic world from which there is no apparent escape. Race is not in fact the central reality of the play, which is akin to late Tennessee Williams in its vision of individuals distorted by their settings and in its apocalypticism.

Given Bullins's own statement about the function of black art, his plays are curiously pessimistic. The simple determinisms seem rooted not merely in the brutal realities of ghetto life but in a more profound conviction about human passivity. His is a naturalist's vision. Environment and heredity provide the determining axes for individuals whose freedoms are illusory and whose dreams and visions are as shaped by these forces as anything else in their lives. It is true that both *In the Wine Time* (1967) and *The Corner* (1968), like *Clara's Ole Man*, are set in the 1950s but the contrast, which might have been expected, between a decade in which racial oppression seemed unrelieved and one in which cultural, political and social rebellion were central facts of the black experience, is never made. The parameters of the lives of his characters are defined by a brutal sexuality, a persistent resort to alcohol and a constant potential for violence. No other possibilities are identified except, in *In the Wine Time*, a lyricism represented by a young woman, half real, half fantasy, who constitutes the possibility of a world elsewhere. But this proves no more than an illusion. The world of his characters is closed. No escape to the white suburbs is envisaged. The only possible response seems to be narcosis or an act of anarchic violence. And yet these are less social plays, indictments of American urban life and racism, than metaphysical laments. The central figure in *In the Wine Time* identifies the barren choice: 'There's a big rich world out there . . . I'm going to get me part of that world or stare your God in the eye and scream *Why*. I am not a beast . . . or animal to be used for the plows of the world. But if I am then I'll act like one. I'll be one and turn this fucken world of dreams and lies and fairy tales into a jungle or a desert.'[31]

The third work in what turned out to be a sequence of plays, *In the New England Winter*, projects the action into the 1960s, but nothing has changed. The same frustrations are enacted, the same absurdity detected. As one of the characters laments, struck by the irony of his position: 'this isn't it . . . there must be order . . . perfection . . . there must be form . . . there must be reason and absolutes . . . There can't be only madness and reaching out and never touching the sides . . . There *has* to be something for me besides this emptiness . . . this living death . . . this white coldness.'[32] Ghetto life exacerbates this absurdity; it does not create it. The limitations imposed on black possibilities are plainly greater than those imposed on whites but they are not different in kind. *In the Wine Time* even demonstrates the degree to which a white family is as subject to this demeaning absurdity as any of the black characters. Bullins's naturalism is misleading. His marginal figures are no less the

406

victims of metaphysical absurdity than Gelber's characters in *The Connection* or Beckett's in *Waiting for Godot*. The realistic surface, fractured occasionally by a disruptive fantasy, is itself evidence of that desire for order which drives his own characters but it proves deceptive as a means of asserting a reassuring coherence.

By 1969 it was possible to detect something of a shift of emphasis in Bullins's work. *The Gentleman Caller*, which was his contribution to *A Black Quartet* (four plays by black writers presented at the Chelsea Center), was an ironic comedy in which a black maid is changed into a revolutionary fighter for black rights. A consciousness-raising piece on a par with LeRoi Jones's revolutionary plays, it ends with a call for black solidarity. Though this was in part a concession to the times and his next play, *The Duplex*, reverted to the mode of his earlier work, this now also bore the marks of a more overt commitment to black emancipation. Once again the play's action identifies no means of escaping the cycle of drink, drugs, and sexuality enacted against a background of urban collapse but he now feels obliged to incorporate a critique of white society, an articulate (too articulate, as it turns out, since such articulateness transcends the consciousness of the character to whom the speech is ascribed) statement of the impossibility of teaching the white world its own enormities. He also hints, though I suspect less consciously, at the ambiguity involved in the act of writing. As one of the play's characters asks,

> where in the hell are we going, brother? Where? Into the machine image of IBM . . . Into the confines of teaching the slavemaster's offspring . . . into the insanity of thinking we can teach them their own language . . . my poor brother, language is more than word . . . it is deeds and gestures . . . and silence . . . what history can we teach those who hide from history . . . those who believe their lies and fears create history . . . can we teach them their own sterility of soul that we slaves learned better than they that call it their civilization.[33]

The problem is that not only is this speech not rooted in character, it also has no correlative in terms of action; it remains simple rhetoric.

Like LeRoi Jones in *Dutchman* and *The Slave*, he feels obliged to acknowledge the ambiguity of his own position as a user of words, as someone trapped in a language whose determinisms are no less real than those of the ghetto which he sets out to describe. Thus, in another play dating from 1970, *Death List*, he apparently produces a black revolutionary play, an agit-prop sketch, in which a black man enumerates those fellow blacks whose views have made them enemies of black men around the world. As he does so he loads a rifle. But Bullins undercuts the simplicities of his own image by introducing a woman who attacks the male character for his arrogant assumption of the right to define and police the nature of blackness. Bullins tends to be absolute in his public statements but equivocal in his art. Having set himself the task of faithfully rendering the nature of black experience he seemingly feels unable to deny complexity to that experience by reducing it to ideological formula, believing that to do so would merely be to compound the forces which he wishes to indict.

Bullins, who had worked with Baraka, Sonia Sanchez, Marvin X and Eldridge Cleaver in Black House, San Francisco, left it following a dispute with Cleaver who wished to see it integrated, and in 1966–7 he joined with Robert Macbeth and others to form the New Lafayette Theatre in Harlem, the name deriving from the old Lafayette which had been famous in the 1930s. Three months later the building burned down and the company moved from 132nd to 137th Street (and Seventh Avenue), opening there with Bullins's *In the Wine Time*. It was this company which produced *The Duplex* in 1970.

Bullins once remarked that 'The revolutionary nature of this theater is not of style and technique but of theme and character.' The function of the black writer, he believed, lay in 'uncovering the reality of his art, his humanity, his existence as an intelligent and moral entity in the universe'. He 'makes the entire universe an audience of this transformation of the psyche and spirit'.[34] He was, indeed, no innovator. His departures from naturalism are tentative. But despite the pressure exerted by the realities of ghetto life and the exigencies of political revolt he has never made his art simply a blunt weapon. Ambiguity and a deep suspicion of facile optimism seem to be part of the reality which he is intent on rendering. Politically an optimist but philosophically a determinist he has created a series of plays dramatising the ironies which result from an attempt to chase the phantoms of coherence and meaning. His subject is the nature of the struggle which he believes must be rendered honestly if it is to offer any element of transcendence. But, a victim of language itself, he seems to doubt the reality of that transcendence, outside of the momentary and fallible coherences offered by personal relationships and art itself.

The fear, for Bullins as for so many other black writers, is always that the word leads away from the act, that a literary shaping is a social betrayal. It is a fear deep in black writing – a fear of selling out, of accommodating oneself to language which shapes rather than describes experience. It is an anxiety visible in Baldwin no less than in Jones. That very detachment which is arguably a prerequisite of art, the ability to see the parameters of experience and to mould contingency into form, is liable to be seen as evidence of desertion. This may account for the curious rhythms of black drama – a brittle rhetoric alternating with subtle lament, a harsh naturalism being drawn towards compassionate utterance. On the one hand there is a necessity to escape that political and social silence imposed by historical fiat, a fiat which had effectively denied blacks access to the theatre no less than to the political system. On the other hand the available language is that of the oppressor. Hence it becomes necessary simultaneously to speak and to subvert speech. The only justification for turning to the theatre lies in the conviction that this will be a drama of praxis in which to speak is to act. Bullins seems to have felt this problem less acutely than Baraka, but then his vision is essentially a darker one. He does not subscribe to the mythicising of black experience. He tends, on the contrary, to see virtue in presenting it as it is rather than as it might become once granted the grace of revolutionary conversion.

There is an exultance and a potential guilt awaiting those who suddenly find a voice after a period of suppression. As the Northern Ireland Catholic poet Seamus Heaney observed, 'Dan Jacobson [the South African writer] said to me once, "You feel bloody well guilty about writing", and there is indeed some part of me that is entirely unimpressed by the activity, that doesn't dislike it, but it's the generations, I suppose, of rural ancestors – not illiterate, but not literary.'[35]

Bullins's fascination with the pathology of the ghetto, the sensual pleasure with which he dramatises the closed avenues of thought and imagination which trap and mark his characters, suggests a writer drawn to the romantic almost as much as to naturalism. Death, decay and violence bloom in his work. His characters run their fingers down the edge of a life whose very resistant qualities are the source of its authenticity. It is the rock to which they are chained. It is equally the rock to which Bullins himself is chained and therein, perhaps, lies an element of self-indulgence. He refuses to discharge creative energy through endorsing myths of escape. His truth lies in describing and even celebrating the trap.

Despite the initial success of Lorraine Hansberry, black drama has been dominated by male writers (of the twenty-two writers represented in Woodie King and Ron Milner's *Black Drama Anthology* only two are women. In Ed Bullins's *New Plays for the Black Theatre*, two out of eleven are women). Much the same, of course, could be said of American drama as a whole but in the context of black theatre this is perhaps not unconnected with the role pressed upon male and female by the myths of black revolution (though this plainly does not apply to black poetry where women have played a central role). In a curious respect LeRoi

Jones, in his black revolutionary plays – along with such writers as
Marvin X (*The Black Bird*), Ben Caldwell (*Family Portrait*), Charles F.
Fuller Jr (*The Rise*) and Ron Milner (*Who's Got His Own*) – ironically
generated a myth which was a black counterpart of the Southern
chivalric code. The male is seen as the warrior, the female as the
irreproachable icon or a race-mingling whore. While the process of
consciousness-raising in the black community required the recuperation
of an image of black womanhood degraded by the realities of slavery and
the pressures of ghetto life, it also tended to turn her into an object. On
the one hand she is presented as tempted by the values of white society; on
the other she is a madonna of the revolution. In either role, however, she
is essentially passive, relegated to a secondary position. As the mood
began to change, however, and the urgencies of black revolt were
blunted by a growing conservatism of both right and left, a turn from
public to private issues, from racial to sexual liberation, so the tone of
black drama began to change, and, in particular, black women playwrights began to turn to feminist issues.

Not that there had been a complete dearth of black women playwrights. The poet Sonia Sanchez wrote several plays, one, *Uh, Uh; But
How Do It Free Us?*, for the New Lafayette, while Adrienne Kennedy
won an Obie in 1964 for *Funnyhouse of a Negro*. Influenced by both
Tennessee Williams and Edward Albee, whose Playwrights' Workshop
she attended, she is an inventive writer whose work was widely produced, appearing, for example, at the National Theatre in England and at
the New York Shakespeare Festival Public Theatre. But in the 1970s
issues of racial identity tended to defer to questions of sexual identity.
And the black woman playwright most associated with this change of
emphasis was Ntozake Shange. A graduate of Barnard College and the
University of Southern California, she worked in the Women's Studies
Programme at Sonoma State College. As she has explained,

> Courses designed to make women's lives and dynamics familiar to us, such
> as: Woman as Artist; Woman as Poet; Androgynous Myths in Literature;
> Women's Biography I and II; Third World Women Writers, are inextri-
> cably bound to the development of my sense of the world, myself, and
> women's language. Studying the mythology of women from antiquity to
> the present day led directly to the piece *Sahita* in which a dance hall girl is
> perceived as deity, as slut, as innocent and knowing.[36]

At the same time she attended dance classes in San Francisco:

> with dance I discovered my body more intimately than I had imagined
> possible. With the acceptance of the ethnicity of my thighs and backside,
> came a clearer understanding of my voice as a woman and as a poet . . .

> Just as Women's Studies had rooted me to an articulated female heritage and imperative, so dance . . . insisted that everything African, everything halfway colloquial, a grimace, a strut, an arched back over a yawn, was mine. I moved what was my unconscious knowledge of being in a colored woman's body to my known everydayness.[37]

She watched the dance group perform to contemporary Senegalese music or recreating the dance routines of the 1920s. She then joined Halifu Osumane's The Spirit of Dance – a group of half a dozen black women who enacted the history of black dance.

In 1974, she began to write a series of seven poems, modelled, as she explained, on Judy Grahn's *The Common Woman*, which were to examine the lives of seven women. Working with two local bands she began to perform these in local cafés and poetry centres. The full choreopoem/play was first presented at a women's bar outside Berkeley in December 1974. In a revised form it was then performed in New York, again in a bar. It then moved firstly to Henry Street, and then to the Public Theatre in June 1976 and from there to Broadway in September of the same year.

For colored girls who have considered suicide/when the rainbow is enuf has been described by Ntozake Shange as 'a young black girl's growing up, her triumphs and errors, our struggle to become all that is forbidden by our environment, all that is forfeited by our gender, all that we have forgotten'.[38] The essence of black poetry, particularly in the 1960s and early 1970s, had lain in its public nature, its performatics. It was never a closet poetry (unless, as LeRoi Jones once observed, the closet be 'as wide as God's eye'). Sonia Sanchez, Nicki Giovanni and many others performed their poetry at large public gatherings in which the symbiosis between audience and performer was a vital part of the aesthetic. Such occasions shared something of the atmosphere of the store-front church. They trembled, in other words, on the brink of ritual and of theatre. Shange's choreopoem is a natural extension of this. Poems with music and dance, forming a narrative account, become a play whose purpose is announced in the opening section by a figure called the Woman in Brown: 'sing a black girl's song / bring her out / to know herself / to know you / but sing her rhythms / carin / struggle / hard times / sing her song of life / she's been dead so long / closed in silence so long / she doesn't know the sound / of her own voice / her infinite beauty / she's half notes scattered / without rhythm / no tune / sing her sighs / sing the song of her possibilities / sing a righteous gospel / let her be born.'[39]

Through a combination of movement, lights and music Shange seeks to present a collage of experiences which are not the experiences of a single woman but of women in general, ranging from love to abortion to rape; from ecstasy to despair. The sense of racial oppression remains – a pressure to betray a sensuality which is not a value endorsed by the larger world in which they move – 'we deal with emotion too much / so why don't we go on ahead and be white then / and make everythin dry and abstract wit no rhythm and no / feeling for sheer sensual pleasure / yes let's go on / and be white / We're right in the middle of it / no use holdin out / holdin onto ourselves / lets think our way outta feelin / lets abstract ourselves some families.'[40] The brutality of the Harlem environment is delineated in a poem whose form exemplifies the constricting reality which is its subject: 'I usedta be in the world / a woman in the world / i hadda right to the world / then I moved to Harlem / for the set-up / a universe / six blocks of cruelty piled up on itself / a tunnel / closin.'[41] Race, indeed, is presented in a historical perspective, time being dissolved with a change of light and costume. But race remains only one dimension of the experience which the play engages. It is a work of patent sentimentality at times but that sentimentality is contained by the structure of the verse as it is amplified by the music. Its originality lies less in its sentiments, its celebration of an embattled feminine sensibility and experience, than in a form which manages to find a correlative for the variegated and yet unified nature of that sensibility and that experience.

If the form of the play grew out of its history, developing from the various facets of her experiences as a poet and dancer in San Francisco and New York, she came eventually to see its originality as a necessary gesture of revolt against models of drama which she saw as alien to her own situation. Thus she insisted, in 1979, that 'for far too long now afro-Americans in the theater have been duped by the same artificial aesthetics that plague our counterparts' since 'a truly European psychology / cannot function efficiently for those of us from this hemisphere'.[42] While it is by no means clear how her aesthetic was any less 'artificial' or in what way European psychology was 'inefficient' for the American sensibility, or even what the word 'efficient' means in such a context (quite apart from the obvious fact that much of the American psychiatric profession works if not efficiently then highly profitably on precisely the opposite assumption), she feels it necessary to choose to counterpose an assumed model of European art to a spontaneity of appeal: 'I am interested solely in the poetry as a moment / the emotional and aesthetic impact of a character or a line.'[43]

But her own concern with a musical theatre left her in an ambiguous position, more especially in a context in which Broadway had capitalised on the achievements of black musicians in shows such as *Eubie, Bubbling Brown Sugar, Ain't Misbehavin'* and *Mahelia,* and the clichés of black rhythm threatened to reduce her to stereotype. Her response was to insist that the fact was that 'most of us can sing and dance / and the reason that so many plays written to silence and stasis fail / is cuz most black people have some music and movement in our lives. we do sing and dance. This is a cultural reality. this is why i find the most inspiring theater among us to be in the realms of music and dance.'[44] To sacrifice music, in a general sense, to words was, in her view, to sacrifice a cultural heritage and an essential part of black life. Accordingly, she quotes approvingly the line from a song, 'here's a chance to dance our way out of our constrictions' because, as she insists, '"we ourselves" are high art. our world is honesty / and primal response'.[45]

She was also supremely conscious of the irony of working in a language which could never be made to express a selfhood warped by that language: 'i can count the number of times i have viscerally wanted to attack deform n maim the language that I waz taught to hate myself in / the language that perpetuates the notions that cause pain to every black child as he / she learns to speak of the world and the "self". yes / being an afro-American writer is something to be self-conscious abt'. Her strategy, therefore, was to disassemble that language and then reconstruct it. She set out to create 'space to literally create our own image'.[46]

Spell 7: geechee jibona quik magic trance manual for technologically stressed third world people, which was produced in 1979 by the New York Shakespeare Festival, begins with a parody of a minstrel show, the price which had formerly been paid by the black for involvement in the theatre and which, given the nature of the Broadway hits of the time, is still in some degree the price. The stage is dominated by a huge minstrel mask which is then lifted as the pains, hopes and anguish of the actor/characters are exposed. The dance element and the music provide a resonance for the main action. The 'theatre piece' ends ambiguously, however, as the mask once again descends, asserting its power as one of the characters chants: 'crackers are born with the right to be / alive / i'm making ours up right here / in yr face / and we gonna be colored and love it'.[47] The same ambiguity is apparent in *a photograph: lovers in motion*, first performed in New York in 1977 and then in revised form at the Equinox Theatre in Houston in 1979. Besides exposing the realities of a life circumscribed and infiltrated by racism, in the figure of a photographer she creates an image of the black artist who observes, who takes pride in the shaping power of art, who is deflected from ethics into aesthetics, and yet who is never immune to the forces which he or she captures.

boogie woogie landscapes (presented as a one-woman piece at the New York Shakespeare Festival's 'Poetry at the Public' series in December 1978, and in play form at the Symphony Space Theatre in June 1979) brought her back more exclusively to that concern with the plight of women, though more especially black women, which had brought her into the theatre in the first place. A lament for the forces which conspire to limit the freedom of women, to deform their sensibility and damage their spirit, it is, nonetheless, a lyrical celebration. And this is the paradox with which Ntozake Shange has saddled herself. The grace of movement, the polyphony of sound, the shaping power of poetry inevitably resist the threat of anarchy which she observes. And if her verse thereby exemplifies the struggle between disorder and order which typifies the life of the individual no less than the work of the artist, it also blunts the edge of her social critique. Shange has developed a very personal form of theatre, a long way removed from the verse drama of Maxwell Anderson, Robert Lowell and James Scheville. It is a form which does, indeed, draw on those elements of black cultural life – music, dance, publicly performed poetry – which have always been deeply rooted in the community. I doubt that she could have created such a theatre ten years earlier. It is the very distance which writers like Hansberry, Baldwin, Baraka and Bullins created between themselves and the clichés of black life, the very confidence with which they laid claim to hegemony over black experience, which enables Shange to reclaim a genuine tradition without embarrassment. Where Baraka and Baldwin had at times embraced a simplified model of black life they had done so as calculated but inherently ambiguous gestures of defiance, forging conscious symbols of revolt in which the black man became the image of revolution. In the case of Shange the revolt takes more subtle form. It lies in the urge to lay claim to the whole gamut of experience and to transform it not with brutal gestures of rebellion but with resources genuinely rooted in the feminine black sensibility. Rather than deny such qualities she places them at the very centre of her work. Her confidence in the strength and authenticity of these qualities and her authority as a writer and performer enable her to present her plays outside the black community and to accept Joe Papp as producer – a gesture which few black writers in the 1960s or early 1970s would have contemplated.

A close relationship between performer and audience, art and life, proposed as an innovative aspect of theatre in America in the 1960s, had rather more substance for a racial minority which had no need to invent notions of community. An increasing number of community drama groups addressed the problems of their communities, shaping that experience into political or cultural form. The revolutionary models of Baraka's theatre, the rituals of Barbara Ann Tear, the naturalistic undertow of Bullins's work and the lyrical choreopoems of Shange addressed experiences which had seldom penetrated the American theatre in the

414

past. Certainly, as Shange implied, when they did it was all too often in the deeply ambiguous form of the black revues and musicals of the 1920s revived in the 1970s and 80s to catch the general mood of nostalgia. And Broadway did absorb some of the energy and vitality of black theatre; what it could not do was recreate the relationship between the black writer and his community – a relationship which emerged out of shared values and experience. The theatre was, admittedly, not a popular form in the black community, any more than in the white. Indeed the achievements of black theatre in the 1960s and 70s lay, to some extent, in the degree to which it created its own audience. But, whether as conscious polemic or sensitive account of ghetto life, whether performed in community centre, on the street, in Black Arts theatres or on Broadway, such works have played their part in reflecting and defining the nature of black experience in late twentieth-century America. They have existed as social facts rather than simply cultural artifacts.

15 Gay theatre

Before examining the emergence of women's theatre as an influential movement in the 1970s and 80s it is worth recalling that another group which suffered discrimination of a legal and social kind for reasons of sexual identity was also turning to the stage – namely homosexuals. Constantly harassed and demeaned, they had suffered from prejudice in all areas of American life but, like so many other minorities, they, too, began to assert those very qualities which had once invited censure. And if Broadway and Hollywood had once been content to parody their particular sensibility then they set out, on the one hand, to subvert the stereotype, and, on the other, to expand it, to revel in self-parody, a gesture of defiance which was in itself a social act. For if they wished to lay claim to a simple human dignity, which Broadway had played its role in denying, they were unwilling to do so at the price of surrendering the very qualities which distinguished them. As a result some gay theatre is an attempt to examine the special conflicts and anxieties which afflict the gay community, and some is a celebration, a flamboyant display, a carnival, which is both an assertion of identity and a refusal to be cowed.

Where homosexuality had appeared in the American theatre it had tended to be as a convenience of plot, a carefully calculated disruption of moral and psychological norms. Thus, in Lillian Hellman's *The Children's Hour* an accusation of lesbianism is enough to dislocate the moral and social world, while in both Robert Anderson's *Tea and Sympathy* and Arthur Miller's *A View from the Bridge* a false accusation of homosexuality is sufficient to make the victim vulnerable. Certainly in the context of Cold War America in the 1950s deviancy of any kind was likely to prove dangerous. There is a special irony in this, of course, in that the homosexual has always tended to be over-represented in the theatre, though the homosexual playwright has not always chosen to address the issue directly, neither Tennessee Williams nor Edward Albee, for example, focussing on the homosexual in their published work (though Sebastian, in *Suddenly Last Summer*, is a disturbing exception, predatory and self-consuming, a writer destroyed by experience). More recently, however, sexual identity has become the basis of both subject and style.

As Charles Ludlam, founder of the 'ridiculous' theatre, has said, 'Gay people have always found a refuge in the arts, and the Ridiculous theatre is notable for admitting it. The people in it – and it is a very sophisticated theatre, culturally – never dream of hiding anything about themselves that they feel is honest and true and the best part of themselves.'[1]

And, indeed, in the 1960s the homosexual began to appear as something other than parody or plot convenience; ambiguously, at first, as in Lorraine Hansberry's *The Sign in Sidney Brustein's Window*, and then, in a more positive and dramatically compelling form, in David Rabe's *Streamers*, Michael Cristofer's *The Shadow Box* and even the musical, *A Chorus Line*.

Joe Cino, the founder of one of the more important Off-Off Broadway theatre spaces, the Caffe Cino, was himself homosexual and sponsored a number of plays by and about homosexuals. Genet and Gide gave way to native products, to Lanford Wilson's *The Madness of Lady Bright* (1964) and Robert Patrick's *The Haunted Host* (1964). Cino died in 1967, the year of Mark Crowley's *The Boys in the Band*, a play in which all but one of the characters were homosexual. In 1972 Doric Wilson, who had himself been a member of the Caffe Cino, formed TOSOS (The Other Side Of Silence), a gay theatre which survived for five years. This was followed by others, including the Glines and Medusa's Revenge, the latter a lesbian theatre group (other lesbian groups included the Lavender Cellar in Minneapolis, the Lesbian Community Theatre in East Lansing, the Washington Area Feminist Theatre, and the Whole Works, a collective in Berkeley). In the late 1970s there was an explosion of such groups, more especially and unsurprisingly in San Francisco and Los Angeles. In 1978 the Gay Theatre Alliance was created. By 1981 it had identified twenty-eight lesbian and gay theatre companies in twenty-one cities in five countries. But this was merely one aspect of a new assertiveness which in 1977 had seen the largest ever homosexual rights demonstration to be held in New York City.

For the most part the new homosexual theatre was not, however, militantly or aggressively political. It was largely a question of style which took its inspiration from the camp films of Andy Warhol and Jack Smith. In a sense what Smith and those he inspired were after was an art which could break free of moral function and even the somewhat solemn celebrations that had characterised such groups as the Living Theatre. His early film, *Flaming Creatures*, was a jumble of images and apparently concerned a group of transvestites. In describing his objective he explained that 'What I am urging is that there is not only moral space, by whose laws *Flaming Creatures* would indeed come off badly; there is also aesthetic space, the space of pleasure.'[2] There was something of this, too, in Andy Warhol's work and, indeed, Warhol did play his part in the emergence of one of those most clearly associated with what came to be known as 'ridiculous' theatre – Ronald Tavel. Tavel wrote a script for

Warhol which was subsequently staged by John Vaccaro (himself a graduate of Warhol's movies) at the Coda Gallery in July 1965. He, in turn, involved Charles Ludlam as an actor. This led to the splitting of what Tavel had called the Playhouse of the Ridiculous and, in 1967, Ludlam formed the Ridiculous Theatre Company.

Tavel's explanation for the company's name was that 'We have passed beyond the absurd; our situation is absolutely preposterous.'[3] Style became content. Thus, Ludlam insisted that, 'Psychology must be banished from the theatre',[4] while Tavel, in *Lady Godiva*, observed that 'Words are an art form. Stop using them to communicate with.'[5] Fairly clearly this stands at some remove from the kind of committed theatre which attracted LeRoi Jones and Luis Valdéz. Indeed Ludlam attacked Tavel when he created plays which appeared to have a function beyond pure theatricality. But even a deliberate flaunting of a baroque sensibility is not without its social meaning and the sudden emergence of homosexual theatre was symbolic of a refusal of consensus of which Off-Off Broadway was partly the cause and partly the result.

The first volume of gay plays appeared in 1979. It included plays by both British and American writers and, indeed, by far the most accomplished was by a British playwright, Joe Orton, who, in his brief life, had succeeded in turning camp style into an anarchic farce of genuine wit and subversive power. None of the other plays in the volume matched his, but the book was in itself evidence for a change in the American theatre which was in a sense confirmed in 1982 when Harvey Fierstein's *Torch Song Trilogy* opened on Broadway. Like so many other Broadway successes, of the 1980s, this had begun life elsewhere, its three constituent plays being produced by Ellen Stewart's La Mama Theatre in 1978 and 1979.

Torch Song Trilogy won a Tony Award, was voted best play by the Dramatists' Guild and received the Drama Desk Award. A blend of humour and pathos, which owed some of its success to its author's bravura performance in the principal role, it made no concessions to its Broadway audience beyond a carefully calculated sentimentality. Of rather more significant symbolic importance than dramatic accomplishment, the play nonetheless marked a critical stage in the emergence of gay theatre – far more so than did the award of the Pulitzer Prize in 1983 to Marsha Norman's *'night Mother* signify a similar significance for women's theatre. For the fact is that the public celebration of homosexual relationships on a Broadway stage and in front of a conservative bourgeois audience was simultaneously an assertion of rights, which had not merely been denied and declared illegal but which continued to be threatened, and an assertion of freedom – the freedom to assert, the

418

freedom to imagine, the freedom simply to be. And if it is also a play which flirts dangerously with stereotypes then perhaps that, too, was a freedom which could only be claimed after other battles had been won.

15 Women's theatre

The women's movement was no different from any of the other movements of the 1960s and 70s in its deliberate attempt to reinvent the past and, in particular, in its desire to rescue from obscurity those figures who could be seen as constituting a buried tradition. Thus, in parallel with the emergence of a number of women writers and the consolidation of the women's movement, a series of books collected together women's plays and attempted to reconstruct thereby a tradition of women dramatists beginning, in the case of America, with Mercy Warren in the late eighteenth century.

Mercy Otis Warren, probably the first woman playwright in America, once asked John Adams, in a letter, 'Though from the particular circumstances of our unhappy time, a little personal acrimony might be justifiable in your sex, must not the female character suffer . . . if she indulges her pen to paint in the darkest shades even those whom vice and venality have rendered contemptible?'[1] It was a question which addressed a principal problem for the eighteenth-century woman writer. She herself, reportedly, refused to go to the professional theatre for some years believing that it was in some way the home of a particularly virulent evil, and though John Adams set her mind at rest her question did highlight the problem which a woman writer had in reconciling her vocation as a writer with her role as woman. As Judith Barlow points out, by the mid nineteenth century such worries were dissipating with Anna Cora Mowett producing one of the best and best-known comedies of the century in the form of *Fashion* (1845) – revived by the Provincetown Players some eighty years later.

But still few women chose to write for the theatre and it was not really until the twentieth century that they began to turn in greater numbers to the stage, with the light comedies of Clare Kunner and Lucy France Pierce, and more substantial work by Alice Brown and Rachel Crothers – a case for whose significance Judith Barlow makes in her introduction to *Plays by American Women: The Early Years* (1981). Their impact remained relatively slight despite their involvement in the little theatre movement of the early years of the century, though it is worth recalling that the Provincetown Theatre alone produced the work of Susan Glaspell (now a neglected writer but one of genuine insight and power), Edna St Vincent Millay, Djuna Barnes, Edna Ferber, Neith Boyce and

Louise Bryant.

Judith Barlow argues that with the passage of the women's suffrage amendment in 1920 demand for equal rights diminished, the stage became more conservative and 'Women became increasingly the target of men's wrath.'[2] In support of this argument she invoked Sidney Howard's *The Silver Cord* (1926), George Kelly's *Craig's Wife* (1925) and Anne Nichols's *Abie's Irish Rose* (1922). But, though the myth of the male writer with a tendency to consign women characters to the margin or, worse still, to force them to act as images of repression and cruelty may be useful for polemical purposes, it is not one which is easy to substantiate. There is, to be sure, a marked tendency in the American novel, as in American myth, to do precisely this (see Leslie Fiedler's *Love and Death in the American Novel*); it is less marked in the American theatre because this is more clearly a twentieth-century phenomenon and the tradition which Fiedler identifies is largely a nineteenth-century one. It survives, of course, in the western and the gangster film, which continue to celebrate a masculine world in which women are alternately a convenience, a hindrance and a threat of lost freedom. But this is less powerfully felt in the theatre except, paradoxically, in some aspects of post-war drama. In the pastoral world that Willy Loman creates in his mind there is no real place for women precisely because this is the nineteenth-century world of his father and grandfather. The subordinate role of women is thus less a product of Miller's incapacity than of the necessities of a play which examines Willy's imperfect grasp of reality. Nonetheless, it is true that the moral crux of his plays concerns a world in which women are peripheral. Though they are in some respects all plays about the struggle to define and assert identity, about the need to perceive the self in relation to society, this is seen as a largely masculine concern. Even the apparent exception to this – *After the Fall* – presents a woman who has no inner life. Conflicting behaviour, in her case, is accommodated to a simple model of inconsistency while for the male protagonist it is a clue to moral and metaphysical truth (*Playing for Time*, which does focus directly on women, though sensitive and powerful, is an adaptation of a book by a woman – Fania Fenelon).

According to Harriet Kriegel this is equally true of Tennessee Williams, whose spiritual and emotional conflicts mirror those of a nation 'thrown into sexual hysteria' by the Hollywood glorification of sex, aroused by the eroticism of literature and advertising and 'spurred by psychoanalysis to give up sublimation and express insinctual drives'.[3] Thus his desire, as a homosexual, for some kind of revenge on women is expressed through his treatment of Alma in *Summer and Smoke* and Stella in *A Streetcar Named Desire*; his sense of repression by a smothering mother figure is embodied in the figure of Amanda Wingfield in *The Glass Menagerie*. The problem with this is that it offers a simplified model of Williams's work. The pressures are real enough but misogyny is an inadequate word to apply to their expression. The fact is that Williams's sensibility is such as to lead him, on occasion, to express his own fears, doubts and concerns through his heroines rather than through his male characters. It is simply not true to say, as does Harriet Kriegel, that Stella is a representative of the debilitated aristocracy who is destroyed by a working class male. She is in some large degree her own person, acting decisively, as her sister did not, and having the compassion and intelligence to recognise the death of a way of life without real value. She is damaged by her husband's infidelity. However, this is not presented as a casual affair but as a calculated destruction of someone who threatens his relationship with his wife. Meanwhile, Blanche is at the very centre of the play, concerned, as was Williams, with the ineluctable passage of time, the decay of physical attractiveness, the sense of a system of values slipping into the past. It is true that his heroines tend to seem outside of history, that in many ways they are unable to deflect the path of an implacable positivism. But Williams holds no brief for that positivism and was quite capable, anyway, of switching roles – in *Suddenly Last Summer*, *Sweet Bird of Youth* and *Cat on a Hot Tin Roof* giving women the strength and tenacity to dominate the action or to move on with history while the men are left behind. In other words, any attempt to characterise Williams's response to women has to deal with his own predilection for moving with ease between masculine and feminine sensibilities, associating himself with male and female characters in turn and in the process writing some of the best women's roles in modern drama.

Harriet Kriegel might seem on firmer ground with Edward Albee and LeRoi Jones. Women are, indeed, domineering in much of Albee's work. Mommy, in *The American Dream*, is simply an extreme example of a genuine misogyny which haunts his work. But again, though present and perhaps an aspect of his personal psychology, it does not provide an adequate explanation or elucidation of any of his plays. Even *The American Dream* concedes that the characters therein described are what human beings have become. It is, in other words, not an acceptance of sexual roles but a critique of them just as its account of the spiritual and physical emasculation of the characters is a plea for the substitution of real for artificial values. In *Who's Afraid of Virginia Woolf?* the woman's role as brash and vulgar bully is an act of compensation for which the play itself offers its own explanation. In *A Delicate Balance*, likewise, the subject is the failure of intimacy and communality in which, far from sexual roles being clear, their confusions are primary evidence for the collapse of form and structure.

As far as LeRoi Jones is concerned, when Harriet Kriegel says that 'the white woman is pathologically destructive' she identifies, though does not allow to impinge on the logic of her argument, the interference pattern of race which makes Jones difficult to invoke in a discussion of this kind. Indeed, it is not even a good description of *The Slave* in which the complexities of the racial and even the sexual relationships provide one of the strengths of the play. It is true that in his later work women do exist primarily as ideological markers. But the men are similarly reduced to elements in a dialectical argument in plays which are agit-prop gestures.

In other words it is not easy to identify a process of systematic misrepresentation of women in American drama nor to establish that in some way they were seen as being irrelevant to central cultural concerns. O'Neill's Mary Tyrone, Williams's Blanche Dubois, Miller's Elizabeth Proctor and Albee's Martha are precisely concerned with the failure of the world to accord to their own sense of values and to the pattern which they would wish to impose on reality. If the emphasis of male play-wrights has tended to fall on the dilemma of male protagonists, this has seldom been a debate about maleness. The issue has been a more fundamental one – the collapse of those structures which formerly seemed to imply public and private meaning, the decay of those symbols which once seemed to offer a system of clear interpretations, the disintegration even of that language with which we once attempted to describe our situation to ourselves and reach out to others whom we assumed to share both that language and that situation. But, just as black writers began to reject such a universalising of experience as an attempt to homogenise that experience, so women, too, began to wish to express their own sensibilities and define their own identities outside the terms offered by male writers. Thus, Harriet Kriegel remarks, 'While many women overcame the myths of the time [the 1950s and early 1960s] most of the heroines of modern drama do not. Our interest in them lies in their desire to overcome limitations which seem endemic to being born female.' But, writing in 1975, she observed that 'with the rise of the new feminism new voices began to make themselves heard in the theater. Women have come to insist on the right to speak for themselves and to create their own portraits. New models are demanded.'[4]

In 1558, John Knox published *The Monstrous Regiment of Women*, an attack on women which was offered as an indirect assault on the power of Queen Elizabeth I. Over four hundred years later a feminist group in England called itself The Monstrous Regiment. It was a deliberate attempt to challenge male arrogance by engaging the past and creating the future. Among the groups listed in *The New Women's Survival Catalog*, published in New York in 1973, were such groups as It's All Right to be Women and Womansong Theatre; they were theatres, in other words, that openly announced their position. Theirs was a movement which attempted not so much to project a positive image of women, in the sense of developing a counter myth, as to stress a freedom of action and imagination which they believed to have been too often denied in the theatre.

It is true that in the absence of women writers there were men – most notably Ibsen and Shaw – who took entirely seriously the necessity for women to define their own experience and to escape the constrictions of social life as defined by law and custom, but there were equally those who, for reasons of personal psychology or social orthodoxy, saw women in terms of a series of entrapping clichés – the pure mother, the corrupting seductress, the threatening emasculator. These had certainly been the stock in trade of nineteenth-century melodrama. They seemed equally a central resource of Strindberg. But whatever the force of his misogyny he granted women an autonomy which went beyond that of his contemporaries, even Ibsen. It was an autonomy which he found threatening; the male role was menaced, as was his own sanity. But he conceded a force to the feminine sensibility which few other dramatists were prepared to acknowledge. For Bernard Shaw, Strindberg's *The Creditors* was 'the terrible play with which Strindberg wreaked the revenge of the male for *A Doll's House* . . . it is the man who is the victim of domesticity, and the woman who is the tyrant and soul destroyer. Thus *A Doll's House* did not dispose of the question: it only brought on the stage the endless recrimination of idealistic marriage.'[5] But, for all this, Strindberg saw the woman as an equal to man at least in her capacity to wage this relentless battle and to deploy intellectual as well as emotional powers.

For Harriet Kriegel, after Shaw the rational woman all but disappears from drama while women are dealt with, if at all, usually as predators bordering on caricature. And, in her view, American drama provides an apt example of this. It is a view which is not easy to sustain. If the stereotype persists in O'Neill's work – in, for example, *Anna Christie* – then this was often a conscious element, an attempt to reproduce the reductive power of modern existence. Indeed, he has described the extent to which he saw Anna's weakness, in that play, her character and language, as a product of a system which gave her no more space for personal freedom than it gave the male Yank, in *The Hairy Ape*: 'with dumb people of her sort, unable to voice strong, strange feelings, the emotions can find outlet only through the language and gestures of the heroics in the novels and movies they are familiar with – that is, that in moments of great stress life copies melodrama'.[6]

O'Neill was vitally alive to the achievements of the European theatre seeing Nazimova's *Hedda Gabler* ten times and being powerfully drawn to Strindberg. But, despite his professed admiration for the latter, it does little justice to see him merely as Strindberg's heir in his portraits of women, as Harriet Kriegel suggests, for if they are seen as destructive in their parental influence, their fragility and their emotional confusions, if they dominate and possess men and urge them to act against their own best interests, then much the same could be said of men. They are mutual victims. It is true that in *Strange Interlude* the woman's reproductive capacity is made the agent of irony but this irony is not generated by any specifically feminine cruelty or callousness. On the contrary, such passion as occurs in the play is viewed deeply ambiguously and the woman is as much an expression of continuity, the race's will to survive, as she is of a sheer determinism – and both qualities equally attach to men. He did admittedly derive some rather strange ideas about women from Schopenhauer – in particular seeing the menopause as the effective end of personal meaning as well as of biological purpose, but, for the most part, he cannot be indicted for providing merely a travesty of women. The mechanical application of the Electra myth in *Mourning Becomes Electra* is balanced by an equally mechanical application of the Oedipus myth. If the mother in *Long Day's Journey Into Night* has been broken by events then so, too, have the other members of the family. If the women in *The Iceman Cometh* are simple caricatures, golden-hearted whores, then the male characters are no less stereotyped. Indeed they have all consciously retreated to a simplistic model of character and action as a primary defence against a knowledge of their own failure.

Indeed, a far more convincing case could be made out for a woman playwright producing female characters who are cruel and emasculating, which is perhaps why Harriet Kriegel's essay, which introduces *Women in Drama*, contains no reference to Lillian Hellman or Lorraine Hansberry and also why, while speaking of Susan Glaspell's play *Trifles*, she makes no reference to *The Outside*, in which for much of the play men represent a persistent life force (albeit giving way to an association of female characters with continuity), or to *The Verge*, in which a woman's desire to rebel against her roles as wife and mother transforms her into a destroyer. The fact is that it is difficult quite so casually to assign attitudes to male and female playwrights simply on the basis of their sex.

And the work of Ntozake Shange highlights the extent to which feminists acknowledged a parallel between their own concerns and those voiced by generations of black activists, for the women's movement drew attention to the degree to which women, no less than blacks, were encysted in myth (Betty Friedan's *The Feminine Mystique* appeared as early as 1963 while the National Women's Political Caucus was formed in July 1971). Communal action, which had been invoked in an attempt to release the black American not only from legal constraints but also from the hardly less destructive limitations imposed by convention, was now invoked to release women from their status as home-makers, sexual objects, models of passivity. For much of history, of course, women had been no less disenfranchised than blacks, the victims of history rather than its shapers. They, too, were seen as manifesting a sensibility – intuitive, sensual, spontaneous – which made them ill-fitted for the task of government. Both blacks and women were seen in some sense as playing the id to the (white) man's ego.

Ellen Moers begins her book *Literary Women* with a quotation from Emerson: 'The poet is representative. She stands among partial women for the complete woman . . . The young woman reveres women of genius, because, to speak truly, they are more herself than she is . . . all women live by truth and stand in need of expression.'[7] It is in part this role to which some of today's women writers lay claim. Like the black writers of the 1960s and early 1970s, they become exemplary figures. And the women's movement did borrow consciously from the civil rights movement. The very word 'sexism' was derived from 'racism'. And this was, indeed, a connection made early. It was Margaret Fuller who wrote, 'As the friend of the negro assumes that one man cannot by right hold another in bondage, so should the friend of Woman . . . assume that Man cannot by right lay even well-meant restrictions on Woman. If the negro be a soul, or the woman be a soul, to one Master only are they accountable.'[8] Or, in the words of Elizabeth Cody Stanton, daughter of the nineteenth-century Congressman, and quoted in a feminist play of the 1970s, 'The custom of calling women Mrs. John This and Mrs. Tom That, and colored men Sambo and Zip-coon, is founded on the principle that white men are the lords of all.'[9]

A necessary part of all revolutions consists in the identification of new heroes (or heroines) and an assertion that they, in a sense, contain the essence of those qualities so long suppressed in the group as a whole. It was this impulse which created contemporary black historiography and the critical recovery of those writers previously disregarded or accommodated to an alien tradition. A second stage followed naturally from this, with the publication of material from the past and present, evidence on the one hand that a tradition does exist, no matter how disregarded, and on the other that there are those who now feel able to speak – hence the publication of Harriet Kriegel's *Women in Drama*, Honor Moore's *The New Women's Theatre* and Julia Miles's *The Women's Project*. The English playwright Michelene Wandor, in her book about women in theatre, *Understudies*, has suggested that in America feminism has been far less a part of radical politics than it has in Europe. As a consequence, relatively few of the plays written by American women have been consciously concerned with changing women's role in society. Some of them, indeed, like the works of Lillian Hellman and Lorraine Hansberry, have shown no particular concern with examining a specifically feminine sensibility. But, more recently, there has clearly been a very conscious attempt to explore precisely this area and if it produces an analysis which is not primarily radical in a political sense, or even in a theatrical sense, it does mark a fundamental break with the masculine-oriented history of American drama.

The first political theatre group to take a feminist stance was Anselma Dell'Ollio's New Feminist Repertory in New York. This was followed in the 1970s by a number of other groups, including Womanspace Theatre and Interart Theatre in New York, the Washington Area Feminist Theatre and Circle of the Witch in Minneapolis. Feminist drama of one kind or another then began to appear at the Public Theatre, always sensitive to new directions and energies in the theatre, and on Broadway itself. As indicated above, by no means all the plays generated by this theatre were militantly feminist, though Lavonne Mueller's *Killing on the Last Line*, written for the American Place Theatre and given a full production in 1980, was a protest against the conditions in which women are required to work (being set in a nuclear reactor parts factory in which low wages are combined with a considerable health risk). However, such works clearly offered a new sense of dignity and selfhood to those involved in this theatre. As Paula Wagner remarked, 'I feel, acting certain roles, that I have to deny parts of myself . . . like my intelligence. *Out of Our Father's House* allowed me to use all of myself as an actress – my mind, my talent, my feelings.'[10]

Mary Ellman, in her book *Thinking About Women* (1968), observed that 'for women writers, as for the Negro, what others have said bears down on whatever they can say themselves'.[11] It is this which creates the necessity to speak as it does the need to re-examine the past. It is not that this literature creates a shift in sensibility but that a shift in sensibility and consciousness creates the necessity for this literature. And in a sense it is possible to see the social turmoil of the 1960s, the determined experimentalism of much of the writing of the period, the eclecticism, the heterogeneity of social and artistic life, as symptoms of anxiety and of a changing perception of personal and public relations. As Virginia Woolf observed in her essay, 'Mr Bennett and Mr Brown' (1924):

> All human relations have shifted . . . and when human relations change
> there is at the same time a change in religion, conduct, politics, and
> literature . . . At the present moment we are suffering not from decay,
> but from having no code of manners which writers and readers accept as a
> prelude to the more exciting intercourse of friendship . . . signs of this are
> everywhere apparent. Grammar is violated; syntax disintegrated . . . The
> sincerity (of modern writers) is desperate, and their courage tremendous;
> it is only that they do not know which to use, a fork or their fingers.[12]

For a generation of committed individuals this doubt was crucial. Even
the act of writing was ambiguous and language was at the very heart
of that ambiguity. The violation of grammar was, indeed, a correlative
of other acts of violation. Feminist art responded to a shift in definitions
of human relations even as it wished to precipitate such a shift. Its
sincerity is real enough, if a touch desperate, and it is no less subject to the
general sense of insecurity than is the work of male writers. The ultimate
objective remains that dangerous friendship to which Virginia Woolf
refers, but it is to be an objective which can be secured only after the social
and moral flux has subsided a little when perhaps it will be clearer
whether fork or fingers will prevail.

In an essay on 'American Fiction' Virginia Woolf once compared the
plight of women writers to that of Americans, remarking that

> one is reminded constantly of the attitude of another race, till lately subject
> and still galled by the memory of its chains. Women writers have to meet
> many of the same problems that beset Americans. They too are conscious
> of their own peculiarities as a sex; apt to suspect insolence, quick to avenge
> grievances, eager to shape an art of their own. In both cases all kinds of
> consciousness – consciousness of self, of race, of sex, of civilization – which
> have nothing to do with art, have got between them and the paper.[13]

But this she regarded as inevitable, an element entering women's writing
'which is entirely absent from a man's, unless, indeed, he happens to be a
working man, a negro, or one who for some reason is conscious of
disability'.[14] And just as the black writer has to struggle with and yet in
some way work within a language which is not merely alien but an
expression of the repressive forces against which he is struggling, so the
woman writer, according to Virginia Woolf, has to face the fact that 'the
very form of the sentence does not fit her' because 'it is a sentence made
by man; it is too loose, too heavy, too pompous for a woman's use'. The
desire to reshape language is an aspect of women's desire, identified by
Virginia Woolf in 1929 but ironically still being asserted in the 1970s, to
'explore their own sex, to write of women as women have never been

written of before; for of course, until very lately, women in literature were the creation of men'. As she asked, in *A Room of One's Own* (1929), 'Suppose, for instance . . . that men were only represented in literature as the lovers of women, and were never the friends of men, soldiers, thinkers, dreamers; how few parts in the plays of Shakespeare could be allotted to them.'[15] The point, of course, is only in part a literary one. It is a comment on the woman's role in society no less than in art but there is a logical connection between the two worlds. This connection is the justification for women's theatre.

The revolt, when it came, was in part strident, as the black revolt had been, and it was also a battle fought partially on a historical battleground. It is, after all, impossible to gain control over the present unless some retrospective claim can be staked to the past. As a result, women's role in history was re-examined; a search was instituted for those unsung heroines of the past who could be redeemed to constitute a recognisable tradition to which the contemporary woman could relate (see Ellen Moers's *Literary Women: The Great Writers*, and Louise Bernilow *The World Split Open: Four Centuries of Women Poets in England and America 1552–1950*). It is for this reason that in her introduction to a collection of plays entitled *Women's Theatre*, published in 1977, Honor Moore begins with a survey of women in the theatre. It is necessarily a brief introduction, for the truth is that, with certain exceptions – Aphra Benn's work in the late seventeenth century being one such – women have indeed played remarkably little role in the development of drama. It is not entirely easy to see why this should be so, at least in so far as the twentieth century is concerned. The association between theatre and immorality, which had some real basis in the theatre of antiquity and which continued to lend a certain notoriety to the acting profession, was doubtless a factor in keeping women away prior to this time but arguments for their relative absence in the modern theatre are largely unconvincing. Honor Moore suggests that the problem lies in the communal nature of theatre which requires that the writer should involve him or herself with the production process, a cameraderie which has proved hostile to women. Hence, she argues that 'Male exclusion of women from this cameraderie, perhaps more than any other single factor, has been responsible for the lack of a female tradition in playwriting similar to that which exists in both fiction and poetry.'[16] But not merely is this cameraderie not a purely male phenomenon but women have played a vital role in the emergence of theatre in America in its modern form. One of the founders of the Provincetown Theatre and the Washington Square Players, from which the modern American theatre was born, was a woman – Susan Glaspell – and she was both an accomplished writer and actress and a forceful proponent of the new theatre. The whole Federal Theatre, fraught with problems of an aesthetic and political kind, was overseen by a woman – Hallie Flanagan – while one of those responsible for the blossoming of the Off-Broadway movement of the 1960s was Ellen Stewart. Nancy Fischandler similarly played an important role in the emergence of the regional theatre as the founder of Arena Stage in Washington. Indeed women were to be found where the battles were most brutal. But they were less visible as writers. Perhaps it is true that Susan Glaspell to some degree subordinated her own talents to those of her less able, though more visionary husband, though there is little evidence for this, but Lillian Hellman has suggested that it was actually Dashiell Hammett who urged her to write for the theatre and helped to shape her work (much the same could be said of George Eliot's encouragement by her husband in the nineteenth century). Arguments for a feminine sensibility being ill-suited to a public art thus seem unconvincing, though writers who have made their name in the novel have admittedly not always found it easy to switch to the theatre (namely Doris Lessing and Iris Murdoch). On the other hand the demands of domesticity may prove incapacitating, as the English dramatist Pam Gems has suggested. Virginia Woolf, for example, insisted that 'Fiction was, as fiction is, the easiest thing for a woman to write' because it 'is the least concentrated form of art. A novel can be taken up or put down more easily than a play or a poem.'[17] It is a dubious statement. Possibly the suggestion that women had begun to claim their rights while the novel itself was still a comparatively new and open genre may go some way towards explaining the attraction of that form but it remains unconvincing. Perhaps the most that can be said is that it is a self-perpetuating problem. And, though with the emergence of the women's movement a number of new writers have appeared, a report still found that in the period 1969–75 only 7 per cent of playwrights and 6 per cent of directors in funded non-profit theatres in America were women. And according to Julia Miles, who worked at the American Place Theatre from 1964 to 1978, only 10 per cent of scripts submitted were by women.

When the relative absence of women playwrights was raised as an issue by *The New York Times* in 1973 a number of explanations were offered. For Gretchen Cryer, author of the book and lyrics for *The Last Sweet Days of Isaac*, it was a problem of family responsibility: 'Who knows how many potential playwrights there may be out there fixing bag lunches for their children who would be attempting to write their plays and get them on, were it not for the fact that they would guiltily consider their efforts self-indulgent folly.'[18] Lillian Hellman explained that she had left the theatre because 'the fun ran out and the raw-money stuff came in'. Adrienne Kennedy suggested that playwriting is 'an arena of glory and power like bullfighting, like boxing' which had necessitated, in her own case, a divorce in order to dedicate herself to her work. The problem, as she saw it, was that 'We feel children tugging at our skirts or blue jeans or whatever, we want a man to protect us.' Indeed, she came to feel that 'that long dedication of art, the perfecting of the skill and the craft, the long listening to the one voice of the muse is unnatural to a woman'.[19] Like Rosalyn Drexler's observation that 'The female play is open and passive', however, this seems something less than persuasive.

The American theatre has, of course, generated women playwrights. As Honor Moore points out, one of the longest-running plays in American theatrical history, *Abie's Irish Rose*, was by Anne Nichols, while Zona Gale won a Pulitzer Prize in 1921 for her adaptation of her own novel *Miss Lulu Bett*, and Zoë Akins another, in 1935, for her adaptation of Edith Wharton's *The Old Maid*. And it is true that Gertrude Stein also wrote for the theatre, some of her theories, indeed, being invoked by Richard Foreman and others in the 1970s. But it is a fragile tradition and the addition, beyond Susan Glaspell and Lillian Hellman, of Carson McCullers does little to make it seem less so. But things began to change with the Off-Broadway movement of the 1960s and the increasing importance of black theatre. Figures like Adrienne Kennedy and Maria Fornes emerged, while dance – presided over by such figures as Martha Graham and Ann Halprin – no longer seemed quite so tangential to theatre. And then, in the middle and late 1970s, a more conscious effort was made not merely to encourage work by women playwrights but to develop a theatre which, unlike the work of Hellman or, indeed, for the most part, Glaspell or McCullers, would attempt to examine the feminine sensibility, to perceive and address the specific situation and emotional realities of women.

In 1978, Julia Miles established the Women's Project at the American Place Theatre with the aid of an $ 80,000 grant from the Ford Foundation. This consisted of rehearsed readings, developmental work and studio productions, two of the plays in the second series going on to full productions at the American Place. In the words of one woman playwright, 'The Women's Project gives to me and to all writers and directors a place to raise their voices *without* apology, not to be heard *above* anyone else, but to be heard! And I think that more and more, with the time and encouragement the Project offers, they will learn to use those voices to explore and evangelize the beautiful and the true, and even the bestial visions to which the feminine principle is heir.'[20]

However, women writers had been staking out their own territory throughout the 1970s and, indeed, in the late 1960s, and in this work

431

certain anxieties seem to have come to the surface. Alice Childress's *Mojo: A Black Love Story* (1971), Honor Moore's *Mourning Pictures* (1974), Anne Burr's *Mert and Phil*, Phyllis Purscell's *Separate Ceremonies* and Joan Schenkar's *Signs of Life* are all concerned in part with cancer. Cancer also occurs in Corinne Jacker's *Bits and Pieces*, though here it is the man who suffers, the play concentrating on the plight of the woman left behind, though the work was inspired by what she thought to be her own impending death. As another character explains, her response to the death is 'a little sense of panic' because 'I can't remember if I have a life outside of Dad's sickness.'[21] Though another observes that 'There is more freedom on this side of death',[22] there is a sense that death precipitates a crisis in which questions of freedom as well as mortality become central. Here we seem to be moving into an area in which basic feminine insecurities and anxieties emerge. Not in any way militantly feminist, such plays probe into experiences in which the subject is not language but the conventionalised responses which it is designed to reinforce. It is a communal theatre not in the degree to which it wishes to shape the nature of women's responses but to the extent that, in the communality of theatre, it recreates the condition of mutuality which is born out of a shared experience and invoked as a possible response to that experience.

These plays are not necessarily innovatory in technique or subject. Indeed, a number of the writers now claimed for the feminist theatre had in fact been around for some time and their work bore the marks of this. They did, however, indicate a shift of emphasis from the early work of a writer like Alice Childress, for example.

Alice Childress was born in North Carolina but brought up in Harlem. She was involved in theatre from an early age and for ten years was an actress, writer and director with the American Negro Theatre, performing in *Anna Lucasta*. In 1952, her music revue, *Gold Through the Trees*, became the first play by a black woman to receive a professional production on the American stage while, in 1955, her *Trouble in Mind* was awarded an Obie, the first such award going to a woman playwright.

In *Mojo* she presents a slight and sentimental drama in which a black man and his ex-wife are reunited as she learns that she has cancer. In *Wedding Band* (1972–3), a melodrama of inter-racial love which could have been written at any time in the previous fifty years, the tragic love of a black woman and a poor white man ends with his convenient death from influenza. But, then, Alice Childress refused to bow to the new orthodoxies of black art. Indeed, she remained acutely aware that art itself risks distorting reality. In *Wine in the Wilderness*, first presented on television in 1969, she creates a simple allegory in which an artist sets out to paint a triptych called *Wine in the Wilderness* – the first component showing an innocent girl, the second the Queen of the Universe and the third, a 'messed up chick'. A young black woman, dispossessed by riots, is, unbeknown to her, recruited to sit for the final panel of the triptych. In fact her name is Tomorrow and she represents the reality of black womanhood. Her vitality refuses to shape itself to serve the purposes of black dogmatists or artists any more than of the white world. 'If a black somebody is in a history book, or printed on a pitcher, or drawed on a paintin' . . . or if they're a statue . . . dead, and outa the way, and can't talk back', she observes to the black artist, 'then you dig 'em and fulla so much a damn admiration and talk 'bout "our" history. But when you run into us livin' and breathin' ones, with the life's blood still pumpin' through us . . . then you comin' on 'bout how we ain't never together.'[23] She accuses him of ignoring the contribution of those he attacks as assimilationists and who created the basis for his freedom; of talking in abstractions and dictating the nature of black individuality: 'If my hair is straight, or if it's natural, or if I wear a wig, or take it off . . . that's all right . . . They're just . . . Accessories . . . The real thing is takin's place on the inside . . . that's where the action is.'[24] As a result of her complaint the artist redesigns his triptych to place her at the centre: 'Look at Tomorrow. She came through the biggest riot of all . . . somethin' called "slavery", and she's even comin' through the "now" scene, folks laughin' at her, even her own folks laughin' at her. And look *how* . . . with her head high like she's poppin' her fingers at the world.'[25] Childress's humanism is evident, and her resistance to ruling political and cultural orthodoxies apparent. Her drama, however, operates on a simple level. Allegory is signalled, conflicts are overt, characters simple and vivid. Though her plays have been produced at the Public Theatre, on Broadway and on television, her audience, like her material, is still, in effect, the black community. Her plays place the woman at the heart of experience less out of an assertive feminism than because this was the experience which she knew and which she chose to dramatise, in *Wine and the Wilderness* consciously resisting the reduction of woman to a symbol in the revolutionary battle, though thereby, ironically, con- structing a symbol of resistance herself.

Corinne Jacker began writing *Bits and Pieces* believing herself to have a terminal disease. It was thus to be a contemplation of mortality and desertion – the desertion of those who remain alive by those who die. Like several other of the new women playwrights she is a graduate in theatre studies (Joanne Russ and Joanna Halpert Kraus are two others).

Her play, which, like her *Harry Outside*, won an Obie award when performed at the Manhattan Theatre Club, is based on the Egyptian Osiris myth. Osiris is filleted by his brother Seth and pieces of his body scattered around the world. His wife, Isis, locates these and buries them. In Corinne Jacker's play Philip, husband to Iris, dies and his donated organs are distributed to those who need them. His wife, unable to come to terms with the fact of his death, elicits a list of those who have received the various component parts of her husband and visits them. Curiously, from this somewhat ludicrous premise Miss Jacker creates a play that is not without its strengths. Though the process of the play seems to be a somewhat elaborate means of arriving at the conviction that life must go on, that from death comes life, it is an articulate work in which the construction mirrors the protagonist's attempt to pull the threads of her life together. Past and present mingle. The dead man remains a present actor in her life, a reality to which she has to adjust. He is in a sense a ghost which has to be laid (and the pun seems to be a conscious one). The burial of the past is more difficult not merely because he has disobligingly disassembled himself but because of the depth of her feeling. Her survival is signalled when she chooses to spend the anniversary of his birthday constructing a bookcase.

Corinne Jacker has said that 'It seems to me that what women are doing now is letting their own sensibilities come through – you don't write like a man any more, you write like yourself . . . I want to be able to . . . write like a woman, but I don't write only for women.'[26]

The fear of being alone seems to link many of these plays as though death were some ultimate act of personal desertion. It dominates the final moments of *Wedding Band*, provides the generative action of *Bits and Pieces*, and echoes through Honor Moore's *Mourning Pictures*, first produced at the Lenox Arts Centre and then moved to the Lyceum Theatre on Broadway in November 1974. Inspired by her own mother's death from cancer, it is a contemplation of death and dying. Originally to have been a book of poems, it bears the marks of this, much of it being set in verse form, with a series of interpolated songs which accompany and comment on the action – resonating the sense of loss which lies at the heart of the piece: 'What will she leave me / Except alone by myself? / No one to have the final word!'[27] The emotional pressure of the play, which is at times genuinely moving, is contained in part by the verse form and in part by a structure which works by a series of controlled juxtapositions, both within and between scenes, as well as by the songs which offer a perspective that locates the personal emotion in a wider context. The play ostensibly focusses on the dying woman; in fact it is concerned with the struggle of the living to face the evidence of their own mortality.

434

The relationship of mother and daughter is equally at the centre of Ursula Molinaru's *Breakfast Past Noon*, which consists of two intercut and juxtaposed monologues that expose the hostilities, rivalries and cruelties of such a relationship – the play ending with the two strangling one another, the hostility of their thoughts being translated into action. A bitter piece, the play probes the tensions deriving from a generational gap. A slight work, like several in the anthology *New Women's Theatre*, it is at best a sketch whose method and subject implies the need to penetrate beyond the conventions of role.

And in so far as sexual stereotypes are in large part an inheritance from a real and fictional past that past becomes a necessary subject of concern. So it is that in *Signs of Life* Joan Schenkar turns to that past in order to examine the distortions of the feminine sensibility which have resulted from social pressure. Joan Schenkar was by no means new to theatre when her play received a studio production at the American Place Theatre in 1979. She had been a playwright in residence for Joseph Chaikin's experimental Writers' Project and had had her work performed at the Public Theatre, the WPA Theatre, La Mama and many others.

Signs of Life is not a realistic play. Its characters include Henry and Alice James, Alice's real companion, Katherine Loring, Dr Simon Sloper, a character from Henry James's *Washington Square*, Jane Merrill, a female version of the elephant man, and P.T. Barnum. These characters combine in a play in which the distortions of the woman's social position are given form in the physically grotesque Elephant Woman and the mentally damaged Alice James. Both are presented as being victims of the play's male characters who capitalise on them – exhibiting one in a museum for freaks and using the other as the source of material for art – itself, of course, a Jamesian moral dilemma, though curiously a dilemma which her version of James is not himself permitted to perceive. And it is, perhaps, the assumptions which Joan Shenkar makes about the causes of Alice James's mental state and her brother's reaction to it which are the source of a certain disquiet. The damage to her mental health is almost wholly ascribed to the male society of the James household into which she is born, while James himself, in reality supremely conscious of the moral charge generated by an art derived from life (as shown, for example, in *The Aspern Papers*), is made insensitive to the issue. The accusation, of course, is that what he perceives in his art he is blind to in life. Thus he creates women who are free in his art but denies them freedom in the world which he chooses to endorse with his authority as head of the house and public figure. It is a paradox, or simply a contradiction, which is not, however, examined.

The chief accusation is that in the context of the world which she summons up the woman is an object – manipulated by the writer, displayed by the showman, dissected by the doctor. Her own needs are never examined or considered. She serves the purposes of others, the writer commandeering her experience, the showman her suffering and the doctor her body. Henry James values her insights only in so far as he can transform and use them. Her own attempts to write, to express the obscenities, even, of the world of which she is a victim, are buried. The Elephant Woman's scream has to be turned to a smile to please the paying customers. In this play to be a woman is, in a sense, already to be a freak, a victim. Women are shown as imprisoned in gilded cages in the form of tastefully designed bedrooms. They are, as Barnum announces the Elephant Woman to be, 'gen-u-wine, home grown, American freak[s]'.[28] Even their sexuality is not theirs to control. The sinister Dr Simon Sloper probes the sexual organs of both the Elephant Woman and Alice James, anxious to cut into their flesh, to use them for his own experiments – an image of the 'use' to which they were put by a system which saw them as simple chattels. Indeed his Uterine Guillotine, used to remove women's sexual organs, is, Joan Schenkar tells us in a note, based on an actual device perfected by an American doctor who 'performed' countless clitoridectomies and reportedly referred to himself as 'the architect of the vagina'. And Schenkar places the word 'performed' in quotation marks because performance and theatre are central terms in the play itself. Not merely is the theatricality itself deliberately foregrounded in a play whose episodic structure and subtle harmonics are of primary importance, but there is a sense in which she is concerned with male/female relations as a matter of role-playing, of social theatre. In this sense she is not primarily interested in creating carefully individualised characters. In a note to the actors, indeed, she suggests:

> It might be helpful to imagine the characters in this play as each an aspect of a *shared* consciousness, rather than each an exponent of a *separate* consciousness. They do have in common certain prejudices and inclinations which make even the most opposed characters in this play seem to share – however stealthily – a kind of identity. The effect this identity (or these identities) should have on the audience is a constant and nervous recollection of familiarity; a shudder of recognition in the most incongruous places. The actors must do everything possible to increase the audience's discomfort in this respect.[29]

Alice James and the Elephant Woman are presented as living out their lives in a world created by men who throughout the play repeatedly drink toasts to 'the ladies' while sustaining a system which warps and destroys them and which denies them the right to speak for themselves.

The former has her journal destroyed; the latter is warned against giving voice to her inner fears and despairs for fear that it will offend her audience. Now, however, in this play, they are contained by a fiction created by a woman, and this is plainly presented as a crucial stage in their liberation. The past has to be exposed and reclaimed both at the level of history and fiction. The theatre, which engages both, thus becomes a homeopathic device.

The women's plays gathered together in the principal collections thus far published are intensely concerned with family relationships. So, too, of course, were O'Neill's and Miller's – indeed almost excessively so. But, unsurprisingly, here it is the women who have moved to centre stage, with the emphasis falling on the relationship between daughter and father (Phyllis Purscell's *Separate Ceremonies* and Myrna Lamb's *I Lost a Pair of Gloves Yesterday*), or mother and daughter (Rose Leiman Goldenberg's *Letters Home*, Honor Moore's *Mourning Pictures* and Ursula Molinaru's *Breakfast Past Noon*). Repeatedly the pressure which precipitates self-examination is the death of a relative, and cancer again provides the starting-point for both *I Lost a Pair of Gloves Yesterday* and *Letters Home*. On one level this is perhaps a case of writers who are looking for a dramatic charge associated with an extreme situation. But beyond this it seems to reach down to a level of profound anxiety – to touch on an experience of abandonment that is both desired and feared. For if a buried theme of many recent plays by women has been the emergence of the female self into full possession of identity, a realisation of an autonomy denied equally by social fiat and conditioned psychology, a necessary precondition for this lies in a rejection of the determining authority of parent and husband. All too often it has been the literal death of these authority figures which has precipitated this realisation, so that the severing of the bond has been the painful route to an autonomy both longed for and shunned. Thus, while there is an element of homage in the work of such authors as Myrna Lamb and Honor Moore, whose ostensible subject is the death of a parent, their underlying concern is with the painful construction of an identity which can function in the world without reference to others. Indeed, there is a line in Phyllis Purscell's *Separate Ceremonies* (1979) which, though given to a male character, expresses precisely this double feeling of betrayal and liberation: 'They die on you – leave you to go it alone – to figure it out for yourself.'[30]

Few of these plays are strident demands for social or political rights. Their concern is antecedent to that. It is to come to terms with the emotional truths of daily existence, to acknowledge the emotive power and centrality of family relationships and to address the question of survival, independence of mind and action within that context. In Tina Hawes's *Birth and After Birth* (1974) the threat is constituted by a child—presented as a grotesque played by an adult actor. But in whatever form such pressures are central.

In March 1983, Marsha Norman's second play, *'night, Mother*, reached Broadway. It had been given its first reading by the Circle Repertory Company in New York in 1981 and was first produced the following year by the American Repertory Theatre in Cambridge, Massachusetts. Her first play, *Getting On*, originally produced at the Actors' Theatre of Louisville, before moving to the Mark Taper Forum in Los Angeles and the Theater des Lys in New York, had been voted Best New Play Produced in the Regional Theatre in 1978; *'night, Mother* won the Pulitzer Prize for 1983, an award which, together with *The New York Times*'s celebration of the play as symbolising a major breakthrough for women in the theatre, provoked an immediate and acerbic debate.

'night, Mother is concerned with the desperate attempt by Thelma Cates to prevent her daughter's suicide. Emotionally unstable for years, Jessie Cates now discovers a rare serenity as she faces the failure of her life and calmly outlines the details of her impending death to an increasingly frantic mother. The play's tension lies in Jessie's evident need to pass through the door of her bedroom, where her revolver awaits, and her mother's equally evident need to prevent this. Its dramatic resolution lies in the moment when the mother can finally release her daughter to the peace which she seeks, the moment when, for virtually the first time, they are able to face one another with honesty and clear an emotional space in which love, for a brief and ironic moment, can find expression.

The disquiet expressed by some of those who worked in the women's movement was a product in part of the play itself and in part of its ready assimilation by commercial theatre and the whole apparatus of the Establishment. Thus the playwright Elizabeth Wray deplored Marsha Norman's co-option by Broadway while Colette Brooks, former Associate Artistic Director of Interart Theatre, denounced *The New York Times* for elevating a relatively undistinguished work whose celebration of the loser she saw as closing off the possibility of genuine analysis. To canonise such work, she felt, was to suppress alternative visions. The playwright and critic Karen Malpede argued that the play's theme pandered to those who believe that women, left to their own devices, are merely self-destructive and neurotic, while Roberta Sklar, writer and director, saw *'night, Mother* as being accommodated to a male tradition of playwrighting, a tradition which concentrated on the isolated self rather than the strength born out of communal action and creativity of the kind which she saw as evidenced in theatres such as At the Foot of the

Mountain, the Women's Experimental Theatre, New Cycles Theatre, Spiderwoman and Split Britches.

Meanwhile, others addressed the question of whether the play's success could really be said to mark a breakthrough for women writers. Anne Cattaneo, dramaturg and translator, was impressed by the number of women playwrights both on and Off-Broadway but the playwright Joan Schenkar pointed out that the Playwrights' Committee in New York had admitted thirty-eight men but only eight women to membership, while Julia Miles, writing of the New York theatre as she found it in June 1983, could point to only one play by a woman on Broadway and two Off-Broadway (both by the English playwright Caryl Churchill).

The responses are less interesting for what they say about Norman's play, which is alternately traduced or ignored, than for the fact that in the 1980s it should still be the cause of a debate of this kind, that it should still call forth a celebration of ancestors, an assault on the assumptions of drama reviewers and the values of commercial theatre and a debate about the role and responsibility of the woman writer. In terms of this debate women's theatre found itself in the position that the black theatre had found itself in twenty years earlier. The writer is charged with an exemplary role which she may or may not wish to embrace or with which she may wish to quarrel. Conventional success is treated with suspicion because it smacks of betrayal. Individual achievement is counterposed to group creativity, as though the act of aesthetic abstraction were an equivalent of social desertion. Male praise of women's theatre tends to be seen as evidence of a desire to patronise, divert or co-opt. But what may appear as paranoia has its own historiography. For whatever cause, women have found it difficult to create sufficient space within the American theatre for their own concerns. Women characters have tended to be voiced by their male creators. Women have not been faced, in the theatre, with images commensurate with their own feelings, needs and social aspirations. It is not that the theatre is charged with fulfilling a function in which the social system itself has failed but that the right to articulate one's own sense of selfhood and group identity is as real in drama as it is in the society of which that drama is an image or for which it may stand as model. Male authority is not challenged because identity comes from rebellion but because it is necessary to reclaim hegemony over one's experience; the symbolic system which is theatre is no less a part of that experience than is the daily struggle to imprint evidence of one's own existence on the sheer flux of events.

Perhaps the play that addresses the need to escape the power of male authority most directly is *Out of Our Father's House*, arranged for the stage by Eve Merriam, Paula Wagner and Jack Offsis and produced at the

439

Lenox Art Centre in 1975. It consists of a collage of historical material which relates to the necessary acts of resistance which are the basis of female identity on a personal and historical level. In the words of Elizabeth Gertrude Stern, born in 1890 in the Jewish ghetto of a midwestern city, 'I remember looking down at the face of my father, beautiful and still in death, and for a brief moment feeling my heart rise up . . . Surely it was in a strange suffocating relief . . . Now I am free!'[31] The struggle of all the women whose experiences are gathered together in this play is to achieve a voice in their own fate, to assert the right to speak – as ministers, advocates, union workers. And this is the essence of women's theatre no less than of black theatre – to speak with the authentic voice of a self no longer determined by the language and assumptions of others. In the words of the character in *Out of Our Father's House*, 'We must make the voyage of life alone. / It matters not whether the solitary voyager be a man or a woman . . . It is the height of cruelty to rob the individual of a single natural right. / Our inner being, which we call our self, no eye nor touch has ever pierced. / Such is individual life. Who can take / . . . dare take / . . . on himself / herself / the rights, / the responsibilities, the duties / of another human soul?'[32]

It is this responsibility to free the self that lies at the heart not only of women's theatre but in a sense of all drama. For what else is the theatre but a place where we encounter a world of possibility? The many voices of the actor are a constant reminder of the fact that transformation is not only a credible goal but a present fact. For the woman playwright, for the Chicano, the Indian, the Chinese and the black dramatist this was equally a social and political fact. But such a conviction is surely never far away from the mind of that writer who chooses what is, after all, the most public of arts, while to meet together, actors all, if only for a matter of hours, is already to assert the possibility of creating at least a provisional sense of community. It is, perhaps, a tenuous basis for hope but it is the fundamental promise of theatre and, anyway, we live at a time when the smallest of gestures must be made adequate to the greatest of needs.

Afterword

In 1978 I was invited to write a seventy-five thousand word critical study of twentieth-century American drama. It seemed a not unreasonable project. Over half a million words later I am all too conscious of having barely touched the surface of the subject. So many names are missing, so many groups absent, so much in the way of achievement unacknowledged. The American musical theatre – a major contribution to world drama – finds no place. This is a consequence of a deliberate strategy whereby I have chosen to deal at greater length with a few key figures and companies. The price of that strategy is clear. I hope that the advantages may be also. I feel that I should offer a litany of names but, of course, that, too, would be incomplete. I can only hope, therefore, that these volumes may have done some justice to the living art of the American theatre and to those who, in the course of a mere seventy years, have brought it from a disregarded and parochial art to a central expression of national consciousness and a major force in world culture.

The growth of non-profit professional theatre

This appendix is reproduced by permission of the Theatre Communications Group. Years refer to dates of the first public performance, or, in a few cases, the company's formal incorporation.

1915
Cleveland Play House

1925
Goodman Theatre

1931
Westport Country Playhouse

1933
Barter Theatre

1935
Oregon Shakespearean Festival

1937
Old Globe Theatre

1946
Stage One: The Louisville
    Children's Theatre

1947
Alley Theatre

1949
New Dramatists

1950
Arena Stage

1951
Circle in the Square

1953
Phoenix Theatre

1954
Milwaukee Repertory Theater
New York Shakespeare Festival

1955
Honolulu Theatre for Youth
Virginia Museum Theatre
Williamstown Theatre Festival

1956
Academy Theatre
Philadelphia Drama Guild

1958
The Paper Bag Players

1959
Dallas Theater Center

1960
Asolo State Theater
The Cincinnati Playhouse in the
    Park

Appendix

1961
The Children's Theatre Company
Theatre Arts of West Virginia
Theatre Three

1962
Great Lakes Shakespeare Festival

1963
Center Stage
The Guthrie Theater
The National Shakespeare Company
New Jersey Shakespeare Festival
Peoples Theatre
Periwinkle Productions
Seattle Repertory Theatre

1964
Actors Theatre of Louisville
The American Place Theatre
Hartford Stage Company
Lovelace Theatre
Missouri Repertory Theatre
O'Neill Theater Center
South Coast Repertory
Theatre by the Sea
Trinity Square Repertory Company

1965
A Contemporary Theatre
American Conservatory Theatre
Detroit Repertory Theatre
East West Players
El Teatro Campesino
Julian Theatre
Long Wharf Theatre
Looking Glass Theatre
Roundabout Theatre Company
Studio Arena Theatre

1966
Arizona Theatre Company
The Harry Chapin Theatre Center
INTAR
The Living Stage Theatre Company
Repertory Theatre of St. Louis

Yale Repertory Theatre

1967
CSC Repertory
Magic Theatre
Mark Taper Forum
The Negro Ensemble Company
The Ridiculous Theatrical
    Company
StageWest
The Wooster Group

1968
Berkeley Repertory Theatre
The Changing Scene
Hudson Guild Theatre
National Black Theatre
Odyssey Theatre Ensemble
Playhouse on the Square

1969
AMAS Repertory Theatre
Body Politic Theatre
Circle Repertory Company
The First All Children's Theatre
    Company
Omaha Magic Theatre
Performance Community
Repertorio Espanol
Theatre X

1970
American Theatre Company
BoarsHead Theater
Folger Theatre Group
Interart Theatre
Mabou Mines
Manhattan Theatre Club
Medicine Show Theatre Ensemble
Music-Theatre Group/Lenox Arts
    Center
New Federal Theatre
The Street Theater
Theater for the New City

443

1971
The Cricket Theatre
Dell'Arte Players Company
The Empty Space
Ensemble Studio Theatre
The Invisible Theatre
Jean Cocteau Repertory
The Old Creamery Theatre
    Company
Playwrights' Center
Playwrights Horizons

1972
The Acting Company
Alabama Shakespeare Festival
GeVa Theatre
Indiana Repertory Theatre
Intiman Theatre Company
McCarter Theatre Company
New American Theater
New Playwrights' Theatre
Provisional Theatre
Starry Night Puppet Theatre
Theater of the Open Eye

1973
Florida Studio Theatre
The Hippodrome Theatre
L.A. Public Theatre
The Play Group
The Whole Theatre Company

1974
Berkeley Stage Company
George Street Playhouse
Germinal Stage Denver
Hartman Theatre Company
The Independent Eye
L.A. Theatre Works
North Light Repertory Company
Palisades Theatre
The People's Light and Theatre
    Company
Portland Stage Company
Roadside Theater
St. Nicholas Theater Company

Syracuse Stage
Victory Gardens Theater
Wisdom Bridge Theatre
Worcester Foothills Theatre
    Company

1975
American Stage Festival
Boston Shakespeare Company
Fairmount Theatre of the Deaf
Los Angeles Actors' Theatre
Pittsburgh Public Theater
The Road Company
Soho Repertory Theatre
Theatre Project Company

1976
Alaska Repertory Theatre
American Theatre Arts
Arkansas Repertory Theatre
Attic Theatre
BAM Theater Company
The Great-American Children's
    Theatre Company
The Iron Clad Agreement
Nebraska Theatre Caravan
One Act Theatre Company of San
    Francisco
Playmakers Repertory Theatre
San Diego Repertory Theatre

1977
Actors Theatre of St. Paul
Horse Cave Theatre
New Jersey Theatre Forum
The Next Move Theatre
North Carolina Shakespeare Festival
Pennsylvania Stage Company
Players State Theatre

1978
Crossroads Theatre Company
Pilgrim Theater
Round House Theatre
Steamboat Repertory Theatre
Tacoma Actors Guild

Appendix

Reprinted from **Theatre Profile 5**, edited by Laura Ross, published by Theatre Communications Group, 355 Lexington Avenue, New York, NY 10017.

Notes

Part I. Beyond Broadway: introduction

1 John Updike, *Rabbit Redux* (New York, 1971), p. 24.
2 Quoted in Charles S. Holmes, *The Clocks of Columbus* (London, 1973), p. 251.
3 Erich Fromm, *The Sane Society* (Greenwich, Conn., 1955), p. 111.
4 Quoted in William Barrett, *Irrational Man* (New York, 1962), p. 33.
5 In Tennessee Williams, *Where I Live* (New York, 1978), p. 9.
6 Erich Fromm, p. 42.
7 William and Jane Stott, *On Broadway* (London, 1979), p. 310.
8 *Ibid.*, pp. 311–12.
9 *Ibid.*, p. 401.
10 William Inge, *Four Plays* (New York, 1979), p. vii.
11 *Ibid.*, p. vi.
12 *Ibid.*, p. viii.
13 *Ibid.*
14 *Ibid.*, p. 280.
15 *Ibid.*, p. 299.
16 Neil Simon, *The Comedy of Neil Simon* (New York, 1973), p. 7.
17 Herbert Blau, *Take Up the Bodies: Theatre at the Vanishing Point* (Urbana, 1982), p. 57.
18 Stuart Little, *Off-Broadway: The Prophetic Theatre* (New York, 1972), p. 38.
19 *Ibid.*, p. 42.
20 *Ibid.*, p. 54.
21 Gerald M. Berkowitz, *New Broadways: Theatre Across America 1950–1980* (Totowa, New Jersey, 1982), p. 29.
22 *Ibid.*, p. 27.
23 Stuart Little, p. 187.
24 Mindy Levine, *New York's Other Theatre: A Guide to Off-Off Broadway* (New York, 1981), p. xi.
25 Ellen Stewart, 'La Mama Celebrates 20 Years', *Performing Arts Journal*, VI, ii (1982), 12.
26 *Ibid.*, 9.
27 Spalding Gray, 'About Three Places in Rhode Island', *The Drama Review*, XXIII, i (March 1979), 34.
28 *Ibid.*, 36.
29 *Ibid.*, 37.
30 Richard Schechner, *The End of Humanism* (New York, 1982), p. 18.
31 *Ibid.*, p. 53.

1. Zen, Happenings, Artaud, Grotowski

1 Martin Duberman, *Black Mountain: An Exploration in Community* (New York, 1972), p. 60.
2 *Ibid.*, pp. 390–1.
3 Alan Watts, *This Is It and Other Essays on Zen and Spiritual Experience* (New York, 1958), p. 11.
4 Richard Kostelanetz, *The Theatre of Mixed Means* (London, 1970), p. 59.
5 Alan Watts, *This Is It*, p. 11.
6 Alan Watts, *In My Own Way: An Autobiography 1915–1965* (London, 1973), p. 263.
7 Michael Kirby, *The Art of Time* (New York, 1969), pp. 196–7.
8 Alan Watts, *Beat Zen, Square Zen and Zen* (San Francisco, 1959), p. 85.
9 Alan Watts, *This Is It*, pp. 32–3.
10 Alan Watts, *Beat Zen*, p. 10.
11 Peter Brook, 'From Zero to the Infinite', *The Encore Reader*, edited by Horowitz, Milne and Hale (London, 1965), p. 250.
12 Alan Watts, *This Is It*, pp. 93–4.
13 Alan Watts, *Beat Zen*, p. 11.
14 Alan Watts, *This Is It*, p. 98.
15 Martin Duberman, p. 350.
16 Jill Johnston, '"Happenings" on the New York Scene', *The Encore Reader*, p. 262.
17 Allan Kaprow, *Happenings* (New York, 1965), p. 49.
18 *Ibid.*
19 Allan Kaprow, *Assemblages, Environments and Happenings* (New York, n.d.), p. 165.
20 *Ibid.*, p. 162.
21 Allan Kaprow, *Happenings*, p. 200.
22 *Ibid.*, p. 202.
23 Allan Kaprow, *Assemblages, Environments and Happenings*, p. 196.
24 *Ibid.*, pp. 188–9.
25 *Ibid.*, p. 193.
26 *Ibid.*, p. 196.
27 *Ibid.* p. 26.
28 *Ibid.*, pp. 207–8.
29 Adrian Henri, *Environments and Happenings* (London, 1974), p. 101.
30 *Ibid.*, p. 174.
31 *Ibid.*, p. 175.
32 Carolee Schneeman, 'American Experimental Theatre: Then and Now', *Performing Arts Journal*, II, ii (Fall, 1977), 22.
33 Richard Kostelanetz, p. viii.
34 *Ibid.*, p. 67.
35 *Ibid.*, p. 68.
36 *Ibid.*, pp. 69–70.
37 *Ibid.*, p. 88.

38 Susan Sontag, *Against Interpretation* (New York, 1966), p. 7.
39 Antonin Artaud, *The Theatre and Its Double*, translated by Mary Caroline Richards (New York, 1958), p. 2.
40 *Ibid.*, p. 13.
41 *Ibid.*, p. 13.
42 *Ibid.*, p. 41.
43 *Ibid.*
44 *Ibid.*, pp. 46–7.
45 *Ibid.*
46 *Ibid.*, p. 70.
47 *Ibid.*, p. 116.
48 *Ibid.*, p. 48.
49 *Ibid.*, p. 70.
50 *Ibid.*
51 *Ibid.*, pp. 70–1.
52 *Ibid.*, p. 72.
53 *Ibid.*, p. 74.
54 *Ibid.*, pp. 76–7.
55 *Ibid.*, p. 77.
56 *Ibid.*, p. 96.
57 Tadeusz Burzynski and Zbigniew Osinski, *Grotowski's Laboratory* (Warsaw, 1979), p. 59.
58 *Ibid.*, p. 55.
59 *Ibid.*, p. 103.
60 *Ibid.*, p. 94.
61 *Ibid.*, p. 101.
62 John Cage, *A Year from Monday* (London, 1968), p. 32.
63 *Ibid.*

Part II. Performance theatre: introduction

1 Karen Taylor, *The People's Theatre in Amerika* (New York, 1972), p. 206.
2 John Cage, *Silence* (Cambridge, 1966), p. xii.
3 Julian Beck, *The Life of the Theatre* (New York, 1972), Section 45.
4 *Ibid.*, Section 35.
5 *Ibid.*, Section 13.
6 Norman O. Brown, *Love's Body* (New York, 1966), p. 125.
7 John Cage, *A Year from Monday: New Lectures and Writings* (London, 1968), p. 9.
8 John Cage, *Silence*, p. 174.
9 Julian Beck, *The Life of the Theatre*, Section 74.
10 Peter Brook, *The Empty Space* (London, 1968), p. 141.
11 Norman O. Brown, *Life Against Death* (New York, 1959), p. 269.
12 *Ibid.*, p. 271.
13 Herbert Marcuse, *Eros and Civilization* (New York, 1955), p. 13.

14 *Ibid.*, p. 15.
15 *Ibid.*, p. 16.
16 *Ibid.*, p. 34.
17 Quoted in Michael Kirby, *Total Theatre* (New York, 1969), p. 7.
18 Julian Beck, *The Life of the Theatre*, Section 121.
19 *Ibid.*, Section 35.
20 Ann Halprin, 'Community Art as Life Process', *The Drama Review*, xvii, iii (September 1973), 65.
21 Richard Schechner, ed., *Dionysus in 69* (New York, 1970), n.p.
22 Herbert Marcuse, pp. 85–6.
23 Richard Schechner, ed., n.p.
24 *Ibid.*
25 *Ibid.*

2. The Living Theatre

1 Edward Braun, *The Theatre of Meyerhold: Revolution on the Modern Stage* (London, 1979), p. 98.
2 *Ibid.*, p. 126.
3 Jack Gelber, *The Connection* (New York, 1960), p. 15.
4 *Ibid.*, p. 21.
5 *Ibid.*, p. 22.
6 *Ibid.*, p. 23.
7 *Ibid.*, p. 25.
8 *Ibid.*, p. 26.
9 *Ibid.*, p. 27.
10 *Ibid.*, p. 59.
11 *Ibid.*, p. 60.
12 *Ibid.*, p. 62.
13 *Ibid.*
14 *Ibid.*, p. 23.
15 Ralph Ellison, *Shadow and Act* (New York, 1972), pp. 189–90.
16 William Spanos, *A Casebook on Existentialism* (New York, 1964), p. 149.
17 Julian Beck, *The Life of the Theatre* (New York, 1972), n.p.
18 Kenneth H. Brown, *The Brig: A Concept for Theatre and Film* (New York, 1965), p. 3.
19 *Ibid.*
20 *Ibid.*, pp. 3–4.
21 *Ibid.*, p. 7.
22 *Ibid.*, p. 26.
23 *Ibid.*, p. 18.
24 *Ibid.*, p. 21.
25 *Ibid.*, pp. 21–2.
26 Paul Goodman, *Three Plays* (New York, 1965), p. 62
27 Julian Beck, n.p.

28 Kenneth H. Brown, p. 48.
29 *Ibid.*, p. 34.
30 Antonin Artaud, *The Theatre and Its Double*, translated by Mary Caroline Richards (New York, 1958), p. 70.
31 *Ibid.*, p. 79.
32 *Ibid.*, p. 81.
33 *Ibid.*, pp. 82–3.
34 *Ibid.*, p. 82.
35 *Ibid.*, p. 87.
36 *Ibid.*, p. 90.
37 *Ibid.*, p. 91.
38 *Ibid.*, p. 92.
39 *Ibid.*, p. 102.
40 *Ibid.*, p. 103.
41 Julian Beck, n.p.
42 *Ibid.*
43 *Ibid.*
44 John Lahr and Jonathan Price, eds., *The Great American Life Show* (New York, 1974), p. 348.
45 Julian Beck, n.p.
46 *Ibid.*
47 *Ibid.*
48 *Ibid.*
49 *Ibid.*
50 Julian Beck and Judith Malina, *Paradise Now* (New York, 1971), p. 5.
51 *Ibid.*, p. 140.
52 Renfreu Neff, *The Living Theatre: USA* (New York, 1970), p. 110.
53 Arthur Sainer, *The Radical Theatre Notebook* (New York, 1975), p. 6.
54 *Ibid.*
55 Renfreu Neff, p. 235.
56 Judith Malina, *The Enormous Despair* (New York, 1972), p. 57.
57 Arthur Sainer, p. 78.

3. The Open Theatre

1 Robert Pasolli, *A Book on the Open Theatre* (Indianapolis, 1970), p. xiii.
2 Joseph Chaikin, *The Presence of the Actor* (New York, 1972), p. 52.
3 *Ibid.*, p. 3.
4 *Ibid.*, p. 6.
5 *Ibid.*
6 *Ibid.*, p. 4.
7 *Ibid.*, p. 15.
8 Robert Pasolli, p. 23.
9 Joseph Chaikin, p. 57.
10 *Ibid.*, pp. 131–2.

11 Robert Pasolli, pp. 50–1.
12 Megan Terry, 'Viet Rock', *Tulane Drama Review*, xi, i (Fall, 1966), 197.
13 Joseph Chaikin, 'Closing the Open Theatre', *Theatre Quarterly*, xvi (November 1974–January 1975), 38.
14 *Ibid.*
15 *Ibid.*
16 Megan Terry, 197.
17 Joseph Chaikin, 'Closing the Open Theatre', 38.
18 *Ibid.*, 34.
19 *Ibid.*, 35.
20 *Ibid.*, 36.
21 *Ibid.*, 34.
22 Pasolli, p. 52.
23 Jean-Claude Van Itallie, 'A Reinvention of Form', *Tulane Drama Review*, xxi, iv (December 1977), 67.
24 Jean-Claude Van Itallie, *America Hurrah!* (New York, 1967), pp. 30–1.
25 *Ibid.*, p. 35.
26 *Ibid.*, p. 39.
27 *Ibid.*, p. 44.
28 *Ibid.*, p. 45.
29 *Ibid.*, pp. 79–80.
30 Joseph Chaikin, p. 75.
31 *Ibid.*, p. 70.
32 *Ibid.*, p. 73.
33 *Ibid.*, p. 103.
34 *Ibid.*, pp. 105–6.
35 Jean-Claude Van Itallie, 'A Reinvention of Form', 67.
36 Antonin Artaud, *The Theatre and Its Double*, translated by Mary Caroline Richards (New York, 1958), p. 97.
37 *Ibid.*, p. 125.
38 *Ibid.*, pp. 115–16.
39 *Ibid.*, p. 113.
40 *Ibid.*, p. 116.
41 Jean-Claude Van Itallie, *The Serpent* (New York, 1969), p. ix.
42 *Ibid.*, p. xvi.
43 *Ibid.*, pp. 12–13.
44 *Ibid.*, p. 41.
45 *Ibid.*, p. xiv.
46 John Lahr and Jonathan Price, eds., *The Great American Life Show* (New York, 1974), p. 66.
47 *Ibid.*, p. 67.
48 Jean-Claude Van Itallie, 'A Reinvention of Form', 72–3.
49 Susan Yankovitz, *Terminal* in *Scripts*, 1 (November 1971), 17–45.
50 *Ibid.*
51 *Ibid.*

52 Edward Braun, *The Theatre of Meyerhold* (London, 1979), p. 165.

53 Keir Elam, *The Semiotics of Theatre and Drama* (London, 1980), p. 22.

4. The Performance Group

  1 Mark Fumarole, 'External Order, Internal Intimacy: An Interview with Jerzy Grotowski', *Tulane Drama Review*, xiv, i (Fall, 1969), 172–3.

  2 *Ibid.*, 174.

  3 *Ibid.*, 177.

  4 Richard Schechner, ed., *Dionysus in 69* (New York, 1970), n.p.

  5 Richard Schechner, *Public Domain: Essays on the Theatre* (Indianapolis, 1969), p. 228.

  6 Richard Schechner, ed., *Dionysus in 69*, n.p.

  7 *Ibid.*

  8 *Ibid.*

  9 *Ibid.*

 10 Arthur Sainer, *The Radical Theatre Notebook* (New York, 1975), p. 218.

 11 *Ibid.*, pp. 218–19.

 12 Theodore Shank, *American Alternative Theatre* (London, 1982), p. 99.

 13 Richard Schechner, 'The Decline and Fall of the (American) Avant-Garde', *Performing Arts Journal*, v, ii (1981), 55.

 14 *Ibid.*, 58.

 15 *Ibid.*, 11.

 16 *Ibid.*, 16.

 17 *Ibid.*, 12.

 18 Richard Schechner, *The End of Humanism* (New York, 1982), p. 54.

 19 Elizabeth LeCompte, 'Who Owns History?' *Performing Arts Journal* vi, i (1981), 50.

 20 Richard Schechner, *The End of Humanism*, p. 45.

 21 Spalding Gray, 'Perpetual Saturdays', *Performing Arts Journal*, vi, i (1981), 48.

 22 *Ibid.*

 23 Elizabeth LeCompte, 52.

 24 Richard Schechner, 'The Decline and Fall of the (American) Avant-Garde: Why It Happened and What We Can Do About It', *Performing Arts Journal*, v, iii (1981), 17–19.

 25 Richard Schechner, *Public Domain*, p. 190.

 26 *Ibid.*

 27 *Ibid.*, p. 196.

 28 *Ibid.*, p. 197.

 29 *Ibid.*, p. 201.

 30 *Ibid.*, p. 202.

 31 Richard Schechner, *Ritual, Play and Performance: Readings in the Social Sciences* (New York, 1976), p. 214.

 32 *Ibid.*, pp. 217–18.

33 R.G. Davis, 'The Radical Right in the American Theatre', *Theatre Quarterly*, v, xix (September–November 1975), 68.

34 *Ibid.*, 72.

35 *Ibid.*

36 Quoted in Ronald Hayman, *Theatre and Anti-Theatre: New Movements Since Beckett* (London, 1979), p. 198.

37 *Ibid.*, pp. 200–1.

38 Charles Marowitz, 'Notes on the Theatre of Cruelty', *Tulane Drama Review* XI, No. 34 (Winter, 1966).

39 Quoted in Ronald Hayman, p. 226.

40 *Ibid.*, p. 214.

41 Edward Braun, *The Theatre of Meyerhold* (London, 1979), p. 46.

42 *Ibid.*, p. 146.

43 John D. Margolis, *T.S. Eliot's Intellectual Development* (Chicago, 1972), p. 181.

44 Quoted in Susan Sontag, *Against Interpretation* (New York, 1966), p. 39.

45 Ronald Hayman, p. 181.

Part III. The theatre of images: introduction

1 'The American Experimental Theatre: Then and Now', *Performing Arts Journal*, II, ii (Fall, 1977), 18.

2 *Ibid.*, 14.

3 Colin Naylor and Genesis P. Orridge, *Contemporary Artists* (London, 1977), p. 347.

4 *Theatre Quarterly*, IV, xv (August–October 1974), 20.

5 Stefan Brecht, *The Theatre of Visions: Robert Wilson* (Frankfurt-am-Main, 1978), p. 421.

6 Mike Gold, *Hoboken Blues* in *The American Caravan* (London, 1927), ed. Van Wyck Brooks, Lewis Mumford, Alfred Kreyborg and Paul Rosenfeld, pp. 548–9.

7 Martin Friedman and Graham W.J. Beal, *George Segal* (New York, 1975), p. 60.

8 *Ibid.*, p. 49.

9 Max Beckman, 'Reality and Artifice: An Arts Council Exhibition', University of East Anglia, 1982.

10 Gregory Babcock, *Super Realism: A Critical Anthology* (New York, 1975), p. 98.

11 Friedman and Beal, p. 38.

12 Alain Robbe-Grillet, *Snapshots and Towards a New Novel*, translated by Barbara Wright (London, 1965), pp. 52–4.

13 Kate Davy, ed., *Richard Foreman: Plays and Manifestos* (New York, 1976), p. 141.

14 Alain Robbe-Grillet, p. 146.

15 *Ibid.*, p. 54.

16 *Ibid.*, p. 98.
17 Peter Conradi, *John Fowles* (London, 1982).
18 Alfred Sohn-Rethel, *Intellectual and Manual Labour: A Critique of Epistemology* (London, 1978), p. 25.
19 Gregory Babcock, p. 32.
20 *Ibid.*, p. 108.
21 Friedman and Beal, p. 51.
22 Kate Davy, ed., *Richard Foreman*, p. 141.
23 Donald Barthelme, *Unspeakable Practices, Unnatural Acts* (London, 1969), p. 44.
24 Sam Shepard, *The Tooth of Crime and Geography of a Horse Dreamer* (New York, 1974), p. 38.
25 Susan Sontag, 'On Art and Consciousness', *Performing Arts Journal*, II, ii (Fall, 1977), 29.
26 Alain Robbe-Grillet, pp. 138, 152.
27 Richard Foreman, p. 30.
28 Samuel Beckett, *Endgame*, trans. by the author (London, 1958), p. 47.
29 Gregory Babcock, p. 102.
30 Friedman and Beal, p. 24.
31 Gregory Babcock, p. 98.

5. Robert Wilson

1 Stefan Brecht, *The Theatre of Visions: Robert Wilson* (Frankfurt-am-Main, 1978), p. 18.
2 *Ibid.*
3 *Ibid.*, p. 32.
4 *Ibid.*, p. 28.
5 *Ibid.*
6 Quoted in Malcolm Bradbury, *The Novel Today* (Manchester, 1977), p. 7.
7 Alain Robbe-Grillet, *Snapshots and Towards a New Novel*, translated by Barbara Wright (London, 1965), pp. 60, 63.
8 Stefan Brecht, p. 393.
9 *Ibid.*
10 *Ibid.*, pp. 392–3.
11 *Ibid.*, p. 417.
12 *Ibid.*, p. 419.
13 *Ibid.*, pp. 420–1.
14 *Ibid.*, p. 421.
15 *Ibid.*, p. 429.
16 *Ibid.*, p. 431.
17 *Ibid.*, p. 439.
18 Ishmael Reed, *Yellow Back Radio Broke Down* (New York, 1973), p. 40.
19 William Hoffman, ed., *New American Plays* (New York, 1970), pp. 144–5.
20 Frontisek Deak, 'Robert Wilson', *Tulane Drama Review*, XVIII, ii (June 1974), 67.

21 Stefan Brecht, p. 274.

22 *Ibid.*, p. 334.

23 *Ibid.*, p. 353.

24 *Ibid.*, p. 368.

25 *Ibid.*, p. 373.

26 Theodore Shank, *American Alternative Theatre* (London, 1982), p. 134.

27 Robert Wilson, *The Golden Window* (Munich, 1982), p. 50.

6. Richard Foreman

1 Harold Rosenberg, *The Tradition of the New* (London, 1970), p. 36.

2 Christopher Butler, *After the Wake* (Oxford, 1980), p. 46.

3 *Ibid.*, p. 162.

4 Richard Foreman, *Plays and Manifestos*, ed. Kate Davy (New York, 1976), p. ix.

5 Michael J. Hoffman, *Gertrude Stein* (Boston, 1976), p. 112.

6 Richard Foreman, p. xi.

7 *Ibid.*, p. xiii.

8 *Ibid.*

9 *Ibid.*, p. 66.

10 *Ibid.*, p. 67.

11 *Ibid.*, p. 68.

12 *Ibid.*, p. 70.

13 *Ibid.*, p. 71.

14 *Ibid.*, p. 72.

15 *Ibid.*, p. 73.

16 *Ibid.*, p. 75.

17 *Ibid.*, p. 77.

18 *Ibid.*, p. 135.

19 *Ibid.*, p. 136.

20 *Ibid.*, p. 137.

21 *Ibid.*, p. 138.

22 *Ibid.*, p. 140.

23 *Ibid.*, p. 141.

24 *Ibid.*, p. 147.

25 *Ibid.*, p. 192.

26 *Ibid.*, p. 193.

27 *Ibid.*, p. 34.

28 *Ibid.*, p. 112.

29 Gregory Babcock, *Super Realism: A Critical Anthology* (New York, 1975), p. 51.

30 *Ibid.*, p. 88.

31 Richard Foreman, 'C'est une pièce sur quoi?' *Café Amérique* (Gennevilliers, 1981), p. 51.

32 *Ibid.*

33 *Ibid.*, p. 52.

34 *Ibid.*

7. Lee Breuer

1 Bonnie Marranca, ed., *Animations: A Trilogy for Mabou Mines* (New York, 1979), p. 32.
2 *Ibid.*, p. 67.
3 *Ibid.*, pp. 66–7.
4 *Ibid.*, p. 59.
5 *Ibid.*, p. 61.
6 *Ibid.*, p. 63.
7 *Ibid.*, p. 66.
8 *Ibid.*, p. 146.
9 *Ibid.*, p. 21.
10 *Ibid.*, p. 22.
11 *Ibid.*, p. 154.
12 *Ibid.*, p. 99.
13 *Ibid.*, p. 100.
14 'Interview with Lee Breuer', in *TCG: New Plays USA* (New York, 1982), p. 29.
15 *Ibid.*, pp. 5–6.
16 *Ibid.*, p. 7.
17 *Ibid.*
18 *Ibid.*, p. 28.
19 *Ibid.*, p. 29.
20 *Ibid.*

8. Sam Shepard

1 Sam Shepard, *Hawk Moon* (New York, 1978), p. 12.
2 Gerald Weales, 'The Transformations of Sam Shepard', in Bonnie Marranca, ed., *American Dreams: The Imagination of Sam Shepard* (New York, 1981), 12.
3 Sam Shepard, *Five Plays by Sam Shepard* (London, 1969), p. 79.
4 Bonnie Marranca, ed., *Animations: A Trilogy for Mabou Mines* (New York, 1979), p. 190.
5 *Ibid.*, p. 191.
6 *Ibid.*
7 *Ibid.*, p. 72.
8 *Ibid.*, p. 197.
9 *Ibid.*, p. 198.
10 Sam Shepard, *Five Plays*, p. 46.
11 Bonnie Marranca, p. 196.
12 *Ibid.*, p. 195.
13 *Ibid.*, p. 201.

14 Sam Shepard, *Five Plays*, pp. 54–5.
15 Bonnie Marranca, p. 59.
16 Sam Shepard, *Five Plays*, p. 90.
17 Sam Shepard, *Seven Plays* (New York, 1981), p. 260.
18 Quoted in Malcolm Bradbury, *The Novel Today* (Manchester, 1977), p. 7.
19 Kenneth Chubb, 'Fruitful Difficulties of Directing Shepard', *Theatre Quarterly*, IV, xv (August–October 1974), 20.
20 Bonnie Marranca, pp. 202–3.
21 Sam Shepard, *Operation Sidewinder* in *The Great American Life Show: Nine Plays of the Avant-Garde*, ed. John Lahr and Jonathan Price (New York, 1972), pp. 156–7.
22 *Ibid.*, p. 146.
23 Bonnie Marranca, p. 214.
24 *Ibid.*, p. 217.
25 *Ibid.*, p. 216.
26 *Ibid.*
27 *Ibid.*
28 *Ibid.*
29 *Ibid.*, pp. 216–17.
30 Bonnie Marranca, p. 216.
31 *Ibid.*, p. 217.
32 Sam Shepard, *The Tooth of Crime and Geography of a Horse Dreamer* (New York, 1974), p. 4
33 *Ibid.*, p. 24.
34 *Ibid.*, p. 29.
35 *Ibid.*, p. 37.
36 *Ibid.*
37 *Ibid.*, p. 38.
38 *Ibid.*
39 *Ibid.*, p. 46.
40 *Ibid.*, pp. 49–50.
41 *Ibid.*, p. 71.
42 Bonnie Marranca, p. 166.
43 *Ibid.*, p. 200.
44 Sam Shepard, *The Tooth of Crime and Geography of a Horse Dreamer*, p. 98.
45 *Ibid.*, p. 105.
46 *Ibid.*, p. 128.
47 *Ibid.*, p. 97.
48 Sam Shepard, *Angel City, Curse of the Starving Classes and Other Plays* (London, 1978), p. 104.
49 *Ibid.*, p. 6.
50 *Ibid.*, p. 13.
51 *Ibid.*, p. 6.
52 *Ibid.*, p. 32.
53 *Ibid.*, p. 45.

54 Bonnie Marranca, p. 216.
55 Sam Shepard, *Angel City, Curse of the Starving Classes and Other Plays*, p. 104.
56 Sam Shepard, *Buried Child, Seduced, Suicide in B♭* (New York, 1979), p. 107.
57 *Ibid.*, p. 111.
58 *Ibid.*, p. 116.
59 *Ibid.*, pp. 146–7.
60 *Ibid.*, p. 150.
61 *Ibid.*, p. 155.
62 Sam Shepard, *Seven Plays*, p. 61.
63 *Ibid.*, p. 118.
64 *Ibid.*, p. 109.
65 Bonnie Marranca, p. 157.
66 *Ibid.*
67 Albert Camus, *The Collected Plays of Albert Camus*, translated by Stuart Gilbert (London, 1965), p. 119.
68 Sam Shepard, *Seven Plays*, p. 36.
69 *Ibid.*, p. 27.
70 *Ibid.*
71 *Ibid.*, p. 60.
72 *Ibid.*, p. 302.
73 Bonnie Marranca, p. 139.
74 *Ibid.*, p. 141.
75 *Ibid.*, p. 145.
76 *Ibid.*, p. 137.
77 Søren Kierkegaard, *The Present Age*, translated by Alexander Dru (New York, 1962), p. 68.
78 Kenneth Chubb, 'Fruitful Difficulties of Directing Shepard', 24.
79 *Ibid.*
80 *Ibid.*

9. David Mamet

1 *Current Biography*, August 1978, p. 27.
2 David Mamet, *American Buffalo, Sexual Perversity in Chicago and Duck Variations* (London, 1978), p. 78.
3 *Ibid.*, p. 81.
4 *Ibid.*
5 *Ibid.*, p. 82.
6 *Ibid.*, p. 84.
7 *Ibid.*, p. 85.
8 *Ibid.*, pp. 85–6.
9 *Ibid.*, p. 86.
10 *Ibid.*, p. 88.
11 *Ibid.*, p. 91.
12 *Ibid.*, p. 92.

13 *Ibid.*, p. 93.
14 *Ibid.*, p. 94.
15 *Ibid.*, p. 53.
16 *Ibid.*, p. 57.
17 *Ibid.*, p. 63.
18 *Ibid.*, p. 71.
19 *Ibid.*, p. 67.
20 *Contemporary Authors*, vols. 81–4, p. 353.
21 Richard Gottlieb, 'The "Engine" That Drives Playwright David Mamet'', *The New York Times*, 15 January 1978, p. D4.
22 David Mamet, p. 9.
23 *Ibid.*, p. 35.
24 *Ibid.*, p. 37.
25 *Ibid.*, p. 10.
26 *Ibid.*, p. 41.
27 *Ibid.*, p. 33.
28 *Ibid.*, p. 41.
29 Brendan Gill, *The New Yorker*, 28 February 1977.
30 Gordon Rogoff, *The Saturday Review*, 2 April 1977.
31 *Contemporary Authors*, vols. 81–4, p. 353.
32 Richard Gottlieb, p. D4.
33 David Mamet, *Reunion* (New York, 1976), p. 21.
34 *Ibid.*, pp. 23–4.
35 *Ibid.*, p. 26.
36 *Ibid.*, pp. 23–4.
37 *Ibid.*, p. 26.
38 *The New York Times*, 16 October 1977, p. D7.
39 David Mamet, *A Life in the Theatre* (New York, 1978), p. 7.
40 *Ibid.*, p. 35.
41 *Ibid.*, pp. 66–7.
42 *Ibid.*, pp. 19–20.
43 *Ibid.*, p. 81.
44 *Ibid.*, p. 80.
45 *Ibid.*, p. 95.
46 *Ibid.*, p. 94.
47 Richard Gottlieb, p. D4.
48 *Ibid.*, p. 1.
49 *Ibid.*, p. 4.
50 *Ibid.*
51 David Mamet, *The Water Engine and Mr Happiness* (New York, 1978), n.p.
52 *Ibid.*, p. 23.
53 *Ibid.*, pp. 26–7.
54 *Ibid.*, p. 25.
55 *Ibid.*, p. 54.
56 *Ibid.*, p. 61.

57 *Ibid.*, p. 64.
58 *Ibid.*, p. 71.
59 David Mamet, *Reunion* (New York, 1976), p. 22.
60 Mel Gussow, 'The Daring Visions of Four New, Young Playwrights', *The New York Times*, 30 November 1977, p. 13.
61 David Mamet, *The Woods* (New York, 1979), pp. 3–4.
62 *Ibid.*, p. 10.
63 *Ibid.*, p. 17.
64 *Ibid.*, p. 11.
65 *Ibid.*, p. 20.
66 *Ibid.*, p. 22.
67 *Ibid.*, p. 30.
68 *Ibid.*, p. 55.
69 *Ibid.*, p. 62.
70 *Ibid.*, p. 64.
71 *Ibid.*, pp. 69–70.
72 *Ibid.*, p. 93.
73 *Ibid.*, p. 95.
74 *Ibid.*, p. 97.
75 *Philadelphia Inquirer*, 1 October 1978, p. F3.
76 David Mamet, *Lakeboat* (New York, 1981), p. 51.
77 Mel Gussow, p. 13.

Part V. The theatre of commitment: introduction

1 Alain Robbe-Grillet, *Snapshots and Towards a New Novel*, translated by Barbara Wright (London, 1965), p. 70.
2 *Ibid.*, p. 141.
3 *Ibid.*, p. 73.
4 In Walter Wager, ed., *The Playwright Speaks* (New York, 1968), p. 200.
5 Peter Brook, 'Introduction', *The Persecution and Assassination of Marat as performed by the inmates of the asylum of Charenton under the direction of the Marquis de Sade* by Peter Weiss, translated by Geoffrey Skelton, verse adaptation by Adrian Michell (London, 1965), p. 5.
6 Rolf Hochhuth, *The Representative*, translated by Robert David MacDonald (London, 1963), pp. 205–6.
7 *Ibid.*, p. 269.
8 Baruch Hochman, 'Robert Lowell's *The Old Glory*', *Tulane Drama Review*, XI, iv, 136.
9 Rolf Hochhuth, *Soldiers*, translated by Robert David MacDonald (London, 1968), p. 53.
10 Robert Lowell, *Near the Ocean* (London, 1967), p. 9.
11 *Ibid.*, p. 16.
12 Jonathan Miller, 'Director's Note', *The Old Glory* (London, 1966), p. x.
13 Nathaniel Hawthorne, *Selected Tales and Sketches* (New York, 1962), p. 143.

14 Robert Lowell, *The Old Glory* (London, 1966), p. 21.
15 *Ibid.*, p. 32.
16 Robert Lowell *et al.*, 'The Cold War and the West', *Partisan Review* XXIX, i (Winter, 1962), 47.
17 Robert Lowell, *The Old Glory*, p. 36.
18 *Ibid.*, p. 37.
19 Baruch Hochman, 'Robert Lowell's *The Old Glory*', 127–38.
20 Robert Lowell, *The Old Glory*, p. 95.
21 Jonathan Miller, 'Director's Note', p. xiii.
22 Robert Lowell, *The Old Glory*, p. 94.
23 *Ibid.*, p. 98.
24 *Ibid.*, p. 69.
25 *Ibid.*, p. 107.
26 *Ibid.*, pp. 95–6.
27 *Ibid.*, p. 100.
28 *Ibid.*, p. 72.
29 *Ibid.*, p. 103.
30 *Ibid.*, p. 99.
31 *Ibid.*, p. 111.
32 *Ibid.*, p. 109.
33 Richard W. Van Alstyne, *The American Empire: Its Historical Pattern and Evolution* (London, 1960), p. 11.
34 Washington Irving, *Selected Prose* (New York, 1962), p. 101.
35 Quoted in *The Observer*, 1 December 1968, p. 11.
36 A. Alvarez, 'A Talk with Robert Lowell', *Encounter* (February 1965), 41.
37 Herman Melville, *Mardi: And a Voyage Thither*, vol. II (New York, 1963), p. 224.
38 Robert Lowell, *The Old Glory*, p. 137.
39 Herman Melville, *Short Novels of Herman Melville* (East Lansing, 1962), p. 81.
40 Merrell R. Davis and William H. Gilman, eds., *The Letters of Herman Melville* (New Haven, 1960), p. 125.
41 Robert Lowell, *The Old Glory*, p. 161.
42 Herman Melville, *Moby Dick* (New York, 1950), p. 422.
43 Robert Lowell, *The Old Glory*, p. 194.
44 *Ibid.*, p. 120.
45 R.W. Van Alstyne, p. 60.
46 Robert Lowell, *The Old Glory*, p. 104.
47 *Ibid.*, p. 186.
48 Anon., 'The Curse and the Hope', *Time*, 17 July 1964, p. 40.
49 Robert Lowell, *The Old Glory*, p. 99.
50 *Ibid.*, p. 187.
51 *Ibid.*, p. 166.
52 Arthur Miller, *After the Fall*, *The Saturday Evening Post*, 12 February 1964, p. 58.

Notes

53 A. Alvarez, p. 42.

54 Herbert Blau, *Take Up the Bodies: Theatre at the Vanishing Point* (Urbana, 1982), p. xi.

55 *Ibid.*, p. xii.

56 *Ibid.*, p. 130.

57 *Ibid.*, p. 132.

58 James F. Mersmann, *Out of the Vietnam Vortex: A Study of Poets and Poetry Against the War* (New York, 1974), pp. 72–3.

59 *Ibid.*, p. 93.

60 *Ibid.*, p. 182.

61 Cecil Woolf and John Bagguley, eds., *Authors Take Sides on Vietnam* (London, 1967), p. 24.

62 James F. Mersmann, p. 123.

63 *Ibid.*, p. 138.

64 Gilbert Adair, *Hollywood's Vietnam* (New York, 1981), p. 35.

65 Robert Lowell, *Prometheus Bound* (New York, 1969), pp. v–vi.

66 *Ibid.*, p. vi.

67 *Ibid.*

68 *Ibid.*

69 *Ibid.*, p. 41.

70 *Ibid.*

71 *Ibid.*, p. 45.

72 *Ibid.*, p. 47.

73 *Ibid.*, p. 59.

74 Robert Brustein, *Making Scenes: A Personal History of the Turbulent Years at Yale 1966–1979* (New York, 1981), p. 43.

75 *Ibid.*, p. 45.

76 *Ibid.*, p. 46.

77 *Ibid.*

78 Françoise Kourilsky, 'Approaching Quetzalcoatl: the Evolution of El Teatro Campesino', *Performing Arts Journal*, VII (Fall, 1973), 37–8.

79 David Rabe, *The Basic Training of Pavlo Hummel and Sticks and Bones* (Harmondsworth, 1978), p. xxv.

80 *Ibid.*, p. 110.

81 *Ibid.*, p. 107.

82 *Ibid.*

83 Stuart W. Little, *Enter Joseph Papp: In Search of a New American Theatre* (New York, 1974), p. 141.

84 David Rabe, p. 225.

85 *Ibid.*, p. 145.

86 *Ibid.*, p. 150.

87 *Ibid.*

88 *Ibid.*, p. 163.

89 *Ibid.*

90 *Ibid.*, p. xxii.

91 *Ibid.*, p. 226.
92 David Rabe, *Streamers* (New York, 1977), p. 50.
93 Tom Cole, *Medal of Honor Rag* (New York, 1977), p. 20.
94 Amlin Gray, *How I Got That Story* (New York, 1981), p. 38.
95 James McLure, *Pvt Wars* (New York, 1980), p. 18.
96 *Ibid.*, p. 39.

10. The San Francisco Mime Troupe

1 R.G. Davis, *The San Francisco Mime Troupe: The First Ten Years* (Palo Alto, 1975), p. 19.
2 *Ibid.*, p. 40.
3 *Ibid.*, p. 42.
4 *Ibid.*, p. 18.
5 Theodore Shank, 'Political Theatre as Popular Entertainment', *Tulane Drama Review*, xviii, i (March 1974), 113.
6 R.G. Davis, p. 82.
7 Theodore Shank, p. 113.
8 R.G. Davis, p. 125.
9 *Ibid.*, p. 250.
10 Theodore Shank, p. 115.
11 R.G. Davis, 'Politics, Art, and the San Francisco Mime Troupe', *Theatre Quarterly*, v, xviii (June–August 1975), 26.
12 *Ibid.*
13 Joan Holden, 'Collective Playmaking: the Why and How', *Theatre Quarterly*, v, xviii (June–August 1975), 28.
14 Theodore Shank, 'The San Francisco Mime Troupe's production of "False Promises"' *Theatre Quarterly*, vii, xxvii (Autumn, 1977), 50.
15 *Ibid.*, 73.

11. Bread and Puppet

1 Martin Esslin, *Brecht: A Choice of Evils* (London, 1965), p. 109.
2 *Ibid.*, p. 117.
3 Karen Taylor, *The People's Theatre in Amerika* (New York, 1972), p. 251.
4 *Ibid.*, p. 260.
5 *Ibid.*, pp. 263–4.
6 Helen Brown and Jane Seitz, 'With the Bread and Puppet Theatre: An Interview with Peter Schumann', *Tulane Drama Review*, xii, ii (Winter, 1968), 64.
7 *Ibid.*
8 *Ibid.*, 69.
9 Erika Munk, 'TDR Comment', *Tulane Drama Review*, xiv, iii (1970), 34.
10 Edward Braun, *The Theatre of Meyerhold: Revolution on the Modern Stage* (London, 1979), p.

11 *Ibid.*, p. 74.
12 Keir Elam, *The Semiotics of Theatre and Drama* (London, 1980), p. 69.
13 *Ibid.*, p. 22.
14 Joseph Chaikin, *The Presence of the Actor* (New York, 1972), p. viii.
15 Françoise Kourilsky, 'Dada and Circus: Bread and Puppet Theatre', *Tulane Drama Review*, XVIII, i (March 1974), 105.
16 *Ibid.*, 107.
17 *Ibid.*
18 *Ibid.*, 106.
19 Edward Gordon Craig, *On the Art of the Theatre* (London, 1911; reprinted 1962), p. 82.
20 *Ibid.*, p. 84.
21 Jean-Paul Sartre, *Situations*, translated by Benita Eisler (London, 1965), pp. 216–17.
22 Florence Falk, 'Bread and Puppet Domestic Resurrection Circus', *Performing Arts Journal*, II, i (Spring, 1977), 22.
23 *Ibid.*, 27.

12. El Teatro Campesino

1 Luis Valdéz, *The Drama Review*, XI, iv (September 1967).
2 Henry Lesnik, ed., *Guerilla Street Theatre* (New York, 1973), p. 195.
3 *Ibid.*, p. 196.
4 *Ibid.*, p. 190.
5 Joan Harrop and Jorge Huerta, 'The Agitprop Pilgrimage of Luis Valdéz and El Teatro Campesino', *Theatre Quarterly*, V, xvii (March–May 1975), 38.
6 Richard Wright, 'Blueprint for Negro Literature', *Amistad 2* (New York, 1971), p. 11.
7 Luis Valdéz, 'Notes on Chicano Theatre', *Chicano Theatre I* (Spring, 1973), 7.
8 W.E.B. Dubois, *The Seventh Son: The Thoughts and Writings of W.E.B. Dubois*, vol. II, ed. Julius Lester (New York, 1971), p. 313.
9 Françoise Kourilsky, 'Approaching Quetzalcoatl: the Evolution of El Teatro Campesino,' *Performance*, VII (Fall, 1973), 39.
10 'Tenaz Manifesto', *Tulane Drama Review*, XVII, iv (December 1973), 89.
11 Susan Bassnett-McGuire, 'Luis Valdéz: Two Views of How the Barrio came to Broadway: El teatro Campesino: From Actos to Mitos', *Theatre Quarterly*, IX, xxxiv (Summer, 1979), 20.
12 Henry Lesnik, ed., p. 239.
13 *Ibid.*, p. 190.
14 *Ibid.*
15 Carlos Morton, 'The Teatro Campesino', *Tulane Drama Review*, XVIII, iv (December 1974), 73.
16 *Ibid.*, 75.
17 Marsue Cumming, ed., *Theatre Profiles 3* (New York, 1977), p. 85.

Notes

18 *Ibid.*

13. American Indian theatre

1 Francis Paul Prucha, *Documents of United States Indian Policy* (Lincoln, Nebraska, 1975), p. 256.
2 Vine Deloria Jr, *Behind the Trail of Broken Treaties* (New York, 1974), p. 249.
3 Hanay Geiogamah, *New Native American Drama: Three Plays by Hanay Geiogamah* (Norman, Oklahoma, 1980), p. 8.
4 *Ibid.*, p. 49.
5 *Ibid.*, p. 52.
6 *Ibid.*, p. 87.
7 *Ibid.*
8 *Ibid.*, p. 132.
9 *Ibid.*, p. 89.
10 James Leverett, ed., *TCG: New Plays USA* (New York, 1982), p. 112.
11 *Ibid.*

14. Black theatre

1 Ethel Pitts Walker, 'The American Negro Theatre', in *The Theatre of Black Americans*, vol. II, ed. Errol Hill (Englewood Cliffs, New Jersey, 1980), p. 53.
2 *Ibid.*, p. 54.
3 Harold Cruse, *The Crisis of the Negro Intellectual* (New York, 1969), pp. 209–10.
4 *Ibid.*
5 Loften Mitchell, *Voices of the Black Theatre* (Clifton, New Jersey, 1975), p. 131.
6 Harold Cruse, p. 233.
7 *Ibid.*, p. 532.
8 Edith J.R. Isaacs, *The Negro in the American Theatre* (New York, 1947), pp. 122, 125.
9 Theodore Ward, *Our Lan'* in *Black Drama in America: An Anthology*, ed., Darwin Turner (New York, 1971), p. 130.
10 Douglas Turner Ward, 'American Theatre: For Whites Only', *The New York Times*, 14 August 1966, Section II, pp. D1, D3.
11 Negro Ensemble Programme.
12 *The Free Southern Theatre Newsletter* (December 1964), p. 3.
13 Quoted in *ibid.*, n.p.
14 *Ibid.*, p. 3.
15 LeRoi Jones, *Dutchman and The Slave* (New York, 1964), p. 35.
16 LeRoi Jones, 'Exaugural Address', *Kulchur*, III iii (Winter, 1963), 86.
17 LeRoi Jones, *Dutchman and The Slave*, p. 44.
18 *Ibid.*
19 *Ibid.*, p. 45.

20 *Ibid.*, p. 53.
21 *Ibid.*, pp. 55–6.
22 *Ibid.*, p. 61.
23 *Ibid.*
24 Ed Bullins, *New Plays for the Black Theatre* (New York, 1969), p. xv.
25 *Ibid.*, pp. viii–ix.
26 *Ibid.*, p. xiv.
27 Ed Bullins, *How Do You Do* in *Black Fire* (New York, 1969), ed. LeRoi Jones and Larry Neal, p. 603.
28 *Ibid.*, p. 596.
29 Ed Bullins, *The Theme is Blackness: The Corner and Other Plays* (New York, 1973), p. 11.
30 *Ibid.*, p. 14.
31 Ed Bullins, *The Electronic Nigger and Other Plays* (London, 1970), pp. 138–9.
32 Ed Bullins, *New Plays for the Black Theatre*, p. 167.
33 Ed Bullins, *The Duplex* (New York, 1970), pp. 120–2.
34 William Couch Jr, *New Black Playwrights* (Baton Rouge, 1968), p. xxi.
35 Blake Morrison, *Seamus Heaney* (London, 1982), p. 24.
36 Ntozake Shange, *For colored girls who have considered suicide/when the rainbow is enuf* (New York, 1977), p. x.
37 *Ibid.*, p. xi.
38 *Ibid.*, p. xv.
39 *Ibid.*, p. 5.
40 *Ibid.*, pp. 44–5.
41 *Ibid.*, p. 39.
42 Ntozake Shange, *Three Pieces* (New York, 1981), p. ix.
43 *Ibid.*
44 *Ibid.*, p. x.
45 *Ibid.*, p. xi.
46 *Ibid.*, p. xii.
47 *Ibid.*, p. 52.

15. Gay theatre

1 Gautam Dasgupta, 'Interview: Charles Ludlam', *Performing Arts Journal*, III (1978), 75.
2 Stefan Brecht, *Queer Theatre* (Frankfurt-am-Main, 1978), p. 75.
3 Bonnie Marranca, *Theatre of the Ridiculous* (New York, 1979), p. 6.
4 Stefan Brecht, p. 34.
5 Bonnie Marranca, p. 8.

16. Women's theatre

1 Judith E. Barlow, *Plays by American Women: The Early Years* (New York, 1981), p. x.

Notes

2 *Ibid.*, p. xxii.
3 Harriet Kriegel, *Women in Drama: An Anthology* (New York, 1975), p. xxxiv.
4 *Ibid.*, p. xxxv.
5 *Ibid.*, p. xxviii.
6 Isaac Goldberg, *The Theatre of George Jean Nathan* (New York, 1968), p. 135.
7 Ellen Moers, *Literary Women: The Great Writers* (New York, 1978), p. 3.
8 *Ibid.*, p. 15.
9 Honor Moore, *The New Women's Theatre* (New York, 1977), p. 512.
10 *Ibid.*, p. 507.
11 Mary Ellman, *Thinking About Women* (New York, 1968), p. 97.
12 Vivian Gornek, *Essays in Feminism* (New York, 1978), p. 216.
13 Virginia Woolf, *Collected Essays*, vol. II (London, 1966), p. 113.
14 *Ibid.*, p. 114.
15 Quoted in Herbert Marder, *Feminism and Art: A Study of Virginia Woolf* (Chicago, 1968), p. 122.
16 Honor Moore, p. xiv.
17 Virginia Woolf, p. 143.
18 'Where Are the Women Playwrights?' *The New York Times*, May 1973, Section 2, p. 1.
19 *Ibid.*, p. 3.
20 Julia Miles, ed., *The Women's Project: Seven New Plays By Women* (New York, 1980), p. 13.
21 *Ibid.*, p. 265.
22 *Ibid.*, p. 288.
23 Alice Childress, *Wine in the Wilderness* (New York, 1969), p. 35.
24 *Ibid.*, p. 37.
25 *Ibid.*, p. 38.
26 Honor Moore, p. 3.
27 *Ibid.*, p. 197.
28 Julia Miles, ed., p. 316.
29 *Ibid.*, p. 313.
30 *Ibid.*, p. 261.
31 Honor Moore, p. 511.
32 *Ibid.*, p. 537.

BIBLIOGRAPHY

Adair, Gilbert. *Hollywood's Vietnam*. New York, 1981

Alvarez, Al. 'A Talk with Robert Lowell', *Encounter*, February 1965, 39–43

Anon. 'Where Are the Women Playwrights?' *The New York Times*, May 1973, Section 2, p. 1

Anon. 'Tenaz Manifesto', *Tulane Drama Review*, xvii, iv (December 1973), 89

Artaud, Antonin. *The Theatre and Its Double*, trans. Mary Caroline Richards. New York, 1958

Babcock, Gregory. *Super Realism: A Critical Anthology*. New York, 1975

Barlow, Judith E. *Plays by American Women: The Early Years*. New York, 1981

Barrett, William. *Irrational Man*. New York, 1962

Barthelme, Donald. *Unspeakable Practices, Unnatural Acts*. London, 1969

Bassnett-McGuire, Susan. 'Luis Valdéz: Two Views of How the Barrio came to Broadway: El Teatro Campesino: From Actos to Mitos', *Theatre Quarterly*, 14, xxxiv (Summer, 1979), 18–20

Beck, Julian. *The Life of the Theatre*. New York, 1972

Beck, Julian, and Malina, Judith. *Paradise Now*. New York, 1971

Beckman, Max. 'Reality and Artifice: An Arts Council Exhibition', University of East Anglia, 1982

Berkowitz, Gerald M. *New Broadways: Theatre Across America 1950–1980*. Totowa, New Jersey, 1982

Blau, Herbert. *Take Up the Bodies: Theatre at the Vanishing Point*. Urbana, 1982

Bradbury, Malcolm. *The Novel Today*. Manchester, 1977

Braun, Edward. *The Theatre of Meyerhold: Revolution on the Modern Stage*. London, 1979

Brecht, Stefan. *Queer Theatre*. Frankfurt-am-Main, 1978

  The Theatre of Visions: Robert Wilson. Frankfurt-am-Main, 1978

Breuer, Lee. 'Interview with Lee Breuer', *TCG: New Plays USA*. New York, 1982

Brook, Peter. 'From Zero to the Infinite', *The Encore Reader*, ed. Horowitz, Milne and Hale. London, 1965

  The Empty Space. London, 1968

  'Introduction', *The Persecution and Assassination of Marat as Performed by the inmates of the asylum of Charenton under the direction of the Marquis de Sade* by Peter Weiss, trans. Geoffrey Skelton, verse adaptation by Adrian Michell. London, 1965

Brown, Helen, and Seitz, Jane. 'With the Bread and Puppet Theatre: An Interview with Peter Schumann', *Tulane Drama Review*, xii, ii (Winter, 1968) 62–73

Brown, Kenneth H. *The Brig: A Concept for Theatre and Film*. New York, 1965

Bibliography

Brown, Norman O. *Life Against Death*. New York, 1959
Brustein, Robert. *Making Scenes: A Personal History of the Turbulent Years at Yale 1966–1979*. New York, 1981
Bullins, Ed. *How Do You Do?* in *Black Fire*, ed. LeRoi Jones and Larry Neal. New York, 1969
   New Plays for the Black Theatre. New York, 1969
   The Duplex. New York, 1970
   The Electronic Nigger and Other Plays. London, 1970
   The Theme is Blackness: The Corner and Other Plays. New York, 1973
Burzynski, Tadeusz, and Osinski, Zbigniew. *Grotowski's Laboratory*. Warsaw, 1979
Butler, Christopher. *After the Wake*. Oxford, 1980
Cage, John. *A Year from Monday*. London, 1968
   Silence Cambridge, 1966
Camus, Albert. *The Collected Plays of Albert Camus*, trans. Stuart Gilbert. London, 1965
Chaikin, Joseph. 'Closing the Open Theatre', *Theatre Quarterly*, xvi (November 1974–January 1975), 36–42
   The Presence of the Actor. New York, 1972
Childress, Alice. *Wine in the Wilderness*. New York, 1969
Chubb, Kenneth. 'Fruitful Difficulties of Directing Shepard', *Theatre Quarterly*, iv, xv (August–October, 1974), 17–26
Cohn, Ruby. *New American Dramatists*. London, 1982
Cole, Tom. *Medal of Honor Rag*. New York, 1977
Conradi, Peter. *John Fowles*. London, 1982
Couch, William, Jr. *New Black Playwrights*. Baton Rouge, 1968
Craig, Edward Gordon. *On the Art of the Theatre*. London, 1911, reprinted 1962
Cruse, Harold. *The Crisis of the Negro Intellectual*. New York, 1969
Cumming, Marsue, ed. *Theatre Profiles 3*. New York, 1977
Dasgupta, Gautam. 'Interview: Charles Ludlam', *Performing Arts Journal*, iii, i (1978), 69–80
Davis, Merrell R., and Gilman, William H., eds. *The Letters of Herman Melville*. New Haven, 1960
Davis, R.G. 'Politics, Art and the San Francisco Mime Troupe', *Theatre Quarterly*, v, xviii (June–August 1975), 26–7
   'The Radical Right in the American Theatre', *Theatre Quarterly*, v, xix (September–November 1975), 67–72
   The San Francisco Mime Troupe: The First Ten Years. Palo Alto, 1975
Davy, Kate, ed. *Richard Foreman: Plays and Manifestos*. New York, 1976
Deak, Frontisek. 'Robert Wilson', *Tulane Drama Review*, xviii, ii (June 1974), 67–73
Deloria, Vine, Jr. *Behind the Trail of Broken Treaties*. New York, 1974
Duberman, Martin. *Black Mountain: An Exploration in Community*. New York, 1972
Dubois, W.E.B. *The Seventh Son: The Thoughts and Writings of W. E. B. Dubois*, vol. ii, ed. Julius Lester. New York, 1971

Bibliography

Elam, Keir. *The Semiotics of Theatre and Drama*. London, 1980

Ellison, Ralph. *Shadow and Act*. New York, 1972

Ellman, Mary. *Thinking About Women*. New York, 1968

Esslin, Martin. *Brecht: A Choice of Evils*. London, 1965

Falk, Florence. 'Bread and Puppet Domestic Resurrection Circus', *Performing Arts Journal*, II, i (Spring, 1977), 19–30

Fierstein, Harvey. *Torch Song Trilogy*. New York, 1981

Foreman, Richard. *Café Amérique*. Gennevilliers, 1981

  Plays and Manifestos, ed. Kate Davy. New York, 1976

Foster, Rick. *West Coast Plays* 10. Berkeley, 1981

Free Southern Theatre Newsletter, December 1964

Friedman, Martin, and Beal, Graham W.J. *George Segal*. New York, 1975

Fromm, Erich. *The Sane Society*. Greenwich, Conn., 1955

Fumarole, Marc. 'External Order, Internal Intimacy: An Interview with Jerzy Grotowski', *Tulane Drama Review*, XIV, i (Fall, 1969), 172–7

Geiogamah, Hanay. *New Native American Drama: Three Plays by Hanay Geiogamah*. Norman, Oklahoma, 1980

Gelber, Jack. *The Connection*. New York, 1960

Gill, Brendan. *The New Yorker*, 28 February 1977

Gold, Mike. *Hoboken Blues* in *The American Caravan*, ed. Van Wyck Brooks, Lewis Mumford, Alfred Kreyborg and Paul Rosenfeld. London, 1927

Goldberg, Isaac. *The Theatre of George Jean Nathan*. New York, 1968

Goodman, Paul. *Three Plays*. New York, 1965

Gornek, Vivian. *Essays in Feminism*. New York, 1978

Gottlieb, Richard. 'The "Engine" That Drives Playwright David Mamet', *The New York Times*, 15 January 1978, p. D4

Gray, Amlin. *How I Got That Story*. New York, 1981

Gray, Spalding. 'About Three Places in Rhode Island', *The Drama Review*, XXIII, i (March 1979), 31–42

  'Perpetual Saturdays', *Performing Arts Journal*, VI, i (1981), 46–9

Gussow, Mel. 'The Daring Visions of Four New, Young Playwrights', *The New York Times*, 30 November 1977, p. 13

Halprin, Ann. 'Community Art as Life Process', *The Drama Review*, XVII, iii (September 1973), 64–80

Harrop, Joan, and Huerta, Jorge. 'The Agitprop Pilgrimage of Luis Valdéz and El Teatro Campesino', *Theatre Quarterly*, V, xvii (March–May 1975), 30–9

Hawthorne, Nathaniel. *Selected Tales and Sketches*. New York, 1962

Hayman, Ronald. *Theatre and Anti-Theatre: New Movements Since Beckett*. London, 1979

Henri, Adrian. *Environments and Happenings*. London, 1974

Hill, Errol. *The Theatre of Black Americans*. 2 vols., Englewood Cliffs, 1980

Hochhuth, Rolf. *The Representative*, trans. Robert David MacDonald. London, 1963

Hochman, Baruch. 'Robert Lowell's *The Old Glory*', *Tulane Drama Review*, XI, iv

Hoffman, Michael J. *Gertrude Stein*. Boston, 1976

470

Bibliography

Hoffman, William, ed. *New American Plays*. New York, 1970
Holden, Joan. 'Collective Playmaking: the Why and How', *Theatre Quarterly*,
    v, xviii (June–August 1975), 28–36
Holmes, Charles S. *The Clocks of Columbus*. London, 1973
Inge, William. *Four Plays*. New York, 1979
Irving, Washington. *Selected Prose*. New York, 1962
Isaacs, Edith J.R. *The Negro in the American Theatre*. New York, 1947
Johnston, Jill. '"Happenings" on the New York Scene', *The Encore Reader*, ed.
    Horowitz, Milne and Hale. London, 1965
Jones, LeRoi. 'Exaugural Address', *Kulchur* iii, iii (Winter, 1963), 86
    Dutchman and the Slave. New York, 1964
Jones, LeRoi, and Neal, Larry. *Black Fire*. New York, 1969
Kaprow, Alan. *Assemblages, Environments and Happenings*. New York, n.d.
Kierkegaard, Søren, *The Present Age*, trans. Alexander Dru. New York, 1962
Kirby, Michael. *The Art of Time*. New York, 1969
    Total Theatre. New York, 1969
Kourilsky, Françoise. 'Approaching Quetzalcoatl: The Evolution of El Teatro
    Campesino', *Performance*, vii (Fall, 1973), 37–46
    'Dada and Circus: Bread and Puppet Theatre', *Tulane Drama Review*, xviii, i
    (March 1974), 104–9
Kriegel, Harriet. *Women in Drama: An Anthology*. New York, 1975
Lahr, John, and Price, Jonathan. *The Great American Life Show: Nine Plays of the
    Avant-Garde*. New York, 1972
    eds., *The Great American Life Show*. New York, 1974
LeCompte, Elizabeth. 'Who Owns History?' *Performing Arts Journal*, vi, i
    (1981), 50–3
Lesnik, Henry, ed. *Guerilla Street Theatre*. New York, 1973
Leverett, James, ed. *TCG: New Plays USA*. New York, 1982
Levine, Mindy. *New York's Other Theatre: A Guide to Off-Off Broadway*. New
    York, 1981
Little, Stuart W. *Enter Joseph Papp: In Search of a New American Theatre*. New
    York, 1974
    Off-Broadway: The Prophetic Theatre. New York, 1972
Lowell, Robert. *Near the Ocean*. London, 1967
    Prometheus Bound. New York, 1969
    The Old Glory. London, 1966
Lowell, Robert, *et al*. 'The Cold War and the West', *Partisan Review*, xxix, i
    (Winter, 1962), 9–89
McLure, James. *Pvt Wars*. New York, 1980
Malina, Judith. *The Enormous Despair*. New York, 1972
Mamet, David. *A Life in the Theatre*. New York, 1978
    American Buffalo, Sexual Perversity in Chicago and Duck Variations. London,
    1978
    Lakeboat. New York, 1981
    Reunion. New York, 1976
    The Water Engine and Mr. Happiness. New York, 1978

The Woods. New York, 1979

Marcuse, Herbert. *Eros and Civilization*. New York, 1955

Marder, Herbert. *Feminism and Art: A Study of Virginia Woolf*. Chicago, 1968

Margolis, John D. *T.S. Eliot's Intellectual Development*. Chicago, 1972

Marowitz, Charles. 'Notes on the Theatre of Cruelty', *Tulane Drama Review* XI, No. 34 (Winter, 1966)

Marranca, Bonnie. *Theatre of the Ridiculous*. New York, 1979

Marranca, Bonnie, ed. *American Dreams: The Imagination of Sam Shepard*. New York, 1981

Animations: A Trilogy for Mabou Mines. New York, 1979

Melville, Herman. *Mardi: And a Voyage Thither*. New York, 1963

Moby Dick. New York, 1950

Short Novels of Herman Melville. East Lansing, 1962

Mersmann, James F. *Out of the Vietnam Vortex: A Study of Poets and Poetry Against the War*. New York, 1974

Miles, Julia, ed. *The Women's Project: Seven New Plays by Women*. New York, 1980

Miller, Arthur. *After the Fall, The Saturday Evening Post*, 12 February 1964

Mitchell, Loften. *Voices of the Black Theatre*. Clifton, New Jersey, 1975

Moers, Ellen. *Literary Women: The Great Writers*. New York, 1978

Moore, Honor. *The New Women's Theatre*. New York, 1977

Morrison, Blake. *Seamus Heaney*. London, 1982

Morton, Carlos. 'The Teatro Campesino', *Tulane Drama Review*, XVIII, iv (December 1974), 71–6

Munk, Erika. 'TDR Comment', *Tulane Drama Review*, XIV, iii (1970), 33–4

Naylor, Colin, and Orridge, Genesis P. *Contemporary Artists*. London, 1977

Neff, Renfreu. *The Living Theatre: USA*. New York, 1970

Norman, Marsha. *'night, Mother*. New York, 1983

Pasolli, Robert. *A Book on the Open Theatre*. Indianapolis, 1970

Prucha, Francis Paul. *Documents of United States Indian Policy*. Lincoln, Nebraska, 1975

Rabe, David. *Streamers*. New York, 1977

The Basic Training of Pavlo Hummel and Sticks and Bones. Harmondsworth, 1978

Reed, Ishmael. *Yellow Back Radio Broke Down*. New York, 1973

Robbe-Grillet, Alain. *Snapshots and Towards a New Novel*, trans. Barbara Wright. London, 1965

Rogoff, Gordon. *The Saturday Review*, 2 April 1977

Rosenberg, Harold. *The Tradition of the New*. London, 1970

Sainer, Arthur. *The Radical Theatre Notebook*. New York, 1975

San Francisco Mime Troupe. *By Popular Demand: Plays and other Works by the San Francisco Mime Troupe*. San Francisco, 1980

Sartre, Jean-Paul. *Situations*, trans. Benita Eisler. London, 1965

Schechner, Richard. *Public Domain: Essays on the Theatre*. Indianapolis, 1969

Ritual, Play and Performance: Readings in the Social Sciences. New York, 1976

'The Decline and Fall of the (American) Avant-Garde', *Performing Arts*

Journal, v, iii (1981), 9–19

The End of Humanism. New York, 1982

ed. *Dionysus in 69.* New York, 1970

Schneeman, Carolee. 'American Experimental Theatre: Then and Now', *Performing Arts Journal*, ii, ii (Fall, 1977), 21–2

Shange, Ntozake. *For colored girls who have considered suicide/when the rainbow is enuf.* New York, 1977

Three Pieces. New York, 1981

Shank, Theodore. *American Alternative Theatre.* London, 1982

'Political Theatre as Popular Entertainment', *Tulane Drama Review*, xviii, i (March 1974), 110–17

'The San Francisco Mime Troupe's production of "False Promises"', *Theatre Quarterly*, vii, xxvii (Autumn, 1977), 41–52

Shepard, Sam. *Angel City, Curse of the Starving Classes and Other Plays.* London, 1978

Buried Child, Seduced, Suicide in B^b. New York, 1977

Five Plays by Sam Shepard. London, 1969

Hawk Moon. New York, 1978

Operation Sidewinder in *The Great American Life Show: Nine Plays of the Avant-Garde*, ed. John Lahr and Jonathan Price. New York, 1972

Seven Plays. New York, 1981

The Tooth of Crime and Geography of a Horse Dreamer (New York, 1974)

Sam Shepard *et al.* 'The American Experimental Theatre: Then and Now', *Performing Arts Journal*, ii, ii (Fall, 1977), 13–24

Simon, Neil. *The Comedy of Neil Simon.* New York, 1973

Sohn-Rethel, Alfred. *Intellectual and Manual Labour: A Critique of Epistemology.* London, 1978

Sontag, Susan. *Against Interpretation.* New York, 1966

'On Art and Consciousness', *Performing Arts Journal*, ii, ii (Fall, 1977), 25–32

Spanos, William. *A Casebook on Existentialism.* New York, 1964

Stewart, Ellen. 'La Mama Celebrates 20 Years', *Performing Arts Journal*, vi, ii (1982), 6–17

Stott, William and Jane. *On Broadway.* London, 1979

Taylor, Karen. *The People's Theatre in Amerika.* New York, 1972

Terry, Megan. 'Viet Rock', *Tulane Drama Review*, xi, i (Fall, 1966), 196–227

Turner, Darwin. *Black Drama in America: An Anthology.* New York, 1971

Updike, John. *Rabbit Redux.* New York, 1971

Valdéz, Luis. *The Drama Review*, xi, iv (September 1967)

'Notes on Chicano Theatre', *Chicano Theatre*, 1 (Spring, 1973)

Van Alstyne, Richard W. *The American Empire: Its Historical Pattern and Evolution.* London, 1960

Van Itallie, Jean-Claude. 'A Reinvention of Form', *Tulane Drama Review*, xxi, iv (December 1977), 65–74

The Serpent. New York, 1969

Wager, Walter, ed. *The Playwright Speaks.* New York, 1968

Walker, Ethel Pitts. 'The American Negro Theatre', in *The Theatre of Black Americans*, vol. II, ed. Errol Hill. Englewood Cliffs, New Jersey, 1980

Ward, Douglas Turner. 'American Theatre: For Whites Only', *The New York Times*, 14 August 1966, Section II, pp. D1, D3

Ward, Theodore. *Our Lan'* in *Black Drama in America: An Anthology*, ed. Darwin Turner. New York, 1971

Watts, Alan. *Beat Zen, Square Zen and Zen*. San Francisco, 1959
  In My Own Way: An Autobiography 1915–1965. London, 1973
  This Is It and Other Essays on Zen and Spiritual Experience. New York, 1958

Williams, Tennessee. *Where I Live*. New York, 1978

Wilson, Robert. *The Golden Window*. Munich, 1982

Woolf, Cecil, and Bagguley, John, eds. *Authors Take Sides on Vietnam*. London, 1967

Woolf, Virginia. *Collected Essays*, vol. 2, London, 1966

Wright, Richard. 'Blueprint for Negro Literature', *Amistad 2*. New York, 1971

Yankovitz, Susan. *Terminal* in *Scripts* 1 (November 1971), 17–45

INDEX

Index

476

Index

Index

Index

Index

Index

Index

Index

Index

Index